Time Out
Boston

Penguin Books

PENGUIN BOOKS

Published by the Penguin Group
Penguin Books Ltd, 27 Wrights Lane, London W8 5TZ, England
Penguin Books USA Inc., 375 Hudson Street, New York, New York 10014, USA
Penguin Books Australia Ltd, Ringwood, Victoria, Australia
Penguin Books Canada Ltd, 10 Alcorn Avenue, Toronto, Ontario, Canada M4V 3B2
Penguin Books (NZ) Ltd, 182-190 Wairau Road, Auckland 10, New Zealand

Penguin Books Ltd, Registered Offices: Harmondsworth, Middlesex, England

First published 1999
10 9 8 7 6 5 4 3 2 1

Colour reprographics by Precise Litho, 34-35 Great Sutton Street, London EC1
Printed and bound by William Clowes Ltd, Beccles, Suffolk NR34 9QE

Edited and designed by
Time Out Guides Limited
Universal House
251 Tottenham Court Road
London W1P 0AB
Tel + 44 (0)171 813 3000
Fax+ 44 (0)171 813 6001
Email guides@timeout.com
http://www.timeout.com

Editorial
Editor Caroline Taverne
Editorial Director Peter Fiennes
Consultant Editor Matt Ashare
Deputy Editor Lily Dunn
Researchers Susie Goldring, Amy Traverso
Proofreader Rhonda Carrier
Indexer Jackie Brind

Design
Art Director John Oakey
Art Editor Mandy Martin
Designers Benjamin de Lotz, Scott Moore, Lucy Grant
Scanner Operator Chris Quinn
Picture Editor Kerri Miles
Picture Researcher Olivia Duncan-Jones
Picture Admin Kit Burnet

Advertising
Group Advertisement Director Lesley Gill
Sales Director Mark Phillips
Advertisement Director North American Guides Liz Howell
(1-800 920 1974, access code 11)
Advertising co-ordinated in the US by Time Out New York:
Alison Tocci (Publisher), Andy Gersten (Advertising Production Manager),
Lisa J Turenchalk (Assistant to the Publisher).

Administration
Publisher Tony Elliott
Managing Director Mike Hardwick
Financial Director Kevin Ellis
Marketing Director Gillian Auld
General Manager Nichola Coulthard
Production Manager Mark Lamond

Features in this guide were written and researched by:
History, **Boston Today**, **Architecture**, **Literary Boston** Art Corriveau; **Campus Culture** Chuck Kapelke; **Boston by Season** Art Corriveau; **Sightseeing** Andrew North, Rachel O'Malley, Jonathan Perry, Susan Ryan-Vollmar, Dan Tobin; **Museums & Galleries** Matt Ashare, Christopher Millis; **Accommodation** Art Corriveau; **Pubs & Bars** Chris Wright; **Restaurants & Cafés** Stephen Heuser, Theresa Regli, Clea Simon; **Shops & Services** Robin Vaughan; **Children** Susie Goldring; **Film** Jon Garelick; **Gay & Lesbian Boston** Art Corriveau; **Media** Andrew North; **Nightlife** Carli Carioli, Jon Garelick, Robin Vaughan; **The Performing Arts** Jon Garelick, Dan Tobin; **Sport & Fitness** Susan Ryan-Vollmar; **Trips Out of Town** Steve Ellman; **Directory** Susie Goldring.

The Editors would like to thank the following:
Katie Anderson; Fred Appel; Anne Bartlet at the Regal Bostonian; Monique Cuvelier; Denise at Virgin Atlantic; Guy Dimond; Jonathan Dyer; Sarah Guy; Ruth Jarvis; Laura Johnson; Ranger Lisa Marsh and the Boston Park Rangers; Ferne Mintz at Bed & Breakfast Agency of Boston; Simon Moore; Aimee O'Brien at the Greater Boston Convention & Visitors Bureau; Nicholas Royle; Greg Selkoe; Angela Smalley at the Four Seasons.

The Editor flew to Boston with Virgin Atlantic (UK reservations 01293 747747).

Maps by JS Graphics, 17 Beadles Lane, Old Oxted, Surrey RH8 9JG.
Map on page 298 reproduced by kind permission of the MBTA.

Photography by Eric Antoniou except for: pages 5 & 11 Hulton Getty; page 7 US Navel Academy, Annapolis/Bridgeman Art Library; pages 7, 8 & 26 AKG; pages 11, 12, 13, 27 & 30 Corbis; page 35 Mark Garfinkel; pages 15 & 36 Popperfoto; pages 38 & 65 Karen Sparcio; page 40 Miro Vintoniv; page 43 Travel Ink/Chris Stock; pages 45, 57, 80 & 86 Greater Boston Convention and Visitors Bureau; page 69 Associated Press; page 79 David A Foster; page 212 Richard Feldman; page 216 M. Lutch; pages 221 & 222 Fayfoto; page 225 Boston Red Sox; page 233 Monarch Novelty; page 237 David Malloy; page 246 Alan Solomon; page 248 Rhode Island Tourism Division; pages 254 & 255 Kindra Clineff/Mott.
The following photographs were supplied by the featured establishments: pages 73, 74, 75, 89, 90, 92, 101, 103, 105, 155, 181, 186, 187, 215, 235, 239, 241, 243, 251, 257 & 259.

Contents

About the Guide

The *Time Out Boston Guide* is one of an expanding series of city guides, produced by the people behind London and New York's successful listings magazines. Other guides in the series include London, Paris, Dublin, Rome, Prague, New York, Los Angeles and San Francisco. Our hard-working team of local writers has striven to provide you with all the information you'll need to explore Beantown, providing up-to-date advice on which sights to see (and which to avoid), where to eat, drink, shop, stay or dance the night away. And we've also included a chapter covering the highlights of New England, from the Green Mountains of Vermont and the White Mountains of New Hampshire, to the beaches and islands of Cape Cod.

CHECKED AND CORRECT

Above all, we've tried to make this book as useful as possible. Addresses, telephone numbers, transport information, opening times, admission prices and credit card details are all included in our listings. And, as far as possible, we've given details of facilities, services and events, all checked and correct at the time we went to press. However, owners and managers can change their arrangements at any time. Before you go out of your way, it's always best to telephone and check opening times, dates of exhibitions and other particulars.

ADDRESSES

We've included the city of Cambridge along with Boston in this guide, as well as neighbouring suburbs like Brookline and Somerville. If a venue is outside central Boston, however, we've indicated this by including the area name in its address – to avoid confusion between the Beacon Street in Boston and the one in Brookline, for example. Where relevant, cross streets are also included, so you can find your way about more easily. We've added zip codes for any venue you might want to write to, as well as e-mail and website addresses where possible. At the back of the guide are 14 pages of colour maps covering Boston and Cambridge in detail, as well as the surrounding countryside. There's also a guide to the local subway system.

PRICES

The prices we've supplied should be treated as guidelines, not gospel. Fluctuating exchange rates and inflation can cause charges, in shops and restaurants particularly, to change rapidly. If prices vary wildly from those we've quoted, ask whether there's a good reason. If there isn't, go elsewhere. Then please write and let us know. We aim to give the best and most up-to-date advice, so we always want to know if you've been badly treated or overcharged.

CREDIT CARDS

The following abbreviations have been used for credit cards: **AmEx**: American Express; **DC**: Diners' Club; **Disc** (Discover); **JCB**: Japanese credit cards; **MC**: Mastercard (Access); **V**: Visa (Barclaycard). Virtually all shops, restaurants and attractions will accept dollar travellers' cheques issued by a major financial institution.

TELEPHONE NUMBERS

The area code for Boston is 617. All telephone numbers printed in this guide take this code, unless otherwise stated. Numbers preceded by 1-800 can be called free of charge from within the US, and some of them can be dialled (though not all free of charge) from the UK.

RIGHT TO REPLY

The information we give is impartial. No organisation has been included in this guide because its owner or manager has advertised in our publications. We hope you enjoy the *Time Out Boston Guide*, but we'd also like to know if you don't. We welcome tips for places you think we should include in future editions and take notice of your criticism of our choices. If you'd like to send us your views please fill in the card at the back of this book.

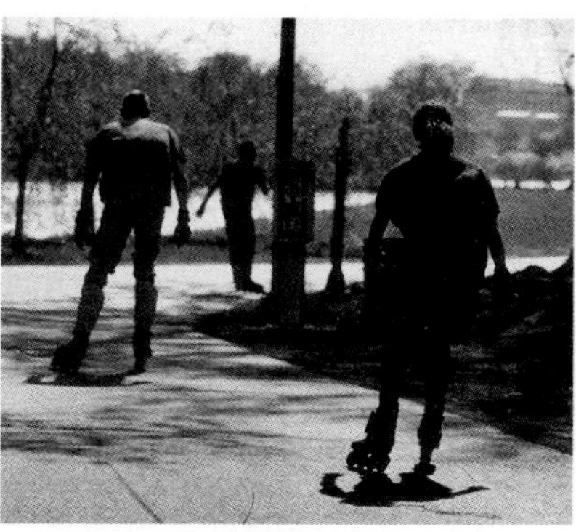

There is an online version of this guide, as well as weekly events listings for several international cities, at **www.timeout.com**

Introduction

If you want to see skyscrapers, you go to New York. If you're looking for presidential monuments, you go to Washington DC. You want sun? Miami. But if it's American history you're after – nearly 400 years of it – you head for Boston. Boston's past is America's past. It's where the Pilgrims first landed, where the flames of revolution were first fanned, where the first battles for independence were fought. Boston is also home to America's first college, first public school, first public library, first public garden. It's known as the Cradle of Liberty, the Athens of America, the Hub of the Universe.

It even *looks* the part. Just take a stroll along the Freedom Trail from the cobbled streets of Beacon Hill through the lively stalls of Quincy Marketplace to Paul Revere's half-timbered house in the North End. It'll make you wonder if the city of Boston isn't just one big, tastefully done theme park. No other American city has a higher concentration of monuments, markets and museums per acre. Few are in better repair, cleaner or safer to explore. And, at barely three miles across, very few are as explorable on foot. Even Disney's Magic Kingdom in Orlando is substantially larger than Boston in size.

But Boston isn't a theme park. It's the real thing – every red brick of it. And though its tangle of narrow brick streets lined with even narrower brick townhouses may remind you more of Europe than America, make no mistake: Boston is all-American. In fact, Boston is *the* American city, having reinvented itself every hundred years or so to keep pace with the country's growth – from tiny religious outpost of the seventeenth century to teeming shipping port of the eighteenth; from manufacturing centre of the nineteenth century to high tech capital of the twentieth.

Boston also tells the story of America's growing pains. In the mid-nineteenth century, the industrial revolution caused it to double in population. The city rose to the challenge by filling in the Back Bay in order to double its size – the greatest engineering feat of its day. Unfortunately, no amount of urban planning could prevent the racial and ethnic tensions that resulted from its transformation from a white Protestant city into a multi-cultural one. By the mid-1950s, these tensions had caused Boston to slump into such economic depression that it actually shrank in population – the only US city to do so during the baby boom. But by the mid-1980s, high tech and tourism had once again made Boston a boom town. And suddenly four million people were commuting into a city that only housed a half million. Boston rose to the challenge again, by undertaking the 'Big Dig', a widening and submersion of its major traffic arteries underground – the greatest engineering feat of our day.

The epitome of the American city, maybe; but damn quirky after 400 years. Yankee homespun traditions mix with highbrow international tastes to produce some bewildering contradictions. Though the city rolls up its sidewalks at midnight, it still manages to produce world-class theatres, museums and restaurants. It's home to America's best seafood and worst drivers, most loyal sports fans and worst professional teams. On Beacon Hill, tweedy *Mayflower* bluebloods live alongside African-Americans, Latino and Asian immigrants, gay and lesbian couples, and a large percentage of Boston's 100,000 college students. Yet a single spirit seems to unite them all: a deep-rooted nostalgia for the past, a sophisticated irony regarding the present, a bruised optimism for the future.

To experience Boston today is perhaps to experience what the rest of America will be like one day when it grows up.

Art Corriveau

In Context

Key Events

c7500 BC Artefacts found in Ipswich date human occupation back to this point.
cAD 500 Native clans begin banding together into tribes.
c1000 Leif Eriksson establishes the colony of Vinland, possibly in present-day Cambridge (unproven).
c1100 The great Algonquin nation is formed, stretching from the Carolinas to Quebec.
1497-1524 Explorations of the Massachusetts Bay by John Cabot, Miguel Corte Real and Giovanni Verrazano – among others.
1614 Captain John Smith explores the Massachusetts Bay area, mapping it and calling it a 'Paradise' in his memoirs.
1620 Puritans set sail aboard the *Mayflower* to establish the first colony in New England. They land on 9 November on Cape Cod. They found Plymouth on 10 December.
1630 John Winthrop and his Puritans establish Boston on the Shawmut peninsula.
1632 Boston is named capital of the Massachusetts Bay Colony.
1636 The first college in the New World is established; it's given the name Harvard College in 1638.
1648 Charlestown witch trials.
1665 Boston witch trials.
1675 Chief Metacomet (King Philip) raids several Massachusetts Bay Colony settlements. A year later he is captured, drawn and quartered and then beheaded.
1692 Salem witch trials.
1764 Parliament imposes the Revenue Act on silk, sugar and wine from the West Indies.
1765 Parliament imposes the Stamp Act on all commercial and legal documents, including newspapers. It's repealed one year later.
1767 The Townshend Acts are passed by Parliament, placing duties on any glass, lead, paint, paper and tea imported to the colonies.
1768 Troops are dispatched to Boston by George III to quiet civil unrest.
1770 George III repeals all duties levied in the Townshend Act except those on tea. Clash on 5 March between Bostonians and English soldiers results in the 'Boston Massacre'.
1773 Parliament imposes the Tea Act on the Colonies, exempting the East India Company from duties on tea. Sons of Liberty host the 'Boston Tea Party' on 16 December by dumping 342 chests of East India tea into the harbour.
1774 Boston port is closed and Massachusetts colonists are prohibited from meeting publicly. Delegates from Massachusetts are sent to the First Continental Congress in Philadelphia, convened on 5 September.
1775 Battle of Lexington and Concord take place on 19 April, when British march to Concord to take an arms store. Patriots are defeated. Battle of Bunker Hill takes place on 17 June. Patriots again defeated but the British suffer twice the casualties.
1776 British troops evacuate Boston in March. Declaration of Independence signed in Philadelphia on 4 July.
1783 Slavery is abolished in Massachusetts.
1793 Eli Whitney introduces his cotton gin in Boston.
1796 John Adams elected second president of the USA.
1806 The African Meeting House is erected, the first in the country.
1807 The Boston Athenaeum is founded, America's first library and art gallery open to the public.
1814 Beacon Street is created to seal Back Bay off from the Charles River.
1822 Boston is granted a city charter.
1824 John Quincy Adams elected sixth president of the USA.
1831 William Lloyd Garrison publishes first issue of abolitionist newspaper *The Liberator.*
1832 New England Anti-Slavery Society is formed.
1835 Abiel Smith School is opened, the first black schoolhouse in the USA.
1839 Charles Goodyear invents vulcanised rubber.
1845 Elias Howe invents the first sewing machine.
1854 Boston Public Library opens, the first free public library in the USA.
1858 Work begins on filling in Back Bay with gravel from Needham.
1862 54th Massachusetts, the first black regiment of the Union Army, is commissioned, trained and sent to battle in the Civil War.
1863 Construction begins on the Museum of Natural History (and is interrupted by the Civil War).
1872 The Great Fire of Boston destroys most of what is now downtown Boston.
1876 Alexander Graham Bell introduces the telephone. The Museum of Fine Arts is opened.
1881 Boston Symphony Orchestra is established.
1887 Park Street and Boylston Street stations open, part of the first subway in the USA.
1897 First Boston Marathon is run.
1903 First World Series game is played between the Boston Pilgrims and the Pittsburgh Pirates.
1912 Fenway Park opens. The Red Sox win the World Series for the first and only time.
1905 James Curley begins political career as alderman, campaigning from jail.
1915 Custom House is erected, Boston's first skyscraper.
1928 World's first computer is developed at MIT.
1946 John F Kennedy is elected congressman.
1947 Curley serves final term as mayor from a federal penitentiary.
1950 Boston is the only major city in the USA census to decline in population.
1955 Beacon Hill Historical District is established.
1957 Boston Redevelopment Authority (BRA) is established to oversee major re-urbanisation projects in the West End, Scollay Square and Back Bay railyards.
1960 John F Kennedy becomes 35th president of the USA.
1963 John F Kennedy is assassinated.
1969 Boston City Hall opens.
1974 Federal district court orders the desegregation of Boston schools. Cross-town busing begins.
1976 Quincy Marketplace opens at Faneuil Hall.
1980 City celebrates its 350th anniversary.
1988 Governor Mike Dukakis runs unsuccessfully as Democratic candidate for president.
1990 Boston's population increases in the census for the first time in four decades.
1993 Thomas Menino is elected mayor, the first non-Irishman to hold the post in 63 years.
1996 Boston Marathon celebrates its 100th anniversary.
1998 200th birthday of *USS Constitution* ('Old Ironsides'), commemorated by its first sail in over a century.

History

The history of Boston – from the Puritans to the Pru.

Strictly speaking, Boston was never truly 'settled' until the arrival of the Puritans in 1620. That doesn't mean that Massachusetts wasn't inhabited, however. Artefacts found in nearby Ipswich date human occupation back to as early as 7500 BC.

NATIVE OCCUPATION

It is believed that these nomadic hunters began banding together into tribes around 1,500 years ago, gathering in the summer to plant crops and to fish for cod. They lived communally – up to ten families together – in permanent longhouses shingled in bark. In the winter months they tended to splinter off into family clans to hunt game, living in collapsible wigwams made of saplings covered in skins.

Little else is known about these early inhabitants, however. Theirs appears to have been an oral culture with no written language, and their beliefs don't seem to have encouraged the accumulation of personal property or riches. About 500 years before European occupation, most of the nomadic tribes incorporated themselves into the Greater Algonquin nation, extending from the Carolinas to Quebec. Those most frequently inhabiting Massachusetts Bay were the Massachusett, Narragansett, Wampanoag, Nauset, Pamet and Pautucket.

EUROPEAN EXPLORATION & SETTLEMENT

Leif Eriksson's fabled colony of Vinland was actually located in Cambridge – if turn-of-the-century historian Eben Horsford is to be believed. In 1889, Horsford announced to the American Geographical Society that he had found the remains of Eriksson's 1,000-year-old settlement along the banks of the Charles River, in an area known for centuries to local tribes as Norbega – which, in his mind, was an obvious corruption of Norvega, or Norway. Though his theory was never really proved or disproved, it was popular enough in the early 1900s for Bostonians to have erected a statue in Eriksson's honour at the head of the Commonwealth Mall.

Perhaps a bit better documented is John Cabot's explorations of Massachusetts Bay during his 1497 quest for the Northwest Passage to the Orient. He claimed Massachusetts (and much of the East Coast of America) for Henry VII of England. Giovanni Verrazano, passing through in 1524, claimed the same land for his employer, Francis I of France (something Miguel Corte Real had apparently also done for Portugal a few years earlier).

No real interest in colonising the Massachusetts Bay area developed, however, until John Smith mapped out its coastline in 1614. His glowing report of a 'Paradise' eventually led James I to charter the Plymouth Company, a commercial trading venture formed with the purpose of colonising 'New England' (the American coastline from Virginia to Newfoundland). Word of the Plymouth Company reached John Brewster, leader of the strict Protestant sect known as the Puritans. Weary of persecution by the Church of England, Brewster convinced the Plymouth Company to fund a Puritan attempt at establishing a colony in America. And so the *Mayflower*, laden with 102 passengers, set sail in September 1620 bound for 'some place about the Hudson River'.

Leader of the pilgrim settlers, John Winthrop.

It landed on the tip of Cape Cod 65 days later, well north of its mark, at what is now Provincetown. Finding it inhospitable, the Puritans crossed the bay and, about a month later, established the colony of Plymouth on a protected stretch of sandy beach – not on the fabled rock, alas – but close to several Indian cornfields. Nearly half of these first 'Pilgrims' (as they have come to be called in American history books) died of pneumonia and smallpox that first winter. But in the spring, local bands of Narragansett and Wampanoag took pity on them and taught them how to plant corn, dig clams and fish for cod. By harvest time, the settlers were well enough established to host a three-day feast in their honour, and it is still celebrated today as Thanksgiving.

ESTABLISHMENT OF BOSTON

Word eventually spread back in England about the new Puritan Utopia. By 1630, 1,000 more willing settlers had arrived in the New World under the sponsorship of the Massachusetts Bay Company. They established Salem, on the north shore of Massachusetts Bay. Under the leadership of John Winthrop, many of these colonists eventually migrated south to a peninsula that later became Charlestown. Lack of fresh water, however, forced them to relocate to the neighbouring peninsula, known to the natives as Shawmut. Winthrop's settlers bought the narrow 440-acre (177-hectare) peninsula from a hermit bachelor named William Blaxton. Securing friendly relations with the neighbouring natives by means of a few gifts and trinkets, they renamed it Tremontaine after its three surrounding hills (hence today's Tremont Street). But the village that Winthrop's Puritans subsequently established became known as Boston, after the Lincolnshire village that many of them were from. Boston was made capital of the Massachusetts Bay Colony in 1632.

INDIAN WARS, RELIGIOUS INTOLERANCE & TRADE

By 1636, there were some 12,000 colonists, primarily Puritans, spread between the townships of Plymouth, Salem and Boston, with new settlements springing up on a monthly basis. (In fact, a lack of qualified ministers led Puritan elders to establish America's first training college, which they later named Harvard after a young minister who died and left the college his library.) Early colonists found Massachusetts curiously easy to settle and rather empty of the anticipated hostile Indians – not realising that epidemics of smallpox and influenza brought over by early explorers had decimated the native population.

Relations with what few tribes remained in Massachusetts deteriorated rapidly, however. The Puritan notion of a righteous life leading naturally to the accumulation of spiritual, as well as material, wealth clashed with native beliefs that it was impossible to own land or anything offered up by it. And, unlike the French to the north, who converted native populations to Catholicism in their attempts to expand the boundaries of Christianity, the Puritans preferred simply to rid Christianity of the heathen devil by burning out their settlements and appropriating their land. The Algonquin nation, under the leadership of Chief Metacomet (known to colonists as King Philip), retaliated in 1675 by raiding several outlying English settlements – all in vain. Metacomet was betrayed by one of his own warriors the following year and gruesomely executed. His head was publicly displayed on a stick in Plymouth for the following 20 years, serving as a very successful deterrent against further attack.

The Indians were by no means the sole targets of Puritan intolerance. They persecuted with equal severity any other religious sects that failed to meet their strict standards of worship. Many a Quaker and Baptist arriving in the colony in the seventeenth century were prevented from even leaving their ships; those who practised their faith publicly were sometimes hanged for heresy or, at the very least, forced to move south, where the more tolerant colonies of Rhode Island, Pennsylvania and Maryland were eventually established. It was little wonder, then, that this sort of religious paranoia gave rise to the witch trials of Charleston (1648), Boston (1665) and – most notably – Salem (1692), where 55 colonists were tortured and 20 were hanged for consorting with the devil.

By 1700, Boston had nonetheless grown into the third largest port of the burgeoning British Empire. Many of the Puritans grew exceedingly rich, thanks primarily to the export of dried cod to the Caribbean and Mediterranean (to this day, a carved pine cod – known as 'the Sacred Cod' – hangs above the entrance to the House of Representatives in the State House, pointing to the party in power). Some got even richer in a notorious triangular shipping trade where sugar cane was harvested by slaves in the West Indies and shipped to Boston to be distilled into rum. These Puritans didn't seem to find the manufacture of rum to be in conflict with their religion's rather narrow views on alcohol – perhaps because they shipped most of it to West Africa to be traded for more slaves who were, in turn, delivered to the Caribbean sugar plantations. In any case, one of the by-products of the city's rum production was molasses (Boston was the largest American producer of the stuff until the early twentieth century). Another was the introduction of slavery to American soil. By 1705, there were more than 400 black slaves – and a small number of free blacks – living in Boston.

REVOLUTIONARY BOSTON

Britain began taxing its wealthy American colonies quite heavily in the mid-eighteenth century. The Empire had incurred enormous expenses during its lengthy (and inconclusive) border wars with France. And as many of these were fought on New England soil, Parliament felt justified in establishing the Revenue Act in 1764, which placed heavy duties on silk, sugar and wine from the West Indies.

Colonists – especially those from Boston and involved in the Triangle Trade – were furious. They quickly organised a boycott of these goods. Undaunted, Parliament established the Stamp Act a year later, placing a tax on all commercial and legal documents, including newspapers. Outraged, the colonists began a boycott of all English goods, unifying themselves under the slogan 'No taxation without representation'. Though the Stamp Act was hastily repealed a year later, Parliament levied another series of taxes in 1767, called the Townshend Acts, on imported lead, glass, paint, paper and tea.

For the first time, Bostonians such as Samuel Adams, Daniel Webster and James Otis began to speak out about the obvious benefits of separating from the British Empire at public meetings in venues such as Faneuil Hall (now known as 'the Cradle of Liberty'), the Old South Meeting House and the Old State House. In 1768, George III reluctantly sent troops to Boston to quiet the growing civil unrest. Military occupation, however, had the opposite effect. On 5 March 1770, it precipitated a clash between English soldiers and a small group of anti-royalists at the Old State House that resulted in the death of five colonists.

Paul Revere's version of the Boston Massacre.

News of this 'Boston Massacre' spread throughout the colonies and galvanised anti-royalist sentiment. Fearing the worst, George III abolished the Townshend Acts – except for the tax on tea, the most widely drunk beverage in the colonies. Imported tea was promptly boycotted. Unfortunately, the East India Company (the Empire's chief

Robert Salmon's depiction of Constitution Wharf in the mid-eighteenth century.

The 'Sons of Liberty' get the party rolling, 16 December 1773.

exporter of tea) was close to collapse in 1773. In an attempt to save it from bankruptcy, Parliament exempted its tea from taxation, hoping to flood the colonial markets with it. Every American city closed its ports to English tea ships – except occupied Boston. In fact, the British Governor, Thomas Hutchinson, insisted that the tea ships remain docked in Boston Harbor until local agents accepted shipment.

On the night of 16 December, 60 men, identifying themselves as the 'Sons of Liberty' and dressed as Indians, boarded the blockaded ships and dumped 342 chests of tea into the harbour. In retaliation, Boston's port was closed and Massachusetts colonists were prohibited from meeting publicly without permission from the governor. Such punishments were far too little, too late. Boston's defiant 'Tea Party' electrified the colonies. The first Continental Congress for independence was convened in Philadelphia on 5 September 1774. Massachusetts sent prominent delegates such as John Adams and John Hancock. And local militia everywhere began training in earnest for a fight.

That fight began in Boston on 19 April 1775. The British, who were billeted on Boston Common, got word of an arms store in the nearby township of Concord. When they crossed the Charles River to march to Concord from Cambridge, sexton Robert Newman hung two lanterns in the steeple of the Old North Church, signalling that the troops' route was to be 'by sea'. Paul Revere, William Dawes and Samuel Prescott set out on horseback to warn local militia that the British were indeed coming. (In fact, both Revere and Dawes were quickly apprehended; it was Prescott who ultimately got the message through, though his name, unfortunately, had fewer rhyming possibilities for Henry Wadsworth Longfellow when he immortalised the event in his celebrated 1861 poem 'Paul Revere's Ride'.) It remains a mystery who fired the 'shot heard round the world', but it was touched off on Lexington Green, where 77 Minutemen – as the local militia were called – crouched waiting for the British Redcoats. The Redcoats quickly put an end to the skirmish, killing eight rebels as they marched on to secure Concord. But the war had begun.

The first real battle – and one of the bloodiest – took place a few months later, on 17 June in Charlestown. The colonists had fortified themselves at the top of Breed's Hill. The British suffered enormous casualties – double that of the Minutemen – before they were able to relay their victory back to England (where it was mistakenly reported as Bunker Hill, the next hill over). From a propaganda point of view, however, victory was clearly with the colonists. Reports of their enormous bravery in battle until ammunition ran out helped inspire insurrection all over the colonies. It ultimately resulted in the Declaration of Independence. On 4 July 1776, John Hancock of Boston allegedly signed his name to the document, large enough for George III to be able to read without spectacles. Though Boston continued to be occupied by the British until the following March, it was not the scene of another battle for the remainder of the war. And when independence was finally won in 1781, Massachusetts numbered among the original 13 United States of America, though technically (along with Virginia and Pennsylvania) it chose commonwealth status over statehood. Massachusetts remains a commonwealth to this day, though the difference is largely symbolic.

INDUSTRIALISATION & IMMIGRATION

Outspoken patriots such as Boston's Samuel Adams fanned the flames of unrest that ultimately led to independence. Unfortunately, this left diplomats such as Sam's cousin, John Adams (the second US president), with the formidable task of rebuilding political and trade relations with England after the war. Massachusetts's shipping-based economy was particularly hard hit by the loss of the English market at the turn of the nineteenth century. Boston barely grew until its economy diversified into whaling and trade with the Far East. Soon after this, however, the demand for fishing clippers from towns such as Nantucket, New Bedford and Salem grew so great that Boston's shipyards mushroomed into some of the largest in the world. Boston mushroomed along with them, and was granted a city charter in 1822.

Though shipbuilding made several wealthy families on Beacon Hill even wealthier, its general effect on the economy was shortlived. Clippers were soon replaced by the newfangled steamship, a vessel that conservative Bostonians refused to build. This put the city into another decline until its economy was once again able to diversify into manufacturing raw goods from Southern plantations. It was in Boston that Eli Whitney first introduced the cotton gin; Charles Goodyear invented vulcanised rubber there, Elias Howe invented the first sewing machine, and Alexander Graham Bell introduced his first telephone. Factories, hungry for workers to process cotton, lumber and tobacco, began welcoming European immigrants – diluting Boston's Puritanism forever.

In the mid-nineteenth century, Boston, like New York, accepted several great waves of immigration. The first brought the Irish in 1845, escaping the great potato blight. They were shortly followed by German Jews seeking asylum from persecution in Europe, and then by Eastern European Jews escaping the fall of tsarist Russia. Mixed in were smaller waves of Poles, Italians, Portuguese and French Canadians. It is estimated that by 1860, more than 60 per cent of Boston's population had been born abroad.

NEW NEIGHBOURHOODS & ETHNIC GHETTOISATION

Boston's narrow peninsula could hardly accommodate such an enormous influx of new citizens. By the early 1800s, it was all too clear that the fetid swamps of Back Bay would make desirable real estate. Two of Boston's three hills were levelled to begin this process and several feet were shaved off the top of Beacon Hill. In 1814, Beacon Street was created to close Back Bay's tidal flats off from the Charles River. Next, the Public Garden was added to the 'shores' of Boston Common (though the authorities considered selling it off as commercial real estate until as late as 1859). But the real work of filling in Back Bay wasn't really begun until 1858, when 3,500 loads of gravel a day were railed in from nearby Needham and dumped into the muck. It took more than 30 years to complete the project – the largest engineering feat of its day. But the result was 450 more acres (181 hectares) of land, which doubled the city's size. The creation of two entirely new neighbourhoods – the South End and Back Bay – gave city planners the opportunity to design streets on a grid system rather than continue with the messy tangle of cow paths and Indian trails that characterised colonial Boston.

Unfortunately, the new neighbourhoods only encouraged more of the process of ethnic ghettoisation that was already well underway. As waves of immigrants poured into the North End, the original colonial port, the alarmed First Families of Boston (or FFB as the Cabots, Lodges, Codmans and Lowells would later refer to themselves) all moved to elegant isolation on Beacon Hill, causing local wit JC Bossidy to declare of them:

This is good old Boston
The home of the beans and the cod
Where the Lowells speak only to Cabots
And the Cabots speak only to God.

They were later dubbed the 'Boston Brahmins' by Oliver Wendell Holmes.

The city's merchant class also took flight, claiming the newly created South End. But the waves of immigrants kept coming and slowly they began to creep up the 'wrong' side of Beacon Hill. The upper classes promptly abandoned the 'right' side and began building mansions in Back Bay as quickly as acres were added (the Back Bay's alphabetical cross streets are apparently named after English ducal palaces: Arlington, Berkeley, Clarendon, Dartmouth). Always the least desirable neighbourhood, the North End was to change population several times during the nineteenth century, from black to Irish to Jewish to Portuguese. Only in the past 60 years has the North End become the lively Italian quarter of the present day.

THE ATHENS OF AMERICA

The original Puritan leaders discouraged the arts as un-Christian. In fact, the first legitimate theatre wasn't built until the late eighteenth century. Colonial Bostonians weren't much more interested in poetry and painting than their forebears, devoting most of their energy to gaining independence from England. ('I must study politics and war so that my sons may have liberty to study mathematics and philosophy in order to give their children a right to study painting, poetry, music, architecture' wrote John Adams to his wife Abigail in 1780.)

Economic prosperity in the nineteenth century, however, brought cultural awakening. The Cabots and Lowells began to travel abroad and, in doing so, realised just how unenlightened their city was. It didn't take them long to rectify the situation. In the short span between the 1840s and 1880s – primarily through private patronage and donorship of the FFB – Boston was graced with a Music Hall (now the Orpheum Theatre), a Public Library, a Museum of Natural History (now the Louis Department Store), a Museum of Fine Arts and a Symphony Orchestra. Boston also built the first subway system in America, opening Park Street and Boylston stations in 1887. The city's unheard-of number of public institutions, coupled with the astonishing literary, artistic and political figures those institutions attracted, soon earned it the sobriquet 'the Athens of America'.

The late nineteenth century also marked the beginning of Boston's love affair with sport. In 1897, the first Boston Marathon was run from the nearby town of Hopkinton to Copley Square. Meanwhile, the newly invented game of baseball was taking the city by storm. Boston's first professional team, the Pilgrims, hosted the Pittsburgh Pirates at the first World Series game in 1903. By the time Fenway Park opened in 1912, the Pilgrims had become the Red Sox. In fact, the Sox won the World Series that year – their first and only time.

ABOLITION & CIVIL WAR

Slavery was abolished in Massachusetts in 1783. By 1800, Boston was home to the oldest and largest black community in America (a full five per cent of its total population of 25,000). The community already had its heroes – Crispus Atticus had been a martyr of the Boston Massacre, Peter Salem a hero of Bunker Hill – and the north slope of Beacon Hill was its home. Though the black population did not yet have the right to vote, they were allowed to earn good wages as servants, street cleaners, shipbuilders, blacksmiths and barbers. They were also allowed to meet freely, worship as they pleased and educate themselves. The first African Meeting House in America was built on Beacon Hill in 1806, as was the first school, Abiel Smith, in 1835.

It wasn't surprising, then, that Boston also became the centre of Abolition, as tensions over slavery mounted between the North and South. The New England Anti-Slavery Society was founded in 1832, and prominent blacks such as Frederick Douglass, William Nell and Maria Miller Stuart began condemning slavery publicly. Their cause was greatly supported by wealthy whites such as William Lloyd Garrison (who first published his Abolitionist paper *The Liberator* in 1831), Wendell Phillips, Charles Sumner and Angelina Grimké (who was, in fact, of mixed heritage).

Boston, by any other name...

(would taste as sweet).

Before there was a Boston, the narrow peninsula on which it was built was known by the Algonquians as **Shawmut**, or 'unclaimed land'. When John Winthrop and his weary band of Puritans laid claim to Shawmut in 1630, they renamed it **Tremontaine** ('three mountains') after the three local hills that dominated the place. But the village they built quickly became known as Boston (a corruption of 'St Botolph's Town') after the Lincolnshire village that most of them hailed from.

Over the course of its 370-year history, however, the city has picked up a few colourful nicknames. Take **Beantown**, for example. In the eighteenth century Boston was fairly awash with molasses, a by-product of rum production. Molasses was naturally used by colonial housewives to sweeten most ordinary foods. A favourite dish of the day was beans which had been stewed in the syrupy stuff for hours. You need only to have glanced at any tavern menu to see that Boston was a bean town. (The recipe, by the way, is said to have been adapted by the Puritans at the first Thanksgiving, from one taught to them by the Wampanoag Indians.)

Boston was America's undisputed capital of culture by the mid-nineteenth century. It boasted a number of cultural firsts: the first public library, the first art museum and the first symphony orchestra, to name but a few. It's little wonder, then, that Boston became known as the 'Athens of America'. In fact, Oliver Wendell Holmes was so proud of the city's artistic and civic achievements that he asserted that Boston's State House was at the 'hub of the Solar System' in his 1858 essay 'The Autocrat of the Breakfast Table'. It took Bostonians no time at all to expand the idea of being at **The Hub** to include the rest of the Universe.

Author and Abolitionist, Frederick Douglas.

Anti-slavery efforts in Boston had become more than mere rhetoric by the mid-nineteenth century. Lewis and Harriet Hayden's house at 66 Phillips Street became a station on the Underground Railroad (*see page 52* **Sightseeing**). And when the Civil War broke out, the first free black regiment of the Union Army – the 54th Massachusetts – was organised on Beacon Hill, trained in Jamaica Plain and sent off to battle in the Carolinas. Their story is immortalised in a sculpture in the Public Garden (*see page 91* **Museums & Galleries**) and in a 1989 film, *Glory*.

TWENTIETH-CENTURY ECONOMIC DECLINE

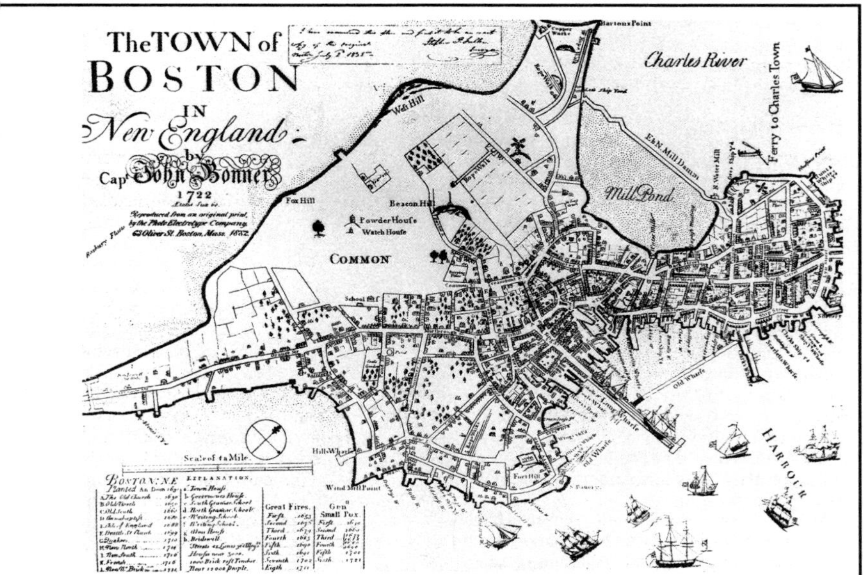

Boston's Irish Catholics, freed from the political oppressions of Britain, took full advantage of their right to hold office in America. The early part of the twentieth century saw the rise of the Irish political machine in the city, with 'Boss' James Curley as its champion. Curley was without doubt the city's most colourful politician. He actually won his first campaign as alderman from jail (where he was serving time for impersonating a friend at a civil service exam). Over a checkered 40-year career, he served as congressman, governor and mayor. And true to form, he spent much of his fourth and last term as mayor in a federal penitentiary for mail fraud. Though Boss Curley set the standard for political corruption in America, he was wildly popular with voters for championing the causes of the poor. Several public parks and hospitals were built during his administration, for example; and when Curley was fined $30,000 in a 1938 fraud case, thousands of Boston's poorer citizens donated the money to pay it off.

Unfortunately, Curley's Irish Catholic administration did not mix well with the lawmakers from long-established Puritan families on Beacon Hill. The inability of the city's Protestant and Catholic politicians to work together prevented Boston from keeping pace with the times. By the late 1940s, it had lost its major port status to those on the West Coast and much of its manufacturing to the South. What's more, Boston became the only major US city in the post-World War II baby boom to decline in population (plummeting from 800,000 to 560,000). Both its middle and upper classes migrated to the suburbs. Most of the single-family townhouses of Beacon Hill, Back Bay and the South End were carved up into apartments and boarding houses. The city's tax base began to crumble, and then its infrastructure along with it.

The only industry that flourished at this time was education. Colleges and universities had cropped up everywhere, thanks to the city's excellent libraries, well-established cultural resources and incredibly cheap rents for students. But institutions such as Harvard, MIT and Boston University were also becoming centres of political turbulence, as America's youth underwent the transformations of the 1960s, questioning government and the status quo. Unrest, sparked off by issues such as the Vietnam War, flourished at the city's 40 or so campuses. With downtown crime on the rise and student demonstrations blocking the streets, tourism began to suffer. By the mid-1960s, Boston had officially become one of the worst places to live in America.

URBAN RENEWAL

Panicked by Boston's decline, city officials attempted to jam on the brakes. Under the direction of Mayor John B Hynes and the newly established Boston Redevelopment Authority (BRA), officials began a 'clean up' of Boston's problem neighbourhoods. The 1960s saw the completion of three massive urban renewal projects – with very mixed results. The West End, Boston's only ethnically mixed neighbourhood, was razed to make way for a luxury apartment complex called Charles River Park. Colourful Scollay Square, home to Boston's few gay bars and jazz joints at that time, was levelled to make way for Government Center. The Prudential Tower rose up out of Back Bay's abandoned Boston & Maine railyards.

However inept, these first efforts at re-urbanisation had their positive side. Organisations such as the Beacon Hill Historical Society were established to protect other neighbourhoods from befalling the fate of the West End. Public outcry caused subsequent developers to be much more wary of an area's architectural and historical significance. This was definitely the case when the rundown warehouses of Quincy Market were transformed into the present-day shopping and entertainment complex for tourists. In fact, Quincy Market was so well converted that it set the standard for revitalisation efforts all over the world.

DESEGREGATION OF SCHOOLS

Racial tensions, never far from the surface in Boston, bubbled over in 1974 when a federal district court order ruled that the city desegregate its schools. Under heavy police escort, the Board of Education began busing white students into black neighbourhoods and black students into white neighbourhoods. Violence erupted everywhere – though it was particularly pronounced in Irish South Boston and black Roxbury.

During the first few years of desegregation, school buses were constantly pelted with rocks and students were beaten in hallways and stabbed in playgrounds. The issue was far more complex than pure racism, however. Over time, Boston's ethnic ghettos had evolved into closely-knit communities. Both blacks and whites were afraid: of losing the neighbourhoods they had worked so hard to build and of losing their cultural identities. Neither had any choice in the matter of where their children were bused, unless they could afford to send them to private school. Resistance to forced integration persisted for the next decade. But over time, 415 court orders were issued and the city's schools were fully integrated.

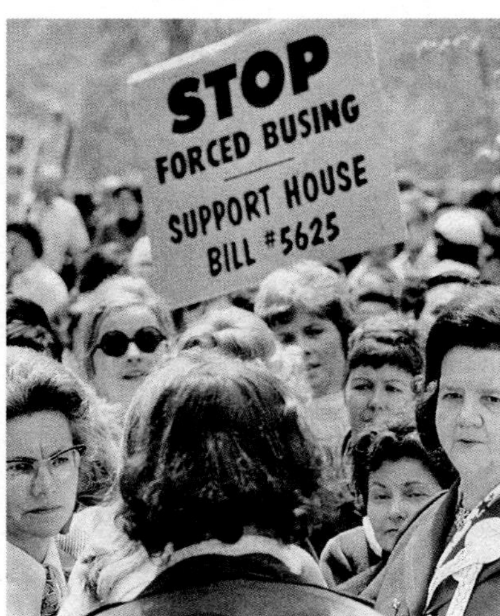

Tensions mount over desegregation.

American royalty

America's love affair with the Kennedy family is admittedly odd – given that the United States was founded on such anti-royalist principles. Yet the country is as obsessed with the comings and goings of the family (will John-John finally pass the bar? Will his magazine succeed? Who will he marry? Will the marriage last?) as some people are with the British Royal Family. For many, the Kennedys epitomise the American Dream.

Patrick J Kennedy arrived penniless in Boston in 1848 at the age of 25, from County Wexford in Ireland. By the age of 35, he had made his mark in saloons and banking. He had also served in the state legislature and befriended Mayor John F 'Honey Fitz' Fitzgerald. His son Joseph attended Harvard, married Fitz's daughter Rose and then amassed a fortune as a stockbroker, film financier and – some say – prohibition bootlegger.

In a single generation, the Kennedy family had moved from a modest three-storey house in East Boston to mansions on Cape Cod and Palm Beach. But that was only the beginning of Joe's ambitions for the clan. He began grooming his good-looking, charismatic sons for national politics. John F (*pictured*) took James Curley's empty seat in the House of Representatives in 1946. He ran for Senate in 1952 and won. He ran for president in 1960 and won. The press dubbed his enormously popular presidency 'Camelot' and hailed his first lady, Jacqueline Bouvier, as one of the most beautiful women in the world. John's brother Robert served as his Attorney General and ran for president himself in 1968. John's other brother Edward filled his vacated seat in Congress and has served in the US Senate ever since.

But like all great mythological dynasties, the Kennedys seem to be star-crossed. Joe Kennedy Jr died a hero in World War II. John F was assassinated during his presidency, Robert was assassinated while running for his. Edward's career was ruined one fateful night on Martha's Vineyard when his companion drowned in his car. But tragedy only seems to make America love the Kennedys – and their children – even more. In addition to elevating their lives to the stuff of legend, tragedy also makes them very, very human.

For the whole story, visit:

John F Kennedy Birthplace
National Historic Site, 83 Beals Street, Brookline (566 7937). Coolidge Corner T, then 66 bus.
Open *summer* 10am-4.30pm Wed-Sun. **Admission** $2. **No credit cards.**

John F Kennedy Library & Museum
See p92 **Museums & Galleries** *for listings.*

1980s RENAISSANCE

Though Boston had been lax in keeping manufacturing alive at the outset of the twentieth century, it would not repeat its mistake in the 1970s with the emerging high tech industry. City officials courted computer companies aggressively and, by the mid-1980s, Boston had reinvented itself once again. 'The Massachusetts Miracle' – as Boston's economic renaissance was touted in the media – was due largely to the leadership of mayors such as Kevin White and Raymond Flynn, and the vision of Mike Dukakis, who served as governor twice and ran as the 1988 Democratic candidate for president.

Ironically, economic decline in the early part of the century had saved Boston's colonial and Victorian neighbourhoods from the sort of badly-planned, baby-boom development suffered by cities such as New York, Detroit and Chicago. By the time the city was once again a boomtown, its codes for historical preservation were well entrenched. Today, the South End and Back Bay comprise the largest complete Victorian neighbourhood left in the world. Restored townhouses and brownstones quickly became desirable places for young urban professionals to live. Boston's middle and upper classes slowly began to return to the city. In the 1990 census, Boston showed a growth in population – its first in four decades.

Today, coffeeshops and restaurants, wine bars and nightclubs abound in nearly every neighbourhood. Boston's arts scene is more vibrant than ever, and it boasts a world-class ballet company and symphony orchestra. There are some 60 colleges and universities in the metropolitan area. And few other American cities can claim such a beautifully restored and socially vibrant downtown.

Boston Today

Despite rising homelessness and crumbling schools, there's no doubt that Boston's a boomtown.

Industry is up, tourism is up and crime is down. In this chapter, we explore some of the blessings – and curses – of living in one of America's hottest cities.

INDUSTRY & EMPLOYMENT

Recent statistics place Boston's unemployment at an astonishingly low three-and-a-half per cent (especially astonishing if you consider that the normal process of people switching jobs accounts for two per cent of the figure). High-tech continues to be one of Boston's biggest employment industries, though most of the jobs are actually located in suburban 'office parks'. The big news in the past couple of decades, however, has been finance. Boston has become the king of the mutual fund, and companies such as Fidelity, Putnam and John Hancock Investments have their headquarters within the city limits. In fact, in 1998, Boston became the world's third largest city for money management, after New York and London.

TOURISM

Another big industry – and one that's getting bigger all the time – is tourism. In warmer months, you can't cross the street without either being clanged out of the way by a bright red sightseeing trolley or quacked at by a boatful of noisy Duck Tourists (*see page 86* **Sightseeing**). Today, an estimated $60 million a year is generated by tourism in America's most historic city.

Most hotels in town now hover at an occupancy rate of around 80 per cent all year round, and they're often completely sold out during Boston's busiest tourist period in the autumn. With so much to see and do, and such a low crime rate, Boston is consistently ranked among America's top ten convention destinations. So in spite of the fact that the Hynes Convention and Exposition Center was enlarged as recently as the early 1990s, plans are underway to build a state-of-the-art convention complex on the waterfront.

PERPETUAL CONSTRUCTION

There hasn't been this much construction in town since Back Bay was filled in. Cranes and scaffolding are permanent fixtures on the skyline and in addition to the new convention centre already mentioned, the city's development plans include revitalising the waterfront along Fort Point Channel, giving the Downtown Crossing shopping area a complete makeover, and turning the area around Dudley Square near Roxbury Crossing into a mini-tech district (*see page 25* **Architecture**).

These projects all pale in comparison, however, to the 'Big Dig' – Boston's attempt to drive its central traffic artery underground while keeping the elevated expressway open to traffic. Begun in 1991, the Big Dig will take about a dozen years to complete. Meanwhile, Bostonians have grown fairly resigned to the inconvenience: the constant pounding and digging, the huge mountains of sand and gravel, the displaced water rats, the inexplicable traffic jams at odd times of the day. Locals have grown to expect exit ramps that open and close without warning, one-way systems that shift daily, ruined suspension on their cars, flat tyres and the need to weave in and out of stark cement towers and under ominous-looking steel girders that seem to lead nowhere. Most Bostonians just sigh and carry on with their daily lives. They may as well. The project is only about half finished (*see page 16*).

LIVING IN BOSTON

In spite of the traffic nuisance, Boston is a very popular place to live, especially among that high-profile breed – young urban professionals. There have never been more restaurants to enjoy, sidewalk cafés to hang out in or theatre performances to attend. These days, almost all of the city's older neighbourhoods are in a Disney-quality state of repair. Strolling through the streets of Beacon Hill or Back Bay is like being on the set of some movie. And sometimes you are: film-makers often use Louisburg and Union Squares for period dramas set in Victorian London or New York.

But utter quaintness also has its irritating sides. Boston is basically a small town trapped in a big city's body. Though it offers all the essentials of urban living – sophisticated shopping, good museums, reliable public transport, a vibrant nightlife – it still tends toward the primness of its Puritan heritage. Most restaurant kitchens close at 10pm and the city rolls up the sidewalks by 2am. Then there are the Blue Laws (deriving, some say, from the blue paper they were written on; others claim the name comes from the shortening of 'bloody laws', or refers to how your skin looked after a public beating for disobeying them). Until 1994, it was

Boston's mayor Tom Menino shares a joke with Bill Clinton.

illegal for most shops to open on Sunday. As a concession to the twentieth century, most places are now able to open from noon until 6pm. But you can forget about trying to buy a bottle of wine to take to Sunday brunch – much less anything stronger. The sale of alcohol is still strictly forbidden, except in restaurants and in the period between Thanksgiving and New Year. And the rest of the time you can forget about trying to buy beer or wine in any establishment besides a licenced 'package store' or liquor store.

Regardless of these frustrations, Boston is the place to live – if you can afford it. But even when you can, finding an apartment is no mean feat. Real estate vacancy is said to be only about two per cent and prices are approaching those in New York and San Francisco. A modest one-bedroom apartment in Back Bay, for example, rents for about $1,600 a month and sells for about $250,000. The going rate for parking spaces alone is $25,000. And parking, of course, is an absolute nightmare. Even with a resident's permit, locals find themselves circling their neighbourhood for 45 minutes looking for a spot. Most parking garages charge upwards of $25 a day.

But the compensations make all this worthwhile. There are all the lovely things you get for free – from concerts every summer night at the Hatch Memorial Shell to a recreational park along the Charles River that stretches to Cambridge and beyond – or the fact that you can live in a building where history was made.

THE BATTLE FOR BEACON HILL

The November 1998 election for Massachusetts governor was one of the closest in the commonwealth's history. Acting Governor Paul Celucci, the Republican candidate, defeated his Democratic opponent, Lt Governor Scott Harshbarger, by less than a two per cent margin. Why was the election so close? Neither candidate was terribly inspiring. Celucci had sort of fallen into the job of governor when William Weld left it 18 months earlier to become US Ambassador to Mexico (which never happened; Weld's nomination was vetoed by Congress). The slight edge Celucci's incumbent status might have given him was eaten away by public doubt about a well-publicised $70,000 personal debt. He was also up against a state that votes overwhelmingly Democratic.

So why didn't Harshbarger, the Democrat, win? To most voters, he seemed incapable of taking a firm stance on any issue, changing positions at a bewildering rate throughout the race. Besides, his campaign wasn't nearly as well-funded as Celucci's. He was only able to spend $3.7 million on nasty, mud-slinging advertising, as opposed to Celucci's whopping $5.7 million. By election day, the public was so fed up with both candidates that the biggest challenge was getting people to come out and vote at all. In the end, less than half of them could be bothered.

THE MOST POPULAR MAYOR SINCE CURLY

When Thomas M Menino was elected mayor in November 1993, he was the first non-Irish man to hold the position in 63 years. During the race, Menino gained popularity for his frank, get-tough attitude to the many challenges facing the city – unemployment, crime, education – and he won by a landslide, carrying 18 of the city's 22 ward districts. And even Menino's most strident critics have to admit that it was results that got him reelected in 1997. During his first term the unemployment rate dropped to almost zero, crime plummeted to its lowest levels in 30 years and school test scores finally began to climb. Menino

The Big Dig

When the Central Artery (the section of the I-93 that runs through the Downtown area) opened in 1959, Boston was in economic crisis. The six-lane elevated highway carried a comfortable 75,000 vehicles a day. No one ever dreamed that by the 1990s the city population would swell to three million people during the working day, nor would they have imagined that the Central Artery would be carrying more than 200,000 vehicles a day. It became all too clear by the late 1980s that something drastic needed to be done. Traffic along the expressway was bumper-to-bumper for ten hours a day and an estimated $500 million had already been wasted in fuel, accidents and late delivery charges.

The solution? What has become known as the 'Big Dig': submersion of the Central Artery below ground; the addition of at least four more lanes of traffic; an extension of I-95 from its present terminus below the Prudential Center to Logan Airport by digging beneath Downtown, South Boston and Boston Harbor; the creation of two new suspension bridges across the Charles River. And all this

seemed to be everywhere: cutting ribbons at new homes for the elderly, marching in the Gay Pride parade, meeting other mayors in Washington and speaking to the city's youth at graduation.

Menino has been criticised for stealing the ideas of others and passing them off as his own. But most Bostonians don't care where the ideas come from, as long as they're effective: the city will probably continue to re-elect Menino as long as he's willing to run. Why fix something that isn't broken?

A DRAMATIC DROP IN CRIME

When city officials decided to make Boston a leading tourist destination, they knew their first job was to make the streets safer for visitors. Crime prevention has been a major priority ever since. In the past decade or so, the Boston Police Department has put more police officers on the street, neighbourhoods all over the city have organised crime watches, and schools have instituted anti-gang programmes. The crime hue-and-cry has also been taken up by state legislators, who have provided Massachusetts with the toughest gun control laws in the country. The results have been pretty spectacular: violent- and property-crime levels are at their lowest in 30 years. Homicide is at its lowest level in 40 years, with a 75 per cent reduction in homicides involving a firearm. Burglary is at its lowest level in the entire history of the state and Boston's juvenile crime prevention strategies have been hailed as a model for the nation. Today, few major metropolitan areas are safer.

FORTIFYING THE CRUMBLING SCHOOLS

It's ironic that Boston was the first American city to establish a public school – Boston Latin Academy – given that it has one of the worst public school systems in the country. And it's doubly ironic, given that there are some 60 colleges and universities in the metropolitan area.

A promise to improve the state of Boston's public schools was what put Menino in office, and his without stopping the flow of daily traffic above ground. In other words, one of the greatest engineering feats of the twentieth century.

Construction began in 1991. It will continue until 2004, when the existing Central Artery will be dismantled and taken away. The total cost of the project is estimated at almost $11 billion, more than 70 per cent of which will be paid up by the US government; the rest will be funded by Massachusetts taxpayers. In 1999 the project entered its peak phase, employing 4,000 workers a day and completing $3 million worth of construction a day. And the Big Dig is still only about half dug.

No one can deny how wonderful it will all be when it's over. For one thing, carbon monoxide emissions in the city will be reduced by some 12 per cent. Neighbourhoods – such as the North End and Charlestown – that have long been isolated by the Central Artery will once again be connected to Downtown. And as soon as the elevated highway is torn down, about 30 acres (12 hectares) of land in the very heart of Boston will open up – most of which has been set aside for parkland. And that's without the 100 or so acres (40.5 hectares) that will be added to Boston Harbor's Spectacle Island using all the displaced earth.

But for most Bostonians, 2004 seems like a very long way away. And when it comes to the Big Dig, they tend to agree with congressman Barney Frank, who complained right at the beginning that it would have been faster and cheaper to raise the city.

administration seems to have risen to the challenge. A new superintendent was hired and an aggressive five-year plan was developed to repair Boston's crumbling schools as well as improve the quality of teaching. Three years into the plan, things are slowly beginning to turn around. The city has sunk $35 million into badly needed renovations; nearly every school has been provided with student computers, raising the total number from 2,000 to 7,000, and teacher contracts have become tougher about the basic skills required for the job. Extracurricular programmes have been added everywhere to keep the schools open after the final bell. And, since 1998, Boston students have been required to pass competency tests in the fourth, eighth and tenth grades (at the ages of 9, 13 and 15). The results so far? Aptitude tests in middle schools are finally on the rise. But even Mayor Menino knows there's a long way to go. If today's high school seniors were to take the tenth grade test, half of them – and many of their teachers – would fail it.

HOMELESSNESS ON THE RISE

In comparison with many other US cities, Boston's homelessness problem has been negligible. Statistics in 1997 placed the total homeless population at about 5,000 – a little under one per cent of the total population. But you need only enter Boston Public Library on a rainy day or pass by the portico of the First Baptist Church on Commonwealth Avenue to realise how inadequate the city's policy is for dealing with the problem.

Long-established shelters such as the Pine Street Inn and St Francis House are always booked to capacity. Though the city added 400 beds in 1997, it seemed to have little effect on the street. And the situation is only going to get worse. The state has set a two-year limit on welfare benefits received by individuals who are not actively searching for jobs. More than 7,100 families will be refused aid as a result. In anticipation of a dramatic rise in homelessness, the city has entered into negotiations with the YMCA and YWCA for more beds. But no one believes these measures will be enough to cover the overflow.

RACISM & GHETTOISATION

Little remains of the racial violence brought on by forced desegregation in the 1970s (*see page 12* **History**). In the end, cross-town busing appears to have been a good thing. It familiarised a whole generation of young Bostonians with the customs and culture of other ethnic groups living in the city. Now grown up, this generation is pretty much free to live where it wants, though there are still ethnic strongholds such as South Boston, Dorchester, Roxbury and Mattapan. But ever so slowly, Boston's neighbourhoods have begun to mix. Today, the South End and Jamaica Plain are two of the most multicultural. It's not at all uncommon to find black families, yuppies, gay couples and Latinos all living in the same house. Just over half of Boston's residents are white, nearly a quarter are black, ten per cent are Hispanic and ten per cent are of Asian descent.

For most ethnic neighbourhoods the biggest problem is no longer racial, it's economic. With moneyed classes pouring back into the city, fringe neighbourhoods are getting younger and wealthier. The result is that working-class families and the elderly are being pushed further away from the centre of city life and the neighbourhoods they once called home are losing their ethnic flavour. So, the North End feels much less Italian these days, the South End less black, Chinatown less Chinese.

A GAMBLE FOR NATIVE AMERICANS

And here we come full-circle back to native occupation. The Wampanoag Indians of Massachusetts may very well be getting their own back. Recent federal legislation exempts reservations of recognised native tribes from standard federal and state laws. This has provided a way for the gambling industry to circumvent prohibition in many states.

Local lingo

They have wicked good frappes with jimmies at that spa next to the packie on Comm Ave.

Understanding a Bostonian can, at times, be hard. Over time, the Hub has developed its own distinctive dialect, so below we've provided you with a brief primer. When it comes to pronunciation, there are a few things to remember: AR sounds are pronounced almost like the British AH (*pahk* for *park*; *cah* for *car*). Ts are pronounced as Ds (*budder* not *butter*). Rs are removed entirely from the ends of words (*buddah* not *budder*) – unless of course the word ends in a vowel, in which case an R is added (*idear* not *idea*). So: 'Pahk the cah ovah by the stoah', 'My motha got this idear in huh head she needs moah buddah'. Got it? Pissa!

Nouns

brew beer, singular or plural. The plural for beer, by the way, is 'some beers': *what did you do last night? We watched the game and a) drank brew b) had some beers.*
frappes milkshakes with ice-cream. They make them at the spa (qv) and the 'e' is silent.
grinder a submarine or french bread sandwich, also made at the spa.
jimmies those little chocolate or multi-coloured sprinkles (hundreds and thousands) on top of a frappe.
packie not a derogatory racist term, but a package or liquor store. Where you can buy brew or some beers. The act is known as a packie run.
quahog (pronounced CO-hog) a type of clam, usually eaten raw.
rotary traffic circle or roundabout (aka suicide circle).
scrod not a type of fish but a size, which is small, usually haddock or cod – whatever's cheaper at the fish market that day.
spas little corner grocery stores with a soda fountain, these days mostly found in South Boston and Jamaica Plain.

Modifiers

killer excellent: *killer brew, man!*
mint excellent: *that place is mint for drinking killer brew.*
pissa excellent: *that place was pissa. We drank killer brew.*
wicked excellent, often used with good: *this brew is wicked good.*

Verbs

bang to make, specifically, right (roger) turns: *bang a roger.*
book to leave in haste: *they booked when they saw the cops.*
hook to make, specifically, left (louie) or U-(euie) turns: *hook a louie.*
pound to drink, often used with back: *that place is mint for pounding back brew.*
skeeve to be grossed out by: *the bathroom in that place really skeeved me.*

Place names

The Cape Cape Cod. There are actually two capes in Massachusetts, but Cape Ann is called the North Shore.
The Combat Zone the once-thriving red-light district, on Washington Street north of Chinatown.
Comm Ave Commonwealth Avenue; also **Mass Ave** Massachusetts Avenue and **Dot Ave** Dorchester Avenue.
The Garden the FleetCenter, which is where Boston Garden used to be before it was torn down.
JP Jamaica Plain (aka Poor Man's Cambridge).
The People's Republic Cambridge (aka Across the River).
The Pike the Massachusetts Turnpike.
The Pru Prudential Tower.
Southie South Boston; **Eastie** East Boston;
Rozzie Roslindale.
The Yard Harvard Yard.

Organisations

The Basement the automatic-markdown bargain basement at Filene's department store.
The Bs the Boston Bruins hockey team.
The Coop the Harvard Cooperative store (nonetheless pronounced like the pen for chickens).
The General Massachusetts General Hospital.
The Sox the Boston Red Sox baseball team (aka the fuckin' Sox).
The T the MBTA subway system (aka the fuckin' T).

Take the case of the Mashantucket Pequots in neighbouring Connecticut. Their casino, Foxwoods, is now the world's largest, bringing in $27 million in revenue a day (*see chapter* **Trips Out of Town**). The state of Connecticut, which receives 25 per cent of Foxwoods' slot machine revenues, couldn't be happier with the arrangement, though gambling is technically illegal there. Meanwhile, the Pequot communities boast the highest per capita incomes in the state, the best-equipped schools and the most technologically advanced public services. The Wampanoag Reservation of Gay Head, Massachusetts (taking its cue from the Pequots) is in the process of proposing a similar relationship with state legislators for the construction of a casino south of Boston. Though the topic is very much still under debate, the thought of a potential $90 million a year in revenue has got many law-makers talking. If all goes well, the Wampanoag who welcomed the *Mayflower* Puritans may very well have something to be thankful for in the end.

Architecture

There's more to Boston than Federal or Victorian red brick: the city's architectural past runs from wooden saltboxes to mirrored skyscrapers.

WHEN SALTBOXES REIGNED & SPARKS FLEW

Imagining Boston as it was in the seventeenth century may require a daytrip to Plymouth or Salem. The original township, located at the tip of the Shawmut Peninsula (today's North End), was a maze of two- and three-storey wooden houses covered in pine clapboards and called saltboxes. It wasn't thoughtless reurbanisation that removed them from Boston's landscape forever; it was fire. The entire North End burned to the ground in 1676, which was one of the main reasons that builders were required by city code to use red brick from then on. As a result, only one example of seventeenth-century wooden architecture remains within Boston's city limits – but at least it's an illustrious one.

The **Paul Revere House** (*see page 56* **Sightseeing**) was originally built in 1680 for a well-to-do merchant named Robert Howard. Though the two-storey, grey clapboard building seems quite modest by modern standards, its leaded diamond panes and extravagant Elizabethan overhang indicate a family of means. During silversmith and famous patriot Paul Revere's residency between 1770 and 1800, a third storey was added to accommodate several of his 16 children, but the nineteenth century saw the house fall into disrepair and it suffered a series of humiliations as a flop-house and souvenir shop. It was saved from the wrecking ball in 1902 by one of Revere's descendants and fully restored to its original two-storey frame; everything but one door of the interior is now reproduction. Today the house stands as a National Historic Landmark and is furnished with period antiques and displays of Revere's remarkable silverwork.

EARLY COLONIAL ERA

Before there were architects, there were housewrights: master builders who followed patterns, usually brought over from England, which they adapted to a family's particular needs. In the early part of the eighteenth century, these patterns were Georgian – the most popular style in England at the time. Unfortunately, most of Boston's early colonial buildings were either destroyed by fire or razed to make way for the building of Government

The much-restored **Paul Revere House** *– one of Boston's oldest.*

Beacon Hill and Boston landmark: Charles Bulfinch's gold-topped **State House**.

Center. However, a few excellent examples – both domestic and public – do remain.

The three-storey brick building adjacent to Revere's house, the **Pierce/Hichborn House** (*see page 56* **Sightseeing**), was built in 1810 for glazier Moses Pierce and later owned by Revere's cousin, a shipbuilder named Nathaniel Hichborn. The contrast of architectural styles is remarkable, given that both houses were built a mere 30 years apart. Organic Tudor gives way to orderly English Renaissance; clapboard to brick; diamond to gridded panes; a cramped winding staircase to one that is extravagantly straight. The Pierce/Hichborn House was painstakingly restored during the 1950s and four of its rooms are now open to the public.

The **Old State House** (*see page 47* **Sightseeing**), another National Historic Landmark, has suffered as many renovations and remodellings as it has had purposes since its construction in 1713. A three-storey brick building topped with a richly ornamented steeple, it first served as the colonial governor's offices – hence the lion and unicorn ornamentation. It was then used as a public meeting place – proclamations and speeches were read from its balcony – until the Revolution, when it became the headquarters of the British Army. The hated lion and unicorn were removed in 1776 – the day the Declaration of Independence was read – and replaced when the Bostonian Society took over in 1881 and restored the building to its original glory.

Today the Old State House serves as the Bostonian Society's museum, where you can view images that chronicle its long history. And, continuing its multi-purpose past, it also serves as the State Street T station.

BULFINCH'S BOSTON

Charles Bulfinch (1763-1844) is America's first architect of note, though he never formally trained as one. Born in Boston to extreme wealth, he travelled extensively in England and Europe and developed a strong affinity for the Greek Revival style of architecture and furnishings that were then in fashion. On his return, he happily designed most of his friends' houses for free. This led to public commissions such as the remodelling of **Faneuil Hall** (*see page 50* **Sightseeing**) and the design of the **State House** (*see page 21*). Today Bulfinch is best known for the development of the Federal style – an Americanisation of Georgian Greek Revival – and his crowning glory outside Massachusetts was the US Capitol building in Washington, DC. Ironically, he died bankrupt from investing in a bad real estate deal.

Not only did Bulfinch design the austere, three-storey brick **Harrison Gray Otis House** for his close friend (*see page 54* **Sightseeing**), but also Otis's second home at 85 Mount Vernon Street and his third at 45 Beacon Street. Completed in 1796, the first of the Otis houses is a masterpiece of symmetry and proportion. Rooms contain false doors, intricately carved fireplaces and shockingly garish colour schemes – all typical of the period. Though the house was nearly condemned in the early 1900s – after suffering for years under various guises as rooming house, bathhouse and

Chinese Laundry – it was rescued in 1916 by the Society for the Preservation of New England Antiquities and painstakingly restored to its original state. Most of the rooms are now open to the public, offering a rare glimpse into colonial life.

The only Bulfinch church left in Boston, **St Stephen's Church** (*see page 58* **Sightseeing**), dates from 1804 and was originally built as the New North Church, a structure that typifies Bulfinch's obsession with Palladian neo-classical themes. Its most notable feature is a campanile-like steeple, domed in copper by Paul Revere, who also cast the bell; the interior boasts beautiful fluted pillars, balconies, Palladian windows and an 1830 pipe organ. Over the years, the church has been raised six feet (1.8 metres), moved back 12 feet (3.65 metres), renovated to resemble an Italian palazzo, and – by order of Cardinal Cushing in 1960 – re-lowered and restored to its original design.

Boston decided it needed a proper State House after the Revolution. A site was chosen for the **State House** (*see page 54* **Sightseeing**) on top of Beacon Hill, so that the building could be seen from anywhere in the city. Bulfinch was commissioned in 1795 and he did not disappoint. The red-brick façade, supported by white Corinthian pillars and flanked by Palladian windows, is considered one of his best works. Over the years the bricks have been painted white and yellow to match the various extensions that were added, but they were mercifully restored to their original colour in 1928. Bulfinch's (now signature) dome was originally clad in white wood shingles; these were later replaced with copper sheeting by Paul Revere in 1802 and painted grey. The present-day 23-carat gold leafing was first applied in 1874.

BEACON HILL: FEDERAL RESERVE

Until the State House was built, Beacon Hill was little more than a brambly pasture criss-crossed by cowpaths. Afterwards, it became Boston's most fashionable neighbourhood. The sunny southern slope was quickly covered in rows of townhouses with reserved, strictly symmetrical façades. And since Bulfinch served as chairman of the Board of Selectmen from 1797 to 1818, it's hardly surprising that the houses he didn't design look very much like those he did. Bulfinch-approved adornments include paned windows, green wooden doors topped with fanlights, wrought-iron grillwork and bay windows – a Boston invention. The preponderance of black shutters you see today are a Victorian afterthought. An anglophile to the end, Bulfinch tried to convince the planners of Beacon Hill to adopt the English style of arranging houses around squares. Only one of these ever materialised, however: Louisburg Square off Mount Vernon Street. Bullfinch would no doubt be gratified to know it has long been the city's most prestigious address.

The best way to experience the hushed Federal atmosphere of Beacon Hill is to wander along its steep, tree-lined streets and make your own discoveries. Louisburg Square is as good a starting point as any. But don't miss the highly coveted free-standing mansions of Mount Vernon Street, or the restrained elegant townhouses of Chestnut Street. For contrast, have a look at tiny Acorn Street – though top real estate now, it was once where the help lived. It's also one of the few cobbled streets left in Boston.

When wandering the streets of Beacon Hill, look out for purple panes in the windows: several bum shipments of glass, in which unstable manganese turned purple as it oxidised, were sent from Hamburg between 1818 and 1824. Though the original purchasers wanted their money back, the windows are now priceless. Needless to say, shameless imitations abound. The real McCoy can be seen at 39-40 Beacon Street, 64 Beacon Street and 24A Chestnut Street.

One of the few Beacon Hill houses you can get inside is the **Charles Nichols House Museum** (*see page 54* **Sightseeing**). Though the exterior is typical Bulfinch, the interior is a cluttered hotchpotch of styles, representing the eccentric taste of Boston's first female landscape architect, Rose Standish Nichols.

VICTORIAN BOSTON

Given all the artifice associated with the Victorian era, it's only fitting that Boston's exquisite Victorian neighbourhoods, the South End and Back Bay, should be entirely the work of human hands. Until 1858 neither neighbourhood existed. 'Back Bay' originally referred to the fetid tidal flats where Bostonians dumped their trash. But over the course of 30 years, the thousands of loads of gravel tipped there every day changed all that and Boston doubled in size.

The South End area was the first to be created, so its architecture tends to follow on from the Federal tradition established on Beacon Hill. Red

The **Harrison Gray Otis House**.

brick and bay windows are in abundance here, and many of the side streets off the main avenues make use of Bulfinch's beloved English square design. Two wonderfully preserved examples can be seen at Union and Rutland Squares. The South End is architecturally different from Beacon Hill in several notable ways, however. The first is the large scale of its townhouses – to accommodate taller nineteenth-century individuals. But high ceilings, soaring windows and mansard roofs also speak of a Victorian preoccupation with verticality. There's no such thing as a ground floor in this upwardly mobile, middle-class neighbourhood. Parlour level is now a half-floor above the street and the kitchen and servants' quarters are a half-floor below it, at garden level.

Back Bay, on the other hand, takes most of its cues from France's Second Empire. This is where Boston's upper class moved when Beacon Hill became crowded with immigrant and black families. The area favours Parisian avenues over English squares and the house façades tend towards marble and sandstone rather than red brick. Small public alleys were added between streets so that deliveries could be made directly to the servants' entrance at the back.

Ostentatious ornamentation is the order of the day. The **Ames-Webster House** (306 Dartmouth Street), for example, sports an elaborate porte cochère that kept the ladies dry as they descended from their carriages. The **Burrage Mansion** (314 Commonwealth Avenue) is a grotesque neo-Gothic confection modelled on the Vanderbilt mansion in Newport, which was itself modelled on Château Chenonçeau in the Loire.

Public architecture in Victorian Boston bears witness to a similar taste for ostentation. The favoured styles were Italian Renaissance, neo-Gothic and neo- Romanesque. One of the first parcels of land set aside in Back Bay was meant to showcase several of Boston's fledgling cultural institutions. It was called Art Square and later renamed Copley Square after the Boston painter. Around it rose great confections of institutional architecture, such as the Museum of Fine Arts (later torn down to make way for what is now the **Fairmont Copley Plaza**, *see page 104* **Accommodation**), the Museum of Natural History (now the **Louis** clothing shop, *see page 163* **Shops & Services**), and the **Boston Public Library** (*see below*).

Though the 1859 façade of **Gibson House** (*see page 65* **Sightseeing**) is rather restrained for its time, the interior offers a rare glimpse of how moneyed Bostonians lived 100 years ago. Its six floors of pure Victoriana are original to the house (a member of the Gibson family lived here until the 1950s) and are now open to the public. For an upstairs/downstairs perspective, take a look at the kitchen and servants' quarters.

Charles McKim's (1847-1909) original wing of the **Boston Public Library** (*see page 62* **Sightseeing**) is usually attributed to the Italian Renaissance style, though he claimed its ornate stone façade was equally inspired by a library in Paris, a temple in Rimini and the Marshall Fields department store in Chicago. Finally completed in 1895, it cost the city a fortune. McKim certainly didn't spare any expense when it came to the library's interior either, commissioning murals by Sargent, paintings by Copley and sculptures by Saint-Gaudens. These days, the McKim wing is well worth a look: its grand staircase, vaulted reading room and enchanting cloistered garden have all been meticulously restored.

RICHARDSON'S BACK BAY

Henry Hobson Richardson (1838-86) was to Victorian Boston what Charles Bulfinch was to Colonial Boston. Though Richardson lived in New York and only built two major buildings in Boston – Trinity Church and the First Baptist Church – Trinity is often cited as the most successful piece of architecture in America.

A student of the Ecole des Beaux Arts in Paris, Richardson was influenced by the heavy lines and solid arcs of medieval French architecture, which he masterfully tempered with delicate Byzantine detailing. Flagrant copies of his neo-Romanesque style abound in Back Bay, including the **New Old South Church** (645 Boylston Street), the **Exeter Theater** (now Waterstones Bookstore at 26 Exeter Street), and the **Flour & Grain Exchange Building** (off Quincy Market). The **Robert Treat Paine House** in suburban Waltham (577 Beaver Street) makes a nice daytrip for Richardson enthusiasts interested in his domestic creations.

Though commissioned in 1872, **Trinity Church** (*see page 62* **Sightseeing**) didn't open until 1877, at a cost of almost four times the original budget – few question the added expense today, however. Exquisite Moorish details abound inside this cruciform church, highlighted by windows and frescoes by John LaFarge and sculptures by Saint-Gaudens. Richardson modelled the central tower after one in Salamanca, though unfortunately it had to be built considerably shorter than the original or the weight of it would have sunk the entire structure into Back Bay. The front porch and minor towers were added 20 years later by Charles McKim.

Some say the **First Baptist Church** (*see page 65* **Sightseeing**) was Richardson's warm-up for the main event. Completed in 1871, it offers a similar mix of stone and wood surfaces. Never one to economise, Richardson commissioned the bas-relief encircling the top of the belltower from Frédéric Auguste Bartholdi – sculptor of the Statue of Liberty.

Richardson's Romanesque **Trinity Church**.

FREDERICK LAW OLMSTED & THE EMERALD NECKLACE

Green space was incorporated into Boston's urban plan from the outset. By 1634, the Puritans had already set aside the 48 acres (19.4 hectares) of **Boston Common** as the perfect place to graze their sheep, train their militia and hang their heretics. In fact, it's the oldest public park in America (*see page 42* **Sightseeing**). The **Public Garden** is also the country's oldest botanical gardens (*see page 64* **Sightseeing**) and practically the first thing built on reclaimed land, in 1837. There was such an uproar when city officials considered selling it off to developers in 1857 that they decided to incorporate even more green space into the design of Back Bay – hence the Commonwealth Avenue mall.

By the time Back Bay had been completed, the Metropolitan Parks Commission (now the Metropolitan District Commission, or MDC) had been established and Frederick Law Olmsted (1822-1903), designer of New York's Central Park and father of landscape architecture in America, had been hired to create an 'Emerald Necklace' – a park system stretching from Boston Common to Jamaica Plain. To Boston Common, the Public Gardens and Commonwealth Avenue, Olmsted added the Back Bay Fens, Olmsted Park, Jamaica Pond, Franklin Park and the Arnold Arboretum (*see page 74* **Sightseeing**). The Charles River Esplanade, although conceived by Olmsted, wasn't developed until well after his death, in the 1930s. And when the Orange Line subway was extended through the South End, the Southwest Corridor Park was added in the 1980s to complete Olmsted's vision.

WELL-INTENTIONED (BUT NOT SO SUCCESSFUL) URBAN RENEWAL

Boston's first attempt to scrape the sky was in 1915, when a 30-storey, neo-Gothic tower was inexplicably added to the **Customs House** (*see page 50* **Sightseeing**). But shortly thereafter the city slumped into a depression and virtually no important construction occurred until the highly controversial urban renewal projects of the 1960s. The first of these was the Prudential Center, whose tower, rising up out of the Boston & Albany railyards, has consistently been voted Boston's ugliest building. Next came **Charles River Park**, a completely anonymous group of apartment buildings for which most of the West End was razed (popularly known as the most regrettable act perpetrated by US public officials in modern history). Colourful Scollay Square was also demolished to make way for Government Center, where 56 acres (23 hectares) were paved over in red brick and 22 city streets were reduced to six. Though many Bostonians have grown used to – and even fond of – these first awkward attempts to modernise the city, the buildings are today most often regarded as the instruction manual of what not to do. But if urban renewal in the 1960s has given rise to other very successful reurbanisation schemes – Quincy Market, for example – then it was probably worth the effort in the end.

With the **Prudential Tower** (*see page 61* **Sightseeing**) Charles Luckman and Associates were going for a sort of Le Corbusier thing, but missed by a mile. The 27-acre (11-hectare) shopping complex at its base had become so dated by the early 1990s that most Bostonians forgot there were shops inside. So the whole thing was gutted and completely redesigned. Nothing much could be done, however, about the 52-storey tower; and anyway, preservationists had grown quite protective of 'The Pru' by then.

The fact that the best architects in the country worked on the **Government Center** complex (*see page 47* **Sightseeing**), completed in 1968, is proof that the road to hell is paved with good intentions – and red brick. IM Pei was responsible for the master plan as well as the infamous Plaza. Kallman, McKinnel and Knowles designed City Hall itself, and Architects Collaborative (Walter Gropius's firm) created the JFK Buildings. Despite such a distinguished pedigree, few Bostonians have taken to Government Center's stark, uninviting planes. In fact, a trust was ultimately established in 1995 to raise funds to renovate the Plaza by adding trees, an enclosed winter garden and an interactive fountain for children.

Some 14 million visitors a year converge on the vast shopping and entertainment complex that is **Quincy Market** (*see page 50* **Sightseeing**). But in 1974 the domed and columned hall, originally designed by Alexander Parris in 1826, was crumbling to the ground. Benjamin Thompson & Associates began a very respectful renovation of the existing market buildings, maintaining much of its cobbled and brick character – and thereby setting the standard by which the rest of the world now converts old buildings to modern use.

The **John Hancock Tower**.

Boston 2000

As if Boston hasn't already got its hands full with the Big Dig, there are several major redevelopment plans in the pipeline for the next millennium. Here's the line-up.

NEW CONVENTION CENTRE

Boston busts at the seams with conventioneers and tourists, so city officials decided in May 1998 to build a new convention and exhibition centre. They promptly signed the paperwork for a $700-million project and broke symbolic ground in the Fort Point Channel area of South Boston (in doing so they got into immediate trouble for the procedure they used in selecting the project's construction management team). How this convention centre will actually look – not to mention which hotel and restaurant chains will be allowed to build around it – is yet to be decided. There's a lot of talk about a river walk along the channel, a new contemporary art museum and lots of condominiums. Residents from South Boston and Fort Point Channel are mounting some formidable resistance to the project: both feel they are being left out of the decision-making process and want it to be slowed down. No one, they claim, wants another Government Center.

THE REURBANISATION OF DOWNTOWN CROSSING

What city officials really mean here is 'we're getting rid of the Combat Zone once and for

BOSTON'S SKYLINE TODAY

Today, most of the city's skyscrapers are located in the Downtown area. That part of town – some 65 acres (26 hectares) – was destroyed by the Great Fire of 1872. Most of the buildings that replaced the colonial architecture were hastily put together; the city then went into decline and virtually nothing was built at all. In terms of historically interesting Downtown buildings, there are only a few. **The Batterymarch** (60 Batterymarch Street) is as nice an art deco building as you're likely to find and **The Winthrop** (276 Washington Street) was Boston's first building to make use of a steel frame.

With the 1980s economic boom came a forest of new skyscrapers, many of which were designed by America's most prominent architects. Three firms in particular have been responsible for shaping modern Boston's appearance: IM Pei Associates, Graham Gund Associates and Philip Johnson.

IM Pei's most spectacular – and controversial – contribution is, of course, the Hancock Tower.

all', to which most people's answer is 'good riddance'. Now that porn videos are easily available at every corner Blockbuster, who needs the couple of rundown peep joints and adult entertainment shops that the once-busy strip on Washington Street offers? Millennium Partners has recently broken ground, with the city's blessing, on a multi-purpose complex near Chinatown including shops, cinemas, a fitness centre, a hotel and luxury condominiums. Plans are also afoot to revamp and re-open Lafayette Place, the boarded-up shopping mall next to Macy's. The BRA (Boston Redevelopment Authority) is confident that redevelopment will put Downtown Crossing and Chinatown back on the map. The inhabitants of Chinatown are less sure of this, fearing that smaller, local businesses won't be able to compete with mall chains. What's clear to everyone is how extremely careful the city must be about over-building. Boston needs a Chinatown far more than it needs another shopping mall.

CROSS-TOWN BUSINESS INITIATIVE

The Dudley Square-City Hospital area, south of Massachusetts Avenue and east of Roxbury, is presently one of the most economically depressed – as well as dangerous – parts of the city. The mayor's office would like to see new life pumped into 'Cross-town', as they've coyly renamed it, in the form of a 'mini-tech corridor', where new computer hardware and software firms might be wooed into opening their urban headquarters or at least branches. The project is meeting with little opposition in the community; there's not much in the way of notable architecture there, anyway. And development would bring more traffic into this traditionally black and Latino neighbourhood. Even if the project drives rents up, it will create thousands more jobs – and reconnect Roxbury to the rest of the city.

NEW BALLPARK FOR THE SOX

Red Sox fans are up in arms about the baseball club's present plans to build a larger park. But Red Sox officials claim that Fenway Park, built in 1912, offers neither enough seating nor sufficient opportunities for off-season events to meet their income objectives. Currently, officials are debating four possible sites for a new park: Charlestown, South Boston (as part of the waterfront redevelopment package), Dudley Square (as part of the Cross-town redevelopment package) or the existing site – that is, tearing Fenway Park down and rebuilding it more or less where it is. The fact that the Sox got into the 1998 playoffs only complicates the issue (*see chapter* **Sport & Fitness**). The more interest in the game, the more fans will be divided over whether Fenway Park should be saved for posterity or abandoned for a more comfortable venue.

But he is also responsible for the new wing of the **Museum of Fine Arts** (*see page 89* **Museums & Galleries**), **Harbor Towers** on the waterfront (off Atlantic Avenue), the master plan for the **Christian Science Center** (175 Huntington Avenue), the **John F Kennedy Library** (Columbia Point, Dorchester), and **MIT's Media Lab** (on the MIT campus, Massachusetts Avenue, Cambridge).

According to IM Pei, the big idea behind the severe rhomboid shape and 62 storeys of the **John Hancock Tower** (*see page 62* **Sightseeing**) is that it doesn't overwhelm Copley Square's older buildings because only a sliver of it shows when viewed from the square. But even the broad sides don't seem terribly monolithic, their mirrored glass reflecting images of Back Bay and the sky. Though instantly more popular than 'The Pru' with most Bostonians, the Hancock did not escape controversy. While it was still under construction in 1973, its windows began popping out and crashing into the street below because of a structural flaw. Every single one of its 10,344 panes had to be replaced – at an additional cost of $8 million. Trinity Church was also damaged during the tower's construction and the resulting law suit has yet to be fully resolved.

Philip Johnson's most important – and controversial – contribution to Boston architecture is the 1972 addition to the **Boston Public Library**. A guru of postmodernism, Johnson also master minded **500 Boylston Street** and **International Place** (on Atlantic Avenue), which is said to contain more Palladian windows than the whole of Italy.

Graham Gund is most noted for his 1978 renovation – also controversial – of the Mount Vernon Church into condominiums called **Church Court** (490 Beacon Street). Other Gund buildings include the gaudily gilded **75 State Street** office complex, the more sedate **Boston Ballet** building (19 Clarendon Street) and the **Inn at Harvard** (*see page 113* **Accommodation**).

Literary Boston

The city's literary luminaries, past and present.

When American literature finally reached world attention in the nineteenth century, many of its authors – Hawthorne, Melville, Emerson, Dickinson – hailed from Massachusetts. This was not by accident. Boston's superb libraries, bookshops and cultural institutions had already earned it the sobriquet 'the Athens of America'. Here are just a few of the authors who walked among its hallowed temples, from Puritan poet Ann Bradstreet to today's Poet Laureate Robert Pinsky.

Nathanial Hawthorne (1804-64).

THE PURITAN POETS

The Puritans who first settled the Massachusetts Bay Colony had little use for literature. Their strict standards of moral conduct did not include wasting time on imaginative pursuits. Anything written down needed to have a purpose. It's not surprising then, that most of the prose coming out of the New World in the seventeenth century took the form of personal journals, histories or sermons.

Fine examples of all three do, nonetheless, exist. William Bradford (1590-1657), *Mayflower* Puritan and second Governor of Massachusetts, kept a detailed account of those first harsh years which was eventually published in 1856 as *Of Plymouth Plantation 1620-1647*. The first governor, John Winthrop (1588-1649), also recorded his impressions in *The History of New England*, which was also published posthumously in 1790. The most successful author of his day, however, was Cotton Mather (1663-1728). Credited for having penned an astonishing 459 histories, treatises and sermons, Mather is most respected for his chronicle of the American Protestant movement, *Magnalia Christi Americana* (1702), though he is best remembered for fanning the flames of the Salem witchcraft hysteria.

There were a handful of early Puritans who, in complete secrecy, did try their hand at verse. Anne Bradstreet's (1612-72) poems fell into the hands of a cousin while she was visiting England and he published them without her knowledge as *The Tenth Muse Lately Sprung up in America* (1650). An authorised volume with her corrections, *Poems* (1678), was eventually published after her death. Edward Taylor (c.1642-1729) was not known as a poet in his lifetime, either. Though he did publish a few elegies while he ministered to his congregation and raised his family, the majority of his more domestic and spiritual musings were not published until 1937. The only poet, in fact, whose work was published while he was alive was Michael Wigglesworth (1631-1705). Curiously, his treatise on Calvinistic theory, *Day of Doom* (1662) – a sort of *Paradise Lost* of the New World – was enormously popular; one copy is said to have been printed for more than 36 colonists living in New England.

THE COLONIAL ERA

The popularity of Wigglesworth indicates how hungry early colonists were for reading material that wasn't strictly utilitarian. Yet Massachusetts was virtually devoid of what we would consider literature throughout much of the eighteenth century. Puritanism had too firm a hold on the colony during the first half of the century, and gaining independence from England became the preoccupation of the second half.

What little literature was read by Bostonians was imported from either England or continental Europe. A notable exception to all this is Royall Tyler (1757-1826). Born in Boston, educated at Harvard and a veteran of the Revolution, Tyler's chief occupation was law, which he practised and taught in Massachusetts, Maine and Vermont. What he's best remembered for, however, is authorship of the first theatrical comedy ever produced in America, *The Contrast* (1787). Writing under the pseudonym of Spondee, Tyler also wrote satirical verse, a novel entitled *The Alergrine Captive* (1797) and a series of letters known as *Yankey in London* (1809).

If Boston legend is to be believed, another literary luminary of the colonial era was Mother Goose. Elizabeth Foster (d.1758), the second wife of Isaac Goose, is credited locally with writing *The Tales of Mother Goose* (1719), the stories and nursery rhymes with which she entertained her own ten children and the ten Isaac already had. None of this is certain, however; nor is it even certain that her final resting place is the Granary Burial Ground, though the grave of Isaac's first wife – Mary Goose – is often pointed out as hers by local tour guides.

THE NEW ENGLAND RENAISSANCE

After the revolution, many Americans – and many Bostonians in particular – turned their attention to the creation of a new cultural life for their brand new country. In 1807, a group of wealthy Beacon Hill Brahmins took it upon themselves to establish 'a reading room, a library, a museum and a laboratory'. They called it the **Athenaeum**, after a temple devoted to the goddess Athena where poets converged to read their works. The Athenaeum served as a model for **Boston Public Library**, which was the first in the country when it opened. In turn, its magnificent art collection formed the nucleus of Boston's **Museum of Fine Arts** (*see page 90* **Museums & Galleries**). And most importantly, it became a meeting place in Boston for anyone with literary ambitions. By 1811, the Athenaeum was already publishing the influential *North American Review* and, over the course of the century, claimed Daniel Webster, Ralph Waldo Emerson, Henry Wadsworth Longfellow and Amy Lowell as members.

In 1829, Timothy Harrington Carter opened the Old Corner Bookstore at the corner of Washington Street and School Street downtown. It quickly became another locus for Boston's fledgling literary scene – especially between 1845 and 1865, when it was owned by William Tichnor and Jamie Fields. The latter dedicated themselves to publishing local authors such as Emerson, Longfellow, Oliver Wendell Holmes and James Russell Lowell. They were also the first to bring European authors such as Charles Dickens to America, the first to publish literary magazines such as *The Atlantic Monthly* and the first to pay their authors royalties on sales rather than a flat fee.

When the local literati weren't reading at the Athenaeum or gossiping over the stacks at the Old Corner Bookstore, they were probably lunching at the **Parker House** hotel (*see page 107* **Accommodation**). Many of Boston's best-known writers – the men, anyway – met there on the last Saturday afternoon of every month. This Saturday Club (as it became known) counted among its members Hawthorne, Emerson, Longfellow, Holmes and John Greenleaf Whittier; and it was probably over Parker House's famous rolls that *The Atlantic Monthly* magazine was first launched.

HAWTHORNE, MELVILLE & DICKINSON

One of the first great authors to come out of the New England Renaissance was Nathaniel Hawthorne (1804-64). A native of Salem, Hawthorne is said to have changed the spelling of his last name to distance himself from his infamous ancestor, Judge John Hathorne, who presided over the 1692 witch trials. He was encouraged by his family to attend Bowdoin College instead of entering the family business because of his delicate health. Here he developed the passion for reading and writing that would sustain him for the rest of his life.

Living as a recluse in early adulthood allowed him to absorb the local history and legends that resulted in his first literary success, *Twice Told Tales* (1837) – a success due to warm reviews from Hawthorne's Bowdoin classmate Henry Wadsworth Longfellow and from Edgar Allen Poe (who, by the way, was born in Boston). Today, Hawthorne's novel *The Scarlet Letter* (1850) is considered one of the finest in American literature. In his own day, however, Hawthorne was hard-pressed to support his family. Financial need drove him to manoeuvre himself into a political appointment at the Salem Customs House, though – as it turned out – he didn't prove particularly well suited to government work. His drafting of *The Scarlet Letter* was nearly jeopardised by a politically-motivated dismissal from his post for alleged malfeasance. During the time he lived in Concord, his home became a gathering place for

Herman Melville (1819-91).

many of the area's Transcendentalist writers, although he never fully endorsed their ideas.

To escape the Customs House controversy, Hawthorne fled with his family to the village of Lenox in western Massachusetts, where he wrote *The House of the Seven Gables* (1857) and made the acquaintance of Herman Melville (1819-91) who was living in the nearby township of Pittsfield. Melville had achieved moderate literary success in New York with the publication of his first two novels of the sea, *Typee* (1846) and *Omoo* (1847). His close friendship with Hawthorne so inspired him to finish *Moby Dick* (1851) that he dedicated the novel to him. Unfortunately, *Moby Dick* wasn't recognised as the quintessential American novel until the 1920s – well after Melville's death.

Also writing in western Massachusetts at the time was Emily Dickinson (1830-86), acknowledged today as the greatest American poet of the nineteenth century. Dickinson lived her entire life in Amherst (*see chapter* **Trips Out of Town**). She never married and spent many of her later years in complete seclusion. Though only seven of her poems were published in her lifetime, she wrote more than 1,800 – only 24 of them with titles. Dickinson was inspired by the rhythm of Protestant hymns and Emerson's Transcendentalism. Though her primary subject was always herself, there are a number of love poems where the object of her affection remains unknown.

THE NEW ENGLAND TRANSCENDENTALISTS

The popularity of Unitarianism in the mid-nineteenth century, combined with the theories of Kant and the German Transcendentalists, gave rise to a hybrid form of Transcendentalism in New England that was liberally dosed with Hinduism and Confucianism. According to the New England Transcendentalists, spirituality was as essential to the human body as food, intuition was more important than intellectual knowledge and the purest ideas came from reason and not sensual discovery.

Their chief prophet was Ralph Waldo Emerson (1807-82). Born in Boston to a long line of Unitarian ministers, Emerson was elected class poet at Harvard (after six other students declined the honour). The journals he kept there, combined with his

Writers in the house

The Boston area boasts more literary sites than just about any other US city. An hour's train ride to Concord will allow you to tour the homes of **Hawthorne**, **Emerson** and **Alcott**, or follow in the footsteps of **Thoreau** around Walden Pond. If you prefer to stay in town, you can view rare books at the **Athenaeum** (America's first lending library), and then see even more rare books at **Boston Public Library**. You can even make pilgrimages to the final resting places of many of Boston's literary giants.

Writers' houses

Emerson's House

Ralph Waldo Emerson Memorial House, 28 Cambridge Turnpike, Concord (1-978 369 2236). **Open** *Apr-Oct* 10am-4.30pm Thur-Sat; 2-4.30pm Sun. **Admission** $3-$4.50. **No credit cards**.

Emerson and his family lived here from when the writer was in his thirties until his death in 1882. Though the house is unremarkable architecturally, it was the scene of many a Sunday lunch that included the likes of Hawthorne, Thoreau and Alcott. The museum's guides do a nice job of bringing Emerson to life by referring to him as Ralph and telling gossipy stories as though he were a distant cousin – which, for some of them, he is. *See also chapter* **Trips Out of Town**.

Hawthorne's House

The Old Manse, 269 Monument Street at North Bridge, Concord (1-978 369 3909). **Open** *late Apr-late Oct* 10am-5pm Mon-Sat; noon-5pm Sun. **Admission** $3-$5.50. **Credit** MC, V.

Originally built by Ralph Waldo Emerson's grandfather in 1770, The Old Manse was where Emerson wrote his first book, *Nature*. In 1842, Nathaniel Hawthorne and his new bride Sophia Peabody took up residence and stayed for three years. The house contains memorabilia from both the Emersons and the Hawthornes. *See also chapter* **Trips Out of Town**.

Longfellow's House

Longfellow National Historic Monument, 105 Brattle Street, Cambridge (876 4491). Harvard T. **Closed for refurbishment**.

A wedding present from Longfellow's second father-in-law, the magnificent Craigie house was also where George Washington was headquartered during the Revolutionary War. Longfellow lived, wrote and hosted lavish literary get- togethers here for 45 years. The décor is much the same as when he died here in 1882. Currently closed for renovation, the house is due to re-open sometime in 2000. *See also p81* **Sightseeing**.

Louisa May Alcott's House

Orchard House, 399 Lexington Road, Concord (1-978 369 3909). **Open** *late Apr-late Oct* 10am-5pm Mon-Sat; noon-5pm Sun. **Admission** $3.50-$5.50. **Credit** MC, V.

Little Women comes to life in this house where Louisa May Alcott penned the semi-autobiographical novel sitting at her bedroom window. Built by her eccentric Transcendentalist father, Amos Bronson Alcott, Orchard House is actually two eighteenth-century homes joined together. Many of its quirky angles and corners are adorned with artwork by Louisa's sister, May, who was freely encouraged to draw on the walls. *See also chapter* **Trips Out of Town**.

extensive travels in England and Europe, provided the inspiration for his first book, *Nature* (1836), in which he espoused the belief that nature serves as a metaphor for the human mind. Emerson is most noted, however, for his collections of *Essays* (1841, 1844) on 'Self-Reliance', 'Compensation' and the 'Oversoul'.

Though it took 12 years to sell the initial 500 copies of *Nature*, the book resonated immediately with a diverse group of writers who had formed the Transcendental Club in 1836. Usually meeting at Emerson's house, the club produced *Dial* (1840-42), a quarterly of poetry and essays dedicated to explaining their views. Among *Dial*'s most noted contributors were Margaret Fuller (journalist, critic and feminist), Amos Bronson Alcott (founder of Boston's controversial Temple School, founder of the short-lived Utopian community Fruitlands and father of Louisa May), George Ripley (founder of the Utopian artist's community Brook Farm), Emerson, and Henry David Thoreau (1817-62).

Thoreau, who lived in Emerson's house on and off, was probably the best literary artist of the group. The two years, two months and two days that Thoreau spent in isolation on Walden Pond resulted in *Walden* (1854), a book that has remained more or less in print ever since its publication. A brief jail sentence for refusing to pay his taxes (an Abolitionist protest against the expansion of slavery into western territories) gave rise to Thoreau's most famous essay, *Civil Disobedience* (1849).

THE CAMBRIDGE POETS

The Transcendentalists were not nearly as popular in their day, however, as a group of writers that became known as the Cambridge Poets. Primarily well-heeled academics, the Cambridge Poets were associated with Harvard in some way and influenced by the work of English Romantic poets such as Wordsworth and Coleridge. Chief among them was Henry Wadsworth Longfellow (1807-82). Though Longfellow's singsong verse has fallen out of fashion, he was the first literary artist in America to support himself completely by his own pen (and the first to earn a place in Poet's Corner in Westminster Abbey). His enormous following gave him the power of myth-making. No one had ever heard of Paul Revere until he penned 'Paul Revere's Ride' in 1863.

Thoreau's Walden Pond

Walden Pond State Reservation, 924 Walden Street, Route 126, Concord (1-978 369 3254). **Open** *park* 7am-dusk daily; *shop* 10am-6pm Mon-Fri. **Admission** £2.25. **No credit cards**.

The 62-acre (25-ha) pond has become a little tatty from the visits of so many tourists over the years, but is still well worth the trip for Thoreau enthusiasts. Though the re-creation of Thoreau's tiny cabin at the main entrance is not on the original site, a marker along the wooded paths encircling the pond indicates where he lived and wrote for two years, two months and two days. *See also chapter* **Trips Out of Town**.

Literary institutions

Boston Athenaeum

See p90 **Museums & Galleries** *for listings.*

Only the first two floors of the Athenaeum are open to the public, but it's worthwhile arranging a special tour. Buried among the 750,000 volumes here are some of the rarest books in America: the King's Chapel library (a gift of William III in 1698), George Washington's personal library, and imprints from the Confederate States, to name but a few.

Boston Public Library

See p62 **Sightseeing** *for listings.*

The building itself is an architectural masterpiece and registered national landmark (*see p22* **Architecture**). Its Italian Renaissance rooms and galleries contain work by all the leading artists of the nineteenth century including Sargent and Saint-Gaudens. Among the library's six million books are rare first editions by many of the authors mentioned in this chapter.

Old Corner Bookstore

1 School Street, at Washington Street. State Street T.

This unassuming little brick building opened as a bookstore in 1829. In its heyday, the building was the literary nexus of the city and published, under the ownership of Ticknor and Fields, the work of such local luminaries as Emerson, Holmes, Longfellow and Lowell – not to mention the *Atlantic Monthly* and *North American Review*.

Final resting places

Mount Auburn Cemetery

580 Mount Auburn Street, Cambridge (547 7105). Harvard Square T, then 71, 73 bus. **Open** 8am-5pm daily. **Admission** free.

America's oldest garden cemetery – and many say its most beautiful. Among the 174 acres (70.5ha) here, are the graves of Henry Wadsworth Longfellow, Oliver Wendell Holmes, Charles Eliot Norton, publishers Little and Brown and even Fanny Farmer (of cookbook fame). Other arts are equally well represented by Winslow Homer, Charles Bulfinch and Isabella Stewart Gardiner. *See p82 chapter* **Sightseeing**.

Sleepy Hollow Cemetery

Bedford Street, off Route 62, Concord (1-978 318 3233/tours 1-978 369 3642). **Open** 7am-dusk daily.

The archetypal spooky-looking New England graveyard, where you'll find the gravestones of Nathaniel Hawthorne, Ralph Waldo Emerson, Henry David Thoreau and Louisa May Alcott. To reach them, enter the cemetery through the Pritchard Gate; 'Author's Ridge' is well marked and the location of the stones is clear from all the flowers left by local English students.

Louisa May Alcott (1832-88).

The same applied to the love affair between Priscilla and John Alden in 'the Courtship of Miles Standish' (1858) and to 'The Song of Hiawatha' (1855) which was not even based on American Indian lore but on the Finnish epic *Kalevala*.

Often seen at Longfellow's magnificent house at 105 Brattle Street were his Cambridge cronies Oliver Wendell Holmes and James Russell Lowell. Holmes (1809-94) was a master of light verse. His 'Breakfast Table' pieces for the *Atlantic Monthly* (1858) combined fictional settings, characters and dialogue with poems and essays. (It was Holmes, in fact, who suggested the name for the magazine). A graduate of Harvard Medical School, Holmes also practised medicine – when he wasn't writing occasional poems or dedication speeches. Though James Russell Lowell (1819-91) was actually suspended from Harvard in his senior year (he spent the time with Emerson and Thoreau in Concord), he ultimately returned there to take Longfellow's professorship when the poet retired to write full-time. In the interceding years, he wrote for the *National Anti-Slavery Standard* in Philadelphia, became the first editor of the *Atlantic Monthly* and co-edited the *North American Review* with Charles Eliot Norton.

Also influenced by the English Romantics (but not considered nearly as urbane as the Cambridge Poets) were John Greenleaf Whittier (1807-92) and William Cullen Bryant (1794-1878). Whittier's somewhat sentimental and homespun poems became the texts for several hymns. Bryant was regarded as the leading American poet of the 1830s, though his best-known poem, 'Thanatopsis' (1815), is one of his first. Bryant's popularity eventually garnered him the position of the New York *Evening Post*'s most influential editor.

WOMEN WRITERS

There were other women besides Emily Dickinson writing in Massachusetts in the nineteenth century. Some say that Amy Lowell (1874-1925) was responsible for popularising Ezra Pound's Imagist style in the USA. Though remembered today for little more than being the black sheep of her prominent Boston family (her many social eccentricities included cigar-smoking), her collection of poems *What's O'Clock* (1925) won her a posthumous Pulitzer prize.

Concord native Louisa May Alcott (1832-88) achieved worldwide fame for her novel *Little Women* (1868) and its sequel *Little Men* (1871). The fact that she had no formal education (she was tutored at home by both Emerson and Thoreau) did not stop her from making a career of novel writing. When Alcott wasn't in residence at her Louisburg Square home on Beacon Hill, she was travelling the world.

Another part-time Beacon Hill writer was Sarah Orne Jewett. Dividing her time between Boston and her native Maine, she wrote stories about the New England character seen from its most attractive side. Jewett is today associated with the Local Color Movement that included authors such as Willa Cather (a great friend and frequent visitor to Boston) and Harriet Beecher Stowe.

BANNED IN BOSTON

If Boston was the 'Hub of the Solar System' in the nineteenth century, it became the epicentre of the literary Dark Ages in the early twentieth century. When it came down to it, Boston's Puritan fabric did not take to the Flapper Era. A city censor was hired by the Mayor's Office in 1904. Using laws and statutes for decency that dated back to the eighteenth century, the city censor forbade publication of any morally corrupt books and plays for an astonishing 40 years. These included works by Ernest Hemingway, Sinclair Lewis and Eugene O'Neill. Lillian Hellman's award-winning play, *The Children's Hour* (1935), wasn't even allowed to open in Boston because it contained lesbian undertones. It's not surprising that the focus of writing and publishing in America shifted to New York; that Bostonian Henry James moved to England and became a British citizen; and that the most celebrated Boston author of the time was Robert McCloskey, famous for his children's book set in the Public Garden, *Make Way for the Ducklings* (1941).

By the 1950s, the city's universities were the sole remaining bastions of artistic life. Writers like Wallace Stevens and TS Eliot found their voices at Harvard, under the tutelage of teachers such as George Santayana. But then they moved on to more welcoming literary climes. Sylvia Plath and Anne Sexton were both students at Boston University in the late 1950s, part of Pulitzer prize-winning poet Robert Lowell's graduate poetry workshop.

This university-based literary scene remains much the same today. Boston University, for example, boasts Nobel Prize-winning authors Saul Bellow, Elie Weisel and Robert Pinsky. There are also literary greats living within a stone's throw: John Updike lives in Beverly, Norman Mailer in Provincetown. But the city is no longer the great literary hub it was in the nineteenth century.

Campus Culture

'The Boston gig has been cancelled. I wouldn't worry about it though, it's not a big college town.' (A manager to his band, 'This is Spinal Tap'.)

Of Boston's 550,000 residents, an estimated 250,000 are students: in other words, no town's more of a college town than Beantown. Yet without paying close attention, a visitor to the city might not even notice the academic glut. Most of the city's campuses – including the two largest, Boston University and Northeastern – blandly blend into the urban scene. Students who live off campus tend to dwell in inexpensive ghettoes not found on most tourist maps, while those inhabiting campus residences move ghostlike between dorm hall, dining hall and lecture hall – with frequent pit stops at the beer hall.

But even while tucked into ivory towers across the city's landscape, students leave their mark on every aspect of Boston life. The arts community relies on cutting-edge campus perspectives; the economy feeds on an estimated $10 billion and 125,000 jobs generated by students each year; nightlife falls flaccid during exam periods; and city officials shamelessly appropriate bragging rights from top institutions such as Harvard and the Massachusetts Institute of Technology (MIT).

Real Bostonians know that student life in Boston is a double-edged sword, however: together with spending and brain power come reckless partying, crowds and higher rents. Amid housing

Autumn in leafy **Harvard Yard**.
For the university, see page 34.

MIT*'s Lewis Music Library.* *See page 34.*

and parking shortages, late-night noise and festering trash and heavy traffic, some neighbourhood leaders have started to complain. In the Allston-Brighton area – a popular student neighbourhood seemingly as densely populated as New York City – permanent residents have tried to get rid of student 'party houses' by demanding higher levels of on-campus student housing. Advocates argue that the area's disproportionate number of pizza joints, bars and cheap furniture stores cater nicely to one-year renters, but not to families settled in for the long haul. The students, meanwhile, remain comfortably oblivious to their impact on the city, fretting more about parties and mid-term exams than the state of their temporary homes.

What students and residents both know is that superimposed onto the normal change of city seasons are the four-year, two-semester cycles of scholarship. In Boston, the new year begins in September – with the annual influx of bright-eyed freshmen – and ends in June – with the purging of sullied futons and the dispensing of diplomas.

It's a process that dates back to the benefaction of Harvard College in 1636 (in appropriately scholastic-sounding Cambridge). The cycle today – with 35 degree-granting colleges in Boston alone – thrives stronger than ever. Several US presidents, including John F Kennedy, sought their education in Boston; future kings, presidents and leaders undoubtedly still roam the city's campuses, which forever abound with Nobel Prize laureates, top research facilities and some of the brightest students anywhere.

AUTUMN: THE INVASION BEGINS

Every **1 September**, sure as a riptide and loaded with flotsam, moving vans flood into Boston, choking city streets and skirting mountains of trash left over from summer renters. Professional movers refer to the period as 'the Rush'; residents think of it more as 'the Hell'. Music blares, drivers seethe and parents weep ('baby's finally left us'): the cycle begins anew.

Because a large percentage of Boston's students come from outside the state (and even the country), the next few weeks bring widespread disorientation. Like all visitors, out-of-state students marvel at the brashness of Bostonians, while fretting secretly about the next four years of incomprehensible locals, harsh drinking laws and angry drivers. During the fall season especially, freshmen seem to stumble around in large, menacing clusters.

Geography is only one component of the colleges' remarkable diversity. Although the city of Boston is generally plagued with tribalism, the campuses manage to seek (and find) students from all walks of life who live together in harmony. Boston University alone enrolls more foreign students than any other American university – an estimate of more than 4,400 from 138 countries in 1998 – though critics claim that foreigners are recruited because they're more able than their American counterparts to pay the full tuition fees. Whatever the case, Boston benefits from these microcosmic campuses and much of the city's international renown stems from the schools' ability to recruit from afar.

With the changing colours of the foliage comes the wane of queues in poster and book stores – the first sign of the fall season's progression. In their first few months, freshmen students might rush fraternities, find and desert the love of their life, or learn the hard way that tequila shots and history papers don't mix. Other perennial fall student activities take place in October: tens of thousands of students gather at Hynes Convention Center for '**Collegefest**,' a marketing orgy for companies targeting college-aged consumers; and the **Head of the Charles Regatta** (*see page 40* **Boston by Season**), a major annual rowing event, heralds the arrival of still more student visitors from around New England.

WINTER: SNOWBALLS & THEATRICALS

Following the first substantial snowfall each winter, Harvard freshmen swarm Harvard Yard for a free-for-all snowball fight. For these students, the event, together with the annual **Harvard-Yale football game** (on the Saturday before Thanksgiving), marks the start of winter in Boston. 'The Game,' as it's known, is guaranteed not to impress, but enough spirited, drunken alumni make the event worth experiencing. For other students, winter arrives with **Thanksgiving**, which for the rest of the city means airport chaos and four days off, as many students take their first trip home.

Boston takes it for granted that the city's students are its most ardent community volunteers; young idealists help out at shelters, inner-city schools and non-profit organisations. This activism reaches a peak during the period prior to **Christmas**. On campus, meanwhile, the holiday spirit never truly breaks through the tension surrounding **first-term's final exams**, except at haughtily obstinate Harvard, where exams take place after the holiday break.

Boston's long winter season is the best time to take advantage of the students' artistic endeavours. Throughout the year, dozens of top-name performers strut their stuff in campus theatres.

Berklee College, one of the best schools in the world for aspiring jazz and rock musicians, sponsors superb concerts in its performance hall; Harvard's majestic **Sanders Theater** hosts some of the city's best world, folk and jazz concerts, as well as the **Harvard-Radcliffe Orchestra**; and the **New England Conservatory** also presents prodigious classical performances.

Boston University's in-residence **Huntington Theater Company** and Harvard's **Loeb Drama Center** (which houses the American Repertory Theatre Company) offer some of the best theatre in the city; Emerson College and Tufts University also produce excellent student plays. In February, Harvard's legendary **Hasty Pudding Theatricals**, the oldest drag show in America, present their 'Man and Woman of the Year Awards' to two bewildered movie stars (*see chapter* **The Performing Arts**).

For fans of the visual arts, the **School for the Museum of Fine Arts**' annual **December Sale** offers an extraordinary chance to snap up works by up-and-coming artists. You can check out the top notch museums and galleries tucked into the larger campuses at the same time: MIT's **List Visual Arts Centre** and Harvard's **Fogg Art Museum** are especially notable (*see chapter* **Museums & Galleries**).

Boston residents also tend to forget that students run some of the best radio stations in the city; spin toward the bottom end of the dial to hear cutting-edge stations such as WERS (88.9FM), WMBR (88.1FM) and WZBC (90.3FM). As winter trudges on, note how these stations devote more airtime than usual to Boston's favourite sport, hockey, and to its favourite hockey event, 'the Beanpot'.

Hockey is the only sport played well by almost all of Boston's major colleges; the **Beanpot Tournament**, deriving its name from the winner's trophy, brings to the (icy) surface a full term's worth of hostile rivalries. Northeastern, Harvard and the particularly contentious Boston University and Boston College teams compete for two weekends in some of the most exciting on-ice action in town.

MIT doesn't really play hockey. Then again, students at that formidable technical school tend to be perpetually stronger in mind than body and most don't play much of anything – except pranks. In that arena, though, no school's finer. The university's wily brainiacs have been known to drop pianos off rooftops (in the name of science, of course), defile the John Harvard Statue and other landmarks at local colleges and slide dorm furniture across the frozen Charles River. In one legendary prank during a break in the 1982 Harvard-Yale game, a huge weather balloon erupted from the centre of the field and swelled to a six-foot diameter before bursting with talcum powder. Players and fans stood aghast and amazed; the prank literally had MIT written all over it. To learn more about this tradition of trickery, visit the Hall of Hacks at the **MIT Museum** (*see page 95* **Museums & Galleries**).

SPRING: AND A YOUNG STUDENT'S FANCY TURNS TO LUST

Springtime in Boston arrives in an orgasmic burst, with one perfect day melting away several months' worth of stress and dreariness. Naturally, mating and dating in Boston are also shaped by the collegiate hordes, although students tend not to fraternise beyond their campuses. Representatives of the state's all-female schools (for example Smith and Wellesley) have traditionally mixed with Harvard men, though in the past years they've been lured away by the (more or less) all-male MIT. Tolerant attitudes on all campuses foster active gay and lesbian student communities.

Come the weekend, students find each other at campus parties, as well as in Allston-Brighton bars, the **Lansdowne Street clubs** (*see chapter* **Nightlife**), Harvard Square (especially the Crimson Sports Grille and the Hong Kong restaurant), the Faneuil Hall/Quincy Market area and at scattered bars downtown (near Emerson College and Suffolk University) and everywhere else.

Getting in a few rounds at the aptly named **Thirsty Scholar**. *See page 34.*

Graduate students tend toward mellower pubs such as the **Thirsty Scholar** in Somerville (*see page 124* **Pubs & Bars**), while wealthy foreign students (referred to as 'Eurotrash', even those of Asian and Middle Eastern descent) mingle in dark, trendy lounges such as Aria, in the Theater District and M-80.

Many of Boston's strict regulations about alcohol (*see page 115* **Pubs & Bars**) can be blamed on the city's students, who insistently flaunt their underage drinking. The city has cracked down particularly hard since 1997, when an 18-year-old MIT freshman drank himself to death at a fraternity party.

These efforts are unlikely to curb 'senioritis' though – the city-wide phenomenon that occurs when final-year students completely destroy all the brain cells they've been nurturing for four long years. **Spring Break**, a week-long holiday in March or April, sends students dashing off to warmer, gentler locales to screw, drink and smoke themselves silly.

By early May, **graduation fever** falls over the city and the next five weeks bring yet another deluge of (still weeping) relatives. Universities deck out their campuses to create an impression of tuition money well spent, hotel rates soar and streets are sometimes closed off to accommodate alumni reunions and high-powered commencement (graduation) speakers.

Graduation season may be Boston's most glorious. Well-wishing wisdom emanates from campuses across the city and, as is so often said, the ceremonies mark a beginning more than an end. For Boston, each June marks the end of the scholastic cycle, but also the beginning of summer (and summer school) and the rejuvenation of the churning, temporary population. Meanwhile, local industries, aware that Boston serves as receptacle to a worldwide brain drain, neatly pluck the fresh crop of learned scholars as, once again, the city reaps the rewards of academia – for better or worse, Boston's most important export.

The colleges

The following are the basic facts about some of Boston's largest colleges and universities:

Boston College

40 Commonwealth Avenue, Chestnut Hill, MA 02467 (552 8000).

Founded in 1863, BC is one of the oldest Jesuit universities in the USA. Boasting top athletic programs and high-quality academics, BC hosts more than 13,000 undergrads and graduate students on its 115-acre (46-ha) campus, which is located in the suburbs six miles (9.7km) from downtown Boston.

Boston University

930 Commonwealth Avenue, Boston, MA 02215 (734 0015).

BU is the largest university in Boston and the third largest independent university in the United States. With more than 30,000 students from all 50 US states and 135 other countries, BU offers a range of degrees and programs, as well as 52,000sq ft of bathroom space in its largest residences. It sprawls along Commonwealth Avenue, west of downtown Boston. Famous alumni include Dr Martin Luther King Jr, Geena Davis, Nina Totenberg and Jason Alexander. Annual tuition costs, including fees, room and board, exceed $31,000.

Emerson College

420 Beacon Street, Boston, MA 02116 (824 8600).

The nation's only four-year college devoted to the study of the performing arts and communication, Emerson links education with hands-on experience in studios, editing booths and workshops. Its radio station, WERS (88.9 FM), consistently earns awards as a college programme. Tuition alone costs $17,376 a year.

Harvard University

Massachusetts Hall, Harvard Yard, off Massachusetts Avenue, Cambridge, MA 02138 (495 1000).

The oldest and most prestigious university in America, enrolling about 6,600 undergrads (in Harvard College) and more than 11,000 graduate students. The Harvard Law, Medical and Business schools are also among the best in the world and the university's massive endowment ($11 billimon) and reputation have guaranteed its steady growth and excellence. Undergraduate tuition costs more than $21,000; the total expense per year is more than $33,000.

Massachusetts Institute of Technology

77 Massachusetts Avenue, Cambridge, MA 02139 (253 1000).

MIT is considered one of the top science and technology universities anywhere. More than 4,300 undergrads pay tuition in excess of $33,000 each year. Men at the school bemoan the 61:39 male-female ratio. Students are required to take a six-subject core course-load that includes calculus, physics, chemistry and biology; eight terms of humanities; plus laboratory and writing classes. Undergrads may also cross-register in courses at Wellesley and Harvard.

Northeastern University

360 Huntingdon Avenue, Boston, MA 02115 (373 2000).

The second-largest school in Boston, enrolling nearly 12,000 undergrads, Northeastern fits neatly into Back Bay between the Museum of Fine Arts and Symphony Hall. Tuition costs $18,000 per year and students are encouraged to participate in 'co-operative education', which combines study with paid, professional employment.

Suffolk University

8 Ashburton Place, Boston, MA 02108 (573 8000).

Located on Beacon Hill, Suffolk sits plum in the heart of Boston. More than 6,000 full- and part-time graduate and undergraduate students are enrolled; Suffolk's Law School is especially renowned.

Tufts University

Bendetson Hall, Medford, MA 02155 (628 5000).

Enrolling more than 8,000 students on three campuses, Tufts is based in Medford, just north-west of Boston proper. It was founded in 1852; here, too, tuition plus room, board and other costs exceeds $30,000 a year.

University of Massachusetts at Boston

100 Morrissey Boulevard, Dorchester, MA 02125 (287 5000).

Established in 1964, UMass Boston represents one of several branches of the state-wide University of Massachusetts. Situated on Columbia Point peninsula, one of the prettiest campus locations in the city, UMass Boston enrolled 12,499 students for the 1998-9 academic year. More than 37% of the university's students are 30 or older; 'students of colour' make up 35% of the population.

Boston by Season

The yearly roster of red-letter days in Boston and Massachusetts.

Weatherwise, the best time of year in Boston is the autumn, or fall. Temperatures are generally in the low 70s°F and the skies are clear for days. Of course, this also means that the city is packed to bursting-point. Prices soar and booking a hotel room or an event becomes a near impossibility. It's the time of year when 60 colleges-worth of students are returning to town, often escorted by their parents (*see chapter* **Campus Culture**); at least half a dozen conventions are in full swing; and fall foliage 'leaf-peepers' are arriving by the busload (*see chapter* **Trips Out of Town**).

Summer is much quieter: Bostonians are more relaxed and it's a lot easier to get around town. But the downside is that temperatures can soar to the 80s°F and 90s°F with almost 100 per cent humidity. Spring is also a quieter time of year, when the blossom appears and the city can be quite beautiful. But the weather's very unpredictable and temperatures can range, day-by-day, from the high 40s to the low 70s°F. Winter tends to be grey and dreary, which is why the hotel rates drop. But there's nothing more magical than a snowstorm in December – the city looks downright Dickensian. Unfortunately rain is far more typical between December and April, when temperatures usually hover around freezing.

Whichever season you choose to visit Boston, make sure you pack layers of clothing. The old chestnut 'If you don't like the New England weather, wait ten minutes' is an old chestnut for a reason. An umbrella is a good idea, too. And if

Public holidays

New Year's Day (1 Jan)
Martin Luther King Day (third Mon in Jan)
Evacuation Day (17 Mar)
Presidents' Day (third Mon in Feb)
Memorial Day (last Mon in May)
Independence Day (4 July)
Labor Day (first Mon in Sept)
Columbus Day (second Mon in Oct)
Veterans' Day (11 November)
Thanksgiving Day (last Thur in Nov)
Christmas Day (25 Dec)

An autumnal storm lights up the Boston night sky.

Latter-day 'Sons of Liberty' turn Boston Harbor into one giant brew every December.

Follow the fathers

Gathering for a Thanksgiving meal on the final Thursday of November is one of America's oldest and most unique traditions. If you're in Massachusetts, why not go to the source? No one else in the world does Thanksgiving like Plymouth, where it all began and where descendants of those who were at the original feast still live within the town limits.

Events in Plymouth are kicked off by a traditional parade that wends its way through the township to The Rock at the waterfront: there are marching bands, festive floats, dozens of costumed 'pilgrims' and the local militia toting muskets. And throughout November, there are guided walking tours of Plymouth's 'historic' homes, covering three centuries of Thanksgiving tradition.

And for the complete costumed experience, **Plimoth Plantation** (*see chapter* **Trips Out of Town**) is a re-creation of the Puritans' first settlement where all the employees dress up and adopt 'characters'. (There's even a Wampanoag village now, to give the original inhabitants their fair due.) The really dedicated can learn what the original Thanksgiving meal entailed – it featured cod and baked beans – and then eat a more familiar, Victorian version with turkey and all the trimmings.

Plymouth Chamber of Commerce
225 Water Street, Plymouth (1-508 830 1620).
Open 9am-5pm daily.
Website www.plymouthchamber.com

Plymouth Visitors' Center
130 Water Street, Plymouth (1-508 747 7533/ 1-800 872 1620). **Open** *summer* 9am-5pm Mon-Fri, 9am-7pm Sat, Sun; *winter* 9am-5pm Mon-Sat.

you're staying in the Back Bay area, you can forecast the weather the way Bostonians do, by checking the top of the Old John Hancock Tower (the one that looks like the Empire State Building next door to the glass one). As the local rhyme goes: *Solid blue, clear view; flashing blue, clouds are due; solid red, rain ahead; flashing red, snow instead.* Except in summer, when solid red means that the Red Sox game has been cancelled. For a list of average annual temperatures, *see chapter* **Directory**.

Information

The events and festivals listed below are held annually. Precise dates are difficult to list in advance because they're often weather-dependent. The best way to confirm when and where a particular event is happening is by phoning the **City of Boston Special Events Line** (1-800 822 0038). You can also get more information by writing to or phoning one of the tourist organisations, or by visiting a Visitor Information Center.

Massachusetts Office of Travel & Tourism

10 Park Plaza, Suite 4510, Boston, MA 02116 (727 3201).
Website: www.mass-vacation.com

Greater Boston Convention & Visitors' Bureau

Box 990468, Prudential Center Towers, Suite 400, Boston, MA 02199 (536 4100/1-888 733 2678).
Website: www.bostonusa.com

Visitor Information Centers

Boston Common *147 Tremont Street (426 3115/advance information 1-800 888 5515). Park Street T.* **Open** 9am-5pm Mon-Fri.
Prudential Center *between Boylston Street & Huntington Avenue (advance information 1-800 888 5515). Prudential or Hynes/ICA T.* **Open** 9am-5pm daily.
Cambridge Information Booth *Harvard Square (497 1630). Harvard T.* **Open** 9am-5pm Mon-Sat.

Winter

Winter is a time when Bostonians tend to hibernate – if they're not out Christmas shopping at Copley Place or along Newbury Street. Not a whole lot happens after the credit card bills arrive in January. **Black History Month** lasts for most of February, offering various events and lectures around town (phone 742 5415 for details). The Park Service usually organises special tours and programmes around the **Black Heritage Trail** to coincide with it (*see page 52* **Sightseeing**).

December

The **Christmas Tree Lighting** ceremony takes place at the Prudential Center on the first Saturday of the month (starting at 4.15pm). The Pru usually has the most magnificent tree in town, absolutely covered in colourful lights. It's the semi-official kick-off for the holiday season and there's usually a sing-a-long if the weather's not too cold (phone 236 3744 for details).

Boston Common Tree Lighting

(Information 635 4505). Park Street T. **Date** 1st weekend in Dec.
Fifty of the Common's trees are strung with lights and a nativity scene and menorah are usually set up near the Park Street Station. Then a local dignitary (usually the mayor) flicks the switch to the accompaniment of local choral groups.

Boston Tea Party Re-enactment

(Information 482 6439/338 1773). **Date** 13 Dec (or the nearest Sun).
'Patriots' gather for a town meeting at the **Old South Meeting House** (*see p47* **Sightseeing**) to debate what they're going to do about nasty old King George. Then they march with fife and drum to a replica tea ship on the waterfront (the **Boston Tea Party Ship and Museum**, *see p92* **Museums & Galleries**) and do the dirty deed.

January

Chinese New Year

(Information 536 4100/1-888 733 2678). **Date** late Jan or early Feb, depending on lunar calendar.
Three weeks of festivities take place in Chinatown, complete with dragon dancing and fireworks. It's the nation's third largest celebration and centres mainly around Beach and Tyler Streets.

First Night

(Information 542 1399). **Date** 31 Dec.
Boston was the first city in the country to offer this alcohol-free alternative to ringing in the New Year, back in the 1970s. First Night is celebrated citywide with hundreds of pageants, parades, music and theatre performances and outdoor art. Main events include the Grand Procession (best seen from Boylston's side streets) and the Perrier Irrepressible Laser Light Show which takes place on Boston Common. It all culminates in a midnight fireworks display at the harbour. For details of events celebrating the new millennium, consult the First Night website.
Website: www.firstnight.org

February

Beanpot Hockey Tournament

(Information 624 1000). **Date** 1st & 2nd Mon in Feb.
The varsity hockey teams from Harvard, Northeastern, Boston University and Boston College vie to be top of the Hub. The winner gets a trophy shaped like, well, a beanpot. Hosted by the **FleetCenter** (*see chapter* **Sport & Fitness**).
Website: www.fleetcenter.com

Boston Wine Expo

(Information 1-800 544 1660). **Date** 23-24 Jan.
More like a gigantic cocktail party, this trade show hosted by the harbourside **World Trade Center** (*see chapter* **Directory**) features tastings from 400 domestic and international wineries, celebrity chef demonstrations and educational seminars.

New England Boat Show

(Information 242 6092). **Date** last week in Feb.
This trade show focuses on the latest in sailing and motorised craft, though vintage and antique boats are also on display in abundance. It's the largest show in the Eastern USA and takes place at the Bayside Exposition Center on Mount Vernon Street.

Skating on Boston Common's Frog Pond: a much-loved winter tradition.

March

Boston Massacre Re-enactment

(Information 720 3290). **Date** 5 Mar.
A gathering to watch the cowardly Redcoats take potshots from the balcony of the **Old State House** (*see p47* **Sightseeing**) at five Patriot heroes below. Costumes, muskets and – hopefully – blanks are supplied courtesy of the Massachusetts Council of Minutemen and Militia.

New England Spring Flower & Garden Show

(Information 536 9280). **Date** 2nd week in Mar.
This has been a spring tradition in Boston for more than a century. The Massachusetts Horticultural Society sponsors 5 acres (2 ha) of landscaped gardens, flower arrangements and horticultural displays at the Bayside Exposition Center on Mount Vernon Street.

St Patrick's Day Parade & Evacuation Day

(Information 536 4100). **Date** 17 Mar.
The Irish community of South Boston hosts one of the largest St Patrick's Day parades in America, complete with floats, marching bands, war veterans and, of course, waving politicians. Then everybody heads for the pub. A smaller ceremony usually takes place to commemorate the day the British left town in 1776. Cynical Bostonians insist it's just an excuse to give city officials – many of them Irish – St Paddy's Day off.

Spring

Spring is more metaphoric than meteorological in Boston. The city usually just goes from cold to hot with a weekend or two of mild weather sandwiched in-between. Boston's annual rebirth starts in April, when the **Red Sox** begin playing again (*see chapter* **Sport & Fitness**) and the **Swan Boats** start up in the Public Garden (*see chapter* **Sightseeing**). In May, magnolias burst into bloom all along Commonwealth Avenue and Marlborough Street, the **Boston Pops** return to Symphony Hall (*see chapter* **The Performing Arts**), and the humpback whales to the Stellwagen Bank – followed by the **whale-watching** cruise ships (*see chapter* **Sightseeing** *and chapter* **Trips Out of Town**). May is also **Museum-goers Month**, in which all 40 of the local museums offer special exhibitions, events and lectures.

April

Lantern Hanging

(Information 523 6676). **Date** Sun before 19 Apr.
Two lanterns are hung in the steeple of the **Old North Church** (*see p58* **Sightseeing**) to commemorate sexton Robert Newman's warning that the British troops were headed for Concord 'by sea' – crossing the Charles River to get from Boston Common to Cambridge (*see also chapter* **History**).

Patriot's Day Re-enactments

(Information 1-508 362 6993/862 1450). **Date** 3rd Mon in April.
In Boston, Paul Revere rides again with the warning that the British are coming. On Lexington Green, there's a full-scale re-enactment – complete with uniforms and muskets – of the skirmish that produced the shot 'heard round the world' (*see p8* **History**). For Lexington, *see chapter* **Trips Out of Town**.

Boston Marathon

(Information 236 1652). **Date** 3rd Mon in April.
Most Bostonians think they get Patriot's Day off to watch the marathon. Thousands line the 26.2 mile (2.2km) route from Hopkinton (just southwest of Boston) to Copley Square in order to cheer on world-class runners and loved ones.
Website: www.bostonmarathon.org

May

Lilac Sunday

(Information 524 1717). **Date** 3rd Sun in May.
Bostonians descend on the Arnold Arboretum (*see p73* **Sightseeing**) to stroll among the 400 or so varieties of fragrant lilacs in bloom. Actually, most of the other flowering trees are in bloom then as well. It's sort of what you've always pictured heaven to look like.

Boston Kite Festival

(Information 635 4505). **Date** mid-May.
Kite flyers are somewhat a breed unto themselves. But they show their colours full-force during this weekend in May at Franklin Park in Roxbury. These people can fly things you've never dreamed of.

Salem Seaport Festival

(Information 1-978 741 3252/1-877 725 3662).
Date mid-May.
At one point, Salem was a more important port than Boston. The locals prove this with an annual festival of live music, food and children's activities. There are also more than 100 exhibitors of arts, crafts and antiques. For Salem, *see chapter* **Trips Out of Town**.

Summer

The high cost of living in Boston pays off during the summer months. Beginning in June, the city hosts free concerts and movies at the **Hatch Memorial Shell** on the Esplanade (*see chapter* **The Performing Arts**). There's a different style of music nearly every night of the week; people generally pack a picnic and spread a blanket. At the end of June the **Boston Globe Jazz Festival** kicks in, with various free or ticketed events throughout the city (*see chapter* **Nightlife**). Then, almost every weekend throughout July and August, the North End hosts an **Italian street festival** (phone 536 4100 for information). Various saints are honoured with macabre parades, activities and food stalls.

Western Massachusetts becomes the epicentre of the arts in the late summer, hosting the **Tangle-wood Music Festival** in Lenox, the **Jacob's Pillow Dance Festival** in Becket and the **Williamstown Theater Festival** (*see chapter* **Trips Out of Town** for further details of all three).

June

Lesbian & Gay Pride Festival

(Information 522 7890). **Date** 1st week in June.
Usually beginning with an AIDS Walk around the Charles River Basin, the week's festivities include lectures, concerts, readings, performances and dance parties. It all culminates in a parade through the South End on the Saturday, and a carnival on the Sunday.

Nantucket Film Festival

(Information 1-508 228 1700). **Date** 2nd week in June.
Agents, actors and fans converge on Massachusetts' most exclusive vacation island for an insider's look at the silver screen. Screenwriting workshops and social events are punctuated by screenings of participant movies. For Nantucket, *see chapter* **Trips Out of Town**.

Bunker Hill Celebrations

(Information 242 5669). **Date** 3rd weekend in June.
A re-enactment of the famous battle – complete with military costumes and muskets (*see p8* **History**). The event kicks off with a parade in Charlestown and carries on with various activities over at the Charlestown Naval Yard.

Massachusetts Special Olympics

(Information 1-978 774 1501). **Date** 3rd week in June.
Physically and mentally challenged athletes get out there and show their stuff. Competition categories include aquatics, sailing, track and field, gymnastics, volleyball and tennis. The event is jointly hosted by Boston University and Massachusetts Institute of Technology.

Boston Harborfest

(Information 227 1528). **Date** 4th week in June.
A maritime festival of fireworks, open-air concerts and (yet more) historical re-enactments. More than 30 different venues offer activities all along the waterfront. Whichever other ones you choose, don't miss the chowderfest.

July

Boston Pops Fourth of July Concert

(Information 266 1492). **Date** 4 July.
It's a party of about a million picnickers and boaters stretching all along the Esplanade on the banks of the Charles River. The Pops begin playing at the Hatch Shell in the early evening and their performance always ends with the '1812 Overture' and the best fireworks you've ever seen. *See also chapter* **The Performing Arts**.

Turning of USS Constitution

(Information 426 1812). **Date** 4 July.
'Old Ironsides', still a commissioned naval vessel, makes her annual sail around Boston Harbor to turn around and redock in the opposite direction at the Charlestown Naval Yard – undertaken to insure the ship weathers evenly.

Bastille Day

(Information 266 4351). **Date** on or near 14 July.
Marlborough Street in Back Bay closes for this annual fête, hosted by the French Library. The evening of traditional French food, wine and song may be a little on the expensive side, but it's worth experiencing at least once.

Edgartown Regatta

(Information 1-508 627 4361). **Date** 2nd weekend in July.
The Edgartown Yacht Club sponsors races with prizes in four categories of vessel. It's a nice excuse to take the ferry out to Martha's Vineyard (*see chapter* **Trips Out of Town**) and wander around the holiday island.

Boston Antique & Classic Boat Festival

(Information 666 8530). **Date** 3rd weekend in July.
Marina Bay in Quincy puts on a show of New England vessels, both old and new. Meet skippers and crews and vote for your favourite boat display; there's even a blessing of the fleet.

Lowell Folk Festival

(Information 1-978 459 1000). **Date** 4th weekend in July.
Lowell is a factory town north of Boston that attracted a lot of immigrant workers during the Industrial Revolution (*see chapter* **Trips Out of Town**). They're honoured annually with a festival of traditional music, dance, storytelling, food and crafts.

Feast of the Blessed Sacrament

(Information 1-508 992 6911). **Date** last weekend in July.
The largest Portuguese cultural event in America. The harbour town of New Bedford (*see chapter* **Trips Out of Town**) hosts this citywide celebration – it features a parade, entertainment, music and performance, as well as a giant funfair.

August

Gloucester Waterfront Festival

(Information 1-781 283 1601). **Date** mid-Aug.
One of the towns that put Boston's fishing industry on the map (*see chapter* **Trips Out of Town**). The festival boasts a Yankee Lobster Bake, whale watches, musical entertainment and stalls selling nautical crafts.

Provincetown Carnival Week

(Information 1-508 487 2313/1-800 637 8226).
Date 3rd week in Aug.
A Mardi Gras-like celebration with an extravagant costume parade down Commercial Street. Though the Carnival is not strictly gay, you have to be up for a lot of drag queens and high camp. *For* **Provincetown**, *see chapter* **Trips Out of Town**.

The Boston Pops' Fourth of July concert.

King Richard's Faire

(Information 1-508 866 5391). **Date** weekends from Labor Day to 17 Oct.
Return to the Renaissance by heading for Carver's long-standing medieval fair. Packed with period revelry, theatricals, sword-play, jousting and food, it's wildly popular with children.

US Pro Tennis Championship

(Information 1-508 620 1847). **Date** 4th week in Aug.
World-class tennis, hosted by the prestigious Longwood Cricket Club in Brookline. You'll need to book tickets well in advance if you want to see the stars volley.

Caribbean Carnival

(Information 282 2605). **Date** Sat before Labor Day.
Franklin Park hosts a celebration of Caribbean culture that runs to ethnic foods, arts, crafts and dance. Make the trip to Roxbury to hear calypso, soca, steel drum and other kinds of music.

Autumn

Boston is the perfect starting point for fall foliage tours of western Massachusetts and Vermont (between mid-September and mid-October). Autumn is also harvest time for apples, pumpkins and cranberries. September marks the kick-off of the **Boston Bruins**'s hockey season at the FleetCenter and the **New England Patriots**, football season at Foxboro Stadium (*see chapter* **Sport & Fitness** *for both*). In October, the **Ringling Brothers Circus** always comes to the FleetCenter – it begins with a traditional parade. And it's **open studio** season for the city's various art communities (*see page 93* **Museums & Galleries**).

September

Cambridge River Festival

(Information 349 4380/4382). **Date** Sun after Labor Day.
An international festival erupts along the Cambridge side of the Charles. There's music and dance, an international bazaar, visual arts and crafts and various children's activities.

Art Newbury Street

(Information 267 7961/859 8500). **Date** end Sept.
Newbury Street closes for a little sidewalk art, music and food. More than 30 of the city's most prestigious galleries host special exhibitions.

Harwich Cranberry Festival

(Information 1-508 441 3199/1-800 432 6389).
Date mid-Sept.
If you've never seen a cranberry bog in bloom (an amazing sight) here's your chance. Harwich's festival includes a family picnic on the beach, a parade, country jamboree and fireworks.

Boston Film Festival

(Information 266 2533). **Date** 2nd week in Sept.
An annual festival of lectures, panels and screenings that showcases both feature-length and independent works. There's a strong, local contingent of participants, many from nearby colleges (*see chapter* **Film**).

October

Boston Fashion Week

(Information 695 8116). **Date** 2nd week in Oct.
Boston's established and fledgling designers get a chance to strut their stuff during this week-long celebration of style. Fashion shows, parties, panel discussions and displays take place at various venues around town.

Harvard Square Oktoberfest

(Information 491 3434). **Date** mid-Oct.
Harvard Square is transformed for a weekend into a Bavarian township, with bands, dancers, ethnic food and – of course – beer gardens. Some 200 regional artisans and merchants display their wares.

Head of the Charles Regatta

(Information 864 8415). **Date** 2nd weekend in Oct.
One of the largest boat races anywhere: thousands of rowers converge on Cambridge for this world-class regatta. Fans bring blankets and picnic baskets to the banks of the Charles to cheer their favourite teams on to victory.

Salem's Haunted Happenings

(Information 1-978 744 0013). **Date** 2nd half of Oct.
No other place in Massachusetts gets into Hallowe'en like Salem (*see chapter* **Trips Out of Town**). Two weeks of celebration are kicked off by a huge costumed parade. Then there are haunted house tours by candlelight, magic shows, a psychics' fair, the Bizarre Bazaar and 'demonstrations' of modern witchcraft.
Website: www.salemweb.com

November

Thanksgiving at Old Sturbridge Village

(Information 1-508 347 3362/1-800 733 1830).
Date 25-27 Nov.
See how families celebrated the holiday 150 years ago at this re-creation of a nineteenth-century New England town. You can stroll through village homes and have dinner at the Bullard Tavern. Reservations are essential. *For* **Old Sturbridge**, *see chapter* **Trips Out of Town**.

Christmas on Cape Cod

(Information 1-516 261 2777). **Date** 4th week in Nov.
If you're not going to be around in December, experience an old-fashioned New England Christmas ahead of time, by attending the series of open houses, parades and lighting of the Pilgrim Monument in P-Town, Cape Cod (*see chapter* **Trips Out of Town**).

Sightseeing

Sightseeing

Explore the big city trapped inside the body of a small town.

The benefit of Boston's modest size is that it's relatively easy to cover a lot of historical ground without having to cover much actual ground. The 2.5-mile (4-kilometre) Freedom Trail, which connects 16 major sites and several different neighbourhoods, is an excellent example of this, especially if you're short of time. But equally, it would be easy to spend an entire day at Faneuil Hall, strolling the streets of Charlestown, visiting Paul Revere's old neighbourhood (the Italian North End), shopping and people watching on Newbury Street, hiking the Emerald Necklace or exploring within the ivy-covered walls of Harvard Yard. However you decide to approach the city, bear in mind that walking and using the excellent local public transport are almost always preferable to driving.

Downtown & the Financial District

See map 5

Much of Boston's downtown retains its original early eighteenth-century street pattern, and in most cases the street names too, since few of them changed after the Revolutionary War. Both the commercial and the historical heart of the city, the downtown area combines colonial red-brick with twentieth-century glass-and-steel, with Boston Common at its heart and the waterfront at its edge.

Around Boston Common

As hard as it may be to believe, given the lush greenery that is its signature, the 48-acre (19-hectare) **Boston Common** – America's oldest public park, established in 1634 – originally had no trees at all, save one giant specimen that served as a central meeting place for the Puritans who settled here. The 'Great Elm', as it was called, was handy for hangings, but the park was originally used as a grazing pasture for cattle, then as a military site. The tree eventually fell victim to a series of ferocious storms that blew it down in the late 1860s or early 1870s, though that didn't put an end to the park's role as a rallying point.

Today, it's a place for public events, protests and baseball games. Stroll the intersecting byways, past the playground, the various statues and the ever-popular Frog Pond (urbanites teeter in circles around it during the winter skating months). Office workers seek a respite from the daily grind on the common, which is also famous for its Christmas lights and loud-mouthed pan handlers.

On the northeastern edge of the common, at One Park Street, is the **Park Street Church** where William Lloyd Garrison gave his first anti-slavery address in 1829 (Sunday services are still held here). Next to the famous church is the **Granary Burying Ground**. Looking like something from a horror movie, this graveyard was established in 1660 and lay adjacent to Boston's first granary (hence the name). Among the famous figures buried here are Paul Revere, John Hancock, Samuel Adams, Peter Faneuil, Ben Franklin's parents, the victims of the Boston Massacre and Samuel Sewall (famous because he was the only Salem Witch Trial magistrate to admit later that he was wrong).

Further north, heading towards Government Center, is the **King's Chapel & Burying Ground**, on the corner of Tremont and School Streets. Originally the first Anglican church in Boston (there was never enough money to give it a steeple), it became the First Unitarian church after the Revolution. The adjoining burial ground is Boston's oldest. Laid to rest here – among other notable Bostonians – is Elizabeth Pain (supposedly the model for Hester Prynne in Nathaniel Hawthorne's *The Scarlet Letter*). The statue of one of the most famous Americans in history, **Benjamin Franklin**, stands in front of the site of Boston's **first public school** (on School Street). Author, inventor, scientist, patriot and scholar, Franklin attended this school, which was built in 1635, with Sam Adams, Cotton Mather and John Hancock – the school masters must have had their hands full. It later became the Boston Latin School.

Also on School Street, at Washington Street, is the site of what was once the **Old Corner Bookstore** (*see page 29* **Literary Boston**). Emerson, Dickinson, Hawthorne, Longfellow, Harriet Beecher Stowe and Thackeray all thumbed through tomes in this scholarly nook at one point or another when it was a bookshop. *Walden*, *The Scarlet Letter* and 'The Song of Hiawatha' were all published in the building.

Two unmissable symbols of the city: the **Pru** *(see page 63) and* **Boston Duck Tours** *(see page 87).*

DEPARTING FROM PRUDENTIAL CENTER
BOSTON ★ DUCK ★ TOURS
LAND & WATER

Old Ironsides (USS Constitution*) takes a rare turn around the harbour. See page 59.*

The Freedom Trail

The red brick line of the Freedom Trail covers Boston's most well-known historical sites. A pretty good starting-point for viewing the city (particularly if your time is limited), the 2.5-mile (4-kilometre) trail links 16 different sites starting in downtown Boston and ending in Charlestown, across the river.

It begins on Boston Common at the **Visitor Information Center** on Tremont Street, where you can pick up maps of the trail. The sites on it are as follows (in this order):

The **State House** (*see page 54*); **Boston Common** (*page 42*); the **Park Street Church** (*page 47*); the **Granary Burying Ground** (*page 47*); the **King's Chapel Burying Ground** (*page 47*); the **First Public School/ Benjamin Franklin Statue** (*page 42*); the site of the **Old Corner Bookstore** (*page 42*); the **Old South Meeting House** (*page 47*); the **Old State House** (*page 47*); the **Boston Massacre Site** (*page 47*); **Faneuil Hall** (*page 50*); the **Paul Revere House** (*page 56*); **Old North Church** (*page 58*); **Copp's Hill Burying Ground** (*page 58*); the **Bunker Hill Monument** (*page 59*); **USS *Constitution*** (*page 59*).

Visitor Information Center

Boston Common, 147 Tremont Street (426 3115/advance information 1-800 888 5515). Park St T. **Open** 9am-5pm Mon-Fri. **Map 5 G4**

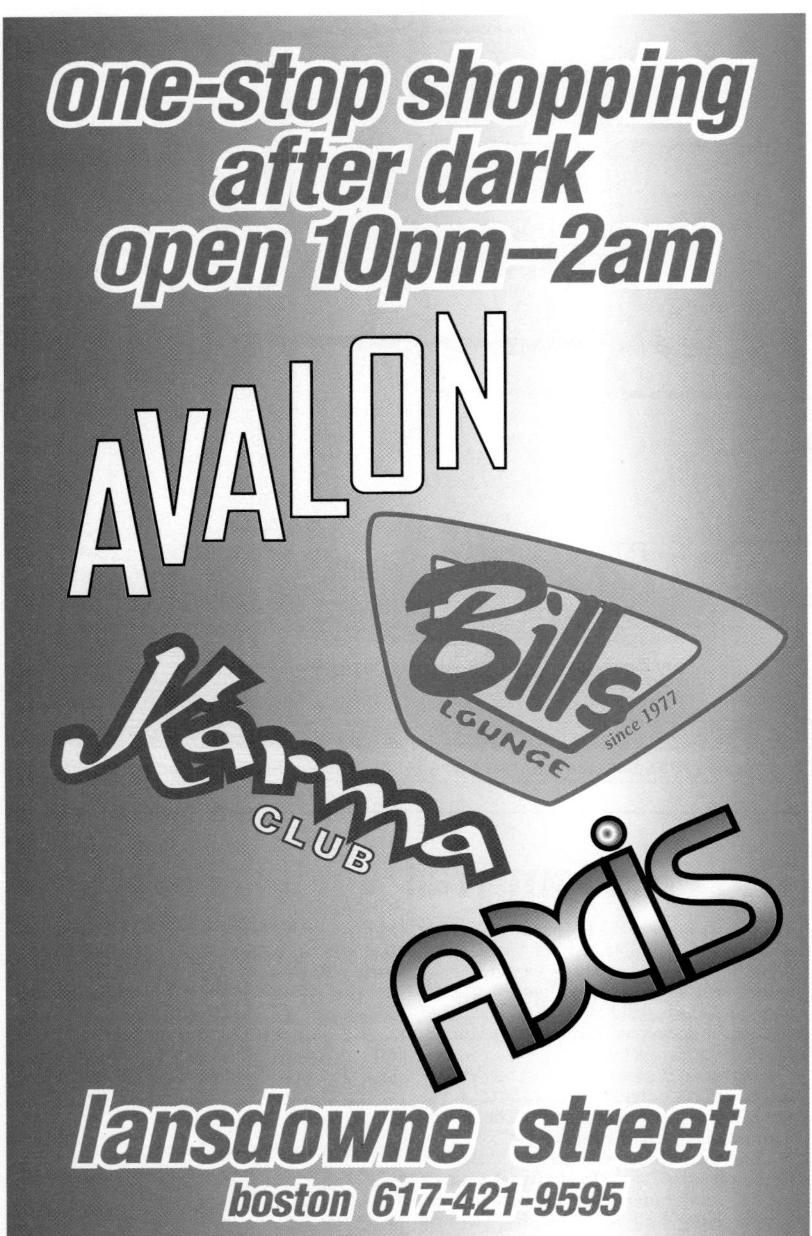
one-stop shopping
after dark
open 10pm–2am
AVALON
Bills
LOUNGE
since 1977
Karma
CLUB
Axis
lansdowne street
boston 617-421-9595

Across the street is the **Old South Meeting House** – the largest building in colonial Boston and a hotspot for anti-British debate before the Revolution. The building was the departure point for the enraged 'Mohawk Indians' who chucked 342 crates of tea into Boston Harbor on the night of 16 December 1773 (*see page 8* **History**).

Perhaps one of the most striking historical sites in the area is the **Old State House**. Elegantly placed in the midst of skyscrapers and traffic, the former legislative house is the oldest surviving public building in Boston – built in 1713 for the Massachusetts Bay Colony governmental offices. Proclamations, including the Declaration of Independence, were read in this building, often from the balcony on the east side . The area below the balcony was the scene of the **Boston Massacre** on 5 March 1770 (commemorated by a ring of cobblestones), when British soldiers fired on an unruly crowd, killing five men. After the Revolution, the State House continued as the seat of Massachusetts government until Bulfinch finished his new legislative building on Beacon Hill. Today, it serves as a museum of the city's history.

Continuing further north along Washington Street takes you to the famous **Faneuil Hall** (*see page 50*), a colonial market and meeting place.

Granary Burying Ground

at Tremont & Bromfield Streets (635 4505). Park St T. **Open** dawn-dusk daily. **Admission** free. **Map 5 G4**

King's Chapel & Burying Ground

58 Tremont Street, at School Street (227 2155). Gov't Center T. **Open** *15 Apr-15 June* 9am-4pm Mon, Fri, Sat; *16 June-Labor Day* 1pm-3pm Sun; *Labor Day-15 Oct* 9am-4pm Mon, Thur-Sat; *16 Oct-14 Apr* 10am-2pm Sat; also by appointment. **Admission** free. **Map 5 G4**

Old South Meeting House

310 Washington Street, between Milk & Water Streets (482 6439). Downtown Crossing or State/Citizen's Bank T. **Open** 9.30am-5pm daily. **Admission** $1-$3. **Credit** MC, V. **Map 5 G4**
Disabled: toilet.

Old State House

206 Washington Street, at State Street (720 3290). State/Citizen's Bank T. **Open** 9am-5pm daily. **Admission** $1-$3. **Credit** AmEx, DC, MC, V. **Map 5 G4**

Park Street Church

1 Park Street, at Tremont Street (523 3383). Park St T. **Open** *July-Aug* 9am-3pm daily. **Map 5 G4**
Disabled: toilet.

Government Center

Government Center, the area roughly bordered by Beacon Hill, Downtown Crossing and Faneuil Hall, is dominated by **City Hall Plaza**. This open brick plaza, anchored by the hulk of City Hall, was the result of the 1960s urban renewal scheme that levelled the West End (*see page 22* **Architecture**).

The **Old State House** *(above) and the* **Old South Meeting House** *(below).*

City planners had wanted to banish the seedy red-light district Scollay Square. In its place, a vast, brick expanse was created for public performances and special events.

City Hall, where the mayor's office and those of other city officials are based, resembles something out of *Star Wars* – all boxy concrete pillars and beams. It was designed by the architectural firm of Kallman, McKinnel and Knowles and is alternatively described as one of the ugliest buildings in Boston and one of its most important architectural achievements. IM Pei was responsible for the master plan of the complex, which was completed in 1968. Significantly, plans are underway to transform the sparse brick plaza into something on a more human scale, by adding trees and benches.

Bordering the area is the **Haymarket** (by the Central Artery), where an open-air fruit, veg and fish market operates on Fridays and Saturdays.

City Hall Plaza
Congress Street, at Court Street. Gov't Center T.
Map 5 G4

Faneuil Hall & Quincy Marketplace

Faneuil Hall, the other side of Congress Street from City Hall, stands in stark contrast to the modern architecture of its neighbours. It was built for the city by the wealthy merchant Peter Faneuil in 1742 and later remodelled by Charles Bulfinch. It played a crucial role in the Revolution (colonial hero Samuel Adams, among others, regularly roused the Boston populace against the British in the first-floor public meeting hall) and so became known as the 'Cradle of Liberty'. Today rabble-rousers can rent the hall (political debates are still held here) and the ground floor market hall is full of tacky souvenir shops.

The **Bunker Hill Monument**. *See page 59.*

The hall stands as a companion piece to **Quincy Market**, adjacent. This Greek Revival building (the Boston equivalent of London's Covent Garden market) was built at the beginning of the nineteenth century as the city's meat, fish and produce market. Nowadays, the innermost hall of the central building is lined with different fast food stands, where tourists and local office workers can grab platefuls of dim sum, sushi, clam chowder or burritos and eat them in the indoor courtyard or on benches outside.

On either side of the central hall (which gives its name to the whole complex), rows of carts loaded with souvenirs and 'crafts' attempt to lure tourists

Colonial marketplace and now tourist mecca: **Quincy Market**.

*The **Charles River** at night (page 78) – one of the city's countless waterfront viewpoints.*

to part with yet more dollars, as do the street performers who flock to the place, some of whom are pretty good. Flanking Quincy Market on either side are the North and South Markets, which are likewise filled with shops ranging from Gap and Disney to local oddities such as 'Kites of Boston'. **Durgin-Park** – famous for its grumpy staff – is nearby (*see page 133* **Restaurants & Cafés**). On a pleasant weekend day, the marketplace, which is confusingly referred to by locals both as Faneuil Hall and Quincy Marketplace, is one of the most vibrant spots in the city.

Walk north up Congress Street and you come to **Blackstone Block** (the block of streets off Blackstone Street, between Hanover Street and North Street). Cosy pubs (including another famous restaurant, the **Union Oyster House**; *see page 133* **Restaurants & Cafés**) line this cobblestoned area, making it an agreeable place to recover with a pint of Guinness after a long afternoon's touring. One of the city's newest landmarks, the **New England Holocaust Memorial**, is directly across the street in Carmen Park (at Congress and Union Streets). Six glass towers covered with six million etched numbers stand as a memorial to those who died in the Holocaust. Steam rises out of the towers and at night gives the monument a particularly haunting effect.

Faneuil Hall

15 State Street, at Congress Street (242 5642). Gov't Center or State/Citizen's Bank T. **Open** 9am-5pm daily. **Admission** free. **Credit** *shop* AmEx, MC, V. **Map 5 G4**

Quincy Market

Chatham & Quincy Streets (338 2323). Gov't Center or State/Citizen's Bank T. **Open** *food hall* 10am-9pm Mon-Sat; noon-6pm Sun. **Map 5 G/H4**
Disabled: toilet.

Long Wharf & the Aquarium

Almost directly behind the Faneuil Hall area lies **Long Wharf** – known as Boston Pier in 1710, when a group of merchants first built brick warehouses here. The shoreline has changed since then: when the **Customs House** was built (in 1847 in the style of an Italian Renaissance campanile and Boston's first skyscraper), it stood on the edge of the water. The landmark now lies on State and

The city is at its most picturesque during the fall foliage season.

India Streets, several streets inland. The scenic space at the border of Long Wharf is **Christopher Columbus Park**, which lies next to the large brick Long Wharf Marriott (one of Boston's fancier hotels). A huge wooden arbour, with vine-covered trellises and benches from which to admire the waterfront views gives the spot an unexpectedly romantic air; it forms the border with the nearby Italian neighbourhood, the **North End** (*see page 55*). An offshoot of the Marriott, **Tia's on the Waterfront** (200 Atlantic Avenue, at Commercial Street; 227 0828) is a popular summertime bar that spills out almost into the park. Its location just about makes up for the pricey beer.

Another watering-hole, steak and seafood restaurant, the **Boston Chart House** (60 Long Wharf, off Commercial Street; 227 1576) is behind the Marriott and sandwiched between the Boston Waterfront Marina and the dock from which most of the harbour cruise ships depart. Long Wharf is the place to come for a ticket for a whale-watching cruise, a tour of the harbour islands, or just a ride around the harbour (*see page 76* **On the waterfront** *and page 85* **Organised tours**). Another courtyard at the very end of the wharf offers great waterfront views of construction cranes, barges, sailing boats and planes flying in and out of Logan airport. And lots of swooping sea gulls.

The striking glass **New England Aquarium** sits on neighbouring Central Wharf and is one of the country's best – it's worth a trip even if you don't like fish. There's a seal tank outside, a huge penguin exhibit indoors (geared so that almost all of the balconies overlook it) and a huge 187,000-gallon salt-water replica of a Caribbean coral reef. Forty feet in diameter and three stories tall, this cylindrical tank is alive with moray eels, sharks, sting rays and huge sea turtles. There's also a display where you can stick your hands into the cold water of a tidal basin and get up close and personal with starfish, sea urchins and hermit crabs.

Whale-watching trips aboard the specially-designed *Voyager II* depart daily from the aquarium dock and provide an excellent commentary on local sea birds and other marine mammals as well as whales. The aquarium also runs a programme called 'Science at Sea,' which is a 90-minute educational tour of Boston Harbor aboard the *Doc Edgerton* and includes an introduction to marine research and various local species of marine life.

For more on Boston's waterfront beyond the downtown area, *see page 76* **On the waterfront**.

New England Aquarium

Central Wharf, at Atlantic Avenue & Milk Street (973 5200). Aquarium T. **Open** *1 July-Labor Day* 9am-6pm Mon, Tue, Fri; 9am-8pm Wed, Thur; 9am-7pm Sat, Sun. *Day after Labor Day-30 June* 9am-5pm Mon-Fri; 9am-6pm Sat, Sun. **Admission** $5.50-$12.50. **Credit** AmEx, DC, MC, V. **Map 5 H4**

Downtown Crossing

Bostonians don't go shopping in Quincy Marketplace – they spend their money in the far less touristy **Downtown Crossing**, the shopping and business area between Boston Common, the Theater District, the Financial District and Government Center. City dwellers search here for basics such as CDs, boots and toasters. Just follow the smell of sweet, roasted peanuts being hocked by street vendors. Walk down **Washington Street**, where Winter Street becomes Summer Street, which is closed off to cars during the day, making it more like an open air mall. Pushcart vendors park their wares – cheap jewellery, Boston T-shirts, sweaters – in front of department stores such as the famous **Filene's Basement** (*see page 162* **Shops & Services**), established by William Filene back in 1881.

The Financial District

The Financial District is roughly bordered by State Street, Washington Street, Atlantic Avenue and Summer Street, where Downtown Crossing takes over. It's a maze of quirky, often picturesque streets whose buildings combine modern skyscrapers with a maze-like street layout that dates back to the city's early days. Don't bother to bring a car to explore: those numbered streets in downtown New York are nothing like the zig-zag of intersections here.

During the day, Boston's business types fill the byways of this money-making district, the heart of America's trust fund industry. Quirky squares dot the area, the most prominent being **Post Office Square Park** (between Pearl and Congress Streets), where you can watch suits nibble their sandwiches and grab a breath of fresh air during their lunch break. At 185 Franklin Street is the giant edifice of the **New England Telephone** building (it now belongs to NYNEX), which contains the world's first telephone exchange.

Tourists mill through the streets during the day on their way to Faneuil Hall or to catch a glimpse of the waterfront, and though the Financial District used to empty pretty quickly after hours, hip restaurants and bars like the **Vault** (*see page 135* **Restaurants & Cafés**) and the **Exchange** (148 State Street; 617 726 7600) have begun popping up recently, giving outsiders an incentive to enter the area after nightfall.

Chinatown

Originally known as South Cove, Chinatown is a small neighbourhood lined with Asian bakeries, tailors, antique shops and, of course, restaurants. Towards the end of the nineteenth century Chinese immigrants began arriving in the city to work on the railroads and as cheap labour in factories. By the early twentieth century there were over a 1,000 residents in Chinatown, and the number expanded hugely after World War II. Today the area is contained within a few blocks next door to the Theater District, and roughly based around Kneeland, Essex, Beach and Tyler Streets.

It's still the best place in the city to get a taste of authentic Asian cuisine. Because of its proximity to the Theater District, the restaurants are often packed with theatre-goers before and after shows and many stay open late into the night to catch the after-hours trade. Vestiges of the **Combat Zone** (the red-light district that was once located around Washington Street between Essex and Kneeland Streets) linger, however, so be on the alert after dark. For a recommended selection of restaurants in the area, *see page 129* **Restaurants & Cafés**.

The Theater & Leather Districts

Next door to Chinatown, based on Tremont Street, is what's known as the **Theater District** (*see chapter* **The Performing Arts**). You can find almost any sort of entertainment within this meagre block, be it comedy, dance, musicals, cabaret or drama. The almost stadium-like **Wang Center** is the most well-known theatre and is where performances of hit shows such as the Boston Ballet's *Nutcracker* or productions of *Phantom of the Opera* play. More intimate and elegant theatres include the **Wilbur**, **Colonial** and **Shubert**. And there's a smattering of restaurants in the area, too, among them the brewpub **Brew Moon** (*see page 118* **Pubs & Bars**), **Jae's Cafe and Grill**, **Pignoli** and a branch of **Legal Sea Foods** (*see chapter* **Restaurants & Cafés**).

Lodged between South Station and Chinatown is Boston's recently revitalised **Leather District** (based around Kneeland, Lincoln and South Streets). After a huge fire in 1872, which started on the corner of Summer and Kingston Streets, most of the downtown, commercial heart of Boston was ravaged and the leather industry was particularly hard-hit. But by the 1880s the demand for leather goods was so high that local manufacturers decided to move to temporary quarters along Lincoln and South Streets. The 1900s marked a decline in urban industry and many of the leather factories moved out to the suburbs. The building of the Central Artery in 1959 added to the area's demise, by cutting it off from the rest of downtown Boston.

In the 1970s, artists began moving back into the Leather District, converting the empty loft spaces into galleries and workshops. The area became known as 'Boston's Soho' or 'NoSo' (North of South Boston) as more galleries and chic restaurants began popping up. A renovated South Station and the addition of the Federal Reserve building at 600 Atlantic Avenue also saved this otherwise forgotten corner from obscurity. And with the revitalisation came some of Boston's trendiest restaurants.

The Black Heritage Trail

During the early nineteenth century, Boston's African-American community lived on the western slope of Beacon Hill. The contributions this community made in the struggle for equality are mapped out in the form of a freedom trail. The National Park Service offers free guided tours of the 1.6-mile (2.5-kilometre) trail for groups (phone 742 5415/1854 to book a place) but you can pick up a map at the Boston Common **Visitor Information Center** (*see page 45*) and cover the ground in your own time.

The first site on the trail is the **Shaw Memorial**, on the corner of Beacon and Park Streets. The 54th Regiment of the Massachusetts Volunteer Infantry was the first black regiment to be recruited in the North after President Lincoln admitted black soldiers into the Union forces during the American Civil War. On 18 July 1863, the regiment became famous for leading an assault on Fort Wagner in South Carolina. Robert Gould Shaw and 62 soldiers were killed during the battle when the regiment managed to save the American flag from Confederate capture.

Other sites include the **George Middleton House**, at 5-7 Pinkney Street, and the **Phillips School** on the corner of Anderson and Pinkney Streets. George Middleton, a veteran of the American Revolution, lived in what is thought to be the oldest house built by African-Americans on Beacon Hill (built in 1797), which he shared with Louis Glapion, a French mulatto hairdresser. The Phillips School – a prototype for all Boston schoolhouses – became one of the city's first racially mixed schools when the segregation of schools was abolished in 1855. Neither site is open to the public.

Abolitionist senator Charles Sumner was a regular at the Beacon Hill barber shop of **John J Smith**, a free-born black whose shop was a base for Abolitionists in Boston and a meeting point for fugitive slaves on the run. Smith also worked as a recruiter in Washington during the Civil War

Beacon Hill & the West End

See map 5

Beacon Hill

Rising up between Boston Common and the Charles River is Boston's most prestigious neighbourhood, Beacon Hill (fictional home of television's Ally McBeal). Because of its views of the Common and the Charles, as well as its proximity to the downtown area, from Boston's earliest days this incline has been the home of well-to-do, moneyed New England families, or the 'Boston Brahmins' as Oliver Wendell Holmes first dubbed them.

A nucleus of wealth and power, the Hill has been home, at one point or another, to famous folk like John Hancock, Louisa May Alcott, Nathaniel Hawthorne and architect Charles Bulfinch. Bulfinch, who designed the State House and part of the Massachusetts General Hospital and enhanced the original Faneuil Hall, left a lasting imprint on the city's architecture as his style continued to be imitated by those who followed in his wake (*see chapter* **Architecture**). Today, Boston's elite continue to occupy the Hill. Carly Simon has recently bought a house here and writers James Carroll, Robin Cook and Robert

The monumental **State House** *(page 54).*

and was elected to the Massachusetts legislature several times after the end of the war. He moved to a house at 86 Pinkney Street (near West Cedar Street) in 1878 and lived there for 15 years.

Further along the trail is the church where blacks fought for religious equality, the **Charles Street Meeting House** (on the corner of Mount Vernon and Charles Streets), and the homes of Abolition leaders and stations along the Underground Railroad, the network of hiding places through which escaped slaves passed on their route to freedom. The **Lewis Hayden House** (66 Phillips Street) is one of the most intriguing and inspiring of these. Occupied by Lewis Hayden and his wife Harriet, the house continued to shelter fugitive slaves even after the Fugitive Slave Act of 1850 gave slave-owners the right to recapture their slaves. Harriet Beecher Stowe, author of *Uncle Tom's Cabin*, visited the Hayden home to witness the number of runaways sheltered there. Rumour has it that the couple kept two kegs of gunpowder under their front step and would greet bounty hunters with lit candles, saying that they would rather blow up the whole house than surrender their guests.

Coburn's Gaming House (2 Phillips Street) was the home of John P Coburn, who was not only an active member in the New England Freedom Associates, the Boston Desegregation campaign and the Boston Vigilance Committee, but also someone who enjoyed some good gambling (in his house, no less). Over on Joy Street, the **Smith Court Residences** (3-10 Smith Court) are typical of the houses occupied by black families in nineteenth-century Boston. A few stops down is the **Abiel Smith School** (at 46 Joy Street, but currently closed for renovation), a community school established by black families in 1834 after their children were denied access to public schools. The final stop on the trail is the **African Meeting House**, one of the oldest black churches still standing. Often referred to as the black Faneuil Hall, this house was a centre for educational, political and Abolitionist gatherings during the nineteenth century.

African Meeting House

8 Smith Court (742 5415). Bowdoin, Charles/MGH or Park St T. **Open** *summer* 10am-4pm daily; *winter* 10am-4pm Mon-Fri. **Admission** free. **Credit** *shop only* AmEx, MC, V. **Map 5 G4**

Acorn Street, *on Beacon Hill.*

Frost have also been Hill residents. If you want further evidence of high-brow society, just note the healthy ratio of Saabs, BMWs and pearl-necked, loafer-bound natives around.

Explore the byways of the hill, beyond the brick townhouses with their overflowing window boxes and gas lamps, to appreciate the other-worldly atmosphere Beacon Hill exudes. In 1955 the Beacon Hill Historic District came into being and began to enforce architectural restraints that allow (well, force) the neighbourhood to keep its colonial, rustic charm. **Acorn Street** (between Mount Vernon and Chestnut Streets), probably one of the tiniest and quaintest, still has some of its original cobblestones.

The most central and largest of three inclines on a larger hill once known as 'Tremontaine,' Beacon Hill earned its name during colonial times. A look-out would be posted at the top of the hill and would light a beacon if enemy ships were sighted out at sea. Before the American Revolution even concluded, Bulfinch had begun designing a new seat for the Massachusetts legislature, to replace the old building at the corner of Washington and State Streets. When word spread that the site of the new **State House** was to be on the southern slope of Beacon Hill (where John Hancock's livestock once grazed), everyone who was anyone began to relocate to the new hub of the Hub (*see page 10* **History**). Bulfinch's State House, with its 23-carat gold dome, was commissioned in 1795 and today the impressive structure is one of Boston's best-known landmarks and continues to house the Senate and House of Representatives of the Massachusetts State legislature.

Other historical and architectural points of interest on Beacon Hill include the **Harrison Gray Otis House** and the **Charles Nichols House Museum** as well as the **Boston Athenaeum** (*see page 90* **Museums & Galleries**). A Harvard graduate, Otis had his house built by Bulfinch in 1796 and was fortunate to inhabit what was considered at the time one of the finest homes in Boston. The Charles Nichols House Museum, also a Bulfinch design, was the home of the slightly wacky spinster, Rose Standish Nichols who lived a Hill life of leisure and wealth. You can wander around her halls and learn in depth how the other half lived.

Charles Street

At the foot of the hill lies the neighbourhood's main thoroughfare, Charles Street. Lined with antique shops and gourmet restaurants, the street contributes considerably to the village-like charm of the area and is the ideal end point of an exploration. If you can swing it, splash out on dinner at one of the local restaurants: perhaps the **Hungry I** – down a positively medieval alleyway – or **Artu**; or drop in for a cup of coffee at **Panificio** or **Curious Liquids** (*see chapter* **Restaurants & Cafés** for all four). And for a real touch of local colour, try the **Sevens Pub** (*see page 118* **Pubs & Bars**).

Charles Nichols House Museum

55 Mount Vernon Street, at Joy Street (227 6993). Park St T. **Open** *1 May-31 Oct* 12.15-4.15pm Tue-Sat; *Nov, Dec, 1 Feb-Apr* 12.15-4.15pm Mon, Wed, Sat; closed Jan. **Admission** $5. **No credit cards.**
Map 5 G4
See also page 21 **Architecture**.

Harrison Gray Otis House

141 Cambridge Street, at Staniford Street (227 3956). Gov't Center T. **Open** *tours only* 11am-4pm Wed-Sun. **Admission** $2-$4. **Credit** MC, V.
Map 5 G4
See also page 20 **Architecture**.

State House

Beacon & Park Streets, Beacon Hill (727 3676). Park St T. **Open** 9am-5pm Mon-Fri; 10am-4pm Sat. **Admission** free. **Map 5 G4**
See also page 20 **Architecture**.
Disabled: toilet.

The West End

Ask Bostonians today about the West End, and many of them will look confused before they say that it no longer exists. And in fact, much of what was the West End does no longer exist. Once a large residential area between the North End and Beacon Hill, the West End housed a considerable low-income population who inhabited winding streets and cramped tenements. Despite the problems that such neighbourhoods tend to endure – overcrowding and a run-down infrastructure – the West End was a gritty but solid niche for minority families. In the 1960s, urban planners decided to give the area a face-lift, levelling the neighbourhood in favour of luxury high-rises and the expanding Massachusetts General Hospital (*see page 22* **Architecture**). This 'urban renewal' displaced thousands of residents – many of them African-American and Hispanic families. The memory of the destruction sticks sharply in Boston's collective memory, and is made worse by the lifeless high-rises that dominate what's left of the West End today.

Although it's not exactly a tourist hotspot, a few of the original neighbourhood buildings remain, such as the **West End Public Library** (151 Cambridge Street) and the synagogue, **Vilna Shul**, at 14 Phillips Street. Bordering what remains of the neighbourhood is the new **FleetCenter** (*see chapter* **Sport & Fitness**) on the former site of the Boston Garden sports arena where the Boston Celtics won numerous NBA Championships in the 1980s and Boston Bruins legend Bobby Orr ruled the hockey rink. Lacking the history, individuality, chipped seats and obscured views of the Garden, the FleetCenter is an impersonal structure, but remains the only place in town to see major sporting events as well as pro wrestling matches and Disney 'Icecapades', among other shows.

The complex that houses the **Museum of Science & Hayden Planetarium** is on the banks of the West End side of the Charles River (*see page 78* **On the waterfront**).

Beacon Hill's only square, Louisburg.

The North End

See map 5

New York's Little Italy comes across as somewhere between a genuine haven for Italian-Americans and an ethnically-themed Disney theme park – a tourist trap by way of Ragu. It's very different in Boston, where the largest community of those of Italian descent lives in the city's most genuine neighbourhood. The North End is the real deal, the oldest residential neighbourhood in the city, a tightly-knit community that has thus far managed to resist the gentrification that has touched almost every other corner of the city.

The area brims with history that extends back to pre-Revolutionary days, from its settling shortly after the Puritans landed on Plymouth Rock to resident Paul Revere's famous ride and the birth of the Kennedy clan. The North End was a locus of

The US Post Office is at the heart of the village-like **Charles Street**.

great wealth before the Revolution, but as the wealthy moved out, various waves of immigrants moved in and today the area's mostly Italian.

The North End has survived many fires, as well as the great and significantly more bizarre 1919 molasses flood, when a tanker truck exploded and sent 2.5 million gallons of molasses coursing through the streets. The disaster killed 24 people, injured 60, and left countless others extremely sticky. Some claim you can still smell the molasses on Commercial Street on a hot day.

Like much of the rest of Boston, the North End is best navigated by foot (although be prepared to fight your way past construction work on the Big Dig if you're walking from the downtown area). One of the best ways to experience the neighbourhood vibe is to check out some of the myriad summer street fairs. Every weekend, residents hold religious-inspired parades, set up food carts and sell locally-made crafts, each household trying to outdo the next in good-natured competition. They're hard to miss because they involve lots of noise and colour (*see page 38* **Boston by Season**).

North Square

Three of the celebrated Freedom Trail's sites (*see page 45*) are in the North End. The most well-known of these is the house of one of the area's big stars, and certainly its most famous former resident, Paul Revere. Every year, 200,000 people visit the **Paul Revere House**. Of course, this isn't the house he was born in. Or the house he died in. Or the house that the Beastie Boys wrote their song 'Paul Revere' about. But it's a house Revere owned for 30 years of his life and it was the house he lived in when he set off on his famous midnight ride through the streets of Boston.

He worked as a silversmith in a workshop on nearby Clark's Wharf and much of his handiwork remains in the house today. What has not lasted is the third storey he added to accommodate his many children – 16, although 30 years separated the oldest and youngest and no more than eight lived under the roof at one time.

The house is interesting as a piece of seventeenth-century architecture (*see page 19* **Architecture**), but its value is far greater as history. Revere snuck out of this very house to alert his fellow patriots that the British were coming and even though we now know that Longfellow's poem may have unjustifiably lionised Revere (*see page 8* **History**) he remains the big star.

More impressive architecturally is the three-storey brick mansion next door, the **Pierce/Hichborn House**. It was built in 1810 and Revere's cousin Nathaniel Hichborn bought it to be closer to his silversmith relative. The contrast between the two houses is fascinating – Revere's being far more primitive than Hichborn's, although only a few years older. While you're here, pay a visit to Walt Whitman's old house of worship, the **Sacred Heart Church**, as well as the **Mariners' House** at 11 North Square (between Moon and Prince Streets), a hotel that rented rooms to sailors for $3.75 a night from the 1870s up until 1997.

The North End can boast other famous sons and daughters. Congressman and Boston mayor John 'Honey Fitz' Fitzgerald was born here on Ferry Street and later lived at 4 Garden Court, where he reared a daughter named Rose who later married a fellow named Kennedy. Her sons included President John F Kennedy, Attorney General Robert F Kennedy and Senator Ted Kennedy, who still serves today. Despite many personal ups and downs, especially among the younger generations, the liberal Kennedy clan remains undefeated in Massachusetts elections (*see page 13* **History**).

Paul Revere & Pierce/Hichborn House

19 & 29 North Square, between Richmond & Prince Streets, North End (523 2338). Haymarket T. **Open** *15 Apr-31 Oct* 9.30am-5.15pm daily; 1 Nov-14 Apr 9.30am-4.15pm daily. **Admission** $1-$2.40; *combined ticket* $1.50-$4. **Credit** *shop only* AmEx. **Map 5 H3**
Website: www.paulreverehouse.org

Sacred Heart Church

12 North Square, at Prince Street, North End (523 5638). Haymarket T. **Open** 7am-8pm daily. **Map 5 G3**

Hanover Street

No visit to the North End would be complete without a good Italian meal, and chances are that exploring Hanover Street will produce one or two…hundred. The menus are posted outside and waiters come out to sell you their restaurant. 'I have the best table for you', they might say, or 'Our spaghetti carbonara is not to be missed'. Try to resist. You'll fail – they've played this game before and their job is to lure you inside. There are also dozens of coffee and pastry shops lining the streets, particularly Hanover Street; for our recommendations, *see chapter* **Restaurants & Cafés**.

One of the more notorious sites in the area is the **Langone Funeral Home** (383 Hanover Street). This is where Nicola Sacco and Bartolomeo Venzetti were executed in 1927, following a controversial robbery and murder trial that preyed on the xenophobia of the era. A nicer memory lies at **168 Hanover Street**, where in 1851 Eben Jordan started a store that evolved into the Jordan Marsh empire. A few years later, Rowland H Macy began his own store nearby, called Macy's. All went well for over a century until Macy's absorbed Jordan Marsh in 1996 – maybe this isn't such a nice story after all.

Nearby on Prince Street is **St Leonard's**, the first Italian Catholic church in New England. It houses a beautiful flower garden and still functions as a place of worship. **St Stephen's** is the only remaining church in Boston designed by master architect

Paul Revere mounts guard over the **Old North Church**. *See page 58.*

Hanging out on **Hanover Street**. *See p56.*

Charles Bulfinch (*see page 20* **Architecture**). Bulfinch remodelled an existing structure in 1804, and it contained a set of church bells cast by Paul Revere. The church also has a part in the history of the Kennedys, serving as the bookends for Rose Kennedy's life, from baptism to burial.

St Leonard's Church

Prince Street, at Hanover Street, North End (523 2110). Haymarket T. **Open** *16 Oct-14 May* 7.30am-1pm Mon-Fri; 7am-6pm Sat, Sun; *15 May-15 Oct* 7am-10pm daily. **Map 5 G3**

St Stephen's Church

24 Clark Street, at Hanover Street, North End (523 1230). Haymarket T. **Open** 7am-dusk daily. **Map 5 H3**

The Prado

In 1933 the North End's star got his own park. The **Paul Revere Mall**, located in an area known as 'The Prado', features as its centrepiece a statue of Revere designed by Cyrus E Dallin in 1865 and finally cast in 1940, when the cash finally came though. The mall (between Hanover and Unity Streets) serves as a social epicentre of the North End, with neighbourhood folks doing neighbourhood things, from playing cards to gossiping or arguing over sport scores. Another social spot further towards the waterfront and on the very edge of the North End is **Christopher Columbus Park**, named after someone who did not live in the North End (*see page 51* **Downtown & the Financial District**).

Another Freedom Trail landmark in the North End is the **Old North Church**. It was originally called Christ Church in Boston, but local custom dictated that the oldest church in the area be known as Old North. It was built in 1723 in the style of Christopher Wren and its famous steeple, from which lanterns were hung to signal the movements of British troops, was added in 1740. Further steeples were added in 1806 and 1954 after a pair of hurricanes knocked the largest one in Boston to the ground. In the original window where the two lanterns were hung sits a third lantern, lit by President Ford on 18 April 1975, symbolising hope for the nation's next century of freedom.

The last Freedom Trail stop in the North End is **Copp's Hill Burying Ground** on Charter Street, the final resting place of roughly 10,000 early Bostonians. It's the highest point in the North End, and an especially good spot for taking pictures of the USS *Constitution* and the Bunker Hill Monument across the harbour in Charlestown. Puritan preachers Cotton and Increase Mather are buried on Copp's Hill, as is black slave and soldier Prince Hall, an early African-American leader in Boston. The British used the site to launch cannon balls at the rebel army during the Battle of Bunker Hill; they warmed up by using some of the gravestones for target practice.

Nearby is the site of the Brinks job, the unsolved 1950 armoured-car heist that inspired a string of movies. And also in the vicinity is a symbol of the sometimes eccentric rudeness of some Bostonians. You'll note that **44 Hull Street** barely looks like a house. After all, it's the narrowest one in Boston – only ten feet (three metres) wide – and its sole purpose was apparently to annoy the neighbours by blocking their view. Welcome to Boston, pal.

Copp's Hill Burying Ground

Charter Street, at Snowhill Street. North Station T. **Open** dawn-dusk daily. **Admission** free. **Map 5 G3**

Old North Church

193 Salem Street, at Hull Street (523 6676). Haymarket T. **Open** *Nov-May* 9am-5pm daily; *June-Oct* 9am-6pm daily. **Map 5 G3**

Charlestown

Charlestown is famous among locals as having been home to the Mob. And it remains the last Boston stronghold for organised crime. It used to have a reputation, ironically enough, as one of the safest areas to live in town (along with the North End) because the Mob kept petty criminals in line. Nowadays this is probably more legend than truth and, like the North End, its prime areas of real estate are being snapped up by young professionals rather than two-bit mobsters. Whatever the case, the local architecture and much older history of the area are what's most likely to strike the casual visitor to Charlestown.

The area was first settled in 1628; in 1847 it became a city in its own right and 27 years after that was annexed to the city of Boston, of which it is now a neighbourhood. One of its most famous residents was John Harvard; when he died in 1638 he bequeathed half his money – along with his collection of classical and theological literature – to a newly-created school in the neighbouring village of Newtowne (now Cambridge). The school, of course, became Harvard College (*see page 79* **Cambridge & Somerville**).

Charlestown Navy Yard

A trip to Charlestown wouldn't be complete without a visit to the Charlestown Navy Yard, which opened in 1800. By the beginning of World War II, the Navy Yard employed 47,000 workers, almost as many people as lived in the city. Today it serves as a museum to American naval history. Start with the **Commandant's House**, which accommodated Navy Yard commandants for 169 years until 1974. Visitors can explore the first floor of this brick house, where photos and other memorabilia are displayed.

You can also tour the USS *Cassin Young*, a World War II destroyer docked at the Navy Yard. It was built in 1943 and has since been restored. The most famous ship at the Navy Yard, however, is the **USS *Constitution***. In 1794 the US Congress authorised the construction of six frigates to protect American merchant ships from pirates as well as French and British forces. One of these contracts, for the USS *Constitution*, was given to a shipyard in Boston. In 1797, the *Constitution*, constructed from more than 1,500 trees and with copper fastenings crafted by Paul Revere, set sail; because it has remained part of the US Navy, it's now the oldest commissioned war ship in the world.

The ship earned its nickname 'Old Ironsides' during a battle with HMS *Guerrière* during the war of 1812, when shots fired by the *Guerrière* supposedly bounced off the hull of the *Constitution*, leading a sailor to remark that the sides of the *Constitution* were made of iron. 'Old Ironsides' has largely remained in dry dock since the late nineteenth century, although she did set sail for the first time in 116 years in 1997 – the year of her bicentennial – and she is towed out into the harbour and turned once a year, to ensure that her hull weathers evenly. Free tours are given of the ship and its 44 guns daily. The **USS Constitution Museum** (*see page 93* **Museums & Galleries**) includes an interactive gallery in which visitors get to load and fire a cannon or simulate steering a square-rigger at sea.

The **Charlestown Visitor's Center** is located in the Navy Yard near the USS Constitution Museum, in which 'The Whites of Their Eyes', a video re-enactment of the Battle of Bunker Hill is shown every 30 minutes. The name refers to the battle orders given to Revolutionary soldiers: in order to save their precious ammunition, the troops – who had dug into Breed's Hill to resist British occupation of Charlestown – were told not to fire on the approaching red coats until they saw the whites of their eyes.

The **Bunker Hill Monument**, in Monument Square, is a memorial to that battle. The obelisk, with 294 steps (it takes about 15 minutes to climb to the top) was dedicated in 1842 by Daniel Webster to commemorate one of the first battles of the Revolutionary War. Although the Patriots lost the battle, the British suffered devastating losses and the fight proved that the British were vulnerable and could be resisted (*see page 8* **History**). The monument is part of the Boston National Historical Park and park rangers give tours of the area.

There is more to local history than the Revolutionary War, however. A walk around the heart of Charlestown reveals a number of older houses that range in architectural style from the late eighteenth-century Federal to the Greek Revival and later nineteenth-century Queen Anne style (the latter two styles can be seen particularly in **Thompson Square** and **Monument Square**). You can create your own tour, or simply pick up the Freedom Trail from North Station to Warren Street.

End your tour at the **Warren Tavern**. It was built just after most of the city was burnt following the Battle of Bunker Hill, which makes it one of the oldest structures (if not the oldest) in Charlestown. Named after Joseph Warren, one of the Revolutionaries who died in the Battle of Bunker Hill, the tavern was where Paul Revere presided over Masonic meetings as a grand master. After he became president, George Washington also visited the place. Its most recent claim to fame was as the watering hole of the main character in TV's *Spencer: For Hire*. The building re-opened as a bar and restaurant in 1972 and has thrived ever since.

Charlestown Navy Yard Visitor's Center & Bunker Hill Pavilion

Outside Gate 1 of the Charlestown Navy Yard, Constitution Road, Charlestown (241 7575). North Station T/92, 93 bus. **Open** *summer* 9am-6pm daily; *winter* 9am-5pm daily. **Admission** free.

Commandant's House

Charlestown Navy Yard, Constitution Road, Charlestown (information 242 5601). North Station T. **Open** 10am-4pm Sat. **Admission** free.

USS *Constitution*

Charlestown Navy Yard, Charlestown (242 5671). Community College T. **Open** 9.30am-3.50pm (last tour 3.30pm) daily. **Admission** free.

Warren Tavern

2 Pleasant Street, at Main Street, Charlestown (241 8142). Community College T. **Open** 11.15am-1am Mon-Fri; 10.30am-1am Sat, Sun. **Credit** AmEx, Disc, MC, V.

Back Bay & the South End

See map 3

Back Bay

Back Bay did not exist 150 years ago: the area was just marshland created by the Charles River. But by the late 1850s, Boston was running out of space and city chiefs decided to fill it in. 'Noxious odors and stagnation' given off by the marsh ever since the completion of a dam along its northern edge in 1821 provided an extra incentive.

That dam became what is today's Beacon Street and, together with the waterfront, it forms the northern boundary of the Back Bay. To the south, the district stretches to the edge of the Southwest Corridor and the Massachusetts Turnpike (I-90), with Massachusetts Avenue and Arlington Street forming its western and eastern boundaries respectively.

If Paris comes to mind when you walk along major Back Bay streets such as Commonwealth Avenue, Arthur Gilman would be pleased. He was the architect who laid the initial street plans for the area and he modelled them on the grand boulevards of Paris. But unlike Paris, the streets of Back Bay are organised on a strict grid pattern, with the major avenues running northeast to southwest and crossed by a series of smaller streets named in alphabetical order. Arlington is closest to the downtown area, while at the far end is Hereford Street, just before Massachusetts Avenue. Strict building codes ensured that only 'grand' designs were approved, resulting in the almost uniform look of Back Bay today. But if you look closely, you'll see a gradual evolution in architectural styles from east to west.

Despite the Parisian inspiration, it seems that Bostonians still retained some affection for their former English cousins and gave the streets of Back Bay names such as Marlborough, Commonwealth and Newbury. For what was once a malodorous marsh, the area didn't take long to establish itself. By the end of the nineteenth century, the city's elite were queuing up to build townhouses here. Today, Back Bay is one of Boston's most expensive areas and contains its glitziest shopping street – Newbury. This, together with Copley Square, is the area's principal attraction, though to get a feel for the neighbourhood you should wander round the quieter back streets too.

Copley Square

Roughly defined, Back Bay's centre is the area stretching from Copley Square up to Newbury Street. It's the obvious starting point for exploring both Back Bay and the South End. If you are coming by T, take the green line and exit at Copley.

Copley Square is one of Boston's most attractive places, with Trinity Church on one side and the public library on the other. Music festivals often take place in the square on spring and summer weekends, and it's also the finishing point for the annual **Boston marathon** (*see page 38* **Boston by Season**).

No coffee-table book on Boston would be complete without its picture of the neo-Romanesque **Trinity Church**, completed in 1877. This was where Boston's elite worshipped in the late nineteenth century. An imposing structure, it somehow also manages to look a bit quaint and fussy. It's surprising that the staid Boston Brahmins of the nineteenth century approved of all that Romanesque flamboyance (*see page 22* **Architecture**). Today, the church has to struggle for space with that glass giant, the John Hancock Tower, Boston's tallest building. Directly opposite the church is the magnificent **Boston Public Library**. Begun in the 1840s, it is America's oldest public library. Go inside to explore its courtyard gardens and imposing reading rooms. On the way up the stairs are murals by Puvis de Chavannes, and there are others elsewhere in the building by Sargent. The star attraction is probably the Bates Hall, which features a majestic barrel-arched ceiling enclosed by half domes at each end and busts of famous writers and Bostonians. The library currently holds more than 7 million books, including over 1 million rare manuscripts covering many key moments in US history (*see also chapters* **Architecture**, **Literary Boston** *and* **Museums & Galleries**).

On the corner of Copley Square, next to Boylston and Dartmouth streets, is **BosTix**, a discount ticket agency, which sells half-price tickets after 11am on the day of the performance (*see page 211* **The Performing Arts**).

Just across St James Avenue from Copley Square is the entrance to the observatory deck at the top of the 62-storey **John Hancock Tower**. On a good day, you can see landmarks more than 100 miles (160 kilometres) away from the top floor, although only from three sides. But it is not just the view that is the attraction here. The top floor also has an audio-visual show tracking the development of Boston from its beginnings as a thin strip of land jutting into the sea – the Shawmut Peninsula. Interspersed with flowery accounts of the 1773 Boston Tea Party and the Revolution that followed, it shows how Boston gradually reclaimed land from the Charles and the ocean.

Looking every inch the sacred institution: the **Boston Public Library** *(see page 62).*

Boston Public Library
700 Boylston Street, at Copley Square (536 5400). Copley T. **Open** 9am-9pm Mon-Thur; 9am-5pm Fri, Sat; 1-5pm Sun. **Admission** free.
Map 3 F5
Disabled: toilet. Website: www.bpl.org

John Hancock Tower
200 Clarendon Street, at Copley Square (247 1977). Copley T. **Open** *Apr-Oct* 9am-10pm Mon-Sat; *Nov-Mar* 9am-5pm Mon-Sat. **Admission** $3-$5. **Credit** AmEx, MC, V.
Map 3 F5
Website: www.hancock.com

Trinity Church
236 Clarendon Street, Copley Square (536 0944). Copley or Back Bay T. **Open** 7am-6pm daily. **Admission** free.
Map 3 F5

Copley Place

A short walk from Copley Square, across Huntington Avenue, is the Copley Place shopping mall. Situated next to the Mass Pike, it's geographically on the boundary between Back Bay and the South End. Psychologically, though, it's in the Back Bay, since it is devoted to shopping (*see chapter* **Shops & Services**). It houses a wide range of shops and cafés, as well as a cinema complex (*see page 186* **Film**) and branches of the **Westin** and **Marriott** hotel chains (*see page 112* **Accommodation**) and the **Hynes Convention Center** (*see page 266* **Directory**).

Boylston Street

Heading towards Newbury Street from Copley Square, you have to cross Boylston Street. Although not in the Newbury league, it is a major shopping street, with a few good bars and restaurants. Architecturally, it's a bit of a mish-mash – where traditional Back Bay style meets modern concrete brutalism, especially at its southwestern end, around the **Prudential Center**, an undercover shopping mall and apartment complex centred around the huge tower known as 'The Pru'. There's a bar and a 'Skywalk' viewing platform in the **Prudential Tower** itself. The Prudential Center is also the starting point for the boisterous **Boston Duck Tours** (*see page 86*).

Not all the area is encased in concrete, however. Also at this end of Boylston is the characterful **Boylston Fire Station** (955 Boylston, at Massachusetts Avenue; 343 3550) dating from 1887, with the same Romanesque style as Trinity Church. It still houses two fire engines. Part of the building was a police station, but in 1976 that section became the **Institute of Contemporary Art** (*see page 88* **Museums & Galleries**). It displays work by lesser-known US as well as big-name artists.

If you like your buildings chintzy, take a look at **The Berkeley**. On the southern side of Boylston, on the corner with Berkeley Street, this early twentieth-century edifice looks like a giant wedding cake, with gleaming white spires and fussy adornments. Looking onto the Public Garden is the **Arlington Street Church**, one of the Back Bay's first buildings, built by Arthur Gilman and containing 16 Tiffany stained glass windows inside. Boylston carries on towards the downtown area, but beyond the **Public Garden** (*see below*) there is little to interest the visitor.

At 500 Boylston is a branch of the **Globe Corner Bookstore** (*see chapter* **Shops & Services**), a good place to pick up local maps and guides. Just opposite is perhaps the most imposing building on Boylston, a giant marble edifice called **The New England**, headquarters to a financial company – although for some tastes, all that marble is a bit too Italian fascist. There are a couple of good bars and restaurants on Boylston. With names like Freedom Trail IPA and Boston Massacre Lager, the microbrew beers at the **Back Bay Brewing Company** may sound like a joke, but they taste good and the bar has won several awards in recent years. For this and watering-holes in the area, *see page 115* **Pubs & Bars**.

South End gardens

The South End (*see page 68*) is famous for its community gardens, which are dotted throughout the area. Some are urban allotments used by nearby residents to grow vegetables. Others are more ornamental, providing a beautiful contrast with the red-brick houses. They originated in the 1950s, when the city authorities were trying to reinvigorate the area by tearing down substandard buildings. Some of the space was reclaimed and turned into gardens. Often these are tiny – slipped into a gap between two houses, but providing a tranquil green space for locals to sit outside in. Two of the prettiest gardens are on **West Concord Street** and **East Rutland Street**, between Tremont Street and Shawmut Avenue.

On the third Saturday in June, many South Enders open up their private gardens to public viewing. The tours are organised by the **South End/Lower Roxbury Open Space Land Trust** (437 0999), which is responsible for most of the community gardens in the area.

Victorian mansions run the length of **Commonwealth Avenue** *(see page 64).*

Arlington Street Church
351 Boylston Street, at Arlington Street (536 7050). Arlington T. **Open** 10am-6pm Mon-Thur; 10am-2pm Sun. **Admission** free.
Map 5 F5
Disabled: toilet.

Prudential Center & Tower
800 Boylston Street, between Dalton & Exeter Streets (236 3318). Prudential T. **Open** *Skywalk* 10am-10pm daily; *stores* 10am-8pm Mon-Sat; 11am-6pm Sun; *food court* 7am-9pm Mon-Sat; 9am-7pm Sun. **Admission** *Skywalk* $3-$4. **No credit cards.**
Map 3 E5
Disabled: toilet.

Newbury Street

The city's hype merchants like to call Newbury Street 'Boston's Rodeo Drive', after the exclusive street in Beverly Hills. There's no doubt that Newbury is the priciest shopping avenue in Boston, and it's the place to find most of the international fashion outlets in the city – names such as Armani and DKNY (*see chapter* **Shops & Services**). Commercial art galleries have also made Newbury their home. There are cafés, restaurant and bistros the length of the street, many as well-known for their intimidating hostesses as for their food and drink.

At the Arlington Street end Newbury has a more reserved atmosphere, with more conservative fashions and traditional stores, as well as the old-fashioned **Ritz-Carlton** hotel (*see page 104* **Accommodation**). As you go southwest along the street towards Massachusetts Avenue, the shops and the prices become less exclusive, while the number of posers increases. So does the traffic, especially in summer, when convertibles and SUVs (sports utility vehicles) crawl along the street, rollerbladers and skateboarders zipping between them. One of the ultimate Newbury shopping experiences is a visit to **Louis Boston** (*see chapter* **Shops & Services**), a grand clothes shop based in a four-storey mansion. The building stands alone, between Boylston and Newbury Streets, with mannequins in glass cabinets outside.

The far end of Newbury Street, near Massachusetts Avenue, is almost hip, thanks to an interesting mix of cafés and shops. **Trident Booksellers and Café** (338 Newbury Street; 267 8688) specialises in 'alternative' books – on anything from medicine to lifestyles to the environment. It's got a good café, and is a useful place to pick up free sheets and details of alternative events around town.

Directly opposite is the second-hand **Avenue Victor Hugo Book Shop** (*see chapter* **Shops & Services**), which, as its name suggests, stocks a wide range of foreign-language titles. Other shops in the area include **Back Bay Bikes & Boards** where you can hire bikes and rollerblades (336 Newbury Street; 247 2336), **Condom World** (*see chapter* **Shops & Services**) and just above it **Newbury Comics** (*see chapter* **Shops & Services**), **Patagonia**, an army surplus shop (346 Newbury Street; 424 1776), and **CD Spins** (*see chapter* **Shops & Services**), a second-hand music store. At the very end of the street is **Tower Records** (*see chapter* **Shops & Services**), open until midnight daily. The entrances to the Hynes/ICA T are right underneath.

'Make Way for Ducklings': feeding the real ones in the ***Public Garden****, and ...*

Around Commonwealth Avenue

Running parallel with Newbury is Commonwealth Avenue, the grand boulevard of Back Bay and easily the most imposing street in Boston. A wide, tree-lined mall and gardens runs along its centre, splitting the traffic. Statues and memorials are dotted along the length of the mall, beginning near Massachusetts Avenue and ending at Arlington Street. It is a popular stroll for locals, who try not to get too close to the many homeless who also enjoy the mall in the warmer months. Classic Victorian mansions run the length of the avenue on both sides, although not all are as exclusive as they look – some serve as student accommodation. One house, at **72 Commonwealth**, is the Boston centre of the International Society for Krishna Consciousness. Not far away, on the corner with Clarendon Street, is another Back Bay landmark – Henry Richardson's 1871 **First Baptist Church** with its striking tower. And, not surprisingly, it was designed in the Romanesque style.

Stroll along the Commonwealth Avenue mall and you'll encounter the granite likeness of **Alexander Hamilton**, the first secretary of the Treasury and an aide to George Washington and whose visage graces the ten-dollar bill. Hamilton, who was responsible for financing the Revolutionary War, met his end the old-fashioned way: he was killed in a duel with US vice-president Aaron Burr after Hamilton reportedly badmouthed him. Further along the mall is a monument that chronicles a more recent tragic piece of Boston history: a dramatic memorial to the nine **Boston firefighters** who lost their lives battling a blaze that broke out at the Hotel Vendôme in 1972. The poignant tribute features a curving, oblong structure detailing the chronology of events that led to the fatalities and a firefighter's coat and helmet, which lie draped over the monument.

Going northwards from Commonwealth Avenue towards the river, the next major street is **Marlborough**. It has no specific sights, but it is the quietest of the Back Bay's grand streets because of traffic restrictions. Consequently, the residences seem just that bit more exclusive on Marlborough. Starting just opposite the Public Garden, it runs in parallel with Commonwealth Avenue and **Beacon Street**. Beacon is one of Boston's longest streets, stretching from the heart of downtown, near the State House, all the way out through Brookline to Cleveland Circle – over four miles (6 kilometres) away. The section that passes through Back Bay is largely a residential street, but it's a major thoroughfare. It is a classic Back Bay grand avenue, with almost uniform Victorian mansions on either side, often encased in ivy. The local branch of the German **Goethe Institute** is between Clarendon and Berkeley Streets (170 Beacon Street; 262 6050), and offers lectures, films, exhibitions and events, focusing on all aspects of German culture and society.

At **150 Beacon Street** is the mansion where the art-collector Isabella Stewart Gardner lived in the late 1800s until her move to a palazzo in the Fenway in 1902 (*see page 72*). Then it was number 152, but when Gardner moved she ordered that

... the bronze versions inspired by Robert McCloskey's children's tale.

the number never be used again – and apparently she was obeyed. The building is now a college. If you want to know what these mansions look like inside, **Gibson House**, at 137 Beacon, will give you a taste. The six-storey brownstone has been turned into a 'Victorian House Museum'.

From the Back Bay section of Beacon Street, there are four entry-points to the waterfront – at the western end, via the ramp from the Harvard Bridge, and then from footbridges at Fairfield Street, at Clarendon Street and from David G Mugar Way at the eastern end, at Charles Street.

You don't just have to see the area from the front. You can also see the Back Bay from the back. A network of alleys runs behind many of the blocks, used for parking and garbage collection. Most have their own street signs, such as Public Alley 422. But they also allow the curious to get a look at the huge decks, balconies and roof gardens at the back of many of the residences.

First Baptist Church

110 Commonwealth Avenue, at Clarendon Street (267 3148). Copley T. **Open** 11am-2pm Tue-Fri. **Admission** free. **Map 5 F5**

Gibson House

137 Beacon Street, between Arlington & Berkeley Streets (267 6338). Arlington T. **Open for tours** *1 May-31 Oct* 1pm, 2pm, 3pm Wed-Sun; *1 Nov-30 Apr* 1pm, 2pm, 3pm Sat, Sun. **Admission** $5. **No credit cards. Map 5 F5**

The Public Garden

The 25-acre (10-hectare) Public Garden sits shoulder-to-shoulder with Boston Common on the other side of Charles Street. But it is much younger than the common, dating from 1837 and the first attempts to reclaim the marsh of the Back Bay. It was an integral part of architect Arthur Gilman's vision for the area, acting as the end-point for the grand expanse of Commonwealth Avenue. It was America's first public botanical garden, a bursting-with-colour showcase for burgeoning greenhouse technology. The dazzling display of floral firepower continues today, albeit with a few newer attractions. One of them, a statue tribute to Robert McCloskey's Boston-based children's story Make Way For Ducklings, features eight of his characters following their quacking mother. A more sombre monument of a Good Samaritan holding an individual under the influence of ether commemorates the 'discovery that the inhaling of ether causes insensibility to pain'. This landmark in medicine – first demonstrated at Boston's Massachusetts General Hospital – was apparently the source of a skirmish between two individuals who each claimed credit for the discovery. So the decision was made to offer a tribute to neither individual, but rather, to ether itself.

A third attraction that stands centre stage in the garden, surrounded by a brilliant yellow bed of dandelions, is a regal-looking bronze statue of **General George Washington** sitting astride his horse. It has been said that the statue features one of the most detailed, true-to-life examples of a horse (the only part of the animal missing is its tongue), but this hasn't stopped late-night pranksters from regularly removing the good general's sword as a souvenir, keeping the statue sword-makers in steady business.

In winter, you can skate on the pond in the garden and in summer, if you're looking for a cheesy tourist experience, take out one of the famous Swan Boats. Just opposite the garden on Beacon Street is another tourist experience, the **Bull and Finch Pub**, better known as the inspiration for *Cheers* (*see page 118* **Pubs & Bars**).

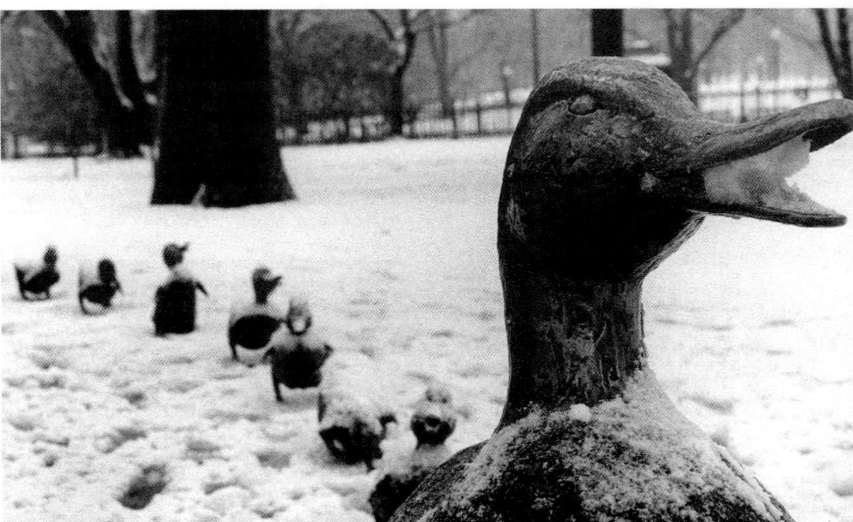

Massachusetts Avenue

From Beacon Street as far as Boylston Street, the section of Massachusetts Avenue that forms the western boundary of Back Bay is a motley mixture of shops, bars, restaurants and colleges. Just after Boylston (going south), at 136 Massachusetts Avenue is the **Berklee Performance Center** (266 7455), linked with the adjacent music college, which puts on shows by its students and members, and occasionally hosts big-name acts. Trendy Berklee Music College next door is the place to go to study pop and all kinds of contemporary music (*see page 208* **Nightlife**).

Further down, the triangle of space formed by Massachusetts Avenue and Huntington is dominated by the world headquarters of the Christian Scientists, officially known as the **First Church of Christ, Scientist** (175 Huntington Avenue; 450 2000). It's an ugly collection of buildings, with a muscular office building on one side and a concrete tower on the other, and an ornate pastiche basilica looking onto Massachusetts Avenue. The long 'Reflecting Pool' redeems the scene – and despite the architecture, it is a relative sanctuary from the noise and dirt of the surrounding roads.

Behind the church, next to Massachusetts Avenue, is the Christian Science Publishing Society building, which contains one of the more unusual attractions in Boston – the **Mapparium**. This is a 30-foot (nine-metre) globe made up of more than 600 stained-glass panels, which allows you to get 'inside' the earth by means of a glass bridge through the middle. National boundaries are drawn to scale, although you'll notice a few things have changed since the Mapparium was constructed in the 1930s. The whole complex was being renovated as this guide went to press, but was due to re-open again shortly.

Across Massachusetts Avenue and a little further down is **Symphony Hall**, headquarters of the Boston Symphony Orchestra (*see page 216* **The Performing Arts**) and completed in 1900. Seiji Ozawa celebrated his 25th year as its conductor in 1998. Opposite, on the same side as the Christian Science church, is the beautiful **Horticultural Hall**, which houses the Massachusetts Horticultural Society as well as a huge library of gardening literature. *Boston Magazine* is also based in this building.

To the east

The area between the southern section of Arlington Street and Copley Place is an unappealing mix of impersonal office blocks split by busy roads. But just at the point where Columbus Avenue meets Arlington Street there is an incongruous castle-like building that breaks up the monotony of the area a little. In the early 1900s, this was the armoury of the **First Corps of Cadets**, who gained fame – or notoriety, depending on your point of view – from their role in taking the place of Boston's cops during the police strike of 1911. Today the building is just a meeting hall. Next door, on Columbus Avenue, is the popular restaurant **Grillfish** (162 Columbus Avenue; 357 1620).

Just opposite, on the other side of Columbus Avenue, is the classic edifice of Boston's **Park Plaza** hotel (*see page 108* **Accommodation**). Nearby is the **Emancipation Group** statue on Park Plaza, situated in the small triangle of space between Charles Street and Columbus Avenue. Set up in 1879, it depicts President Abraham Lincoln and a freed slave and is a replica of a statue in Washington DC that emancipated slaves paid to have erected four years earlier.

Bay Village

Traffic roars through this area, but just a short walk southwards down Charles Street from the Park Plaza is a relative oasis that somehow has managed to shut out the city. It's Bay Village, one of Boston's more unusual neighbourhoods. Squeezed between Arlington, Stuart and Charles Streets and the Turnpike, its small, intimate houses and buildings give the area an almost European village-like atmosphere. Bay Village's reputation is one of genteel bohemia and it has a significant gay population, many artists and media types, as well as more reserved law offices and quite a few senior citizens. At night, the transvestites come out to play – heading for **Jacque's Cabaret**, a drag bar near the Charles Street end (*see page 193* **Gay & Lesbian Boston**). Only since the 1960s has the area been known as Bay Village. Before that it was the Church Street district. But it has been around since 1815 – another stretch of land that was reclaimed from the Charles River mudflats.

Fayette Street is one of the prettiest roads through the area. On the corner of Fayette and Church Streets is what must be Boston's tiniest bar and café, **Twelve Church** (12 Church Street; 348 0012). With the counter, there's room for just three small tables and chairs. In June or July, Bay Village holds an annual street party, although the date varies from year to year. If you can catch it while you're in town, go along to get a feel for this eclectic area.

The South End

To Bostonians who never bother to go there – and there are many – the South End means only one thing: the gay area. In fact, it's probably the city's

South End landmark: the **Boston Center for the Arts**. *See page 68.*

ARTS
CYCLORAMA
539

most ethnically and socially mixed district, with large Puerto Rican, African-American and Chinese populations, and there's much more to the area than a thriving gay scene. It's a neighbourhood where high-price condos and low-rent housing projects stand cheek-to-cheek and where – by some estimates – more than 70 languages are spoken. Its flavour can change dramatically from street to street.

Roughly speaking, the South End's boundaries are the Mass Turnpike (I-90), with Northampton Street/Massachusetts Avenue forming its western side and the area around Albany Street its eastern limit – although at the end it's fairly industrial. At its northeastern end, the South End merges into **Chinatown** (*see page 51*).

The area has had a Cinderella-like history – which makes it all the more interesting. Like so much of Boston, what is now the South End started life as a mudflat around the area known as 'the Neck', the narrow stretch of land (just 100 feet/30 metres wide in places) linking central Boston to the mainland. That was in the late eighteenth century, and at the time there was another South End, around Summer Street, which is now very much part of the downtown area.

In those days, the Neck was best known as an execution ground. By the 1860s, the area around the Neck had been filled in and the 'New' South End had become one of Boston's grander neighbourhoods. The distinctive Victorian houses and squares date from this time. But then the Back Bay stole the show. By the late-1870s, the South End was no longer the place to be and instead had become a district of lodging houses, developing a low-life reputation. Despite – or maybe because of – this, many churches also moved into the area, and you will see them dotted throughout the South End, although several now serve other purposes. Different ethnic minorities moved in, tempted by the low rent, and distinct communities developed. It was from this base that the South End emerged as the centre of jazz music in Boston in the 1950s, although not much of that scene remains.

Today, though, Cinderalla is definitely back at the ball. Since the late 1970s, the old brownstones have gradually been restored and it has become a hip neighbourhood. The area's designation as a historic preservation district in 1983 helped, and it has been recognised as the largest complete Victorian neighbourhood in the whole of the USA.

But it was the adoption of the area by the gay community that really got the renewal process going. The seedier side of the South End remains, however, especially in its further reaches, from Washington to Albany Streets. Gentrification hasn't really touched this area, and prostitution and drug-dealing are common – you'll get the picture from reading Officer John Sacco's column in the *South End News* (*see page 197* **Media**). Don't be put off – there are a few sights down this way, too.

We have divided the neighbourhood roughly into two areas – north and south of Tremont Street, the South End's main street.

North of Tremont

The South End's core is around the junction of Clarendon and Tremont Streets, with Union Park just opposite. Here, a cluster of trendy cafés and fancy stores create a hip urban-village identity. Many of the businesses are either gay-owned or gay-aimed and at Pride time (*see page 39* **Boston By Season**) rainbow flags are everywhere.

The landmark around these parts is the **Boston Center for the Arts** (*see page 88* **Museums & Galleries**). The BCA has three theatres and a large, airy gallery that displays a wide range of contemporary and experimental art. Its Black Box Theatre has won a national reputation for its cutting-edge gay drama. The BCA's centrepiece is the **Cyclorama**: a circular, domed structure built in 1884 to exhibit the huge painting of the Civil War battle of Gettysburg, by Dominique Philoppoteaux. The painting went on tour five years later, but never returned – it's now on display in Gettysburg. The Cyclorama itself has served as all sorts of things, including a roller-skating arena, flower market and factory – one Albert Champion invented the spark plug here in 1907. Today, it's a great exhibition space and venue for special events, among them different kinds of flea markets – antiques one week, fetish paraphernalia another.

Many artists also have their studios in the BCA complex and in September they open them up to the public as part of the annual **South End Open Studios** weekend. More than 200 artists across the South End participate (it's organised by United South End Artists, 267 8862). Right next door to the BCA is the Tremont Estates building, which was an organ factory in the mid-nineteenth-century, when the South End was the centre for US organ and piano manufacture. It now houses **Hamersley's Bistro** (*see page 139* **Restaurants & Cafés**), one of Boston's swankiest restaurants. At night, its valet service employees lounge around outside like models from a fashion show.

Just behind the BCA (at the junction of Clarendon Street and Warren Avenue) is the headquarters of the **Boston Ballet**, although this is a rehearsal and admin centre, not a performance venue. The ballet usually performs at the **Wang Center** (*see page 213* **The Performing Arts**). A short walk up Clarendon Street is a cheaper and deservedly popular local watering hole called the **Delux Café** (*see page 116* **Pubs & Bars**).

Roxbury & the black Civil Rights Movement

Roxbury has always had one of the highest proportions of African-Americans of any Boston district. And it was in Roxbury that a young preacher named Martin Luther King Junior (*above*) started to build his reputation.

From 1951 to 1953, King studied at Boston University's School of Theology and on Sundays he would often preach at the **Twelfth Baptist Church** in Roxbury. It's still there, at 160 Warren Street. When he came to Boston in 1965 to bring his campaign against racial discrimination to the North, thousands of Roxbury residents turned out to greet him. King then marched to Boston Common at the head of a procession of over 20,000 people, almost as many white as black. His assassination in Memphis just three years later provoked serious rioting in Roxbury, as it did in many other American cities. Martin Luther King Jr Boulevard runs through the heart of Roxbury, joining onto Warren Street.

He was not the only black leader with ties to Boston. Malcolm 'Red' Little spent part of his life in Boston. After being convicted for burglary in 1946, he was imprisoned at the Charlestown jail where he converted to Islam and called himself Malcolm X (*below*). He joined the Nation of Islam, but in 1963 was suspended from the movement and two years later he was assassinated in Harlem. New Dudley Street in Roxbury is also known as Malcolm X Boulevard. One of Malcolm X's key associates was Louis X, who grew up in Roxbury under the name Gene Walcott. Today, he is Louis Farrakhan, the controversial leader of the Nation of Islam.

Twelfth Baptist Church
160 Warren Street, at Moreland Street, Roxbury (442 7855). Jackson Square T. **Open** 10.30am-5pm Mon-Fri; 10am-5pm Sat; 2pm-5pm Sun.
Disabled: toilet.

From Clarendon Street take a walk up **Appleton** or **Chandler Streets**, two of the most desirable in the neighbourhood. The Victorian architecture manages to look good in any season and just about any weather. The South End is a great neighbourhood in which to simply wander, stumbling across tiny little parks or the occasional public garden sandwiched between buildings. The very active neighbourhood associations work hard to keep up the area's drive towards gentrification and no parcel of land is allowed to simply fester. If you're on Appleton Street, stop by the **Appleton Bakery Café** (123 Appleton Street; 859 8222), which sells just about the best bread in Boston and a good selection of sandwiches and salads.

When you reach Columbus Avenue, it's hard to believe that this drab main road was once touted as the finest residential avenue in the city. But that was 1869 and today it lacks soul. However, there are several great restaurants in the section between Dartmouth Street and Concord Square (*see page 138* **Restaurants & Cafés** for a selection). And if you are in the neighbourhood anywhere close to brunch time, **Charlie's Sandwich Shoppe** (429 Columbus; 536 7669) is worth a visit. The classic diner décor and menu have barely changed since the 1930s. Charlie's turkey hash is a divine way of clogging your arteries.

The Southwest Corridor

If you continue towards the Back Bay from Columbus Avenue, you have to cross the South End's northern boundary – the Southwest Corridor. It's an open, tree-lined strip running from Copley Place at Dartmouth Street to Massachusetts Avenue. Underneath is the Orange Line, running from the distinctive concrete Back Bay/South End T stop opposite Copley Place to the Massachusetts Avenue T stop. From there, the Southwest Corridor continues for over four miles (six kilometres) into **Roxbury** (*see page 83*), with the Orange Line and the Commuter Rail running through the middle of it. Originally, a railway ran along the route of the corridor above ground. The city authorities wanted to turn the space over to another main road, but a Massachusetts State Governor won office with a campaign against the plan. It is now a relatively quiet place to walk, rollerblade or cycle. You can cycle the Corridor on a designated route all the way out to Roxbury. Within the South End section, there are public tennis and basketball courts and a children's playground, near where West Newton Street crosses the Corridor.

Just a short walk down from the Massachusetts Avenue T stop, near Columbus Avenue, is one of the South End's surviving jazz bars, **Wally's Café** (*see page 210* **Nightlife**). It dates from 1947 and puts on a pretty broad range of jazz acts.

South of Tremont Street

Getting a feeling for the South End requires some serious hanging out. Two good cafés for that are on the south side of Tremont: **Mildred's Coffeeshop** at 552 Tremont and **Francesca's Expresso Bar** at 565 Tremont (*see page 189* **Gay & Lesbian Boston** for both) – although the service in both can be haphazard. They stock some useful reading matter: the gay weeklies *Bay Windows* and *In Newsweekly* and *The South End News*, as well as other local listings info. Just down the street is the **We Think the World of You** bookshop, aimed at the gay community (*see page 189* **Gay & Lesbian Boston**).

Further along the street the other way, between Union Park Street and Upton Street, are two other popular restaurants – **Geoffrey's Café & Bar** (578 Tremont; 266 1122) and the **Metropolis Café**, which also owns **Aquitaine** opposite (*see pages 141 and 138* **Restaurants & Cafés**). But take the time to wander down **Union Park** into the little elliptical 'square' there, the best-looking of all the South End's manicured Victorian spaces. Dating from 1851, the garden is overlooked by iron-railing fronted brownstones.

Beyond Union Park is Shawmut Avenue, which runs from Berkeley Street southwest across Massachusetts Avenue and into Roxbury. It's named after the original peninsula that connected Boston to the mainland. Between here and Washington Street – the gateway to Boston – you can be pretty sure you are standing on real dry land.

At the junction with Union Park, there are some good eating places: **On the Park** at 1 Union Park, the **To Go Bakery** at 314 Shawmut Avenue and the **Purple Cactus Café** opposite at 312 Shawmut (*see page 191* **Gay & Lesbian Boston** for all three). They are often at their busiest at

The elliptical **Union Park**.

6.30am, when locals sit outside having a quick cup of coffee before heading to work. If you take a left down Shawmut towards Berkeley Street, you'll come to another popular South End bar and eatery – the **Franklin Café** (*see page 139* **Restaurants & Cafés**).

Between Shawmut Avenue and Tremont Street is almost entirely residential all the way up to Massachusetts Avenue. However, a few streets linking these two main roads are worth a look, if only for their gardens (*see page 62*). Also, on West Newton Street, between Shawmut Avenue and Tremont, is the **Jorge Hernandez Cultural Center** (85 West Newton Street; 247 7604) in the Villa Victoria Community Center, formerly a Lutheran Church – a sure sign of Boston's shifting communities. The centre is well-known for its Latino music.

From the junction of Shawmut Avenue and Union Park Street, stay on Union Park until you hit Washington Street and you'll see New England's largest cathedral just to your right: the **Catholic Cathedral of the Holy Cross** and seat of New England's cardinal. Its designer originally intended it to be much larger, with a 300-foot (91-metre) tower – but there were concerns that the landfill site would not take the weight. As it is, the cathedral looks a bit stunted and forlorn, although there are plans to give the outside a facelift. The inside has recently been restored.

If you feel like exploring and really want to get off the tourist track, head southwest down Washington Street (away from downtown). On either side are two old South End green spaces, **Franklin Square** and **Blackstone Square**. Then you will reach an early nineteenth-century burial site for Boston's working classes: the **South Burying Ground** on Washington Street. It's a small space, especially when you discover that more than 11,000 people were buried here, most of them too poor to afford a headstone. You need an appointment to go in (phone the Boston Parks Department for one, on 635 4505), but a look through the gate will be enough for all but the most morbid.

A bit further on, just before Massachusetts Avenue, is Worcester Street, which leads to another classic Victorian South End space: **Worcester Square**. It joins onto Harrison Avenue. It's the same age as Union Park, but has suffered from being a bit out of the way and has only recently been restored. When the 'New' South End was first laid out, the hope was that squares like Worcester and other grand spaces nearby would attract people away from downtown. In fact, the oldest buildings in the South End are found in this western part of the district. But despite the authorities' best efforts, people preferred to live in the area closer to the centre.

From Washington Street, turn right onto Massachusetts Avenue and head back towards Tremont Street. Between Shawmut Avenue and Tremont Street, you'll come to another grand Victorian space – **Chester Square**. Or rather it was a square, until the 1950s when the city put six lanes of Massachusetts Avenue right through the middle. Perhaps hoping to redeem themselves, the authorities are now considering submerging Massachusetts Avenue beneath Chester Square. The **South End Historical Society** has its office here (532 Massachusetts Avenue; 536 4445). Every October, the Society organises a tour of South End houses. Now more than 30 years old, this annual event offers a way to get inside some of the area's more impressive homes and marvel (in horror or envy) at the tastes of South Enders. The tour costs around $20 and you must book a place in advance.

Next door to the South End is Roxbury. Massachusetts Avenue forms the rough boundary between the two districts, although many South End addresses actually have a Roxbury zip code. For more on Roxbury, *see page 83* **Further afield**.

Isabella Stewart Gardner Museum *(page 72).*

Catholic Cathedral of the Holy Cross

1400 Washington Street, at Union Park Street (542 5682). Back Bay or Copley T.
Open 9am-3pm Mon-Sat; 8am-3pm Sun.
Map 5 F6
Disabled: toilet.

The Emerald Necklace

See map 8

It's impossible to talk about, or traverse, Boston's Emerald Necklace without mentioning a name that is all but inseparable from the Boston park system: Frederick Law Olmsted (1822-1903). Generally acknowledged to be the father of landscape architecture, Olmsted is perhaps best known as the designer (along with Calvert Vaux) of New York's Central Park.

After he moved his offices from New York to the Boston suburb of Brookline in 1883, however, Olmsted undertook one of his greatest endeavours – designing the Boston park system known as the Emerald Necklace, a continuous string of nine parks that stretch through, and offer a respite from, some of the city's busiest districts.

It should be noted that although Olmsted did not design the Necklace's first three parks (**Boston Common** *page 42*, the **Public Garden** and the **Commonwealth Avenue mall**, *page 64*), he incorporated them into his overall vision. Not surprisingly, the parks that make up the Emerald Necklace (a total of 1,338 acres/542 hectares) are listed in the National Register of Historic Places and the name fits: the Emerald Necklace is indeed one of Boston's most striking jewels.

It is feasible – even for more sedentary types – to walk the Necklace from end-to-end (it's about a seven-mile/11-kilometre trek from Boston Common to Franklin Park), although sensible walking shoes and a motivated frame of mind are advisable at the outset of such a journey. The **Boston Park Rangers** (*see page 87* **Organised tours**) offer a walking and biking tour of the Necklace every season that is both spirited and thoroughly informative. Less ambitious perhaps, but easier on the feet, is the Emerald Necklace slide presentation, which is also offered by the Park Rangers by appointment.

For Olmsted's former house in Brookline, *see page 85* **Frederick Law Olmsted National Historic Site**.

The Back Bay Fens

The marshy 113 acres (46 hectares) that make up the Back Bay Fens play host to some of the city's most intimate, off-the-beaten-path charms. Among them are the **Victory Gardens** (near Kenmore T), which got their start during World War II as a place where food was grown and shipped overseas to US troops. These days, the area serves as a kind of paean to community expression and visitors can wander through individually maintained gardens where fresh vegetables and flowers are grown. Some of the gardens are quite elaborate, with trimmed and sculpted hedges, stone walkways and wagon wheels, wooden fences, and strategically situated lawn chairs facing tenderly cared for flower beds.

Walking through the rose-vined archways of the **James P Kelleher Rose Garden** – also in the Fens and established in 1930 – can be a sumptuous experience, especially if you happen to be travelling in late April or May, when the flowers explode into blushing shades of crimson and pink.

Inspiration comes in many forms, and both the **Museum of Fine Arts**, and the nearby **Isabella Stewart Gardner Museum** (*see page 90* **Museums & Galleries** *for both*) offer plenty. The 1998 'Monet in the Twentieth Century' show, organised by the MFA and the Royal Academy of Arts in London, shattered all MFA records for attendance. Masterpieces by Degas, Renoir, Rembrandt, Sargent and Picasso are also on display, as well as art ranging from African sculpture to sixteenth-century Chinese furniture and Egyptian artifacts.

The palatial Isabella Stewart Gardner Museum is an equally impressive showcase, with three floors of galleries that house an array of antique furnishings and masterpieces by Rembrandt, Botticelli and Whistler, among others.

In nearby Kenmore Square is **Fenway Park** famous home to the Boston Red Sox (*see page 84* **Further afield**).

Olmsted Park & the Muddy River

Continuing along the Riverway portion of the Emerald Necklace is the Olmsted-designed, man-made **Muddy River** (it isn't actually that muddy), which leads towards the posthumously named Olmsted Park. With its strategically steep banks designed to block out what were once carriageways (and are now roadways) and its inviting paths, the 28-acre (11-hectare) Muddy River remains one of the purest examples of Olmsted's vision of rural sanctuary in an urban setting.

Olmsted Park, once known as Leverett Park after the man-made Leverett Pond, features a well-travelled path for cyclists and pedestrians and its 180 acres (73 hectares) provide ample space in which to pedal or walk.

Olmsted Park

Between Jamaica Way & Riverdale Parkway/ Perkins Street, Jamaica Plain. Heath T/ 39 bus.

The **Back Bay Fens** *are the very picture of tranquillity.*

Rangers at work. In snow ...

Jamaica Pond & the Arnold Arboretum

The two most celebrated sites of the Jamaica Plain neighbourhood are the 265-acre (107-hectare) Arnold Arboretum and the 120-acre (49-hectare) stretch of Jamaica Pond, and for good reason. **Jamaica Pond**, a kettlehole caused by an ancient glacier, is routinely appreciated and celebrated as the largest body of water in Boston by a steady stream of joggers, walkers and picnickers who populate its paths and sit on the grassy slopes leading to the water's edge. Although most people prefer to fish it rather than drink it, one could down a glass of the stuff: Jamaica Pond's water is so clean that Boston has designated it as its back-up city reservoir.

The pond lured Boston's wealthiest people to build lavish summer homes facing it, and although Olmsted subsequently convinced the city to buy out – and demolish – many of these properties in the late nineteenth century, when he wanted to incorporate the area into the Emerald Necklace, at least one remains standing, albeit in dilapidated condition. Sadly holding out against the elements on the northern side of the pond, the **Perkins Estate** is a three-storey brick affair named after its former owner. It exists in limbo, awaiting restoration that it is estimated will cost somewhere between $3 million and $4 million. Other, far more upbeat, sights along the pond include a **boathouse** (where canoes and rowing boats can be hired) and an outdoor **bandstand**, which regularly hosts live jazz bands and small-piece orchestras.

With 15,000 trees and shrubs dappling its gently rolling hills and lush expanses of lawn and marshland, the **Arnold Arboretum** is a magnificent study in science (courtesy of scientist Charles Sprague Sargent, who collected and catalogued the plant specimens) and design (Olmsted – who else?). The Arboretum is named after James Arnold, who financed its development and left his fortune (including the Arboretum) to Harvard University, which subsequently sold it to the city. The city in turn leased it back to the university for one dollar a year for 1,000 years. Today, the place looks like a spectacular, three-dimensional painting of peaceful water lily decorated ponds, exotic bonsai trees and intoxicating lavender-coloured lilac trees, among other numerous seasonal delights. The Arboretum is more than just a showplace, however. Its living, breathing tree museum is a bountiful resource for botanists and other scholars, students and teachers.

Arnold Arboretum

125 Arborway, at Routes 203 & 1, Jamaica Plain (524 1718). Forest Hills T. **Open** *grounds* dawn-dusk daily; *building* 9am-4pm Mon-Fri; noon-4pm Sat, Sun. **Admission** free.

Jamaica Pond

Jamaicaway, at Pond Street, Jamaica Plain (635 7383). Back of the Hill T, then 39 bus.

A country park within the city: the **Arnold Arboretum**.

Franklin Park

The sprawling 527-acre (213-hectare) **Franklin Park** was rightfully considered by Olmsted to be his Boston masterwork – a scenic 'country park' intended, first and foremost, to be used for recreation and enjoyment by city dwellers seeking escape from the pressures of workaday life. The park, which features a woodland preserve, golf course and zoo (a new baby gorilla was born there in 1998), took several years to build and the effort shows: inside the park, medieval-looking stone steps lead to picture-perfect vistas of colour and detail; splashes of yellow and orange dominate the treescapes in autumn. Seemingly endless lawns roll out into other distant wonders and there's not one car to be seen for what, quite literally, is miles of unbroken country.

Franklin Park & Zoo

1 Franklin Park Road (park 635 7383/zoo 541 5466). Forest Hills T, then 16 bus. **Open** *park* dawn-dusk daily; *zoo* winter 10am-4pm daily; summer 10am-5pm Mon-Fri, 10am-6pm Sat, Sun. **Admission** *park* free; *zoo* $3-$6. **Credit** AmEx, MC, V.
Disabled: toilet.

... and on mounted patrol.

Jamaica Plain

Ask the people who reside in the area to describe Jamaica Plain and they'll usually say it's like living in the country within the city. It's an apt description of a place once known as 'the Eden of America' because of the wealth of green space that all but surrounds it. Several tales – some of them quite tall – surround the naming of the village that was originally a part of the neighbouring town of Roxbury. One of the stories claims Jamaica Plain earned its moniker because residents in the northern part of Roxbury happened to enjoy Jamaican rum – and what's more, they liked it 'plain'. The Jamaica Plain Historical Society, however, puts the name down to a Native American woman called Jamaica who once lived on the shores of Jamaica Pond.

The area, settled in 1639, blossomed into a farming community during the eighteenth century and was eventually annexed to the city of Boston in 1874. During the nineteenth century, JP – as it's known today – became increasingly industrialised, as tanneries, shoe factories and breweries were built following a wave of German and Irish immigration. Jamaica Plain was also the area that many of Boston's most wealthy and powerful movers-and-shakers chose as an idyllic getaway from city life. Walk along Jamaica Pond and you'll be able to see the imposing Victorian mansions that once dominated the landscape. James Michael Curley, Boston's flamboyant four-term mayor, two-term congressman and one-term governor, built a majestic Georgian Revival mansion at 350 Jamaicaway, which had shamrock shutters to identify its owner as being of Irish descent.

Other notable sites include the granite **Monument**, which pays tribute to the 23 residents of West Roxbury who died in the service of the Union during the Civil War. This is in **Eliot Square** (considered the heart of JP), an area bordered by Centre and South Streets. The Footlight Club, the oldest amateur theatrical group in the United States, still calls **Eliot Hall** home, and produces plays and musicals in the building that served as West Roxbury's first town hall (7A Eliot Street; 524 3200). The **Loring-Greenough House** is where British loyalist Joshua Loring once lived and was later used as a hospital for General Washington's troops. The home was bought in 1924 (and saved from demolition) by the Jamaica Plain Tuesday Club, an organisation formed in 1868 devoted to 'the improvement of female minds in the neighbourhood'. A host of other progressive-minded notables have lived in JP, including Judith Windsor Smith, an Abolitionist and suffragist who voted for the first time at the age of 99 when women were finally granted that right in 1919.

Jamaica Plain's tradition of liberal politics continues today. The area has a reputation for being a bastion of racial, ethnic, sexual and class diversity – although it has become increasingly gentrified as city dwellers seek to escape congestion and concrete, a phenomenon that has inevitably driven real estate prices through the roof and forced some longstanding residents out. In recent years, a bevy of boutiques, cafés, healthfood shops and upmarket restaurants catering to a younger, more affluent clientele has moved in alongside the older bars and five-and-dime shops that were once staples of Centre Street, JP's main thoroughfare.

But the area retains an eclectic mix of cultures. **Hyde Square** and the area around **Egleston Street** and **Jackson Square**, for example, is widely considered one of the main hubs of activity for New England's Latino community. Of the roughly 45,000 residents who live here, census figures show, 52 per cent are white, 27 per cent Latino, 17 per cent African-American and four per cent Asian. JP is also home to a significant gay and lesbian population and, in recent years, has attracted a younger network of artists, musicians and writers, all attracted to this jewel within the Emerald Necklace.

Loring-Greenough House

12 South Street, at Centre Street (524 3158). Forest Hills T, then 39 bus or Green St T. **Open** by appointment; *tours in summer* noon-3pm Sat. **Admission** $3 donation. **No credit cards**.

On the waterfront

See maps 5 and 7

Boston's waterfront area is one of the country's hottest development spots, and private and public interests are battling over the future of the 180 miles (290 kilometres) of undeveloped shoreline, 46 square miles (74 square kilometres) of water surface and 5,000 acres (2,023 hectares) of underutilised land. A grandiose **Federal Courthouse** was recently built on the waterfront, sparking much controversy among those who wanted to see the land go to the highest bidder (a hotel developer, perhaps), those who wanted to see the waterfront retained for public use and those who didn't think public use included the construction of federal property. Still, the courthouse – located at the tip of Fort Point Channel on the east side of the Northern Avenue bridge – with its signature semicircular wall of glass reflecting the water, is a majestic site and one best appreciated from aboard a harbour cruise.

While the various factions continue to fight over the future of Boston's waterfront, the area remains one of the best sightseeing spots in the city. Until the late 1860s, the city of Boston survived on maritime activities: ship-building, water commerce and fishing. Although today the economics of the city have little to do with water-based activities, the Port of Boston remains active. Boston Harbor received container ships carrying more than 16 million tons of goods and 70,000 automobiles in 1997. The port is also one of just five worldwide to import Volkswagen's wildly popular redesigned VW Bug. And Boston's Fish Pier (Pier 6), constructed in 1914, is the oldest working fish pier in the country.

Boston Harbor Islands

One of the finest introductions to the harbour is a visit to the Boston Harbor Islands – small islands left by a retreating glacier about 12,000 years ago – of which there are about 30 in the harbour. Seventeen of them make up the **Boston Harbor Islands National Park**; of these just six are open to the general public. Together, they form a nature-lover's paradise. And thanks to the massive Boston Harbor clean-up effort, wildlife is thriving in the water and on the islands. Rare and endangered species of birds such as the plover and osprey have been spotted. And grey and harp seals live in the harbour. Calf Island, which is not open to the public, contains a colony of about 100 harbour seals.

The islands were designated a national park by President Clinton a few years ago, but they don't seem to have been discovered by the general public: in 1997, for instance, only 120,000 people visited the park. This means they can still be enjoyed in relative comfort, even on a sunny summer day.

Take a ferry cruise from Long Wharf to the islands (with **Boston Harbor Cruises**). The 28-acre (11-hectare) **George's Island** is where you'll land first. The front part of the island is dominated by Fort Warren, a massive structure that was used during the Civil War as a training base for Union soldiers. It also served as a prison for captured Confederate soldiers including, most famously, the vice-president of the Confederacy, Alexander Hamilton Stephens. Today, the Fort is said to be haunted. You can attend a guided tour or explore it on your own and find out for yourself.

A free shuttle service takes you to other islands in the park. **Bumpkin Island**, covering about 35 acres (14 hectares), is tucked away in Hingham Bay and doesn't see much traffic. From the early part of the century to the 1940s, it was used to quarantine children with polio. It's one of four harbour islands where camping is permitted. (**Peddock's**, **Grape** and **Lovell's** also allow camping. In all cases, reservations must be made in advance with the Boston Harbor Islands National Park. Also note that alcohol is not permitted on the islands).

Gallop's Island, just 16 acres (six hectares), is the smallest of the harbour islands open to the public. In the mid-nineteenth century it served as a popular summer resort. During the Civil War, the island and its buildings were taken over by the

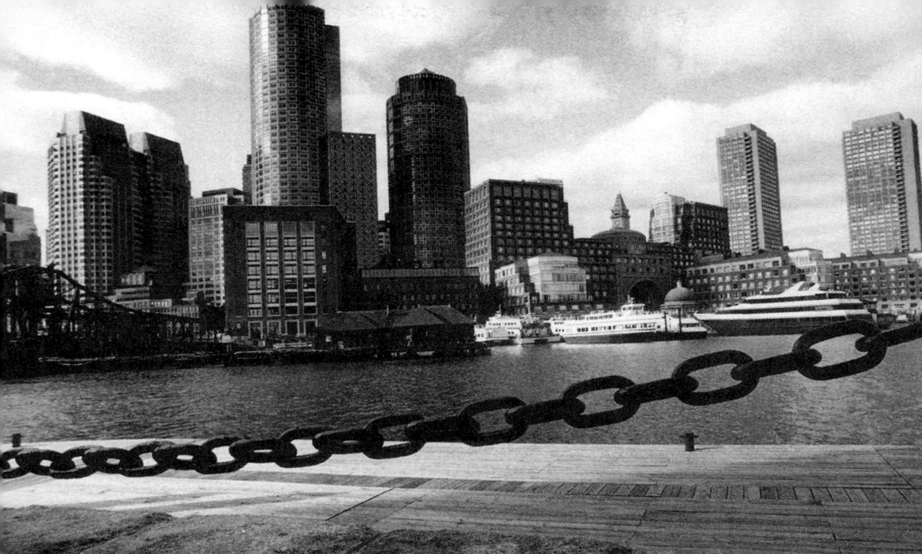

Ferries and cruise ships line up to take passengers on a tour of Boston Harbor.

government and put to use by Union soldiers. Today it offers hiking trails, picnicking spots and some of the best views of the Boston skyline.

Grape Island has never been developed; the remains of a nineteenth-century farmhouse are the only clue that the 50-acre (20-hectare) island was once inhabited. The island has pristine shell and gravel beaches, campsites, and berries to pick (including strawberries, blueberries, huckleberries and raspberries). Spend some time here and you'll forget you're touring the sites of a city.

Lovell's Island covers 62 acres (25 hectares) and has a public swimming beach, hiking trails, wooded hills and dunes. **Peddock's Island**, at 188 acres (76 hectares), is the largest of the harbour islands. During the 1960s a 4,100-year-old skeleton was excavated on it. It's the only island with residents all year round; when the harbour islands were first turned into a state park, the state granted these residents, almost all of them fishermen, life-long leases, which means that on their death the land reverts back to state ownership. Peddock's also allows camping, picnicking and hiking. With its salt marshes, wildlife sanctuary and heavily wooded inlands, the island is a mini paradise.

Boston Harbor Cruises

1 Long Wharf, next to New England Aquarium (227 4321). Aquarium T. **Rates** *sightseeing & whale-watching* $8-$28. **Map 5 H4**

Boston Harbor Islands National Park

408 Atlantic Avenue, suite 228, Boston MA (223 8666).
Website: www.nps.gov/boha/

Touring Boston Harbor

If a trip to the islands is a bit rustic for your taste, the harbour can be enjoyed on a cruise. There are a number of private companies that offer tours, including educational narrated tours arranged by the **New England Aquarium** or fine dining and musical entertainment aboard the luxurious ***Odyssey***. More modest entertainment can be had on an **AC Cruise Line** tour with county & western music and line-dancing. **Bay State Cruises** offers daily trips from Boston to Provincetown. And **Boston Harbor Cruises** (which take you to the islands) also offers hour-long sightseeing tours of the harbour with a commentary; there are lunchtime and sunset cruises. For details of all these, *see page 85* **Organised tours**.

If you'd rather stay on land, you can stroll along the harbourfront between the Boston Tea Party Ship and Museum and Long Wharf. For the **New England Aquarium**, *see page 51* **Downtown & the Financial District**.

Fort Point Channel

In 1773, about 150 colonists, disguised as Mohawk Indians, dumped 342 chests of tea into Boston Harbor in protest at the tea tax imposed by George III (*see page 8* **History**). This crucial moment in American history, which precipitated the American Revolution, is commemorated by the **Boston Tea Party Ship and Museum** (*see page 92* **Museums & Galleries**). The actual ships used to dump the tea are long gone, but the *Beaver II* is a full-size working 'replica' with costumed guides who re-enact the Tea Party daily.

Fort Point Channel. *See page 77.*

Complimentary cups of 'tax-free tea' are provided. If you want something to go with your cup of tea, visit **The Bottle** nearby at 312 Congress Street. It's a giant milk bottle that's been serving fast food since 1934.

The area on the eastern side of Fort Point Channel, between Northern Avenue and Summer Street, has become known as Museum Wharf because of the museums located along the harbour front. The **Computer Museum** (*see page 92* **Museums & Galleries**) claims to be the world's only computer museum. Exhibits include a multimedia show featuring data and videos from robots including NASA's Mars Rover, R2-D2, Shakey and Sea Rover. The museum also houses a collection of vintage computers and robots and has over 150 hands-on displays illustrating how computers have affected modern society. One of the highlights is the 1970s 'Hacker's Garage', which includes an Apple I and a Pong.

The **Children's Museum** (*see chapter* **Children**) is the perfect place to visit if you're travelling with kids. It focuses on early childhood education and teaching resources, and has hands-on displays for children of all ages. Continuing along Northern Avenue, you come to Boston's **Fish Pier** (Pier 6), as well as the site of the **World Trade Center** (*see page 266* **Directory**), one of the city's newest convention centres. This is also the place to come for various harbourside fish shacks, including **Jimmy's Harbourside** (242 Northern Avenue; 451 3663) and **Anthony's Pier 4** (140 Northern Avenue; 423 6363), where baked cod, finnian haddie and oyster crackers can be eaten among driftwood and fishing nets, with sweeping views of the harbour beyond.

The Charles River Basin

Boston Harbor waterfront is hard to beat, but it's not the only waterfront. The Charles River Basin runs from the river's end at the Museum of Science to the Boston University Bridge. The entire river runs from the end of the basin out to Hopkinton, Massachusetts – a distance of just 26 miles (42 kilometres). If you count the river's many twists and turns, however, it's more than 64 miles (103 kilometres) long. All types of craft under 35 feet (10.6 metres) are allowed on the water. And it's here that you can get the best view of the annual Fourth of July concert on the Esplanade, provided you can find a boat. Bicycle paths and grassy banks hug either side of the river; on sunny summer days sun-worshippers lie out on towels, along with frisbee players, dog walkers, cyclists and rollerbladers. At the weekends it can get quite crowded. One of the best views of the city skyline is from the Cambridge side of the basin along **Memorial Drive** between the Boston University and Longfellow Bridges. On a temperate evening, it's one of the best strolls in the city.

The **Charles River Esplanade** is located on the Boston side of the basin just after the Harvard Bridge as you head toward Boston. It's a grassy field criss-crossed by numerous walking paths and anchored by the **Hatch Memorial Shell**, a beautiful permanent pavilion most famously connected with the annual Fourth of July concert by the Boston Pops (*see page 38* **Boston by Season** *and page 216* **The Performing Arts**), an extravaganza which attracts hundreds of thousands of concert-goers. During the day, sunbathers and other outdoor types make use of the paths, but at night the Esplanade becomes a cruisey place, especially for gay men. During the summer, evening concerts, film screenings and other special events take place at the Hatch Shell.

Further up the path behind the Hatch Shell is **Charlesbank Park**. There are tennis courts and a playground for children here as well as the **Community Boating Center** (*see chapter* **Sport & Fitness**), where sailing boats can be hired during the summer.

Hatch Memorial Shell

Charles River Esplanade, between Longfellow & Harvard Bridges (Boston Symphony Hall 266 1492). Arlington or Charles/MGH T. **Map 5 F4**

Museum of Science

If you continue north along the path, you'll come to Science Park and the **Museum of Science** (*see page 92* **Museums & Galleries**). Located in a dome-topped building, the Museum of Science is the modern-day descendent of the New England Museum of Natural History, which relocated to Science Park in 1953.

It prides itself on making science accessible to the average person, and has hundreds of interactive displays and exhibitions – there's even one on that bane of Boston life, the Big Dig. Although some of the better examples of taxidermy were retained from the old Museum of Natural History and are stored in the Colby Room (named after Francis Colby, a hunter who donated most of the animals), the Museum of Science is as far removed from its origins as modern day medicine is from the ancient practice of blood-letting. Among its countless exhibits is the Theater of Electricity and the permanent display of a life-sized replica of the skull of a Giganotosaurous in the lobby. An entire weekend could be spent exploring the place. The museum also houses the Charles Hayden Planetarium, which puts on psychedelic laser shows set to rock music as well as more educational shows on astronomy. The Omni Theater shows films in the giant IMAX format.

JFK Library & Museum

Located on the windswept Columbia Point peninsular on Dorchester Bay overlooking Boston's waterfront, this museum is housed in an IM Pei-designed building. There are 25 displays commemorating the 1,000 days John F Kennedy served as the nation's 35th president. The historic candidates' debate between Kennedy and Richard M Nixon (which many believe won the election for the telegenic Kennedy) can be seen here, and there are recreations of the Oval Office and the office of Attorney General Robert F Kennedy. Historical documents and interactive computer displays also illustrate the programmes of the Kennedy Administration. Special exhibitions are regularly scheduled: the most recent focused on the Civil Rights struggle and included a display of the telegram sent by Martin Luther King Junior to President Kennedy regarding the Birmingham church bombings. The museum also houses a research library, gift shop and café (*see page 91* **Museums & Galleries**) and offers splendid views of the water.

Cambridge & Somerville

See map 4

Boston is famous for being a college town, but Cambridge and Somerville are the real academic centres. World-class institutions such as Harvard and MIT are based in Cambridge, but increasing gentrification of the area has begun to force poorer residents into other locales, including Somerville, which has only recently begun to evolve as a destination in its own right. With the well-respected but poorly publicised Tufts University as its major university and Davis Square its flagship 'cool' area, Somerville is beginning to give Cambridge a run for its money. Both areas are the suburbs that aren't quite suburbs – part of Boston yet cities in their own right.

Cambridge, originally called Newtowne, was founded in 1630 by one of the first waves of Puritans who came to settle the Massachusetts Bay Colony. It was a farming community before the city elders established the country's first college there in 1636, which was later named after the clergyman John Harvard when he left the school half his estate and all of his library on his death in 1638. Newtowne was then renamed after that other famous university town in England, where many of the settlers had received their education.

It became a city in 1846, its population swelled by an influx of immigrants fleeing the Irish potato famine. Settlers from other countries followed,

The Head of the Charles Regatta is an annual Cambridge bonanza.

establishing the pattern of cultural diversity that remains today: it is estimated that Cambridge's public schools currently educate children from 82 different countries.

Harvard University

It was the oldest college in the USA that brought settlers to Cambridge in the first place. Harvard has more than 400 buildings scattered around 360 acres (146 hectares) in Boston and Cambridge, but its nerve centre is **Harvard Yard**, where some buildings date back to the early eighteenth century. Entering the Yard (opposite Harvard T stop) by the gate on Massachusetts Avenue opposite Dunster Street, you'll see **Massachusetts Hall** diagonally opposite, to the left. Built from 1718 to 1720, it still houses freshmen and the president of Harvard. It just edges out the 1726 Georgian **Wadsworth House** as the oldest building in the yard, though the latter, yellow clapboard structure, is the more beautiful.

University Hall, designed by Charles Bulfinch in 1813, lies directly in front of what is probably the biggest tourist magnet in Harvard: the 1848 statue of **John Harvard** which is known as the 'three lies statue'. Its inscription reads 'John Harvard – founder – 1638', three times inaccurate since John Harvard was a donor, not a founder, the college was set up in 1636, and nobody knows what he really looked like, so the face of the statue was based on a friend of the sculptor Daniel Chester French.

One of the most impressive collegiate libraries anywhere (containing over 12 million volumes) is **Widener Library**, though getting through the doors is as difficult as getting a place at the college itself. But even those without the requisite student ID can appreciate the *Titanic* tie-in of the place. Harry Elkins Widener graduated from Harvard in 1907, then died on the famous ship when he couldn't swim 50 yards to a lifeboat. The following year, his mother donated $2 million to Harvard for this library. Legend has it that she stipulated all undergraduates must pass a 50-yard swimming test.

Another vital part of the university is the **Harvard Museums** (*see page 95* **Museums & Galleries**), which range from the expansive **Fogg Art Museum** and the Eastern works of the **Arthur M Sackler Museum** to the more scientific **Mineralogical and Geological Museums**.

Harvard Yard

Harvard University Campus, Cambridge/Harvard University Events & Information Center, Holyoke Center Arcade, 1350 Massachusetts Avenue, at Holyoke Street, Cambridge (495 1573). Harvard T. **Tours** *Sept-May* 10am, 2pm Mon-Fri; 2pm Sat; *June-Aug* 10am, 11.15am, 2pm, 3.15pm Mon-Sat; 1.30pm, 3pm Sun. **Map 4 B2/3**

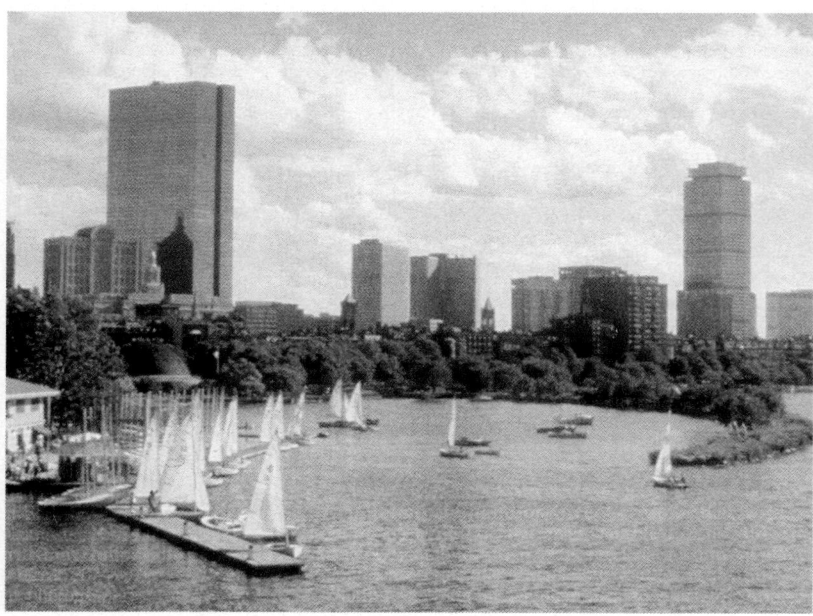

Messing about on the Charles River, at the **Community Boating Center** *(page 78).*

Outside the yard

Radcliffe Yard is on a separate plot of land: the entrance is where Brattle Street and James Street fork. Harvard's college for women was founded in 1879 and the school became fully co-educational and part of Harvard in 1970, although it continues to offer courses relating to women's issues. Beyond the confines of both yards lies the **Harvard Lampoon Castle**, a haven for writers and editors of the satirical publication the *Harvard Lampoon*, which continues to spawn countless Hollywood comedy writers. The building is wedged into a corner, but architects Wheelwright & Haven have made the most of the awkward site, adding a turret and constructing windows that form a human face.

Harvard Lampoon Castle

44 Bow Street, at Mount Auburn Street, Cambridge. Harvard T. **Not open to the public. Map 4 B3**

Harvard Square

Cambridge and Somerville are all about squares. The cities are divided up into neighbourhoods designated by this geometric shape – though most of the so-called 'squares' are just glorified intersections. The most well-known, and certainly one of the most popular tourist destinations, is **Harvard Square**.

The winding streets surrounding it are best navigated by foot – lanes suddenly merge or disappear without warning and free parking is only for those with Zen-like patience and eagle eyes. The streets are lined with shops and restaurants, once independent but now predominately part of national chains. The recent demise of Tasty, a tiny greasy-spoon once admired by JFK and featured more recently in the film *Good Will Hunting*, is yet another indication of the widespread gentrification of the area.

One business worth checking out is the **Harvard Coop** on Mass Ave (499 2000), the university's book- and souvenir shop. It's one of 24 bookshops in Harvard Square – Cambridge has the most per square mile in the whole of the USA. Another good one is the **Grolier Poetry Book Shop** (6 Plympton Street; 547 4648), which has stocked rare and hard-to-find works of verse for over 30 years.

Harvard Square is also a people-watchers' paradise. Coming out of the T station, the biggest local landmark is **Out of Town News** (*see page 199* **Media**), which stocks a wide selection of periodicals from all over the world. Right next to it is a pedestrianised space known as 'the Pit' – not much to look at when nobody's around, but it has been a haven for street kids since punk-rock broke in the 1970s.

There are usually plenty of street performers in the Pit, as well as on every corner of the square when weather allows. The magicians and jugglers may seem familiar, but the area's less touristy than Faneuil Hall, and more musically focused. Another favourite spot for street musicians is outside the local branch of **Au Bon Pain** (Massachusetts Avenue, at Harvard Square; 354 4144). Despite the sometimes mediocre coffee and pastries, this is the ideal spot for relaxing outdoors and observing the local streetlife.

Just outside the square at the intersection of Garden Street and Massachusetts Avenue is **Cambridge Common**, a beautiful 16-acre (six-hectare) stretch of grass during the day and a bad place to walk at night. William Dawes rode across it before the battles of Lexington and Concord (*see page 8* **History**); it's also where George Washington took control of the Continental Army in 1775 and a plaque now marks the elm tree under which it was mustered. Established in 1631, the common is the only surviving element of colonial Cambridge.

Nearby **Christ Church** was designed in 1761 by the country's first trained architect, Peter Harrison. George and Martha Washington worshipped here, and it became a focus of Revolutionary War activity. The walls are still peppered with bullet-holes and the original organ's pipes were melted down to make bullets in the war. Right next to the church is the **Old Burying Ground**, also known as 'God's Acre'. It began life as a cemetery in 1635 and contains the remains of several early Cambridge settlers as well as Revolutionary War veterans.

Brattle Street was once called Tory Row and several of the grand mansions of its former wealthy merchant residents remain. The Cambridge poet lived at what is now the **Longfellow National Historic Site** (*see page 28* **Literary Boston**), a 28-room Georgian mansion where he resided from 1837 until his death in 1882. This is also one of the many spots in Cambridge where George Washington spent time during the Revolutionary War. Appropriately enough, a few doors down is the headquarters of the Cambridge Historical Society, who've set up shop in the oldest house in Cambridge, the 1688 **Hooper-Lee-Nichols House**.

Modern commerce still thrives in this neighbourhood, too. The **Brattle Theatre** (*see page 185* **Film**) is an independent cinema that screens art movies and film classics and has been a fixture for more than 100 years, first as a social hall and later as a theatre. The other top-line arts venue in the area is the legendary **Club Passim** (*see page 204* **Nightlife**) which helped launch the careers of Joan Baez and Jimmy Buffet, among others.

Christ Church

Zero Garden Street, at Massachusetts Avenue, Cambridge (876 0200). Harvard T. **Open** 7.30am-6pm Mon-Fri, Sun; 7.30am-3pm Sat. **Map 4 B2**
Disabled: toilet.

Hooper-Lee-Nichols House
159 Brattle Street, at Sparks Street, Cambridge (547 4252). Harvard T. **Open** 2-5pm Tue, Thur. **Admission** $3-$5. **No credit cards. Map 4 A2**

Old Burying Ground
Massachusetts Avenue, at Garden Street, Cambridge (Cambridge Historical Commission 349 4683). Harvard T. **Open** dawn to dusk daily. **Map 4 B2**

Kendall & Central Squares

Harvard notwithstanding, some of the smartest people in the world come out of that other school in Cambridge, **Massachusetts Institute of Technology** in Kendall Square. MIT was founded in 1861 and rose to prominence during World War II when radar was invented in its labs.

The architecture of its various buildings is wildly diverse, ranging from the neo-Classical **Building 10**, the main administration building, to the **Wiesner Building**, on which IM Pei collaborated. MIT also boasts its fair share of impressive museums, from **Doc Edgerton's Strobe Alley** to the multimedia **MIT Museum** (*see page 94* **Museums & Galleries**). One of the most amusing of these is the 'MIT Hall of Hacks' installation at the MIT Museum, a permanent exhibition that chronicles the various pranks pulled by wacky MIT students over the years.

MIT doesn't have the same symbiotic relationship with Kendall Square that Harvard has with its square so Kendall doesn't really have its own identity. It does have some great restaurants, however, and a popular if overpriced art house cinema (the **Kendall Square Cinema**, *see page 185* **Film**). It also has a few shops worth checking out, such as the vintage and second-hand clothing emporium known as the **Garment District** (*see page 171* **Shops & Services**). But despite all this, Kendall lacks personality.

This is not the case with **Central Square**, which continues to resist gentrification and retain an air of urban seediness. It's a lower-income section of Cambridge, and as such has attracted a young, alternative population. It's also an international neighbourhood, with several Indian, Ethiopian and Middle Eastern restaurants (*see chapter* **Restaurants & Cafés**). The local **World's Fair** features fantastic food and music and attracts some of the most diverse crowds you'll ever see in Boston (contact the Cambridge Information Booth in Harvard Square, 497 1630, for information). **Cambridge City Hall** is also in Central Square.

The best live-music scene in Boston is also based in Central Square, crammed into one small alley. The **Middle East** on Massachusetts Avenue (*see page 206* **Nightlife**) is a top-notch restaurant with three different stages – an intimate venue to catch rising stars of the local music scene as well as big names in alternative and indie rock. All this and belly-dancing on Wednesday nights, too. Next door is **TT the Bear's Place** (*see page 208* **Nightlife**), which has served up a similar helping of rock excellence for the past 25 years. And for something completely different, it's only a short distance to goth paradise at **Man Ray** (*see page 202* **Nightlife**).

Mount Auburn Cemetery

Another Cambridge destination worth visiting on foot is **Fresh Pond**, at the end of Fresh Pond Parkway (take bus 72 from Harvard T). The Pond was discovered in 1805 as an ice source and today is a beautiful reservoir with a 2.5-mile (4-kilometre) perimeter and constantly changing, gorgeous scenery. To its south lies **Mount Auburn Cemetery**, the country's first garden cemetery and the final resting place for Oliver Wendell Holmes, Winslow Homer, Charles Bulfinch, Henry Wadsworth Longfellow, and over 86,000 others. In fact the cemetery is now so full that locals who want to spend the afterlife at Mount Auburn have to settle for cremation. There are 4,000 kinds of trees and 130 species of shrub alone on its 174 acres (70 hectares) and excellent free guided tours to help you distinguish them.

Mount Auburn Cemetery
580 Mount Auburn Street, Cambridge (547 7105). Harvard T, then 71, 73 bus. **Open** *cemetery* 8am-5pm daily; *greenhouse* 8am-3.30pm Mon-Fri; 9am-1pm Sat. **Admission** free. **Map 4 A3**

Somerville & Davis Square

Somerville was originally part of Charlestown in the seventeenth century, but became its own city in 1842. Now it's a working-class suburb that has attracted a young community, lured by the low rent and increasingly hip lifestyle. Many of the local twentysomethings arrive straight from of **Tufts University** (*see page 34* **Campus Culture**), which straddles Medford and Somerville.

Tufts was founded in 1852 and ranks among the top 25 schools in the country. Circus impresario PT Barnum developed an affinity for the place, donating both money and his pet elephant Jumbo. The original (stuffed) Jumbo was consumed in a fire but a concrete version now stands in the academic quad. And the Tufts sports teams are called the Jumbos in tribute.

Beyond Tufts lies **Davis Square**, which has developed a reputation as a burgeoning bohemia and has become increasingly commercialised as a result. This is where to come for **The Burren** (*see page 124* **Pubs & Bars**), as well as one of the best local second-hand CD stores, **Disc Diggers** (*see page 166* **Shops & Services**), and the **Rosebud**

The fast and efficient MBTA system makes travelling beyond the centre of town easy.

Diner (381 Summer Street; 666 6015) which looks like a train caboose and hasn't changed much since it opened in 1941.

Right outside Davis Square is **Powder House Park**, where the first hostile act of the Revolutionary War took place when the British raided 250 barrels of gunpowder from the West Somerville Powder House in 1774. The shack still stands. A few years later, on the first day of 1776, colonists raised the country's first flag at Prospect Hill in defiance of British rule. A small castle built in 1903 now marks the site.

Powder House Park

Powder House Square, at College Avenue & Broadway, Somerville (Somerville Museum 666 9810). Davis T.

Further afield

Roxbury

This area of the city, next door to the South End, once served as a port of entry to Boston (first for Irish immigrants, then Jewish immigrants and then African-Americans). Today, Roxbury is populated mostly by long-settled African-American families and has a small immigrant population.

In its heyday, Roxbury was a bustling hub of activity, but in the 1970s and 1980s it fell into poverty, the victim of 'white flight' to the suburbs, poor investment in the public schools, and institutional neglect. Today, there is a growing middle class, but residents still face higher rates of unemployment than in other areas of the city, as well as a higher crime rate. Federal government- and city-sponsored urban renewal/investment plans are underway, however: Dudley Square, which for a century was one of the city's centres of commerce and transportation, until the mid-1980s when the MBTA re-routed its Orange Line, has recently been revamped.

For the adventurous tourist, a slice of life can be seen in Roxbury that simply doesn't exist elsewhere in Boston, and the area provides a view of what the city must have looked like at the turn of the nineteenth century. One of the area's sights worth visiting is the beautiful **First Church of Roxbury** (the oldest wooden church in Boston). This is about eight blocks from the Prudential Center in downtown Boston and sits on a slight hill overlooking John Eliot Square; Paul Revere cast the bell in its tower.

The **Shirley-Eustis House**, one of the city's hidden gems – largely unknown to all but a small group of preservationists and historians – is also here. It was built in 1747 and in 1867 was moved 60 feet (18 metres) to make way for a new street and divided into small apartments. Over the years, it has housed two Massachusetts governors (William Shirley, who served as the royal governor of the Massachusetts Bay Colony, and Dr William Eustis, who served as governor from 1823 to 1825) and received visits from George Washington, Benjamin Franklin and Daniel Webster. During the Revolutionary War, it served as a barracks and hospital for the British. In 1970, work began on restoring the house to what it looked like in the Federal era and it remains open as a museum.

In 1900 there were no less than 30 active breweries in full operation in Boston. In fact, the city had more breweries per capita than anywhere else in the country. Today, there are just two (the Samuel Adams Brew House in Jamaica Plain and Tremont Ale in Charlestown). But the ornate brick buildings that once housed the breweries (owned and operated mostly by Irish and German immigrants) are still standing. Many of them were located along the banks of Stony Brook in Roxbury. Of particular interest is the **American Brewing Company** building at 235 Heath Street, an ornate, 107-year-old brick building that still retains its original granite sign. The structure is topped with a pointed tower and there are two false clocks built into its façade: one is set at seven o'clock and the other at five o'clock – brewers' hours.

Just down the street is the former home of the **Alley Brewing Company** at 123 Heath Street. It's a massive brick structure, though it lacks the interesting architectural details of the American Brewing Company. There were several other breweries in this area (including the AJ Houghton Co/Vienna Brewery at 125 Halleck Street and the Union Brewing Company at 103 Terrace Street), but their buildings are hollowed out, graffiti-covered shells of their former selves.

Other streets in the area worth exploring include Alleghany, Calumet and Iroquois Streets, and Parker Hill Avenue. These reveal a mix of once-grand houses, some of then painstakingly restored, but others suffering the rude fate of a century of neglect – or worse, vinyl siding. The overwhelming impression is one of a neighbourhood struggling to regain its lost glory.

First Church of Roxbury

10 Putnam Street, at Dudley Street (445 8393). Roxbury Crossing T. **Open** tours by appointment only.

Shirley-Eustis House

33 Shirley Street, at Massachusetts Avenue (442 2275). JFK/UMass T. **Open** *June-Sept* 10am-4pm Thur-Sun; *Oct-May* by appointment only. **Admission** $3-$5. **No credit cards**.

Kenmore Square

Kenmore is home to Boston University. And the triangular area bordered by Commonwealth, Brookline and Massachusetts Avenues is a haven for college students. The 15-block area houses a McDonald's, countless pizza joints, a fast food Chinese restaurant, a sit-down Thai restaurant, sandwich bars and smoothie shops, at least two coffee shops and about 15 bars/nightclubs. There's a huge branch of **Barnes & Noble** (*see page 159* **Shops & Services**) selling classbooks for BU's 20,000 students, all manner of BU paraphernalia including sweatshirts and coffee mugs, dorm room accoutrements, a well-stocked magazine/newspaper area and a café.

Appropriately enough, the offices of the *Boston Phoenix*, the weekly arts and entertainment newspaper aimed at the city's twentysomethings, are located about two blocks outside Kenmore Square. The giant **Citgo sign** that sits high above the Barnes & Noble bookstore dominates the area. This 33-year-old neon sign has been a steady beacon (except during the four years of the energy crisis between 1979 and 1983, when it was turned off) drawing nightclubbers to the city. In 1983, when Citgo announced plans to dismantle the sign, thousands of citizens signed a petition to keep it in place. Today, it's such a fixture that it figures prominently in any picture postcard of the area.

Most of the local nightclubs are on **Lansdowne Street**, across the street and up one block from the Citgo sign. In fact, nightlife for young twentysomethings doesn't get much better than this small stretch of the city. Among others here, there's **Avalon**, with one of the largest dance floors in the city, the upmarket, Indian-themed **Karma Club**, the alternative **Axis**, with its changing theme nights, and **Mama Kin**, spawn of Aerosmith (*see chapter* **Nightlife** for details of all four).

You can also visit **Fenway Park** (*see also chapter* **Sport & Fitness**), home of the Boston Red Sox, while in Kenmore Square. Located one block from Lansdowne Street at 4 Yawkey Way, the park, which opened on 20 April 1912 (the same day the *Titanic* sank), has seen generations of baseball greats including Babe Ruth, Cy Young, Jimmy Foxx, Ted Williams and Roger Clemens. But despite all the Hall of Famers who have at one time or another worn the Red Sox uniform, Fenway Park – with its foreboding 37-foot (11-metre) left-field wall affectionately known as 'the Green Monster' – just might be more famous than any of its players. As most New Englanders know all too well, the Red Sox haven't won a World Series since 1918. The baseball park is one of the last in the country still located in the heart of a team's home town, as opposed to the suburban outskirts.

Brookline

If you follow **Beacon Street** out of the middle of Kenmore Square, it will take you to Brookline. You can either walk or take the 'B' Line of the MBTA Green Line. The stretch of Beacon Street immediately outside Kenmore Square accommodates a number of excellent restaurants (*see chapter* **Restaurants & Cafés**). There's the gourmet Cambodian **Elephant Walk**, the Japanese sushi eaterie **Ginza** and the American **Providence**. This stretch also includes a number of more modest, but no less delicious, bars and restaurants

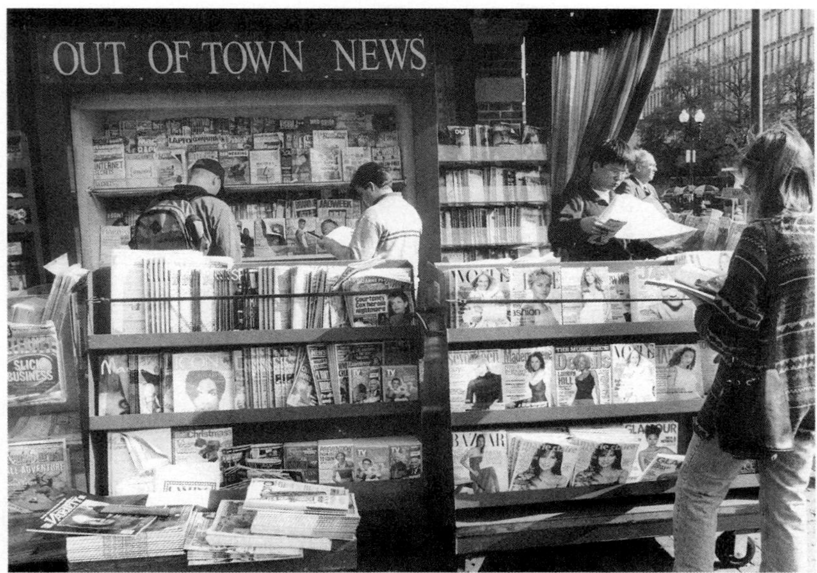

For magazines and newspapers of every stripe, head for **Out of Town News**. *See page 81.*

including **Audubon Circle** (*see page 115* **Pubs & Bars**), a cosy wood-panelled bar for local denizens and the Irish **RíRá** (*see page 117* **Pubs & Bars**) which serves excellent fish and chips. Further up Beacon Street is Coolidge Corner and the **Coolidge Corner Theater** (*see page 185* **Film**), housed in a beautifully-restored art deco building. The Coolidge screens excellent foreign and independent films rarely shown in mainstream cinemas. It also has special events and concerts. Next door is **Grand Opening!** (*see page 171* **Shops & Services**), a sex shop staffed by friendly, non-threatening sexperts. The shop's proprietor, Kim Airs, is also president of the Brookline Chamber of Commerce.

Reflecting the tastes of the neighbourhood's local Jewish population, there are countless bagel shops along **Harvard Avenue**, as well as a couple of kosher delis. One of the country's best independent bookshops, the **Brookline Booksmith**, is also located in Coolidge Corner (279 Harvard Street; 566 6660).

Brookline also has its share of historical sites. Between the Beacon Street food stretch and Coolidge Corner is **Beals Street** (off Beacon Street). Number 83 is the birthplace and boyhood home of **John F Kennedy** (*see page 13* **History**).

Also in the area is the **Frederick Law Olmsted National Historic Site**, the former house and office of the father of US landscape architecture and creator of Boston's Emerald Necklace. Guided tours are available.

The **Museum of Transportation** (*see page 93* **Museums & Galleries**), at the Carriage House in Larz Anderson Park, houses antique cars in an 1889 carriage house (including the British-built 1905 'electromobile' and an 1908 Bailey that still runs). There's also a fully-restored tack room, vehicles that children can climb on and picnic areas. Displays change seasonally.

Frederick Law Olmsted National Historic Site

99 Warren Street, at Dudley Street, Brookline (566 1689). Brookline Hills T. **Open** 10am-4.30pm Fri-Sun. **Admission** free.

Organised tours

By bus

Exploring the city on your own can be fun, but occasionally you want somebody to do the work for you, somebody who can provide strange insights, esoteric facts and really bad puns. Or maybe you just like to feel like a tourist, swept away from walking or thinking or knowing exactly what you're looking at. Whatever the reason, organised bus tours thrive in Boston. Be

One of the many floating tour options in Boston and Cambridge.

forewarned – as much fun as some of these are, almost all are fairly tacky and overpriced. If you accept this fact at the outset and commit yourself not to care what you're getting into, they can be a lot of fun. Put on your 'I'm with Stupid' T-shirt, strap the 35mm around your neck and take to the streets.

Locals may laugh at you, but the best ride in the city is an amphibious adventure so unique you shouldn't pass it up: the well-publicised **Boston Duck Tours**. The vehicles are impossible to miss on the streets (and rivers) of Boston and have an interesting historical genesis as World War II amphibious landing-craft. Code-named DUKW, these vehicles greatly helped in the Normandy invasion. Today, they tackle the Newbury Street invasion, restored, painted in bright colours and manned by so-called 'conDUCKtors'.

Another kitsch tour worth subjecting yourself to is one on a **Boston Old Town Trolley**. These trolley-cars would seem more appropriate in San Francisco. Their conductors spend 100 minutes explaining all there is to know about Boston – well, maybe not everything, but they probably know their stuff better than any other tour conductors in town. Reboarding is free if you want to get off and wander through the Paul Revere House or shop at the Prudential Center, so you can tour at your own pace.

The **JFK Tour** (run by Boston Old Town Trolley Tours) follows major sites in the life of the 35th president. From his birthplace to his childhood hangouts to the library and museum built in his honour, this is a Camelot-obsessive's dream come true.

The beer-minded will be pleased to know that despite the recent decline of American microbrews, Boston is still home to many small independent breweries. A good way to investigate a few is on the **Boston Brew Pub Tour**. You'd think they could hit more than three brew pubs in the three hours allotted to the tour, but it would probably be dangerous to customers' livers. So instead of more beer, they pour on the history. Unfortunately, this tour only runs a few times a year (it's also run by Boston Old Town Trolley Tours).

If you have an extremely limited time in which to see Boston and Cambridge, hop on the whirlwind **Minuteman Boston Trolley Tour**, which covers over 100 sites in just two hours. And for those more comfortable hearing bad puns in Spanish, French, Italian, German or Japanese, the **Discover Boston Multilingual Trolley Tours** are perfect.

Boston Duck Tours

Huntington Avenue, at Prudential Center (723 3825). Prudential T. **Rates** $11-$21. **Map 3 E5/6**

Boston Old Town Trolley Tours

Old Atlantic Avenue, at New England Aquarium (269 7150). Aquarium T. **Rates** *Trolley Tours, Brew Pub Tour, JFK Tour* $8-$25. **Map 5 H4**

Discover Boston Multilingual Trolley Tours

66 Long Wharf, at New England Aquarium, or 73 Tremont Street, at Visitors' Information Center, Park Street (742 1440). Aquarium or Park St T. **Rates** $14-$21. **Map 5 H4**

Minuteman Trolley Tours

Old Atlantic Avenue, at New England Aquarium (269 3626). Aquarium T. **Rates** $10-$23. **Map 5 H4**

By boat

Boston's surrounding waters are an essential part of its image (*see page 76* **On the waterfront**) and taking to the sea on an organised boat cruise is one of the best ways of appreciating this. They're seasonal and don't offer nearly as much history as the bus tours. They do, however, offer plenty of water.

Boston Harbor Cruises take you through the scenic yet once notoriously dirty body of water, and some even take you up to the USS *Constitution* itself. **Bay State Cruise Lines** offers jazz, blues and rock cruises featuring local talent, plus voyages to points along Cape Cod and around the Boston coastline. The enormous boat *The Spirit of Boston* features a daily clambake lunchtime cruise. **Massachusetts Bay Lines** also runs cruises with live musical entertainment and tours of the harbour, as does **Odyssey Cruises**.

The Cambridge area gets covered by the **Charles River Boat Company**, which tours the Charles River basin and even offers tours that head back toward the harbour. To check out a water-friendly suburb, try the trip to scenic Gloucester on **AC Cruise Lines**. And the **New England Aquarium** organises educational tours aboard the specially designed research ship *Voyager II* (*see page 51* **Downtown & the Financial District**).

Most of these companies also offer whale-watching trips; for more of these, *see chapter* **Trips Out of Town**.

AC Cruise Lines

290 Northern Avenue, at World Trade Center (261 6633). South Station T, then 7 bus. **Rates** *whale-watching & trips to Gloucester & Salem* $12-$19. **Map 3 J5**

Bay State Cruise Lines

164 New Northern Avenue, at World Trade Center (457 1428). South Station T, then 7 bus. **Rates** *lunch & dinner cruises* $21-$30. **Map 3 J5**

Boston Harbor Cruises

1 Long Wharf, next to New England Aquarium (227 4321). Aquarium T. **Rates** *sightseeing & whale-watching* $8-$28. **Map 5 H4**

Charles River Boat Company

Galleria Mall, 100 Cambridgeside Place, Cambridge (621 3001). Lechmere T. **Rates** *sightseeing of Charles River & Boston Harbor* $6-$8. **Map 4 F3**

Massachusetts Bay Lines

60 Rowes Wharf, at Boston Harbor Hotel (542 8000). Aquarium or South Station T. **Rates** *Boston Harbor cruise & whale-watching* $8-$25. **Map 5 H4**

Odyssey Cruises

Rowes Wharf (654 9700). Aquarium T. **Rates** *lunch & dinner cruises* $40-$99. **Map 5 H4**

By foot

New England isn't known for consistently fair weather, but about half of the year is surprisingly beautiful, or at least tolerable. The period from May to September is the best time to navigate the city by foot, and plenty of organisations set up shop in those months to help tell you what you're walking past. **Boston by Foot** runs an impressive selection of walking tours through various neighbourhoods every day of the walking season. People who know their history lead, often shaping the path to a particular theme, such as women's history or examples of art deco in Boston. Tours cover areas of Boston such as the Back Bay, North End and the waterfront; most begin at the Sam Adams statue at Faneuil Hall.

Another geographically-based walking tour comes courtesy of the **Historical Neighbourhoods Foundation**, which runs different programmes every year that cover architecture and history around the city. For those interested in exploring the scenery of the Emerald Necklace, the **Boston Park Rangers** offer a free tour. **WalkBoston** sponsors occasional tours of areas outside Greater Boston; and in Cambridge, **Mount Auburn Cemetery** (*see page 82* **Further afield**) offers frequent tours on which guides point out the graves of historical figures and show you round the grounds, which look more like an arboretum than a final resting place.

Boston by Foot

(367 2345/recorded information 367 3766). **Rates** $6-$9. *Website: www.bostonbyfoot.com*

Boston Park Rangers

145 Tremont Street, at West Street (635 7383). Park St T. **Open** 9am-5pm Mon-Fri. **Tours** *include Freedom Trail Starter, the Hike, the Necklace Tour, Women's History Tour.* **Map 5 G4/5**

Historic Neighbourhoods Foundation

(Information 426 1885). **Rates** vary; phone for details

WalkBoston

(Information 451 1570). **Rates** vary; phone for details.

Museums & Galleries

From a culture of world-class but conservative collections, a vibrant modern art scene is beginning to emerge.

Visual arts museums

An emblematic anecdote that still captures something of the spirit of Boston involves a young woman, a newcomer to town, who is introduced to one of the established Brahmins from Beacon Hill. 'Madame,' asks the new arrival, 'where did you get your hat?' 'In Boston,' sneers the silver-haired blue blood, 'we do not get our hats, we have our hats.'

Until recently, the same could be said about the visual arts in Boston. With the permanent collections at a small handful of major institutions outstripping anything resembling the avant-garde, Boston had its art, it didn't get it. But all of that has changed, not in number – Boston remains an art-poor town – so much as in the quality of the work being done, particularly in painting and sculpture. In fact, the museums and galleries of Boston, especially the smaller museums and some of the less well-known galleries, rank as among the most ground-breaking venues in the United States. Boston's beginning, after all, to get it.

For the **Children's Museum**, *see chapter* **Children**.

Boston Center for the Arts

Mills Gallery, 539 Tremont Street, at Clarendon Street (426 5000/Cyclorama 426 7700). Back Bay or Copley T. **Open** for exhibitions only 1-4pm Wed, Sun; 1-4pm, 7-10pm, Thur-Sat. **Admission** free.
Map 5 F6

The BCAs' Mills Gallery in the South End defines its mission more humbly than the **ICA** (*below*), showcasing Boston and New England artists primarily. Group shows at the Mills (it has not hosted a solo exhibition in recent memory) tend to be organised around material or conceptual themes. The Mills Gallery also plays host to large, experimental installation works, both within its own space and in the remarkable Cyclorama next door: a huge brick rotunda of a building constructed in the latter part of the last century in which historic and clumsy tableaux vivants could be enacted. In the Cyclorama's case, its re-enactments originally centred on the Civil War (*see also p68* **Sightseeing**).
Disabled: toilet.

Institute of Contemporary Art

955 Boylston Street, at Massachusetts Avenue (266 5152). Hynes/ICA T. **Open** noon-5pm Wed, Fri-Sun; noon-9pm, Thur. **Admission** $4-$6 (under-12s & 5-9pm Thur, free). **Credit** AmEx, MC, V.
Map 3 E5

Another venue that rounds out the city's major non-commercial, public showcases. The ICA, housed in a converted nineteenth-century fire station, sees its mission as the importing of works by contemporary European, Asian and American artists – generally in that order – working in non-traditional materials. The downside of such a posture is that exhibitions often suffer from a didactic, heavy-handed feel. On the other hand, the ICA remains unique in Boston for its parade of international artists.
Disabled: toilet.

Don't miss...

Fogg Art Museum: for all the major travelling exhibitions (*see page 94*).
Genovese/Sullivan Gallery: outstanding contemporary art in an art-friendly space (*page 98*).
Hamill Gallery of African Art: a comprehensive collection which makes essential viewing (*page 98*).
Harvard University Museums: for noteworthy time-travelling and globe-trotting collections (*page 98*).
Howard Yezerski Gallery: a provocative Newbury Street stalwart (*page 98*).
MIT Museums: covering anything from high-speed photography to holographic art (*page 95*).
Museum of Fine Arts: the grand-daddy of them all (*page 90*).
Museum of Science & Hayden Planetarium: (*page 92*) for hands-on displays that prove science *is* fun.
John F Kennedy Library & Museum: everything there is to know about JFK (*page 92*).

The central courtyard of the palatial **Isabella Stewart Gardner Museum**. *See page 90.*

Isabella Stewart Gardner Museum

280 The Fenway, at Palace Road (566 1401). Museum of Fine Arts T. **Open** 11am-5pm Tue-Sun. **Admission** $3-$10. **Credit** AmEx, Disc, MC, V. **Map 3 D6**

Based in a charming structure not far from the Museum of Fine Arts, this museum can boast such unlikely holdings as the city's only Michelangelo. Though significantly attenuated by the greatest art theft in history a number of years ago, the idiosyncratic Gardner collection, together with the Venetian villa housing it, offers a variety of unexpected delights, from Renaissance Italian masters to the famous portrait of Gardner herself by John Singer Sargent. What's more, the Gardner has recently begun an artist-in-residence programme, for the first time in its history, allowing it a chance to mount important solo shows by the living artists it has invited as its guests.

Museum of Fine Arts

465 Huntington Avenue, at Museum Street (267 9300). Museum of Fine Arts T. **Open** 10am-4.45pm Mon, Tue; 10am-9.45pm Wed-Fri; 9am-5.30pm Sat, Sun. **Admission** $8-$10 (under-17s free). **Credit** AmEx, Disc, MC, V. **Map 3 D6**

The place you're most likely to hear about, though not necessarily the first place to seek out, is the Museum of Fine Arts, the largest, oldest, in some respects still the most expansive, of Boston's mainstream institutions. With extensive holdings in a range of areas, from the art of Asia to American Colonial and Federal portraits, and with smaller collections studded by gems (European Impressionists and ancient Egyptian artifacts significant among them) the MFA earns a place on most itineraries. While its widely-marketed blockbuster shows tend to be disappointments (in its efforts to seem youthful, the museum's often caught looking like von Aschenbach at the end of *Death in Venice* – some recent atrocities have included a giant exhibition of the fashion photographer Herb Ritts and a similarly spellbinding display of the cartoon figures Wallace and Gromit), it remains a repository of significance. Think of a visit here as you would a call on an ancient relative.

John Singer Sargent's 'Carnation, Lily, Lily, Rose' in the **Museum of Fine Arts**.

Art schools

Particular attention deserves to be paid to the exhibition spaces connected with a special subset of Boston's post-secondary schools, namely its art schools. Foremost is the **Massachusetts College of Art**, the only publicly-funded school in the USA solely dedicated to the fine and decorative arts. Not only do its galleries showcase artists with deserved international reputations, its student and faculty shows can offer the same quality excitement without the name-recognition. The **School of the Museum of Fine Arts**, an institution largely independent of the museum, sponsors a yearly competitive exhibition called 'Travelling Scholars'. Although the show does not actually travel, the select alumni and alumnae as well as the fifth year students that it features are invariably provocative. Finally, the **Art Institute of Boston**, which has recently joined forces with Lesley College, continues to become a more exciting location for contemporary art. Recent exhibitions have ranged from folk art of the Andes to the art of the political satirist Edward Sorel.

Art Institute of Boston

700 Beacon Street, at Commonwealth Avenue (262 1223). Kenmore Square T. **Open** 9am-6pm Fri, Sat. **Admission** free. **Credit** MC, V. **Map 3 D5**
Disabled: toilet.

Massachusetts College of Art

Bakalar, Huntington & President's Galleries
621 Huntington Avenue, at Longwood Avenue (232 1555). Longwood T. **Open** 10am-6pm Mon-Fri; 11am-5pm Sat. **Admission** free. **Map 3 7D**
Disabled: toilet.

School of the Museum of Fine Arts

230 The Fenway, next to the Museum of Fine Arts, Huntington Avenue (267 6100). Museum of Fine Arts T. **Open** varies according to exhibition. **Admission** free. **Map 3 D6**
Disabled: toilet.

Other museums

Around Boston & Cambridge

Boston Athenaeum

10½ Beacon Street, between Bowdoin & Somerset Streets (227 0270). Park St T. **Open** 8.30am-5.30pm Tue-Fri; 9am-4pm Sat; 8.30am-8pm Sun. **Admission** free. **Map 5 G4**

The Boston Athenaeum is a private institution with a long and distinguished history of serving the public good. Founded in the early nineteenth century as a literary society, the Athenaeum published America's first literary magazine and began acquiring an extensive library of books and collecting works of art. By the dawn of the twentieth century, the Athenaeum had helped establish Boston's Museum of Fine Arts and moved into its current home, a giant five-storey building on Beacon Street that serves mainly as a library and research facility for its members. The first and second floor of the building is, however, open to the public, and although most of the society's art collection has been transferred to the MFA, the Athenaeum still has some works of interest on display, including nineteenth-century paintings by John Singer Sargent and Chester Harding and books that once belonged

The **Boston Athenaeum**: *distinguished library, museum and gallery.*

Public art

Public art in Boston falls into two distinct categories: the execrable and the extraordinary. Some of the very best monuments in the city are concentrated on the mall on Commonwealth Avenue and in the Boston Public Garden. For example, Olin Levi Warner's statue of the abolitionist **William Lloyd Garrison** on Commonwealth Avenue captures the spirit of a man who burned a copy of the Declaration of Independence on the State House lawn to protest against slavery and was then dragged by horse at the end of a rope over Boston's cobbled streets until his flesh tore away. When he recovered, he returned to Constitution burning.

One of the outstanding figures in the Public Garden depicts the writer and minister **Edward Everett Hale**. Bela Lyon Pratt's 1913 statue caused a stir at the time of its erection because Mr Hale is shown with a walking stick and wearing no hat, as if he were strolling in the Garden along with the rest of us.

On the lawn of the State House, overlooking the Public Garden, is one of the city's most poignant statues, Sylvia Shaw Judson's 1959 memorial to the Quaker martyr **Mary Dyer**. Dyer was hanged on nearby Boston Common for challenging Puritan religious laws and her seated figure suggests the unimaginable strength of her spirit.

Directly across the street from Mary Dyer is arguably the most outstanding work of public art in the United States, Augustus Saint-Gaudens' tribute to **Colonel Robert Gould Shaw** and his infantrymen. Shaw, a white man and Abolitionist who came from a wealthy Boston home, is seen leading a regiment of African-American men, all of whom were killed in the assault on Fort Wagner, South Carolina, in July 1863. Although the marching soldiers and the horse-riding Shaw crowd the space they're allotted in the towering bas relief, Saint-Gaudens' memorial renders each man with a haunting peculiarity.

Somewhat off the beaten path, along the Southeast Expressway in fact, which heads out of the city towards Cape Cod, stands Boston's most peculiar and genuinely arresting public monument, a huge gas tank that Corita Kent turned from a typical urban eyesore into something magnificent when she painted it in 1971. At first glance, the tank appears to have had alternating colours of paint poured over it from the top so that it resembles a crude rainbow. It took people a long time to realise that the seemingly randomly dripping blue band actually had the outline of the face of **Ho Chi Minh**, leader of the North Vietnamese forces with whom the United States were at war in 1971. Despite all sorts of protests, the piece remains, a pleasure for all.

Getting to grips with the **Museum of Science**.

to George Washington. A gallery on the second floor hosts monthly exhibitions of works by regional artists.

Boston Public Library

See p62 **Sightseeing** *for listings.*

This is America's oldest public library. The original structure, an Italian Renaissance-style building designed by Charles McKim, was extended when an annex designed by Philip Johnson was built in the early 1970s. Along with plenty of books and periodicals, the BPL features several galleries for exhibiting everything from rare books and manuscripts to photographs of Boston's changing cityscape. Of more interest, perhaps, are permanent fixtures such as the bronze doors designed by Lincoln Memorial architect Daniel Chester French and several newly restored religious-themed murals by John Singer Sargent (*see p21* **Architecture**).

Boston Tea Party Ship and Museum

Congress Street Bridge (338 1773). South Station T. **Open** *1 Mar-30 Nov* 9am-6pm, *1 Dec-28 Feb* 9am-5pm, daily. **Admission** $4-$8. **No credit cards. Map 5 H5**

They'll actually serve you a cup of tea here. And it's of a quality that encourages a certain kind of historical re-enactment from visitors, who toss the tea into Boston Harbor from the brig *Beaver II*, a 'replica' of the *Beaver*, one of the ships vandalised by Colonists in protest at the British tea tax back in December 1773 (*see p8* **History**). In fact, before it became a tourist attraction, *Beaver II*, which is docked opposite the museum, was a Danish ship built in the early twentieth century. And the museum part of the Boston Tea Party Ship and Museum includes a video about it's 'historic' voyage to Boston in 1972, as well as exhibits about the tea industry and shipbuilding, a model of Boston c1773, and a tea crate thought to have been part of the real Boston Tea Party.

Disabled: toilet.

Computer Museum

300 Congress Street, at Sleeper Street (423 2800). South Station T. **Open** *winter* 10am-5pm Tue-Sun; *summer* 10am-6pm daily. **Admission** $5-$7. **Credit** AmEx, MC, V. **Map 5 H5**

A giant walk-through computer is the main attraction at this warehouse-sized facility dedicated to the machine that's caused its own share of pre-millennial tension. The museum features dozens of other interactive exhibits about computers aimed mainly at curious kids and geared more towards exploring the early evolution of computer technology than more recent, cutting-edge developments.

Disabled: toilet.

John F Kennedy Library & Museum

Columbia Point, at Morrissey Boulevard, Dorchester (929 4500). JFK/UMass T. **Open** 9am-5pm daily. **Admission** $4-$8. **Credit** AmEx, Disc, MC, V.

A looming concrete-and-glass monolith designed by IM Pei, the Kennedy Library overlooks the outer harbour from high on top of the Columbia Point peninsula. Inside, you'll find displays dedicated to the memory of the 35th President of the United States, including a time-line of the Kennedy family, films of JFK press conferences, and the president's desk. Along with JFK memorabilia, the museum also features a room containing books and manuscripts that once belonged to Ernest Hemingway.

Longyear Museum

(Information 267 6688). **Open** by appointment.

A museum and historical society dedicated to exploring the life and work of Christian Science founder Mary Baker Eddy. The museum contains manuscripts and biographical material about Eddy and offers tours of several nearby houses she lived in. It is due to move premises in the year 2000, but a limited collection can be viewed by arrangement in a temporary address at 271 Huntington Avenue until then.

Museum of Afro American History

See **African Meeting House** *p53* **Sightseeing** *for listings.*

The Museum of Afro American History is essentially two structures of historical significance – the **African Meeting House**, which once housed the first classroom for black children in Boston and remains the longest standing black church in the country; and the **Abiel Smith School**, which is where the New England Anti-Slavery Society was founded in the 1830s. Though there are exhibitions about African-Americans in New England on display at the African Meeting House, the museum is primarily a historic landmark and the launching point for the National Park Service's Black Heritage Trail (*see p53* **Sightseeing**).

Museum of Science & Hayden Planetarium

Science Park, Charles River Dam (723 2500). Science Park T. **Open** 9am-5pm Mon-Thur, Sat, Sun; 9am-9pm Fri. **Admission** $7-$9. **Credit** AmEx, MC, V. **Map 5 F3**

From the Gemini Space Ship capsule (which orbited the Earth more than 200 times in 1965) to the Thomson Theatre of Electricity (which houses a giant Van de Graaf generator), Boston's Museum of Science is committed to providing an interactive and educational experience. It justifiably prides itself on making science accessible to the average person, through exhibitions that explain all things scientific in straightforward terms and via hundreds of different hands-on installations. At the **Charles Hayden Planetarium** (admission $5.50-$7.50) audiences relaxing in ergonomic seats watch the dome-shaped ceiling as the Zeiss Star Projector creates a believable night sky before their eyes. 'The Sky Tonight' gives viewers a tour of the stars, planets and constellations visible in New England each night. And to keep the teenagers happy, there are psychedelic, rock 'n' roll laser shows such as the 'Laser Hendrix/Doors' and the 'Laser Beatles'. Alternatively, there's the **Mugar Omni Theater** (Larz Anderson Park, 15 Newton Street, Brookline; 522 6547; admission $3-$5), where the five-storey screen and incredible sound system combine to make the viewer feel as if they really are flying over the Great Barrier Reef, riding the rapids of the Grand Canyon or dangerously speeding down a Boston expressway. Other shows have focused on climbing Mount Everest, exploring Antarctica, or negotiating the Amazon.

Disabled: toilet. Website: www.mos.org

Open studios

Every autumn, more than a dozen artist studio complexes (ranging in size from single buildings to entire city blocks) in and around Boston host 'open studios'. Artists working in a range of media and at every level of accomplishment open their work spaces, which are often also their homes, for a public viewing and buying bonanza.

The open studios season takes place from mid-September to late November, and while a great deal of what's on show is the output of weekend sculptors and greetings-card painters, you can also discover the work of strong artists, some unaffiliated and undiscovered, others with major national galleries behind them.

A list of open studio locations and schedules can be obtained by phoning the office of the arts commissioner at **Boston City Hall** (635 3245).

Museum of Transportation

Larz Anderson Park, 15 Newton Street, Brookline (522 6547). Cleveland Circle or Reservoir T. **Open** 10am-5pm Tue-Sun. **Admission** $3-$5. **No credit cards.**

Located in Brookline's Larz Anderson Park, the Museum of Transportation is at its best in the warmer months, when it hosts weekend get-togethers for classic car buffs and the parking lot fills with rare automobiles. Inside you'll find displays detailing the history of America's favourite form of transport.

Disabled: toilet.

USS Constitution Museum

Charlestown Navy Yard (426 1812). Community College T. **Open** 10am-5pm daily. **Admission** free.

In 1974 Charlestown Navy Yard was decommissioned by the US Navy and turned into a historic site. But for the better part of the previous two centuries, the yard had been one of the American Navy's most important facilities – a place where new warships could be built under cover and old warships kept in dry dock. One of the Navy Yard's most celebrated guests was the *USS Constitution*, a battleship built in Boston and nicknamed 'Old Ironsides' when it emerged victorious from a battle with the British Navy during the War of 1812. These days, the restored *Constitution* is one of the prime attractions at the Navy Yard, which also houses a museum that features historical exhibitions about shipbuilding and life on board the *Constitution* back in 1812.

Disabled: toilet.

Further afield

The following is a selection of museums within easy reach of Boston – as part of a daytrip within Massachusetts for instance. For museums and sights in the further reaches of New England, *see chapter* **Trips Out of Town**.

American Textile History

491 Dutton Street, Lowell (1-978 441 0400). **Open** 9am-4pm Tue-Fri; 10am-4pm Sat, Sun. **Admission** $3-$5. **Credit** AmEx, Disc, MC, V.

Based in the former mill-dominated town of Lowell, this museum contains permanent exhibitions about the American textile industry, as well as more contemporary one-off displays such as a collection of dresses belonging to Diana, Princess of Wales.

Disabled: toilet.

Boott Cotton Mills Museum

Lowell National Historical Park, 400 Foot of John Street, Lowell (1-978 970 5000). **Open** 9.30am-5pm Mon-Sat; 11am-5pm Sun. **Admission** $2-$4. **No credit cards.**

Located in Lowell National Historical Park, which hosts a folk festival every summer and participates in the annual celebration of native son Jack Kerouac's birthday, the Boott Cotton Mills Museum contains exhibitions on the Industrial Revolution in America and the textile industry in Lowell. *See also chapter* **Trips Out of Town**.

Disabled: toilet.

Cape Ann Historical Museum

27 Pleasant Street, Gloucester (1-978 283 0455). **Open** *Mar-Jan* 10am-5pm Tue-Sat. **Admission** $2.50-$4. **No credit cards.**

Gloucester was once a thriving fishing village on Massachusetts' North Shore. The Cape Ann Historical Museum contains photographs and other memorabilia commemorating that history, as well as a large collection of maritime paintings. *See also chapter* **Trips Out of Town**.

Disabled: toilet.

Concord Museum

Cambridge Turnpike, Concord (1-978 369 9763). **Open** 9am-5pm daily. **Admission** $4-$10. **Credit** AmEx, MC, V.

A lantern hung at the Old North Church to warn the local Minutemen of the British Army's approach is on display here, as are furniture and other artifacts documenting life in Concord as far back as the pre-Revolutionary War era. *See also chapter* **Trips Out of Town**.

Higgins Armory Museum

100 Barber Avenue, Worcester (1-508 853 6015). **Open** 10am-4pm Tue-Sat; noon-4pm Sun. **Admission** $5-$5.75. **Credit** MC, V.

A unique institution that specialises in the history of arms and armaments. The collection goes all the way back to the medieval chain-mail-and-lance, which never got much use in America.

The **John F Kennedy Library & Museum**.

University collections

An entirely different and rich category of museums exists in Boston, making it unique among American cities. As the hub of perhaps the single greatest concentration of institutions of higher learning in the world, Boston is also home to numerous museums associated with colleges and universities.

By far the most noteworthy is the complex associated with **Harvard University**, particularly the **Fogg Art Museum**. With a permanent collection that ranges from the African to the European Baroque, the Fogg regularly hosts important exhibitions travelling the USA and Europe. Contiguous to the Fogg is Harvard's **Busch-Reisinger Museum**, the only museum in the western hemisphere devoted to the art of German-speaking Europe, and which contains in its permanent collection works by Klee, Kandinsky, Beckmann and Klimt. No less compelling are the Asian collections at the **Arthur M Sackler Museum**, which houses the widest collection of Chinese jades outside China, an unrivalled collection of Korean ceramics, sculptures and paintings, as well as an outstanding collection of Thai illuminated manuscripts.

Along with its three impressive art museums, Harvard is also home to several other important exhibition spaces. The Harvard University Museum is itself essentially four museums in one: the **Botanical Museum**, which features the famous Ware Collection of glass flowers; the **Museum of Comparative Zoology**, where you'll find 'the world's oldest reptile egg and largest turtle shell', among other delights; the **Mineralogical and Geological Museums** – both home to thousands of mineral specimens as well as exhibitions on volcanoes and meteorites; and the **Peabody Museum of Archaeology and Ethnology**, an anthropological museum featuring fossils and artifacts from as far back as the Paleolithic period. The **Semitic Museum** is an institution best known for its rotating exhibitions of early photographs of the Middle East.

While it comes as little surprise that the wealthiest American university encompasses first-rate smaller museums, what is surprising is the high quality of those museums and galleries associated with other local schools. **MIT** (Massachusetts Institute of Technology), for instance, encompasses not only the **List Visual Arts Center** but also the galleries of the **MIT Museum** – entirely different enterprises.

The List Visual Arts Center constructs its exhibitions within a clear, perhaps flagrant, political agenda. Its tendency is toward displays by artists who can boast coming from – or at least having been to – war-torn countries. Recent shows have included works by Alfredo Jaar (Rwanda), William Kentridge (South Africa) and Kiki Smith (the war between the sexes).

As with other venues in this category, the university museums do not need to indulge in the quick turnover of their more commercial counterparts. Currently on indefinite show at MIT Museum's **Strobe Alley** are photographs of Harold ('Doc') Edgerton, the pioneer of high-speed photography (Edgerton was the first to capture a bullet in flight and the first stage of an exploding balloon on film). Also on display are the kinetic sculptures of Arthur Ganson – ingenious, frequently hilarious machines that seem to have minds of their own. And since you might expect a little eccentricity from one of the world's finest institutions of scientific research, the museum also features an outstanding collection of holographic art, as well as an exhibition about the exciting evolution of the slide rule.

The **Hart Nautical Museum**, by contrast, is dedicated not to the study of marine biology but to a collection of model ships; and the **Compton Gallery** features rotating shows that draw on the MIT's historical collection of art and scientific objects.

Also worth seeking out are the galleries associated with **Tufts University**, whose curators stand out for their willingness to take exciting and meaningful risks. A recent show of photos depicted the people and landscape of Nagasaki after its bombing in WWII.

The **McMullen Museum of Art**, connected with **Boston College**, proves a more conservative but genuinely erudite place. It was the only North American venue, for instance, to show the recently discovered Caravaggio *The Taking of Christ*, which was on display until May 1999.

Finally, **Boston University** offers a number of affiliated spaces, from the gallery associated with its School for the Arts, the **Boston University Art Gallery**, to two galleries specialising in photography. One, the **Panopticon Gallery**, is unique as both a developing centre for the city's commercial photographers, as well as an informal space for artists. The other BU gallery, the **Photographic Resource Center**, tends to be strongest for its historic shows and weakest when it shows photos by celebrity rock stars.

One of Harvard's highlights: the **Arthur M Sackler Museum**.

Boston College

McMullen Museum of Art, 140 Commonwealth Avenue, at College Road, Newton (552 8587). Chestnut Hill T. **Open** *Sept-May* 11am-4pm Mon-Fri, noon-5pm Sat, Sun; *June-Aug* 11am-3pm Mon-Fri. **Admission** free.
Disabled: toilet.

Boston University

Boston University Art Gallery
855 Commonwealth Avenue, at Boston University Bridge (353 3329). Kenmore T. **Open** 10am-5pm Tue-Fri; 1-5pm Sat, Sun. **Admission** free. **Map 4 C5**

Panopticon Gallery *187 Bay State Road, at Sherbourn Street (267 8929). Kenmore T.* **Open** 9am-5pm Mon-Fri; by appointment Sat. **Admission** free. **Map 4 D5**
Disabled: toilet.

Photographic Resource Center
602 Commonwealth Avenue, at Blandford Street (353 0700). Blandford Street T. **Open** noon-5pm Tue, Wed, Fri-Sun; noon-8pm Thur. **Admission** $2-$5 (free Thur). **Map 4 C5**
Disabled: toilet.

Harvard University Museums

Arthur M Sackler Museum *485 Broadway, at Quincy Street, Cambridge (495 9400). Harvard T.* **Open** 10am-5pm Mon-Sat; 1-5pm Sun. **Admission** *with Busch-Reisinger & Fogg* $3-$5. **Credit** AmEx, Disc, MC, V. **Map 4 B2**

Busch-Reisinger Museum & Fogg Art Museum *32 Quincy Street, at Broadway, Cambridge (495 2397). Harvard T.* **Open** 10am-5pm Mon-Sat; 1-5pm Sun. **Admission** *with Sackler* $3-$5. **Credit** AmEx, Disc, MC, V. **Map 4 B2**

Harvard Semitic Museum *6 Divinity Avenue, at Kirkland Street, Cambridge (495 2123). Harvard T.* **Open** 10am-4pm Mon-Fri; 1-4pm Sun. **Admission** free. **Map 4 C2**

Harvard University Museum *Oxford Street, at Kirkland Street, Cambridge (495 3045). Harvard T.* **Open** 10am-5pm Mon-Sat; 1-5pm Sun. **Admission** $3-$5. **Credit** AmEx, Disc, MC, V. **Map 4 B2**

MIT Museums

Compton Gallery *77 Massachusetts Avenue, at MIT Campus, Cambridge (253 4444). Kendall/MIT T.* **Open** 9am-5pm Mon-Fri. **Admission** free. **Map 4 D2**
Disabled: toilet.

Hart Nautical Galleries *55 Massachusetts Avenue, at MIT Campus, Cambridge (253 5492). Kendall/MIT T.* **Open** 9am-8pm daily. **Admission** free. **Map 4 D4**.

List Visual Arts Center *20 Ames Street, at Main Street, Cambridge (253 4680). Kendall/MIT T.* **Open** noon-6pmTue-Thur, Sat, Sun; noon-8pm Fri. **Admission** free. **Map 4 E4**.
Disabled: toilet.

MIT Museum *265 Massachusetts Avenue, at Front Street, Cambridge (253 4444). Kendall/MIT T.* **Open** 10am-5pm Tue-Fri; noon-5pm Sat, Sun. **Admission** $1-$3. **No credit cards**. **Map 4 D4**
Disabled: toilet.

Strobe Alley *Fourth floor, Building Four, 77 Massachusetts Avenue, at MIT Campus, Cambridge (253 4629). Kendall/MIT T.* **Open** 24 hours daily. **Admission** free. **Map 4 D4**.

Tufts University Gallery

Aidekman Arts Center, Tufts University, Talbot Avenue, Somerville (627 3518). Davis T. **Open** noon-8pm Wed-Sat; noon-5pm Sun. **Admission** free.
Disabled: toilet.

Hull Lifesaving Museum

1117 Nantasket Avenue, Hull (1-781 925-5433).
Open *Sept-June* 10am-4pm Fri-Sun; *July, Aug* 10am-4pm Wed-Fri; 10am-5pm Sat, Sun. **Admission** $1.50-$4. **Credit** MC, V.
A restored nineteenth-century US Lifesaving Station on Massachusetts' South Shore, this museum contains historical displays relating to lighthouse operation, shipwrecks and boat building.
Disabled: toilet.

Kendall Whaling Museum

27 Everett Street, Sharon (1-781 784 5642).
Open 10am-5pm Tue-Sat; 1-5pm Sun. **Admission** $2.50-$4. **Credit** AmEx, MC, V.
Perhaps it's not the most PC of subjects, but whaling is certainly a part of local history and this museum features a number of items relating to the practice of hunting the great whale, as well as a collection of paintings of whalers in action.
Disabled: toilet.

Museum of Our National Heritage

33 Marrett Road, Lexington (1-781 861 6559). **Open** 10am-5pm Mon-Sat; noon-5pm Sun. **Admission** free.
An institution primarily dedicated to chronicling the town of Lexington's importance in the days of the Revolutionary War through a permanent show entitled 'Lexington Alarm'd'. The museum also features temporary displays exploring other periods in America's history, and historical exhibits about various aspects of American life. *See also chapter* **Trips Out of Town**.
Disabled: toilet.

Basketball Hall of Fame

1150 West Columbus Avenue, Springfield (1-413 781 5759). **Open** 9am-6pm daily. **Admission** $5-$8.
No credit cards.
Springfield doesn't have its own NBA team, but it is home to the official Basketball Hall of Fame, a giant three-level facility featuring a cinema and various displays about the game. *See also chapter* **Trips Out of Town**.
Disabled: toilet.

New England Quilt Museum

18 Shattuck Street, Lowell (1-978 452 4207). **Open** *Dec-Apr* 10am-4pm Tue-Sat; *May-Nov* 10am-4pm Tue-Sat, noon-4pm Sun. **Admission** $3-$4. **Credit** *shop only* MC, V.
It may not sound like the most exciting premise for a museum, but in an old textile town like Lowell, quilts are a big deal. The New England Quilt Museum puts quiltmaking in proper perspective as a folk art, with a collection of quilts old and new.
Disabled: toilet.

Norman Rockwell Museum

9 Glendale Road, Stockbridge (1-413 298 4100).
Open *May-Oct* 10am-5pm daily; *Nov-April* 10am-4pm Mon-Fri, 10am-5pm Sat, Sun. **Admission** $2-$9.
Credit AmEx, MC, V.
The world's largest collection of Norman Rockwell's paintings is housed here, in a museum dedicated to exploring the life and work of one of America's most respected illustrators. *See also chapter* **Trips Out of Town**.
Disabled: toilet.

Peabody Essex Museum

East India Square, Salem (1-800 745 4054). **Open** *1 June-31 Oct* 10am-5pm Tue-Sat; noon-5pm Sun.
Admission $5-$8.50. **Credit** AmEx, MC, V.
If you're looking for a more scholarly, less Disney-style examination of the Salem Witch Trials than you're likely to get at 'historical' landmarks such as the **House of Seven Gables** (*see chapter* **Trips Out of Town**), the Peabody Essex Museum is your ticket. Featuring 30 galleries and a research library, the museum contains displays that explore American history on land and sea, as well as artifacts from the infamous trials. *See also chapter* **Trips Out of Town**.
Disabled: toilet.

Words and Pictures Museum

140 Main Street, Northampton (1-413 586 8545).
Open noon-5pm Tue-Thur; noon-8pm Fri, Sat.
Admission $1-$3. **Credit** AmEx, Disc, MC, V.
Probably the only institution in the world dedicated solely to the oft-maligned medium of comic book art. The Words and Pictures Museum contains permanent displays of the work of *Teenage Mutant Ninja Turtles* co-creator Kevin Eastman, works by other important comic book artists, and temporary exhibitions that explore the work of mainstream and underground sequential-art specialists. *See also chapter* **Trips Out of Town**.
Disabled: toilet.

Galleries

Newbury Street

More dynamic than the museum scene in Boston is the gallery scene, which can basically be divided into two parts, Newbury Street and everywhere else. Newbury Street in Boston's Back Bay is home to at least three-quarters of all the commercial spaces for art in the Boston area. It's also the most exclusive street for shopping in Boston, studded alternately with art galleries and designer boutiques, designer hair salons and expensive eateries. Unlike other major American cities, Boston is unusually concentrated and peculiarly ghettoised: families stay in their neighbourhoods and businesses are expected to do the same. As a result, a former Newbury Street gallery that dared defect by moving 15 blocks away is still talked of in scandalous tones in the art world.

However, while the equal mixture of pricey shops and art galleries in places like the West Village and Soho in Manhattan signals the death throes of the art scene, Boston's a different story: they've been side-by-side forever, and it's likely to stay that way a while. And the irony is, that for every schlock gallery on Newbury Street (beware any place that calls itself a 'guild' or 'society' or shows the work of anyone sharing the gallery's name) there's another type, often tucked away on the upper floor of a converted brownstone, that's urbanely, demurely providing a showcase for intense, unsettling and lastingly engaging work.

In addition to those listed below, other Newbury Street galleries of note – places where the odds are less than even of a great show, but where great shows happen nevertheless – include the **Pepper Gallery** (38 Newbury Street, at Berkeley Street; 236 4497) – keep an eye on the rising star portrait painter Dafne Confar; the **Robert Klein Gallery** (38 Newbury Street, at Berkeley Street; 267 7997), which shows only well-known photographers; the **Chase Gallery** (129 Newbury Street, at Clarendon Street; 859 7222), which shows work by

Newbury Street – the heart of Boston's commercial art scene.

prominent American and European artists; and the **Michael Price Gallery** (285 Newbury Street, at Gloucester Street; 437 1596), where people such as Ann Christensen and Sarah Hutt are helping build a strong reputation for one of Newbury Street's newcomers.

As well as representing the architectural photographer Phillip Jones, the **Mercury Gallery** (8 Newbury Street, at Arlington Street; 859 0054) also shows the work of the last living member of the original Whiteney Dissenters, Joseph Solman, who along with others, such as Ben-Zion and Mark Rothko, were key figures in American Abstract Expressionism.

Barbara Krakow Gallery

10 Newbury Street, at Arlington Street (262 4490). Arlington T. **Open** 10am-5.30pm Tue-Sat. **Admission** free. **Map 5 F5**

The Barbara Krakow Gallery counts among the longest lasting and most prestigious galleries in Boston. While a preponderance of well-known duds shamelessly abound here, the gallery's conservatism also perversely guarantees there's a whole lot worth seeking out. Watch out for the extraordinary, personal, and searingly honest documentary photographs of Nicholas Nixon (a recent show included 20 years of images of his wife's sisters in an identical pose, creating an uncanny time warp) and the mesmerising constructions of Cameron Shaw doing in three dimensions what René Magritte did a century ago in two.

Chappel Gallery

14 Newbury Street, at Arlington Street (236 2255). Arlington T. **Open** 11am-5.30pm Tue-Sat. **Admission** free. **Map 5 F5**

In the same building and one floor down from the **Howard Yezerski Gallery** (*p98*), this gallery shows the work of Asian, European and American artists working in glass. Admittedly, nobody's quite sure yet if glass qualifies as a legitimate medium for artistic expression, but a visit to the Chappel Gallery will help with an answer. Pieces range from what look like the tops of tranquil lakes to totemic carvings, from the meditative and translucent to the playful and brightly coloured, from the comfortingly utilitarian to the disturbingly abstract. And the commitment to an international roster of artists suggests no pretence here; instead, it's a sign of the zeal and knowledge of gallery director Alice Chappel.

Creiger-Dane Gallery

36 Newbury Street, at Arlington Street (536 8088). Arlington T. **Open** 10am-5.30pm Tue-Sat, or by appointment. **Admission** free. **Map 5 F5**

The Creiger-Dane shares with the **Pucker Gallery** (*p98*) both a Newbury Street address and a certain hit-or-miss quality with respect to its shows: as often as they're spellbinding they're lacklustre. Among the most accomplished painters associated with this gallery are some of Boston's very best, including Miroslav Antic (his last show depicted landscapes on make-believe Venetian blinds – you looked at them and through them simultaneously) and Steven Trefonides, an almost 80-year-old artist whose vigour makes most people half his age seem lame.

Gallery NAGA

67 Newbury Street, at Berkeley Street (267 9060). Arlington T. **Open** 10am-5.30pm Tue-Sat. **Admission** free. **Map 5 F5**

One of Boston's greatest artists, the portrait and figurative painter Paul Rahilly, can be counted among this gallery's senior affiliates. However, not every show is informed by the same perspicacity, and those less successful exhibitions are united by their confusion of foolishness and lightheartedness. NAGA is at its worst when it shows artists doing essentially decorative work. It's at its strongest when showcasing symbolists (such as the work of Ken Beck, whose galvanising renditions of children's beach toys are deservedly earning him a national reputation), realists such as Rahilly and experimentalists. A recent show by the pioneer holographer Harriet Casdin-Silver was plainly, breathtakingly historic.

Howard Yezerski Gallery

14 Newbury Street, at Arlington Street (262 0550). Arlington T. **Open** 10am-5.30pm Tue-Sat. **Admission** free. **Map 5 F5**

At one end of Newbury (few of the best galleries have street-level windows; you must seek what you're after, up elevators and down hallways) you come upon this space no bigger than the boardrooms of many banks, divided into two chambers. Howard Yezerski has been a fixture on the Boston art scene for more than 20 years, and his success is attributable in part to the quality of the artists he shows. In addition, his tastes incline him to youthful renegades. Nowhere else on Newbury will you find an entire exhibition given over to steel books or abstract concoctions of cotton and glass, or the gently outrageous photomontages of John O'Reilly. Whether the work on display is to your liking or not, you can count on a Yezerski show to be intelligent and provocative.
Disabled: toilet.

Nielsen Gallery

179 Newbury Street, at Exeter Street (266 4835). Copley T. **Open** 10am-5.30pm Tue-Sat. **Admission** free. **Credit** AmEx, Disc, MC, V. **Map 3 E5**

Another of the Newbury Street elite where the odds are pretty much even for taking in memorable work. Among the Nielsen's most dynamic and unsettling painters is Anne Harris, whose artistic skills are as strong as her boldness of vision: a recent series of work followed her body through pregnancy; the result was a rare combination of the shocking and the tender. Jane Smaldone's neo-naïvety – Henri Rousseau with attitude – also places her among the Nielsen's strong artists.
Website: www.nielsengallery.com

Pucker Gallery

171 Newbury Street, at Dartmouth Street (267 9473). Copley T. **Open** 10am-5.30pm Mon-Sat; 1-5pm Sun. **Admission** free. **Map 3 F5**

This gallery is increasingly making rightful claims to a place on the 'best of Newbury Street' list, despite its occasional indulgences in sentiment. When director Bernard Pucker gets it right, the results can be breathtaking, as with the exquisite mobiles of Mark Davis, the ceramic work of Tatsuzo Shimaoka, who has been designated a national living treasure of Japan, and the evanescent landscapes of Gunnar Norman. Pucker is also distinct on Newbury Street for showing noteworthy unschooled art, particularly Innuit carvings.
Disabled: toilet.

Beyond Newbury Street

Boston's intense provincialism immediately becomes clear when you realise you need only walk a few blocks to be off what's considered the beaten track. But the new paths are worth beating, and they're not that far away from Newbury Street, either. A recent development has seen a small concentration of galleries take hold in Boston's South End, and there are other outposts further afield.

Bernard Toale Gallery

450 Harrison Avenue, at Thayer Street (482 2477). NE Medical Center T. **Open** 10am-5.30pm Tue-Sat. **Admission** free. **Credit** AmEx, DC, Disc, MC, V. **Map 5 G6**

On the same block and of nearly the same calibre as the **Genovese/Sullivan Gallery** (*below*). Bernie Toale's place on the Boston art scene is solid, as much because of his unimpeachable taste as his political manoeuvring. A visit here promises an exposure to riches, including the seditious eroticism of Debra Bright's oversized colour photos of a plastic horse wearing mascara.

Center Street Studio

Third Floor, 369 Congress Street, at A Street (338 1153). South Station T. **Open** 9am-5pm Mon-Fri; by appointment Sat, Sun. **Admission** free. **Map 5 H5**

This gallery in South Boston (not to be confused with the South End), under the direction of master printer James Stroud, earns its appellation as the centre of some of Boston's finest print-making. Don't miss the idiosyncratic, sharp work of Bill Wheelock and the cerebral yet touching prints of the late James Hansen.

Clifford-Smith Gallery

Third floor, 450 Harrison Avenue, Thayer Street (695 0255). NE Medical Center T. **Open** 11am-5pm Tue-Sat. **Admission** free. **Map 5 G6**

The Clifford-Smith Gallery is a new arrival on the scene, and a welcome one; rare is the established space – let alone the unestablished – as willing to take informed, exciting risks as Clifford-Smith. From the hallucinatory paper abstractions of Saul Chernick to the spooky hilarity of Karen Kimmel's installation (she made what she called a 'comfort suit' of thin white sponge, and one was afraid to ask what it's worn for), Clifford-Smith's commitment to quality before sales is as refreshing as it is anachronistic.

Genovese/Sullivan Gallery

47 Thayer Street, at Harrison Avenue (426 9738). NE Medical Center T. **Open** 10.30am-5.30pm Tue-Sat. **Admission** free. **Map 5 G6**

The Genovese/Sullivan deserves to be on everyone's short list of galleries to visit, not only because it occupies the most art-friendly space of any gallery in the city (the rooms are expansive, the ceilings tall), but for the curatorial acumen of its owners, David Sullivan and Camellia Genovese. The insight of most galleries tends to lie in an area or two, an artist or two; with the Genovese/Sullivan it's more like a dozen. Among the outstanding artists affiliated with it is the sculptor Pat Keck, who creates diabolical works of seeming simplicity and extraordinary complexity, like *Big Head*, which appears to be no more than an inanimate four-foot tall decapitated wooden head – until you look into one of its eyes, where there's a headless man drumming his fingers while attempting to play solitaire.

Hamill Gallery of African Art

2164 Washington Street, at Melnea Cass Boulevard (442 8204). Ruggles T. **Open** noon-6pm Wed-Sat; by appointment Mon, Tue, Sun. **Admission** free.

Although somewhat further afield than the other galleries, the Hamill is worth the effort to visit. Apart from some major museums, it's hard to imagine a venue more comprehensive and intelligently managed. Artist and gallery director Tim Hamill has devoted the better part of the last decade to building up a showcase that acts as both gallery and educational centre; collectors come to buy, students come to learn. With textiles that range from the bark cloth of the Mboto pygmy to the exotic, bright cotton weaves of the Asante, with sculpture that ranges from the granary doors of the Dogon to the carved posts of the nomadic Tuareg, Hamill's gallery offers satisfaction of sufficient depth that if you go nowhere else you won't feel guilty.

Kougeas Gallery

88 White Street, East Boston (569 9317). Wood Island or Maverick T. **Open** 2-6pm Thur, Fri, Sat; also by appointment. **Admission** free.

If you are feeling slightly adventurous, pay a visit to this gallery in East Boston. Here you will find gallery director Pamela Sienna reigning over a group of artists, the strongest of whom are working in photography and sculpture. Outstanding among them is photographer Mia Rosenblatt, whose satirical family photos make you half wish our species had never evolved.

Consumer Boston

Accommodation

Where to hang your hat in the Hub City.

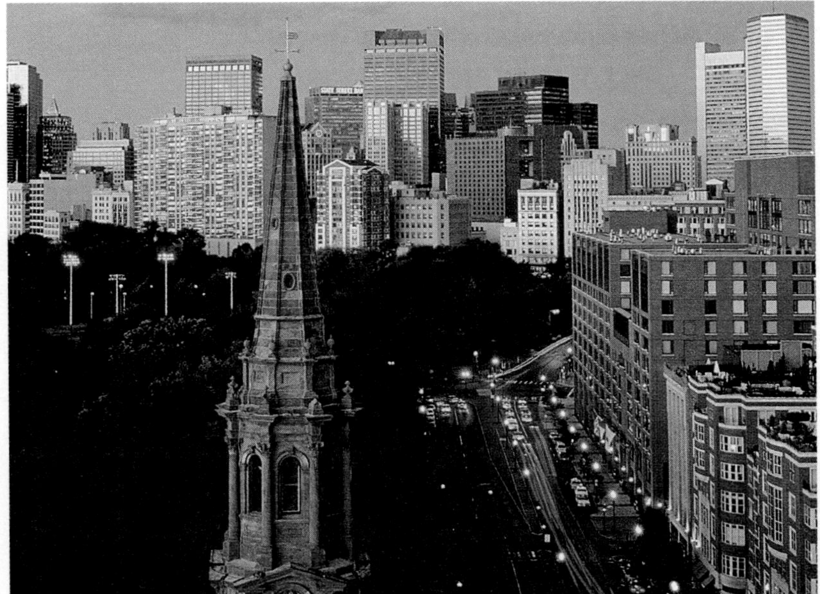

The **Four Seasons** *(page 103) has an enviable location overlooking the Public Garden.*

Boston's historical significance has long made it one of America's most popular tourist destinations. In the past decade or so, however, it has also become one of the country's top ten convention cities. This has left Boston surprisingly short of bed space. Worse, what few hotels there are in the centre are priced for business travellers on expense accounts. Plans are in full swing to build a brand new convention centre on the waterfront to ease some of the space crunch after the millennium, but this won't help prices much, since all of the hotels planned for the complex are in the luxury category.

On average, luxury hotels start at $250 a night and business hotels start at $150. Even 'tourist-class' hotels start at $75. If you're travelling on a budget, finding a good hotel in Boston at a decent price will present a challenge. The entire town operates on an ever-sliding scale of availability, so the rates listed below are only meant to give you an indication of range (and don't forget to add 12.75 per cent state hotel tax on top). Prices might dip well below what we've indicated during low season (December to February) or soar well above during high season (August to October).

We've tried our best to offer economical alternatives. Many of the options listed under 'Practical', for example, offer rooms with kitchenettes so that you can save on eating out. We've also listed a few good bed and breakfast agencies who can do the searching for you.

A few tips, then, for booking a hotel in Boston. Begin looking as early as possible. Enquire about possible fly-and-stay agreements that your airline might have with local hotels. And ask the hotels themselves about any special deals, family rates or weekend packages: they are not always as forthcoming about these as you might expect. Also mention any frequent flyer programmes or business organisations you may belong to: these sometimes get you 'preferred customer' rates.

About location: most of the city's hotels are in Back Bay, although there are a handful in the Financial District and Cambridge. Central Boston is surprisingly empty of cookie-cutter chains, until you get to the suburbs (for hotel chain listings *see page 112* **Spare chains**).

About tipping: it's customary to tip bellhops $1 per bag, room service waiters 10-15 per cent of the total bill (unless a charge has already been added on) and staff members – except maybe the concierge – a token amount for any special favours they do for you.

About parking: unless otherwise indicated, if we have listed parking as being available at a hotel, there is an additional fee involved.

Unless otherwise stated, all rooms have a telephone and a TV.

Top of the Hub

Boston boasts only two world-class hotels – the **Four Seasons** and the **Ritz-Carlton** – and they're both within sight of each other, facing the Public Garden. The Four Seasons consistently makes the 'Top 20' lists of the world's best hotels. The Ritz-Carlton follows close behind. Both also command world-class prices, of course, but they offer two entirely different styles of service.

Four Seasons

200 Boylston Street, Boston, MA 02116, at the Public Garden (338 4400/1-800 332 3442/fax 351 2051). Arlington T. **Rates** *rooms* $435-$565; *suites* $575-$1,200. **Credit** AmEx, DC, Disc, JCB, MC, $TC, V. **Map 5 F5**

Not exactly architecture's gift to Boston, the Four Seasons makes up in assiduous, professional service and luxurious amenities for what it lacks in (exterior) charm. Built on the site of the Playboy Club, bastion of the now defunct Combat Zone, the hotel overlooks the beautiful Public Gardens and is close to the restaurants and shops of Back Bay, Newbury Street and the downtown financial institutions. Inside, all the amenities you'd expect at these prices are present and correct: gleaming public spaces filled with flowers and oil-paintings include the **Bristol Lounge** (for high tea or cocktails) and the much-lauded **Aujourd'hui** restaurant, where chef Edward Gannon produces a classically-French inspired menu (*see p132* **Restaurants & Cafés** *for both*). The extremely classy 24-hour room service even extends to a pet menu (post-prandial dog-walking is an optional extra). The rooftop pool, though on the small side, offers good views over the city, and the adjoining gym has all the basic facilities. The hotel offers several relatively bargain-priced deals tied in with local events, such as art exhibitions and concert series, which are definitely worth asking about.

Hotel services *Air-conditioning. Babysitting. Bar. Business services. Concierge (24-hour). Conference facilities. Currency exchange. Disabled: access; rooms for disabled. Fax. Gym. Interpreting service. Laundry. Limousine service. No-smoking rooms. Parking. Restaurants (2). Safety deposit. Shoeshine (free). Swimming pool.*
Room services *Dataport jack. Hairdryer. Minibar. Radio. Robes. Room service (24-hour). VCR. Voicemail.*

The turn-of-the-century **Lenox** *(above, see p104) and the plush interior of the* **Four Seasons** *(below).*

The **Eliot**: *perfect for families.*

Ritz-Carlton

15 Arlington Street, Boston, MA 02116, at Newbury Street (536 5700/1-800 241 3333/fax 536 1335). Arlington T. **Rates** *rooms* $320-$450; *suites* $470-$2,000. **Credit** AmEx, DC, Disc, JCB, MC, $TC, V. **Map 5 F5**

Truly the Grande Dame of Boston hotels. The Ritz was opened in 1927 with the intention of catering to a very select clientele – the Duke and Duchess of Windsor, Winston Churchill and Charles Lindbergh among them – and the hotel has never deviated appreciably from this policy (although it has long-since stopped screening bookings with the Social Register). If you prefer old-world charm and extremely formal service, this is your place. There are said to be two employees for every guest. Great care is taken to make sure the Ritz feels familiar to loyal customers (though the hotel's 278 French Provincial rooms have been completely overhauled in the past three years, and its façade is presently being restored to its original 1927 splendour). For Beacon Hill Brahmins, tea at the Ritz is an institution, its ballroom the site of legendary evenings. For today's well-heeled travellers, it continues to be the epitome of elegance.

Hotel services *Air-conditioning. Babysitting. Bar. Beauty salon. Business services. Concierge. Conference facilities. Currency exchange. Disabled: access; rooms for disabled. Fax. Gift & flower shop. Gym. Interpreting service. Laundry. Limousine service. No-smoking rooms. Restaurants (2). Safety deposit. Shoeshine. Valet parking.*

Room services *Dataport jack. Fax (suites). Hairdryer. Minibar. Newspaper. Radio. Refrigerator. Robes. Room service (24-hour). Safe. VCR. Voicemail.*

Historic luxury

Boston offers a surprising number of historic hotels that are able to keep pace with their modern counterparts when it comes to room amenities and guest services. If you prefer to stay in places with real character, you might like to consider one of the following.

Eliot

370 Commonwealth Avenue, Boston, MA 02215, at Massachusetts Avenue (267 1607/1-800 443 5468/ fax 536 9114). Hynes/ICA T. **Rates** *rooms* $195-$255; *suites* $225-$550. **Credit** AmEx, DC, Disc, JCB, MC, $TC, V. **Map 3 E5**

Built in 1925 at the outer edge of Back Bay, the Eliot recently renovated its 95 rooms and suites, without losing its original atmosphere. The main lobby is cosy and on a human scale; the front-desk staff few but efficient. Also on the main floor is **Clío**, one of Boston's hottest restaurant/bars (*see p127* **Restaurants & Cafés**), which also provides room service for the hotel guests. Most of the Eliot's accommodation is in suites – bedrooms and sitting rooms equipped with small kitchenettes and fold-out sofas. Perfect for families travelling together.

Hotel services *Air-conditioning. Bar. Business services. Currency exchange. Disabled: access; rooms for disabled. Fax. Laundry. No-smoking rooms. Restaurant. Safety deposit. Valet parking.*

Room services *Dataport jack. Fax. Hairdryer. Iron/ironing board. Kitchenettes. Minibar. Robes. Room service (until 11pm). Radio. Sofabeds. Voicemail.*

Fairmont Copley Plaza

138 St James Avenue, Boston, MA 02116, at Copley Square (267 5300/1-800 527 4727/fax 375 9648). Copley or Back Bay T. **Rates** *singles* $299; *doubles* $329-$419; *suites* $670-$750. **Credit** AmEx, DC, Disc, MC, $TC, V. **Map 5 F5**

Overlooking Copley Square, the Copley Plaza was originally built in 1912 as the sister to New York's Plaza. It has never waned in style or elegance – the mirrored and gilded lobby is nothing short of spectacular. Every US president since Taft has stayed here (except for Clinton), and the **Oak Room** bar (*see p116* **Pubs & Bars**), was recently voted Boston's best steakhouse. In contrast to the over-the-top lobby, all of the hotel's 379 rooms combine a more discreet plushness with every modern amenity, including a personal fax machine. Service is impeccable and no question goes unanswered. Some members of the concierge staff have been with the hotel for 25 years.

Hotel services *Air-conditioning. Babysitting. Bar. Beauty salon. Business services. Concierge. Conference facilities. Currency exchange. Disabled: access; rooms for disabled. Fax. Fitness room. Laundry. Multilingual staff. No-smoking rooms. Restaurant. Safety deposit. Valet parking.*

Room services *Dataport jack. Fax. Hairdryer. Iron/ironing board. Minibar. Newspaper. Radio. Robes. Room service (24-hour). VCR. Voicemail.*

Lenox

710 Boylston Street, Boston, MA 02116, at Copley Square (536 5300/1-800 225 7676/fax 266 7905/ www.lenoxhotel.com). Copley T. **Rates** *rooms* $278-$308; *suites* $358-$498. **Credit** AmEx, DC, Disc, MC, $TC, V. **Map 3 F5**

Recently voted the most improved hotel in Boston, the Lenox originally opened in 1900 and has always boasted a prime location next to the Public Library. But it languished for years as a careworn tourist-class hotel until recent renovation brought it more into line with its neighbour the Copley Plaza. The hotel's new décor has picked up a few design awards, and its restaurant, **Anago**, is one of the most fashionable in town (*see p126* **Restaurants & Cafés**). Several of the Lenox's 212 beautifully appointed rooms boast working fireplaces and there's another in the charmingly restored lobby.

Nothing quite rivals the **Fairmont Copley Plaza** *for sheer glitz.*

Best hotels for...

Overall value: **John Jeffries House** (*page 111*).
Proximity to historic sites: the **Regal Bostonian** (*page 108*).
Killer views: the **Boston Harbor** (*below*).
Backpackers: the **Buckminster** (*page 110*).
Old-world grandeur: the **Ritz-Carlton** (*page 104*).
A romantic getaway: the **Lenox** (*page 104*).
Longer stays: **Copley Inn** (*page 110*).
Families: **Midtown Hotel** (*page 109*).
Proximity to Harvard: **Inn at Harvard** (*page 113*).
Aspiring writers: **Omni Parker House** (*below*).
Fitness buffs: **Charles Hotel** (*page 113*).
Weirdness factor: **Florence Frances Guest House** (*pictured, see page 111*).

Hotel services *Air-conditioning. Bar. Business services. Concierge. Conference facilities. Currency exchange. Disabled: access; rooms for disabled. Fax. Fitness room. Laundry. Multilingual staff. No-smoking rooms. Restaurant. Safety deposit. Valet parking.*
Room services *Dataport jack. Fax. Hairdryer. Newspaper. Radio. Robes. Room service. Voicemail.*

Omni Parker House

60 School Street, Boston, MA 02108, at Tremont Street (227 8600/1-800 843 6664/fax 725 1638). Park St or Gov't Center T. **Rates** *rooms* $245-$315; *suites* $335-$475. **Credit** AmEx, DC, Disc, JCB, MC, $TC, V.
Map 5 G4
First opened in 1855 as Parker House, this is the oldest continuously operating hotel in America (it's also one of the largest in Boston, with 552 rooms). In the city's literary heyday, the Parker House was host to the Saturday Club, a group of distinguished authors that included Longfellow, Hawthorne and Emerson, who all met here once a month for lunch (*see p26* **Literary Boston**). Though the oak walls and burnished brass of Omni Parker's lobby bespeak an elegance of days gone by, its corridors and rooms feel dark and cramped by contrast. The service – and famous Parker House rolls – are completely up to snuff, however.
Hotel services *Air-conditioning. Bar. Business services. Concierge. Conference facilities. Currency exchange. Disabled: access; rooms for disabled. Fax. Laundry. No-smoking rooms. Restaurant. Safety deposit. Valet parking.*
Room services *Dataport jack. Hairdryer. Iron/ironing board. Minibar. Radio. Refrigerator. Robes. Room service (until 11pm).*

Modern luxury

Desperate for more hotel space two decades ago, Boston courted the business of quality hotels willing to build downtown. All of Boston's newer hotels tend to offer better sound-proofing against noise and more sensible room layouts for modern life.

Boston Harbor

70 Rowes Wharf, Boston, MA 02110 (439 7000/1-800 752 7077/fax 345 6799). South Station T. **Rates** *rooms* $260-$510; *suites* $365-$660. **Credit** AmEx, DC, Disc, JCB, MC, $TC, V. **Map 5 H4**
Outside the Boston Harbor, the Big Dig is in full swing (*see p16* **Boston Today**). Inside, the cares of the world melt away. The elegant lobby looks out over the sparkling harbour. Polished wood, marble and brass gleam at you from every angle. But what makes this such a spectacular hotel is its attention to detail. Tiffany designed the restaurant's china; the fitness centre has gym clothes and swimsuits you can borrow. Over half of the hotel's 230 rooms boast harbour views; some have private balconies and all of them feature sound-proof glass and separate seating areas, as well as the little niceties – cotton buds in the bathroom, two pairs of slippers, bottled water at turn-down – that make a difference. All of which more than compensates for being in the middle of what seems like the biggest construction site in history.
Hotel services *Air-conditioning. Babysitting. Bar. Business services. Concierge. Conference facilities. Currency exchange. Disabled: access; rooms for disabled. Fax. Gym. Health spa. Interpreting service. Laundry (24-hour). Limousine service. No-smoking rooms. Parking. Restaurants (2). Safety deposit. Shoeshine. Swimming pool.*
Room services *Dataport jack. Hairdryer. Minibar. Newspaper. Radio. Robes. Room service (24-hour). Video-conferencing (on request). Voicemail.*

Colonnade

120 Huntington Avenue, Boston, MA 02116, at the Prudential Center (424 7000/1-800 962 3030/fax 424 1717). Prudential T. **Rates** *rooms* $225-$315; *suites* $450-$1,050. **Credit** AmEx, DC, Disc, JCB, MC, $TC, V.
Map 3 E5
The best feature of the Colonnade's somewhat sterile 1970s architecture is its rooftop swimming pool – nothing beats it on a sticky summer afternoon. Nothing beats its restaurant, **Brasserie Jo**, for after-theatre dining (according to *Boston Magazine*) either (*see p126* **Restaurants & Cafés**). The Colonnade's 285 rooms are generous in size if somewhat anonymous in décor (despite the complimentary rubber duck

Agencies

Reasonably priced B&Bs do not always have the budget to advertise, which is why many of them sign up with reservation agencies like those listed below. All three agencies offer rooms with continental breakfast and private baths, starting in the $75-$85 price range (suburban locations tend to be even cheaper). All three can also help you with longer-term stays in furnished studios, apartments and house-shares.

Bed & Breakfast Agency of Boston

47 Commercial Wharf, Boston, MA 02110 (720 3540/1-800 248 9262/fax 523 5761/freephone in UK 0800 89 5128).
This agency offers some of the highest-quality accommodation in central Boston. There are nearly 160 possibilities, from waterfront lofts to Victorian rooms in historic Back Bay homes. The agency is especially good at finding short-term studios and apartments.

Bed & Breakfast Associates Bay Colony

PO Box 57166, Babson Park Branch, Boston, MA 02157 (449 5302/1-800 347 5088/fax 449 5958).
This lists accommodation in more than 150 homes with waterfront, Back Bay or Beacon Hill locations. The agency has particularly good listings outside Boston, on the North and South Shores.

New England Bed & Breakfast

PO 9100, Suite 176, Newton Centre, MA 02159 (244-2112).
A one-man operation offering home stays in suburban Boston, most of them within a short walk of public transport. Catering for special needs (no-smoking, no pets, allergies) seems to be a specialty.

for the tub). But what the hotel lacks in charm it makes up for in its location – right next to the Copley Place and Prudential Center shopping malls.
Hotel services *Air-conditioning. Babysitting. Bar. Business services. Concierge. Conference facilities. Currency exchange. Disabled: access; rooms for disabled. Fax. Fitness room. Interpreting services. Laundry (24-hour). Limousine service. Multilingual staff. No-smoking rooms. Parking. Restaurant. Safety deposit. Swimming pool.*
Room services *Dataport jack. Fax (suites). Hairdryer. Minibar. Radio. Robes. Room service (24-hour). Safe. Voicemail.*

Le Méridien

250 Franklin Street, Boston, MA 02110, near Post Office Square (451 1900/1-800 543 4300/fax 423 2844). State/Citizen's Bank T. **Rates** *rooms* $295-$475; *suites* $550-$775. **Credit** AmEx, DC, Disc, JCB, MC, $TC, V. **Map 5 H4**
Le Méridien is Boston's most elegant downtown hotel (its proximity to the Financial District accounts somewhat for its price). Its architects made marvellous use of a former Federal Reserve Bank's Renaissance Revival architecture, and polished bronze, ornate woodwork and coffered ceilings abound. Some 326 guest rooms have been slotted into the space with admirable inventiveness (some of the pricier suites feature duplex lofts with skylights) and there's still plenty of room for a health club, indoor lap pool, two bars and two of the most popular French restaurants in town – **Julien** and **Café Fleuri** (*see p133* **Restaurants & Cafés**).
Hotel services *Air-conditioning. Bar. Business services. Concierge. Conference facilities. Currency exchange. Disabled: access; rooms for disabled. Fax. Gym. Laundry. Multilingual staff. No-smoking rooms. Restaurants (2). Safety deposit. Swimming pool. Valet parking.*
Room services *Dataport jack. Hairdryer. Minibar. Newspaper. Radio. Robes. Room service (24-hour). Voicemail.*

Park Plaza

64 Arlington Street, Boston, MA 02116, at Boston Common (426 2000/1-800 225 2008/fax 423 1708). Arlington T. **Rates** *rooms* $235-$255; *suites* $265-$285. **Credit** AmEx, DC, Disc, JCB, MC, $TC, V. **Map 5 F5**
Few hotels operate on this sort of scale these days – 960 rooms, two ballrooms, two bars, two restaurants and a shopping arcade – yet there's something downright homey about the Park Plaza. Perhaps it's the aura of slightly faded grandeur: the hallways wide enough to accommodate hoop skirts, the tea garden in the lobby, that distinctive swan logo emblazoned on everything. When booking, however, it's best to request one of the newly renovated rooms. Their light colour schemes, rich fabrics and contemporary fixtures justify the price far better than the older, more careworn versions. When all's said and done, it's worth it to be a block away from the Public Garden.
Hotel services *Air-conditioning. Bar. Beauty salon. Business services. Concierge. Conference facilities. Currency exchange. Disabled: access; rooms for disabled. Fax. Fitness room. Laundry. No-smoking rooms. Parking. Pharmacy. Restaurants (2). Safety deposit. Travel agency.*
Room services *Dataport jack. Hairdryer. Radio. Room service (until 10pm). Voicemail.*

Regal Bostonian

Faneuil Hall Marketplace, Boston, MA 02109 (523 3600/1-800 222 8888/fax 523 2454/www.regal-hotels.com). Haymarket or Gov't Center T. **Rates** *rooms* $245-$345; *suites* $500-$775. **Credit** AmEx, DC, Disc, JCB, MC, $TC, V. **Map 5 G4**
The Bostonian prides itself on being one of Boston's 'intimate' hotels (it has 163 rooms, which just goes to show that the city doesn't do small hotels). Housed in a couple of adjoining converted red-brick warehouses, and in the process, as we went to press, of expanding further, the hotel is arranged around a central brick courtyard, and close to the madding crowds of Faneuil Hall and Quincy Market. On Fridays and Saturdays, the costermongers of the Haymarket fruit and veg market add further to the general din outside. Noise aside (ask for a room at the back), the Bostonian's rooms are neutrally decorated with small, awninged balconies, well equipped bathrooms (featuring absolutely vast baths) and the usual expensive minibar/TV/dataport facilities. Nightly 'turndown' includes a card predicting the next day's weather, along with the more familiar chocolates. A fire crackles in the lobby hearth on cooler days and the sound of jazz wafts in from the piano bar. **Seasons**, the hotel's rooftop restaurant, is an ideal spot for a power breakfast or lunch.
Hotel services *Air-conditioning. Babysitting. Bar. Business services. Concierge. Conference facilities. Currency exchange. Disabled: access; rooms for disabled. Fax. Laundry. Limousine service. Multilingual staff. No-smoking rooms. Restaurant. Safety deposit. Valet parking.*
Room services *Dataport jack. Hairdryer. Iron/ironing board. Minibar. Newspaper. Radio. Robes. Room service (24-hour). Safe. Voicemail.*

Business class

If your budget doesn't allow for luxury accommodation but you're not quite ready to go the austerity route, Boston does offer a number of centrally located hotels popular with the business set. Many of these belong to chains and offer pretty much what you'd expect anywhere (*see page 112* **Spare chains**). The hotels listed below, however, offer a bit more individuality.

Copley Square

47 Huntington Avenue, Boston, MA 02116, at Exeter Street (536 9000/1-800 225 7062/fax 236 0351 /www.copleysquarehotel.com). Copley or Back Bay T. **Rates** *rooms* $175-$225; *family rooms* $345. **Credit** AmEx, DC, Disc, JCB, MC, $TC, V. **Map 3 E/F5**

Across the street from the luxury **Lenox** (*see above*) is its more modest turn-of-the century sister, the Copley Square. This understated hotel has a distinctly European feel about it, from the snatches of French and German you'll hear in the comfortable lobby lounge to the traditional Hungarian food served up at Café Budapest. True, the corridors are a bit dark and the décor of the 143 rooms is a bit spare. But with coffee pots, ironing boards and dataports in every room, nothing is lacking for a comfortable stay. And, as the hotel's name suggests, you can't beat the location.

Hotel services *Air-conditioning. Babysitting. Bar. Business services. Concierge. Conference facilities. Currency exchange. Disabled: access; rooms for disabled. Fax. Laundry. Multilingual staff. No-smoking rooms. Parking. Restaurant. Safety deposit.* **Room services** *Coffeemaker. Dataport jack. Hairdryer. Iron/ironing board. Radio. Room service (until 10pm). Safe. Voicemail.*

Tremont House

275 Tremont Street, Boston, MA 02116 (426 1400/1-800 331 9998/fax 338 7881). Boylston T. **Rates** *rooms* $179-$249; *suites* $189-$399. **Credit** AmEx, DC, Disc, JCB, MC, $TC, V. **Map 5 G5**

OK, the hotel was originally built in 1925 as the national headquarters for the Elks Club (note the authentic elk head doorknobs). But the hotel's recent renovators have had a lot of fun with that, softening up the icy marblework and patriotic murals with bright Deco furniture and fixtures. They've carried this playfulness through to the hotel's 322 rooms, making them both hip (with funky fabrics) and cosy (with down quilts). The 'Concierge Level' offers slightly better rooms and free continental breakfast. Ideal for young urban types, the hotel has two popular nightclubs on the premises and a decent restaurant and bar, and the city's nightlife is only a few steps away.

Hotel services *Air-conditioning. Bar. Business services. Conference facilities. Currency exchange. Disabled: rooms for disabled. Fax. Fitness room. Laundry. Nightclubs (2). No-smoking rooms. Restaurant. Safety deposit. Valet parking.* **Room services** *Coffee machines. Dataport jack. Hairdryer. Iron/ironing board. Newspaper. Radio. Robes. Room service (until 11pm). Voicemail.*

Midtown Hotel

220 Huntington Avenue, Boston, MA 02115, at the Christian Science Center (262 1000/1-800 343 1177/fax 262 8739). Prudential or Symphony T. **Rates** *rooms* $99-$199. **Credit** AmEx, DC, Disc, JCB, MC, $TC, V. **Map 3 E6**

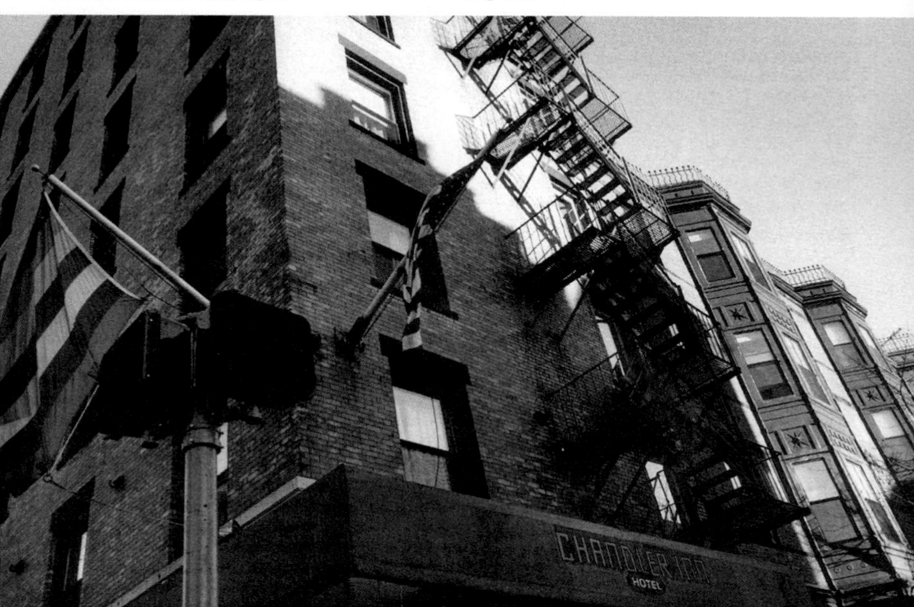

'Straight-friendly' and with an ideal South End location – the **Chandler Inn**. *See page 110.*

The **Eliot and Pickett Houses**. *See p111.*

The Midtown is like one of those 1950s motels you'd expect to stay in on a road trip across America – only you're actually in the heart of Back Bay. If you don't mind high kitsch (and the occasional busload of pensioners), you could probably get into the retro atmosphere here. The 170 rooms are enormous, there's an outdoor pool, kids under 18 stay free, and this is one of the few hotels in town with free parking. The only drawback (apart from the colour scheme) is that there's no bar on the premises, because the land is leased from the Christian Scientists across the street.
Hotel services *Air-conditioning. Babysitting. Beauty salon. Business services. Concierge. Conference facilities. Currency exchange. Fax. Laundry. No-smoking rooms. Parking (free). Restaurant (breakfast only). Safety deposit. Swimming pool (seasonal).*
Room services *Dataport jack. Hairdryer (on request). Iron/ironing board (on request). Radio.*

Practical

If you think that hotels are for sleeping in, not for hanging out in, then any of the 'tourist class' options below will probably satisfy your accommodation needs. They range from basic-but-clean hotels to small guesthouses. The common thread is that most offer some form of self-catering facilities.

Beacon Inn Guest Houses

248 Newbury Street, Boston, MA 02116, between Gloucester & Fairfield Streets (266 7142/262 1771/ fax 266 7276). Copley or Convention Center T.
Rates *singles* $85 per night, $490 per week; *doubles* $99 per night, $575 per week.
Credit AmEx, DC, Disc, MC, $TC, V.
Map 3 E5
This is about as basic as it gets. Though clean, all of the 32 rooms look as if they've been decorated out of a charity shop. Each has a fully equipped kitchenette and private bath but no TV. Also note that there is no maid service (you can, however, request a daily change of bedding). But, hey, you get to claim Boston's most fashionable shopping district as your address. Best for longer-term stays.
Hotel services *Air-conditioning.*
Room services *Kitchenette. Radio. Refrigerator.*

Buckminster

645 Beacon Street, Boston, MA 02215, at Kenmore Square (236 7050/1-800 727 2825/fax 262 0068). Kenmore T. **Rates** *rooms* $89-$129; *suites* $139-$169.
Credit AmEx, DC, Disc, MC, $TC, V.
Map 3 D5
The Buckminster offers great value, if cost is more important to you than quality. None of its 96 rooms is going to win an award for décor but all are equipped with cheaper versions of the amenities that the deluxe hotels offer (air-conditioning, dataport jack, hairdryer, radio). And every floor is equipped with a full kitchen and laundry facilities. Attached to the hotel are a cheap pizza place and a decent Japanese restaurant. Kenmore Square may not be the most stylish neighbourhood in town, but it's relatively safe, right on the subway – and just around the corner from Fenway Park.
Hotel services *Air-conditioning. Bar. Disabled: access; rooms for disabled. Fax. Kitchens (every floor). Laundry room (every floor). Multilingual staff. No-smoking rooms. Parking. Restaurants (2). Safety deposit.*
Room services *Dataport jack. Hairdryer. Iron/ironing board. Microwave (suites). Minibar (suites). Radio. Room service (until 10pm).*

Chandler Inn

26 Chandler Street, Boston, MA 02116, between Columbus & Warren Avenues (482 3450/1-800 842 3450/fax 542 3428/www.chandlerinn.com). Back Bay T.
Rates *rooms* $69-$119. **Credit** AmEx, MC, $TC, V.
Map 3 F5/6
Chandler Inn is what you'd call 'straight-friendly.' Its primary clientele is gay, but heteros are more than welcome – as long as they're cool. The Chandler's location in the South End is as unbeatable as its price. True, the 56 rooms are a little dingy, but they're very clean and border on the tasteful. There's no lobby to speak of, no restaurant, no lounge, but **Fritz**, the gay bar on the ground floor, offers a decent brunch at the weekend and serves coffee to guests in the morning (*see p189* **Gay & Lesbian**).
Hotel services *Air-conditioning. Bar. Disabled: access; rooms for disabled. Fax. No-smoking rooms. Parking.*
Room services *Hairdryer. Radio.*

Copley Inn

19 Garrison Street, Boston, MA 02116, near the Christian Science Center (236 0300/1-800 232 0306/fax 536 0816). Prudential T. **Rates** $85-$135 per night; $510-$810 per week. **Credit** AmEx, MC, $TC, V.
Map 3 E6
One of the best-kept secrets in the city. The Copley Inn is a pretty little townhouse tucked away on a quiet side street, about a 30-second walk from the Prudential Center. Its décor is comfortable and tasteful. Each of its 21 rooms is scrupulously clean and equipped with a fully stocked kitchenette. Smokers be warned, however: the owner insists on a smoke-free environment. There's no parking either. Otherwise the Copley Inn can't be beaten for quality, location and price. If you stay a week, you'll even get the seventh night free.
Hotel services *Air-conditioning. Fax. No-smoking rooms only.*
Room services *Coffee pot. Dataport jack. Hairdryer (on request). Kitchenette. Iron/ironing board. Microwave (on request). Radio. Refrigerator. Voicemail.*

Copley House

239 West Newton Street, Boston, MA 02116, between Huntington & Columbus Avenues (236 8300/ 1-800 331 1318/fax 424 1815). Prudential T.
Rates $85-$125 per night; $375-$675 per week.
Credit AmEx, MC, $TC, V. **Map 3 E6**
Similar to the **Copley Inn** (*p110*) in terms of price, rooming style and neighbourhood, Copley House offers the same sort of good value. But it just isn't, well, as nice. Its 52 rooms are actually spread out over several townhouses in the South End. They tend to vary a little in quality and amenities, but they're all perfectly clean and have small kitchenettes. Note that for longer stays, linen is only changed once a week.
Hotel services *Air-conditioning. Fax. No-smoking rooms only. Parking.*

Room services *Answering machine. Coffee pot. Kitchenette. Iron/ironing board (on request). Radio. Refrigerator.*

John Jeffries House

14 David G Mugar Way, Boston, MA 02114, at Charles & Cambridge Streets (367 1866/fax 742 0313). Charles T. **Rates** *rooms* $80-$110; *suites* $120-$160. **Credit** AmEx, DC, Disc, MC, $TC, V. **Map 5 F4**

This turn-of-the-century hotel should probably, by definition, appear in the bed and breakfast section: a continental buffet is served each morning in the common room on the ground floor. But John Jeffries House really feels more like a proper hotel – and a lovely little one at that. The quality of both the décor and the amenities well exceeds the price. And each of its 46 rooms and suites is furnished with a small kitchenette. Other hotel amenities are basic, however – there's no restaurant, for example, but the shops and restaurants of Charles Street are right on the doorstep. Dollar for dollar, this is one of the best deals in town.

Hotel services *Air-conditioning. Continental breakfast. Disabled: access; rooms for disabled. Fax. Garden. No-smoking rooms. Parking.*
Room services *Dataport jack. Hairdryer. Kitchenette. Iron/ironing board (on request). Radio. Refrigerator.*

Bed & breakfast

The establishments listed below indicate more of a 'family-style' approach to accommodation: they're smaller places with fewer amenities (not all of them guarantee you a private bath, for example). A continental breakfast, however, is usually included in the price of your stay. There are also agencies in Boston that can help you book bed and breakfast accommodation (*see page 108* **Agencies**).

Eliot and Pickett Houses

6-7 Mount Vernon Place, Boston, MA 02108, next to the State House (248 8707/fax 742 1364/www.uua.org/ep). Park Street T. **Rates** *rooms* $85-$160. **Credit** MC, $TC, V. **Map 5 G4**

First the good news: these are two wonderful old brick townhouses joined together into a charming guesthouse. It occupies a prime location on Beacon Hill, where your closest neighbour is the **State House** (*see p54* **Sightseeing**). Each of the 20 rooms is individually decorated with simple, unpretentious antiques – some with four-poster beds. Guests have access to a huge kitchen (breakfast is self-service), a parlour with a piano, a sunny roof deck overlooking Boston Common and a study. Now the bad news: there are no TVs in the rooms, no smoking and no parking. You might also like to know that the guesthouse is run by the Unitarian church (whose headquarters is next door), though everyone is welcome.

Hotel services *Air-conditioning. Breakfast. Fax. Kitchen. No-smoking rooms only. TV in common room.*
Room services *Radio.*

Florence Frances Guest House

458 Park Drive, Boston, MA 02215, at Beacon Street (267 2458/fax 424 1815). Fenway T. **Rates** *rooms* $50-$60. **No credit cards. Map 3 D6**

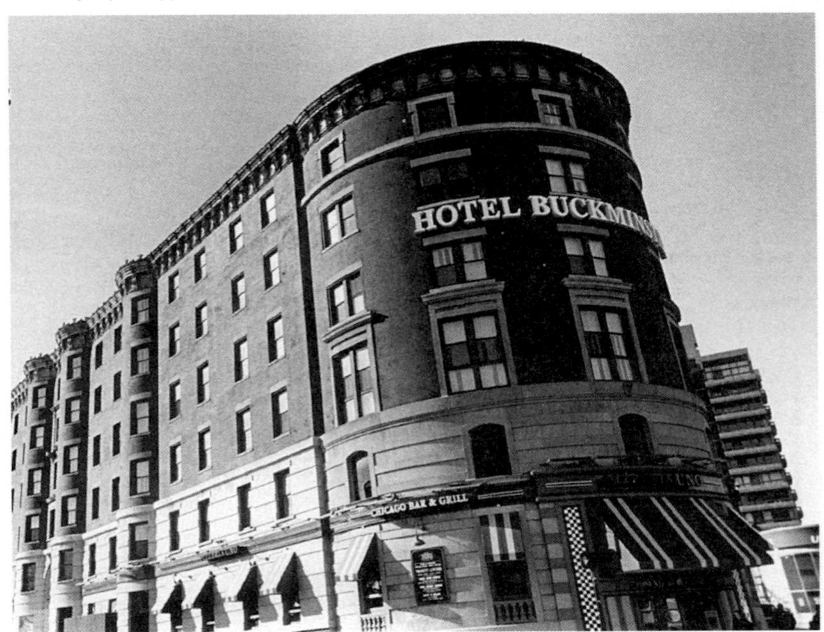

The **Buckminster** *may not win awards for style, but it's strong on amenities.*

We've put Ms Frances' Fenway guesthouse in the B&B section although breakfast is not included in the rates. You are welcome to make yourself at home in her kitchen, however, since this 150-year-old townhouse is, in fact, Florence Frances' home. Each of the four rooms is done up according to a different, and slightly over-the-top, theme (Ms Frances is a decorator as well as former model, world traveller and inveterate collector of china figurines). Each room has a colour TV, but no telephone or private bath. There's a comfortable lounge, a roof terrace, laundry facilities and free parking at the back. The owner herself is an added feature of your stay here – if you don't mind her participating a little in it.

Spare chains

There are a number of chain hotels, mostly business class, in central Boston. Listed below are their locations and toll-free central reservation numbers.

Hilton
Back Bay (Haynes Convention Center) and Dedham (1-800 445 8667).

Holiday Inn
Cambridge Street (Government Center), Beacon Street (Brookline) and Somerville (1-800 465 4329).

Howard Johnsons
Kenmore Square and Fenway Park (1-800 654 2000).

Hyatt
Cambridge Regency and Harborside Logan Airport (1-800 233 1234).

Marriott
Copley Place, Long Wharf, Cambridge, Newton and Burlington (1-800 228 9290).

Radisson
Radisson 57 (Theatre District) and Chelmsford, Marlboro and Milford (1-800 333 3333).

Sheraton
Prudential (Hines Convention Center), Cambridge, Newton and Braintree (1-800 325 3535).

Westin
Copley Place and Waltham (1-800 228 3000).

Motels

Most of the economy hotel and motel chains offer several places to stay in suburban Boston. Here's a list of the most common with their toll-free central reservation numbers. For more details of out of town accommodation, *see chapter* **Trips Out of Town**.

Best Western (1-800 528 1234)
Comfort Inns (1-800 228 5150)
Days Inn (1-800 222 3297)
Motel 6 (1-800 466 8356)
Ramada Inn (1-800 272 6232)
Suisse Chalet (1-800 524 2538)
Travelodge (1-800 255 3050)

Hotel services *Air-conditioning. Kitchen. Laundry (self-service). No-smoking rooms only. Roof terrace.*
Room services *Radio.*

Newbury Guest House

261 Newbury Street, Boston, MA 02116, between Gloucester & Hereford Streets (437 7666/fax 262 4243). Hynes/ICA T. **Rates** *rooms* $100-$140.
Credit AmEx, DC, Disc, MC, $TC, V.
Map 3 E5
There's very little to choose between the Newbury Guest House and the **Beacon Inn Guest Houses** (*see p110*) across the street – especially if you're only staying a few days. The Newbury is actually three refurbished townhouses joined together. Its 32 rooms are very tastefully done out: wooden floors, high ceilings and bay windows abound. Light sleepers, however, should request rooms away from lively Newbury Street. And note that no children aged between two and 13 are allowed. Continental breakfast is served in a sunny little room that opens onto a patio terrace and staff are relaxed and friendly (and gay-friendly – though the clientele is a mix of anyone who appreciates good value). The location is unbeatable.
Hotel services *Air-conditioning. Continental breakfast. Deck. Disabled: access; rooms for disabled. Fax. No-smoking rooms. Parking. Safe.*
Room services *Free local calls. Hairdryer. Iron/ironing board. Radio. Refrigerator.*

Oasis Guest House

22 Edgerly Road, Boston, MA 02115, behind Symphony Hall (267 2262/fax 267 1920/www.oasisgh.com). Hynes/ICA T. **Rates** *rooms* $69-$109. **Credit** AmEx, MC, $TC, V. **Map 3 E6**
The Oasis is aptly named. Though it's just a few blocks from Symphony Hall and the city's hottest nightclubs, its location on a leafy, quiet side street makes you feel as though you're in a small town. The 16 rooms are very comfortably decorated, and most offer private baths. The lounge, where breakfast and afternoon sherry is served, is downright cosy, and the two outdoor decks are the scene of many an impromptu cocktail party in warm weather. The clientele here is a mix, with about half the guests being gay men.
Hotel services *Air-conditioning. Continental breakfast. Decks (2). Fax. No-smoking rooms. Parking. Safe.*
Room services *Dataport jack. Radio.*

Budget

If you're looking for a room for under $50 a night in Boston, you're looking at student accommodation. If you don't positively relish the idea of dormitory rooms, you can at least console yourself that you're saving money.

Boston International American Youth Hostel

12 Hemenway Street, Boston, MA 02115, behind Symphony Hall (536 1027/1-800 909 4776 ext 07/fax 424 6558). Convention Center T. **Rates** *members* $18; *non-members* $23. **Credit** $TC.
Map 3 E6
Before you get all excited about the price, phone up and find out about what an American Youth Hostel is. This one at the edge of Back Bay can accommodate up to 190 people, but the rooms are dormitory style (single sex), with up to six beds each. And you have to bring your own sheets or rent them for $2 a night. Still, there's access to a kitchen, laundry facilities and a TV lounge. You get what you pay for.
Hotel services *Air-conditioning. Kitchen. No-smoking rooms. TV lounge.*

YMCA

316 Huntington Street, Boston, MA 02115, at Northeastern University (536 7800/fax 267 4653). Northeastern T. **Rates** *single* $39; *double* $49. **Credit** MC, $TC, V. **Map 3 E6**

This one's men only. But the Y has a surprisingly friendly atmosphere and its private rooms certainly make it a step up from the Youth Hostel. The rooms look austere, but are comfortable enough. Bathrooms are down the hall. A great advantage to the Y is its excellent gym – popular with locals as well as visitors. Guests also have access to the indoor lap pool, TV lounge, laundry facilities and cafeteria. Cheap and cheerful.

Hotel services *Air-conditioning. Cafeteria. Gym. No-smoking rooms. Swimming pool. TV lounge.*

YWCA/Berkeley Residence

40 Berkeley Street, Boston, MA 02116, between Warren Avenue & Appleton Street (482 8850/ fax 482 9692). Back Bay T. **Rates** *single* $48; *double* $74; *triple* $84. **Credit** MC, $TC, V. **Map 5 F6**

And this is for women only. Not only that, but no men are allowed beyond the public areas. The rooms, as you might expect, are a bit battered but are clean. Bathrooms are down the hall. Breakfast is in a surprisingly pleasant restaurant-cum-cafeteria and is included in the price. Dinner can also be purchased there for $6.50. Guests have access to a TV lounge and laundry facilities. There's even a nice public pool with special women-only swimming hours. Weekly, monthly and permanent rates are available.

Hotel services *Air-conditioning. Kitchen access. No-smoking rooms. Restaurant. Swimming pool. TV lounge.*

Staying in Cambridge

Some travellers, those either associated with Harvard or MIT or those who want accommodation a little outside the urban fray, prefer Cambridge to Boston (which is easily accessible by T). Most of the hotels here belong to one of the chains (*see page 112* **Spare chains**). Listed below is a small range of hotels, from luxury to B&B, with individual character.

Cambridge House Bed & Breakfast

2218 Massachusetts Avenue, Cambridge, MA 02138, north of Harvard Square (491 6300/1-800 232 9989/ fax 868 2848). Porter or Davis T. **Rates** *rooms* $139-$159. **Credit** AmEx, DC, Disc, JBC, MC, $TC, V. **Map 4 B2**

A lovely little Greek Revival house built in 1892, a pleasant walk from Harvard Square. You feel at home the moment you see the fire crackling in the parlour. Each of the 16 rooms is furnished with period antiques and two of them also have working fireplaces. A full, cooked breakfast is included in the room price, along with a hot and cold buffet in the early evening. Not only that, but there's free off-street parking. Very good value for the price.

Hotel services *Air-conditioning. Breakfast. Fax. No-smoking rooms. Parking.*
Room services *Dataport jack. Hairdryer. Radio. Voicemail.*

Charles Hotel

1 Bennet Street, Cambridge, MA 02138, off Harvard Square (864 1200/1-800 882 1818/fax 865 5715). Harvard T. **Rates** *rooms* $275-$295; *suites* $389-$589. **Credit** AmEx, DC, Disc, JCB, MC, $TC, V. **Map 4 B2**

The Charles Hotel bills itself as 'simply elegant'. It is. The theme is American quilts. And the 296 rooms epitomise New England decorative restraint: all are done in blond woods and have white walls, muted carpets and colourful fabrics. That does not mean to imply a lack of luxury, however. Rooms also have nice touches such as stereos, feather beds and bathroom scales. The phones are even equipped with a Children's Story Line. Amenity-wise, the Charles can't be beaten: there's a full-size gym, pool and spa; two exceptional restaurants (**Rialto** and **Henrietta's Table**, *see p153* **Restaurants & Cafés**); and a bar that hosts the hottest jazz ensembles in town. If the Charles were in Boston, it would probably rival the Four Seasons in terms of service – and price.

Hotel services *Air-conditioning. Babysitting. Bar. Beauty salon. Business services. Concierge (24-hour). Conference facilities. Currency exchange. Disabled: access; rooms for disabled. Fax. Gym. Interpreting service. Laundry (24-hour). Limousine service. No-smoking rooms. Parking. Restaurants (2). Safety deposit. Shoeshine. Spa. Swimming pool.*
Room services *Dataport jack. Feather beds. Hairdryer. Iron/ironing board. Minibar. Radio/stereo. Robes. Room service (24-hour). Voicemail.*

Inn at Harvard

1201 Massachusetts Avenue, Cambridge, MA 02138, off Harvard Square (491 2222/1-800 222 8733/ fax 491 6520). Harvard T. **Rates** *rooms* $189-$329. **Credit** AmEx, DC, Disc, MC, $TC, V. **Map4 B2**

A little gem of a place a stone's throw from Harvard Yard. In 1992, Harvard alumnus Graham Gund designed the Inn for the university (it owns the hotel, though the place is run by Doubletree). When you walk through the front door, you feel instantly as though you've been transported to Europe. All 113 rooms are arranged over four floors around a skylit central courtyard reminiscent of a Tuscan palazzo. The atrium is the ideal place for morning coffee, afternoon tea or a quiet dinner. The rooms themselves are somewhat more anonymous but as comfortable as you like, with all the usual amenities. For the same price, there's no question that this hotel wins over the **Sheraton Commander** (*see below*).

Hotel services *Air-conditioning. Bar. Business services. Conference facilities. Disabled: access; rooms for disabled. Fax. Interpreting service. Laundry (24-hour). Limousine service. No-smoking rooms. Parking. Restaurant. Safety deposit.*
Room services *Dataport jack. Hairdryer. Iron/ironing board. Radio. Robes. Room service (until 10pm). Voicemail.*

Sheraton Commander

16 Garden Street, Cambridge, MA 02138, off Harvard Square (547 4800/1-800 325 3535/fax 868 8322). Harvard T. **Rates** *rooms* $160-$324; *suites* $295-$775. **Credit** AmEx, DC, Disc, JBC, MC, $TC, V. **Map 4 A1**

Located on Cambridge Common, the Commander is Harvard Square's oldest hotel ('Commander', as the décor reminds you at every turn, refers to George Washington, who was billeted nearby during the Revolution). For a hotel that claims a recent renovation, it has an odd air of faded luxury about it. The 176 rooms are comfortable but careworn, though some feature four-poster beds and kitchenettes. Most guests here are business travellers, as evidenced by the 'concierge floor', which provides faxes in each room, a lounge and continental breakfast.

Hotel services *Air-conditioning. Bar. Business services. Conference facilities. Disabled: access; rooms for disabled. Fax. Fitness room. Laundry (24-hour). No-smoking rooms. Restaurant. Safety deposit. Valet parking.*
Room services *Coffee pot. Dataport jack. Fax (concierge floor/suites). Hairdryer. Iron/ironing board. Radio. Robes (concierge floor/suites). Room service (until 10pm). Video games. Voicemail.*

Pubs & Bars

Irish pubs, brewpubs, style bars, hotel bars – Boston has no shortage of watering holes.

The 1990s have been kind to Boston's nightlife scene. It seems that every week a new bar, restaurant or club springs out of the city's fertile economic soil. Drinking establishments, in particular, have undergone something of a boom over the past few years. Bars have traditionally been the haunts of students and barflies; these days, though, everyone's getting in on the act. And the range of bars enjoying success is just as impressive as the number. Brewpubs, lounge bars, Martini bars, live music bars, dance club pubs, Irish pubs – all are doing a roaring trade. About the only nightlife scene in Boston that hasn't enjoyed the boom is the adult entertainment industry, which – after years of neighbourhood activism and screw-tightening legislation – has packed its collective bags and moved to the suburbs.

Otherwise, Bostonians are taking to the bars in record numbers, transmuting their famous Protestant work ethic into a couple of elbows propped on a sticky wooden bar-top. But even that image is all wrong: though many of the old-time watering holes are hanging on, the sticky wooden bar-top has frequently given way to the immaculate slate bar-top, the gleaming copper bar-top, the *faux* marble bar-top. Who knows how long the boom will last? Maybe next month the bottom will fall out of the market and locals will revert to their stuffy, reclusive ways. Until then, Bostonians are enjoying the good life while they can.

Note: the legal drinking age in Boston is 21, but carry photo ID and expect to get 'carded' if you look anything under 35.

Best place to...

Do an impression of Robert De Niro: **The Good Life** (*page 118*).
Observe the Boston Brahminry: **Lock-Ober** (*page 119*).
Spot visiting superstars: **The Bristol Lounge** (*page 118*).
Write that screenplay: **Bukowski's** (*page 116*).
Impersonate minor sports celebrities: **Daisy Buchanan's** (*page 116*).
Enjoy a pint and a slab of black pudding: **Irish Embassy** (*page 121*).
Slum it in style: the **Model Café** (*page 121*).
Play liar's poker: **Plough & Stars** (*page 123*).
Tap your foot to Irish fiddlers: **The Burren** (*page 124*).

Back Bay & the South End

Anchovies

432 Columbus Avenue, at Dartmouth Street (266 5088). Back Bay or Prudential T. **Open** 4pm-2am daily.
Credit AmEx, MC, V. **Map 3 F6**

As well as being a place to get good nosh, the bar at Anchovies – small, steamy and inescapably intimate – is known as a place where South Enders go to let their hair down – if they haven't already shaved it all off. One thing's for sure, you won't see too many 'I Love Boston' T-shirts in here.
Disabled: toilet.

Audubon Circle

838 Beacon Street, at Park Street (421 1910). Kenmore T. **Open** 11.30am-1am daily (food served until 11pm).
Credit AmEx, DC, Disc, MC, V.

With its angular slate bar counters, clean wooden bar-back and subdued lighting, Audubon is one of the more stylishly decorated bars in Boston. And its patrons keep their end up, too. Located a comfortable distance from student-riddled Kenmore Square, the bar has an agreeable laid-backness to it. Not to mention terrific food. *See also p137* **Restaurants & Cafés**.
Disabled: toilet.

Back Bay Brewing Company

755 Boylston Street, between Exeter & Fairfield Streets (424 8300). Copley T. **Open** 11.30am-1am Mon-Sat; 11am-1am Sun. **Credit** AmEx, MC, V.
Map 3 E5

The BBBC is two storeys tall – with multiple bars and lots of polished wood – and is pretty stylish for a brewpub. Twentysomethings pack it out on weekend nights, creating a slightly better-bred version of the antic singles scene further up Boylston Street. The dinner menu gets pretty ambitious for a brewpub, even a classy one. There are seats outside in warm weather.

Bill's Bar

5½ Lansdowne Street, at Brookline Avenue (421 9678). Kenmore T. **Open** 9am-2am Tue, Wed, Fri-Sun; 8am-2am Thur. **Credit** AmEx, MC, V.
Map 3 D5

Set among the hip nightclubs dotting Lansdowne Street, Bill's offers welcome respite from the clang and clatter of clubland's dark and sweaty dancefloors. If there's no live music, you can actually hear yourself think in here – not necessarily a good thing for many teenysomething clubgoers. *See also p201* **Nightlife**.
Disabled: toilet.

The cosy and popular **Delux Café**.

Bukowski's

50 Dalton Street, at Boylston Street (437 9999). Hynes/ICA T. **Open** 11.30am-2am daily. **No credit cards. Map 3 E5**

This tiny bar, wedged between the Mass Pike and the Cheri cinema, used to be a dive called Jack Lynch's Webster Lounge. Refurbished and renamed (after the poet Charles Bukowski, the patron saint of the types who used to frequent Lynch's), the bar now caters to a hip, young crowd, plus a smattering of old regulars and the occasional dapper businessman. So large is the bar's beer selection (90 bottled beers, 18 draft, eight cans) the staff have set up a wheel of indecision, which, when spun, will make the choice for you. Though the bar serves wine, there are no spirits. As one employee put it, 'It's all about beer'.

Clery's

113 Dartmouth Street, at Columbus Avenue (262 9874). Back Bay or Copley T. **Open** 11am-2am daily. **Credit** AmEx, DC, V. **Map 3 F6**

Large, labyrinthine and lively, Clery's attracts a refreshingly mixed crowd. Business stiffs and the megahip alike lean over frothing pints and heaped plates of grilled meat. If this place is anything to go by, we can all just get along.

Daisy Buchanan's

248B Newbury Street, at Fairfield Street (247 8516). Copley T. **Open** 11.30am-2am daily. **No credit cards. Map 3 E5**

A favourite haunt of the romantically challenged, Daisy Buchanan's often resembles the set of *The Dating Game* rather than a bar. Though it can be interesting watching guys with enormous pecs pursue gals with enormous eyelashes, if you are not large of pec or lash, you should probably keep walking.

Delux Café

100 Chandler Street, at Clarendon Street (338 5258). Back Bay T. **Open** 5pm-1am Mon-Sat. **No credit cards. Map 3 F5/6**

A shrine to all things kitsch, Delux is a good place if you're in the mood to cosy up with the young and the hip. And cosy up is right, too: the place is as small as it is popular, the latter thanks largely to some fine micro-brews and even finer food. Don't forget to check out the décor in the toilets.

The Oak Room

Fairmont Copley Plaza, 138 St James Street, at Dartmouth Street (267 5300 ext 1638). Back Bay or Copley T. **Open** 4.30pm-1am daily. **Credit** AmEx, Disc, MC, $TC, V. **Map 3 F5**

From the high ceilings to the panelled walls to the plush furniture, the Oak Room (located in the Plaza hotel), simply oozes class. Sink back into an easy chair, light up a cigar (if you are so inclined) and sloop one of the bar's delicious cognacs around a magnificent snifter. Then get the hell out of there before you spend your entire holiday allowance. *For the* **Fairmont Copley Plaza** *see p104* **Accommodation**.
Disabled: toilet.

Other Side Cosmic Café

407 Newbury Street, at Massachusetts Avenue (536 9477). Hynes/ICA T. **Open** 10am-midnight Mon-Wed; 10am-1am Thur-Sat; noon-midnight Sun. **No credit cards. Map 3 E5**

Smoking

You'd have thought it would have happened first over the river, in the so-called 'People's Republic of Cambridge', but, from midnight on 30 September 1998, it was Boston who followed the lead of the well-to-do suburban town of Brookline (which recently banned smoking in bars as well as restaurants) when the Boston Public Health Commission implemented an immediate citywide ban on smoking in its restaurants.

The left-leaning, health-conscious city of Cambridge proposed such a ban back in the 1980s, but has since settled for a law that requires restaurants with more than 25 seats to allot 75 per cent of the seating to non-smoking sections. Meanwhile, the city of Somerville – which borders Cambridge to the north – is moving towards a ban of its own. Traditionally a blue-collar enclave, Somerville has recently undergone a wave of gentrification. In a bid to escape rising rental rates, former Cambridge residents have moved into Somerville in droves, bringing many of their progressive ideals with them. On 30 September, the same day Boston's restrictions went into effect, the Somerville Board of Health voted to implement smoking restrictions of its own. Under the new law, 75 per cent of restaurant seating must be non-smoking and all of the city's restaurants must be fully smoke-free by the year 2000.

But it was the Boston ban that was the shocker. Indeed, the day the new law went into effect, many Boston residents had no idea the issue had even been raised. Even restaurateurs seemed caught off-guard and the early hours of

The Oak Room *at the Fairmont Copley Plaza – for the ultimate cigar-and-brandy experience.*

So called because of its location at the tail end of Newbury Street, cut off from the rest of Boston's trendiest street by Massachusetts Avenue, the Other Side has become a sort of Galapagos Island of Newbury Street bars, attracting a whole different kettle of clientele. Scruffy, bohemian and often goateed, this crowd is equally at home sipping beer or carrot-based cocktails. If you feel that you can't even look at another Martini, this is the place to head for.

The Rattlesnake

384 Boylston Street, at Arlington Street (859 8555). Arlington T. **Open** 11am-2am daily. **Credit** AmEx, DC, MC, V. **Map 5 F5**

A good place to hang out if you want to munch on cheapo Tex-Mex food and mingle with the college crowd. At weekends this place turns into a stop-off for people heading out for a night of dancing at 'The Alley' (*see chapter* **Nightlife**), and making yourself heard above the sound of crunching nachos becomes difficult.

RíRá

835 Beacon Street, at Milner Street (262 2121). Kenmore T. **Open** 11am-1am Mon-Wed; 11am-2am Thur-Sun. **Credit** AmEx, DC, Disc, MC, V.

RíRá is a hybrid of dance club and Irish pub. Do you wave your hands in the air like you just don't care or sit and contemplate the pint before you? Judging by the zillions of exuberant kids who jam themselves in for the nightly festivities, it's definitely the former. Not for the over-60s.

Disabled: access.

Sonsie

327 Newbury Street, between Hereford Street & Massachusetts Avenue (351 2500). Hynes/ICA T. **Open** 7am-1am daily. **Credit** AmEx, DC, MC, V. **Map 3 E5**

Known mainly as a restaurant, the insanely tasteful Sonsie is possibly *the* hangout spot for the Newbury Street elite and those who want to meet them. The bar is often packed to the

1 October saw hundreds of restaurant managers reaching for their protractors as they calculated how to put the ban into effect.

The law seems straightforward enough:

No smoking in restaurants that do not serve alcohol.
No smoking in the dining section of any restaurant.
No smoking en route to the rest rooms or in reception areas.
Smoking permitted in bar sections of restaurants, but only if the bar is not more than one-third of the total seating capacity of the establishment and only if a 6-ft (1.8-m) buffer zone or a floor-to-ceiling barrier separates the bar from the restaurant.
Smoking is allowed in bars whose primary function is to serve alcohol but that also serve food.

In reality, though, the smoking ban has sewn much confusion among restaurant owners, staff and customers. It is not uncommon to be told by one staff member that smoking is permitted in a certain area, only to have another snatch your ashtray away and inform you in no uncertain terms that you are breaking the law. Invisible lines are being drawn and all too often no one seems to know precisely where they are. One popular Boston establishment prohibits smoking the length of its bar, but where the bar-top makes a right-angled turn smoking is permitted. So, when standing at the corner of the bar you can have one foot simultaneously planted in non-smoking territory and the other in smoking territory.

Whether this is the best or worst of both worlds is anyone's guess.

gills with wealthy Europeans and tipsy fashion plates – all firm believers in the virtues of noisy banter. The service here is phenomenal. No matter how busy it is, you can usually hold your breath when you enter and be served before you expire. *See also p131* **Restaurants & Cafés**.
Disabled: toilet.

29 Newbury Street

29 Newbury Street, at Arlington Street (536 0290). Arlington T. **Open** 11.30pm-1am Mon-Sat; noon-1am Sun. **Credit** AmEx, DC, Disc, MC, V. **Map 4 F5**
Though primarily a restaurant, 29 also has a thriving little bar area where Boston's PR and media power players get together to chug Martinis and call each other darling.

Beacon Hill

Beacon Hill Pub Number

53 Charles Street, at Cambridge Street (no phone). Charles/MGH T. **Open** 11am-2am daily. **No credit cards. Map 5 F4**
Tourists who – after a day spent wandering the red-brick wonderland of the Hill – find themselves suffering from charm overload could do worse than park themselves on a barstool at this no-nonsense little neighbourhood bar, not least because one senses that this place will soon become a part of Beacon Hill history itself. Try it before the Paul Revere Bistro or John Hancock Raw Bar takes over.

Hill Tavern

228 Cambridge Street, at Charles Street (742 6192). Gov't Center T. **Open** 11.30am-2am Mon-Fri, Sun; 11am-2am Sat. **Credit** AmEx, DC, MC, V. **Map 5 F4**
A place where young urban professionals and State House denizens gather to compare power suits, the Hill Tavern is something of an upstart among Boston bars, and, judging by the enormous weekend crowds, a surprisingly popular one.
Disabled: toilet.

Sevens Pub

77 Charles Street, at Mount Vernon Street (523 9074). Charles/MGH T. **Open** 11.30am-1am Mon-Thur; noon-1am Fri, Sat. **No credit cards. Map 5 F4**
Though often prohibitively crowded, this unpretentious little pub is also a good spot to seek respite from a day of relentless sightseeing. Find a booth in the corner, settle down with a Guinness or a Bass and you may find that the Freedom Trail ends right here.
Disabled: toilet.

Downtown

Brew Moon

115 Stuart Street, at Tremont Street (523 6467). Boylston T. **Open** 11.30am-12.30am daily. **Credit** AmEx, MC, V. **Map 5 G5**
Every brewery-restaurant has to distinguish itself somehow, and Brew Moon was the first to break from the Brit pack and go modern. Its clean steel tanks and inexpensive New American menu have been so successful that the place has cloned itself in Cambridge and even Hawaii. This is the original, on the corner of Tremont and Stuart Streets, and is still busy and good. As with most brewpub beer, the product tends a little towards the bitter; to play it safe you can order a sampler of five small glasses that come in a steel rack.
Disabled: toilet.
Branch: 50 Church Street, Cambridge (499 2739).

Bishop's Pub

21 Boylston Place, between Charles & Tremont Streets (351 2583). Boylston T. **Open** 7pm-2am Tue-Sat. **Credit** AmEx, MC, V. **Map 5 F5**
Situated in what is known as 'The Alley', Bishop's is in among one of the densest concentration of clubs in Boston. As such, it's something of a pit-stop for the giggling clouds of hair spray that float from club to club. Things don't really get started in here until after 11pm and then you'll be lucky if you can breathe, let alone move.
Disabled: toilet.

Bristol Lounge

Four Seasons Hotel, 200 Boylston Street, at Arlington Street (351 2071). Arlington T. **Open** 11am-11.30pm Mon-Thur; 11.30am-midnight Fri, Sat; noon-11.30pm Sun. **Credit** AmEx, DC, Disc, C, $TC, V. **Map 5 F5**
Situated in the swank Four Seasons Hotel, the Bristol Lounge is a proper-attire-required kind of a place. The bar is full of the sort of antique furniture that low-tier royalty might own. And, this being the Four Seasons, there's no telling who one might see here: Rosie O'Donnell stuffed into one of the bar's plush armchairs, Al Gore sipping a glass of cognac, John Travolta nodding his head to subtle jazz. *See also p133* **Restaurants & Cafés**.
Disabled: toilet.

Bull and Finch Pub

84 Beacon Street, at Arlington Street (227 9605). Arlington T. **Open** 11am-2am daily. **Credit** AmEx, DC, Disc, MC, V. **Map 5 F4**
Though this place is credited with providing the inspiration for the TV sitcom *Cheers*, expect no Sams, Norms or Carlas. Do, however, expect to have your retina seared by endless camera flashes.
Disabled: toilet.

Emily's

48 Winter Street, at Tremont Street (423 3649). Park St T. **Open** 5pm-2am Tue-Sat. **Credit** AmEx, MC, V. **Map 5 G4**
When MTV's the *Real World* filmed in Boston, Emily's was the place the cast chose to hang out. The bar certainly has a Gen-X feel to it, with its *faux* lounge décor and a DJ playing dance hits at ear-splitting volume. If you haven't a cutie to cuddle up to on one of the bar's dimly-lit sofas, you might want to try your hand at playing pool on a table conveniently located three inches from the dance floor.
Disabled: toilet.

The Good Life

28 Kingston Street, at Summer Street (451 2622). Downtown Crossing T. **Open** 11am-2am Mon-Fri; noon-2am Sat; 5pm-2am Sun. **Credit** AmEx, DC, MC, V. **Map 5 G5**
The Good Life is just one of the upmarket bars and restaurants that have transformed downtown Boston from a late-night wasteland into a nightlife Elysium. This place is certainly one of the most popular – and with good reason. With its orange vinyl walls, wood panelling, Rat Pack soundtrack and *Goodfellas* ambience, the Good Life manages to be a smirky tribute to lounge bars and a very good lounge bar at the same time. It's the kind of place where one might feel inadequate for not smoking. Especially downstairs, where there's live jazz from Thursday to Sunday (no cover) and bohemians and business types nurse their drinks while octogenarian drummers beat the hell out of tired-looking drum sets. Yeah.
Disabled: toilet.

Hibernia

25 Kingston Street, at Summer Street (292 2333). Downtown Crossing or South Station T. **Open** 11.30am-2am Mon-Sat. **Credit** AmEx, MC, V. **Map 5 G5**

Small but perfectly formed: **The Littlest Bar.**

Across the road from **The Good Life** (*above*) and adjacent to **JJ Foley's** (*below*), Hibernia is one of the many Irish bars that have popped up in Boston over the past few years. This one, though, has foregone the ubiquitous Irish *seisiún* for a dancefloor and DJs spinning the latest House hits. The décor blends ancient Celtic symbols and modern geometric shapes. And though the bartenders can pour a pint of Guinness with the best of them, they also serve a decent Martini.

JJ Foley's

21 Kingston Street, at Summer Street (338 7713). Downtown Crossing T. **Open** 11am-2am Mon-Fri; 10am-2pm Sat, Sun. **Credit** AmEx, MC, V. **Map 5 G5**

This low-key Irish bar is an institution in Boston, a hangout for bike messengers, the tattooed masses, business suits and borderline bums. Anyone who has lived in Boston for any amount of time has met someone at Foley's, or broken up with someone, or met and broken up with them at the same time – or knows someone who has. At night the place is packed, smoky and brimming with energy. Though the historic Freedom Trail has its merits, this is the place to observe Boston's personal history being forged. There's live music on Sunday nights.

The Littlest Bar

47 Province Street, at Broomfield Street (523 9667). Downtown Crossing or Park St T. **Open** 8.30am-1am daily. **No credit cards. Map 5 G4**

There may be littler bars than the Littlest Bar (which measures 16ft/5m from end to end), but we don't know of any. And it's not just the bar's size that makes it such an intimate setting. The place draws a crowd of doggedly loyal regulars, some of whom are members of Boston's political and cultural elite (note the 'Seamus Heaney peed here' sign outside the men's room). That said, the patrons seem more than willing to make a place at the bar for newcomers – or they would if they could.

Lock-Ober

3 & 4 Winter Place, at Tremont Street (542 1340). Park St T. **Open** 11.30am-3pm, 5.30-10pm, Mon-Fri; 5.30-10pm Sat. **Credit** AmEx, DC, Disc, MC, V. **Map 5 G4**

The first thing to do when you enter Lock-Ober (established in 1875) is resist the urge to run. You will be immediately struck by the must of cigars. You will see smartly – no, ceremoniously – dressed waiting staff, a sea of leather, white linen and the mythical Boston Brahmin. You will hear the clinking of ice, the mumble of deals being made. Sit down at the bar and a bartender will appear before you, offering to cater to your every whim. As in most top-drawer Yankee hangouts, you'll be treated with almost unsettling deference. The only problem is that you'll soon be back outside in the cruel, cruel world.

The Mercury Bar

116 Boylston Street, at Tremont Street (482 7799). Boylston T. **Open** 5pm-2am Mon-Sat. **Credit** AmEx, MC, V. **Map 5 G5**

With its 100-ft (30-m) bar-top, red velvet U-shaped booths and subtle lighting, the Mercury Bar has established itself as one of the prime destinations for the burgeoning Martini set. Though it gets particularly lively from Thursdays to Saturdays when there's a dance club in operation at the back (*see p201* **Nightlife**), there's never really a dull moment here.

Disabled: toilet.

Oskars

107 South Street, at Kneeland Street (542 6756). South Station T. **Open** 11.30am-2am Mon-Thur; 5.30pm-1am Fri; 7pm-1am Sat; 10pm-1am Sun. **Credit** AmEx, DC, MC, V. **Map 5 G5**

Though better known as a restaurant than a bar, it's worth having a drink here just to get a whiff of the good life. The staff are friendly and efficient, and the glasses have an irresistible heft to them. Only someone as important as yourself would drink out of such a glass. Before you get too carried away, Oskars is a prime spot for beautiful-people-watching and an hour or so of sipping cocktails in the bar's ruggedly chic environs may have you silently vowing to contact a plastic surgeon first thing in the morning.

The Mercury Bar. *See page 119.*

Silvertone

69 Bromfield Street, at Tremont Street (338 7887). Downtown Crossing T. **Open** 11.30am-2am Mon-Fri; 5pm-2am Sat; 9pm-2am Sun. **Credit** AmEx, DC, Disc, MC, V. **Map 5 G4**

With its modern – but not tacky – décor, its danceable – but not deafening – music, and its fashionable – but not tragically hip – crowd, Silvertone has made a virtue out of compromise. Tucked away on a gloomy side street near Downtown Crossing, it's not really the kind of place you stumble across. On any given night the clientele consists almost entirely of regulars. A good place to get acquainted with Boston's smart – but not smarmy – set.

Les Zygomates

129 South Street, at Kneeland Street (542 5108). South Station T. **Open** 11.30am-2pm, 6pm-1am, Mon-Thur; 6pm-1am Fri, Sat. **Credit** AmEx, DC, Disc, MC, V. **Map 5 G5**

First, try not to mispronounce the name (Zee-go-maht). Next, get out of those ripped jeans. Now take the plunge into one of Boston's most elegant wine bars. Unless you're a bit of an urbanite yourself, it can be intimidating just walking through Les Zyg's (as nobody ever calls it) door. And this is nothing compared to being confronted with the bar's telephone directory-sized wine list. *See also p135* **Restaurants & Cafés**.

Faneuil Hall

Backstage

245 Quincy Marketplace (726 1110). Gov't Center or Haymarket T. **Open** 11.30am-2am daily. **Credit** AmEx, MC, V. **Map 5 G4**

In the heart of Quincy Market, Backstage is a sign that trendier days are coming to this stuffy old tourist spot. The bar's cavernous space thrums with the sounds of dance music, flickers with a chaos of coloured lights and heaves with the bodies of the young and supple. And that goes for the staff, too, who spend their spare time practising Tom Cruise-like bottle flinging moves (one bartender catches them in her cleavage).

Disabled: toilet.

Bell in Hand Tavern

45-55 Union Street (227 2098). Gov't Center or Haymarket T. **Open** 11.30am-2am daily. **Credit** AmEx, MC, V. **Map 5 G4**

Built in 1795, the Bell in Hand is 'the oldest tavern in the US', as a plaque outside attests. Yet there's little 'Ye Olde' nonsense going on here. The clientele is made up largely of young regulars and you'll find them nose to elbow at weekends, when the bar opens its side room for dancing. Perhaps they're drawn by the, er, unpretentious décor, which has been described as Woolworthian. Oh, and if you look beyond the television, outside the window stands Boston's hauntingly beautiful Holocaust Memorial.

Disabled: toilet.

The Black Rose

160 State Street, at Commercial Street (742 2286). Gov't Center or State/Citizen's Bank T. **Open** 11.30am-1am daily. **Credit** AmEx, DC, MC, V. **Map 5 G4**

Irish Republican proclamations adorn the walls. The faces of Republican patriots gaze down with stern dignity. But don't let that put you off. If you're in the mood for a singsong, this is your place. The bar has live Irish music '364 nights a year' (they take Christmas Day off). And they're certainly not averse to a bit of audience participation. From Thursdays to Saturdays the bar opens its upstairs section for music and dancing.

Disabled: toilet.

The Green Dragon

11 Marshall Street, at Union Street (367 0055). Gov't Center T. **Open** 11am-2am daily. **Credit** AmEx, DC, MC, V. **Map 5 G4**

A stone's throw from the **Bell in Hand** (*see above*), this bar dates back (though not in its present form) to 1773. The spot on which it stands is 'the birthplace of American freedom', a place where the sons of liberty gathered over a few pints to plot the downfall of the British. For doubters, there's a glass case on the wall containing some of the implements – muskets and so on – used to achieve that end. Otherwise, the place couldn't be more congenial, with attentive staff, carpeted nooks and slightly faded wallpaper. If you're lucky you might even catch a bit of English soccer on the telly.

The Purple Shamrock

1 Union Street, at Congress Street (227 2060). Downtown Crossing, Gov't Center or Haymarket T. **Open** 11.30am-11.30pm Mon-Fri; 10am-1.30am Sat; 9am-1.30am Sun. **Credit** AmEx, DC, MC, V. **Map 5 G4**

Nestled between the old world charm of Quincy Market and the stark modernism of City Hall, this bar attracts government employees and tourists in equal measure. As its name suggests, it is something of a hybrid Irish bar, with Murphy's and Guinness on tap and a large mosaic shamrock decorating the floor. Otherwise, it screams America.

Disabled: toilet.

Around North Station

Grand Canal

57 Canal Street, at Causeway Street (523 1112). Haymarket or North Station T. **Open** 11am-1.30am daily. **Credit** AmEx, MC, V. **Map 5 G3**

The Grand Canal boasts one of the finest façades in the city. There's something very English about the place and it doesn't take too much suspension of disbelief to imagine that you're enjoying a pint in deepest West London. Live music

and a cheery pub atmosphere have made this bar enormously popular among young people.
Disabled: toilet.

Irish Embassy

234 Friend Street, at Causeway Street (742 6618). North Station T. **Open** 11.30am-2am daily. **Credit** AmEx, DC, MC, V. **Map 5 G3**
Live English soccer on Saturdays, artery-choking breakfasts and an authentic pub atmosphere draw to the Irish Embassy one of the highest concentrations of English and Irish expats in the city. A good place to overhear people casting colourful aspersions on the proverbial referee.
Disabled: toilet.

McGann's

197 Portland Street, at Causeway Street (227 4059). North Station T. **Open** 11.30am-2am Mon-Sat; noon-2am Sun. **Credit** AmEx, DC, Disc, MC, V. **Map 5 G3**
If you've a hankering for pub grub, McGann's will take care of you. Lacking the loud and ribald banter of the **Irish Embassy** (*above*), this is as good a spot as any to settle down with a paper and chew over the day's news.
Disabled: toilet.

Further afield

Allston

Big City

138 Brighton Avenue, at Harvard Avenue, Allston (782 2020). Harvard T. **Open** 11.30am-1am Mon-Sat; 11am-1am Sun. **Credit** AmEx, MC, V.
Housed in what used to be a bank, Big City lives up to its name. Urban visual gags abound: a working traffic light sits in the corner, parking meters on the raised bench tables. Rooms surrounding the bar contain some of the nicest pool tables in town, but this is also a fun place to just sit and have a drink. Not least for the 82 beers on tap and the bar menu, which consists almost entirely of pizza – including the 'Eye Opener', with bacon, scrambled eggs and home fries, and the peanut butter and (we're not kidding) jelly pizza.
Disabled: toilet.

Model Café

7 North Beacon Street, at Cambridge Street, Allston (254 9365). Washington Sq T. **Open** 11.30am-2am daily. **No credit cards**.
The Model has had an interesting life. It started off as an unpretentious little neighbourhood dive and then one day, through no fault of its own, it was suddenly enormously pretentious, playing host to the cream of the counter-cultural community (who inexplicably started calling it the 'Mow-DELL'). Nowadays, the trendy crowd and the divey neighbourhood crowd share the place. It's quite sweet, really.
Disabled: toilet.

Sunset Grill

130 Brighton Avenue, at Harvard Avenue, Allston (254 1331). Harvard T. **Open** 11.15am-1am daily. **Credit** AmEx, DC, MC, V. **Map 4 A5**
For the no-nonsense ale lover, the Sunset may be the only place in town. Though it's pleasant enough, the bar's décor and clientele are nothing to write home about. The beer menu, on the other hand, is ridiculous: 450 beers in bottles, 111 on tap.
Disabled: toilet.

The White Horse

116 Brighton Avenue, at Harvard Avenue, Allston (254 6633). Harvard T. **Open** 11.30am-2am daily. **Credit** AmEx, MC, V. **Map 4 A5**
Though this pub can get crammed at weekends, its massive size makes it a perfect place for those times when you need privacy. Sit at the huge bar and look around: that couple over in the corner talking in hushed tones could be breaking up or just getting acquainted. The beauty of the White Horse is that you and everyone else are sitting too far away to tell.
Disabled: toilet.

Adding a touch of class: the jazz trio at the **Wonder Bar**. *See page 122.*

Wonder Bar

186 Harvard Avenue, at Commonwealth Avenue, Allston (351 2665). Harvard T. **Open** 5pm-2am daily. **Credit** MC, V. **Map 4 A4**

Though Allston hasn't exactly felt the cleansing fire of progress yet, there are definite signs that the area is picking up – much like the Wonder Bar. On the premises of what used to be a famously grungy music club, Wonder Bar makes no bones about wanting to move in higher circles. At the door a dress code proclaims, among other things, that 'shirts must be tucked and buttoned'. Inside, the bar's black-and-white tiled floor, slo-mo ceiling fans and perennial jazz trio all attest to the encroachment of Martini sensibilities on a Bud Lite neighbourhood.

Jamaica Plain

Brendan Behan Pub

378 Center Street, at Sherridan Street, Jamaica Plain (522 5386). Stony Brook T. **Open** 11am-1am Mon-Sat; 11am-midnight Sun. **No credit cards.**

Whether coming here for a quiet game of afternoon cribbage or for its nightly standing-room-only sessions, fans of Behan rank the small Irish bar alongside the polio vaccine in the benefit-to-mankind stakes. Dimly-lit, smoky, often packed to the gills with a young, lively crowd, the success of this pub paved the way for the spate of Irish bars that subsequently popped up in the JP area. *See also p204* **Nightlife**.

Doyle's

3484 Washington Street, at Williams Street, Jamaica Plain (524 2345). Green St T. **Open** 9am-12.45am daily. **No credit cards. Map 4 D2**

One of the oldest Irish pubs in Boston, Doyle's has been in the business for more than a century and it shows. There is an effortless charm about the place, and it doesn't rely on 'DUBLIN 23 MILES' signs to promote its Irishness, but quietly goes about the business of pulling a great pint and serving hearty food at low prices. It's a rambling place, with high ceilings, huge murals and invariably a large, chatty crowd.

Flann O'Brien's

1619 Tremont Street, at Wigglesworth Street, Jamaica Plain (566 7744). Brigham Circle T. **Open** 11am-1am Mon-Sat; noon-1am Sun. **No credit cards.**

Though somewhat out of the way in the Brigham Circle area of Boston, O'Brien's is worth the trip. Irish immigrants and locals alike have found this an ideal spot in which to let their hair down and have a bit of mad fun. Portraits of Irish literary heroes festoon the walls, often lit up by flickering disco lights. The sounds of laughter and loud music compete for air space. Dancers and drinkers somehow commingle with barely a drop of spillage.

James's Gate

5 McBride Street, at South Street, Jamaica Plain (522 5386). Forest Hills T. **Open** 11.30am-1am daily. **Credit** AmEx, MC, V.

Irish bars

Not too long ago, the words 'Irish bar' brought to mind something in the Irish-American vein, old-time bars such as Mulligan's or O'Malley's. According to conventional wisdom, the old Irish-American bars were musty, vaguely frightening places with dim lighting, shabby pool tables and neighbourhood geezers slumped over mugs of Bud Lite. While there were long-standing establishments such as the **Plough & Stars** in Cambridge (*see page 123*) and **Doyle's** in Jamaica Plain (*see page 121*) – places that captured the feel of an authentic Irish pub (which has much to do with the hospitality of the staff, the layout of the pub, and, of course, the quality of the ale) – on the whole, the Irish bar scene was a pretty joyless one. And then, about five years ago, all that changed – a new breed of Irish pub started popping up all over the place.

Many of Greater Boston's most successful Irish pubs can be traced back – through a convoluted and contiguous scribble of association – to the inception of **Brendan Behan Pub** in Jamaica Plain (*see page 122*). Here (deep breath) is the abridged story:

Behan was opened a little more then ten years ago by Irish natives Butch Murray and Jerry Brennan. Butch went on to open **Flann O'Brien's** in Roxbury (*see page 122*) and **The Field** in Cambridge (*see page 123*), which he owns with Jerry Coleman. Behan owner Jerry is also one of the owners of the **Thirsty Scholar Pub** in Somerville (*see page 124*). Kevin Treanor of the **Phoenix Landing**, also in Cambridge (*see page 123*), used to be a bartender at Behan and at the Druid in Cambridge (1357 Cambridge Street, 497 0965). The Druid is owned by John Flaherty and Pedro Smyth, who are now also co-owners of **Hibernia** in downtown Boston (*see page 118*). Patsy Long used to work at Behan as well and Joe McCabe worked at the Druid, before the pair went on to open the Phoenix Landing with Kevin Treanor. John Broderick used to be a regular at Behan; he went on to open **The Burren** in Somerville (*see page 124*) with Tommy McCarthy and Louise Costello, who are close friends of the Phoenix Landing's Patsy Long, and who used to be resident musicians at Behan. Pauly Byrne, of Behan, and Christy Page, who is friends with Tommy and Louise, opened up **James' Gate** in Jamaica Plain (*see page 122*).

So it is that Butch, Jerry, Jerry, Kevin, John, Pedro, Patsy, Joe, Kevin, John, Tommy, Louise, Pauly and Christy helped establish the humble Irish pub as one of the great successes of Greater Boston's nightlife boom. Those of us who like good beer, comfortable surroundings and a friendly atmosphere thank them heartily.

Perhaps the only spot in Boston where one can sit next to a crackling hearth while listening to loud techno music, James's Gate also sports one of Boston's more interesting décors, a mix of quirky art and the overall feel of a Mexican restaurant. One sip of the Guinness, though, should be enough to quell lingering doubts that this is anything but an Irish pub, even if there is a young trendy type bobbing along to the music a millimetre from your left elbow.
Disabled: toilet.

Cambridge & Somerville

Cambridge

Cambridge Brewing Company

1 Kendall Square, at Hampshire Street, Cambridge (494 1994). Kendall/MIT T. **Open** 11.30am-12.30am daily. **Credit** AmEx, MC, V. **Map 4 E4**
Located in the industrial-turned-entertainment complex of One Kendall Square (the Kendall Landmark Theater is a stone's throw away, as are a number of very good restaurants), this bar boasts some of the finest home-brew in the region – the Cambridge Pale Ale is to die for. In the summertime you can sit at the bar's outside tables, where trees adorned with twinkling fairy lights create a lovely romantic setting. Or maybe that's just the beer.
Disabled: toilet.

Cambridge Common

1667 Massachusetts Avenue, at Sacramento Street, Cambridge (547 1228). Harvard or Porter T.
Open 11.30am-1am Mon-Wed; 11.30am-2am Thur-Sat; 11am-midnight Sun. **Credit** AmEx, DC, Disc, MC, V.
Map 4 B1
Perched above one of the quirkier live act clubs in Boston, the **Lizard Lounge** (*see p206* **Nightlife**), Cambridge Common itself is a fairly low-key, get-a-couple-down-you kind of place. Somewhat off the beaten track (halfway between Harvard and Porter Squares), it attracts mostly regulars, as well as the poets, jazz players and Marlene Dietrich lookalikes who frequent the downstairs club. *See also p149* **Restaurants & Cafés**.

The Cellar

991 Massachusetts Avenue, at Dana Street, Cambridge (876 2580). Central or Harvard T. **Open** 4pm-1am daily. **No credit cards**. **Map 4 C3**
If anthropologists wanted to examine the habits of the elusive Cantabrigian, the Cellar might be the place to do it. Not only does everybody know your name here, they know a fair bit about your personal history too. With unfinished, whitewashed walls, the snug little subterranean pub was recently extended to include a second-floor bar area, where food is served. Downstairs, though, is where you'll find many of Cambridge's most colourful characters.

The Field

20 Prospect Street, at Massachusetts Avenue, Cambridge (354 7345). Central T. **Open** 11am-1am Mon-Sat; noon-1am Sun. **No credit cards**. **Map 4 C3**
Outside Dublin, the Field may be as close as you get to the feel of a real Dublin pub, precisely because it doesn't go overboard to achieve that feel. Irish and American kids get together to jostle happily in the front room, bobbing about to a soundtrack of blaring popular music, or to sit in the considerably more sedate back room and have a natter.
Disabled: toilet.

Grafton Street

1280 Massachusetts Avenue, between Linden & Plympton Streets, Cambridge (497 0400). Harvard T.
Open 11am-1am daily. **Credit** AmEx, DC, MC, V.
Map 4 B2
This fairly new Irish pub overflows in summer, when its big French windows allow interaction with Harvard Square's ongoing parade. Foodwise, however, it is still a pub. Just because the menu offers shrimp scampi is no reason to venture beyond fish and chips.
Disabled: toilet.

Green Street Grill

280 Green Street, between Pearl & Magazine Streets, Cambridge (876 1655). Central T. **Open** 3pm-1am daily. **Credit** AmEx, DC, MC, V. **Map 4 C3**
This unpretentious restaurant/bar/club has steadily become a staple of Cambridge nightlife. Attracting a young, local crowd, Green Street is a perfect place for a relaxed, though not soporific, drink. Tuesday is Spirits & Magicians night: a free show in which quippy conjurers work their magic at the bar. *See also p152* **Restaurants & Cafés** *and p204* **Nightlife**.

John Harvard's Brew House

33 Dunster Street, at Massachusetts Avenue, Cambridge (868 3585). Harvard T. **Open** 11.30am-1am Mon-Thur; 11.30am-1.30am Fri, Sat. **Credit** AmEx, DC, MC, V.
Map 4 B2
Long a favourite of Harvard's student body, this large underground bar offers basic American cooking, delicious microbrewed beer and the opportunity to be surrounded by – well, the bodies of Harvard's large student body.
Disabled: toilet.

Miracle of Science Bar & Grill

321 Massachusetts Avenue, at State Street, Cambridge (868 2866). Central T. **Open** 11.30am-1am daily.
Credit AmEx, DC, Disc, MC, V. **Map 4 D4**
Sister bar to **Audubon Circle** in Boston (*see p115*), the Miracle of Science has huge windows looking out onto Mass Ave, an ultra-mod design, good beer and a comfortable (though perhaps too well-lit) atmosphere. In honour of the many MIT students who frequent the place, the bar serves drinks in laboratory beakers. It's an MIT thing.

The People's Republik

880 Massachusetts Avenue, at Lee Street, Cambridge (492 8632). Central or Harvard T. **Open** noon-1am Mon-Wed, Sun; noon-2am Thur-Sat. **No credit cards**.
Map 4 C3
Located in the spot that used to house the divey little bar Drumlins, the People's Republik has jazzed things up considerably. With inspirational posters from Russia and Red China on the walls and a giant bomb above the window, the bar plays around with a revolutionary theme, which has led local wags to rename the place 'Kremlins'.
Disabled: toilet.

Phoenix Landing

512 Massachusetts Avenue, at Brookline Street, Cambridge (576 6260). Central T. **Open** 11am-1am daily. **Credit** AmEx, DC, MC, V. **Map 3 D3**
Invariably packed, loud and steamy, the Phoenix was one of the first Irish pubs in the area to realise the potential of combining a dance club with an Irish pub. It offers live music as well as showcasing some of the area's up-and-coming young DJs. And the bartenders pull a pretty decent pint, too.
Disabled: toilet.

Plough & Stars

912 Massachusetts Avenue, at Hancock Street, Cambridge (441 3455). Central T. **Open** 11.30am-1am daily. **No credit cards**. **Map 4 C3**
The spiritual forefather of Greater Boston's thriving pub business, the Plough has been going for 30 years and many of the regulars who line the bar (and whose ink-on-napkin portraits adorn the walls) have been around since the beginning. In the daytime the Plough offers the best pub grub in town, contentious games of cribbage and live soccer. At night the tiny

Shirts may be worn untucked and unbottoned at the **Plough & Stars**. *See page 123.*

bar is transformed into a hotbed of smoke, elbows and live music. Getting to the bathrooms when a band is on can be an interesting challenge, not least because you have to push your way through the band to get there. *See also p208* **Nightlife**.

Rialto

1 Bennett Street, at the Charles Hotel, Cambridge (661 5050). Harvard T. **Open** 5-11pm Mon-Thur, Sun; 5-11.30pm Fri, Sat. **Credit** AmEx, DC, MC, V. **Map 4 B2**

Not your let's-pop-in-for-a-quickie kind of place, Rialto serves hefty cocktails (not to mention excellent food) and has prices to match. Nestled in the elegant Charles Hotel and a stone's throw from the John F Kennedy School of Government, it's a place where you're equally likely to find yourself sipping a G&T beside foreign dignitaries, expense account-wielding out-of-towners and well-heeled locals. *See also p153* **Restaurants & Cafés**.

Disabled: toilet.

Shay's Lounge

58 John F Kennedy Street, at Mount Auburn Street, Cambridge (864 9161). Harvard T. **Open** 11.30am-1am daily. **Credit** AmEx, DC, MC, V. **Map 4 B2**

Owned and operated by English expats, Shay's is one of the nicer bars in Harvard Square. Sunk a few feet below the sidewalk and with a nifty outdoor patio, the bar itself is rather pokey. Conversation at Shay's, though, is more expansive – the bar attracts a lively brew of academics, artists and die-hard regulars, and barside banter can range from the Middle East peace talks to why the Red Sox suck. Though many take advantage of Shay's extensive beer menu, this is primarily a wine bar and there are no spirits.

Toad

1912 Massachusetts Avenue, at Porter Square, Cambridge (497 4950). Porter T. **Open** 5pm-1am Mon-Wed, Sun; 5pm-2am Thur-Sat. **No credit cards**. **Map 4 B1**

You'd miss Toad if you blinked. But if you want to get intimate with Cambridge residents, this friendly, low-key little bar is an indispensable venue. Toad flies in the face of physical laws, successfully combining live music, enormous popularity and minuscule size.

Disabled: toilet.

Somerville

The Burren

247 Elm Street, at Davis Square, Somerville (776 6896). Davis T. **Open** 11.30am-1am Mon-Fri; 10am-1am Sat, Sun. **Credit** AmEx, Disc, MC, V.

Since its opening a few years ago, the Burren has enjoyed enormous success – so much so that it has expanded, opening up a huge back room to accommodate the pub's many devotees. In the daytime, a scattering of people can be found eating Guinness-and-beef stew at the bar's wooden tables. At night the place is packed with crowds (including students from nearby Tufts University) who show up to hear world-class Irish musicians jam in the pub's incomparable *seisiúns*.

Disabled: toilet.

Joshua Tree

256 Elm Street, at College Avenue, Somerville (623 9910). Davis T. **Open** 11.30am-1am daily. **Credit** AmEx, Disc, DC, MC, V.

The Davis Square area has steadily thrown off its blue collar traditions over the past few years, becoming one of Greater Boston's prime nightlife destinations. Hence the inception of trendy bars such as the Joshua Tree, which consistently draws young, noisy crowds into its ultra-modern fold. Perhaps the bar's best feature (because it sure ain't the food) is the large window that, in the summer, opens the rumpus up to the street.

Disabled: toilet.

Thirsty Scholar Pub

70 Beacon Street, at Washington Street, Somerville (497 2294). Harvard T. **Open** 11am-1am daily. **Credit** AmEx, MC, V. **Map 4 C2**

With its exposed brick and little nooks and crannies, the Thirsty Scholar is the perfect place for an intimate, or simply private, drink. Not that you'd particularly want to shut yourself off from this pub's patrons, who rank among the friendliest in the area. And they may just be the most literate pub-goers in the area, too. Once a month, distinguished local writers have an informal get-together, and, true to its name, the pub plays host to many readings.

Disabled: toilet.

Tir na nog

366A Somerville Avenue, at Union Square, Somerville (628 4300). Washington Sq T. **Open** 3pm-1am Mon-Wed; 11.30am-1am Thur-Sat; noon-1am Sun. **Credit** MC, V.

This is a terrific little pub, with bookcases lining the walls and a marvellous mahogany bar. But it's tiny and on nights when it hosts live Irish or folk music the place can begin to feel like the inside of a bean burrito. And yet you couldn't hope to have the life squeezed out of you by a nicer bunch of people.

Disabled: toilet.

Restaurants & Cafés

The best of Boston's eateries: from cafés, caffes and cantinas to bistros and upmarket dining rooms.

Boston has seen its share of cultural shifts in recent years, but maybe none more pronounced than the one that has turned 'the home of the bean and the cod' into a hive of fusion grills and New American bistros. The burgeoning economy has helped fuel a parallel rise in dining-out budgets; meanwhile, conservative Yankees are being edged out by hungry omnivores who moved to the area for college, stayed for high-tech jobs, and have the money and curiosity to keep the grills fired.

Admittedly, it took a while for Boston to enter the ranks of America's serious restaurant cities. Perhaps because New England inherited its cooking traditions from Old England, perhaps because the thrifty Puritans were discomfited by anything so pleasurable and decadent as eating well, Boston spent years in the grip of overcooked indifference.

Don't miss:

South End hot spot, **Aquitaine** (*page 138*).
Audubon Circle: the last word in chic good value (*page 137*).
Brown Sugar (*page 137*) – for the best Thai food in town.
The essence of gastronomic Boston: **Clío** (*page 127*).
Elephant Walk (*page 137*), for French-Cambodian fusion in a colonial-chic setting.
Ginza: worship at the fish-lovers' temple (*page 129*).
L'Espalier: for the ultimate *prix fixe* blow-out (*page 127*).
Marcuccio's: for some of the best Italian-inspired food in the North End (*page 137*).
Bistro of the moment, **No.9 Park** (*page 135*).
Olives, stalwart of the Todd English empire (*page 132*).
Tapéo: for the best tapas in town (*page 131*).

The city then spent a few years enslaved by a new-cuisine explosion that had the feel of sudden adolescent freedom – exciting but untethered. Now things have settled down a little: new restaurants are still opening at a remarkable pace, but increasing competition means they have to be *good*, not just different. Which is great news for diners.

The city's legendary reserve hasn't totally dissipated; you won't find a lot of grand gestures or radical-looking theme restaurants here. The tight zoning laws of Boston's nineteenth-century neighbourhoods mean that the standard model is a low-key, almost informal bistro. Which is not to say inexpensive: most of the new flash and sizzle comes at what for most diners is the high end of the market. The city's good restaurants tend to have main course prices in the high teens and low $20s, and a handful are creeping into the $30s. To be fair, some of this is due to high rents and some to the difficulty of getting unusual ingredients to New England from the regions where they're grown.

Still, you'll hardly notice a shortage of ingredients eating out in Boston: a Mediterraneanised version of bistro cooking, with massive plates of meat, starch and vegetables, has ruled 'scene' restaurants for a few years, only recently starting to give way to some newer trends. The most influential (and outrageous) practitioner of this style is Todd English, whose remarkable work at **Olives** (*see page 132*) inspired a series of chefs to open their own restaurants. In the right hands, this approach yields amazing, generous washes of flavour (try Olives or the Back Bay newcomer **Anago**, *page 126*); in the wrong hands you get indiscriminate excess, which has led a national restaurant writer to refer to the city's cuisine as the 'Boston glob'.

Unfair? Probably. Especially in light of the new wave of spruced-up, New Yorky French cooking appearing around the city. New bistros are rolling out steak frites, foie gras, savoury tartlets and the occasional brilliant green bowl of vichyssoise. And all the while a cadre of flavour-happy grill cooks, led by Chris Schlesinger of Cambridge's quirky **East Coast Grill** (*see page 151*), has been spreading the spice-and-smoke gospel of the Caribbean.

For all its contrasts, Boston's food scene is also characterised by a remarkable spirit of bonhomie and even conscience. Chefs join together in hunger benefits, food festivals and even a summer camp-out meant to encourage farmers to grow heirloom apples, tomatoes and other traditional produce. The idea – a sensible one – is to bring a little of New England back into New England cooking – but this time on far more flavourful terms.

For brewpubs, many of which have excellent food as well as local ales, *see* **Back Bay Brewing Company**, **Brew Moon** *and* **Cambridge Brewing Company** *in chapter* **Pubs & Bars**. For an index of restaurants by cuisine, *see page 155*.

Back Bay

It's hard to generalise about a neighbourhood whose main shopping thoroughfare, Newbury Street, begins at the starchy **Ritz-Carlton** (*see page 104*) and ends eight blocks later at the duelling nose-ring hangouts **Tower Records** (*page 175*) and **Urban Outfitters** (*page 171*). The eating starts out schmancy, at the dressed-up hotel dining rooms near the Public Garden, and never quite descends to funky, though there are bargains to be found on the side streets. Most of Newbury Street's sidewalk cafés and restaurants are known more for high-visibility summertime patio dining than for anything revolutionary in the kitchen, but in the mix are a handful of stellar ethnic menus, especially at **Kashmir** (*see page 127*), **Tapéo** (*page 131*), and **Gyuhama** (*page 127*). Back Bay's very best restaurants are also some of the city's most expensive: pace-setter **Biba** (*below*), elegant **L'Espalier** (*page 127*), hot **Anago** (*below*), and stylish, exquisite **Café Louis** (*page 127*).

Also in the area

Davio's (*see page 151*); **Legal Sea Foods** (*see page 135*) *and* **Pho Pasteur** (*see page 129*); **29 Newbury** (*see page 117* **Pubs & Bars**).

Ambrosia on Huntington

116 Huntington Avenue, at Garrison Street (247 2400). Park St T. **Lunch served** 11am-2pm Mon-Fri. **Dinner served** 5.30-10pm Mon-Thur; 5.30-11pm Fri; 5-11pm Sat; 5-10pm Sun. **Main courses** $25. **Credit** AmEx, DC, MC, V. **Map 3 E6**

Chef Michael Ambrose won a recent edible-art competition by painting Gustav Klimt's *The Kiss* in miso and gold flake. Half chef, half sculptor, Ambrose turns out elaborate Asian-inflected fusion dishes in a stylish dining room presided over by a surreal, fairytale green pastry-oven.
Disabled: toilet.

Anago

Lenox Hotel, 65 Exeter Street, at Boylston Street (266 6222). Copley T. **Dinner served** 5.30-10pm Mon-Thur; 5.30-11pm Fri, Sat; 5.30-9pm Sun. **Main courses** $18-$33. **Credit** AmEx, Disc, MC, V. **Map 3 E5**

Bob Calderone and Susan Finegold's previous restaurant in Cambridge was a little place whose reputation outgrew its size. They closed it down not long ago and opened this tall, red-drenched dining room in the Lenox Hotel – a success from the start among the Back Bay set. The kitchen produces layered, globalised, classy bistro food: potato bisque is drizzled with bright green chive oil and served with a salmon cake; 'trio of carpaccio' is a lush plate of raw beef, tuna and scallop with a different topping for each. This is an unusually adept version of anything-goes Boston bistro cooking and one suspects that each of the dishes touches at least three food groups and two continents.
Disabled: toilet.

Angelo's Ristorante

575 Boylston Street, between Dartmouth & Clarendon Streets (536 4045). Copley T. **Lunch served** 10.30am-3.30pm, **dinner served** 5pm-midnight, Mon-Sat. **Main courses** $22-$30. **Credit** AmEx, DC, Disc, MC, V. **Map 3 E5**

Angelo Caruso's powerful, big-city Italian food always seemed out of place in the quirky strip-mall restaurant where he started out. Now, at this new place in the heart of Back Bay, it feels more at home. It's harder to enforce consistency in a bigger restaurant, but when he's on he's on: the bow-tied waiters deliver an amazing salad of roast portobello mushrooms and shaved Parmesan; perfectly *al dente* pasta; or a buttery-rich lobster bisque with a whole rock lobster in the bowl. There's outdoor seating in warm weather.
Disabled: toilet.

Armani Café

214 Newbury Street, between Exeter & Dartmouth Streets (437 0909). Copley T. **Open** 11.30am-midnight Mon-Wed, Sun; 11.30am-1am Thur-Sat. **Main courses** $15-$20. **Credit** AmEx, DC, Disc, MC, V. **Map 3 E/F 5**

Dense, salty risotto; clinking Martini glasses; waiters in black, black, black: Giorgio Armani's restaurant doesn't sell clothes – the boutique is next door – but it does sell attitude by the tableful. It's where to go when you want to feel rich and European and 20 years old, and where rich European 20-year-olds go to feel at home. The city's recent restaurant smoking ban (*see p116*) means an unusually large cluster of people around the bar here. Outdoor seating in warm weather.
Disabled: toilet.

Biba

272 Boylston Street, at Arlington Street (426 7878). Arlington T. **Lunch served** 11.30am-2.30pm Mon-Fri; 11.30am-3pm Sat. **Dinner served** 5.30-10pm Mon-Thur, Sun; 5.30-11pm Fri, Sat. **Main courses** $20-$39. **Credit** AmEx, MC, V. **Map 3 F5**

Stylish, pricy and still playful after a decade in business, this is one of the cornerstones of the city's growing culinary reputation. A well-heeled clientele soaks up a beautiful view of the Public Garden and orders from a menu divided humorously into categories such as 'legumina', 'offal' and 'starch'. Chefs Lydia Shire and Susan Regis pull off neat tricks with quirky ingredients such as skate wing, garlic shoots and oxtail, still setting the standard for creative, eclectic cooking in Boston.
Disabled: toilet.

Brasserie Jo

Colonnade Hotel, 120 Huntington Avenue, at Massachusetts Avenue (425 3240). Prudential T. **Open** 6.30am-1am Mon-Fri; 7am-1am Sat, Sun. **Main courses** $6-$25. **Credit** AmEx, DC, Disc, MC, V. **Map 3 E6**

The Boston sequel to a successful Chicago restaurant, Brasserie Jo is big, busy and French in a way you don't necessarily expect in an American city: in addition to quirky specialities such as shrimp in a pastry bag, the menu includes kidney, omelettes and blood sausage. Desserts are to die for. For the Colonnade Hotel *see p107* **Accommodation**.

Café Louis

234 Berkeley Street, between Newbury & Boylston Streets (266 4680). Arlington T. **Open** 11.30am-10pm Mon-Sat. **Main courses** $20. **Credit** AmEx, MC, V. **Map 3 F5**

There is something exquisite and un-Bostonian about this tiny restaurant, built into the back of the imposing men's clothing store **Louis** (*see p163* **Shops & Services**). The spare, steel-and-green interior is straight out of a European design magazine and the food comes from Rhode Island – more specifically, from the legendary Providence restaurant Al Forno, whose chefs George Germon and Johanne Killeen act as executive chefs here. The menu is a remarkable trip through New Italian cooking: the antipasto Louis contains pretty dollops of white bean paste, stewed red onion and a tiny quiche over translucently thin slices of prosciutto; pastas are intense without being oversauced; the wood-grilled pizza tastes smoky and fresh all at once.

Disabled: toilet.

Capital Grille

359 Newbury Street, at Hereford Street (262 8900). Hynes/ICA T. **Lunch served** *Nov, Dec* noon-2pm daily. **Dinner served** 5-10pm Mon-Thur, Sun; 5-11pm Fri, Sat. **Main courses** $20-$30. **Credit** AmEx, DC, Disc, MC, V. **Map 3 E5**

There's a carpenter in Vermont who makes a living simply by providing these restaurants with their wood panelling. You can imagine the rest: giant Martinis in the bar; porterhouse steaks dry-aging in a meat locker; a list of major-league and expensive red wines. In classic steakhouse fashion, you order vegetables separately, if at all.

Disabled: toilet.

Branch: 250 Boylston Street, Newton (928 1400).

Clío

Eliot Hotel, 370 Commonwealth Avenue, at Massachusetts Avenue (536 7200). Hynes/ICA T. **Dinner served** 5.30-10pm Mon-Thur, Sun; 5.30-10.30pm Fri, Sat. **Main courses** $25-$34. **Credit** AmEx, MC, V. **Map 3 E5**

Chef Ken Oringer's cooking is a nose-thumbing to the profuse and ingredient-intensive cuisine that earned Boston its spot on the gastronomic map. It's also very, very good. His focused flavours and small, sculptural presentations wouldn't be out of place in New York: a dramatically spare plate of foie gras; steak seared with spices and served over a little vegetable ragoût; two perfect scallops on two pedestals of salt. The dining room is quiet and attracts an older crowd than the trendy Newbury Street spots nearby. For the Eliot Hotel, *see p103* **Accommodation**.

Disabled: toilet.

Cottonwood Café

222 Berkeley Street, at St James's Street (247 2225). Arlington or Copley T. **Open** 4-9.30pm Mon; 4-11pm Tue-Thur; 4pm-midnight Fri; 3pm-midnight Sat; 3-9.30pm Sun. **Main courses** $14-$29. **Credit** AmEx, DC, Disc, MC, V. **Map 3 F5**

This groovy Nu-Mex standby still turns out capable, fun dishes in a trendy space that resembles an updated Margarita bar. Sunday brunch is excellent and inexpensive.

Disabled: toilet.

Branch: 1815 Massachusetts Avenue, Cambridge (661 7440).

L'Espalier

30 Gloucester Street, at Newbury Street (263 3023). Hynes/ICA T. **Dinner served** 6-10pm Mon-Sat. **Set menus** $65, $82. **Credit** AmEx, DC, Disc, MC, V. **Map 3 E5**

Chef-owner Frank McClelland serves toweringly exquisite food at towering prices in a Back Bay brownstone. Known for its intimacy, hyperattentive service and an unequalled seven-course *prix fixe* meal, L'Espalier is the location of up to three marriage proposals a night and is not quite matched by anything else in the city.

Grill 23 & Bar

161 Berkeley Street, at Stuart Street (542 2255). Arlington T. **Open** 5.30-10.30pm Mon-Thur; 5.30-11pm Fri, Sat; 5.30-10pm Sun. **Main courses** $25-$29. **Credit** AmEx, MC, V. **Map 3 F5**

A power-suited crowd eats steak and swordfish surrounded by wood panelling, marble pillars and clinking Martini glasses. You get the picture.

Disabled: toilet.

Gyuhama

827 Boylston Street, at the Prudential Center (437 0188). Copley T. **Lunch served** 12.30-2.30pm, **dinner served** 5.30pm-1.30am, daily. **Main courses** $15-$20. **Credit** AmEx, MC, V. **Map 3 E6**

One of the two best sushi restaurants in the city (the other is **Ginza**, *p129*, with branches in Brookline and Chinatown). There's a full menu of Japanese items such as tempura and udon, and even a hamburger. But the sushi – generous and glossy-fresh – is the real attraction here. Décor is nicer (and quieter) than the garish green sign outside would indicate. There's usually a queue at night, especially at the weekend, but a party of two can often sneak into a spot at the sushi bar.

Kashmir

279 Newbury Street, at Gloucester Street (536 1695). Hynes/ICA T. **Open** 11.30am-11.30pm Mon-Fri; 11.30am-midnight Sat, Sun. **Main courses** $12.95-$18.95. **Credit** AmEx, MC, V. **Map 3 E5**

Sonsie *(p131): for the scene, not the food.*

Eating in Chinatown

Food is cheap in Chinatown's snarl of streets and tends toward traditional Hong Kong seafood and Mandarin sauces; though Asian inflections are showing up on menus across town, the arrival of New Anything hasn't been felt here. Nonetheless, you can eat well if you know where to look. At one end of Chinatown, the city's ebbing red-light district, the Combat Zone, has been colonised by super-cheap Vietnamese soup shops and the island-themed Malaysian restaurant **Penang** (*see below*); at the other end, not far from Chinatown's Beach Street gate, two fine and different places gaze across at each other: **Ginza** (*below*), a sushi wonderland where Japanese businessmen give way to a late-night crowd of clubbers; and **New Shanghai** (*below*), with its precise traditional Chinese cuisine. In-between are too many noodle houses, seafood joints and walk-up cafeterias for us to list here.

Buddha's Delight

5 Beach Street, at Washington Street (451 2395). Chinatown T. **Open** 11am-10pm Mon-Thur, Sun; 11am-11pm Fri, Sat. **Main courses** $5.50-$8. **No credit cards. Map 5 G5**

One of the city's few vegan restaurants, this serves very good Vietnamese and Chinese food (complete with imitation chicken, shrimp and pork) in a standard Chinatown setting of linoleum and mirrors.

Chau Chow

52 Beach Street, at Washington Street (426 6266). Chinatown T. **Lunch served** 10am-2pm Mon-Thur, Sun; 10am-4pm Fri, Sat. **Main courses** $10. **No credit cards. Map 5 G5**

The Luu family keeps upping the ante on excellent, low-cost cooking. The original Chau Chow is small and busy, with red vinyl booths and tables you might be forced to share; its 'Grand' brother across the street is handsome, with mirrored walls and tanks of fresh fish; and nearby Chau Chow City is a three-storey palace of neon and etched-glass dragons open until 4am. All serve a knock-out salt-and-pepper squid and a full menu of zingy Southeast Asian-influenced Chinese food.

Branches: **Grand Chau Chow** 45 Beach Street (292 5166); **Chau Chow City** 83 Essex Street (338 8158).

Ginza

16 Hudson Street, at Beach Street (338 2261). Chinatown T. **Lunch served** 11.30am-2.30pm daily. **Dinner served** 5pm-2am Mon, Sun; 5pm-4am Tue-Sat. **Main courses** $14. **Credit** AmEx, DC, Disc, MC, V. **Map 5 G5**

A fish-lover's temple. From the genteel sushi chefs of these modest, spare Japanese restaurants come the most radical sushi combinations in the city, with names such as 'B-52 maki' and 'caterpillar maki' (the latter named after its appearance, not ingredients). The straightforward nigiri is excellent, too, and the bar stocks 20 brands of sake. This branch is one of the city's prime late-night destinations.

Branch: 1002 Beacon Street, Brookline (566 9688).

New Shanghai Restaurant

21 Hudson Street, at Kneeland Street (338 6688). Downtown Crossing or South Station T. **Open** 11am-10pm Mon-Thur, Sun; 11am-11pm Sat, Sun. **Main courses** $8-$10. **Credit** AmEx, Disc, V. **Map 5 G5**

CK Sau is the only chef in Chinatown with any name recognition: even the *New York Times* has got wind of his elegant work with seafood and the formal cuisine of Shanghai. One of the better-looking and dressier restaurants in Chinatown.

Disabled: toilet.

Pearl Dynasty

25 Tyler Street, at Kneeland Street (422 0664). Chinatown T. **Open** 11am-midnight daily. **Main courses** $6-$8. **Credit** Disc, MC, V. **Map 5 G5**

Pearl serves up a sharp blend of Malaysian and Chinese cooking in an unassuming walk-up space.

Penang

685-681 Washington Street, at Kneeland Street (451 6372). Chinatown T. **Open** 11.30am-11.30pm Mon-Thur, Sun; 11.30am-midnight Fri, Sat. **Main courses** $10-$20. **Credit** MC, V. **Map 5 G5**

This branch of a New York Malaysian restaurant is island- themed, dressed mostly in bamboo and netting. Like all Boston's Malaysian restaurants, it leans towards the Chinese rather than the Indian side of Malaysian cookery, producing food that's more sharp than hot. The menu gets as familiar as pancakes with curry dip and as exotic as various treatments of fish heads. Desserts are very strange, but don't let that put you off.

Pho Bolsa Restaurant

1 Stuart Street, at Washington Street (695 1843). Chinatown T. **Open** 10.30am-11pm daily. **Main courses** $6.85-$7.50. **Credit** MC, V. **Map 5 G5**

This corner shop sells pho, the fragrant Vietnamese beef broth, along with a huge number of Chinese and Thai dishes. The menu does a spirited job of explaining the myriad variations of pho. An uncharitable Western critic might call the décor achingly tacky, but it's no worse than the rest of Chinatown's pho shops.

Pho Pasteur

8 Kneeland Street, at Washington Street (451 0247). Chinatown T. **Open** 8am-9pm daily. **Main courses** $5-$10. **No credit cards. Map 5 G5**

Vietnamese food is to Boston what Mexican food is to Los Angeles and curry is to London: the best value in high-flavour ethnic cooking. Duyen Le has almost single-handedly brought Vietnamese cooking out of Chinatown with his formula of fresh ingredients, spot-on cooking and low prices. The branches have become fancier as they've moved into high-rent districts such as Harvard Square and Newbury Street, but the quality has stayed constant and no dish is even remotely expensive. The enormous menu includes huge bowls of elegant beef soup, excellent spring rolls and sharp-tasting plates of grilled pork, beef and shrimp.

Branches: 119 Newbury Street (262 8200); 682 Washington Street (482 7467); 35 Dunster Street, Cambridge (864 4100); 137 Brighton Avenue, Allston (783 2340).

This below-street-level spot is probably the best Indian restaurant in the city – not quantum distances beyond the competition, but still the most handsome with the finest food. Curries are delicate, balanced and energetic; specials such as tandoori rack of lamb are presented with all the flair of a good French dish.

Mucho Gusto

1124 Boylston Street, at Massachusetts Avenue (236 1020). Hynes/ICA T. **Open** 5-10pm Wed; 5-11pm Thur; noon-11pm Fri, Sat; noon-10pm Sun. **Main courses** $12-$15. **Credit** MC, V. **Map 3 E5**

There are restaurants and then there are crazy little outposts of aesthetic. This Cuban storefront just outside Back Bay is decorated entirely with 1950s American kitsch, all for sale. It fills up at night with locals, students, musicians and arty types who sit at 1950s kitchen tables, drink sangria, eat fried plantains, chicken dumplings and Cuban sandwiches, and trade pleasantries with the effusive owner, Oz Mondejar. Opening hours vary seasonally, so phone to check.
Disabled: toilet.

Sonsie

327 Newbury Street, between Hereford Street & Massachusetts Avenue (351 2500). Hynes/ICA T. **Breakfast/lunch served** 7am-2.30pm, **dinner served** 6-11.30pm, daily. **Brunch served** 11.30am-3pm Sat, Sun. **Main courses** $13-$27. **Credit** AmEx, DC, MC, V. **Map 3 E5**

Restaurants this successful eventually become a kind of cliché, and at this point it's hard to tell if Sonsie still draws the city's nightlife mavens or just those who want to be near them. People come for that scene more than for the food, though the latter is capable enough – there's an eclectic menu of gourmet pizzas, Northern Italian pasta dishes and the like. The front of the restaurant is a café where tables face the windows, so everyone can keep an eye on who's promenading along this stretch of chic Newbury Street. In warm weather, the windows louvre sideways to create a cappuccino- (or Martini-) sipping spot that's partly indoors, partly out. *See also p117* **Pubs & Bars**.
Disabled: toilet.

Tapéo

266 Newbury Street, between Gloucester & Fairfield Streets (267 4799). Copley or Hynes/ICA T. **Dinner served** 5.30-10.30pm Mon-Wed, Sun; 5.30-11.30pm Thur-Sat. **Main courses** $19; *tapas* $5.40-$7.50. **Credit** AmEx, DC, MC, V. **Map 3 E5**

Tapéo – run by the same family as Somerville's wonderful **Dalí**, *p154* – is *the* place to go for tapas in Boston. Downstairs is a kitschy-fun Spanish sherry bar. Upstairs is a more spacious dining room with witty décor. The menu is consistently excellent, especially if you like garlic; tapas are as simple as marinated olives and as outré as an $18 plate of baby eels. You don't really need to order entrées, though there's a spectacularly presented fish baked in salt. The list of Spanish wines is extensive and very nicely presented. The place is often crowded, so arrive early or book a table.
Disabled: toilet.

Travis Restaurant

135 Newbury Street, between Dartmouth & Clarendon Streets (267 6388). Copley T. **Open** 7am-4.30pm daily. **Main courses** *sandwiches* $4.50. **No credit cards**. **Map 3 F5**

A lunch counter that has managed to survive from the days before Newbury Street was a synonym for chi-chi. The walls are given over to paper memorabilia, but the real memento is the Travis itself, which serves grilled cheese sandwiches and lime rickeys without seeming self-conscious or retro.

Beacon Hill

Also in the area

Figs *(see below)*.

Artu

89 Charles Street, at Pinckney Street (227 9023). Charles/MGH or Park St T. **Open** 11.30am-10pm Mon-Thur, Sun; 11am-11pm Sat, Sun. **Main courses** $7.95-$11.95. **Credit** AmEx, MC, V. **Map 5 F4**

Peer through the street-level windows of this little Beacon Hill trattoria and you'll see platters of marinated mushrooms, grilled red pepper and mozzarella cheese. A leg of lamb, studded with garlic, turns on a spit. Walk down the stairs and you'll be served the best lamb sandwich in the city, along with some very good versions of other Italian standards and an excellent home-made tiramisu.
Branch: 6 Prince Street (742 4336).

Hungry I

71 Charles Street, at Mt Vernon Street (227 3524). Charles/MGH T. **Brunch Served** 11am-2pm Sun. **Dinner served** 6-9pm Mon-Thur, Sun; 6-10pm Fri, Sat. **Main courses** $22-$32. **Credit** AmEx, MC, V. **Map 5 F4**

It's easy to hit your head ducking into the little alley that leads to the door of this quirkily intimate restaurant on Charles Street. The colonial layout is all nooks, wood, brick, and candlelight. Indeed, the Hungry I trades more on romance than on its menu, which is continental and competent, if not surprising.

Istanbul Café

37 Bowdoin Street, at Beacon Street (227 3434). Gov't Center or Park St T. **Open** 11am-10pm Mon-Wed; 11am-11pm Thur-Sat; noon-10pm Sun. **Main courses** $11.50. **Credit** MC, V. **Map 5 G4**

There isn't much Turkish food in Boston, but even without competition this basement café behind the State House does a nice job with Turkish favourites such as börek, houmous and a fine kebab plate: shawarma-style meat layered with tomato sauce and yoghurt over toasted cubes of bread. Turkish posters adorn the walls; Efes beer comes in bottles.

The King & I

145 Charles Street, at Cambridge Street (227 3320). Charles/MGH T. **Open** 11.30am-9.45pm Mon-Thur, Sun; 11.30am-10.45pm Fri, Sat. **Main courses** $7.95-$9.95. **Credit** Disc, MC, V. **Map 5 F4**

Among the sharper Thai restaurants in the city, the King & I is located in a pleasant room on picturesque Charles Street.

Lala Rokh

97 Mount Vernon Street, at Charles Street (720 5511). Charles/MGH or Arlington T. **Dinner served** 5.30-10pm daily. **Main courses** $14-$18. **Credit** AmEx, DC, MC, V. **Map 5 F4**

A remarkable warren of rooms on a Beacon Hill sidestreet, serving pretty, piquant food from the Persian recipes of the owner's mother, who also mails packets of hard-to-find spices over from the Middle East. Dishes feature unusual ingredients such as pomegranate juice and sturgeon; service is helpful and the experience is one of the most unique and romantic in the city.

Charlestown

Figs

67 Main Street, at Monument Avenue (242 2229). Community College T. **Open** 5.30-10pm Mon-Thur; 5.30-10.30pm Fri, Sat; 5.30-9pm Sun. **Main courses** $10-$18. **Credit** AmEx, DC, MC, V.

Coffee connections

Though Bostonians aren't quite as obsessed with coffee as Seattlites, in the 1980s the city had its own, perhaps more sophisticated, version of the upmarket coffee chain Starbucks. Simply known as the **Coffee Connection**, the company sold its specially roasted products at several branches in the Boston and Cambridge area, introducing Bostonians to the wonders of the French press, steamed milk and high-priced, custom-ground beans from around the world. At the height of its success, the Coffee Connection was even supplying its quality joe to local branches of the *faux* French national café chain **Au Bon Pain**. So Boston, having already made the adjustment from the 35¢ cup of coffee to the $2.50 cappuccino grande, was well primed for the great **Starbucks** invasion of the 1990s.

Rather than competing with Coffee Connection, Starbucks wisely bought the company. And to this day you'll find local coffee connoisseurs sore about Starbucks' departure from their original intention to leave Coffee Connection locations alone – particularly the branch in Harvard Square. Instead, they were all transformed into Starbucks, the wide variety of roasts that the Coffee Connection once offered replaced by Starbucks' uniformly dark beans and more bitter brews and the Big Green Machine rapidly took over the city.

You can still find pre-packaged Coffee Connection coffee in some local supermarkets. But anyone who remembers the chain will tell you that it's just not the same. Meanwhile, Starbucks has opened dozens of branches and remains virtually unchallenged, a fact that has put the continued existence of independently-owned coffee houses in jeopardy. One can still get a passable cup of joe at Au Bon Pain; and some swear by the lower-brow pleasures of the coffee served at branches of **Dunkin' Donuts**. But by and large Boston has become a Starbucks town.

In addition to the cafés featured elsewhere in this chapter – most of which offer something more than just a cup of coffee and a pastry – here's a brief list of locations where you can get your daily caffeine fix and perhaps a slice of cake or a sandwich to go with it.

Chains

Au Bon Pain

There are 30 branches in the Boston area; phone 742 8452 for the location of your nearest.

Dunkin' Donuts

There are 56 branches in the Boston area; phone 523 1451 for the location of your nearest.

After Todd English moved his influential bistro **Olives** (*below*) into its current digs in City Square, he opened an upmarket pizzeria in its tiny original space, making connoisseurs of clam-and-oregano pizza very happy. Recent expansions mean he's making them happy in Beacon Hill and Newton. Expect to wait for a table.
Disabled: toilet.
Branches: 42 Charles Street (742 3447); 1208 Boylston Street, Newton (738 9992).

Olives

10 City Square, at Main Street (242 1999). North Station T. **Dinner served** 5.30-10.15pm Mon-Fri; 5-10.15pm Sat. **Main courses** $19-$35. **Credit** AmEx, MC, V.
Todd English has influenced Boston cooking like nobody since culinary *grande dame* Julia Child. His totally unrestrained and powerfully flavoured approach to Italian ingredients and sauces, his layers of taste on taste, create a kind of magic that has kept the house full every night for years and inspired all kinds of imitators. No reservations are taken for parties smaller than six; the insider move is to show up the minute the restaurant opens, put your name on the list and find something else to do for a couple of hours. English's empire is big now – a chain of **Figs** pizzerias (*above*); an Olives in Las Vegas – and his divided attention takes its toll here and there. Still, there's nothing quite like it.
Disabled: toilet.

Downtown

Also in the area

Bertucci's *(see page 148).*

Aujourd'hui

Four Seasons Hotel, 200 Boylston Street, at Arlington Street (351 2071). Arlington T. **Breakfast served** 6.30am-11am Mon-Fri. **Lunch served** 11.30am-2pm Mon-Fri, Sun. **Dinner served** 5.30-10pm Mon-Sat. **Main courses** *lunch* $23, *dinner* $32-$45. **Credit** AmEx, DC, Disc, MC, V. **Map 5 F5**
Along with **L'Espalier** (*see p127*), this represents the teetery-top end of starched-cloth swellegance and updated haute cuisine. Some find the food to be perfection itself; others would like a little more verve in $35 entrées, but very few ever fault the service. For the Four Seasons Hotel *see p103* **Accommodation**; *see also below* **Bristol Lounge**.
Disabled: toilet.

The Barking Crab

88 Sleeper Street, at Northern Avenue (426 2722). South Station T. **Open** 7.30am-10pm Mon-Fri; 11.30am-10pm Sat, Sun. **Main courses** $8.95-$14.95. **Credit** AmEx, DC, MC, V. **Map 3 H5**
Without being outright wacky, the Barking Crab is very much its own kind of fun. Especially in the summertime, when this is an outdoor lobster tent providing bench seating, beer in plastic cups, lobster in a paper basket and

Starbucks
There are 30 branches in the Boston area; phone 720 6340 for the location of your nearest.

Independents

Beacon Hill

Curious Liquids
22B Beacon Street (720 2836). Park St T. **Open** 7am-2am daily. **No credit cards. Map 5 G4**

Panificio
144 Charles Street, at Revere Street (227 4340). Charles/MGH T. **Open** 7am-9pm Mon-Fri; 8am-7pm Sat, Sun. **No credit cards. Map 5 F4**

North End

Caffe Graffiti
307 Hanover Street, between Parmenter & Prince Streets (367 2494). North Station T. **Open** 6am-midnight daily. **No credit cards. Map 5 G/H 3/4**

Caffe Paradiso
255 Hanover Street, between Parmenter & Prince Streets (742 1768). North Station T. **Open** 8am-midnight Mon-Fri; 8am-12.30am Sat, Sun. **No credit cards. Map 5 G/H 3/4**

Caffe Vittoria
296 Hanover Street, between Parmenter & Prince Streets (227 7606). North Station T. **Open** 6.30am-2am daily. **No credit cards. Map 5 G/H 3/4**

Back Bay & the South End

Hazel's Cup and Saucer
130 Dartmouth Street (262 4393). Back Bay T. **Open** 7am-11pm Mon-Fri; 8am-11pm Sat, Sun. **Credit** AmEx, MC, V. **Map 5 F5**

Mildred's
552 Tremont Street, at Waltham Street (426 0008). Back Bay T. **Open** 7am-11pm Mon-Fri; 8am-11pm Sat, Sun. **Credit** AmEx, MC, V. **Map 5 F6**

Other Side Cosmic Café
407 Newbury Street, at Massachusetts Avenue (536 9477). Hynes/ICA T. **Open** 10am-midnight Mon-Wed; 10am-1am Thur-Sat; noon-midnight Sun. **No credit cards. Map 4 E5**
(*See also p116* **Pubs & Bars**.)

Fenway

Designs for Living
52 Queensbury Street, at Jersey Street (536 6150). Kenmore T. **Open** 7am-9pm Mon-Fri; 8am-9pm Sat; 9am-9pm Sun. **Credit** Disc, MC, V. **Map 3 D6**

Cambridge

Algiers Coffee House
40 Brattle Street, at Harvard Square, Cambridge (492 1557). Harvard T. **Open** 8am-midnight daily. **Credit** AmEx, MC, V. **Map 4 B2**

1369 Coffee House
1369 Cambridge Street, at Hampshire Street, Cambridge (576 1369). Central T. **Open** 7am-10pm Mon-Thur; 7am-11pm Fri; 8am-11pm Sat; 8am-8pm Sun. **No credit cards. Map 4 D2**
Branch: 757 Massachusetts Avenue (576 4600).

steamer clams in a bucket. In winter, the food moves indoors to a marine-themed room with a fireplace. Either way, it's a quintessential New England road-trip experience in the middle of the city, with an unparalleled view of Downtown.
Disabled: toilet.

Blue Diner
150 Kneeland Street, at South Street (695 0087). South Station T. **Open** 24-hours daily. **Main courses** $6. **Credit** AmEx, Disc, DC, MC, V. **Map 5 G5**
This hasn't been a diner for years, not since it moved out of the dining-car space it once occupied on the next corner. It's not even very blue, either. But where else can you get a big barbecue meal at 3am? The food is updated American roadhouse cooking, not quite plain-folks but close enough to make the name work.
Disabled: toilet.

Bristol Lounge
Four Seasons Hotel, 200 Boylston Street, at Arlington Street (351 2071). Arlington T. **Open** 11am-11.30pm Mon-Thur; 5-11pm Fri, Sat; noon-11.30pm Sun. **Main courses** $14-$35. **Credit** AmEx, DC, Disc, MC, V. **Map 5 F5**
The hamburger that keeps being voted the best in Boston is almost worth the $14 price tag here: perfectly grilled, served with amazing fries and a ducky view of the Public Garden as a bonus. The rest of the upmarket 'home cooking' is good, especially if you're amused by the idea of eating fried chicken and meatloaf among Ming vases and Martini-drinking powerbrokers. *See also p103* **Accommodation**, *p117* **Pubs & Bars** *and page 132* **Aujourd'hui**.
Disabled: toilet.

Café Fleuri & Julien
Le Méridien, 250 Franklin Street, near Post Office Square (451 1900/1-800 543 4300). State/Citizen's Bank T. **Open** *Café Fleuri* 7am-10pm daily; *Julien* noon-2pm, 6-10pm, Mon-Fri; 6-10pm Sat. **Main courses** *Café Fleuri* $10-$18; *Julien* $22-34. **Credit** AmEx, DC, Disc, JCB, MC, $TC, V. **Map 5 G4**
Famous for the most extensive (and expensive) Sunday brunch menu in the city, the first floor Café Fleuri, in the atrium of the Le Méridian hotel, feels not unlike an office building, with white walls, pink marble and a vast paned skylight. The rest of the week, sandwiches and New American entrées offer a slightly less expensive alternative to the hotel's elegant main dining room, **Julien** – which may be the city's grandest restaurant and produces an expensive but noteworthy menu of consistently excellent continental dishes. For **Le Méridien**, *see p108* **Accommodation**.

Durgin-Park
30 North Market Street, between Clinton & Congress Streets (227 2038). Gov't Center T. **Open** 11.30am-10pm Mon-Thur; 11.30am-10.30pm Fri, Sat; 11.30am-9pm Sun. **Main courses** $16. **Credit** AmEx, MC, V. **Map 5 G4**
Durgin-Park is famous for two reasons. Firstly, because no other restaurant still specialises in traditional Yankee dishes such as scrod, pot roast, baked beans and Indian pudding.

VISIT
Cheers®
® & © 1998 Par. Pic.
The Inspiration For The Setting Of The TV Series

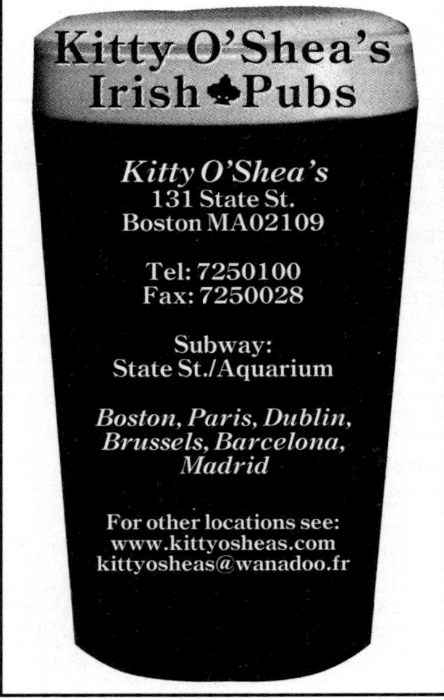
Kitty O'Shea's
Irish Pubs
Kitty O'Shea's
131 State St.
Boston MA02109
Tel: 7250100
Fax: 7250028
Subway:
State St./Aquarium
Boston, Paris, Dublin, Brussels, Barcelona, Madrid
For other locations see:
www.kittyosheas.com
kittyosheas@wanadoo.fr

Secondly, because the service is a bit like Boston traffic: appalling and fearsome, but somehow all part of the fun. The communal long-table seating, bullying waitresses and slam-your-food-down service have become a kind of gimmick, amusing most visitors and upsetting the occasional tourist who expects that a 150-year-old restaurant will be run as a kind of Disney exhibit. For everyone else, the only real disappointment is how little traditional Yankee cooking has improved in the last 150 years.

Galleria Italiana

177 Tremont Street, at Boylston Street (423 2092). Boylston T. **Breakfast/lunch served** 7am-2.30pm Mon-Fri. **Dinner served** 5.30-10.30pm Tue-Sat. **Main courses** $20. **Credit** AmEx, DC, Disc, MC, V. **Map 5 G5**

The Galleria owners come from Abruzzi, but their menus roam the Italian countryside, delivering smart, fresh renditions of regional cooking styles. The restaurant is hidden in a building just outside the Theater District; it's a testament to the cooking that so many people find it night after night.
Disabled: toilet.

Maison Robert

Old City Hall, 45 School Street, between Tremont & Washington Streets (227 3370). Gov't Center or State/ Citizen's Bank T. **Lunch served** 11.30am-2.30pm Mon-Fri. **Dinner served** 5.30-10pm Mon-Sat. **Main courses** $18-$24. **Credit** AmEx, DC, MC, V. **Map 5 G4**

This stalwart of haute-cuisine Boston is now on its second generation of French Robert family. The food recently went through a period of almost-fusion and now seems to have settled back into a classic style.

No-Name

17 Fish Pier, off Northern Avenue (338 7539). South Station T. **Open** 11am-10pm Mon-Sat; 11am-9pm Sun. **Main courses** $10. **No credit cards. Map 3 J5**

A big, crazy waterfront joint serving basic Greek-style seafood (grilled, with oil and lemon) and beer in plastic cups. It's fun and not terribly expensive, though the quality that once made this place special has long since been surpassed by **Legal Sea Foods** (*below*) among others.
Disabled: toilet.

No.9 Park

9 Park Street, at Beacon Street (742 9991). Park St T. **Lunch served** 11.30am-2.30pm, **dinner served** 5.30-10pm, Mon-Sat. **Main courses** $15-$35. **Credit** AmEx, DC, Disc, MC, V. **Map 5 G4**

This spare and pretty restaurant, chef/owner Barbara Lynch's first solo effort, is the city's inventive-bistro-of-the-moment; the walls are clean and moss-coloured, but plates are crowded with fancy things such as lobster vol-au-vents and pheasant served with chanterelle flan.
Disabled: toilet.

South Street Diner

178 Kneeland Street, at South Street (350 0028). South Station T. **Open** 24 hours daily. **Main courses** $5-$6. **Credit** AmEx, Disc, DC, MC, V. **Map 5 G5**

If you sat in a booth here for 24 hours, you'd see the whole city go by in shifts: cops and construction workers early in the morning, Downtown types at lunch and club kids after hours. The food is the usual diner stuff with a home-made twist (omelettes, French toast, big, ragged hamburgers) and the singular building, tiled in blue, dates from the 1920s.

The Vault

105 Water Street (292 9966). State/Citizen's Bank T. **Open** 11.30am-10.30pm Mon-Wed; 5-11pm Thur, Fri. **Main courses** $17-$28. **Credit** AmEx, DC, Disc, MC, V. **Map 5 G4**

Chef Rebecca Esty does a knockout job walking the line between tradition (oyster stew with huge buttermilk crackers) and novelty (melon soup with crème fraîche). It's appropriate in this flatiron-shaped space, which updates the grand, oaky, linen-tablecloth feel of a Financial District restaurant through contemporary fittings and a groovy little corkscrew logo on the menus, doors and curtain pulls. One of the co-owners is the proprietor of a Back Bay wine shop, so the wine list is wide-ranging and interesting, including a number of pre-selected 'tasting flights'.

Ye Olde Union Oyster House

41 Union Street, at Faneuil Hall (227 2750). Gov't Center or Haymarket T. **Open** 11am-9.30pm Mon-Thur; 11am-10pm Fri, Sat. **Main courses** $15-$18. **Credit** AmEx, DC, Disc, MC, V. **Map 5 G4**

A recent survey by the *Boston Globe* found that this 170-year-old seafood restaurant is where most hotel concierges send tourists for a Real Boston Experience. It's debatable whether baked scrod is a contemporary experience or not, but the semi-circular oyster bar, whitewashed booths and open lobster pound here fit undeniably well with the traditional tourist view of the city as a slice of living American history.
Disabled: toilet.

Les Zygomates

129 South Street, at Kneeland Street (542 5108). South Station T. **Lunch served** 11.30am-2pm Mon-Fri. **Dinner served** 6-10.30pm Mon-Thur; 6-11.30pm Fri, Sat. **Main courses** $13-$28. **Credit** AmEx, DC, Disc, MC, V. **Map 5 G5**

This Francophile bistro, complete with tile floor and zinc bar, has two owners: one, a Parisian-trained American cook who turns out straightforward versions of French classics such as rabbit pâté, venison and sweetbread vol-au-vents; the other, a European oenophile who keeps the wine list stocked with new names and unusual varietals and hosts weekly wine tastings on Tuesdays. Wine is available by the 'taste' (two ounces) as well as by the glass and by the bottle, so a good bet is to sit at the bar, order a few appetisers and taste your way down the list.

Theater District

Also in the area

Jae's Cafe and Grill (*see page 141*).

Legal Sea Foods

Park Square, between Columbus Avenue & Stuart Street (426 4444). Park St T. **Open** 11.30am-10pm Mon-Thur; 11.30am-10.30pm Fri, Sat; 11.30am-9pm Sun. **Main courses** $13.95-$34.95 **Credit** AmEx, DC, Disc, MC, V. **Map 5 F5**

Legal is that rare thing, a tourist magnet that hasn't lost credibility with locals. This huge and thronged restaurant has enjoyed years of success by following a simple rule: start with something fresh out of the ocean and don't screw it up. Decorating the place like the bar in *Cheers* and opening a branch in every upmarket mall doesn't seem to have hurt it, either. The Legal C Bar, near the giant Columbus Street restaurant beneath the Park Plaza Hotel, trades the typical Legal brass-and-oak for a more festive décor and a Caribbean-themed menu focusing on grilling and smoking.
Disabled: toilet.

Branches: Prudential Center, 800 Boylston Street (266 6800); Copley Place, 100 Huntington Avenue (266 7775); 5 Cambridge Center, Kendall Square, Cambridge (864 3400); Chestnut Hill Shopping Center, 43 Boylston Street, Newton (277 7300);
Legal C Bar 27 Columbus Avenue, at Arlington Street (426 5566).

Pignoli

79 Park Plaza, at Arlington Street (338 7500). Arlington T. **Lunch served** 11.30am-2.30pm daily. **Dinner served** 5.30-10pm Mon-Thur, Sun; 5.30pm-midnight Fri, Sat. **Main courses** $20. **Credit** AmEx, DC, Disc, MC, V. **Map 5 F5**

The owners of nearby **Biba** (*p126*) opened this as a less expensive, more Italian version of their creative vision. The room is a cool, high-ceilinged space with Zeppelin-like light fixtures (the smart money says they're giant pignoli nuts). The food uses Italian country cooking as a jumping-off point for a pretty style that's not quite as zany as Biba's.

Fenway

Audubon Circle

838 Beacon Street, at Park Drive (421 1910). Kenmore T. **Open** 11.30am-1am daily (food served until 11pm). **Main courses** $12. **Credit** AmEx, DC, Disc, MC, V.

The only outdoor sign for this sleek, modern bar is a cryptic circle and a dot, and the interior is just as understated. The food is a complete miracle for the price: an excellent pressed turkey and bacon sandwich; white bean paste with grilled bread; a thick pork chop with garlic butter and grits. Everything works, and nothing's expensive. The low-profile approach meant business was originally slow to build, and now everyone packing the bar on Friday night thinks it's his or her little discovery. Audubon Circle is within walking distance of Fenway Park, but miles away from the beer-soaked baseball crowd in mood. *See also p115* **Pubs & Bars**.

Disabled: toilet.

Brown Sugar

129 Jersey Street, at Boylston Street (266 2928). Kenmore T. **Open** 11am-10pm Mon-Thur; 11am-11pm Fri, Sat. **Main courses** $9. **Credit** MC, V. **Map 3 D6**

The best Thai food in town is served in this pretty-but-casual room in the quiet West Fens, just across the park from the Museum of Fine Arts. Appetisers are particularly vivid and sharp and the Thai iced coffee and tea are absolutely standard-setting. The small amount of free parking is a real bonus in a small neighbourhood of residents-only spaces.

Disabled: toilet.

Elephant Walk

900 Beacon Street, at Park Drive (247 1500). Kenmore T. **Lunch served** 11am-2.30pm Mon-Sat. **Dinner served** 5-10pm Mon-Thur; 5-11pm Fri; 4.30-11pm Sat; 4.30-10pm Sun. **Main courses** $16-$18. **Credit** AmEx, Disc, MC, V.

It's hard to find someone who doesn't like Elephant Walk's fresh, lively versions of classic Cambodian dishes and French-Cambodian fusion. Authentic fish sauce and dried shrimp are just two of the piquant elements in an excellent cuisine served in a colonial-chic setting.

Disabled: toilet.

Branch: 2067 Massachusetts Avenue, at Russell Street, Cambridge (492 6900).

Sol Azteca

914 Beacon Street, at Park Drive (262 0909). Kenmore T. **Dinner served** 5-10.30pm Mon, Tue; 5-11pm Fri, Sat; 5-10pm Sun. **Main courses** $11-$15. **Credit** AmEx, MC, V.

Mexican cooking in Boston doesn't exactly reach dizzying heights, but Sol Azteca is pretty far up the hill. It's among the few restaurants that focus more on real Mexican food (such as pollo con mole) than big cheesy Tex-Mex stuff.

Branch: 75 Union Street, Newton (964 0920).

North End

The North End's steadily rising rents and influx of young professionals hasn't affected the feel of this old neighbourhood's narrow, shop-lined streets, or the Italian chatter in the back rooms of little pasta houses. The area can be a food-lover's treat, as you browse through beautifully stocked Italian provisioners, or a food-lover's nightmare, as the indistinguishable 'red sauce' joints menace you with rubber gnocchi and sandpaper veal. But plenty of new-school food is here if you know where to look, and for every tourist trap there's a creative trattoria such as **Marcuccio's**, **Antico Forno** or **Sage** working magic with herbs and polenta and striped bass. Many North End restaurants operate on a cash-only basis, many don't take reservations and some don't serve dessert. The last is the easiest to deal with: after your meal, just stop by for an espresso and pastry at one of the renowned little caffes on Hanover Street (*see page 133*).

Antico Forno

93 Salem Street, at Parmenter Street (723 6733). Haymarket T. **Open** 11.30am-10pm Mon-Thur, Sun; 11.30am-10.30pm Fri, Sat. **Main courses** $11-$16. **Credit** MC, V. **Map 5 G3**

Excellent upmarket pizza, outstanding roasted vegetables and other tasty rustic fare emerge from the brick-clad wood-burning oven of this appealing Italian restaurant.

Disabled: toilet.

Daily Catch

323 Hanover Street, at Prince Street (523 8567). Haymarket T. **Open** 11.30am-10pm daily. **Main courses** $10-$38. **No credit cards**. **Map 5 G/H3**

Not cheap, and so small you're practically eating in the kitchen. But that's all part of the fun at this bustling little seafood joint with powerful red sauces, super-fresh fish and pasta that comes to your table still in the skillet. Don't miss the excellent stuffed squid or clam linguine.

Branches: 261 Northern Avenue (338 3093); 441 Harvard Street, Brookline (734 5696).

Mamma Maria

3 North Square, at North & Prince Streets (523 0077). Haymarket T. **Open** 5-10pm Mon-Thur, Sun; 5-11pm Fri, Sat. **Main courses** $20-$22. **Credit** AmEx, DC, Disc, MC, V. **Map 5 G3**

Top-notch Italian food is cooked extraordinarily well at this romantic three-storey corner restaurant. There are flower-boxes in the windows, candles on the tables and chairs upholstered in rich flowered tapestry.

Disabled: toilet.

Marcuccio's

125 Salem Street, at Prince Street (723 1807). Haymarket T. **Dinner served** 5-10pm daily. **Main courses** $13-$17. **Credit** MC, V. **Map 5 G3**

By day, rising-star chef Charles Draghi grows his own herbs in the sun by the front windows; by night, he uses those herbs and whatever he finds in the local markets to confect novel, powerful Italian-inspired food that's more interesting than anything else in the North End. Don't be put off by the goofy post-modern décor: in the kitchen, the man knows what he's doing.

Disabled: toilet.

Pomodoro

319 Hanover Street, at Prince Street (367 4348). Haymarket T. **Open** 11am-11pm daily. **Main courses** $13-$17. **No credit cards. Map 5 G/H3**

The smell of sizzling garlic permeates this tiny storefront restaurant, owned by unlikely Italian-food maven Siobhan Carew. The simple, excellent specials and pasta dishes stand out from those found at the run-of-the-mill Italian joints that clutter Hanover Street.

Sage

69 Prince Street, at Hanover Street (248 8814). Haymarket T. **Open** 5.30-10pm Mon-Thur, Sun; 5.30-11pm Fri, Sat. **Main courses** $17-$26.
Credit AmEx, DC, MC, V. **Map 5 G/H3**

Chef Tony Susi may not be famous, but he has attracted a cult following for the bright, herb-happy Italian food he serves in this tiny (eight-table) North End eatery.
Disabled: toilet.

Terramia

98 Salem Street, at Parmenter Street (523 3112). Haymarket T. **Open** 5.30-10pm Mon-Sat; 1-10pm Sun. **Main courses** $22-$28. **Credit** AmEx, DC, MC, V. **Map 5 G3**

Another of the handful of restaurants pushing up the quality level of the North End, this perky trattoria is loud, crowded and always interesting.
Disabled: toilet.

Trattoria Il Panino

11 Parmenter Street, at Hanover Street (720 1336). Haymarket T. **Open** 10.30am-11pm daily.
Main courses $9.95-$17.95. **No credit cards. Map 5 G3**

This, the original Panino, is a no-frills trattoria that raised the standard for basic North End food: nothing gourmet, but a cut above the bland red sauce and leaden polenta served at your average tourist trap. The various sequels include **Tutto Mare**, a Salem Street seafood storefront joint (63 Salem Street; 557 6064); **Il Panino Express**, a cafeteria-style pasta-and-sandwich shop on the corner of Parmenter and Hanover Streets (266 Hanover Street; 720 5720); and the dressy five-story **Il Panino** bistro and nightclub in the financial district (295 Franklin Street; 338 1000).

South End

Back Bay may be richer and the North End more touristy, but no Boston neighbourhood beats the South End for pure density of stylish bistros. On broad avenues that cut through blocks of recently renovated brownstones, see-and-be-seen restaurants such as **Mistral** (*see page 143*), **Aquitaine** (*below*) and **Hamersley's** (*page 139*) provide grist for local gossip columnists while low-key gems such as the **Metropolis Café** (*page 141*), **Franklin Café** (*page 139*), and the funky **Delux Café** (*see page 116* **Pubs & Bars**) fill up with a smart local walk-in trade. The young chefs of **Truc** *(page 143)*, on Tremont Street, and **La Bettola** (*below*), on Columbus, have received national attention for their (respectively) French and Italian-Asian fusion menus. To some, the South End is the centre of gay Boston; to others, the heart of the arts community. Nobody, however, considers it an easy place to park, so take a taxi or walk the 10 minutes from Back Bay.

Also in the area

Bertucci's (*see page 148*).

Addis Red Sea

544 Tremont Street, at Clarendon Street (426 8727). Back Bay or Copley T. **Open** 5-10.30pm Mon-Fri; noon-10.30pm Sat, Sun. **Main courses** $11.
Credit AmEx, DC, V. **Map 3 F6**

This ten-year-old veteran of Tremont Street may still be Boston's most exotic place to eat. Low wooden stools surround woven-grass tables; food is delivered on wide plates without silverware. Injera, the spongy sourdough bread of Ethiopia, serves as both utensil and mild-tasting foil for the spicy chicken, lamb and lentil stews. Don't miss the red pepper cottage cheese as an appetiser and use the diced tomato salad to cool your palate off a little.
Disabled: toilet.

Aquitaine

569 Tremont Street, at Union Park (424 8577). Back Bay or Copley T. **Dinner served** 5.30-10pm Mon-Thur, Sun; 5.30-11pm Fri, Sat. **Main courses** $16-$26.
Credit AmEx, DC, Disc, MC, V. **Map 3 F6**

The wine racks stretch to the ceiling and the crowd stretches the imagination at this South End hotspot recently opened by the owners of **Metropolis** (*p141*), just across the street. Floor-to-ceiling windows look across Tremont Street, right at the heart of the South End; the tiny bar fills up with people waiting for a table at the banquette along the wall. The food has an undeniable Continental feel, like a good French restaurant in London. A 'tartlet' takes caramelised onions and rich Gruyère and tops them with richer bacon; big ravioli are filled with minced duck and foie gras, bathed in a dark, compelling sauce of madeira and truffle oil. The wine list is expensive and flashy; the clientele is under 40 and South Endy, which means about as well-dressed as Bostonians get.

Bob the Chef's Café

604 Columbus Avenue, at Massachusetts Avenue (536 6204). Mass Ave T. **Open** 11am-10pm Tue, Wed; 11am-midnight Thur-Sat; 11am-9pm Sun. **Main courses** $20.
Credit AmEx, DC, MC, V. **Map 3 E6**

A few years ago, Bob's was a funky cafeteria-style soul food restaurant and a cult favourite. After a protracted renovation it emerged in almost unrecognisable form, with the sponge-painted walls and four-person tables of a bistro. There are probably better soul food restaurants in the world, but this is the one with the local reputation, and that big hunk of 'glorifried chicken' is still mighty good. The cult still lives, but in a nicer suit. For details of jazz nights *see p210* **Nightlife**.
Disabled: toilet.

La Bettola

480 Columbus Avenue, at Rutland Street (236 5252). Prudential T. **Dinner served** 5.30-10pm Mon-Thur, Sun; 5.30-11pm Fri, Sat. **Main courses** $24-$38. **Credit** AmEx, MC, V. **Map 3 E6**

One of the most lauded new restaurants in the city, this is the second effort from the two women behind that Theater District favourite **Galleria Italiana** (*p133*). They hired chef Rene Michelena to confect a menu of attractive, adventurous dishes that merged Asian and Italian flavours; the result hits the mark enough to have won over nearly all its critics. The menu is a playground of velvet-black risottos, miso-sauced lobster salads and intriguing desserts. The bistro-sized dining room is decorated like the outside of a decaying villa and seating spills out onto the pavement in warm weather.

Cena

14A Westland Avenue, at Massachusetts Avenue (262 1485). Symphony T. **Dinner served** 5-10pm Tue-Thur, Sun; 5-11pm Fri, Sat. **Main courses** $15.50-$22. **Credit** AmEx, DC, Disc, MC, V. **Map 3 E6**

Eclecticism and creativity combine at ***Biba*** *in the Back Bay. See page 126.*

Not quite a vegetarian restaurant, but you still won't find steak or pork on the menu in this global-influenced bistro near Symphony Hall. The flavours here are mostly Italian and eastern Mediterranean, with some Asian dishes thrown in. You won't find cream, either. Most dishes are vegetable-based; a few contain chicken or fish. You don't really notice, though: the flavours are powerful and if the presentation isn't always perfect (and the *faux*-Roman décor a little goofy), the staff and owners are young and energetic enough to carry it all off. It makes an excellent choice for a pre-concert stop.
Disabled: toilet.

Claremont Café

535 Columbus Avenue, at Massachusetts Avenue (247 9001). Mass Ave T. **Breakfast/lunch served** 7.30am-3pm Mon-Fri; 8am-3pm Sat; 9am-3pm Sun. **Dinner served** 5-10pm Mon-Thur; 5-10.30pm Fri, Sat. **Main courses** $8-$20. **Credit** AmEx, MC, V. **Map 3 E6**

The Claremont has been eclipsed in fame by the slew of high-ambition bistros in the neighbourhood, unfairly, as this very consistent restaurant turns out good, sharp-flavoured food – particularly on the appetiser menu – at moderate prices. There's seating outside during warm weather.
Disabled: toilet.

Franklin Café

276 Shawmut Avenue, at Hanson Street (350 0010). Back Bay T. **Lunch served** 10.30am-3pm Sun. **Dinner served** 5.30pm-1.30am Mon-Sat. **Main courses** $12-$15. **Credit** AmEx, MC, V. **Map 3 F6**

Small, full, warm and constantly abuzz. The Franklin Café's South End clientele (both gay and straight) and snappy, updated comfort food give it the feel of the perfect neighbourhood bar in the city's hippest neighbourhood. And it really is easier if you're a neighbour, since parking is nigh-on impossible.
Disabled: toilet.

Le Gamin

550 Tremont Street, at Dartmouth Street (654 8969). Back Bay T. **Open** 8am-midnight daily. **Main courses** $10. **Credit** MC, V. **Map 3 F6**

The crêpe returns to Boston in a very Parisian little incarnation, a below-street-level café where you can eat a very serviceable meal for $10 a head and not feel as though you're slumming. The elaborate cold salads and drinks are good too.

Hamersley's Bistro

553 Tremont Street, at Clarendon Street (423 2700). Back Bay or Copley T. **Dinner served** 6-10pm Mon-Fri; 5.30-10.30pm Sat; 5.30-9.30pm Sun. **Main courses** $23-$29. **Credit** AmEx, DC, Disc, MC, V. **Map 3 F6**

Chef Gordon Hamersley is the most famous alumnus of Todd English's kitchen at **Olives** (*p132*). He struck out on his own several years ago and now runs this spacious first-rate 'bistro' (really a full-on restaurant), with an open kitchen and a middle-aged power-suited clientele. His garlic-roasted chicken is powerfully flavoured and moist throughout; service is informed and not overbearing. Rumoured to be one of chef Julia Child's favourite places to eat.

Clío, *in the Eliot Hotel. See page 127.*

The consummately popular **Olives** *(page 132).*

Harvey's

99 St Botolph Street, at West Newton Street (266 3030). Prudential T. **Open** 5pm-1am Mon-Sat; 11am-1am Sun. **Main courses** $12-$18. **Credit** AmEx, DC, MC, V. **Map 3 E6**

A mellow restaurant and bar tucked between Back Bay and the South End, and a better choice for a drink or a quick bite near Huntington Avenue than the nearby hotels. Brick walls and black-and-white photographs give it a neighbourhoody feel; the New American menu is solid and reasonably priced.

Icarus

3 Appleton Street, at Tremont Street (426 1790). Back Bay T. **Dinner served** 6-9.30pm Mon-Thur; 6-10.30pm Fri; 5.30-10.30pm Sat; 5.30-9.30pm Sun. **Main courses** $20-$30. **Credit** AmEx, DC, Disc, MC, V. **Map 3 F 5/6**

Long before the South End was overrun by bistros *du moment*, Icarus had staked out this distinctive, romantic below-street-level spot for Chris Douglass's fancy-but-not-frivolous New American cooking.

Jae's Cafe and Grill

520 Columbus Avenue, at Worcester Road (421 9405). Mass Ave T. **Lunch served** 11.30am-4pm, **dinner served** 5-11pm, Mon-Fri. **Open** 11.30am-11pm Sat. **Main courses** $10.95-$17.95. **Credit** AmEx, DC, Disc, MC, V. **Map 3 E6**

An endlessly popular and consistently good sushi/Korean/Thai café. Servers speak of 'the Jae's menu' with near-reverence and it is worshipped by a large cult of well-turned-out Bostonians. All four restaurants feature tropical-fish tanks, a wide-ranging sushi selection and delicious pad Thai. The newest is the spectacular three-storey Stuart Street flagship, with a top floor dedicated entirely to tabletop Korean barbecue. The Cambridge branch is open until 1am on Saturdays.

Disabled: toilet.

Branches: 212 Stuart Street (451 7788); 1281 Cambridge Street, Cambridge (497 8380); Atrium Mall, 300 Boylston Street, Newton (965 7177).

Metropolis Café

584 Tremont Street, between Clarendon & Dartmouth Streets (247 2931). Back Bay T. **Dinner served** 5.30-9.30pm Mon-Thur, Sun; 5.30-11pm Fri, Sat. **Main courses** $15-$20. **Credit** AmEx, MC, V. **Map 3 F5**

Nobody had heard of Seth and Shari Woods when they bought the old Tremont Ice Cream Parlour and converted it into this tiny, glittering French-Italian bistro. Now the couple (he cooks, she's the hostess and pastry chef) are ubiquitous in the burgeoning South End food scene and have opened the larger **Aquitaine** across the street (*p138*). Some reports claim the first restaurant has suffered from the expansion, but it would have to suffer a lot before it stopped being worthwhile. The excellent food has strong flavours and exacting presentation: a salmon pavé with seared horseradish crust; rich mussel soup; reliably impressive daily risotto specials. A treat for the largely local crowd that eats here.

The **Barking Crab**: *a quintessential New England experience with a pretty good view. Page 132.*

Italian-inspired food under the aegis of Charles Draghi (left) at **Marcuccio's** *(above). P137.*

Mistral

223 Columbus Avenue, at Clarendon Street (867 9300). Back Bay T. **Dinner served** 5.30pm-midnight daily. **Main courses** $19-$39. **Credit** AmEx, DC, Disc, MC, V. **Map 3 F5**

The opening of this high-ceilinged, high-style showpiece was preceded by a year's worth of gossip and followed by a year in which it seemed nobody could actually score a reservation. Now Mistral – a collaboration between nightlife impresario Seth Greenberg and former Four Seasons chef Jamie Mammano – seems to have settled down as a haunt for the haute bourgeoisie and Prada-wearing international student set. The food is expensive, refined and quite remarkable-looking; if your zillionaire date gets boring, you can always fall back on examining the dome of puff pastry over your lobster bisque.

Disabled: toilet.

Restaurant Zinc

32 Stanhope Street, at Clarendon Street (262 2323). Back Bay T. **Dinner served** 5.30-10.30pm Tue-Fri; 5.30-11.30pm Sat; *bar open* 5.30pm-2am Mon-Sat. **Main courses** $20-$26. **Credit** AmEx, DC, MC, V. **Map 3 F5/6**

The idea behind Restaurant Zinc was to create a chic and tasty Parisian bistro for nightclubbers and an elite South End clique. The star chef has since left, and the club-promoter co-owner is out of the picture, but Zinc's late kitchen hours and quality bartending ensure that the bloom is not yet off the rose.

Disabled: toilet.

Tremont 647

647 Tremont Street, at West Brookline Street (266 4600). Back Bay T. **Dinner served** 5.30-10pm daily. **Main courses** $16-$19.50. **Credit** AmEx, DC, MC, V. **Map 3 F6**

After working as sous chef for Chris Schlesinger at Cambridge's famous **East Coast Grill** (*see p151*), Andy Husbands had a novel idea: why not put a dressier spin on Schlesinger's world-class grilled food? The result is this stylish, Back Bay narrow room. It has an open kitchen, yellow-parchment lampshades and some very interesting flavours on the plate. After one of the city's best breadbaskets (containing flatbread, jalapeño muffins and grilled sourdough, amont others), the nifty dishes follow one another to the table: a banana-leaf packet that opens to steamed Chilean sea bass over jasmine rice; chicken tamales; and a spice-rubbed skirt steak served with truffled tater tots, no less.

Disabled: toilet.

Truc

560 Tremont Street, at Clarendon Street (338 8070). Back Bay T. **Dinner served** 6-10pm Tue-Thur; 6-10.30pm Fri-Sun. **Main courses** $18-$22. **Credit** MC, V. **Map 3 F5**

A treat for lovers of French food with some money in their pockets. Corinna Mozo turns out very accomplished French classics: cassoulet, trout meunière, a buttery-soft rabbit loin, pork rillettes served with a mustard pot and cornichons. There's a nice wine list made up almost entirely of French bottles and décor is understated (green walls, black-and-white paintings) but handsome.

The **Metropolis Café**. *See page 141.*

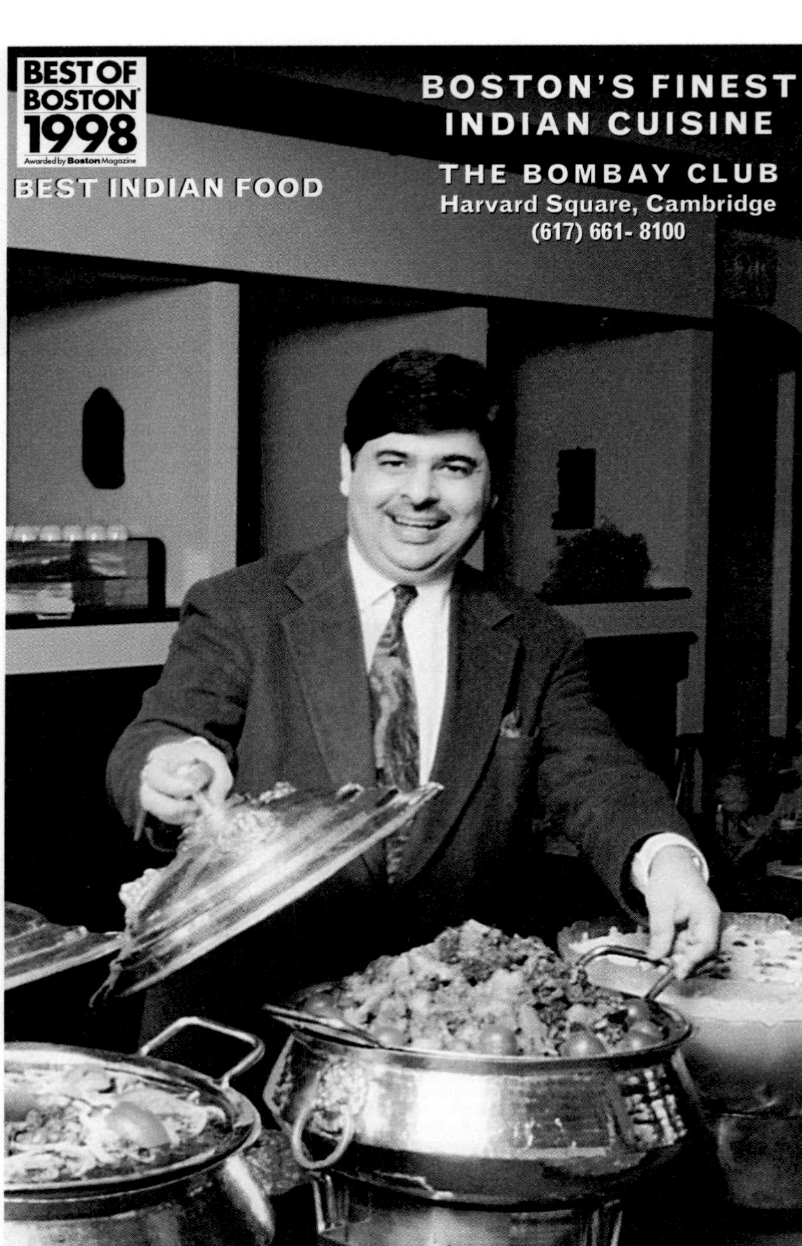
BEST OF BOSTON 1998
Awarded by Boston Magazine
BEST INDIAN FOOD
BOSTON'S FINEST INDIAN CUISINE
THE BOMBAY CLUB
Harvard Square, Cambridge
(617) 661- 8100

Lydia Shire's **Rialto**, *in Cambridge. See page 153.*

Further Afield

Allston

Also in the area

Ginza *and* **Pho Pasteur** (*see page 129 for both*).

Ducky Wok

122-126 Harvard Avenue, at Brighton Avenue, Allston (782 8868). Packards Corner T. **Open** 11am-10pm daily. **Main courses** $7. **Credit** (for orders over $15) AmEx, DC, Disc, MC, V.

Behind a ridiculous name (and silly Japanese cartoon duck sign), this is an attractive Chinese and Vietnamese restaurant with a reputation for good, fresh seafood and sharp cooking.

Rangoli

129 Brighton Avenue, at Harvard Avenue, Allston (562 0200). Harvard Ave T. **Lunch served** 11.30am-3pm Mon-Fri. **Dinner served** 5-10.30pm Mon-Thur; 5-11pm Fri. **Open** 11.30am-11pm Sat; 11.30am-10.30pm Sun. **Main courses** $6. **Credit** AmEx, MC, V.

While most of Boston's Indian restaurants serve North Indian staples such as chicken tikka masala and tandoori dishes, Rangoli – a pleasant but unassuming storefront on busy Brighton Avenue – was the first to make a specialty of South Indian food. Others have followed, but Rangoli is still a bargain and a treat, with foot-long dosai (fried chickpea-flour pancakes) wrapped around potatoes and chicken.

Brighton

Bluestone Bistro

1799 Commonwealth Avenue, at Chestnut Hill Avenue, Brighton (254 8309). Chiswick Rd T. **Open** 10.30am-11pm Mon-Thur; 5.30pm-midnight Fri; 10am-midnight Sat, Sun. **Main courses** $8.35-$12.50. **Credit** AmEx, DC, Disc, MC, V.

The restaurant that brought personal-size gourmet pizzas to

One of Somerville's finest: **Dalí** *(page 154).*

Brunch across the river

The Sunday tradition of midday overindulgence lives on at Cambridge restaurants and makes an ideal prelude to an exploration of the area. Fare varies from the spicy egg dishes of the **East Coast Grill** (*page 151*) to the Italian specialities of **Giannino's** (*page 152*), but some constants remain true. Almost everywhere you'll find staples such as French toast, whether its done with eggy challah bread at the **S&S Deli Restaurant** (*page 154*) or garnished with tropical fruit at **Chez Henri** (*page 150*). And almost everywhere freshly-squeezed orange juice is used to disguise the poor-quality bubbly in the traditional Mimosa. People tend to linger, Sunday papers in hand, so phone ahead to book a table if you can.

Brighton still feels pretty hip several years later, with Californianesque décor, an unusual roster of pizza ingredients and several beers on tap. This is where Boston College students go on dates, and probably where their professors go too. There's usually a crowd, especially from Thursday to Saturday nights.

Tasca

1216 Commonwealth Avenue, at Washington Street, Brighton (730 8002). Washington St T. **Dinner served** 5-11pm Mon-Thur; 5pm-midnight Fri, Sat. **Main courses** $10.95-$14.95. **Credit** MC, V.

What happens when an Irishman opens a tapas bar? You get a friendly, convivial Spanish-looking restaurant serving a slightly blander version of the salty and piquant tapas available downtown. The dishes are a dollar or two cheaper than other tapas bars, and the free valet parking is an enormous convenience in a car-choked stretch of Comm Ave.

Uva

1418 Commonwealth Avenue, between Harvard Avenue & Washington Street, Brighton (566 5670). Waban T. **Dinner served** 5-10pm Mon-Sat. **Main courses** $10-$20. **Credit** AmEx, DC, Disc, MC, V.

The story at this airy, pleasant Italian restaurant isn't the food, which is serviceable but nowhere near as good as you find elsewhere; rather, it's the wine list, which follows the marvellous policy of pricing bottles at about $10 over cost. And the list is a remarkable collection that includes mature wines and rare boutique bottles that you're unlikely to see in shops for this (or any other) price. A find for the oenophile. *Disabled: toilet.*

Brookline

Also in the area

Bertucci's (*see page 148*).

Café St Petersburg

236 Washington Street, at Harvard Street, Brookline (277 7100). Brookline Village T. **Open** noon-midnight Tue-Sun. **Main courses** $11-$12. **Credit** DC, Disc, MC, V.

For French-Cambodian fusion cooking, head for the Fenway and **Elephant Walk** *(page 137).*

A small, quirky place with curtained front windows and (sometimes) classical music coming from the upright piano at the rear of the room. This is the only proper Russian restaurant in the whole of Boston and it makes a strong case that there should be more. There are blinis with caviar (actually salmon roe, but this isn't a beluga kind of place); a streamlined salad of beets, potatoes and vinegar, and excellent dumplings.
Disabled: toilet.

Pandan Leaf

250 Harvard Street, at Beacon Street, Brookline (566 9393). Coolidge Corner T. **Open** 11.30am-10.30pm Mon-Thur; 11.30am-11.30pm Fri, Sat; noon-10.30pm Sun. **Main courses** $7.95-$15.95.
Credit AmEx, MC, V.
This upscale, bistro-like Malaysian restaurant not far from Coolidge Corner has caught on like wildfire among Brookline's adventurous-but-not-flashy restaurant-goers.
Disabled: toilet.

Providence

1223 Beacon Street, at St Paul's Street, Brookline (232 0300). St Paul's T. **Dinner served** 5.30-10pm Tue-Sat. **Main courses** $19.95. **Credit** DC, MC, V.
Chef Paul O'Connell, an alumnus of the **Olives** kitchen (*see p132*) who also owns **Chez Henri** in Cambridge (*see p150*), puts French, Italian and American ideas together in a very good, somewhat formal restaurant not far from Coolidge Corner. If you wanted to get engaged in Brookline, this is where you'd do it.
Disabled: toilet.

Taberna de Haro

999 Beacon Street, at St Mary's Street, Brookline (277 8272). St Mary's T. **Open** 11.30am-2pm, **dinner served** 5.30-11pm, Mon-Sat. **Main courses** $8. **Credit** AmEx, Disc, MC, V.
This new, casual tapas restaurant dispenses with the Madrid-basement kitsch of the city's other top-notch tapas bars (**Dalí** and **Tapéo**, *see p154 and p131*) in favour of a clean, open atmosphere. Tapas come small and smaller, with intense flavours and in consistently interesting flavour combinations.
Disabled: toilet.

Zaftigs

335 Harvard Street, at Babcock Street, Brookline (975 0075). Coolidge Corner T. **Open** 8am-10pm daily. **Main courses** $9. **Credit** AmEx, MC, V.
Maybe the most popular breakfast spot in Brookline, if not the whole Boston area, Zaftigs updates the Jewish deli for a 1990s, slightly more calorie-conscious crowd. There's a huge menu and a 45-minute wait for a table on Saturday or Sunday mornings. Book if you can (a day or two in advance at weekends).
Disabled: toilet.

Jamaica Plain

Also in the area

Bertucci's (*see page 148*).

Jake's Boss BBQ

3492 Washington Street, at William's Street, Jamaica Plain (983 3701). Green St T. **Open** 11am-10pm Mon-Thur, Sun; 11am-11pm Fri, Sat. **Main courses** $10. **Credit** AmEx, DC, Disc, MC, V.
This unassuming corner joint hides a massive smoker at the back that turns out what is probably the best authentic Southern barbecue food in the city, along with spicy 'cowboy beans' and tasty collard greens. It's worth the trip to Jamaica Plain if you're itching for barbecue.
Disabled: toilet.

Cambridge & Somerville

Cambridge

The 'People's Republic' is more yuppie than hippie these days, but that's not bad news for Greater Boston's Left Bank diners. Eclectic cuisines – Asian fusion, New American inventiveness – have finally overtaken the 'crunchy-granola' 1970s Cambridge style, and several celebrity chefs (notably Chris Schlesinger at **Salamander** and Lydia Shire at **Rialto**) have upped the ante further.

That said, Cambridge is still dominated by the universities of Harvard and MIT, and the constant influx of students means that cheap, largely ethnic storefront eateries thrive, particularly in Central and Harvard Squares and Portuguese-dominated East Cambridge. Nor has the older egalitarian ethic quite lost its hold: you'll need reservations for your splurge at **Harvest** (*page 152*), **Rialto** (*page 153*) or **Salamander** (*page 154*) and for some of the smaller 'destination' restaurants too. But gentlemen scholars will rarely be asked to don a tie or jacket, and those stiletto heels (so impractical on the city's charming brick sidewalks) belong strictly across the river.

Also in the area

Cottonwood Café (*see page 127*); **Elephant Walk** (*see page 137*); **Jae's Cafe and Grill** (*see page 141*); **Legal Sea Foods** (*see page 135*); **Pho Pasteur** (*see page 129*).

Bartley's Burger Cottage

1246 Massachusetts Avenue, between Plympton & Bow Streets, Cambridge (354 6559). Harvard T. **Open** 11am-10pm Mon-Sat. **Main courses** $3.90-$7.75. **No credit cards. Map 4 B3**
Beef, beef and more beef all formed into meatball-shaped burgers and topped with everything imaginable. Parties are squeezed onto tiny tables and singles share, but the prices, the options (guacamole, blue cheese, bacon and more) and the marvellous aroma keep pulling the Harvard Square strollers in. Many combos are named after local politicians and the menu humour is invariably bad, but that's all part of the charm.

Bertucci's

21 Brattle Street, at Massachusetts Avenue, Cambridge (864 4748). Harvard T. **Open** 11am-11pm daily. **Main courses** $10. **Credit** AmEx, Disc, MC, V. **Map 4 B2**
This branch of the local Italian chain is hopping, hip and crowded. All locations serve up the signature chewy, tasty wood-oven pizza (and great rolls from the same dough) and a small but choice selection of pasta dishes for gourmet quality on a budget. There are numerous other offshoots in the Boston area: check the phone book or call this branch for their location.

Blue Room

1 Kendall Square, between Hampshire Street & Cardinal Madeiros Avenue, Cambridge (494 9034). Kendall/MIT T. **Open** 5.30-10pm Mon-Thur; 5.30-10.30pm Fri, Sat; 11am-2.30pm, 5.30-10pm, Sun. **Main courses** $17-$22. **Credit** AmEx, DC, Disc, MC, V. **Map 4 D3**
Kendall Square's purple, green and peach-themed Blue Room brings New American fusion to the grill, pairing seared tuna

with tomatillos or enlivening beef skirt with kim chee. The seasonal menu, elegant brunch and lively bar keeps the clientele faithful.
Disabled: toilet.

Bombay Club

57 John F Kennedy Street, at Winthrop Street, Cambridge (661 8100). Harvard T. **Open** 11.30am-11pm daily. **Main courses** $8. **Credit** AmEx, DC, MC, V. **Map 4 B2**
Diners come for the view over Harvard Square and return for the wide range of Indian specialities, particularly vegetarian offerings such as the smoky aubergine-based baigan bharta. The usual tandooris and curries get a fresh kick here from careful spicing.
Disabled: toilet.

Border Café

32 Church Street, at Brattle Street, Cambridge (864 6100). Harvard T. **Open** noon-1am Mon-Thur, Sun; noon-2am Fri, Sat. **Main courses** $15. **Credit** AmEx, Disc, MC, V. **Map 4 B2**
Recent grads and those who want to love them flock to this fancifully decorated Harvard Square cantina. But the focus is more on the bar scene than the Tex-Mex melted-cheese offerings or the ersatz Cajun dishes. Bring proof of age if you're under 35 and be prepared to wait for a table.
Disabled: toilet.

Café Celador

5 Craigie Circle, between Concord Avenue & Brattle Street, Cambridge (661 4073). Harvard T. **Open** 5.30-9.30pm Tue-Thur; 5.30-10pm Fri, Sat. **Main courses** $15.50-$23. **Credit** AmEx, DC, Disc, MC, V. **Map 4 A2**
Chef Patrick Noe's minuscule basement bistro seats only 50, but those smart enough to make reservations can indulge in country French classics, such as cassoulet and duck confit. Touches of Italy, Spain and even nouvelle creativity sneak in – the lemon sole is tied with scallions and surrounded by light-as-air onion rings – but the friendly, relaxed atmosphere makes Celador feel like a country inn in the heart of Cambridge.

The much-discussed **Mistral** *(page 143).*

Cambridge Common

1667 Massachusetts Avenue, at Sacramento Street, Cambridge (547 1228). Harvard or Porter T. **Open** 11.30am-1am Mon-Wed; 11.30am-2am Thur-Sat; 11am-midnight Sun (after midnight bar food only). **Main courses** $5.95-$9.95. **Credit** AmEx, DC, Disc, MC, V. **Map 4 B1**
Handy for comfort food such as chicken pot pie and meat loaf, at family prices. The only frills come in the amount of blue cheese melted on the blue chips or the generous size of the Cosmopolitans, but few complain when they slide into the big wooden booths at this welcoming retreat. *See also p123* **Pubs & Bars**.
Disabled: toilet.

Carberry's Bakery and Coffeehouse

74 Prospect Street, at Massachusetts Avenue, Cambridge (576 3530). Central T. **Open** 6am-8pm daily. **Main courses** *coffee & danish* $3. **No credit cards. Map 4 C3**
For an Icelandic bakery set in a former auto supply shop just off Central Square, Carberry's has caught on fast. It could be the outsize fruit-studded scones, the marzipan-rich pastries or the huge windows, which make the café tables inside almost as light and airy as those lining the parking lot.
Disabled: toilet.

Casa Mexico

75 Winthrop Street, at John F Kennedy Street, Cambridge (491 4552). Harvard T. **Lunch served** noon-2.30pm Mon-Fri. **Dinner served** 6-10pm Mon-Thur, Sun; 6-11pm Fri; 5.30-11pm Sat. **Main courses** $10.50-$14.50. **Credit** AmEx, DC, Disc, MC, V. **Map 4 B2/3**
This cosy Harvard Square basement, with its colourful tiles and stained-glass lights, may have faded over the past decade, but it still serves up very respectable and varied Mexican fare. Velvety mole sauces still enrobe chicken breasts and enchiladas, and the shrimp and steak preparations reflect the cooking of Acapulco, Veracruz and beyond. A definite step above the usual taco-and-burrito joint, although those can be found here too.
Disabled: toilet.

Casa Portugal

12 Cambridge Street, between Prospect & Tremont Streets, Cambridge (491 8880). Harvard or Lechmere T. **Open** 11.30am-10pm Mon-Thur; 11.30am-11pm Fri, Sat; noon-10pm Sun. **Main courses** $12. **Credit** AmEx, DC, Disc, V. **Map 4 D2**
A small, family-run escape into the Old World, with the accent on savoury seafood and shellfish stews, such as tomato-based caldeirada Portuguesa or almond-scented mariscada Costa Brava. Those with smaller appetites should try authentic treats such as the carne de porco a alentajana, which matches marinated pork cubes with the tiniest cherrystone clams.
Disabled: toilet.

Changsho

1712 Massachusetts Avenue, at Shepherd's Street, Cambridge (547 6565). Porter T. **Open** 11.30am-9.30pm Mon-Thur, Sun; 11.30am-10.30pm Fri, Sat. **Main courses** $12.95. **Credit** AmEx, DC, MC, V. **Map 4 B1**

Sooner or later the whole of Boston passes through the **South Street Diner** *near*

Years ago this Chinese place was a favourite student haunt, because within its dim, red interior, amazing Peking duck – with crisp skin and juicy flesh – could be had dirt cheap. Now that the next generation has taken over, the prices have risen and the décor has been redone, with an emphasis on light and minimalism. The food is also lighter, with winter melon and mango showing up in the specials, but the quality (and the duck) remain.
Disabled: toilet.

Chez Henri

1 Shepherd Street, at Massachusetts Avenue, Cambridge (354 8980). Harvard or Porter T. **Open** 6-10pm Mon-Thur; 5.30-11pm Fri, Sat; 11am-2pm, 5.30-9pm, Sun. **Main courses** $16-$22. **Credit** AmEx, DC, MC, V. **Map 4 B1**

Sometimes the French and Cuban fusion comes together wonderfully, for instance when a moist, tangy duck tamale garnishes a meal-sized warm spinach salad. At other times, this popular little bistro splits its dishes with flair – as in the bouillabaisse with a side dish of tostones (fried plantain). Quieter in the summer, with tall open windows, and boisterous in the winter, Chez Henri and its adjoining bar qualify as a first-class neighbourhood secret.
Disabled: toilet.

Christopher's

1920 Massachusetts Avenue, at Porter Square, Cambridge (876 9180). Porter T. **Open** 4pm-midnight daily. **Main courses** $6-$15. **Credit** AmEx, Disc, MC, V. **Map 4 B1**

When you could eat a cow, Christopher's burgers satisfy the craving with a nice selection of brews to wash that big beef down. Fancier dishes can trip themselves up, but the long wooden bar that dominates this big Porter Square room should serve as a signal that here basic is best.
Disabled: toilet.

CityGirl Caffe

204 Hampshire Street, at Inman Square, Cambridge (864 2809). Central or Harvard T. **Open** 11am-9pm Tue-Fri; 10am-9pm Sat; 10am-7pm Sun. **Main courses** $7. **Credit** MC, V.

This tiny Inman Square café serves up some of the best customised calzones in town, as well as soups and sandwiches that the counter staff will grill on request. There's brunch on Sundays, too.

Common Market

1815 Massachusetts Avenue, at Porter Exchange, Cambridge. Porter T. **Map 4 B1**

Actually a conglomerate of six small restaurants, this mini-mall in the Porter Exchange shopping building is the heart of Little Asia for North Cambridge and serves excellent Japanese fare at rock-bottom prices. Sit down at the sushi bar at **Kotobukiya** (492 4655; open noon-8.30pm Mon-Sat; noon-6.30pm Sun) for fast, fresh nori rolls. Or belly up to big bowls of noodle soups at **Tampopo** (868 5457; open noon-9pm Mon-Sat, noon-8pm Sun) or a curried cutlet at

South Station. See page 135.

Café Mami (547 9130; open noon-9pm Mon-Sat, noon-7pm Sun). **Masao's Kitchen** (497 7348; open noon-2.30pm, 4.30-9pm, Tue-Thur, noon-9pm Fri-Sun), Cambridge's only macrobiotic restaurant, is tucked away in here as well.

Davio's

5 Cambridge Parkway, at Royal Sonesta Hotel, Cambridge (661 4810). Science Park T. **Open** 6.30am-11pm Mon-Fri, Sun; 7am-11pm Sat. **Main courses** $8. **Credit** AmEx, DC, Disc, MC, V. **Map 4 F3**

The Cambridge branch of this Boston restaurant produces northern Italian specialities and fanciful gourmet pizzas in understated elegant surroundings, complete with excellent, original artworks.

Disabled: toilet.

Branch: 269 Newbury Street (262 4810).

Dolphin Seafood

1105 Massachusetts Avenue, at Remington Street, Cambridge (661 2937). Harvard T. **Open** 11.30am-9.30pm Mon-Thur; 11.30am-10pm Fri, Sat. **Main courses** $7-$12. **Credit** MC, V. **Map 4 C3**

Straightforward seafood at great prices distinguishes this neighbourhood favourite. Standard grub is spankingly fresh and offered grilled, fried or baked, often with the choice of blackening spices or without butter for the calorie-conscious. Fancier dishes tend towards Mediterranean cuisine, with lots of wine and garlic. Check out the menu board for specials that can include the best deals on lobsters or local bluefish.

Disabled: toilet.

East Coast Grill

1271 Cambridge Street, at Prospect Street, Cambridge (491 6568). Central T. **Open** 5.30-10pm Mon-Thur, Sun; 5.30-10.30pm Fri, Sat. **Main courses** $18. **Credit** AmEx, Disc, MC, V. **Map 4 D2**

This high-minded grill joint began the gentrification of Inman Square, and its shift towards seafood over recent years promises the colourful, always-packed ECG (and its patrons) a long life. Everything is fresh, everything spiced (although not always hot) and the hungry regularly queue up for more than an hour for grilled oysters and ingenious side dishes, such as the Asian-inspired slaws. Regular 'hotter than hell' nights bring out the macho element, as does the Sunday brunch Bloody Mary bar, with its assortment of peppers and salsas.

Disabled: toilet.

Fire and Ice

50 Church Street, at Brattle Street, Cambridge (547 9007). Harvard T. **Open** 11.30am-10.30pm Mon-Sat; 10.30am-2.30pm, 3-10pm, Sun. **Main courses** $13.75. **Credit** AmEx, DC, Disc, MC, V. **Map 4 B2**

High-concept dining in the form of mix-and-match lets the largely student crowd load up on veg, meat (or meat substitutes) and sauces, and then watch as it all gets seared by the pros behind the big grills in the middle. Overenthusiasm (and the ample drinks) can lead to some unsavoury mixtures (portobello mushrooms and tempeh in barbecue sauce anyone?), but you've no one but yourself to blame.

Disabled: toilet.

Forest Café

1682 Massachusetts Avenue, at Sacramento Street, Cambridge (661 7810). Porter T. **Open** 9am-1am Mon-Sat; 11.30am-2.30pm, 5-11pm, Sun. **Main courses** $8-$14. **Credit** AmEx, DC, Disc, MC, V. **Map 4 B1**

The closest many Cantabridgians will come to Mexico's two coastlines is this long, narrow bar room. Here the daily catch comes served with sauces of pumpkin seed and cilantro (coriander) and shrimp soak up garlic and herbs; non-fish-eaters can enjoy a smoky mole chicken or enchilada, all at barroom prices.

Disabled: toilet.

Giannino's

Courtyard of Charles Hotel, 20 University Road, Cambridge (576 0605). Harvard T. **Open** 11.30am-11pm daily. **Main courses** $20. **Credit** AmEx, DC, Disc, MC, V. **Map 4 B2**

Offering northern Italian elegance in the Charles Hotel complex, Giannino's serves up superb risottos and pasta dishes (also available in half portions), often paired with seafood, as well as classics such as osso buco alla Milanese. The now-ubiquitous tiramisu comes in a light and flavourful version.

Disabled: toilet.

Green Street Grill

280 Green Street, between Pearl & Magazine Streets, Cambridge (876 1655). Central T. **Open** 3pm-1am daily. **Main courses** $13.95-$22.95. **Credit** AmEx, DC, MC, V. **Map 4 C3**

Tucked away behind a supermarket, this hot little Caribbean bar serves spicy, big-flavoured food. Rum and various peppers turn the predominately seafood dishes into mouth-watering treats, and even more pedestrian-sounding fare (stews and barbecues) mix fruit and punch with flair. The fixed-price dinners on Monday draw a crowd that stays for the free music, usually local rock. *See also p122* **Pubs & Bars** *& p204* **Nightlife**.

Grendel's

89 Winthrop Street, at John F Kennedy Street, Cambridge (491 1050). Harvard T.
Open 11am-11pm Mon-Thur, Sun; 11am-midnight Fri, Sat. **Main courses** $6. **Credit** AmEx, Disc, MC, V. **Map 4 B2/3**

The last of the hippie hangouts, famous since the Supreme Court case that won this one-time Harvard 'Finals' club a liquor licence over the objection of a nearby church, Grendel's still rules for casual food and ambience. The long salad bar and the burgers and melts provide comfort grub for carnivores and vegetarians alike in a cavernous main room conveniently hunkered down in the middle of Harvard Square. In the bar below a big log fire blazes when winter kicks in.

Harvest

44 Brattle Street, at Church Street, Cambridge (868 2255). Harvard T. **Open** 11.30am-11pm Mon-Thur; 11.30am-midnight Fri, Sat; 5.30-11pm Sun. **Main courses** $20-$27. **Credit** AmEx, Disc, MC, V. **Map 4 B2**

This newly re-opened Harvard Square institution has quickly reclaimed its regular hum of Brattle Street architects and academics of a certain age. Foodies who make it past this bar-crowding crew will find that the refurbished surroundings accompany a new commitment to innovative preparations and fresh, local fare. Surely the city's Puritan forefathers didn't envision Harvest's sea bass over saffron ratatouille or turnip soup garnished with duck confit? But food fads (Maine 'peeky-toe' crab, roasted marrow bones) only add to the flavours of a classic splurge revived.

Disabled: toilet.

Henrietta's Table

Charles Hotel, 1 Bennett Street (661 5005). Harvard T. **Open** 6.30am-3pm, 5-10pm, Mon-Thur, Sun; 6.30am-3pm, 5-11pm, Fri, Sat. **Main courses** $9 lunch, $15 dinner. **Credit** AmEx, DC, MC, V. **Map 4 B2**

Set in the Charles Hotel, this upmarket take on a New England farmers' market focuses on fresh and 'honest' fare, but lots of crisp vegetables do not necessarily make a meal interesting. Nice presentation – great pickles, big comfortable wooden chairs – make dining here pleasant, but unspectacular.

Disabled: toilet.

House of Blues

96 Winthrop Street, at John F Kennedy Street, Cambridge (491 2583). Harvard T. **Open** 11.30am-11.30pm Mon-Sat; 4-11pm Sun. **Main courses** $14. **Credit** AmEx, Disc, MC, V. **Map 4 B2**

The food reflects the music on the first floor of this small Harvard Square club, the first of the national chain. That means Southern, with a rich, if somewhat tomato-packed, jambalaya, jalapeño-studded cornbread and a respectably dark gumbo. The acts upstairs can be seen and heard via video monitors, so you can linger over your bread pudding. *See also p205* **Nightlife**.

Disabled: toilet.

India Pavilion

17 Western Avenue, at Massachusetts Avenue, Cambridge (547 7463). Central T. **Open** noon-11pm daily. **Main courses** $10. **Credit** AmEx, DC, MC, V. **Map 4 C3**

Central Square houses a cluster of decent Indian restaurants, all serving up the standard spinach saags and creamy jalfrezis, but India Pavilion stands a cut above its neighbours, with distinctive flavourings and budget-conscious dishes.

Iruña

56 John F Kennedy Street, at Memorial Drive, Cambridge (354 8576). Harvard T. **Lunch served** 11.30am-2pm Mon-Thur; 11.30am-4.30pm Fri, Sat. **Dinner served** 6-9pm Mon-Thur; 6-10pm Fri; 5.30-11pm Sat. **Main courses** $14. **Credit** AmEx, Disc, MC, V. **Map 4 B2**

Poet Robert Lowell reportedly brought his students here, and locals still flock to this cosy spot for richly fragrant garlic soup, paella and other Castilian treats. Enthusiastically courtly service helps make this inexpensive Harvard Square restaurant a treat, as does the small but romantic backyard patio.

Korea Garden

20 Pearl Street, at Massachusetts Avenue, Cambridge (492 9643). Central T. **Lunch served** noon-3pm Mon-Sat. **Dinner served** 5.30-10.30pm Mon-Fri; 5.30-11pm Sat. **Meals served** 1-10pm Sun. **Main courses** $10. **Credit** DC, Disc, MC, V. **Map 4 C3**

Tucked in among Central Square's ethnic restaurant enclave, this family-run storefront Korean has been delivering cheap and hearty food to garlic-loving locals for almost two decades. With big bowls of the egg, meat and veggie bi bim bap and sweet-hot bulgogi barbecue for comfort, as well as the eye-stinging heat of yuk kai jang soup to fight the winter chill, this fine little restaurant sustains the Seoul of the city.

Magnolia's

1193 Cambridge Street, at Tremont Street, Cambridge (576 1971). Central T. **Open** 6-10pm Tue-Sat. **Main courses** $9.95-$20.95. **Credit** AmEx, DC, Disc, MC, V. **Map 4 D2**

The one-time Cajun Yankee, which introduced Louisiana cuisine to this region more than 15 years ago, now reaches out to the entire South. Fried green tomatoes and Maryland crab cakes join the jambalaya and blackened pork loin on tables

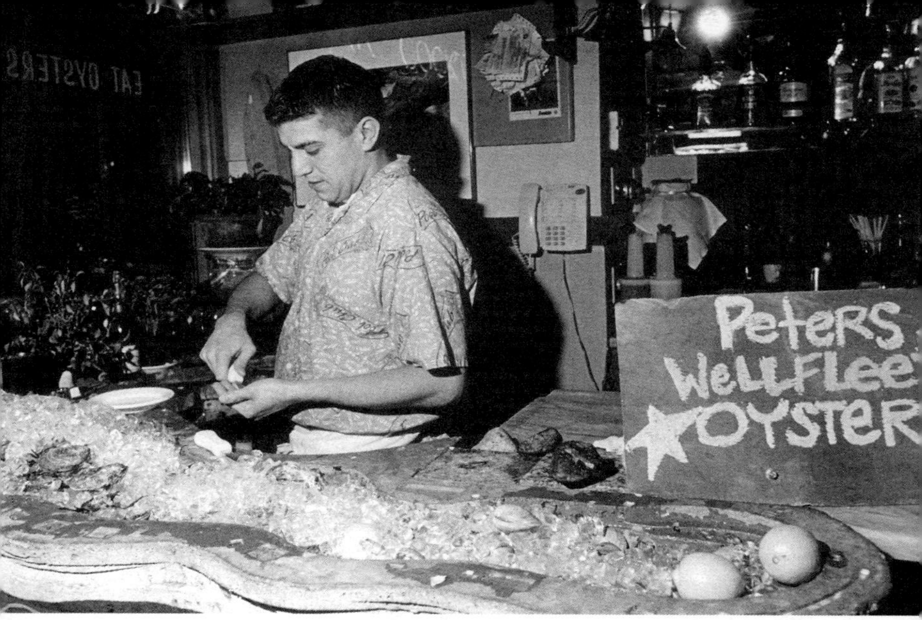

The oysters get snapped up fast at the **East Coast Grill** *in Cambridge. See page 151.*

clustered beneath Mardi Gras beads. Desserts are pure New Orleans, with lots of pecans and butter in the praline parfait and a variety of pies.

Mary Chung

464 Massachusetts Avenue, at Main Street, Cambridge (864 1991). Central T. **Open** 11.30am-10pm Mon, Wed, Thur, Sun; 11.30am-11pm Fri, Sat. **Main courses** $7. **No credit cards. Map 4 D3**

Recently re-opened after a several-year absence, Mary's hasn't missed a beat. MIT brains are still powered by her gaspingly hot suan la chow show 'soup' (really a combination of wonton and bean sprouts in hot oil and soy sauce) and Szechuan specials such as the yang chow chicken, with its lettuce and pine nuts, remain consistently superb. Somehow tang, sweet and hot come together in nearly every generous dish. Those Techies aren't dumb, you know.
Disabled: toilet.

Midwest Grill

1124 Cambridge Street, at Norfolk Street, Cambridge (354 7536). Lechmere T, then 61 bus. **Open** 11.30am-11pm daily. **Main courses** $15. **Credit** AmEx, DC, Disc, MC, V. **Map 4 D3**

The Brazilian Midwest Grill is a carnivore's dream. In the churrascaria tradition of primal dinner theatre, everything is grilled and the spits taken from table to table, where waiters lop off peppery sausages and crispy chicken parts or carve from melting tenderloins and joints. The accompanying salad bar – with rice, beans, and hearts of palm – is the only concession to vegetarians or nutritional balance.
Disabled: toilet.

Porter House Grill

2046 Massachusetts Avenue, at Creighton Street, Cambridge (497 9222). Porter T. **Open** 11.30am-3pm, 5-10pm, Mon-Thur, Sun; 11.30am-3pm, 5-11pm, Fri, Sat. **Main courses** $10.95. **Credit** MC, V.

This popular North Cambridge bar calls itself a Memphis grill and has a ferocious barbecue to prove it. Beef ribs and brisket are on the menu, but it leans appropriately toward pork, in 'pulled' (shredded) sandwiches and meaty chop-like Mississippi ribs, with sauces as hot as you dare.
Disabled: toilet.

Rialto

1 Bennett Street, at the Charles Hotel, Cambridge (661 5050). Harvard T. **Dinner served** 5.30-10pm Mon-Thur, Sun; 5.30-11pm Fri, Sat. **Main courses** $26. **Credit** AmEx, DC, MC, V. **Map 4 B3**

Relax on one of the overstuffed banquettes and enjoy the latest in celebrity chef Lydia Shire's offerings: vaguely European combinations of tuna, veal and what have you, meticulously prepared and fancifully presented. Many swear by desserts such as the hot chocolate cream. *See also p124* **Pubs & Bars**.
Disabled: toilet.

Roka

101 Massachusetts Avenue, at Dana Street, Cambridge (661 0344). Central T. **Lunch served** 11.30am-2.30pm, **dinner served** 5.30-10.30pm, daily. **Main courses** $13-$17. **Credit** AmEx, DC, Disc, MC, V. **Map 4 C3**

Feather-light tempura and generous sushi combos show how Roka, one of the last straight-Japanese restaurants, survives. From the hot towels through the fragrant miso and down to the green tea ice-cream, Roka is a classic.

Royal East

782 Main Street, at Windsor Street, Cambridge (661 1660). Central T. **Open** 11.30am-10pm Mon-Thur, Sun; 11.30am-11.30pm Fri, Sat. **Main courses** $8. **Credit** AmEx, DC, MC, V. **Map 4 D4**

Big enough to accommodate the **Mary Chung** (*see above*) overflow, Royal East offers many of the same Chinese dishes (such as the beansprout-and-wonton suan la chow show) at nearly the same quality and has big round tables that are great for parties.
Disabled: toilet.

Salamander

1 Athenaeum Street, at First Street, Cambridge (225 2121). Kendall/MIT or Lechmere T. **Dinner served** 5.30-9pm Mon-Sat. **Main courses** $25. **Credit** AmEx, DC, MC, V. **Map 4 E3**

Deep-fried lobster with Thai curry sauce? Duck that's half confit, half Peking-style? Hotshot chef Chris Schlesinger's latest project makes indulgence fun, and Salamander gives its diners their (considerable) money's worth in dining-as-theatre. A playful fusion menu and exquisite service are complemented by a low-key arty atmosphere.
Disabled: toilet.

Sandrine's Bistro

8 Holyoke Street, between Massachusetts Avenue & Mount Auburn Street, Cambridge (497 5300). Harvard T. **Lunch served** 11.30am-2.30pm Tue-Sat. **Dinner served** 5.30-10pm Tue-Thur; 5.30-10.30pm Fri, Sat. **Main courses** $16-$30. **Credit** AmEx, MC, V. **Map 4 B2**

More of a brasserie than a bistro, Harvard Square's Sandrine's serves up classic Alsace fare with a twist. Traditional heavy dishes, such as the sausage-and-sauerkraut choucroûte, are also available in seafood versions, and the piquant herring comes piled into a pyramid with slices of apple. With the menu's heavy reliance on meat – venison with spiced raisin sauce, grilled veal chops – diners might be tempted to skip dessert. The sampler of three treats, intensely flavoured with cassis and cocoa, is a good reason not to. Service is impeccable and friendly.
Disabled: toilet.

S&S Deli Restaurant

1334 Cambridge Street, at Prospect Street, Cambridge (354 0777). Harvard T. **Open** 7am-11pm Mon, Tue; 7am-midnight Wed-Sat; 8am-11pm Sun. **Main courses** $5. **No credit cards. Map 4 D2**

A great, basic deli where breakfast is served up until closing time. Join the queue at this 80-year-old Inman Square institution for bagels and overflowing omelettes on Sunday mornings, or slide into a booth for late-night comfort food and ridiculously rich desserts. Fancier daily specials are sometimes over-ambitious and seafood is often overcooked, but basics such as onion-packed chopped liver and piled-on pastrami never fail.
Disabled: toilet.

Shilla

57 John F Kennedy Street, at Winthrop Street, Cambridge (547 7971). Harvard T. **Open** 11.30am-10.30pm Mon-Wed, Sun; 11.30am-1am Thur-Sat. **Main courses** $10-$25. **Credit** AmEx, DC, Disc, MC, V. **Map 4 B2**

Sparkling sushi and slightly tamed Korean dishes make this basement a popular venue. Fusion dishes, such as tuna sashimi with a sweetly incendiary Korean hot sauce, show the flair which this recently relocated Harvard Square spot is capable of.
Disabled: toilet.

Trattoria Pucinella

147 Huron Avenue, at Concord Avenue, Cambridge (491 6336). Harvard T. **Lunch served** 11.30am-2.30pm Tue-Thur. **Dinner served** 5-10pm Mon-Thur, Sun; 5-11pm Fri, Sat. **Main courses** $18-$25. **No credit cards. Map 4 A1**

This tiny trattoria celebrates the full flavours of Naples and its environs, adding pine nuts and raisins to veal 'Siracusana' style and pairing wide pappardella noodles with sardines and fennel. Wait to hear about the numerous specials before ordering, however, since they're invariably inventive.

Up Stairs at the Pudding

10 Holyoke Street, between Mount Auburn Street & Massachusetts Avenue, Cambridge (864 1933). Harvard T. **Lunch served** 11.30am-2.30pm Mon-Sat; 11am-2pm Sun. **Dinner served** 5.30-9.30pm daily. **Main courses** $18-$33. **Credit** AmEx, MC, V. **Map 4 B2**

A cavernous green and red room surrounded by Harvard's theatrical Hasty Pudding Club memorabilia may seem an odd setting for fine, European-inspired cuisine, but even non-Crimson types flock to the Pudding for rare, seared duck breast, rack of lamb and New England bouillabaisse piled high with cherrystone clams. In warm weather, the herb garden patio fills up quickly, particularly at brunchtime.
Disabled: toilet.

Yenching

1326 Massachusetts Avenue, at Holyoke Street, Cambridge (547 1130). Harvard T. **Open** 11.30am-11pm daily. **Main courses** $8. **Credit** MC, V. **Map 4 B2**

Recently renovated and always reliable, this bright Harvard Square Chinese offers specials (such as a buffet lunch) that keep it reasonably packed. The big Mandarin-Szechuan menu can be misleadingly tempting – stick with the Szechuan specials – but a good spice-to-grease ratio and accommodating hours (it's even open on Christmas Day) keep this a local favourite.

Somerville

Also in the area

Bertucci's (*see page 148*).

Dalí

415 Washington Street, at Beacon Street, Somerville (661 3254). Harvard T. **Dinner served** 5.30-11pm daily. **Main courses** $17-$22; *tapas* $2.50-$7.50. **Credit** AmEx, DC, MC, V. **Map 4 C2**

Dalí, decidedly one of the best eateries in the Boston area, also features some of the best flamenco-dancing waiters this side of the Atlantic. The atmosphere is animated, from the chatter at the bar (festooned with cured ham and dried vegetables) to the lively Spanish music. There's usually a queue (reservations are only accepted for large parties) for those waiting to try the dizzying array of savoury and creative tapas. The sangria's great, but there's also an exceptional list of wines and sherries. Ask for one of the two-person booth tables if it's intimacy you're after.

eat

253 Washington Street, at Somerville Avenue, Somerville (776 2889). Central or Harvard T. **Dinner served** 6-10pm Mon-Wed; 6-10.30pm Thur-Sat; 5.30-9.30pm Sun. **Main courses** $12-$18. **Credit** DC, Disc, MC, V. **Map 4 D2**

This cosy American eclectic is so eager to feed that its name insists that you nourish yourself. The menu draws upon various influences, from Cajun-style catfish and jasmine rice to Italian antipasto and pasta. At eat, nothing is fancy. The overall theme is one of comfort – there are even old armchairs to make you feel at home.
Disabled: toilet.

Evoo

118 Beacon Street, at Washington Street, Somerville (661 3866). Harvard T, then 87 bus. **Dinner served** 6-10pm Mon-Thur; 6-11pm Fri, Sat. **Main courses** $16-$23. **Credit** AmEx, Disc, MC, V. **Map 4 C2**

An acronym for extra virgin olive oil, Evoo is the new Mediterranean spot in Somerville, featuring a wild ensemble of tastes in its wide array of dishes. Chef Peter McCarthy cooks up adventurous variations of seafood, quail, soups,

Restaurants & cafés by cuisine

American & New England
Bartley's Burger Cottage *p148*; Blue Diner *p133*; Bob the Chef's Café *p138*; Border Café *p149*; Bristol Lounge *p133*; Café Fleuri *p133*; Cambridge Common *p149*; Capital Grille *p127*; Christopher's *p150*; Durgin-Park *p133*; eat *p154*; Fire and Ice *p151*; Franklin Café *p139*; Gargoyles on the Square *p156*; Grendel's *p152*; Grill 23 & Bar *p127*; House of Blues *p152*; Jake's Boss BBQ *p148*; Magnolia's *p152*; Porter House Grill *p153*; Redbones *p156*; South Street Diner *p135*.

Cafés, coffeehouses & delis
Algiers Coffee House *p133*; Au Bon Pain *p132*; Caffe Graffiti *p133*; Caffe Paradiso *p133*; Caffe Victoria *p133*; Carberry's Bakery and Coffee-house *p149*; Curious Liquids *p133*; Designs for Living *p133*; Dunkin' Donuts *p132*; Le Gamin *p139*; Hazel's Cup and Saucer *p133*; Mildred's *p133*; Other Side Cosmic Café *p133*; Panificio *p133*; Il Panino Express *p138*; S&S Deli Restaurant *p154*; Salt & Pepper Café *p156*; Someday Café *p156*; Sound Bites *p156*; Starbucks *p133*; 1369 Coffee House *p133*; Travis Restaurant *p129*; Zaftigs *p148*.

Chinese
Buddha's Delight *p129*; Changsho *p153*; Chau Chow *p129*; Mary Chung *p153*; New Shanghai Restaurant *p129*; Pearl Dynasty *p129*; Royal East *p153*; Yenching *p154*.

French & Continental
Aquitaine *p141*; Brasserie Jo *p126*; Café Celador *p149*; Chez Henri *p150*; Hungry I *p129*; Les Zygomates *p135*; Restaurant Zinc *p143*; Sandrine's Bistro *p153*; Truc *p141*; Union Square Bistro *p156*.

Good for vegetarians
Bombay Club *p149*; Buddha's Delight *p129*; Cena *p138*; Grendel's *p152*; Masao's Kitchen *p151*.

Haute cuisine
Aujourd'hui *p132*; L'Espalier *p127*; Julien *p133*; Maison Robert *p135*.

Indian
Bombay Club *p149*; India Pavilion *p152*; Kashmir *p127*; Rangoli *p145*.

International
Addis Red Sea *p138*; Café St Petersburg *p147*; Cena *p138*; Istanbul Café *p131*; Lala Rokh *p131*.

Italian & Mediterranean
Angelo's Ristorante *p126*; Antico Forno *p137*; Armani Café *p126*; Artu *p131*; Bertucci's *p148*; La Bettola *p138*; Café Louis *p127*; Davio's *p151*; Evoo *p154*; Galleria Italiana *p135*; Giannino's *p152*; Mamma Maria *p137*; Noodles *p156*; Il Panino *p138*; Pomodoro *p138*; Sage *p138*; Sonsie *p131*; Terramia *p138*; Trattoria il Panino *p138*; Trattoria Pucinella *p154*; Uva *p147*; Vinny's *p156*.

Japanese & Korean
Café Mami *p151*; Common Market *p150*; Ginza *p129*; Gyuhama *p127*; Korea Garden *p152*; Kotobukiya *p150*; Masao's Kitchen *p151*; Roka *p153*; Shilla *p154*; Tampopo *p150*.

Mexican & Tex-Mex
Casa Mexico *p149*; Cottonwood Café *p127*; Forest Café *p152*; Palenque *p156*; Picante *p156*; Sol Azteca *p137*; Taqueria la Mexicana *p156*.

New American & celebrity chefs
Anago *p126*; Audubon Circle *p137*; Biba *p126*; Blue Room *p148*; Claremont Café *p139*; Clío *p127*; East Coast Grill *p151*; Hamersley's Bistro *p139*; Harvest *p152*; Harvey's *p141*; Henrietta's Table *p152*; Icarus *p141*; Metropolis Café *p141*; Marcuccio's *p137*; Mistral *p143*; No.9 Park *p135*; Olives *p139*; Pignoli *p137*; Providence *p127*; Rialto *p153*; Salamander *p154*; Tremont 647 *p143*; Up Stairs at the Pudding *p154*; The Vault *p135*.

Pizza
Bertucci's *p148*; Bluestone Bistro *p145*; Figs *p131*.

Seafood
The Barking Crab *p132*; Daily Catch *p137*; Dolphin Seafood *p151*; Legal Sea Foods *p135*; No-Name *p135*; Tutto Mare *p138*; Ye Olde Union Oyster House *p135*.

South American & Caribbean
Green Street Grill *p152*; Midwest Grill *p153*; Mucho Gusto *p131*.

Southeast Asian & fusion
Ambrosia on Huntington *p126*; Brown Sugar *p137*; Ducky Wok *p145*; Elephant Walk *p137*; Jae's Cafe and Grill *p141*; The King & I *p131*; Penang *p129*; Pho Bolsa Restaurant *p129*; Pho Pasteur *p129*.

Spanish & Portuguese
Casa Portugal *p149*; Dalí *p154*; Iruña *p152*; Neighborhood Restaurant and Bakery *p156*; Taberna de Haro *p148*; Tapéo *p126*; Tasca *p147*.

beef tenderloin and chicken. Abuzz since its opening, this is perhaps the only Somerville restaurant that can get away with charging South End prices.
Disabled: toilet.

Gargoyles on the Square

215 Elm Street, at Russell Street, Somerville (776 5300). Davis T. **Dinner served** 5-10pm Tue, Wed; 5-10.30pm Thur-Sat; 5-8pm Sun. **Main courses** $17. **Credit** AmEx, MC, V.
Perhaps the snazziest restaurant in Davis Square, Gargoyles has a moderately-priced menu of well-presented and excellently prepared American food, leading with squash soup, risotto, salmon, lamb, beef and duck. The intimate tables make this a good spot for a date and the Martinis are a hit.
Disabled: toilet.

Neighborhood Restaurant and Bakery

25 Bow Street, at Walnut Street, Somerville (623 9710). Lechmere T, then 87 bus. **Open** 7am-9pm Mon-Sat; 7am-3pm Sun. **Main courses** $8.99. **No credit cards.**
The breakfasts are gigantic at this inexpensive eatery, where Portuguese food is served up for lunch and dinner.

Noodles

414 Washington Street, at Beacon Street, Somerville (492 1770). Harvard T. **Open** 11am-9pm Mon-Thur; 11am-10pm Fri, Sat. **Main courses** $5.95-$10.95. **Credit** MC, V. **Map 4 C2**
Nestled between the celebrated **Dalí** (*see p154*) and **Evoo** (*see p154*), Noodles is *the* Somerville place for takeaways. While there are about ten tables for two, most people stop by and pick up homemade lasagne, spaghetti or ravioli, or a soul-warming soup full of noodles and fresh vegetables. Lighter fare includes panini and spicy pasta salads full of fresh herbs. Fresh pasta for home cooking is also on sale.
Disabled: toilet.

Palenque

300 Beacon Street, at Eustis Street, Somerville (491 1004). Harvard or Porter T. **Dinner served** 5-10pm Tue-Sat; 5-9pm Sun. **Main courses** $5-$15. **Credit** AmEx, DC, Disc, MC, V. **Map 4 C1**
Named after an ancient Mayan city, Palenque is a casual restaurant (a step up from the usual order-at-the-counter style) featuring pure Mexican fare without the influence of the American Southwest. Fresh, homemade salsa and guacamole back up the roster of meat-centric dishes served on oval platters with refried beans and rice.
Disabled: toilet.

Picante

217 Elm Street, at Cutter Avenue, Somerville (628 6394). Davis T. **Open** 11am-10pm Mon-Thur, Sun; 11am-11.30pm Fri; 11am-11pm Sat. **Main courses** $4-$7. **No credit cards.**
A small Davis Square Mexicali joint that serves huge portions of fresh and flavourful tacos, chips, quesadillas, burritos and enchiladas. Special combo platters come with sides of rice, black beans and salad.
Disabled: toilet.

Redbones

55 Chester Street, at Elm Street, Somerville (628 2200). Davis T. **Open** 11.30am-10.30pm daily. **Main courses** $7-$15. **No credit cards.**
Probably the Boston area's best barbecue, this Davis Square two-floor favourite, which is full of cafeteria-style tables, slow-cooks succulent ribs and brisket in the classic Southern style. Flaky fried catfish, spongy cornbread and spicy corn pudding are among the lighter offerings. Huge platters, such as the nearly foot-high pile of ribs and brisket called the 'Barbecue Belt', will put you in a meat coma. There are two lively bars serving an extensive variety of beers, including a 'barbecued' one. As good as Southern cooking gets this far north.
Disabled: toilet.

Salt & Pepper Café

81 Holland Street, at Irving Street, Somerville (666 1376). Davis T. **Open** 6.30am-7pm Mon-Fri; 7am-7pm Sat; 7.30am-3pm Sun. **Main courses** $5. **Credit** MC, V.
This is where to go when you need items for a picnic or just a quickly prepared and fresh sandwich. Buttermilk biscuits, huge muffins, banana-nut or zucchini bread and coffee cake come straight from the oven. Heartier items include roll-ups, focaccia sandwiches and 'pulled' pork.
Disabled: toilet.

Someday Café

51 Holland Street, at Davis Square, Somerville (623 3323). Davis T. **Open** 7am-11pm Mon-Thur; 7am-midnight Fri; 8am-midnight Sat; 8am-11pm Sun. **Main courses** *coffee & pastry* $2.65. **No credit cards.**
A local writers' haven in the decidedly unromantic Davis Square. Coffee and tea, as well as cold drinks, are served in laid-back surroundings, where laptops are just as prevalent as notebooks. Couches and board games are also on hand for those less creatively inclined.
Disabled: toilet.

Sound Bites

708 Broadway, at Willow Street, Somerville (623 8338). Sullivan Square T, then 89 bus. **Open** 7am-3pm daily. **Main courses** $4-$5. **No credit cards. Map 4 D3**
This cheap and inventive little café's main draw is its excellent breakfasts (try the eggs Benedict). At lunchtime, Middle Eastern food is served.
Disabled: toilet.

Taqueria la Mexicana

47 Washington Street, at Somerville Avenue, Somerville (776 5232). Porter T, then 87 bus. **Open** 9am-10pm Mon-Sat; 10am-9pm Sun. **Main courses** $5. **No credit cards. Map 4 D2**
An inexpensive burrito joint owned and operated by natives of San Luis, Mexico. Choose your preferred combination of beans, vegetables, rice or meat. The enchiladas and nachos are also popular.

Union Square Bistro

16 Bow Street, at Somerville Avenue, Somerville (628 3344). Lechmere T, then 87 bus or Sullivan Square T, then 86, 91 bus. **Lunch served** noon-3pm Sun. **Dinner served** 5-9pm Mon-Thur, Sun; 5-10pm Fri, Sat. **Main courses** $12.95-$19.95. **Credit** AmEx, DC, Disc, MC, V. **Map 4 D1**
This French casual-but-elegant bistro is one of the city's better restaurants and a good spot for a classic but not-overpriced French meal. The menu changes seasonally and there's a reasonably priced wine list. During warm weather there's a pleasant deck for outdoor dining.

Vinny's

76 Broadway, at Hawthorn Street, Somerville (628 1921). Sullivan Square T. **Open** 4.30-10.30pm Tue-Fri; 4.30-11pm Sat, Sun. **Main courses** $10-$20. **Credit** MC, V.
Vinny's Superette café by day, this place transforms itself into a side-street Mediterranean dining room at night, serving savoury stews, meatballs, salads, calamari, pizzas, lobster, roasts, imported smoked cheeses and, of course, big portions of pasta. There are two guys named Vinny: uncle and nephew both cook.
Disabled: toilet.

Shops & Services

Boston and Cambridge offer plenty of opportunities for you to flex your credit card – if you know where to look.

Until the early 1980s, Boston's consumer profile was characterised mainly by its sturdy New England conservatism. Speciality shops, funky boutiques and bohemian shopping outposts have always existed here and there, thanks largely to the city's enormous youth population, but the area's Puritan history and harsh winters tended to foster a no-nonsense aesthetic in fashion and lifestyle among the mainstream, and the majority of shops offered few surprises.

Fortunately, Boston is no longer a bastion of New England anti-style and the marketplace has grown to accommodate its increasingly cosmopolitan consumer demands. You can now wear just about any outrageous thing on the street without shocking the average city dweller (out in the 'burbs it's a different story), and the city's designer boutiques, large urban malls and cross-section of speciality shops provide some satisfying spending opportunities – especially since there's no state tax on clothing in Massachusetts.

The goods may be out there, but finding them isn't always easy. Shopping in Boston can be a lot like driving in Boston: you have to know where you're going, and navigating between destinations can be tricky.

WHERE TO SHOP

Central Boston has several concentrated shopping areas and malls that are well worth visiting, but some of the more unusual finds are scattered all over town, as well as in Cambridge and the suburbs. All the areas listed here are accessible by public transport (sometimes a little walking is involved), but driving is recommended if you're heading towards the fringes of town.

For an easy one-day spree, you might want to stick to the major shopping areas. The **Back Bay** offers the best shopping, with two large malls and the city's most famous shopping strip, Newbury Street, all within steps of each other.

The commercial stretch of **Newbury Street** is nine blocks long. The most expensive upmarket boutiques are at the Arlington Street end of the street, where the venerable Ritz-Carlton is located. A couple of blocks down Arlington Street is Park Square, where you'll find a cluster of designer and classy speciality shops. The top of Newbury Street, at Massachusetts Avenue, represents the funkier, more youthful end of the spectrum. The **Prudential Center** mall, filled mainly with reputable national chain stores, is a short walk away. One of the Pru's best features is that it's connected to the upmarket Copley Place mall by a glassed-in bridge, so you can easily cross from one to the other without dealing with bad weather or traffic.

Copley Place, a posh retail centre decked in marble, features both designer shops and topflight chain stores and boutiques. Continue south from Copley and you come to the **South End**. The shops here are New York-chic, but not always clustered conveniently together.

Downtown Crossing is the first stop for many visitors to town, due partly to the fame of Filene's Basement, an automatic-markdown store in which bargains can be found if you can stand the chaos and confusion. There are also two major mainstream department stores here – Macy's and Filene's (no longer affiliated with the bargain basement store). **Washington Street**, the main drag, is crowded with vending carts and stalls, and old pen shops and bookshops are tucked away on some of the side streets. This is a high-intensity area, so if you're in the mood for a charming window-shopping stroll, head elsewhere.

Across Boston Common, **Beacon Hill** is a neighbourhood of narrow, hilly streets and expensive townhouses. **Charles Street** is the main shopping avenue. Its antique and gift shops, gourmet grocers and boutiques tend to be pricey, but most of what you'll see is impeccably tasteful. Further downtown, near the waterfront, the **Faneuil Hall/Quincy Market** area is one of the region's most popular tourist attractions, so it's often uncomfortably crowded, but the cobblestoned setting is quaint and there are a number of boutiques and stores worth visiting. From here, you can walk to the **Haymarket** to explore the open food stalls, or investigate the old-world Italian charm of the **North End** nearby.

In **Cambridge**, a visit to Harvard Square is recommended. The streets are busy with international crowds, academics, teenage punks, hippies, yuppies and street performers – some of them actually good. **Harvard Square** has branches of many of the same stores you'll find on Newbury Street, as well as a few unique finds. It's a smaller shopping district, but offers a good mix of hip shops and bookstores. Other Cambridge shopping destinations include the **Porter Square** area, where the shops become increasingly interesting as you head north on Massachusetts Avenue but are more spread out than in Harvard Square.

For a decidedly boho shopping experience, visit **Allston**, a Boston neighbourhood currently balanced midway between funky student/artist ghetto and yuppie-gentrified urban village. Along the main thoroughfare of **Harvard Avenue** you'll find Vietnamese grocers, student-quality furniture outlets, music stores, antique shops and subculture shopping spots.

Antiques & collectibles

Antique Revival

1 Harvard Avenue, at Cambridge Street, Allston (787 4040). Harvard Ave T. **Open** 11am-6pm daily. **Credit** AmEx, MC, V. **Map 4 A4/5**

One of Allston's most reliably interesting antique shops, selling wooden furniture, lamps and collectibles from the eighteenth to the twentieth century.

Brodney Gallery

145 Newbury Street, at Dartmouth Street (536 0500). Copley T. **Open** 10am-5.45pm Mon-Sat; noon-5pm Sun. **Credit** AmEx, MC, V. **Map 3 F5**

A classy, well-established gallery selling paintings from the eighteenth to the twentieth century, bronze, jewellery, watches, estate pieces, furniture, fine French antiques, clocks and Oriental art.

Cambridge Antique Market

201 Monsignor O'Brien Highway, Cambridge (868 9655). Lechmere T. **Open** 11am-6pm Tue-Sun. **Credit** Disc, MC, V. **Map 4 F3**

A dusty, five-level warehouse filled with eighteenth- to twentieth-century antique and collectable furniture, houseware, china, toys, ephemera, clothing and various bits and pieces of decorative arts. The London Café on the fourth floor serves light lunches.

JMW Gallery

144 Lincoln Street, at Beach Street (338 9097). South Station T. **Open** 11am-6pm Tue-Fri; 11am-5pm Sat. **Credit** Disc, MC, V. **Map 5 G5**

This gallery specialises in Mission and Arts & Crafts styles: furniture, lighting, American art pottery, metalwork, textiles and woodblock prints.

Website: www.jmwgallery.com

Machine Age

354 Congress Street, at A Street (482 0048). South Station T. **Open** noon-5pm Tue-Sat. **Credit** AmEx, MC, V. **Map 5 H5**

A giant showroom with an exceptional selection of classic, contemporary designs – Herman Miller, Charles Eames, George Nelson and the like – and a variety of twentieth-century artefacts in good condition.

Marcoz Antiques

177 Newbury Street, between Dartmouth & Exeter Streets (262 0780). Copley T. **Open** 10am-6pm Mon-Sat. **Credit** AmEx, Disc, MC, V. **Map 3 E/F5**

Marcoz sells eighteenth- and nineteenth-century French and English furniture and stylish decorative arts.

Mucho Gusto

See page 131 **Restaurants & Cafés** *for listings.*

A Cuban bistro selling vintage 1930s to 1950s Cuban and American kitsch and collectibles such as cigar advertising art, television lamps, bakelite radios, plaster fruit wall decorations and dolls. If you haggle entertainingly enough, you'll be rewarded with a free cup of Cuban coffee.

Sadye & Co

182 Massachusetts Avenue, at Albany Street, Cambridge (547 4424). Central or Kendall/MIT T. **Open** 11am-6pm Mon-Sat; noon-5pm Sun. **Credit** AmEx, MC, V. **Map 4 D4**

An inviting clutter of mostly twentieth-century furniture, housewares and ephemera, with some nineteenth-century pieces and the occasional well-priced, fabulous find.

Army & Navy stores

Generation after generation of American kids and construction workers have outfitted themselves at Army & Navy stores, where the clothes and boots are built to last, in both youth-style and substance.

Harry the Greek's Dover Bargain Store

1136 Washington Street, at East Berkeley Street (338 7511). NE Medical Center T. **Open** 8am-5.30pm Mon-Sat. **Credit** Disc, MC, V. **Map 5 G6**

Now into its 65th year, this family-owned business sells sneakers, sweatshirts, work clothes, work boots and some department-store fashion lines, as well as surplus items, including Army fatigue jackets and Navy watchcaps, at 10% to 20% off.

Mass Army Navy Store

895 Boylston Street, at Gloucester Street (267 1559). Hynes/ICA T. **Open** 9.30am-8pm Mon-Sat; noon-6pm Sun. **Credit** AmEx, Disc, MC, V. **Map3 E5**

A reliable all-round retailer of Navy peacoats, Army jackets, snorkel jackets, Levi jeans, long underwear, Timberland boots, Adidas sneakers and more.

Branch: 698 Massachusetts Avenue, Cambridge (497 1250).

Art supplies

Johnson Paint and Art Materials

355 Newbury Street, at Massachusetts Avenue (536 4244). Hynes/ICA T. **Open** 7.30am-5.30pm Mon-Fri; 8.30am-1pm Sat. **Credit** Disc, MC, V. **Map 3 E5**

Not the cheapest supplier, but convenient to downtown and well stocked with the basics and some speciality items.

Pearl Art & Craft Supplies

597 Massachusetts Avenue, between Essex & Pearl Streets, Cambridge (547 6600). Central T. **Open** 9am-7pm Mon-Thur, Sat; 9am-8pm Fri; noon-6pm Sun. **Credit** AmEx, Disc, MC, V. **Map 4 C3**

The largest art supplier in the Boston area, with three floors of art and crafts supplies in all media except photography, from children's fingerpaints to professional drafting boards.

Packed with collectibles: the **Cambridge Antique Market**. *See page 158.*

Barbers

Gentlemen's Salon

79 Commercial Street, at Richmond Street (523 0112). Haymarket T. **Open** 9am-6pm Tue-Sat. **No credit cards. Map 5 H4**

This salon specialises in men's hairstyling and colour, with licensed barbers doing traditional clipper cuts as well as contemporary styles. Cuts cost $25. First-time clients get a 20% discount.

State Street Barbers

31 State Street, at Congress Street (723 3111). Downtown Crossing or State/Citizen's Bank T. **Open** 8.30am-6pm Mon-Fri; 8.30am-3pm Sat. **No credit cards. Map 5 G4**

Traditional clipping and razor cuts, and men's manicures.

Beauty supplies

Colonial Drug

49 Brattle Street, Cambridge (864 2222). Harvard T. **Open** 8am-7pm Mon-Fri; 8am-6pm Sat. **No credit cards. Map 4 A2**

A unique, family-run business for the last 53 years, this apothecary looks like a typical American corner drugstore, circa 1950, but carries lovelier things than bromides and hot-water bottles. Colonial Drug specialises in fine imported fragrance and beauty lines, some hard to find in department stores. It stocks Cellcosmet, Clarins, Decleor, Orlane, Christian Dior and Stendhal beauty products, fine grooming accessories and men's and women's fragrances by Hermés, Caron, Guerlain, Patou and others.

Fresh

121 Newbury Street, between Clarendon & Dartmouth Streets (421 1212). Copley T. **Open** 10am-7pm Mon-Sat; noon-6pm Sun. **Credit** AmEx, Disc, MC, V. **Map 3 F5**

Lev Glazman and Alina Roytberg's first beauty store, Nuts About Beauty, was everyone's favourite South End find, with an exquisite selection of imported, relatively inexpensive body-care and fragrance items. Their second store and first original collection, Fresh (an all-natural line of fragrance, bath and body products), has been hotter still and the company is booming. Now Fresh Make-Up and Life Fragrances are sold at the Newbury Street boutique, the Madison Avenue flagship store in New York and such prestigious cosmetic counters as Barney's New York and Colette in Paris.

Origins

8 Brattle Street, at Palmer Street, Cambridge (868 8090). Harvard T. **Open** 9am-9pm Mon-Sat; 11am-6pm Sun. **Credit** AmEx, Disc, MC, V. **Map 4 B2**

Sells Estee Lauder's minimally-packaged, chemical-free 'lifestyle' line of cosmetics, skin, hair and body-care products and accessories for women, men, babies – even dogs.

Bookshops

For international newsstands, *see chapter* **Media**.

Barnes & Noble

395 Washington Street, at Bromfield Street (426 5184). Downtown Crossing or Park St T. **Open** 9am-7pm Mon-Sat; 11am-6pm Sun. **Credit** AmEx, DC, Disc, MC, V. **Map 5 G4**

The largest downtown branch of the largest bookseller in the USA.

Branch: 325 Harvard Street, Brookline (232 0594).

Border's Books and Music

10-24 School Street, at Washington Street (557 7188). Gov't Center, Park St or State/Citizen's Bank T. **Open** 7am-9pm Mon-Sat; 10am-8pm Sun. **Credit** AmEx, Disc, MC, V. **Map 5 G4**

A large, well-stocked general-reading chain store with the added bonus of a music department and a café.

One of the oldest antiquarian bookshops in town: the **Brattle Book Shop**.

Globe Corner Bookstore

500 Boylston Street, between Berkeley & Clarendon Streets (859 8008). Arlington or Copley T.
Open 9.30am-8pm Mon-Fri; 9.30am-7pm Sat; noon-6pm Sun. **Credit** AmEx, Disc, MC, V.
Map 5 F5
The Globe is a travel reference shop selling books, maps, globes, atlases and guides.
Branch: 28 Church Street, Cambridge (497 6277).

Rizzoli Bookstore

Copley Place (437 0700). Back Bay or Copley T.
Open 10am-8pm Mon-Sat; noon-6pm Sun.
Credit AmEx, DC, Disc, MC, V. **Map 3 F5**
Specialises in books on art, architecture and photography. Also sells international CDs and tapes.

Waterstone's Booksellers

26 Exeter Street (859 7300). Copley T. **Open** 9am-10pm Mon-Sat; noon-8pm Sun. **Credit** AmEx, Disc, MC, V.
Map 3 E5
A branch of the British chain, this spacious shop housed in a beautiful old theatre building stocks a comprehensive selection of general literature, children's books, history, magazines and study materials. As you might expect, Waterstone's also stocks an exceptional selection of British and Irish fiction.
Branch: Quincy Market, Faneuil Hall Marketplace (589 0930).

WordsWorth Books

30 Brattle Street, at Concord Avenue, Cambridge (354 5201). Harvard T. **Open** 9am-11.15pm Mon-Sat; 10am-10.15pm Sun. **Credit** AmEx, Disc, MC, V.
Map 4 B1/2
A well-stocked discount bookshop with more than 100,000 titles on its shelves. Selected new titles, hardcover bestsellers, trade and paperback books are discounted anything from 10% to 40%.

Second-hand & rare books

Avenue Victor Hugo Book Shop

339 Newbury Street, between Hereford Street & Massachusetts Avenue (266 7746). Hynes/ICA T.
Open 10am-10pm Mon-Sat; noon-10pm Sun. **Credit** MC, V.
Map 3 E5
A dusty retreat complete with sleepy cats lying around, the Victor Hugo sells new and second-hand books on all subjects, rare and first editions and magazines dating back to 1850. Fiction, science fiction and history are a speciality.

Brattle Book Shop

9 West Street, at Washington Street (542 0210). Downtown Crossing or Park St T. **Open** 9am-5.30pm Mon-Sat. **Credit** AmEx, MC, V. **Map 5 G5**
A cosy old general bookshop with an antiquarian floor, established in 1825.

Boston Book Annex

906 Beacon Street, at Park Drive (266 1090). St Mary's T.
Open 10am-10pm Mon-Sat; noon-10pm Sun. **Credit** Disc, MC, V.
Sells second-hand recent releases, first editions, rare books and general reading.

McIntyre and Moore Booksellers

8 Mount Auburn Street, at Putnam Avenue, Cambridge (491 0662). Harvard T. **Open** 10am-10pm Mon-Sat; noon-10pm Sun. **Credit** AmEx, Disc, MC, V. **Map 4 C3**
Sells academic and scholarly books.

Cameras, video equipment & repair

Bromfield Camera and Video

10 Bromfield Street, between Washington & Tremont Streets (426 5230). Park St T. **Open** 8.30am-6pm

For club-friendly lines, head for **Allston Beat**. *See page 163.*

Mon-Fri; 9am-5.30pm Sat. **Credit** AmEx, Disc, MC, V. **Map 5 G4**
Sells and repairs new and second-hand cameras, video and digital equipment. Stocks a good selection of old and hard-to-find photographic equipment and supplies and carries out on-site repairs, sometimes while you wait.

Calumet Photographic

65 Bent Street, at First Street, Cambridge (576 2600). Lechmere T. **Open** 8am-6pm Mon-Fri. **Credit** AmEx, Disc, MC, V. **Map 4 E/F3**
Calumet stocks professional photo equipment for sale or rent, as well as photo supplies.

Campus Camera

636 Beacon Street, at Massachusetts Avenue (236 4400). Kenmore T. **Open** 10am-7pm Mon-Fri; 10am-6pm Sat; noon-5pm Sun. **Credit** AmEx, Disc, MC, V. **Map 3 E5**
A shop which sells still cameras and photo supplies. Enlargements and developing are carried out on the premises, repairs off-premises.

Children's clothes

See chapter **Children**.

Computer rental

Kinko's

187 Dartmouth Street, between Stuart & St James Streets (262 6188). Back Bay or Copley T. **Open** 24 hours daily. **Credit** AmEx, Disc, MC, V. **Map 3 F5**
A full-service copy and print shop with on-site hourly Mac and IBM rentals, Internet-ready. All major Microsoft applications and major graphic-design programmes are offered, including QuarkXPress and Photoshop. Kinko's also does colour laserprints, scanning and transparencies and will make custom greeting cards and calendars if you supply the photos. The round-the-clock opening hours are an added bonus.
Branches: 10 Post Office Square, at Milk Street (482 4400); 2 Center Plaza, Government Center (973 9000); 1 Muffin Place, Cambridge (497 0125).

Department stores

Discount

Filene's Basement

426 Washington Street, at Summer Street (542 2011). Downtown Crossing, Park St or State/Citizen's Bank T. **Open** 9.30am-7.30pm Mon-Fri; 9am-7.30pm Sat; 11am-7pm Sun. **Credit** AmEx, Disc, MC, V. **Map 5 G4**
The world-famous automatic-markdown store, with mid-quality to designer-label clothing, jewellery, housewares and bridal attire discounted from 48% to 70%. The spectacular steals are a matter of luck and fortitude, but there's usually something interesting to be found among the racks and racks of humdrum separates.
Disabled: toilet.

Loehmann's

385 Washington Street, between Winter & Bromfield Streets (338 7177). Downtown Crossing or Park St T. **Open** 9am-7.30pm Mon-Sat; 11am-6pm Sun. **Credit** Disc, MC, V. **Map 5 G4**
With the closing of the treasure-packed Back Room, Loehmann's is not the cache it once was, but it still sells some Calvin Klein and other designer labels with up to 40% off.
Disabled: toilet.

Marshall's

500 Boylston Street, at Clarendon Street (262 6066). Arlington or Copley T. **Open** 9am-9pm Mon-Sat; 11am-7pm Sun. **Credit** AmEx, Disc, MC, V. **Map 5 F5**
Marshall's sells brand-name men's, women's and children's clothing, as well as gifts, fine cutlery, shoes and accessories, at reductions of 20% to 40%. There's a smaller selection of designer labels.

General

Filene's

426 Washington Street, at Summer Street (357 2100). Downtown Crossing, Park St or State/Citizen's Bank T. **Open** 9.30am-7.30pm Mon-Sat; 11am-7pm Sun. **Credit** MC, V. **Map 5 G4**
Brand-name clothing, cosmetics, china, crystal, furniture, bridalwear, housewares and jewellery.

Macy's

450 Washington Street, at Summer Street (357 3000). Park St or State/Citizen's Bank T. **Open** 9.30am-7.30pm Mon-Sat; 11am-7pm Sun. **Credit** AmEx, MC, V. **Map 5 G4**
Brand-name clothing, cosmetics, housewares, china, crystal, furniture, mattresses and shoes. There's a good selection of lingerie and underwear. Alterations available.
Disabled: toilet.

Upmarket

Lord & Taylor

760 Boylston Street, at Exeter Street (262 6000). Copley T. **Open** 10am-9pm Mon-Fri; 10am-8pm Sat; 11am-7pm Sun. **Credit** AmEx, Disc, MC, V. **Map 3 E5**
Shoes, smart dresses, cosmetics, fine jewellery, lingerie, men's suits and accessories. It's a good-quality but fairly conservative selection.
Disabled: toilet.

Saks Fifth Avenue

Prudential Plaza (262 8500). Copley T. **Open** 10am-8pm Mon-Sat; noon-6pm Sun. **Credit** AmEx, DC, Disc, MC, V. **Map 3 E5**
Stocks top-quality clothing, shoes, jewellery and designer labels including Donna Karan, Calvin Klein, Versace and Giorgio Armani.
Disabled: toilet.

Fashion

See also **Department stores** *above.*

Speciality stores

Louis Boston

234 Berkeley Street, at Newbury Street (262 6100). Arlington T. **Open** 10am-6pm Mon, Tue, Fri, Sat; 10am-8pm Wed, Thur. **Credit** AmEx, JCB, MC, V. **Map 5 F5**
Considered by some to be one of the finest men's shops in the country, Louis has three floors of men's clothes and a single-floor women's department. It sells an upmarket house label as well as top designers from around the world, employs a staff of 'personal consultants' and has a chi-chi café frequented by socially prominent locals.
Disabled: toilet.

Neiman Marcus

5 Copley Place (536 3660). Back Bay or Copley T. **Open** 10am-8pm Mon-Sat; noon-6pm Sun. **Credit** AmEx, DC. **Map 3 F5**

Backbone of the Back Bay, Newbury Street is a consumers' and poseurs' paradise.

Neiman's doesn't call itself a department store ('high-end speciality store' is preferred) but has several departments, including furs, precious jewellery and designer clothing (Prada, Chanel, Loro Piana cashmere). The gift shop is referred to as a 'gallery'.

Boutiques

Alan Bilzerian

34 Newbury Street, between Arlington & Berkeley Streets (536 1001). Arlington T. **Open** 10am-6pm Mon-Sat. **Credit** AmEx, MC, V. **Map 5 F5**

An ultra-posh boutique with a selection of the world's top men's and women's designers. Has exclusive Boston selling rights on Yohji Yamamoto, Ann Demeulemeester, John Galliano and Raf Simons.

Bargain hunting at **Filene's Basement***.*

Allston Beat

348 Newbury Street, between Hereford Street & Massachusetts Avenue (421 9555). Hynes/ICA T. **Open** 11am-10pm Mon-Sat; noon-8pm Sun. **Credit** AmEx, MC, V. **Map 3 E5**

The place to shop if you plan to attend a rave. This local alternative institution sells Pimpgear, Doc Martens, Lip Service and other club-friendly lines, as well as glitzy accessories and body jewellery.

Bebe

Copley Place (267 2323). Back Bay or Copley T. **Open** 10am-8pm Mon-Sat; noon-6pm Sun. **Credit** AmEx, MC, V. **Map 3 F5**

If you're feeling sexy but not cheap, check out this line of chic, body-hugging suits, dresses and separates. The company drops client-list celebrity names, including Madonna and Drew Barrymore.

Jasmine Boutique and Sola Men

37 Brattle Street, at Church Street, Cambridge (354 6043). Harvard T. **Open** 10am-7pm Mon-Wed; 10am-8pm Thur, Fri; 10am-7pm Sat; noon-7pm Sun. **Credit** AmEx, DC, Disc, MC, V. **Map 4 B2**

Jasmine, a women's boutique and its brother store, Sola Men, are among the better fashion boutiques in town, with tastefully youthful collections of men's and women's sportswear, suits, shoes and accessories.

Branch: 333 Newbury Street (536 6697).

Riccardi

116 Newbury Street, between Clarendon & Dartmouth Streets (266 3158). Copley T. **Open** 11am-7pm Mon-Sat. **Credit** AmEx, JCB, MC, V. **Map 3 F5**

Caters to a Euro-chic clientele, with men's and women's sportswear, evening wear, coats, shoes and accessories by European and Japanese designers, including Boston exclusives on lines by Vivienne Westwood, Thierry Mugler, Comme des Garçons, D&G and Chrome Hearts.

Jasmine Boutique and Sola Men: *for tasteful accessories and essentials.* *See page 163.*

Serenella

134 Newbury Street, between Clarendon & Dartmouth Streets (262 5568). Copley T. **Open** 10am-6pm Mon-Sat. **Credit** AmEx, MC, V. **Map 3 F5**

Serenella sells up-and-coming as well as already established European designer lines.

Designers

Agnès B

172 Newbury Street, between Dartmouth & Exeter Streets (266 3300). Copley T. **Open** 11am-7pm Mon-Sat; noon-6pm Sun. **Credit** AmEx, MC, V. **Map 3 E/F5**

Well-cut classic Parisian styles in fashionable casual wear, dresses and elegantly understated evening wear.

Betsey Johnson

201 Newbury Street, between Exeter & Fairfield Streets (236 7072). Copley T. **Open** 11am-7pm Mon-Sat; noon-6pm Sun. **Credit** AmEx, MC, V. **Map 3 E5**

Famously funky designer of affordable to top-of-the-range separates, evening wear, shoes, accessories and jewellery. The clothes are known for their body-conscious design and sumptuous colour.

Chanel

5 Newbury Street, at Arlington Street (859 0055). Arlington T. **Open** 10am-6pm Mon-Wed, Fri, Sat; 10am-7pm Thur; noon-5pm Sun. **Credit** AmEx, DC, JCB, MC, V. **Map 5 F5**

Ready-to-wear from the house of the sainted couturier. Also handbags, shoes, jewellery, cosmetics, fragrances and accessories. The service is as gracious as the goods.

Emporio Armani

210 Newbury Street, between Exeter & Fairfield Streets (262 7300). Copley T. **Open** 11am-7pm Mon-Sat; noon-6pm Sun. **Credit** AmEx, DC, JCB, MC, V. **Map 3 E5**

Giorgio Armani's second collection, or 'bridge' line, clothes much of the Euro set in elegant, forward-looking style. When they're not buying clothes, the young internationals convene in the attached café to see and be seen.

Gucci

Copley Place (247 3000). Back Bay or Copley T. **Open** 10am-8pm Mon-Sat; noon-6pm Sun. **Credit** AmEx, DC, JCB, MC, V. **Map 3 F5**

Core and runway-collection pieces from the venerable couture house, all with some variation on the horsebit theme (Gucci originated in the early 1900s as an equestrian house). Traditionally based on a darker palette but now incorporates seasonal colour highlights.

Escada

308 Boylston Street, at Arlington Street (437 1200). Arlington T. **Open** 10am-6pm Mon-Sat. **Credit** AmEx, DC, JCB, MC, V. **Map 5 F5**

Discreetly elegant, upmarket design and couture.

Hermès

22 Arlington Street, at Boylston Street (482 8707). Arlington T. **Open** 10am-6pm Mon-Sat. **Credit** AmEx, DC, JCB, MC, V. **Map 5 F5**

Classic, understated design from the 162-year-old French fashion house. Men's and women's suits, leather goods and the famous Hermès silk scarves.

Spin recycle

You can still find tons of vinyl in Boston, as well as a good selection of second-hand CDs and tapes in every musical genre, most in pristine condition. Old LPs sell for anything from a few dollars to collectors' prices, cassette tapes are usually dirt cheap, and second-hand CDs will cost about half their usual retail prices.

There are more music re-sellers in the Greater Boston area than there's room to list here, so we've devised a walking tour (with a few quick bus and train rides along the way) to get you to selected points of interest. Start on Newbury Street, at **Mystery Train II**, where the staff can discuss arcane details of rock history – and will, if they're in the mood. Headphone set-ups allow you to check out the records for scratches. A few doors away, there's **CD Spins**, which stocks a large selection of recent releases and back-catalogue classics on CD.

Bypassing the street's two main retailers (**Newbury Comics** and **Tower Records** – *see page 175*), take a left at the corner of Massachusetts Avenue and cut over to Boylston Street. You'll recognise **Looney Tunes** (*pictured*) by the bargain-cassette concession on the street outside and the scruffy rock musician who's usually sitting behind it, looking bored. The aisles between the second-hand CDs and the record bins are a bit narrow in here, and working your way to the cassette cases at the back of the shop tends to be an adventure in contortionism, but the selection is worth it and the clientele usually adheres to a polite passing policy. Rare classical and jazz CDs are a speciality here, and the rock, dance and funk inventories are satisfyingly dense.

Head back up Massachusetts Avenue, past Newbury Street to Commonwealth Avenue, and take a left. A few blocks away, in Kenmore Square, **Nuggets** sells used CDs, tapes, records, videos and a ragtag assortment of ephemera, and the layout is relatively browser-friendly. Further into Kenmore, **In Your Ear** sells a good selection of rock and pop from the past few decades. From here you can head to the rich resources of Cambridge.

To get there by train, take the Green Line T inbound from Kenmore to Park Street and switch to the Red Line outbound to Central. Or you can walk back to Massachusetts Avenue and take the No 1 bus over the bridge and into Central Square. Stop at **Skippy White's**, which has specialised in R&B, blues, jazz, gospel, soul and oldies since 1961. Across the street, there's **Cheapo Records**, which has a huge selection of oldies in every category from African to zydeco. Heading further up Massachusetts Avenue towards Harvard Square, you'll hit – in quick succession – another **Looney Tunes**, **Second Coming Records**, **Pipeline Records** and the original **Mystery Train Records** store, all with savvy selections of used music. Off Massachusetts Avenue, just before Harvard Square, is **Twisted Village**, a shop specialising in avant-garde genres including modern composers, acid folk, psychedelia and out-there jazz.

If you still haven't had enough, take the Red Line from Harvard Square to Porter and visit **Stereo Jack's**, where you can poke around in the jazz, blues and nostalgia collections. Then get back on the train and go one stop to Davis, in Somerville, where **Disc Diggers** stocks what they claim to be New England's largest selection of second-hand and discounted CDs and cassettes.

Mystery Train II

306 Newbury Street, between Gloucester & Hereford Streets (536 0216). Hynes/ICA T. **Open** 10.30am-7.30pm daily. **Credit** AmEx, Disc, MC, V. **Map 3 E5**

CD Spins

324 Newbury Street, between Hereford Street & Massachusetts Avenue (267 5955). Hynes/ICA T.

Open 11am-8pm Mon-Wed; 11am-9pm Thur, Fri; 11am-10pm Sat; noon-7pm Sun. **Credit** MC, V. **Map 3 E5**

Looney Tunes

1106 Boylston Street, at Massachusetts Avenue (266 7698). Hynes/ICA T. **Open** 10am-9pm Mon-Sat; noon-8pm Sun. **Credit** AmEx, Disc, MC, V. **Map 3 E5**
Branch: 1001 Massachusetts Avenue, between Dana & Ellery Streets (876 5624).

Nuggets

486 Commonwealth Avenue, at Beacon Street (536 0679). Kenmore T. **Open** 10am-10pm Mon-Sat; noon-7pm Sun. **Credit** Disc, MC, V. **Map 3 D5**

In Your Ear

957 Commonwealth Avenue, at Deerfield Street (787 9755). Kenmore T. **Open** 10.30am-8pm Mon-Sat; noon-6pm Sun. **Credit** Disc, MC, V. **Map 3 D5**

Skippy White's

538 Massachusetts Avenue, between Norfolk & Prospect Streets, Cambridge (491 3345). Central T. **Open** 10am-6pm Mon-Wed; 10am-8pm Thur, Fri; 10am-6pm Sat. **Credit** AmEx, Disc, MC, V. **Map 4 C/D3**

Cheapo Records

645 Massachusetts Avenue, at Prospect Street, Cambridge (354 4455). Central T. **Open** 10am-6pm Mon-Wed, Sat; 10am-9pm Thur, Fri; 11am-5pm Sun. **Credit** MC, V. **Map 4 C3**

Second Coming Records

1105 Massachusetts Avenue, between Remington & Trowbridge Streets, Cambridge (576 6400). Harvard T. **Open** 11am-7pm daily. **Credit** MC, V. **Map 4 C3**

Pipeline Records

1110 Massachusetts Avenue, between Putnam Avenue & Day Street, Cambridge (661 6369). Central or Harvard T. **Open** 10am-8pm Mon-Wed, Sat; 10am-9pm Thur, Fri; 11am-7pm Sun. **Credit** AmEx, MC, V.

Mystery Train Records

1208 Massachusetts Avenue, at Harvard Street, Cambridge (497 4024). Harvard T. **Open** 10am-7pm daily. **Credit** AmEx, Disc, MC, V. **Map 4 B2/3**

Twisted Village

12B Eliot Street, opposite the Charles Hotel, Cambridge, (354 6898). Harvard T. **Open** noon-8pm Mon-Fri; 11am-8pm Sat; noon-6pm Sun. **Credit** MC, V. **Map 4 B2/3**

Stereo Jack's

1686 Massachusetts Avenue, at Sacramento Street, Cambridge (497 9447). Porter T. **Open** 10am-8pm Mon-Fri; 10am-6pm Sat; noon-7pm Sun. **Credit** AmEx, Disc, MC, V. **Map 4 B1**

Disc Diggers

401 Highland Avenue, at Grove Street, Somerville (776 7560). Davis T. **Open** 10am-9pm Mon-Sat; noon-7pm Sun. **Credit** Disc, MC, V.

Get your fruit and veg at the **Haymarket** *farmers' market. See page 157.*

Hubba Hubba *(page 172): for all those Latex and chainmail needs.*

Polo/Ralph Lauren

Copley Place (266 4121). Back Bay or Copley T.
Open 10am-8pm Mon-Sat; noon-6pm Sun.
Credit AmEx, DC, Disc, JCB, MC, V.
Map 3 F5
The landed-gentry line of men's and women's sportswear by the well-known New York cowboy.

Sonia Rykiel

280 Boylston Street, at Arlington Street (426 2033). Arlington T. **Open** 10am-6pm Mon-Sat. **Credit** AmEx, MC, V. **Map 5 F5**
Designs that range from sportswear to black tie, from the French designer known as the 'queen of knits'.

(Almost) all-American

Banana Republic

Copley Place (424 7817). Back Bay or Copley T.
Open 10am-8pm Mon-Sat; noon-6pm Sun. **Credit** AmEx, Disc, JCB, MC, V. **Map 3 F5**
The Gap empire's line of better-quality sportswear and career-wear, heavy on Italian design.
Branches: Faneuil Hall Marketplace (439 0016); 28 Newbury Street (267 3933).

Brooks Brothers

46 Newbury Street, at Berkeley Street (267 2600). Arlington T. **Open** 9am-7pm Mon-Fri; 10am-6pm Sat;

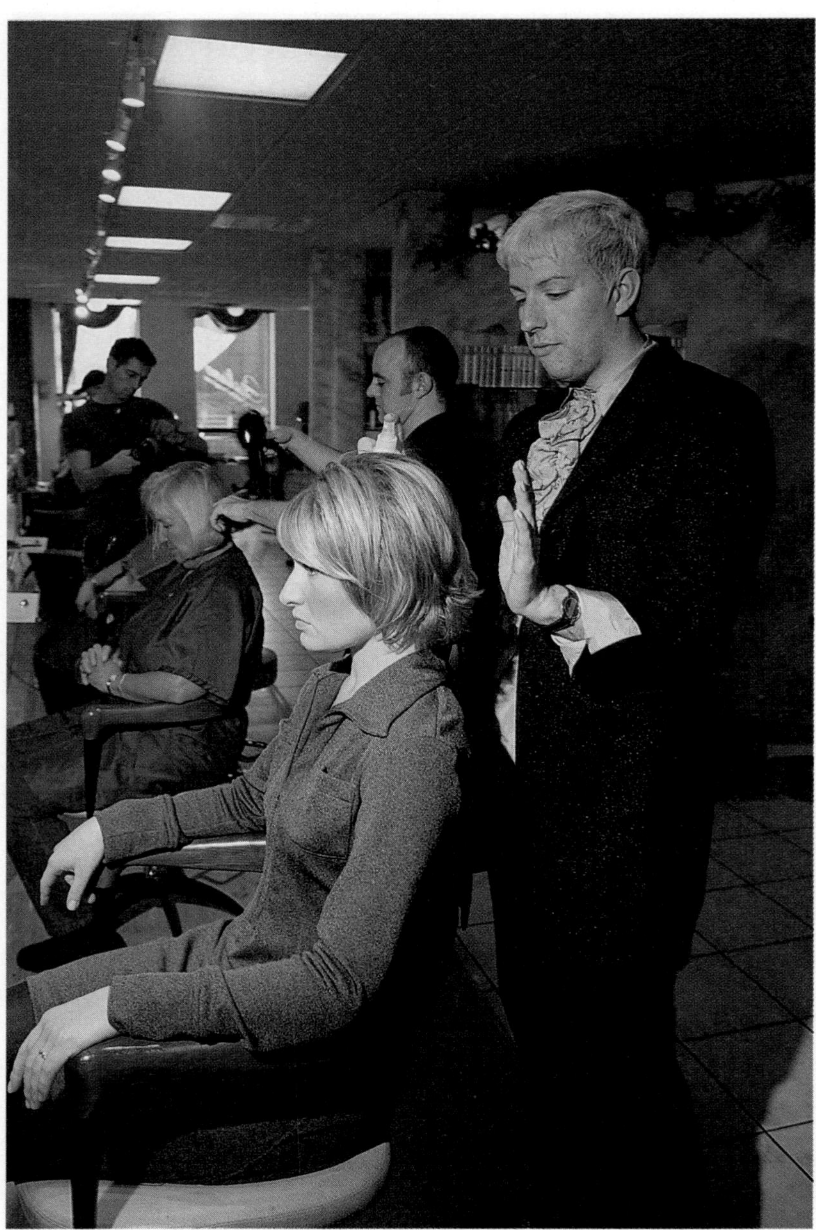

Spa, hair salon and 'wellness center', **Giuliano**. *See page 175.*

noon-6pm Sun. **Credit** AmEx, Disc, JCB, MC, V. **Map 5 F5**
What to wear if you're having lunch at the Harvard Club – fine-quality, conservatively styled men's suits, sports coats and formal wear, with a smaller selection of women's suits and dresses.

Diesel

116 Newbury Street, between Clarendon & Dartmouth Streets (437 7344). Copley T. **Open** 11am-7pm Mon-Sat. **Credit** AmEx, DC, MC, V. **Map 3 F5**
The Italian line of superior-quality jeans and tops that kids love so much.
Branch: 30 John F Kennedy Street (354 5258).

French Connection

Copley Place (424 1819). Back Bay or Copley T. **Open** 10am-8pm Mon-Sat; noon-6pm Sun. **Credit** AmEx, Disc, MC, V. **Map 3 F5**
The English company with a Continental attitude – fitted, youthful sportswear, clubwear, dresses and suits, mostly in black and grey.
Branch: 206-8 Newbury Street, at Exeter Street (247 1301).

The Gap

200 Newbury Street, at Exeter Street (267 4055). Copley T. **Open** 10am-9pm Mon-Sat; noon-6pm Sun. **Credit** AmEx, Disc, MC, V. **Map 3 E5**
Everybody loves the American standard in affordably priced sportswear. By the time you read this, there'll be a Gap on every street corner.
Branches: Copley Place (247 1754); 15 Brattle Street, Cambridge (864 9077).

Guess

80 Newbury Street, between Berkeley & Clarendon Streets (236 4147). Copley T. **Open** 10am-8pm Mon-Sat. **Credit** AmEx, Disc, JCB, MC, V. **Map 5 F5**
Well-known Euro-sleek American sportswear and designer collections.
Branch: Cambridge Side Galleria Mall (621 3432).

The Original Levi's Store

800 Boylston Street, Prudential Center (375 9010). Copley or Prudential T. **Open** 10am-8pm Mon-Sat; noon-6pm Sun. **Credit** AmEx, Disc, JCB, MC, V. **Map 3 E5/6**
Jeans, khakis and tops for men and women by the San Francisco company whose models can beat up Kate Moss. The shop will custom-design jeans for you on request, so you can still get your hands on a discontinued version, add bootlegs or perhaps get a little more (or less) room in the rear.

Replay Jeans

130 Newbury, between Clarendon & Dartmouth Streets (536 0610). Copley T. **Open** 11am-7pm Mon-Sat. **Credit** AmEx, DC, MC, V. **Map 3 F5**
Italian jeans and vinyl pants for the hip college set.

Urban Outfitters

11 John F Kennedy Street, at Massachusetts Avenue, Cambridge (864 0070). Harvard T. **Open** 10am-10pm Mon-Thur; 10am-11pm Fri, Sat; noon-8pm Sun. **Credit** AmEx, Disc, MC, V. **Map 4 B2**
The late store opening hours are a godsend in times of fashion crisis. Come to Urban Outfitters for inexpensive, trendy knockoff designs for hip youngsters and young-at-heart hipsters who don't mind a loose thread or two. The place also sells funky houseware of the plastic-chair variety, cards and silly toys.
Branch: 261 Newbury Street (236 0088).

Maternity wear

Mimi Maternity

10 Newbury Street, between Arlington & Berkeley Streets (262 8012). Arlington T. **Open** 10am-6pm Mon-Sat; noon-5pm Sun. **Credit** AmEx, MC, V. **Map 5 F5**
Mimi Maternity provides upmarket maternity sportswear, dresswear and Italian knits.

Vintage & second-hand

Bertha Cool

Second floor, 528 Commonwealth Avenue, at Brookline Avenue (247 4111). Kenmore T. **Open** 11am-6pm Mon-Sat; noon-5pm Sun. **Credit** AmEx, MC, V. **Map 3 D5**
One of the last vestiges of Kenmore Square's disappearing boho/rocker scene. Sells trendy vintage clothing, leather coats and second-hand Levi's.

Garment District and Dollar-a-Pound Plus

200 Broadway, at Davis Street, Cambridge (876 5230). Kendall/MIT T. **Open** *Garment District* 11am-7pm Mon-Fri, Sun; 9am-7pm Sat. *Dollar-a-Pound Plus* 9am-4pm Mon-Thur; 9am-2pm Fri; 7.45am-2pm Sat; 7.45am-4pm Sun (phone to check first). **Credit** AmEx, Disc, MC, V. **Map 4 D3**
Despite the somewhat obscure location, this offers the area's best selection of 1960s and 1970s gear, lots of jeans and restyled vintage clothing by local designers. The Dollar-a-Pound adjunct is for those who don't mind stains and missing zippers. Friday is 50-cents-a-pound day.

Keezer's

140 River Street, between Massachusetts Avenue & Memorial Drive, Cambridge (547 2455). Central T. **Open** 10am-6pm Mon-Sat. **Credit** MC, V. **Map 4 B/C3/4**
Established in 1895, Keezer's is the oldest used-clothing store in the country and a cherished local institution – members of the Boston Symphony buy their tuxedos here. Max Keezer started the company by going into the Harvard dorms to buy barely-worn fine clothing from allowance-starved heirs. The shop now sells second-hand and end-of-the-line men's suits, tuxedos, sports coats, overcoats and casual wear, in good or mint condition, with at least 50% off.

Oona's

1210 Massachusetts Avenue, between Quincy & Bow Streets, Cambridge (491 2654). Harvard T. **Open** 11am-7pm Mon-Sat; noon-6pm Sun. **Credit** AmEx, MC, V. **Map 4 B2/3**
A landmark of sorts, in its 27th year in the same location. Oona's sells vintage clothes from the 1920s to the 1970s, leather jackets and costume-wear.

Second Time Around Collections

167 Newbury Street, between Dartmouth & Exeter Streets (247 3504). Copley T. **Open** 10am-8pm Mon-Fri; 10am-7pm Sat; noon-6pm Sun. **Credit** AmEx, Disc, MC, V. **Map 3 D/F5**
Contemporary designer re-sale shop.
Branch: 8 Eliot Street, Cambridge (491 7185).

Fetish & sex

Condom World

332 Newbury Street, between Hereford Street & Massachusetts Avenue (267 7233). Hynes/ICA T. **Open** 11am-7pm Mon-Thur; 11am-8pm Fri, Sat; noon-6pm Sun. **Credit** AmEx, Disc, MC, V. **Map 3 E5**
Condoms, party novelties, adult toys and body oils.

Grand Opening!
Suite 32, 318 Harvard Street, at Beacon Street, Brookline (731 2626). Coolidge Corner T.
Open 10am-7pm Tue, Wed; 10am-9pm Thur, Fri; 10am-7pm Sat; noon-6pm Sun. **Credit** AmEx, Disc, MC, V.
A small 'sexuality boutique' selling sex toys and tools (condoms, books, videos, lubricants, oils, vibrators) especially but not exclusively for women. The jolly atmosphere is designed to make women feel comfortable.
Website: www.grandopening.com

Hubba Hubba
534 Massachusetts Avenue, between Brookline & Pearl Streets, Cambridge (492 9082). Central T.
Open noon-8pm Mon-Thur; noon-9pm Fri; noon-7pm Sat. **Credit** AmEx, Disc, MC, V.
Map 4 C/D3
A locally renowned sexual fetish store, catering to every kink. Come here for all your leather, Latex and PVC needs. Also sells corsets, restraints, toys, vibrators, jewellery, accessories, shoes and punk band T-shirts.

Film processing

Most pharmacy chains offer fast, inexpensive film developing and there's an **Osco** or **CVS** conveniently located in just about every part of town (check the phone book for your nearest branch). The following shops offer a complete range of professional photographic services, with one-hour developing options.

Cambridge Street Photo
282 Cambridge Street, at Anderson Street (248 0454). Charles/MGH or Gov't Center T. **Open** 9am-6pm Mon-Fri; 10am-4pm Sat. **Credit** MC, V. **Map 5 F4**
You can try Cambridge Street Photo for one-hour processing, custom enlargements, slides and prints.

Copley Photo
441 Stuart Street, at Dartmouth Street (859 8922). Back Bay or Copley T. **Open** 8am-6pm Mon-Fri; 10am-4pm Sat. **Credit** AmEx, Disc, MC, V.
Map 3 F5
Colour or black-and-white film developing and printing, passport photos, enlargements and a one-hour photo lab. Also does videotape duplication and slides from prints.

Florists

Lotus Designs
482A Columbus Avenue, between West Newton Street & Rutland Square (262 7031). Back Bay or Prudential T.
Open 8am-7pm Mon-Wed; 8am-8pm Thur-Sat; 10am-6pm Sun. **Credit** AmEx, Disc, MC, V.
Map 3 E/F6
A favourite South End neighbourhood shop, Lotus sells only top-quality and exotic flowers – no carnations – and will mix an outstanding bunch for as little as $10.

Winston Flowers
131 Newbury Street, between Dartmouth & Clarendon Streets (541 1100). Copley T. **Open** 8am-6pm Mon-Sat; 9am-5pm Sun. **Credit** AmEx, Disc, MC, V.
Map 3 F5
Winston Flowers specialises in trend-setting flower design and has been family-owned for the past 50 years. There are five different locations of the florist in and around the Boston area; phone this branch to find out the location of your nearest.

Food & drink

Gourmet shops

Cardullo's
6 Brattle Street, at John F Kennedy Street, Cambridge (491 8888). Harvard T. **Open** 8am-8pm Mon-Fri; 9am-9pm Sat; 11am-7pm Sun. **Credit** AmEx, Disc, MC, V.
Map 4 B2
The staff at Cardullo's is so friendly and helpful you won't feel foolish if you don't know your foie gras from your goose liver. The shop sells international gourmet food products, including beer, wine and champagne, has deli and bakery counters, creates gift baskets and offers shipping and delivery.
Website: www.cardullos.com

Cremaldi's
31 Putnam Avenue, between Green & Franklin Streets, Cambridge (354 7969). Harvard T. **Open** 10am-7pm Mon-Sat. **Credit** AmEx, Disc, MC, V. **Map 4 C3**
An old-fashioned speciality food store, selling prepared foods and groceries – produce, meats, fish, barrels of pasta, imported delicacies, fresh herbs and Italian desserts. The staff will also create and ship beautiful gift baskets.

DeLuca's
Back Bay Market, 239 Newbury Street, at Fairfield Street (262 5990). Copley or Hynes/ICA T. **Open** 7am-10pm Mon-Sat; 7am-9pm Sun. **Credit** AmEx, MC, V.
Map 3 E5
Established in 1905, Boston's oldest gourmet grocer sells superior quality produce, meat, fish, caviar, pâté, wine, beer, champagne, fresh baked bread and more. Their motto is 'What we don't have, we get'.

Garden of Eden
577 Tremont Street, between Dartmouth Street & Union Park (247 8377). Back Bay or Copley T. **Open** 7am-9pm Mon-Fri; 7am-6pm Sat, Sun. **No credit cards.**
Map 5 F6
A stylish South End shop with a full selection of imported cheeses and pâtés. Garden of Eden also stocks fine French pastry, readymade meals, a limited gourmet product line, fresh bread, coffee beans and tea.

Tealuxe
Zero Brattle Street, at John F Kennedy Street, Cambridge (441 0077). Harvard T. **Open** 8am-11pm Mon-Wed, Sun; 8am-midnight Thur-Sat. **Credit** Disc, MC, V.
Map 4 B2
This charming shop in Cambridge serves and sells more than 100 different types of tea as well as tea accessories, scones, tea cakes and cookies.

Italian bakeries

Bova's Bakery
134 Salem Street, at Prince Street (523 5601). Haymarket T. **Open** 24 hours daily. **No credit cards.**
Map 5 G3
Owned by the same family for 90 years, this all-day, all-night shop offers classic Italian pastries and cookies, freshly-made pizza and calzone and a full deli counter.

Mike's Pastry
300 Hanover Street, between Prince & Parmenter Streets (742 3050). Haymarket T. **Open** 8am-9pm Mon-Wed; 8am-10pm Thur, Sun; 8am-10.30pm Fri; 8am-11pm Sat. **No credit cards. Map 5 G3/4**
The best-known of the North End bakeries, Mike's is a 54-year-old family business selling traditional Italian pastries. It also has table service.

Noir

If you practise the black arts or just dabble in creepy eccentricity, you might want to check out the local offerings in supplies for witches, weirdos and Goths. In Cambridge, you can visit **Gypsy Moon** (near Porter Square), which sells 'magickal medieval garb for everyday', as well as a selection of incense, tarot cards, crystals, candles and other tools of the trade. The clothing and jewellery line includes Romantic, Gothic and Renaissance designs, many of them original, some subtle enough to mix with more conventional officewear. The accessories collection includes things like chain-mail hairpieces.

In Allston, one of the area's most extensive selections of serious witchcraft supplies can be found at **Ritual Arts**, which sells skulls, spell kits, talismans, herbs, obscure ephemera and a wide range of spooky jewellery, statuary, gargoyles, T-shirts and gift items. Also on Harvard Avenue in Allston is **Flyrabbit**, the freaks' favourite toystore. Riding the 'fine line between novelty and natural history', this shop has been known to stock pig foetuses, stuffed tarantulas and framed bugs and butterflies. It also sells an assortment of cultish novelties and decorative objects – Bettie Paige lampshades, Mexican wrestling masks, rubber eyeballs– you get the picture, and it isn't pretty.

Flyrabbit
155 Harvard Avenue, between Commonwealth & Brighton Avenues, Allston (782 1313). Harvard Ave T. **Open** 11am-7pm Mon-Sat; noon-5pm Sun. **Credit** Disc, MC, V. **Map 4 A5**

Gypsy Moon
1780 Massachusetts Avenue, at Arlington Street, Cambridge (876 7095). Porter T. **Open** 10am-7pm Mon-Fri; 10am-6pm Sat; noon-5pm Sun. **Credit** AmEx, MC, V. **Map 4 B1**

Ritual Arts
153 Harvard Avenue, between Commonwealth & Brighton Avenues, Allston (787 4157). Harvard Ave T. **Open** 10am-6pm Mon-Wed; 10am-7pm Thur, Fri; 11am-5pm Sat; noon-5pm Sun. **Credit** Disc, MC, V. **Map 4 A5**

Modern Pastries
257 Hanover Street, between Cross & Richmond Streets (523 3783). Haymarket T. **Open** 8am-9pm daily. **No credit cards. Map 5 G/H3/4**
The North End old-timers' choice for strictly authentic Italian torrone, cakes and pastries. The goods are not too gooey, sweet or Americanised.

Liquor stores

Blanchard's
103 Harvard Avenue, at Commonwealth Avenue, Allston (782 9500). Harvard Ave T. **Open** 9am-11pm Mon-Sat. **Credit** MC, V. **Map 4 A5**
This full-service superstore takes pride in a comprehensive wine selection and claims to stock the largest selection of beer in New England. There's a wine-tasting room and wine consultants on the staff. It offers radio-dispatched delivery in Greater Boston.

Bauer Wine and Spirits
330 Newbury Street, between Hereford Street & Massachusetts Avenue (262 0363). Hynes/ICA T. **Open** 10am-11pm Mon-Sat. **Credit** AmEx, Disc, MC, V. **Map 3 E5**
Established in 1960, this is one of Boston's most well-respected stores. Howie Rubin, a famous local wine connoisseur, is the general manager. The shop sells fine wines from every (important) region of the world, has a well-stocked liquor department, an international beer selection and sells premium cigars from around the world. Free delivery.

Marty's
193 Harvard Avenue, at Commonwealth Avenue, Allston (782 3250). Harvard Ave T. **Open** 9am-11pm Mon-Sat. **Credit** AmEx, Disc, MC, V. **Map 4 A5**
A large, full-service liquor store with an extensive selection of discounted fine wine, liquor, beer, handrolled cigars and gourmet food, with a full deli and delivery service.

Hair salons

Newbury Street has 70 salons, so if you feel inspired to transform yourself while strolling among the shops, snagging a walk-in appointment somewhere shouldn't be a problem. If you're not a risk-taker when it comes to unknown cutters, however, arrange an appointment at one of these well-respected hair houses.

Ecocentrix
30 Newbury Street, between Arlington & Berkeley Streets (262 2222). Arlington T. **Open** 9am-4pm Mon; 9am-7pm Tue-Fri; 9am-5pm Sat. **Credit** Disc, MC, V. **Map 5 F5**
Local award-winners with a hip reputation for style-savvy cuts and colour.

Mario Russo
9 Newbury Street, at Arlington Street (424 6676). Arlington T. **Open** 9am-5.45pm Mon, Tue; 9am-6.45pm Wed-Fri; 9am-4.45pm Sat. **Credit** AmEx, MC, V. **Map 5 F5**
Getting an appointment with owner Mario Russo at this high-status salon could mean a long, shaggy wait, but you should be able to book one of the other stylists within a week. The salon offers cuts, colour and skin care.

Salon Pini
231 Newbury Street, between Exeter & Fairfield Streets (236 1727). Copley T. **Open** 9am-5pm Mon; 9am-7pm Tue-Sat. **Credit** AmEx, Disc, MC, V. **Map 3 E5**
Owner Pini Swissa is a low-key master who has styled run-

way shows for Chanel and L'Oréal and once styled Hilary Clinton's hair, but keeps regular hours and treats walk-ins like longtime clients. His shop is a full-service salon, offering colour, manicures, pedicures and facials.

Houseware

Bed and Bath

361 Newbury Street, between Hereford Street & Massachusetts Avenue (421 9442). Hynes/ICA T. **Open** 9.30am-9pm Mon-Sat; noon-7pm Sun. **Credit** AmEx, Disc, MC, V. **Map 3 E5**

A regional chain store selling mostly discounted linens and towels, pillows, comforters, bathroom accessories, shower curtains and rugs.

Branch: 1 Porter Square, Cambridge (491 5431).

Crate and Barrel

140 Faneuil Hall Marketplace (742 6025). Gov't Center T. **Open** 10am-9pm Mon-Fri; 10am-8pm Sat; noon-6pm Sun. **Credit** AmEx, Disc, MC, V. **Map 5 G4**

This Chicago-based chain store is the houseware source for the style-conscious yuppie. It sells contemporary furniture, linen, kitchen fixtures, glassware, cutlery as well as decorative objects.

Branches: 1045 Massachusetts Avenue, Cambridge (547 3994); Copley Place (536 9400).

Kitchen Arts

161 Newbury Street, between Dartmouth & Exeter Streets (266 8701). Copley T. **Open** 10am-6pm Mon-Sat; noon-5pm Sun. **Credit** AmEx, MC, V. **Map 3 E/F5**

Affordable and top-of-the-range lines of cookware, cutlery, gadgets and other tools for preparing food, discounted by up to 30%.

Restoration Hardware

711 Boylston Street, at Exeter Street (578 0088). Copley T. **Open** 10am-9pm Mon-Fri; 11am-7pm Sun. **Credit** AmEx, MC, V. **Map 3 E5**

A California-based chain and catalogue store, Restoration Hardware has an emphasis on Mission furniture, retro lamps, accessories and hardware.

Jewellers

See also page 162 **Department stores** *and* **Fashion**.

Dorfman Jewelers

24 Newbury Street, between Arlington & Berkeley Streets (536 2022). Arlington T. **Open** 10am-5.30pm Mon-Sat. **Credit** AmEx, DC, MC, V. **Map 5 F5**

An ultra-elegant boutique selling high-carat, one-of-a-kind jewellery in contemporary and classical Italian styles.

Shreve, Crump & Lowe

330 Boylston Street, at Arlington Street (267 9100). Arlington T. **Open** 10am-5.30pm Mon-Sat. **Credit** AmEx, MC, V. **Map 5 F5**

This venerable old jewellery and luxury-line gift shop is Boston's expression of the 'Breakfast at Tiffany's' attitude – whether you're buying a diamond or a bottle of ink for a fountain pen, your business is welcomed here.

Tiffany & Co

Copley Place (353 0222). Back Bay or Copley T. **Open** 10am-6pm Mon-Sat; noon-5pm Sun. **Credit** AmEx, Disc, JCB, MC, V. **Map 3 F5**

Its mall location in the albeit swanky Copley Place saps some of the glamour from the experience of shopping at Tiffany's, but it's still Tiffany's under the glass.

Watch repair

Alpha Omega

57 John F Kennedy Street, at Winthrop Street, Cambridge (864 1227). Harvard T. **Open** 10am-9.30pm Wed, Thur, Fri; 10am-5pm Sat; noon-5pm Sun. **Credit** AmEx, DC, Disc, MC, V. **Map 4 B2/3**

On-staff watchmakers will make repairs on the premises, sometimes while you wait. Vintage and fine Swiss watches are bought and sold and a large selection of designer jewellery is also stocked.

Small Pleasures

142 Newbury Street, between Clarendon & Dartmouth Streets (267 7371). Copley T. **Open** 11am-6pm Mon-Sat. **Credit** AmEx, MC, V. **Map 3 F5**

Small Pleasures sells, buys and repairs antique, estate and vintage watches.

Time and Time Again

172 Newbury Street, between Dartmouth & Exeter Streets (266 6869). Copley T. **Open** 10.30am-6.30pm Mon-Sat. **Credit** AmEx, Disc, MC, V. **Map 3 E/F5**

Repairs watches on the premises, sometimes while you wait. Second-hand and vintage watches are bought and sold, from Timex to Cartier. Also stocks the largest selection of used Rolexes in Boston.

Watch Hospital

40 Bromfield Street, between Washington & Tremont Streets (542 8332). Park St or State/Citizen's Bank T. **Open** 8.30am-5.30pm Mon-Fri; 9am-3pm Sat. **Credit** AmEx, Disc, MC, V. **Map 5 G4**

A family business for generations, Watch Hospital offers expert Swiss-watch repair and a fast turnaround.

Laundry & dry-cleaning

Back Bay Laundry and Dry Cleaning Emporium

409A Marlborough Street, at Massachusetts Avenue (236 4552). Hynes/ICA T. **Open** 7.30am-11pm daily. **Credit** MC, V. **Map 3 E5**

A coin-operated laundry with dry-cleaning and wash-and-fold service. Pickup and delivery is available in Greater Boston.

Posters

International Poster Gallery

205 Newbury Street, between Exeter & Fairfield Streets (375 0076). Copley T. **Open** 10am-6pm Mon-Sat; noon-6pm Sun. **Credit** AmEx, MC, V. **Map 3 E5**

Stocks a strong collection of original vintage advertising designs, theatre and opera posters and political propaganda, mainly from the turn of the century to World War II, with some more contemporary pieces from the 1960s to the 1980s.

Nostalgia Factory

51 North Margin Street, at Thatcher Street (236 8754). Haymarket T. **Open** 10am-6pm Mon-Sat. **Credit** AmEx, Disc, MC, V. **Map 5 G3**

Movie memorabilia from vintage to the present day, including posters, stills, press kits and cards.

Piercing

Rites of Passage

107 Brighton Avenue, at Harvard Street, Allston (783 1918). Harvard Ave T. **Open** by appointment only. **Credit** MC, V. **Map 4 A5**

A clean, reputable, professional body-piercing salon. The company has lobbied to regulate body-piercing in Massachusetts, where certification is still not required to practise the art, and holds licences in other states.

Records, tapes & CDs

General

These mega-stores regularly discount current top-40 CDs.

HMV

1 Brattle Street, at Mount Auburn Street, Cambridge (868 9696). Harvard T. **Open** 10am-10pm Mon-Thur; 10am-midnight Fri, Sat; noon-9pm Sun. **Credit** AmEx, Disc, MC, V. **Map 4 B2**
The usual variety of music, with a good classical department.
Branch: 24 Winter Street (357 8444).

Newbury Comics

332 Newbury Street, between Hereford Street & Massachusetts Avenue (236 4930). Hynes/ICA T. **Open** 10am-10pm Mon-Sat; 11am-8pm Sun. **Credit** AmEx, Disc, MC, V. **Map 3 E5**
A thriving regional chain that started as a humble comic-book store and still sells comics and underground reading material as well as CDs and tapes.
Branch: 36 John F Kennedy Street, Cambridge (491 0337).

Tower Records

360 Newbury Street, at Massachusetts Avenue (247 5900). Hynes/ICA T. **Open** 9am-12.30pm Mon; 9am-midnight Tue-Sun. **Credit** AmEx, Disc, MC, V. **Map 3 E5**
A multi-level monolith among record stores. The cult-conscious bookstore and magazine department here attracts a late night crowd of young, single men.
Branch: 95 Mount Auburn Street (876 3377).

Techno

Boston Beat

279 Newbury Street, at Gloucester Street (247 2428). Copley T. **Open** 11am-9pm Mon-Thur, Sun; 11am-10pm Fri, Sat. **Credit** AmEx, Disc, MC, V. **Map 3 E5**
A full-service electronic-music shop, selling DJ equipment and international house, techno, progressive dance, downtempo lounge and drum-and-bass music, on vinyl and CD. Also stocks brand new imports.

Shoes

See also page 162 **Department stores** *and* **Fashion**.

Aldo

180 Newbury Street, at Exeter Street (266 0501). Copley T. **Open** 10am-7pm Mon-Thur; 10am-8pm Fri, Sat; noon-6pm Sun. **Credit** AmEx, Disc, MC, V. **Map 3 E5**
Clunky, funky fashion shoes and boots for women and men.

Berk's

50 John F Kennedy Street, at Winthrop Street, Cambridge (492 9511). Harvard T. **Open** 10am-9pm Mon-Sat; 11am-7pm Sun. **Credit** AmEx, DC, Disc, MC, V. **Map 4 B2/3**
Has an exceptional selection of trend-setting shoes, Doc Martens and sneakers in an affordable range.

Cuoio

115 Newbury Street, at Clarendon Street (859 0636). Copley T. **Open** 10am-6pm Mon-Sat; noon-5pm Sun. **Credit** AmEx, Disc, MC, V. **Map 5 F5**
Fine European shoes and hard-to-fine labels.
Branch: 170 Faneuil Hall Marketplace (742 4486).

Helen's Leather Shop

110 Charles Street, between Revere & Pinckney Streets (742 2077). Charles/MGH T. **Open** 10am-6pm Mon-Sat; noon-6pm Sun. **Credit** AmEx, Disc, MC, V. **Map 5 F4**
Top-quality leather for hippies and cowboys – including western boots, Birkenstocks, handsewn moccasins and leather jackets.

John Fluevog

302 Newbury Street, between Gloucester & Hereford Streets (266 1079). Hynes/ICA T. **Open** 11am-7pm Mon-Sat; 1pm-6pm Sun. **Credit** AmEx, Disc, MC, V. **Map 3 E5**
The Canadian-based Fluevog line is fun, funky and sometimes downright silly. All styles of shoes are unisex. The shop holds a huge sale during the entire months of January and July.

Penny Lane

10 Prospect Street, at Massachusetts Avenue, Cambridge (491 5552). Central T. **Open** 10am-8pm Mon-Wed; 10am-9pm Thur, Fri; 10am-7pm Sat; noon-6pm Sun. **Credit** AmEx, MC, V. **Map 4 C3**
Low mark-ups on domestic and European boutique-brand shoes (Steve Madden, Zodiac, Vagabond). Also sells leather jackets and men's and women's clothing.
Website: www.pennycentral.com

Thom Browne

331 & 337 Newbury Street, between Hereford Street & Massachusetts Avenue (266 8722). Hynes/ICA T. **Open** 10am-7pm Mon-Fri; 10am-8pm Sat; noon-7pm Sun. **Credit** AmEx, DC, Disc, JCB, MC, V. **Map 3 D5**
Has a trendy selection of good-quality designs, making it one of the most popular fashion footwear shops in town.

Skecher's

342 Newbury Street, between Hereford Street & Massachusetts Avenue (262 4339). Hynes/ICA T. **Open** 10am-8pm Mon-Thur; 10am-9pm Fri, Sat; 11am-7pm Sun. **Credit** AmEx, Disc, JCB, MC, V. **Map 3 E5**
The local outpost of the trendy California-based footwear line. Sells boots, shoes and sneakers for men, women and even funky infants.

Spas & salons

Candela Laserspa

28 Arlington Street, between Boylson Street & St James Avenue (426 6999). Arlington T. **Open** 5.30am-9pm Mon-Fri; 8.30am-6pm Sat, Sun. **Credit** AmEx, MC, V. **Map 5 F5**
A salon like a private club, Candela Laserspa offers hair and skin services, a laser clinic (as the name implies), manicures and pedicures, whirlpool and lap pool.

Giuliano

338 Newbury Street, between Hereford Street & Massachusetts Avenue (262 2220). Hynes/ICA T. **Open** 9am-6pm Mon; 8am-8pm Tue-Fri; 8am-5pm Sat; 10am-6pm Sun. **Credit** AmEx, Disc, MC, V. **Map 3 E5**
When they call themselves a 'full-service salon and wellness center', they mean it. After your haircut, you can visit a board-certified plastic surgeon or a cosmetic dentist. Other services available include massage, reflexology, waxing,

acupuncture and body wraps. The half- and full-day package prices include parking and all tips.

Le Pli Salon and Day Spa

Charles Hotel, 5 Bennett Street, Cambridge (547 4081). Harvard T. **Open** 9am-5pm Mon-Wed, Sat; 9am-8pm Thur, Fri; 10am-5pm Sun. **Credit** AmEx, MC, V. **Map 4 B2**
Hair and skin treatments in an elegant spa setting.

Saks Fifth Avenue Salon and Spa

Saks Fifth Avenue, Prudential Plaza (262 8500). Copley or Prudential T. **Open** 10am-6pm Mon, Sat; 10am-8pm Tue-Fri. **Credit** AmEx, DC, Disc, MC, V. **Map 3 E5**
Offers all spa skin-care services except massage. Half- and full-day packages include the 'City Escape,' with a skin-illuminating anti-oxidant facial, manicure, pedicure, shampoo, style and makeup refresher, for $140.

Salon Nordic

221 Newbury Street, between Exeter & Fairfield Streets (421 9551). Copley T. **Open** 10am-6pm Mon-Fri; 9am-5pm Sat. **Credit** MC, V. **Map 3 E5**
Facials, massage and body waxing.

Sports shops

See chapter **Sport & Fitness**.

Luggage

Willowbee & Kent Travel Company

519 Boylston Street, between Berkeley & Clarendon Streets (437 6700). Copley T. **Open** 10am-7pm Mon-Sat; noon-6pm Sun. **Credit** AmEx, Disc, MC, V. **Map 5 F5**
A one-stop shop for travel, with a ticket agency and comprehensive retail store selling luggage, travel clothing (lightweight, wrinkle-free, comfortable pieces), adventure gear, backpacks, kids' travel games and travel accessories.

Musical instruments & equipment

Cambridge Music

6 Hemenway Street, at Boylston Street (247 1747). Hynes/ICA T. **Open** 10am-8pm Mon-Thur; 10am-6pm Fri, Sat; noon-5pm Sun. **Credit** AmEx, Disc, MC, V. **Map 3 E5**
This is the adjunct to a bigger Cambridge Music store in Porter Square, but is more conveniently located to the downtown area. The shop stocks mostly second-hand and consignment pieces, with an emphasis on guitars and amps and the occasional rare effects relic.
Branch: 1906 Massachusetts Avenue (491 5433).

Daddy's Junky Music

159-65 Massachusetts Avenue, between Boylston Street & Huntington Avenue (247 0909). Hynes/ICA T. **Open** 11am-8pm Mon-Fri; 10am-6pm Sat; noon-5pm Sun. **Credit** AmEx, Disc, MC, V. **Map 3 E6**
A regional chain store that grew from a single, humble music shop in New Hampshire. There's a large selection of second-hand gear, with best price guaranteed on new keys, drums, guitars, amps, PA systems and more.
Branch: 2238 Massachusetts Avenue, Cambridge (497 1556).

Guitar Center

750 Commonwealth Avenue, at St Mary's Street (738 5958). BU Central T. **Open** 10am-9pm Mon-Fri; 10am-6pm Sat; noon-6pm Sun. **Credit** AmEx, Disc, MC, V. **Map 4 C5**
A music centre selling guitars, keyboards, amps, drums, multi-track recording and pro-audio gear, DJ equipment, lighting systems and accessories. The second-hand and vintage gear selection ranges from cheap beginner guitars to $20,000 rarities. It offers a best-price guarantee and repair service. The vibe in here is a bit chain store, but the service is accommodating.

Jack's Drum Shop

1096 Boylston Street, at Massachusetts Avenue (266 4617). Hynes/ICA T. **Open** 11am-7pm Mon-Fri; 10am-6pm Sat; 1-5pm Sun. **Credit** AmEx, Disc, MC, V. **Map 3 E5**
Jack's has been the source for skinheads since 1945. A friendly staff of drummers will show you a large selection of new drums, cymbals, percussion instruments and accessories as well as vintage snares and kits. The shop undertakes the re-skinning of hand drums and comprehensive on-site repairs.

Mr Music

128 Harvard Avenue, between Commonwealth & Brighton Avenues, Allston (783 1609). Harvard Ave T. **Open** 10am-7pm Mon-Fri; 10am-6pm Sat. **Credit** AmEx, Disc, MC, V. **Map 4 A5**
A funky, independent music shop with a big selection of second-hand guitars, usually including a few to-die-for classic Gibsons and Fenders. Mr Music also sells amps, some drums, CDs, stereo and electronic equipment, and sheet music.

Pop gifts

Buckaroo's Mercantile

858 Massachusetts Avenue, at Sellers Street, Cambridge (864 3637). Central T. **Open** 11am-7pm Mon-Sat; noon-6pm Sun. **Credit** Disc, MC, V. **Map 4 C3**
A pop-culture variety store, selling original clocks, cowboy lampshades, jewellery, mouse pads, T-shirts, clothing by local designers, 1950s pin-ups and nostalgia toys. Custom designs are also available.

Smoking

Buried Treasures

28 Haviland Street, between Massachusetts Avenue & Hemenway Street (247 1011). Hynes/ICA T. **Open** 11am-7pm Mon-Sat; noon-6pm Sun. **Credit** AmEx, MC, V. **Map 3 E5/6**
The tie-dye clothing, Grateful Dead and Bob Marley posters might give you a clue to the kind of smoking supplies you might find here, but be careful what you ask for. 'Water-filtration devices' and 'cigarette papers' are sold, but don't ask for a bong or rolling papers or they'll show you the door.

LJ Peretti Co, Inc

2½ Park Square, at Charles & Boylston Streets (482 0218). Arlington or Boylston T. **Open** 8.30am-8pm Mon-Fri; 8.30am-7pm Sat. **Credit** AmEx, DC, Disc, MC, V. **Map 5 F5**
Established in 1870, Peretti's is the oldest family-owned tobacconist in the USA. It specialises in handblended tobacco, makes and repairs pipes on the premises and sells an exhaustive selection of imported and domestic cigars and cigarettes.

Toys

See chapter **Children**.

Arts & Entertainme

Children

Fun for all the family – come rain, snow or sun.

Boston may be famous for universities, sport and bars, but that doesn't mean it's no place for kids. Not only does it boast the largest teddy bear in the USA (outside the **FAO Schwarz** store, *see page 181*) and the pioneering **Children's Museum** (*see page 179*), it offers plenty of seasonal family activities, including children's day at the Boston Harborfest (*see page 39* **Boston by Season**), winter skating on Boston Common's Frog Pond, surrounded by ice-sculptures and trees bedecked with lights (*see page 180*), and a visit to Robert McCloskey's endearing Mallard family at their home in the Public Gardens (*see page 180*) at any time of the year.

The Calendar section in Thursday's edition of the *Boston Globe* offers a selection of children's activities for the forthcoming week, and a good monthly source of what's hot for young ones is *Parents' Paper* (www.BostonParents.com), available from street booths and selected newsstands and vendors.

For further information on activities suitable for children, contact the **Greater Boston Convention & Visitors' Bureau** (*see page 272* **Directory**), and pick up a copy of *Kids Love Boston* ($3.25) which offers a wealth of information on making a family trip to Boston easier and cheaper.

For the **Ducklings** *tour, see page 180.*

At the airport

Kidport

Logan Airport, Terminal C (561 1212). Airport T.
Open 9am-7pm daily. **Admission** free.
Logan Airport has made travelling with children almost fun with Kidport, its hands-on interactive exhibition centre. Features include an aeroplane climbing structure, a baggage claim slide, an infant and toddler play area, a magnetic poetry wall and a toy shop.
Disabled: toilet.

Babysitting

The monthly *Parents' Paper* provides a list of child-minding services, though it's always essential to enquire about any screening process for employing sitters. Listed below are two licensed, reputable agencies.

Nanny Poppins

(227 5437). **Open** 9am-5pm Mon-Fri. **Rates** $20 call-out fee, then $8-$12 per hour. **Credit** Disc, MC, V.
Nanny Poppins must have one of the most stringent screening processes around. All sitters are investigated by a private detective, and not only are state criminal records checked, but also federal, national and driving records. Nannies who speak a range of languages, including sign language, are on the organisation's books, as are those happy to babysit in hotels.

Parents in a Pinch

(739 5437). **Open** 8am-5pm Mon-Fri. **Rates** *babysitting* $9 per hour per child (50¢ per hour each extra child, plus travel expenses of up to $15); *agency charge* $30 per evening, $40 per day. **Credit** AmEx, MC, V.
This 15-year-old agency can refer up to 150 different nannies offering short-term childcare. Sitters are at least 18 years old and have been trained by the agency.

Eating out

Although many of Boston's restaurants are child-friendly, it may be helpful to phone in advance to check whether they have kid's menus, high chairs or any special entertainment. If you're in a hurry, or want to avoid the decision-making process, try placing your order over the phone.

Bertucci's

See p148 **Restaurants & Cafés** *for listings.*
Even the fussiest of kids won't turn their nose up at pizza or a plate of pasta. At Bertucci's there's the choice of both, while parents can enjoy a relaxing meal. Create your own pizza by adding a variety of toppings or go for one of Bertucci's own tried and tested combinations.

The Blueberry Moose

30 Station Street, at Washington Street, Brookline (277 8133). Brookline Village T. **Open** 11.30am-10.30pm daily. **Credit** MC, V.
There's a superb choice of ice-creams (including a delicious pumpkin flavour) and yoghurt here, along with chalks and a blackboard to keep the offspring amused. Staff are friendly and efficient and accustomed to the influx of hungry young ones from the neighbouring puppet theatre (*see p180*).
Disabled: toilet.

Cybersmith

42 Church Street, at Massachusetts Avenue, Cambridge (492 5857). Harvard T. **Open** 10am-10pm Mon-Thur; 10am-midnight Fri, Sat; 11am-8pm Sun. **Credit** AmEx, Disc, MC, V. **Map 4 B2**
A café that offers most older kids' dream combo – food and computers. Each table has its own terminal, with facilities to surf the net and play computer games. There are also several virtual reality machines ranging from skateboarding and skiing to the usual shoot-'em-dead games. Food consists of everything snacky from cookies to muffins, bagels to scones, and a selection of fresh fruit juices. For more on-line facilities, *see chapter* **Directory**.
Disabled: toilet. Website: www.cybersmith.com

Figs

See p131 **Restaurants & Cafés** *for listings.*
Figs don't have a children's menu, but they do offer macaroni cheese, plain cheese pizzas, and simple spaghetti, as well as a more adventurous menu for adults. It's well worth trying if you're in the area, though you may have to wait for a table.

Friendly's

41 Boylston Street, at Chestnut Hill Plaza, Brookline (731 1095). Chestnut Hill T/60 bus. **Open** 8am-10pm Mon-Thur, Sun; 8am-11pm Fri, Sat. **Credit** Disc, MC, V.
The ever-popular Friendly's chain has a vast menu with something for almost any whim. Ice-cream desserts entitled 'volcano', 'explosion' or 'monster mash' are hard to resist. Also on offer is what must be one of the cheapest children's meals around – food and drink for just $2.79 (4-8pm Monday to Thursday). There are also high chairs, a play area, books and crayons.
Disabled: toilet.

Full Moon

344 Huron Avenue, at Fresh Pond Parkway, Cambridge (354 6699). Harvard T. **Open** 11am-8.30pm Mon-Thur, Sun; 11am-9pm Fri, Sat. **Credit** MC, V.
Twice winner of the *Parents' Paper* Clean Plate Club Award, Full Moon satisfies adults and children with its food and play area. Peanut butter and jelly sandwiches keep most sprogs happy (for a short time anyway) and parents can try dishes such as butternut squash soup with a glass of Chianti. Booking is recommended.
Disabled: toilet.

Hard Rock Cafe

131 Clarendon Street, at Stuart Street (353 1400). Back Bay T. **Open** 11.30am-11pm (bar closes at midnight) daily. **Credit** AmEx, DC, Disc, MC, V. **Map 3 F5**
Join the other tourists and get a hamburger and fries at one of the best-known burger joints in town. On the kids' menu there's a choice of macaroni with cheese, hot dogs, fried chicken or a cheeseburger, for $5.99. Children also get treated to a colouring book and crayons. *See also p205* **Nightlife**.
Disabled: toilet.

JP Licks

674 Centre Street, Seaverns Avenue, Jamaica Plain (524 6740). Green St T. **Open** 11.30am-midnight daily. **No credit cards**.
The giant plastic cow on JP Licks' roof doesn't detract from its great tasting ice-cream. The place is due to relocate at the end of 1999 to the firehouse across the street, which will be converted into a coffee micro-roastery, bakery and play space.
Branches: 311A Harvard Street, Brookline (738 8252); 352 Newbury Street (236 1666).

Papa Razzi

271 Dartmouth Street, between Boylston & Newbury Streets (536 9200). Copley T. **Open** 11.30am-11pm Mon-Wed, Sun; 11.30am-midnight Thur-Sat. **Credit** AmEx, DC, Disc, MC, V. **Map 3 F5**
Well-prepared Italian food is served here and although there's no children's menu, high chairs are available and staff are accommodating.
Disabled: toilet.

Entertainment

Many of Boston's museums cater for children (*see chapter* **Museums & Galleries**), particularly the **Computer Museum**, where, among other activities, kids can climb inside the x-wing of the computer gallery and become Luke Skywalker. The **Museum of Science & Hayden Planetarium** offers live animal presentations and puppet shows, and on a visit to the **New England Aquarium** (*see chapter* **Sightseeing**) you can befriend a penguin, stroke a turtle or handle a starfish. There's even a sealion show that takes place on board the neighbouring ship *Discovery*. More serious stops such as the **Paul Revere House** (*see page 56* **Sightseeing**) offer guided tours especially for kids.

General

Children's Museum

300 Congress Street, at Museum Wharf (426 8855/ 6500). South Station T. **Open** *Sept-June* 10am-5pm Tue-Thur, Sat, Sun; 10am-9pm Fri; *July, Aug* 10am-7pm Tue-Thur, Sat, Sun; 10am-9pm Fri. **Admission** $2-$7; $1 5pm-9pm Fri. **Credit** AmEx, DC, Disc, MC, V. **Map 5 H5**
Whether driving a boat, putting out fires, dressing up, playing with Lego, reading, blowing giant bubbles or just climbing is their thing, this is the place to do it. Exhibitions change regularly, with the emphasis always on having fun and learning at the same time. There's also a theatre and museum shop (all kinds of useful bendy, shiny and plastic objects abound) and a giant milk bottle outside dispensing snacks. Advance booking is recommended in the summer.
Disabled: toilet. Website: www.bostonkids.org

Animals & nature

Franklin Park & Zoo

See p75 **Sightseeing** *for listings.*
The African Tropical Forest, complete with gorillas, leopards, pygmy hippos and monkeys, is the main draw here. But most kids head for the Children's Zoo (even though it's

a long walk from the main gate), where they get a chance to meet horses, porcupines, llamas, peacocks, cows, goats, a variety of reptiles, monkeys, ducks and turtles.

Theatre

Boston Children's Theatre

647 Boylston Street, at Dartmouth Street (424 6634). Copley T. **Open** 9am-5pm Mon-Fri. **Performances** 2pm Sat, Sun. **Tickets** $12-$18. **Credit** MC, V. **Map 3 F5**

The 50-year-old BCT puts on three main stage shows a year in a number of indoor and outdoor venues around the city. Major productions, by kids for kids, are timed to coincide with the school holidays but acting classes are offered all year round. Summer sees regular evening performances in Copley Square.

Puppet Showplace Theatre

32 Station Street, at Washington Street, Brookline (731 6400). Brookline Village T. **Open** *office* 9am-5pm daily; *puppet-making workshop* 4pm Sat, Sun. **Tickets** $6. **Credit** MC, V.

Some of the most popular fairy tales, from *Cinderella* to *Jack and the Beanstalk*, are shown here, along with more contemporary stories – all performed by professional puppeteers. For the curious, there's sometimes the chance to meet the stars of the show after the performance. Although no food or drink is allowed in the auditorium, there's a great ice-cream place next door (*see page 179* **The Blueberry Moose**).

Wheelock Family Theatre

200 the Riverway, at Longwood Avenue (734 4760). Longwood Avenue T. **Open** *box office* noon-5.30pm Mon-Fri. **Performances** *Jan, Feb, Apr, May, Nov, Dec* 7.30pm Fri; 3pm Sat, Sun. **Tickets** $10-$15. **Credit** MC, V.

The Wheelock Theatre offers seasonal shows for all the family; past performances have included an introduction to Shakespeare in a kids' version of *The Tempest*.
Disabled: toilet.

Swimming

During the summer months, the fountains outside the **Christian Science** complex (215 Massachusetts Avenue, at Huntington Street) fill with paddling toddlers. Just outside the **First Church of Christ, Scientist** (*see chapter* **Sightseeing**), the fountains provide a perfect location for cooling off in the middle of the day. For more swimming suggestions *see chapter* **Sport & Fitness**.

Tours

Boston by Little Feet

(367 2345/recorded information 367 3766). **Tours** *May-Oct* 10am Mon, Sat; 2pm Sun. **Tickets** $6-$8. **No credit cards.**

Boston by Little Feet, organised by the Boston by Foot tour group (*see p87* **Sightseeing**), provides a child's-eye view of nine sites along the Freedom Trail. While this is specifically for little feet, bigger feet are obligatory as children must be accompanied by an adult. Buy tickets from the guide at the start of the tour.
Website: www.bostonbyfoot.com

Make Way For Ducklings Tour

(Historic Neighbourhoods Foundation 426 1885). **Tours** *Apr-mid June* 9am, 10am, 11am, Mon-Fri. **Tickets** $5. **No credit cards.**

A tour with plenty of photo opportunities. Children aged 5-8 are encouraged to waddle in the footsteps of the Mallard family, making Robert McCloskey's celebrated book, *Make Way For Ducklings*, come alive. Quacking is essential. The Historic Neighbourhoods Foundation also organises the Ducklings Parade that takes place on Mother's Day in May: up to 1,000 parents and children have been known to trace the route of Jack, Kack, Mack, Nack, Quack, Pack and Mr and Mrs Mallard as they search for a home. Prizes are awarded for the best-looking 'duckling'. Participation costs $10-$25. The Foundation also offers tours for older children (8-12) of the North End, Chinatown and the waterfront.

Swan Boats Lagoon

Public Gardens, opposite the Ritz-Carlton, 15 Arlington Street, at Newbury Street (267 1029). Arlington T. **Open** *mid Apr-June* 11am-4pm daily; *June-Sept* 10am-5pm daily. **Price** 95¢-$1.50. **Map 5 F5**

The Swan Boats, based in the Public Gardens since 1877, usually prove irresistible to children. The Lagoon that they navigate isn't very big, but a trip on one is still an essential Boston tourist experience.

Wearing them out

Bowling alleys are always a great place for the family: check the **Sport & Fitness** chapter for details of Boston's best. If you really want to make sure your children sleep well, walk to the top of the 221-foot (67-metre) **Bunker Hill Monument** (*see page 59* **Sightseeing**).

Ice-skating on Frog Pond

Boston Common, at Park & Beacon Streets (635 2120). Park St T. **Open** *early Nov-mid March* 10am-9pm Mon-Thur, Sun; 10am-10pm Fri, Sat. **Admission** $3. **Skate rental** $5. **Credit** AmEx, Disc, MC, V. **Map 5 G4**

If you're in Boston over the winter, there's no excuse for not hiring a pair of ice-skates and heading down to Frog Pond, illuminated by the Boston Common Christmas lights. Private and semi-private lessons are also available.

Whale-watching

If life in town gets too much, during the summer months you can always head out to sea and try a whale-watching tour. It gets windy on board, though, and it's easy to get sunburnt out on the water, so take plenty of layers and sunscreen. For details of tours, *see chapter* **Trips Out of Town**.

Out of town events

Salem's Haunted Happenings

See p40 **Boston by Season** *for listings.*

If the kids have a morbid fascination with witches, spells and hauntings, it's worth taking a trip to Salem over the Hallowe'en period.

Sandcastle and Sculpture Day

Jetties Beach, Nantucket (Nantucket Chamber of Commerce 1-508 228 1700). **Date** 15 August, noon-4pm. **Admission** $5. **Credit** AmEx, MC, V.

Show off your architectural capabilities in Nantucket. Families, individuals or teams are invited to participate.

Teddy Bear Rally

Amherst Town Common, Amherst (Amherst Rotary Club 1-413 256 8983). **Date** first weekend in August, 9.30am-4pm. **Admission** free.

Taking a break for lunch at the **Children's Museum**. *See page 179.*

A rally that celebrates bears and all related items. The 'teddy bear hospital' will aid the sick and wounded and clothes can be purchased for more stylish bears.
Disabled: toilet.

Turn-of-the-century Ice Cream Social

8 Memorial Street, Old Deerfield (Old Deerfield Craft Fairs 1-413 774 7476). **Date** 4 July, 10.30am-4.30pm. **Admission** $1-$5. **No credit cards**.
The festival includes ragtime, dancing and games, as well as lots of dressing up.
Disabled: toilet.

Shops

Boston has a great choice of children's shops. For a more extensive list, consult the *Baby Resource Guide of Greater Boston* by Aley Lopez O'Toole Smith, which has a chapter devoted to local products and shopping. *See also chapter* **Shops & Services**.

Toys & books

Curious George Goes To WordsWorth

1 John F Kennedy Street, at Harvard Square, Cambridge (498 0062/1-800 899 2202). Harvard T. **Open** 9am-11.15pm Mon-Sat; 10am-10.15pm Sun. **Credit** AmEx, Disc, MC, V. **Map 4 B2**
When WordsWorth Books expanded its children's department into a separate location in 1996, it seemed natural to name it after George, the little monkey whose creator, Margret Rey, often frequented the bookstore. This colourful shop looks like one big party hosted by George, with guests such as Arthur, Madeline, Thomas the Tank Engine and Winnie the Pooh. It's hard not to be drawn in by the selection of books and toys. The staff will accommodate out-of-print searches and worldwide shipping, and gift certificates are available.

FAO Schwarz

440 Boylston Street, at Berkeley Street (262 5900). Arlington T. **Open** 10am-9pm Mon-Sat; 11-7pm Sun. **Credit** AmEx, DC, Disc, MC, V. **Map 5 F5**

'Welcome to our world, welcome to our world, welcome to our world of toys...' If you can deal with the mind-control aspects of the FAO Schwarz shopping experience – that constantly-repeated song won't leave your brain for days – bring the kids here for a romp through toyland. The giant bronze teddy bear outside is a favourite backdrop for tourist snaps. The shop organises special events throughout the year: the last Saturday in October sees the bear's birthday party, celebrated in true style with cakes and balloons (any profit goes to a children's charity) and there are regular book-signings.
Disabled: toilet.

Disney Store

100 Huntington Avenue, at Copley Square (266 5200). Back Bay or Copley T. **Open** 10am-9pm Mon-Sat; noon-6pm Sun. **Credit** AmEx, Disc, MC, V. **Map 3 F5**
Here you'll find all the merchandise plugging the latest Disney extravaganza, along with those Mickey Mouse boxer shorts you've always wanted.
Branch: Quincy Marketplace, Faneuil Hall (248 3900).

Learningsmith

25 Brattle Street, at John F Kennedy Street, Cambridge (661 6008). Harvard T. **Open** 10am-10pm Mon-Thur; 10am-11pm Fri, Sat; 11am-7pm Sun. **Credit** AmEx, Disc, MC, V. **Map 4 B2**
This is an excellent educational toy shop for kids and adults, with toys, games, books and learning kits in every field of art and science.

Learning Express

1290A Beacon Street, at Harvard Street, Brookline (232 5700). Coolidge Corner T. **Open** 9.30am-6.30pm Mon-Wed, Sat; 9.30am-8pm Thur, Fri; 11.30am-5pm Sun. **Credit** AmEx, Disc, MC, V.
Toys, books, funky backpacks, lunch boxes, pencil cases and other essentials are available from this favourite Brookline store.

No Kidding

19 Harvard Street, at Boylston Street, Brookline (739 2477). Brookline Village T. **Open** 9.30am-6.30pm Mon, Wed, Thur, Sat; 9.30am-9pm Tue, Fri; noon-5.30pm Sun. **Credit** MC, V.
A selection of toys and books designed for all ages, from birth through to adulthood. No kidding.

Toys R Us and Kids R Us

200 Alewife Brook Parkway, at Concord Avenue, Cambridge (576 8697). Alewife T. **Open** 9.30am-9.30pm Mon-Sat; noon-6pm Sun. **Credit** AmEx, Disc, MC, V.
A good range of well-priced toys and clothing is available from the ever popular R Us chain.

Warner Bros Store

800 Boylston Avenue, at Prudential Center (859 3770). Prudential T. **Open** 10am-8pm Mon-Sat; 11am-6pm Sun. **Credit** AmEx, Disc, MC, V. **Map 3 E5**
The usual Warner Brothers merchandise and characters are sold here, including the interactive Daffy, Sylvester, Tweetie and Bugs.
Branch: 8 Quincy Marketplace, Faneuil Hall (227 1101).

Clothing

Children's Orchard

807 Boylston Street, just west of Chestnut Hill Reservoir, Brookline (277 3006). Chestnut Hill T. **Open** 9am-6pm Mon-Fri; 10am-5pm Sat. **Credit** Disc, MC, V.
This national chain offers great second-hand clothing for ages 0-8. There are also toys, books and pushchairs on sale, and the friendly owner is always willing to give advice.

Gap Kids/Baby Gap

201 Newbury Street, at Exeter Street (424 8778). Copley T. **Open** 10am-9pm Mon-Sat; noon-6pm Sun. **Credit** AmEx, Disc, MC, V. **Map 3 E5**
You're never too small to join the Gap nation. Miniature jeans, cords, jackets, T-shirts, sweatshirts and other clothes for stylish babies and kids.
Branches: Copley Place (262 2370); Faneuil Hall Marketplace (439 7844).

Gymboree

Copley Place (437 1191). Back Bay or Copley T. **Open** 10am-8pm Mon-Sat; noon-6pm Sun. **Credit** AmEx, Disc, MC, V. **Map 3 F5**
Beautiful designs are sold for boys and girls, from infancy to age seven, including co-ordinated separates, fashion and holiday lines.

Oilily

31 Newbury Street, between Arlington & Berkeley Streets (247 9299). Arlington T. **Open** 10am-6pm Mon-Wed; 10am-7pm Thur; 10am-6pm Fri, Sat; noon-5pm Sun. **Credit** AmEx, Disc, MC, V. **Map 3 F5**
A Dutch-designed line of fun, colourful children's clothes, a little pricier than Gap.

Red Wagon

26 Common Street, at Winthrop Street, Charlestown (242 7402). Community College or Haymarket T. **Open** 10am-6pm Mon-Sat; 11am-5pm Sun. **Credit** AmEx, Disc, MC, V.
Red Wagon makes designer dressing affordable and shopping fun. Creative displays offer a wealth of colour, and labels such as Küda, Rebel Kids and Mulberribush can be picked up at reasonable prices.

Kenzie Kids

Chestnut Hill Mall, 199 Boylston Street, Brookline (965 5566). Chestnut Hill T. **Open** 10am-9.30pm Mon-Fri; 10am-8pm Sat; noon-6pm Sun. **Credit** AmEx, MC, V.
Special-occasion clothing for the parent who wants to dress up their child. There are party dresses for little princesses, waistcoats for page boys, and a mass of top labels, from Chevignon to Kenzo to Calvin Klein.

Shoes

The Kids Barn

25 Kempton Place, at Washington Street (332 6300). Woodland T. **Open** 9.30am-9pm Mon-Fri; 9am-6pm Sat; noon-5pm Sun. **Credit** AmEx, Disc, MC, V.
Knowledgeable staff help parents and children find shoes they both agree on.

Stride Rite

199 Boylston Street, at Hammond Pond Parkway, Newton (244 5251). Chestnut Hill T. **Open** 10am-9.30pm Mon-Sat; noon-6pm Sun. **Credit** AmEx, Disc, MC, V.
The popular line of children's shoes has its own shop and is as reliable as ever when it comes to the classics. You can be assured of good quality and service.
Branch: **Macy's** 450 Washington Street, at Summer Street (357 3303).

Varese Shoes

285 Hanover Street, at Richmond Street (523 6530). Haymarket T. **Open** 10am-6pm Mon-Sat. **Credit** AmEx, Disc, MC, V. **Map 5 G/H3**
To go for the true Italian feel when treading the streets of the North End, what better than to buy your child a pair of perfect-fitting Italian leather shoes? Varese is the antidote to mall shopping, and owner Mario Corsaro has been supplying Boston's youngest with classics for over 40 years.

Film

Where to see Boston on film and films while in Boston.

Like many of the arts in Boston, the film scene is generated mostly out of the city's colleges and universities. The rudiments of film-making are taught at places such as the School of the Museum of Fine Arts ('the Museum School', as it's known), Harvard's Carpenter Center for the Visual Arts, Boston University's College of Communication, and others. In these institutions experienced documentarians provide inspiration for up-and-comers and young cineastes are born.

Although art houses don't necessarily thrive in Boston, they do exist and the typical art house retrospective series devoted to auteurs such as Fassbinder, Ford, Bertolucci and Wenders owes much to the academic climate, where students are first bitten with the 'film as art' bug. As for the film-making scene, it's very indie indeed. Some of the underground leaders of the cinema verité movement have spent their careers here: Robert Gardner, Richard Leacock and Frederick Wiseman among them. Errol Morris (*The Thin Blue Line*) has spent virtually the whole of his career in the city, as have the documentarians Richard Broadman (*Mission Hill* and *The Miracle of Boston*), Ross McElwee (*Sherman's March*) and David Sutherland (*The Farmer's Wife*). Young feature film-makers based in Boston who've recently made a splash are Maureen Foley (*Home Before Dark*), Robert Patton-Spruill (*Squeeze*) and Brad Anderson (*Next Stop, Wonderland*). But Boston ain't Hollywood. It's the home of post-grad indie projects, location shoots and the occasional director who leaves to make it big in Hollywood. (John Paul Anderson's story is somewhat typical: a Hollywood kid, he logged some time at Boston's Emerson College and then went on to make *Hard Eight* and *Boogie Nights*).

On the whole then, Boston is more a city for film-lovers than film-makers and it serves the former fairly well. During the 1960s and 1970s, art houses in Boston boomed. The Orson Welles Cinema, a multi-screen art house on Massachusetts Avenue just outside Harvard Square, almost single-handedly fuelled a national reggae explosion with its long run of *The Harder They Come* (the cinema closed in the 1980s). There was a double-screen art house in nearby Central Square (for years the home of Philippe de Broca's *King of Hearts*). The single-screen Harvard Square Cinema would run film cycles or movies in rep, pairing, for instance, *A Streetcar Named Desire* with *Last Tango in Paris.* It also presented the occasional rock show: Bruce Springsteen made a famous early appearance here and it's where The Clash made their Boston début. There were art houses, too, in Boston's Park Square and Kenmore Square. But now, alas, the national chains have taken over and the art house has become an endangered species. Even the commercial cinemas (owned by Sony) have begun to close and the power has shifted to the big suburban multiplexes.

Seasonal flicks

In the summer, don't miss the Friday Flicks at the **Hatch Memorial Shell**, when the area in front of the stage on the Esplanade fills with picnicking families who come to watch popular movies shown *al fresco* when the sun goes down (phone the Visitors' Bureau information line on 1-800 888 5515 for more details). And in the winter, the **Wang Center for the Performing Arts** (*see chapter* **The Performing Arts**) adds films shown in repertory to its busy schedule.

Art house cinemas

The Coolidge and the Brattle are virtually the last of an art house breed. The **Coolidge Corner Theater** is a glorious double-screen art house in Brookline. Once a church, it was converted into an art deco movie palace in 1933. In 1977 film-lover Justin Freed (who had also programmed the Park Square and Kenmore Square art houses) acquired the cinema and began showing independent and foreign films. He later succumbed to multiplex and video rental pressure and converted the balcony into a second auditorium.

By 1988, however, he was ready to get out of the business. Saving the cinema from demolition, a group of community activists/film lovers got together and eventually formed the Coolidge Corner Theater Foundation. These days, the cinema screens a diverse mix of art and foreign films, revivals and first-runs, and shows special children's movies and Jewish-themed films that cater to the local Jewish community (the cinema also hosts the annual Jewish Film Festival). Despite constant renovations to the exterior of the building and portions of the lobby and the addition of the second screen upstairs, the main auditorium – with its beautiful art deco fixtures and giant screen – remains intact. That screen alone makes the Coolidge worth a visit.

For the past few years, the programmes at the Coolidge have been organised by the Beacon Cinema Group, part of the non-profit-making Running Arts organisation that owns and operates the **Brattle Theatre**. The Brattle is a legend in its own right and since 1998 has been the last single-screen cinema in Boston or Cambridge. In a history written for the Brattle's 100th birthday in 1990, writer John Engstrom traced the building's development from its construction for theatrical events by the Cambridge Social Union in 1890 to its current use as an art house cinema that mixes repertory and first-run films and readings sponsored by nearby Wordsworth Books with occasional musical performances.

The exterior of the Brattle still looks pretty much as historian Engstrom described it on its completion in 1890: 'a simple, unpretentious Queen Anne-style edifice with a gambrel roof of gradual pitch', though the porte cochère for horse-drawn carriages has long since gone.

The history of the Brattle includes not only a series of amateur and professional theatrical productions but the creation, during the 1940s, of a resident theatre company. Those who acted on the Brattle stage included Harvardians such as TS Eliot, as well as Paul Robeson, who made his US début as Othello here in 1942, opposite Uta Hagen and Jose Ferrer. Other performers through the years have included Cyril Ritchard, Jessica Tandy, Hume Cronyn and Zero Mostel.

But it was in the 1950s that the Brattle began to make its mark as a cinema. That's when Harvardians Bryant Haliday and Cyrus Harvey converted it, renovating the auditorium and installing a Translux twin-projector system that is still in use. Harvey, a former Fulbright/Sorbonne student, was inspired by Paris's Cinemathèque to programme a mix of classic and contemporary American and foreign films. The opening season, in 1953, featured WC Fields and Mae West in *My Little Chickadee*, Jean Cocteau's *Orphée* and Serge Eisenstein's *Ivan the Terrible*. Haliday and Harvey revived interest in the films of Humphrey Bogart, which they ran in week-long series during Harvard exam periods, a move that also influenced the naming of a bar/restaurant in the building, the Casablanca.

Haliday and Harvey's influence extended not only to the Boston area, but internationally too. In the mid-1950s they turned New York's 55th Street Playhouse into a cinema and founded Janus Films, Inc, the US distributor for directors such as Bergman, Fellini, Godard, Kurosawa and Truffaut. In 1961 Harvey accepted Bergman's Best Foreign Film Oscar for *The Virgin Spring* on the director's behalf.

Harvey eventually sold the Brattle lease in 1977, but despite several threats of closure and extensive

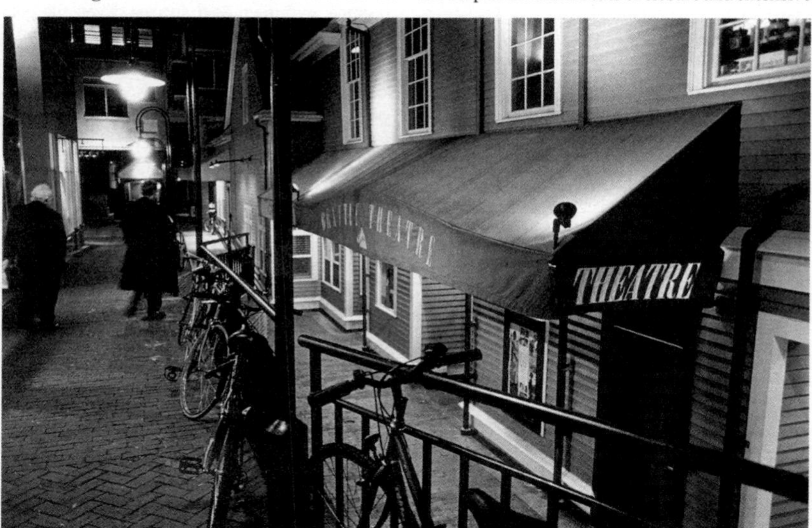

Cambridge legend, the **Brattle Theatre** *– one of the last of the art houses.*

renovation to the building (which also includes retail and restaurant space) the Brattle has maintained its high repertory and first-run standards. Since 1986, Running Arts has operated its 'vertical' calender: film noir on Mondays (including series of restored films from Universal and Columbia), Wordsworth readings and indie film series on Tuesdays, and special showings of newly struck 35mm prints such as *The Lady from Shanghai* or *The Wizard of Oz*, Fellini films, or Cambridge premières of new auteurs such as Tony Gatlif at the weekend. Other days of the week are dedicated to a particular star, director, nationality, or theme (perhaps Hong Kong action flicks, Universal horror films, the movies of Harvey Keitel or Catherine Deneuve).

Brattle Theatre

40 Brattle Street, Cambridge (876 6837). Harvard T. **Tickets** $4-$7. **No credit cards. Map 4 B2**
Disabled: toilet.
Website: www.beaconcinema.com/brattle

Coolidge Corner Theater

290 Harvard Street, Brookline (734 2500). Coolidge Corner T. **Tickets** $4.50-$7.50. **No credit cards.**

Other art house screens

Harvard Film Archive

Carpenter Center for the Visual Arts, 24 Quincy Street, Cambridge (495 4700). Harvard T. **Tickets** $5-$6. **No credit cards. Map 4 B2**
The HFA's auditorium is smaller and less comfortable than that at the **Museum of Fine Arts** (*see below*) and the archive also lacks the MFA's funding, apparently due to the ambivalent attitude of the university of which it is a department. Is the archive a tool for scholarship and research, or an enlightened public exhibitor of world cinema? By 1998 the HFA had been without a permanent curator/director for several years, but temporary curators have nonetheless maintained the compelling series of programmes that mix pop and high art – from Fassbinder to 'Masterpieces of Gay and Lesbian Cinema'. Programmes often include lectures and discussions.
Disabled: toilet.

Kendall Square Cinema

1 Kendall Square, Cambridge (494 9800). Kendall/MIT T. **Tickets** $5-$7.75. **No credit cards. Map 4 E4**
For a steady diet of first-run art films, this is the place to come, though 'art film' can describe any number of commercially-minded Miramax period productions and *The Full Monty* as well as challenging US fare such as *Happiness* or *The Ice Storm*. This 10-screen branch of the Landmark chain has big, comfortable auditoriums, large screens and an equally appealing lobby with neo-deco touches.
Disabled: toilet.

Museum of Fine Arts

465 Huntington Avenue, at Museum Street (369 3770). Museum of Fine Arts T. **Tickets** $6-$7. **Credit** AmEx, MC, V. **Map 3 D6**
Curator Bo Smith and his team present a creative and wide-ranging mix of world premières, locally-made documentaries and series that include screenings for the Boston Jewish Film Festival or new films from Iran. You can also catch occasional long runs of popular movies such as *SlamNation* or *The Jew in the Lotus*. Programmes include lectures and discussions, and personal appearances. Screenings are in the large, comfortable Remis Auditorium.

The **Coolidge Corner Theater** *in Brookline.*

Nickelodeon

34 Cummington Street, off Commonwealth Avenue (424 1500). BU East or Kenmore T. **Tickets** $5-$7.75. **Credit** AmEx, Disc, MC, V. **Map 3 D5**
Its location in the heart of Boston University (and its previous incarnation as a bona fide indie house) means that this six-screen Sony outpost draws arty films (*American History X, Velvet Goldmine*) or big-budget art-minded films that bomb (*Beloved*).
Disabled: toilet.

Other screens

For the location of your nearest cinema or information on films currently on release, call the free **Moviephone** service on 333 3456.

Allston Cinema

214 Harvard Avenue, at Commonwealth Avenue, Allston (277 2140). Harvard Avenue T. **Tickets** $4.75-$7.50. **Credit** MC, V.
A comfortable little two-screener cinema in the heart of Allston's student ghetto, adjacent to nearby bars and clubs. It's off the busy Harvard Avenue/Commonwealth Avenue intersection.
Disabled: toilet.

Capitol Theater

204 Massachusetts Avenue, at Lake Street, Arlington (1-781 648 4340). Harvard Square T, then 77 bus. **Tickets** $3.50-$5. **Credit** AmEx, DC, MC, V.

On location

Boston is most frequently seen as the backdrop for TV shows such as *The Practice* and *Ally McBeal* (*below*) or, in the past, *Cheers* (now in syndication), *Spencer: For Hire* and *St Elsewhere*. But at least since *The Thomas Crown Affair* in 1967 (*below, right*) and *The Boston Strangler* in 1968, the city has been the location for a number of movie productions. In the 1990s, the Massachusetts Film Office reported about a dozen productions a year – of feature films, TV specials and series.

The movies offer a whole range of perspectives of the city. Certainly, in *Ally McBeal*, the sweeping aerial shots of State Street and the Financial District, Charles River, Beacon Hill and Back Bay present the city at its most picturesque. Films such as *Love Story* (1970 – *below, opposite*) and *The Paper Chase* (1973) take in the Harvard scene. *Good Will Hunting* (1997 – *above, right*) does a fairly good job of presenting the town/gown Boston dichotomy in the story of a South Boston prodigy who works as a janitor at MIT, solving maths problems between spells of waxing floors.

Its star, Cambridge-born Damon (and his childhood pal and co-screenwriter and -star Ben Affleck) have the advantage of an inside view and so manage to avoid the pitfall of most Hollywood actors playing Bostonians – they do get the accent. Most actors remember the adage about 'pahking yuh

This little gem of an art deco cinema just outside Cambridge (accessible by bus from Harvard Square) shows a mix of classics and first-run films on its six screens.
Disabled: toilet.

Cheri

50 Dalton Street, opposite the Sheraton Hotel (536 2870). Hynes/ICA T. **Tickets** $5-$7.75. **Credit** AmEx, MC, V. **Map 3 E5**

There are three screens in descending order of size and the Back Bay location is the heartiest recommendation for this Sony house.
Disabled: toilet.

Circle Cinemas

Cleveland Circle, 399 Chestnut Hill, at Beacon Street (566 4040). Cleveland Circle T.
Tickets $5-$7.75. **Credit** Disc, MC, V.

Cleveland Circle is at the nexus of the Boston University/Boston College area as well as the classier enclaves of Brookline and Newton. Accessible by Green Line T, this National Amusements first-run house has the advantage of comfortable high-backed, deep-cushioned tilting chairs.
Disabled: toilet.

Copley Place

100 Huntington Avenue, at Dartmouth Street (266 1300). Copley T. **Tickets** $5-$7.35. **Credit** AmEx, MC, V. **Map 3 F5**

This honeycomb of tiny auditoriums in the Copley Place shopping mall began as an art house complex, but now features all manner of big commercial first-runs. The crowds can make it hellish, especially when kids pack the place for an animated feature such as *Toy Story* or *Antz*, but you can't beat the location on a rainy day and the screens are pretty comfortable, with good sight lines. While watching *There's Something About Mary*, though, be prepared to overhear the occasional screams and explosions from John Carpenter's *Vampires* showing next door.
Disabled: toilet.

Harvard Square Theater

10 Church Street, at Massachusetts Avenue, Cambridge (864 4580). Harvard T.
Tickets $5-$7.75. **Credit** AmEx, DC, MC, V.
Map 4 B2

This Loews four-screener was fashioned out of a former single-screen beauty with wicker chairs in the first row of the balcony and a nice repertory programme. The main

cahr in Hahvahd Yahd' and end up with some stilted approximation of the Kennedys' unrepresentative, aristocratic twang. (Despite Tony Curtis's solid performance in *The Boston Strangler – above, left* – most native Bostonians wince at the Brooklyn-born actor's mangling of 'Jordan Marsh'.)

This makes it worth seeking out the hard-to-find *The Friends of Eddie Coyle*, where Robert Mitchum plays the aging Mafia errand boy of the title. The story, from a novel by former Boston prosecutor-turned-novelist George V Higgins, involves a creaky plot about pseudo-revolutionary arms smuggling, but it offers a compelling view of Boston's seedier side (the Mafia has written some lurid chapters in the city's history). In one of the movie's more telling scenes, the hapless Eddie attends a Boston Bruins hockey game and admires the fancy skate work of the legendary Bobby Orr. Here, and in other scenes, Mitchum portrays Eddie as a simple, frustrated Boston working stiff. Without condescending, he gets the temperament – and the accent – just right.

auditorium still has its huge screen, though poor conditions made it the scourge of first-run fanatics for years. Nonetheless, if you're in Harvard Square and want to see something like *Face/Off*, this is the place to come.
Disabled: toilet.

Festivals

The **Boston Jewish Film Festival** (1-781 899 3830/www.bjff.cyways.com) began in 1989 and now includes as many as 40 films – both documentary and feature – from 15 different countries, all with varying degrees of a Jewish theme. It lasts for two weeks in November and takes place at a variety of venues, including the **Coolidge Corner Theater** and the **Museum of Fine Arts**.

The two-week **Boston Film Festival** (266 2533) takes place from the second week in September, mostly at the Loews Theater (Copley Place). It lacks the prestige of larger, juried festivals and its selections sometimes seem arbitrary, dependent solely on the availability of product in the marketplace. However, the BFF does attract a bit of glitz for its career achievement awards (Al Pacino and Helena Bonham Carter have both received them in the past) and it manages to book interesting items that overflow from the first-class Toronto Film Festival, which takes place at about the same time.

The **Boston Film/Video Foundation** (536 1540) is an important centre for the Boston indie film and video scene. Its annual **New England Film & Video Festival** is small – lasting just six days – and limits its focus to New England artists, but it employs a serious jury and fielded 187 entries in 1998. The festival takes place every spring (between April and May) at the same time as the **International Festival of Women's Cinema**.

Gay & Lesbian Boston

From the Puritans to Pride.

Of course, there were queers in colonial times. Same-sex love landed on Plymouth Rock along with the Puritans. Even the first governor of Massachusetts, John Winthrop, wrote love letters to a man he had left behind in England, one William Springe: 'I loved you truly, before I could think you took any notice of me'. (To be fair, Winthrop also buried three wives and had about 14 children). Much of Puritan poet Michael Wigglesworth's diary was written in code. When these passages were deciphered centuries later, they turned out to be all the naughty thoughts he'd had about his male students.

Dykes from Boston even fought for Independence alongside the Minutemen. Take the case of Deborah Sampson. No one knew she was a woman until she was wounded in battle. Under the guise of Robert Shurtleff, Sampson had drunk ale with the boys and wooed many a maiden. She was even awarded a soldier's pension for bravery.

Boston in the nineteenth century is said to have been rife with literary men loving men. There's all sorts of speculation about Herman Melville and Nathaniel Hawthorne, for example. Ralph Waldo Emerson's diary chronicles a two-year obsession with fellow Harvard classmate Martin Gay. Henry Thoreau's diary describes the emotional attraction he felt to men such as Canadian woodcutter Alek Therian during his long walks around Walden Pond. Perhaps a bit better documented, though, are the 'Boston Marriages' that were socially sanctioned between women. There was actress Charlotte Cushman and Sallie Mercer, for example, writer Sarah Orne Jewett and Annie Adams Fields and poet Amy Lowell and Ada Dwyer Russell.

World War II changed the way most Americans saw the world. Enlisted men began spending a lot of intimate time in the company of men; women entered the workforce and began supporting themselves. Freed from typical social roles, some Bostonians began to identify themselves as homosexual. Several of Boston's first gay bars – the Half Dollar, Light House and Crawford House – sprang up among the strip joints and flophouses of Scollay Square. Lower Washington Street became known as 'Gay Times Square'. Bay Village became a haven for same-sex relationships.

City officials tried their best to get rid of this 'homosexual problem' by razing most of the gay neighbourhoods in the name of urban renewal (*see page 12* **History**). But by then it was too late. Boston's gay network was too well established. It took to the streets after Stonewall, organising one of the country's first Gay Pride parades. It responded to the AIDS crisis by founding the internationally respected AIDS Action Committee. It sent local representatives such as Gary Studds to Beacon Hill and congressmen such as Barney Frank to Washington. It was one of the first gay communities in the country to secure domestic partner benefits for city employees. We're here and we're queer – and we've been that way for almost 400 years now.

For a more in-depth look at Boston's gay history, we recommend *Improper Bostonians: Lesbian and Gay History from the Puritans to Playland* (Beacon Press, 1988).

GAY CULTURE TODAY

Bostonians aren't exactly known for being the warmest population on the planet. Blame it on their restrained, and often disapproving, Puritan heritage. Unfortunately, the city's gay population could be said to suffer from a similar coldness. It's not that Boston queers are unfriendly, exactly; it just takes a while to get to know them. You'll notice that in bars they tend to huddle in small groups of close friends. Don't be put off. They actually like it when strangers come up and introduce themselves; they're just not good at making the effort themselves.

As with every long-established gay community, a sort of class system has sprung up over time. Old and moneyed Bostonians move in a circle known as the A-List, for example. There are A-List parties, and A-List-approved bars, cafés and gyms. The gay middle classes tend to divide into buff, button-down South Enders, jeans-and-leather Fenway dwellers, young and hip JPsters and political Cantabrigians. In the end, however, everyone more or less gets to know everyone else: the town's just too small for too much segmentation.

Curiously, all the barriers seem to come down during Pride (the first week of June, *see page 39* **Boston by Season**). People transform miraculously during the many events, parties and dances that take place, from the AIDS Walk on Sunday to the South End parade and Carnival the following weekend. During Pride, gay Bostonians stroll hand in hand, dance in the street and smile. They actually smile.

NEIGHBOURHOODS

Ten years ago, Boston's gay boys kick-started the transformation of the South End from a somewhat dangerous and rundown neighbourhood into the town's hippest address. Though rental prices have risen accordingly and straight yuppies have moved in in force, the South End is still *the* zip code to have if you're a gay man. A little quieter and smaller is nearby Bay Village. It's a great place to live, though transvestite prostitutes tend to haunt the street corners at night, never venturing far from the lights of Jacque's (*see page 193*). A large contingent of older gay men own homes in the long-established enclave of the Fenway – its Victory Gardens were the site of relentless midnight cruising in pre-AIDS Boston. Jamaica Plain is being hailed as the new South End. It's a pain to get to on public transport but has nevertheless become popular among lesbians and gay men of more modest means. Cambridge, however, still offers the highest concentration of lesbians. The Inman Square area is where most women's cafés and bars seem to spring up.

Queer press

Bay Windows

Free weekly newspaper for lesbians and gay men, focusing on Boston news, politics and the queer art scene. Available on Thursdays in most gay-friendly venues.

Gay Community News

Quarterly news and literary magazine for lesbians and gay men. Available at many gay-friendly venues and by subscription.

In Newsweekly

Another free lesbian and gay weekly, covering news, politics and art in the whole of New England. Available on Thursdays in most gay-friendly venues.

One In Ten

A free monthly supplement to the *Boston Phoenix* for lesbians and gay men. Available towards the end of the month from newsstands and in most gay-friendly venues.

Sojourner

Monthly newspaper for lesbians. Available at most lesbian-friendly venues and by subscription.

Accommodation

Chandler Inn

See p110 **Accommodation** *for listings.*
Really the only proper gay hotel in town. There are no frills here – barely even a lobby – but it's cheap and the 56 rooms offer all the basics and are scrupulously clean, if a little careworn. There's no restaurant, but you're right in the 'hood, where there are dozens. Fritz, the neighbourhood bar on the ground floor, lays on a free continental breakfast buffet and serves a full brunch at weekends.

Newbury Guest House

See p112 **Accommodation** *for listings.*
Three townhouses joined together London-style on Boston's most exclusive shopping street. Though it doesn't bill itself as gay (a large part of the clientele is European), the staff are completely cool and friendly. The rooms are tasteful and Victorian with all the amenities (if you're a light sleeper, request one at the back). A generous continental breakfast is included and parking is available.

Oasis Guest House

See p112 **Accommodation** *for listings.*
This moderately priced B&B is very gay-friendly, offering a 50-50 mix of homos and hets. The rooms are tastefully decorated and quiet, some with bathrooms, some without. There's a cosy lounge in the lobby (where continental breakfast is served) and the outdoor seating at the back is a popular place to drink cocktails in the warmer months. Parking is available.
Website: www.oasisgh.com

Bookshops

Glad Day Bookshop

673 Boylston Street, at the Public Library (267 3010). Copley T. **Open** 9.30am-10pm Mon-Thur; 9.30am-11pm Fri, Sat; noon-9pm Sun. **Credit** AmEx, Disc, MC, V. **Map 3 F5**
Boston's oldest queer bookshop. A nice mix of theory, self-help, pulp and literature, including a surprising number of foreign-language titles. Glad Day also offers a decent range of adult magazines, videos and greetings cards.

New Words: A Woman's Bookstore

186 Hampshire Street, Cambridge (876 5310). Central T. **Open** 10am-8pm Mon-Fri; 10am-6pm Sat; noon-6pm Sun. **Credit** AmEx, Disc, MC, V. **Map 4 D3**
The only queer bookshop in Cambridge, where the emphasis and atmosphere are definitely lesbian. The staff are friendly, smart and helpful. Buy your books here, then leaf through them over a cup of coffee next door at the **City Girl Caffe** (*see below*).

We Think the World of You

540 Tremont Street, between Berkeley & Clarendon Streets (574 5000). Back Bay T. **Open** 10am-7pm daily. **Credit** AmEx, DC, Disc, MC, V. **Map 5 F6**
Just what you'd want from your local homo bookstore: the latest queer novels, studies, biographies and magazines, all attractively displayed in an unapologetically sunny environment. The staff are very knowledgeable and happy to make special orders. The store sponsors a reading series and runs a discount scheme for frequent buyers.

Coffeeshops & lunch stops

City Girl Caffe

See p150 **Restaurants & Cafés** *for listings.*
For all walks of dyke. One of the few places in town where lesbians can go and just hang out over a cup of joe. The City Girl serves fairly light fare, food-wise: bagels, pastries, sandwiches and pizzas.

Everyday Café

517 Columbus Avenue, at Greenwich Park (536 2119). Mass Ave T. **Open** 7am-8pm Mon-Fri; 9am-5pm Sat, Sun. **Main courses** $5. **Credit** MC, V. **Map 3 F6**

A chatty breakfast and lunch hangout for the neighbourhood's mixed clientele. In addition to good coffee, pastries and sandwiches (the curried chicken and cucumber roll-up is pretty fabulous), you can pick up a few gourmet grocery items in the shop.

Francesca's Espresso Bar

565 Tremont Street, at Union Park (482 9026). Arlington or Back Bay T. **Open** 8am-11pm Mon-Thur, Sun; 8am-midnight Fri, Sat. **Main courses** $7. **No credit cards. Map 3 F6**

Francesca's does a respectable range of breakfast fare, soups, roll-up sandwiches and pastries. It features the work of local artists on the walls and is open pretty late. It would be an even nicer place if the employees and regulars would leave their attitudes at home.

Disabled: toilet.

Kettle Café

288 Columbus Avenue, at Clarendon Street (236 0777). Back Bay T. **Open** 7am-3pm Mon-Fri; 8am-3pm Sat. **Main courses** $6. **No credit cards. Map 5 F5**

A cosy neighbourhood café (lesbian owned and run) that serves breakfast and lunch only. Go there just half a dozen times and Joanne and Stephanie start calling you by your name. They brew both light and dark roast coffee, and recently won Best of Boston billing for their wonderful sandwiches.

Disabled: toilet.

Mildred's Coffeeshop

552 Tremont Street, at Waltham Street (426 0008). Back Bay T. **Open** 7am-midnight Mon-Fri; 8am-midnight Sat, Sun. **Main courses** $6. **Credit** AmEx, MC, V. **Map 3 F6**

With its sunny corner location, Mildred's is popular with the Ballet across the street and smokers everywhere (it's one of the few places left in town where you still can). The staff here are gossipy and lighthearted and never think to move you on if you're reading or working. The food's fine, though the lunch specials try too hard sometimes.

Disabled: toilet.

To Go Bakery

314 Shawmut Avenue, at Union Park (482 1015). Back Bay T. **Open** 6.30am-5pm Mon-Fri; 7am-4pm Sat; 7am-3pm Sun. **Average** $5. **No credit cards. Map 3 F6**

Locals swear by the coffee at this tiny corner shop. You can choose from a range of breakfast or lunch goodies, which staff will happily reheat. When the weather's nice, the clientele tends to linger and gossip on the benches outside.

Gyms & spas

Adam Berke Gym

1260-66 Boylston Street, at Massachusetts Avenue, behind Fenway Park (421 5500). Hynes/ICA T. **Open** 5am-10pm Mon-Fri; 8am-5pm Sat, Sun. **Rates** $39 per month. **Credit** AmEx, DC, Disc, MC, V. **Map 3 F5**

If you've got the cash, this is the place to work out. Partly because it's a beautifully designed gym offering the very latest in equipment, personal training, diet consultation and aerobic fitness; mostly because there are so many amazing-looking people wandering around – not the least of whom is Adam Berke himself.

Étant

251 Shawmut Avenue, at Herald Street (423 5040). NE Medical Center T. **Open** 10am-9pm Wed-Fri; 8am-6pm Sat; 11am-5pm Sun. **Rates** *massage* $65; *facial* $65; *manicure* $16. **Credit** AmEx, Disc, MC, V. **Map 3 G5**

Though Étant bills itself as a 'spa for well-being', it's basically a nice little neighbourhood place where you can book a massage, get a facial or have your nails done. There's nothing wrong with that, and it does offer a limited range of alternative treatments in addition, such as reflexology. Make an appointment, though walk-ins can sometimes be accommodated.

Metropolitan Health Club

209 Columbus Avenue, at Berkeley Street (536 3006). Back Bay or Copley T. **Open** 6am-11pm Mon-Fri; 8am-9pm Sat; 9am-9pm Sun. **Rates** *day pass* $12. **Credit** AmEx, MC, V. **Map 5 F5**

This is where the South End boys with attitude work out – if they can't afford Adam Berke. The Met is a fully equipped fitness centre with new weight-training and cardio equipment and a very good aerobics staff. It's best at off-peak hours, if you're the type who just wants to get it over with. Otherwise, it's a little like a gay bar with weights.

Disabled: toilet.

Mike's Gym II

560 Harrison Avenue, at Waltham Street (338 6210). Back Bay T. **Open** 6am-10pm Mon-Fri; 8am-8pm Sat; 9am-6.30pm Sun. **Rates** *day pass* $12; *week pass* $30. **Credit** MC, V. **Map 3 F6**

Where the serious, big boys go (and those who love them). Good if you like places that are a little more ethnically and racially mixed; bad if you're a clean freak. Mike's has all the equipment you could need (with the emphasis on free weights) and a decent aerobics schedule, but the facilities are a little worn and grubby.

Restaurants

Any restaurants or cafés in the South End are, by virtue of their location, gay-friendly. Those listed below are particularly popular with queer patrons.

Appetito

1 Appleton Street, at Tremont Street (338 6777). Back Bay T. **Brunch served** 11am-2.30pm Sun. **Dinner served** 5-10pm Mon-Wed, Sun; 5-10.30pm Thur; 5-11pm Fri, Sat. **Main courses** $14. **Credit** AmEx, DC, Disc, MC, V. **Map 5 F5**

Hearty Italian food is served in a relaxed South End atmosphere. The kitchen does great roasted meat, interesting pasta dishes and good individual pizzas (if you just want something quick). Though the food isn't brilliant, it never gets it really wrong, either – that's why the punters keep coming back. Very good value, Appetito is a favourite for first dates and huge birthday dinners.

Disabled: toilet.

Club Café

209 Columbus Avenue, at Berkeley Street (536 0966). Back Bay T. **Dinner served** 8pm-midnight Wed, Sun; 9pm-2am Thur-Sat. **Main courses** $15-$25. **Credit** AmEx, DC, Disc, MC, V. **Map 5 F5**

This offers formal dining in a very gay atmosphere – a place to see and be seen if you're on the A-List. Chef Julia Brant makes very few mistakes with her international menu, but if you're not up for all the knives and forks, there are plenty of good things to order tapas-style from the bar menu. Expensive, either way.

Franklin Café

See p139 **Restaurants & Cafés** *for listings.*

The Franklin has been voted Best of Boston for 'South End scene'. It produces home cooking – roast chicken, grilled fish, meatloaf – but usually with a worthwhile twist. The bar serves wicked Martinis, which is a good thing because the wait for one of the eight or ten tables can be up to two hours. Surprisingly affordable.

Geoffrey's Café-Bar

578 Tremont Street, between Clarendon & Dartmouth Streets (266 1122). Back Bay T. **Open** 9am-10.30pm Mon-Thur; 9am-11pm Fri, Sat; 9am-10pm Sun. **Main courses** $12. **Credit** AmEx, DC, MC, V. **Map 3 F6**

Extremely popular with the gay boys for some reason, possibly the floor-to-ceiling windows looking out on to Tremont Street. The overpriced menu ranges from burgers to pasta to grilled entrées. It's alwayμs best to keep it simple here. *Disabled: toilet.*

Mario's

69 Church Street, at Park Plaza (542 3776). Arlington T. **Dinner served** 5.30-10.30pm Mon-Thur, Sun; 5.30-11pm Fri, Sat. **Main courses** $13. **Credit** AmEx, DC, Disc, MC, V. **Map 5 F5**

Italian-American fare (with the emphasis definitely on the American) in an enjoyably weird atmosphere – straight out of *Blue Velvet* – where the waitresses all have perms and call you 'hon'. Request one of the plush robin's egg booths. A tad expensive for what it is.

Mucho Gusto

See p131 **Restaurants & Cafés** *for listings.*

Cuban classics are served up in a fabulous 1950s atmosphere. Oswaldo, the owner, claims all the recipes are his mum's. He fusses over you and makes you a little Cuban coffee at the end of your meal. The clientele is pleasingly mixed: a little Latin, a little gay, a little studenty. A terrific place to go if you're looking for something different – and good value as well.

On the Park

315 Shawmut Avenue. at Union Park (426 0862). Back Bay T. **Brunch served** 9am-3pm Sat, Sun. **Dinner served** 5.30-10.30pm Tue-Thur; 5.30-11pm Fri, Sat. **Average** $14. **Credit** AmEx, MC, V. **Map 3 F6**

Lesbian owned and operated, On the Park is a South End standby. Both the summer and winter menus feature interesting updates of classic New England dishes, and it does one of the best Sunday brunches in town (if you don't mind waiting for a table). The place is so charming it's often used as a movie location. Worth the price.

Provincetown

P-Town is queer Boston's summer mecca on Cape Cod (*see chapter* **Trips Out of Town**). Think *Moby Dick* meets *Priscilla Queen of the Desert* – with a little *Beach Blanket Bingo* thrown in on the side.

Everything about P-Town is extreme, from its location at the very tip of Cape Cod to its long history as a landing place for Puritans, haven for pirates, port for erstwhile whalers, colony for artists and – most recently – beach resort for all of gay New England. Even its seasonal shifts are dramatic. In November, P-Town is a sleepy little community of painters and lesbians; in July, it's the homo version of Disneyland. If you're in Boston during the summer, it's well worth an overnight trip. Nothing beats Herring Cove beach on a hot, sunny day. There's no better boy-scouting than at the Boat Slip's tea dance. And what could be more romantic than a sunset stroll past the sun-bleached cottages of Commercial Street with the one you love?

Getting there

Provincetown is a two-and-a-half hour drive from Boston, usually longer in weekend traffic. If you don't feel up to the hassle of renting a car, you can fly there (expensive), catch a bus from South Station (cheap), or take the ferry from the waterfront (the most fun). You don't really need a car once you're there: the town is tiny, and most people either walk or rent bikes (*see chapter* **Trips Out of Town**).

Restaurants

Just about every place in town is gay-friendly, though most queers steer clear of the touristy lobster places. For posh meals, check out the **Martin House** (157 Commercial Street; 1-508 487 1327) or **Front Street** (230 Commercial Street; 1-508 487 9715). For simpler fare, there's **Fat Jack's** (295 Commercial Street; 1-508 487 4822) or the **Post Office Café** (303 Commercial Street; 1-508 487 3892; open summer only).

Accommodation

Though there are any number of queer guesthouses in town, it's always best to book as early as possible for summer stays. A few tried-and-true Victorian B&Bs are **The Sandpiper** (165 Commercial Street; 1-508 487 1928), the **Beaconlite Guest House** (12 Winthrop Street; 1-508 487 9603) and the **Brass Key Guest House** (9 Court Street; 1-508 487 9005).

The routine

Whether you're a girl or boy, there seems to be a ritual that everyone follows. First the beach, then the tea dance at the **Boat Slip** (161 Commercial Street; 1-508 487 1669; open summer only). After-tea at the **Pied Piper** – considered America's best lesbian bar (193A Commercial Street; 1-508 487 1527; open summer only) – for a drink and a bit of a jig. Then you're on your own for dinner and a disco nap before regrouping with friends for drinks at your favourite P-Town bar. At around 10pm, just about everybody ends up at the **Atlantic House** (4-6 Masonic Place; 1-508 487 3821) for dancing. All the bars close at midnight in P-Town, and everyone who hasn't already hooked up strolls over to **Spiritus Pizza** (192 Commercial Street; 1-508 487 2808; open summer only) for a slice and a chat. Nearly half the town's there in the early hours.

Further information

For a free directory of gay- and lesbian-owned hotels, restaurants, bars and services, contact the **Provincetown Business Guild** (115 Bradford Street; 1-508 487 2313/1-800 637 8696).

Reigning supreme: **Jacque's Cabaret** *is the oldest gay bar and drag show in town.*

Purple Cactus Café

312 Shawmut Avenue, at Union Park (338 5675). Back Bay T. **Open** 11.30am-10pm daily. **Average** $6.50. **Credit** AmEx, MC, V. **Map 3 F6**

A welcome oasis in a town that doesn't know how to make Mexican food. It serves mainly burritos and salads – but often made with interesting, super-fresh ingredients (there's a Thai-style burrito with peanut sauce, for example). Though it's mainly a take-out place, the Cactus's few tables are usually crowded with boys, fresh from the gym. Cheap and good.

South End Grill

439 Tremont Street, at Appleton Street (338 8884). Back Bay T. **Dinner served** 5-10pm Mon-Wed, Sun; 5-10.30pm Thur; 5-11pm Fri, Sat. **Average** $11. **Credit** AmEx, DC, Disc, MC, V. **Map 3 F5/6**

Recently opened by the **Appetito** people (*see p190*), the menu is basically diner food – but well prepared. Whether you order the burger or chicken pot pie, you really can't go wrong. The décor is cosy and tasteful, if a little on the dark side, and the staff are friendly. The perfect place to go on a first date. Good value.
Disabled: toilet.

Shops & services

Boomerangs

60 Canal Street (723 2666). Haymarket T. **Open** 11am-6.30pm Mon-Fri; 10am-5pm Sat; noon-5pm Sun. **Credit** AmEx, Disc, MC, V. **Map 5 G3**
A resale store operated by the AIDS Action Committee. It sells all manner of donated treasures, though it can take some dedicated digging to find them. One-stop shopping for glamorous drag outfits at bargain basement prices.
Disabled: toilet.

Liquid Hair Salon

640 Tremont Street, at West Newton Street (425 4848). Back Bay T. **Open** 11am-8pm Tue-Fri; 10am-6pm Sat. **Credit** AmEx, MC, V. **Map 3 F6**
A recently opened salon catering to South End queens who like a little atmosphere and chat, but don't want to (or can't) pay Newbury Street prices. The stylists are experienced professionals who are willing to go just as far as you are.
Disabled: toilet.

Marquis Leather

73 Berkeley Street, between Chandler & Lawrence Streets (426 2120). Back Bay T. **Open** 11am-1am Mon-Thur, Sun; 11am-3am Fri, Sat. **Credit** AmEx, MC, V. **Map 5 F5**
Surprisingly unintimidating for a sex shop. In addition to renting every vid known to male homodom (without even a trace of a sneer), the Marquis happily supplies the neighbourhood with magazines, toys, leather accessories and lube.

Mike's Movies

557 Tremont Street, at Clarendon Street (266 9222). Back Bay T. **Open** 10am-10pm Mon-Thur; 10am-11pm Fri, Sat; 11.30am-10pm Sun. **Credit** AmEx, Disc, MC, V. **Map 5 F6**
The entire neighbourhood, straight and gay, comes to Mike's for the latest Hollywood blockbusters. The gay boys make good use of a very generously stocked porn section at the back. It all works, somehow. Mostly rental.

The Movie Place

526 Tremont Street, at Berkeley Street (482 9008). Back Bay T/43 bus. **Open** 11am-11pm daily. **Credit** *for rentals over $20* AmEx, Disc, MC, V. **Map 5 F6**
This one's more exclusively gay. It's the best place in town for hard-to-find camp classics. Here you can rent both versions of *Giant*: the three-hour one with Liz Taylor and the 40-minute one – well, without her.

Santa Fe Styling Company Hair Salon

528 Tremont Street, at Berkeley Street (338 5095). Back Bay T. **Open** 11am-7pm Tue-Fri; 9am-5pm Sat; 1-5pm Sun. **Credit** AmEx, Disc, MC, V. **Map 5 F6**
Specialising in buff-boy homo cuts. The nice thing about Santa Fe is that everybody's welcome – most of the stylists speak Spanish – and it doesn't cost an arm and a leg to get a few, secret highlights in.

Santa Fe Styling Company Tanning Salon

546 Tremont Street, at Clarendon Street (338 5095). Back Bay T. **Open** 10am-8.30pm Mon-Sat; 10am-6pm Sun. **Credit** AmEx, Disc, MC, V. **Map 5 F6**
Up the street from the hair salon, Santa Fe's tanning centre has both stand-up booths and beds. Products on sale include creams and colour enhancers plus a skimpy line of men's bathing trunks for use in P-Town and beyond.

Boys' night out

Avalon

See p201 **Nightlife** *for listings.*
If you're of a mind to dance on a Sunday night, this is the place. Avalon offers a mix of techno and hip hop and boasts the best sound system in town. You also have access to Axis and DV8, two smaller clubs next door offering more alternative music.

Boston Eagle

520 Tremont Street, at Berkeley Street (542 4494). Back Bay T. **Open** 3pm-2am Mon-Fri; 1pm-2am Sat; noon-2am Sun. **Admission** free. **No credit cards. Map 5 F6**
Most nights, the Eagle is a quiet leather and pool bar offering cheap drinks and loud music. But at weekends, the 'Dirty Bird' has inexplicably become the preferred place for the A-List to hang out – after **Club Café** (*see p190*). Jack, the bartender, just shrugs and takes their cash.

Buzz

See p200 **Nightlife** *for listings.*
Where the buff boys go to dance on Friday and Saturday nights. Buzz offers two floors of fun: the top dancefloor is where you gyrate shirtless to techno, the bottom where you drink and chat.

Chaps

See p200 **Nightlife** *for listings.*
This dance bar's been around forever, though it moved to larger digs a couple of years ago. It even looks the same on the inside. Always dependable, Chaps hires go-go boys at weekends, has a great Latino night on Wednesdays and does a decent tea dance early on Sunday evenings – when you can't stay out till all hours at Avalon.

Fritz

26 Chandler Street, at Berkeley Street (482 4428). Copley T. **Open** noon-2am Mon-Fri, Sun; 11am-2am Sat. **Admission** free. **No credit cards. Map 5 F5**
The closest Boston comes to a neighbourhood pub. Fritz is popular with suits after work, work boot and jeans types at night and just about everybody on Sunday afternoon. It serves a respectable brunch on Saturday and Sundays.

Jacque's Cabaret

See p205 **Nightlife** *for listings.*
Jacque's is the oldest gay bar in town these days (since Playland and Napoleon's closed in 1998, after 60 years of operation). Jacque's has long reigned supreme as the only drag cabaret in town. Its foul-mouthed MCs and discount-store drag queens make for an unusual evening. A couple of tips: go in a group, and laugh with the whole weird experience, not at it.
Disabled: toilet.

Luxor

69 Church Street, at Park Plaza (423 6969). Arlington T. **Open** 4pm-1am daily. **Admission** free. **Credit** AmEx, Disc, MC, V. **Map 5 F5**
This video bar has rather fallen out of fashion in recent years. The VJ is actually pretty good, but the crowd tends to be primarily tourists and suburban types. Downstairs, there's an eternally empty sports bar. A place to go on the way to somewhere else.

Machine

See p202 **Nightlife** *for listings.*
This new dance bar in the basement of the Ramrod leather bar is giving **Buzz** (*see above*) a run for its money at the

Pool and darts **Upstairs (at Hideaway Pub).**

weekends. There's decent music, a good bar, a huge dancefloor and a great pool table/chill-out area. Your cover gives you access to the Ramrod. Kind of a shame, though, that it ruins the atmosphere upstairs.

Man Ray (Campus)

See p202 **Nighlife** *for listings.*

Though this club is only officially gay on Thursdays (men) and Sundays (women), it's popular with the bisexual and homo-friendly student set at all times. You have your choice of two dancefloors: one house, one tending towards boypop.

Moonshine (at Club Café)

209 Columbus Avenue, at Berkeley Street (536 0966). Back Bay T. **Open** 9pm-2am Thur-Sat; 8pm-midnight Wed, Sun. **Admission** free. **No credit cards.** **Map 5 F5**

Moonshine is the back video bar of **Club Café** (*see p190*). On Thursdays, it's the hottest place in town for boy-scouting (it's pretty popular with girls, too). The crowd usually overflows to the front bar, where a pianist and singer run through club standards. At weekends, Club Café tends to be where friends meet before they go off nightclubbing.
Disabled: toilet.

Paradise

180 Massachusetts Avenue, at Albany Street, Cambridge (494 0700). Central T. **Open** 5pm-2am Thur-Sat; 5pm-1am Mon-Wed, Sun. **Admission** free. **No credit cards.** **Map 4 D4**

It closed for a while and now it's back – though it feels exactly the same, with a chatty upstairs bar, cruisy downstairs bar and dancefloor. From Thursday to Sunday nights it features some surprisingly tasty go-go boys. TV sports nuts can watch the game and nibble on free bar food most Sunday afternoons. Not, incidentally, to be confused with the rock venue of the same name.

Safari Club

Second floor, 90 Wareham Street (292 0011). Back Bay T. **Open** 24 hours daily. **Admission** *day pass* $5. **Credit** MC, V. **Map 3 F6**

It bills itself as an athletic club. Yeah, right. What little equipment there is has dust on it an inch thick. Somebody at the Safari Club must be working out, though; the showers and saunas are absolutely teeming. Must be because it's the only gym in town open 24 hours.
Disabled: toilet.

Girls' night out

Man Ray and **Moonshine** (*see above*) also have women's nights.

Club Estelle

888 Tremont Street, at Massachusetts Avenue (1-781 766 2914). Mass Ave T. **Open** 9pm-2am Fri (monthly). **Admission** $10. **No credit cards. Map 3 E6**

A basic neighbourhood bar that becomes a girl joint for one Friday night every month. The atmosphere is friendly enough, and you can dance. The music ranges from reggae to bebop and deep house.

Lava Bar

575 Commonwealth Avenue, at Kenmore Square (267 7707). Kenmore T. **Map 3 D5**

The Lava Bar was scheduled to open as this guide went to press, so we haven't sampled it ourselves, but in a girls' scene offering slim pickings, any new venue should be an asset.

SomePLACE Else (at Ryles)

212 Hampshire Street, at Inman Square, Cambridge (876 9330). Central T. **Open** 7pm-midnight Sun. **Admission** $5-$8. **Credit** AmEx, Disc. **Map 4 D2**

The line-up of musicians and performers changes weekly in this downstairs cabaret space. (Ren Jender's Amazon Slam has been a regular on the last Sunday of the month.) It's primarily a hetero establishment but is reliably gay-friendly, and has regular lesbian nights. There's a DJ upstairs for those who aren't quite ready to go home yet.

Upstairs (at Hideaway Pub)

20 Concord Lane, near Fresh Pond Rotary, Cambridge (661 8828). Alewife T. **Open** 11am-12.30am Mon-Wed, Sun; 11.30am-1am Thur-Sat. **Admission** free. **No credit cards.**

Your basic butch scene with pool tables and darts. You know what you're getting in a comforting sort of way: plenty of loud jukebox music and cheap beer. Tends to be favoured by a more mature clientele.
Disabled: toilet.

Media

Boston's media puts in a determined bid not to be overshadowed by its noisier neighbour New York.

Smug and parochial are two jibes often aimed at Boston's media: but even Bostonians will admit – a tad defensively perhaps – that there's some truth in these criticisms. Life viewed from the front page of the city's biggest daily, the *Boston Globe*, often seems too cosy and suburban, as if there were no social or economic problems in the city worth covering. But then the unrelenting stream of police busts, murders and petty crimes pumped out by local TV news shows is hardly the reality either.

Part of the problem is that the city is just too close to New York and can't escape the shadow of its big and noisy neighbour. It doesn't help that the *Globe*'s 121 years of independent ownership ended in 1993 when it was bought by none other than the *New York Times*. And after a crisis at the *Globe* in 1998 over the firing of two of its columnists, the paper itself is feeling even more insecure. Moreover, Boston's media elite often gets a little chippy about the city's standing nationwide: it should be recognised as America's intellectual capital, they say, rather than as just another big city.

However, if you forget New York and the chippiness, treat the TV news as comedy and go beyond the *Globe*'s front page, Boston's media deserves a second look. The *Globe* and its main competitor, the *Boston Herald*, are interesting in themselves, because of the central role they played in the city's recent history. In addition to these two big dailies, the city supports a sharply-written weekly, the *Boston Phoenix*, as well as a vibrant ethnic press and many other papers in Cambridge, Brookline and other city districts. There are several good freesheets as well. Boston is a key radio and TV production centre and the original home to much of the programming on PBS (America's public television network). There's a good choice of radio stations, broadcasting everything from news and talk shows to music of all kinds. And don't forget the Internet. Bostonians who have easy access to the web find it a crucial source of information on arts, entertainment and events. The best known local site, boston.com, has won nationwide acclaim.

Newspapers & magazines

Daily newspapers

The two main daily newspapers in the greater Boston area are the *Boston Globe* and the *Boston Herald*. The former is a broadsheet and New England's largest paper, selling around 475,000 copies on weekdays and 750,000 on Sundays. The weekly edition costs 50¢, while the bulky Sunday edition is $2. The tabloid *Herald* also costs 50¢ during the week, and on Sunday is $1.75. Both are available across the city, in sidewalk dispensers or from newsagents (*see page 199* **Outlets**).

Over its more than 120-year existence, the *Globe* has taken a cautiously liberal line on most subjects and its stance on some civil rights issues has been crucial. Nonetheless, it is seen as the voice of the city's Yankee establishment and too often, say its detractors, it has ended up vacillating – trying to please everyone but ending up pleasing no one. Its news coverage has also taken a lot of criticism: sometimes stories, whether local or national, that really should be covered, mysteriously aren't.

The *Globe*'s biggest test came during the so-called busing crisis of 1974-5 – the struggle over desegregating Boston's schools, which provoked protests and violence across the city. The *Globe* backed desegregation, which meant busing over 20,000 kids from both white and black communities to schools outside their neighbourhoods in order to achieve a more equal 'racial balance'. The scheme split the city, but the deepest opposition came from Boston's Irish community. In the past, the Irish had seen the *Globe* as their friend. Now they saw it as a standard-bearer for a liberal, middle-class white conspiracy against working-class whites (although ironically, many in the Yankee elite also opposed the busing plan).

The *Herald* and many other newspapers also backed the busing plan, but it was the *Globe* that took the serious flak. On two successive nights in 1974 the *Globe*'s headquarters were raked by gunfire. *Globe* delivery workers were attacked in the streets and in South Boston, the city's Irish heartland, the paper was boycotted. But as the pressure rose, the paper was accused of toning down its unequivocal support for busing in an effort to soften criticism from whites. The *Globe* eventually won a Pulitzer prize for its coverage of the crisis. To its editors and reporters it must have seemed like a military campaign medal.

But this is not some interesting historical diversion. Like the ghosts of fallen soldiers, the strains left by the busing crisis within the *Globe* have come back to haunt the paper almost a quarter of a century later, leaving it bruised and humiliated. The ghosts came in the form of two big-name columnists who were fired in the space of three months in 1998, after being accused of fabricating stories. The sackings made national headlines. First to go was black writer Patricia Smith, who had helped win the paper a new following in Boston's black community. The other was Boston Mike, or Mike Barnicle, who was seen as the voice of 'Joe Sixpack' at the *Globe* and had a particularly strong following among the city's Irish people. He had worked for the paper for more than 25 years, including during the busing crisis. What made the firings such a humiliation for the *Globe* was the revelation that it had been concerned about their just-too-perfect quotes, untraceable interviewees and plagiarism for some time – in Barnicle's case for more than a decade. But because of the paper's desperate desire to rebuild relations with the Irish community and to build a following among blacks, it had turned a blind eye – until it could no longer ignore the problem. Editors also feared the reaction of the paper's ethnically-mixed staff. But critics say that by failing to discipline the two writers earlier, the *Globe*'s management caused much greater turmoil, leaving staff morale at an all-time low. The damage to the paper's reputation will not heal quickly.

The *Globe*'s discomfort was a gift for the *Herald*, and it had weeks of fun at the other paper's expense. The *Herald* is a conservative-leaning tabloid, with a more raucous style than the *Globe* – although by British standards, or those of the *New York Post*, it's pretty tame. The *Herald*'s circulation of 289,000 lags well behind that of the *Globe*, but it has a strong following among working-class Bostonians. It is often described as a paper for Reagan Democrats – traditional supporters of the Democratic Party who backed President Reagan in the 1980s. Ironically, until the 1950s its readers were mostly middle class and it was identified with the Yankee elite. At that time, it was also well ahead of the *Globe* in circulation. But as the suburbs grew outside Boston, the *Globe* made the new commuting classes its own and overtook the *Herald* in circulation.

The *Herald* is still known for its strong news coverage, plus some loud, often controversial columnists. Its commentators took a more aggressive line on President Clinton than the *Globe* during the long investigation into his affair with Monica Lewinsky, joining the 'he should resign' camp early on.

The New England edition of the *New York Times* and America's 'national' paper *USA Today* are also widely available. Boston is also the headquarters for the *Christian Science Monitor*, which focuses on social issues and foreign affairs, though it's only available on subscription.

Weekly newspapers

Another paper that feasted on the *Globe*'s troubles during the Barnicle and Smith scandals was the *Boston Phoenix*, an irreverent weekly which tries to take an alternative line on the city's politics and

Boston online *The best of Beantown's websites*

Boston.com *www.boston.com*: this local news and listings service, run by the *Boston Globe*, is the most comprehensive information service for Boston and the surrounding area. Updated every hour, it provides everything from arts and entertainment listings to the *Yellow Pages* and directions to any business in the area.

Boston Herald *www.bostonherald.com*: the website of Boston's main tabloid paper, with news, features, listings, reviews and ads from the paper. Updated daily.

Townonline *www.townonline.com*: a kind of online local newspaper network, run by the company that publishes the *Tab* series and the *Cambridge Chronicle*, with individual sites for most Boston-area towns and districts. Aimed at residents, it features local news, shopping information and arts listings.

Yahoo! *www.yahoo.local.com*: a local directory service which covers all US states. Click on Massachusetts and from there you can jump to its Boston pages which cover entertainment, arts, restaurants and local news. It also provides a fairly comprehensive list of all the main newspapers as well as television and radio stations.

Sidewalk *boston.sidewalk.com*: a Microsoft-owned local information site focusing on arts, entertainment and going out.

Digital City *home.digitalcity.com/boston*: this is AOL's offering in the already crowded online guide market. It has an arts and entertainment bias.

Online media

Boston Phoenix *www.bostonphoenix.com*
Eagle (93.7 FM) *www.eagle937.com*
Harvard Crimson (Harvard University newspaper) *www.thecrimson.harvard.edu*
Irish Echo *www.irishecho.com*
KISS *www.kissfm.com*
MIX *www.mix985.com*
WBOS *www.wbos.com*
WBUR *www.wbur.org*
WBZ *www.wbz.com*
WCRB *www.wcrb.com*
WFNX *www.wfnx.com*
WGBH *www.wgbh.org*
The World *www.theworld.org*
WRKO *www.wrko.com*
WXRV *www.wxrv.com*
WZLX *www.wzlx.com*

culture. It doesn't cover news exhaustively, preferring longer, opinionated features. The *Phoenix* probably has the best arts, music and entertainment coverage in the city for twenty- and thirty-somethings, and is particularly strong on the nightlife scene, with regular polls of the city's best bars, restaurants and clubs. The paper is linked to the music radio station **WFNX** (*see page 198* **Radio**). Published on Thursday, it costs $1.50 and is available in most newsagents.

Local daily & weekly newspapers

The *Globe* and the *Herald* don't just compete against each other. Cambridge, Somerville, Brookline and all the other Greater Boston cities and towns have their own paper, in some cases several. The *Cambridge Chronicle*, the leading paper in Cambridge (although a fairly average local), is published weekly and costs 75¢.

The same company behind the *Chronicle* also publishes the freesheet *Tab* series – a local paper covering virtually every city and town in the Boston region. It concentrates on community issues, with plenty of crime coverage, as well as having comprehensive arts and entertainment sections, with restaurant, movie and other entertainment reviews. It's available from sidewalk dispensers in each district.

Within Boston itself, there are several local papers. The best of the bunch, however, is one of the freesheets – the *South End News*. It looks pretty average, focusing on community issues and events in the South End, but is really famous for its lurid 'Police Beat' column. Each week, local cop John Sacco reports in a deadpan style on the most salacious or violent incidents in his D-4 precinct. A recent typical extract was entitled 'The Runaway': 'On October 1 at about 1.25am, 28-year-old Dave needed oral. He picked up a 17-year-old from Lynn, a 200-pounder named "Joanne". They parked on Harrison Avenue. Dave paid "Joanne" $43 and dropped his pants. She went to work. Along came D-4 Officers Garcia and Brown. The duo was arrested. In the glove pocket in plain view was a quantity of herb. More trouble for Dave.'

By comparison, the weekly *Beacon Hill,* which covers Massachusetts government and politics, is a big snooze. *Spare Change* is Boston's version of the UK's *Big Issue* (although without the celebrity and style features) and is edited and sold by homeless people. Vendors operate on major pedestrian areas, near T stops.

Magazines

Local magazines include *Boston Magazine*, a conservative monthly general interest glossy with a mix of lifestyle features, profiles and occasional strong pieces on city issues. It costs $3.50 and is available from most newsagents. *Boston Editorial Humour* isn't really a magazine, but the bi-weekly collection of cartoons from newspapers across America isn't really a newspaper either. Look out for it in sidewalk dispensers, where it costs 50¢.

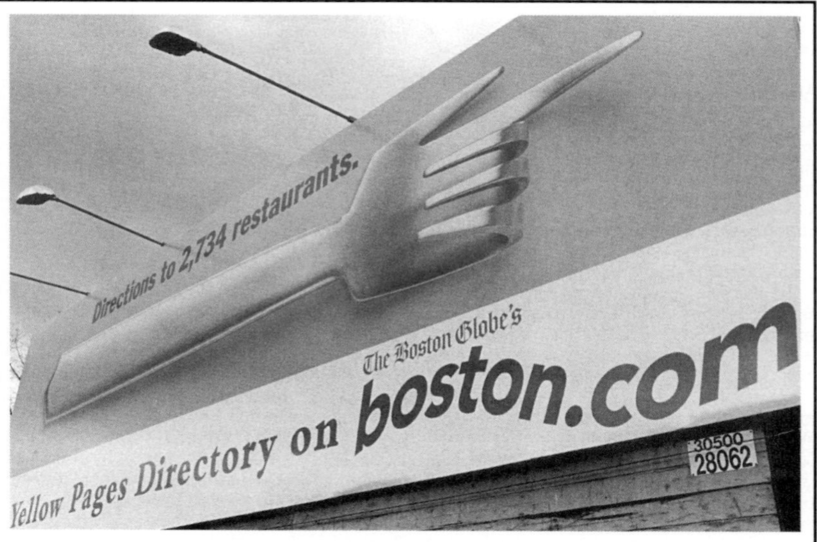

The *Improper Bostonian* is a weekly lifestyle magazine distributed free from sidewalk dispensers on main streets. Newbury Street is the centre of its universe and its desperately enthusiastic style and health features are, well, desperate.

Gay & lesbian

There are two weekly papers aimed at gays and lesbians. Most popular is *Bay Windows*, which costs 50¢ (although it's free from many bars and shops in Back Bay and the South End) and is the best source for what's going on in the city's gay scene. *Newsweekly* covers the gay and lesbian scene across New England; the best place to find it is in the South End. *See also chapter* **Gay & Lesbian**.

Ethnic

Boston's ethnic diversity comes close to rivalling that of New York, and it has an ethnic press to match. In addition to newspapers brought over from Ireland, there are at least four papers aimed specifically at Boston's Irish: the regional edition of the New York-based *Irish Echo*, the *Irish Voice*, the *Irish Emigrant* and the *Boston Irish Reporter*. And local papers in areas such as South Boston, Quincy and Dorchester have a very Irish flavour. The *Bay State Banner* is a weekly aimed at the black community across Massachusetts, with a Boston focus. It has arts and local events listings as well as news.

Among the selection of other papers to target Boston's various ethnic communities are: *El Universal*, the *Brazilian Newspaper*, the *Brazilian Times*, *Boston Chinese News*, the *Jewish Advocate* and the *Boston Russian Bulletin*.

Arts & entertainment coverage

Several newspapers carry good listings and reviews, including the *Globe*. The *Phoenix* is very strong on music, alternative arts and performance and the nightclub scene. Also worth checking out for nightlife is the weekly free magazine *Stuff@Night* – you'll see it in dispenser bins in popular hangouts such as Newbury Street or Central Square in Cambridge.

Another freebie to watch out for is *INsite* – a monthly arts and music review mag with listings and sister publications in five other US cities. But as the web grows in popularity and availability, such freesheets will find it tough to survive.

Radio

Boston has one of the most eclectic selections of radio programmes in America, with at least 50 local stations. Distinguishing between the music stations isn't made easier by the fact that most of them claim to be 'alternative'. But at least the city's airwaves aren't being invaded by hell and damnation bible stations. The selection of commercial stations includes:

WXRV The River (92.5 FM)
An 'alternative' rock music station that plays blues and classic rock.
WBOS (92.9 FM)
A mainstream rock station (with the occasional pop tune slipping onto the playlist).
Eagle (93.7 FM)
If it didn't happen in the 1970s or 1980s, you won't hear it on Eagle. But definitely the first stop for Led Zep, Meatloaf and Bruce Springsteen fans.
MIX (98.5 FM)
Another 'alternative' station, in love with Barenaked Ladies.
WZLX (100.7 FM)
More Meatloaf and Led Zep.
WFNX (101.7 FM)
'Boston's real alternative' (according to their slogan) still can't resist mainstream pop and rock at drivetime.
WOAZ (99.1 FM)
Plays easy-listening jazz, verging on airport toilet.
WCRB (102.5 FM)
Boston's commercial classics station, similar to the UK's Classic FM.
WBCN (104.1 FM)
The Boston home to the loudmouthed *Howard Stern Show* (one of the most popular syndicated radio shows in the USA) on weekday mornings. It also plays a mix of mainstream music.
WROR (105.7 FM)
Plays '60s and '70s oldies.
WXKS (108 FM)
Yet another 'alternative' station, but one that plays a lot of good dance stuff. Playlists range from Oasis to Natalie Merchant.
WRKO (680 AM)
Great for talk and news. It's also Boston's local shock jock station (although not always that shocking). This is where you'll find Rush Limbaugh, the Clinton-hating right-winger whose show is syndicated to stations across the US (weekdays from noon to 3pm).
WEEI (850 AM)
Perfect for sports fans.
WBZ (1030 AM)
A lively, fast-paced news and sports station with regular phone-ins on local and national stories, although sometimes the presenters barely get a word in between the weather and traffic reports, which come every ten minutes during the day. Its best-known programme is the *David Brudnoy Show* (7pm to midnight, Tuesday to Friday). Can that man talk!

Public radio

Only rarely does news from the outside world intrude into commercial radio bulletins. Public radio fills the gap, and Boston has two publicly-funded stations. The trouble with many public radio shows, though, is that they are so desperate not to be like commercial radio that they often end up sounding slow and stodgy.

WBUR (90.9 FM) is the local National Public Radio (NPR) news station – most of its airtime is taken up with news and talk shows. It broadcasts the major nationwide NPR news shows such as *Morning Edition* from Monday to Friday and *Weekend Edition* on Saturday and Sunday. The afternoon show, which airs at 4pm, is *All Things Considered*. Both shows cover a much wider range of domestic and international affairs than you can hear on any other radio or TV outlet. Another popular show on WBUR is *The Connection*, a newsy discussion programme broadcast in two installments every weekday morning – at 10am and 11am, with repeats at 8pm every evening.

WGBH (89.7 FM) airs most of the main NPR news shows, in addition to a mix of classical music and jazz. It is also the production centre for *The World* – a daily one-hour international news show broadcast across the States and co-produced with the BBC and Public Radio International (PRI), a competitor of NPR. *The World* airs at 4pm in Boston. PRI is also responsible for the acclaimed daily business show *Marketplace*, broadcast in Boston on both WGBH and WBUR.

It is not easy to find good radio listings or station frequencies. Not even the *Globe* publishes comprehensive listening schedules, preferring just to highlight a few programmes. The best place to look is on the web at boston.com.

Television

All four major networks – **ABC**, **NBC**, **CBS** and **Fox TV** – have local affiliated stations in Boston. What that means is that you won't miss out on nationwide hit shows such as *Friends* or *E.R.* At times, you might even see them on three channels at once. In addition, there is the usual endless choice of cable and pay-per-view channels, depending on your tastes and pocket. Channels like **CNN** are provided as part of a basic cable package, but you have to pay extra for services such as the **Movie Channel**. The following is only an overview of what's available on Boston TV.

Free **WBZ** on **Channel 4** (CBS) shows a mix of sitcoms, documentaries and movies, as well as the local news show *News 4 New England*. It also broadcasts the nationwide *CBS Evening News* with Dan Rather. **WCVB** on **Channel 5** (ABC) offers a similar mix to **WBZ**. It's also home to shows such as *Good Morning America* and *ABC News* with Peter Jennings. *Channel 5 News* is the daily local news programme and **WHDH TV** on **Channel 7** (NBC) is the place to go for *Dateline NBC* and *Meet the Press*, as well as *E.R.* and *Frasier*. **WFXT** on **Channel 25** (Fox) is the best place for major US sports such as American football, baseball and ice hockey: Rupert Murdoch, the station's owner, has signed exclusive deals with the National Football League and National Hockey League, as well as quite a few baseball teams. It's also the channel to catch *The Simpsons* and *The X-Files*. The Spanish-language station **WUNI** on **Channel 27** broadcasts programmes from across Latin America and **WSBK** on **Channel 38** is the slot for *Seinfeld* and *Frasier* repeats, plus *Star Trek*.

WGBH on **Channel 2** and **Channel 44** is Boston's public TV station. Channel 2 is Boston's PBS station and broadcasts a lot of old BBC shows, such as *Monty Python* and *Are You Being Served?*, perpetuating a strangely mythical view of Britain among some Bostonians. But WGBH is a serious programme-maker in its own right, serving as the base for several prominent PBS shows, including the documentary series *Frontline* and the science programme *Nova,* normally broadcast on Channel 44. Channel 2 broadcasts a regional news magazine show called *Greater Boston* at 7pm on weekdays.

WLVI TV on **Channel 56** is known for its movies and the nightly *Ten O'Clock News*, not to mention *Buffy the Vampire Slayer*. **WABU** on the cable **Channel 68** offers a mix of movies and light documentaries and is also the place to catch broadcast games of local baseball team the Red Sox.

Cable

Channel numbers vafry depending on where you are in the Boston area. All the main national cable channels, such as **CNN**, **MSNBC**, **CNBC** and **A&E** are available, plus quite a few locals, including **NECN** (New England Cable News) and **NESN** (New England Sports News).

Outlets

Barnes & Noble

600 Beacon Street, at Commonwealth Street (267 8484). Kenmore T. **Open** 10am-9pm Mon-Fri; 10am-6pm Sat; noon-6pm Sun. **Credit** MC, V. **Map 3 D5**

Stocks a wide range of domestic and foreign publications and a lot of alternative magazines aimed at students.

Copley Square News

Corner Boylston Street & Copley Square (262 1477). Copley T. **Open** 6am-7pm Mon-Fri; 6am-6pm Sat. **No credit cards**. **Map 3 F5**

This newsstand sells most local papers and magazines, plus many national and international newspapers and magazines. British papers are normally a day behind.

Out of Town Newspapers

Harvard Square, in front of Harvard T, Cambridge (354 7777). Harvard T. **Open** 6am-10.30pm Mon-Thur, Sun; 6am-11.30pm Fri, Sat. **Credit** AmEx, Disc, MC, V. **Map 4 B2**

Carries probably the best range of foreign newspapers and magazines in the Boston area. It also sells a wide range of papers from other US cities, which aren't always easy to find elsewhere. Opposite, on Brattle Street, is **Nini's Corner**, another well-stocked newsagent (1394 Massachusetts Avenue, corner of Brattle Street; 547 3558).

Waterstones Booksellers

26 Exeter Street (859 7300). Copley T. **Open** 9am-10pm Mon-Sat; noon-8pm Sun. **Credit** AmEx, Disc, MC, V. **Map 3 E5**

Stocks a big choice of domestic and foreign papers and magazines, as well as a good selection of alternative publications. **Branch**: Quincy Marketplace, Faneuil Hall (589 0930).

Nightlife

The best of Boston's ever-changing after-hours scene: dance clubs, jazz clubs, rock clubs and more.

For theatre, dance, comedy and classical music, *see chapter* **The Performing Arts**.

Dance clubs

Mark Twain's observation about the New England weather holds true for the dance club scene in Boston: if you don't like it, wait a minute. Many of the dance venues in town feature dramatically different scenes from one night to the next and the formats change as quickly as the trends and promoters.

THE CODE

To get into most clubs you must be over 21 – or at least aged 19; the law allows entry for those over 18, but the clubs usually like to know that their clientele has finished high school, remedially or not. Dress codes are looser than they used to be, before the upmarket trend started slipping. Club managers usually apply the 'no riff-raff' code, which translates as no ripped jeans, baseball caps, sneakers or anything else that identifies you as a dumb jock prone to bar fights.

THE SCENE

There are two main club districts in Boston. **Lansdowne Street**, a one-block stretch bordering Fenway Park and packed with nightclubs, is the main club row, with a neon-lit, carnival-like atmosphere. The street has some great, revamped industrial spaces and hit music programmes, but hordes of college students and suburbanites descend at the weekends, so enter the area with caution.

Boylston Place (also known as 'the Alley'), near the Theater District, is a smaller, more mainstream club mall, with a slightly older clientele of partyhounds and swinging yuppies. Its doors usually open by 8.30pm or 9pm and the queues are long by 10.30pm at the weekend (be prepared to wait from 20 minutes to more than an hour).

Many of the city's wildest dance scenes are gay or gay-oriented, so keeping to the straight and narrow isn't the only option (*see chapter* **Gay & Lesbian Boston**). The traditionally exclusive gay club crowds have become significantly more mixed recently (the gay community is split on whether this is a good or bad thing) but the trend isn't likely to lose momentum. Another way to sidestep the weekend yokel scene is to check music stores and trendy boutiques for flyers – some of the hippest underground dance parties are organised by independent promoters and take place at various lofts around town.

Theater District

Buzz

67 Stuart Street, at Dartmouth Street (267 8969). Boylston or NE Medical Center T. **Open** 10pm-2am Fri, Sat. **Admission** $5. **Credit** AmEx, MC, V. **Map 3 F5**

A former Euro-palace, this downtown space is now equal parts gay disco and international club. Buzz has a funky, bi-level layout with dance floors and cosier alcove lounges, such as the 'Eros' Greek bar. On Friday nights, guest DJs spin Latin and Eurohouse music. The Saturday night 'Killer Dance Club' is a lively gay night. *See also page 193* **Gay & Lesbian Boston**.

Website: www.buzzboston.com

Chaps

100 Warrenton Street (695 9500). Boylston T.
Open 2pm-2am Mon-Wed; noon-2am Thur-Sun.
Admission $3-$5. **No credit cards**. **Map 5 G5**

One of the most famous gay clubs in Boston, Chaps has mellowed from an implicitly exclusive gay men's club to a more mixed scene. A few straights and drag queens now frequent the club, especially on Tuesdays, an oldies dance night with spins from the 1970s to the early 1980s, and on Thursdays, when the hip hop 'Mocha' programme brings in a racially and sexually mixed crowd. The Friday and Saturday DJs spin high-energy dance music. The Sunday 'Tea Dance' (6-10pm), featuring disco classics and modern house spins, is an honoured tradition. *See also page 193* **Gay & Lesbian Boston**.

Roxy

279 Tremont Street, at Stuart Street (338 7699). Boylston T. **Open** 9pm-2am Thur-Sat. **Admission** $10-$15. **Credit** AmEx, MC, V. **Map 5 G5**

Located in the renovated ballroom of the Tremont House hotel (*see p109* **Accommodation**), the Roxy is Boston's grandest dance and live music room. It occasionally hosts hit rock, funk and techno bands on weeknights, but the club's regular schedule is restricted to weekends. Thursday is Latino night, with live bands and DJs playing salsa and merengue. On Fridays, the club's big-band history is revisited in a full-scale swing night, regularly featuring national headliners and a crowd of zoot-suiters. Saturday is a longstanding weekend-warrior scene, when the dressed-up suburban crowd piles in. No sneakers, jeans or T-shirts. *See also p208.*

Boylston Place

The Big Easy

1 Boylston Place, between Charles & Tremont Streets (351 7000). Boylston T. **Open** 8pm-2am Thur-Sat.
Admission $5-$7. **Credit** AmEx, DC, MC, V.
Map 5 G/F5

Gay disco and international club, **Buzz**.

A large, New Orleans-style dance club (wrought-iron railings, bayou-country décor details) with DJs and cover bands playing alternative and top 40 dance music, 1960s Motown and old and new R&B and soul. Two separate lounges upstairs offer cosy nuzzling room and pool tables. No sneakers, ripped jeans, baseball caps or sports wear.
Disabled: toilet.

Envy

25 Boylston Place, between Charles & Tremont Streets (542 3689). Boylston T. **Open** 9pm-2am Fri, Sat. **Admission** free-$5. **Credit** AmEx, MC, V. **Map 5 G/F5**
Recently revamped by a Hollywood set designer, this club features wall murals of the seven deadly sins and attracts a weekend crowd of young executive types. Currently, Friday night offers disco, top 40, R&B and dance sounds, with top 40, trance and house on Saturdays. Smaller rooms within the club offer pool tables, banquette seating and rubbernecking vistas through a glass window. No sneakers, hats or printed T-shirts.

The Mercury Bar

See p119 **Pubs & Bars** *for listings.*
At the back room of this chi-chi Euro-spot is a dark little dancehall called The Club. Name-brand DJs spin international music during the week and modern dance hits at the weekend. The crowd consists mainly of young professionals and rich Euros. No sneakers, jeans or T-shirts.

Sugar Shack

3 Boylston Place, between Charles & Tremont Streets (351 2510). Boylston T. **Open** 9pm-2am Tue-Sun. **Admission** free-$5. **Credit** AmEx, DC, MC, V. **Map 5 G/F5**
The former site of a roughneck pick-up bar for young party animals (think Jell-o shots), this venue has been upgraded to club level. Now a New Orleans-style miniature of its big-brother club, **The Big Easy** (*see p200*), Sugar Shack plays 1970s-90s dance hits, soul, hip hop and R&B for a crowd of yuppies in the 23-33 age bracket.
Disabled: toilet.

Lansdowne Street

Atlas Bar & Grill

First floor, Jillian's, 3 Lansdowne Street, at Ipswich Street (437 0300). Kenmore T. **Open** *club* 10pm-2am Fri, Sat. **Admission** $5. **Credit** AmEx, MC, V. **Map 3 D/E5**
Located on the first floor of Jillian's, a massive entertainment complex with several floors of pool tables, darts, a video arcade that looks and sounds like Vegas, and virtual-reality amusements, Atlas is a modern bar and grill with a Deco-influenced, futuristic décor. The dance floor is in a back room, in front of a wall of giant video screens. The music is a mix of top 40 and 1970-90s dance hits. The atmosphere is casual, in the sense that no one will look at you sideways if you're not dressed in Gucci or Versace. No hats, ripped jeans, or sneakers.
Disabled: toilet.

Avalon

15 Lansdowne Street, at Ipswich Street (262 2424). Kenmore T. **Open** 10pm-2am Mon, Wed-Sun. **Admission** $10-$15. **Credit** AmEx, Disc, MC, V. **Map 3 D/E5**
This is the biggest venue on the street, with a regular schedule of high-profile live shows and regular weekend dance formats. Friday is a strong dance night, with a racially mixed crowd of gay and straight 19-25 year-olds. Saturday is more of a bridge-and-tunnel scene, with a bit of a pick-up vibe. The Sunday gay night, now in its 20th successful year, is the most interesting dance night here. Merging with **Axis** next door (*below*), the club becomes a huge complex with three dance floors – the main room at Avalon tends to be more mainstream; the main room at Axis has a darker, techno edge for hardcore dancers. The night draws a wide range of out-of-staters and a fair number of straight couples and women craving some peace from the weekend muttonhead squad. *See also p204 and p193* **Gay & Lesbian Boston**.

Axis

13 Lansdowne Street, at Ipswich Street (262 2424). Fenway T. **Open** 10pm-2am Mon, Wed-Sun. **Admission** $10-$12. **Credit** AmEx, Disc, MC, V. **Map 3 D/E5**
Axis is one of the cooler venues on the street, with a strong tradition in live music and cutting-edge dance trends. Thursday's 'Chrome' programme draws guest DJs from around the world, serious dance fanatics and a mixed urban/college, gay/straight crowd. Friday's 'Spin Cycle' event features house and progressive dance. The Saturday X-Night is a perennial scene, with contemporary dance and industrial beats downstairs and classic new wave upstairs. Monday's 'Static' gay night features a mixed dance crowd and local drag performers. No hats, hoods or sneakers; 'creative dress' requested. *See also p204.*

Bill's Bar

See p115 **Pubs & Bars** *for listings.*
Bill's, a retro-influenced club with a logo appropriated from a divey 1950s lounge, is mainly a live music club, but Tuesday night's 'Phat Tuesday/Girltown' hip hop event packs in the most consistent crowds, who squeeze together in the rectangular room until they are permitted to spill over into the roomier **Karma Club** next door (*see p202*). Get here by 10pm or you'll be waiting in line for a while. *See also p204.*

Karma Club

9 Lansdowne Street, at Ipswich Street (421 9595). Fenway T. **Open** 10pm-2am daily. **Admission** $10-$15. **Credit** AmEx, MC, V. **Map 3 D/E5**

This remarkable-looking club, decorated in rich fabrics and carved woodwork, much of it imported from India and the East, is constantly undergoing changes in its musical identity. Currently incorporating national-tour live shows into its weekday schedule, the club's relatively hip dance nights at weekends usually include a lot of retro disco and high-energy club hits. *See also p206.*

Disabled: toilet.

Downtown

Il Panino

295 Franklin Street, at Broad Street (338 1000). Downtown Crossing or State/Citizen's Bank T. **Open** 9pm-2am Thur-Sun. **Admission** free. **Credit** *for parties of five or more* AmEx, DC, Disc, MC, V. **Map 3 H4**

A five-storey club with a Latin and international crowd not averse to ordering a bottle of decent champagne at bar prices. On Sunday, there's underground house on the fourth and fifth floors and Latin house on the third floor. On Thursday one dance floor is open, with Brazilian and American club music. On Friday and Saturday, the spins are international, Latin and progressive house music. The crowd's older on Friday and Saturday (about 25 to 55) than the Sunday set (21 to 30).

Disabled: toilet.

Joy Boston

533 Washington Street, at West Street (338 6999). Downtown Crossing T. **Open** 11pm-2am Thur, Sat; 10pm-2am Fri, Sun. **Admission** $10-$12. **Credit** AmEx, MC, V. **Map 4 G5**

When the doors open at 10 or 11pm, the line of good-looking young internationals in expensive black leather coats stretches down to the corner, most of them claiming to be on the guest list. The music programmes include a Greek night, several international and Latin events and a hugely popular hip-house and New York-house night, starring big-name local club DJs. There's valet parking too.

Disabled: toilet.

Central Square

Paradise

180 Massachusetts Avenue, at Albany Street, Cambridge (494 0700). Central T. **Open** 5pm-2am Thur-Sat; 5pm-1am Mon-Wed, Sun. **Admission** free. **No credit cards. Map 4 D4**

One of the hipper hideaways on the gay club scene, this inconspicuous brick building on a quiet corner of Massachusetts Avenue near MIT was a traditional men's bar (as in, 'ladies not welcomed') from the 1930s until the early 1980s, when it became a gay bar. Paradise is now the only full-time gay bar in Cambridge. The main floor is a traditional, low-lit bar room with an old hardwood bar and a pool table. The darker, funkier basement is the top 40 dance club. *See also p194* **Gay & Lesbian Boston**.

Man Ray

21 Brookline Street, at Central Square, Cambridge (864 0400). Central T. **Open** 9pm-1am Wed, Sun; 9pm-2am Thur, Fri; 10pm-2am Sat. **Admission** $5. **Credit** AmEx, MC, V. **Map 4 D3**

Man Ray, named after the avant-garde photographer, is the underground club with the most interesting queues outside on Wednesday and Friday nights – lots of shrouds, corsets, vinyl hip boots and priestly cassocks. In addition to the dedicated Goth/industrial nights, there are two gay nights (Thursdays for men, Sundays for women) and a camp disco/new wave night (Saturdays), but the Goths and fetishists don't always stick strictly to the schedule. Creative dress definitely encouraged. *See also p194* **Gay & Lesbian Boston**.

Website: www.manrayclub.com

Fenway

Machine

Below the Ramrod, 1256 Boylston Street, at Jersey Street (266 2986). Fenway or Kenmore T. **Open** 10pm-2am daily. **Admission** free-$5. **No credit cards. Map 3 D6**

Manly men have been sweating up the famous Ramrod for decades. This ultra-dark, rough-hewn gay landmark features a notorious back room with a strict dress code – if you're not in leather, you must be barechested – and a leather concession selling various implements of bondage. After guarding their domain for decades, the Ramrod crowd has been infiltrated by a more mixed gay dance crowd (pretty boys, a few straights, flashy club kids and flamboyant drag queens) that hangs out at Machine, the futuristic new dance club downstairs. This sprawling basement glitter palace features a games room with pool tables and video games; a cyber-lounge; and an anti-gravity machine next to the dance floor. *See also p193* **Gay & Lesbian Boston**.

Rock, blues & folk

Even back in 1967, you didn't need a PhD to figure out that Boston was one of the most fertile environments for rock 'n' roll anywhere in the country. The area was already home to more than 80 colleges and a quarter of a million students; it was 'with the exception of Berkeley, the hippest town in America', in the estimation of Ray Riepen, who that year founded the Boston Tea Party, now Avalon (the local equivalent of San Francisco's Fillmore, and one of the few places outside New York where the Velvet Underground actually drew an audience). Over the years, this renewable natural resource made Boston a target of promoters as well as bands and music fans themselves. A diverse network of clubs and bars arose to attract the disposable incomes of the area's academic residents – and a dizzying number of those bars, clubs and restaurants support live music. An annual guide to Boston bands published by the *Boston Phoenix* regularly lists in excess of 2,000 active local bands.

Just across the Charles River, Cambridge's Club 47 (now **Club Passim** *see page 204*) was crucial in launching the folk and blues revival of the 1950s, as well as the careers of such prototypical folkies as Bob Dylan and Joan Baez. And the area remains a hotbed of aspiring singer-songwriters – on any given afternoon they spill out onto the street and into the subway stations where Mary Lou Lord got her start – as well as a launching pad for such nationally-acclaimed folkies as Ellis Paul, Dar Williams and Chris Smither. (Cambridge was also the birthplace of modern rock criticism: it was after a show in Harvard

Square that Jon Landua penned the infamous line 'I saw rock and roll future and its name is Bruce Springsteen' for Boston's *Real Paper*.)

A proliferation of college radio stations provide drive-time and prime-time FM-dial access to undergrounds both local and national. Boston has remained for the most part a left-of-centre town, musically – though the exceptions to that rule, Aerosmith and Boston, are pretty big exceptions. You can trace the history of the Boston underground here from the proto-punk of the Remains and the 1970s garage punk of the Lyres and DMZ to the new wave of the Cars and the hardcore of Gang Green; or from the Pixies, Throwing Muses and Lemonheads up to latter-day alterna-pop stars like Juliana Hatfeld, Letters to Cleo, Morphine, Tracy Bonham and the Mighty Mighty Bosstones. Almost all of them have served as perennial premonitions of what's coming next.

Man Ray (*see page 202*), the official home of Boston's committed Goth/S&M subculture, also has occasional, largely unpublicised, live gigs: Alien Sex Fiend are Hallowe'en regulars.

Major venues

FleetCenter

See chapter **Sport & Fitness** *for listings.*
Built next door to the old Boston Garden – the scene of historic concerts by the Who and the Stones, as well as an Alan Freed package bill that turned into one of the first high-profile rock 'n' roll riots – the new home of the Bruins and Celtics leans toward middle-of-the-road megastars such as Billy Joel, Elton John, Celine Dion and Rod Stewart. While most of the rowdier acts end up at the Worcester Centrum, Aerosmith can still be counted on to play here just about every New Year's Eve, and now that Kiss is back in make-up, pyrotechnic action is still guaranteed at least once a year.

Foxboro Stadium

See chapter **Sport & Fitness** *for listings.*
In recent years only the Rolling Stones, U2 and Dave Matthews – an odd trinity – have been ambitious enough to book themselves into the 50,000-plus-seat home of the New England Patriots, who recently signed a deal to move to Connecticut for the 2001 season.
Disabled: toilet.

Great Woods Performing Arts Center

885 South Main Street, Mansfield (1-508 339 2331/ recorded information 1-508 339 2333). **Open** *box office* 1pm-5.30pm Mon-Sat. **Tickets** $25-$75. **Credit** AmEx, MC, V.
One of the prototypical summer-season sheds, Great Woods once backed away from rock 'n' roll – after a particularly rowdy Lollapalooza during which patrons lit bonfires and ripped up the sod on the general-admission lawn for the purpose of lobbing it towards the stage. The kids have since listened to reason and the lawn has remained intact for the subsequent array of summer package tours (Lilith Fair, Ozzfest, Smokin' Grooves), old-timer gigs (Steve Miller, Jimmy Buffett, whoever's doing the big reunion this year), radio station extravaganzas, and big-name alternative and metal acts who've been called in to pay the rent (Pearl Jam, White Zombie).
Disabled: toilet. Website: www.greatwoods.com

Harborlights

Fan Pier, Northern Avenue (374 9000). **Map 3 H5**
On the banks of the Charles River, Harborlights has served as a smaller, upmarket version of Great Woods. Soul reviews and oldie packages stock the summer season with nostalgic memories for the boomer crowd; that Bauhaus played here in the summer of '97 announces Generation X's own coming of age. Otherwise, it caters to the tastes of a much older generation: Bette Midler, Tony Bennett and the late Frank Sinatra have all taken to its stage. Negotiations are underway to relocate the tent to another area in South Boston, so phone to check on progress.

Orpheum Theatre

1 Hamilton Place, at Tremont Street (679 0810/NEXT Ticketing 423 6398). Park St T. **Open** *box office* 10am-5pm Mon-Sat; *NEXT Ticketing* 24 hours daily. **Tickets** $20-$50. **Credit** *NEXT Ticketing* AmEx, Disc, MC, V. **Map 3 G5**
An oddly-situated but long-running opera house located just off the Boston Common and easily accessible by public transport. It's the biggest you can get in Boston without graduating to a hockey rink, and its old-fashioned theatre seating is either considered a relic of more civilised times (to the kind of folks who've seen Dylan, Keith Richards or the Grateful Dead here) or a royal pain in the ass (to the kind of folks who've seen Hole, Pantera, or Motley Crue here).

Paul Tsongas Arena

300 Arcand Drive, Lowell (1-978 848 6900). **Open** *box office* 10am-6pm Mon-Fri; noon-5pm Sat. **Tickets** $20-$35. **Credit** Disc, MC, V.
Boston lacks a suitable mid-size venue for bands that are too big to play the 3,000-seat **Orpheum** (*above*) and are too small for arenas. A series of make-shift suburban sites have been utilised, including the Wallace Civic Center in Fitchburg

For **Bill's Bar**, *see pages 201 and 204.*

(a sweaty high-school hockey rink) and the New Aud in Worcester (an ancient-looking theatre where vendors once tried to sell ice-pops and pizza, arena style, at an Offspring show). This newly-built, 7,800-capacity venue – named after the late US senator Paul Tsongas – is the latest out-of-town solution: closer to Boston than the others and built to accommodate concerts. Marilyn Manson, the Verve and Tori Amos are among those who have made use of it so far.

Somerville Theater

55 Davis Square, Somerville (625 5700/recorded information 625 4088/Ticketmaster 931 2000). Davis T. **Open** *box office* 1-9pm daily. **Tickets** $15-$25. **Credit** *Ticketmaster* AmEx, Disc, MC, V.

A converted movie house that still serves mainly as a second-run cinema, the Somerville Theater is situated in the middle of the chic Davis Square neighbourhood. It enjoys the patronage of New England's hippie jam-rock underground the World Music organisation and is also the gig of choice for top-bill folkies such as Arlo Guthrie.

Worcester Centrum Center

50 Foster Street, at Worcester Center Boulevarvd, Worcester (1-508 755 6800). **Open** *box office* summer 9.30am-4.30pm Mon-Fri; winter 9am-5.30pm Mon-Fri; 9am-4pm Sat. **Tickets** prices vary, phone for details. **Credit** Disc, MC, V.

An arena slightly less sprawling than the FleetCenter – the only regular occupants are the minor-league IceCats hockey team – the Centrum is where you'll see your Korns and Bushes. Although acts who play here often greet their fans with a cheery 'Hello, Boston!', the venue's actually a good hour's drive away, which inevitably leads to a proliferation of parental units and limousines waiting patiently outside. Despite the distance, acts from the Beastie Boys and Puff Daddy to Green Day and Metallica regularly sell the place out.

Still going strong: the legendary **Club Passim**.

Music clubs

Avalon

See p201 for listings.

By night, the massive sound system and slick lighting attract the Euro crowd to one of the biggest dance clubs in the city. But years ago, as the Boston Tea Party, this was one of the first big rock ballrooms, and it still keeps up an impressive schedule of top-notch alternative rock, electronica and punk acts. When it's not roped off for VIPs, the balcony provides one of the best vantage points for big-name rock acts on the East Coast. In the span of a good month, you might see PJ Harvey, Garbage, Sepultura, Cake, Alanis Morissette and the Jon Spencer Blues Explosion.

Axis

See p201 for listings.

Once a punk club known as Spit, Axis has remained a grungey room. The acts tend towards metal, industrial and the (very occasional) progressive hip hop act, though lately there have been some electronic-oriented shows by the likes of Cornelius and Asian Dub Foundation. Major labels often send their latest punk rock acquisition (for example Nashville Pussy) to Axis and the few crossover-minded hip hop acts that get to play Boston (Everlast, Pharcyde, the Roots) usually play here.

Bill's Bar

See p115 **Pubs & Bars** *for listings.*

The smallest of the string of clubs lining one side of Lansdowne Street – the other side is the left-field 'Green Monster' of Fenway Park – Bill's has survived as a low-key joint mostly catering to established local bands. Worth checking out is the weekly swing/lounge/exotica night run by Combustible Edison's Brother Cleve, who keeps abreast of the latest international trends in the electronic/lounge hybrid known as EZ-tune, and imports both live bands and DJs fluent in the genre.

Brendan Behan Pub

See p122 **Pubs & Bars** *for listings.*

The flipside to living in a town overrun by students is the ongoing attempt to find out-of-the-way places to avoid them. Irish bars seem to offer one solution – especially tiny, closet-sized ones such as this local watering-hole, where the only thing thicker than the Guinness is the brogue spoken by the bartender. The pub has a stellar rockabilly night, as well as gigs by cult-fave local singer-songwriters such as Rounder's Dennis Brennan.

Club Passim

47 Palmer Street, at Church Street, Cambridge (492 7679). Harvard T. **Open** 11am-11pm daily. **Admission** $5-$15. **Credit** AmEx, Disc, MC, V. **Map 4 B2**

As CBGBs is to American punk, Club Passim is to the counter-culture folk scene of the 1960s. This legendary spot was the epicentre of the folk revival even before Joan Baez got her start here (renting the room herself and introducing Bob Dylan between sets). First known as Club 47 and later simply as Passim, it served as an irregularly-open but regularly busted jazz joint. Over the past 40 years Passim has been the launching ground for folkies from Baez and Taj Mahal to Suzanne Vega and Shawn Colvin, and has retained an intimate, grass roots atmosphere throughout. After some financial trouble a few years ago, the club is back, re-organised and stronger than ever, still playing host to legions of singer-songwriters in the 1960s tradition, from Patty Larkin and the Nields to Ellis Paul and Chris Smither.

Green Street Grill

See p152 **Restaurants & Cafés** *for listings.*

Central Square's best-kept secret. On Monday nights you can get a terrific Caribbean meal for under $10 and stick around to see acts ranging from the strange to the sublime. It

Bastion of surrealism: **Jacque's Cabaret.**

Johnny D's: *see page 206.*

remains to be seen how the recent departure of Lily Denison – who'd booked the club for over a decade – will affect the mix, which has included Knitting Factory-style experimental jazz and rock as well as avant-folk and indie bands, serious bluegrass and plenty of wild rock 'n' roll. This is also the place most likely to host one-off performances by alt-rock supergroups and rare solo appearances. Elliot Smith Lou Barlow, Morphine's Mark Sandman, Juliana Hatfield, and countless other rock luminaries have been regulars at the bar as well as at the mike. The room has the most revered jukebox in town.

Hard Rock Café

131 Clarendon Street, at Stuart Street (353 1400). Back Bay T. **Open** 11.30am-11pm (bar closes at midnight) daily. **Credit** AmEx, DC, Disc, MC, V. **Map 5 F5**

A typical Hard Rock, with lots of memorabilia and lots of tourists. The music in the downstairs Cavern Club (containing bricks from the club of the same name where the Beatles used to play) tends toward B-list local acts playing acoustic. Occasionally, however, the club lives up to its name: both Megadeth and Van Halen (after the latter picked up Gary Cherone, formerly of local glam-funk-metal dudes Extreme) have performed acoustic gigs here.

Harpers Ferry

158 Brighton Avenue, at Harvard Avenue, Allston (254 9743). Harvard Ave T. **Open** 2pm-2am daily. **Admission** $3-$27. **No credit cards. Map 4 A5**

Situated right in the middle of student hell, this isn't exactly where you'd expect to find Bo Diddley – though it is his preferred joint in town. Other than that, the blues you'll hear (even at the club's annual Battle of the Blues Bands) is a kind of Chicago/patrician mix, mostly played by white guys who make faces when they solo. The sound system is superior, there's plenty of room surrounding the bar and there are pool tables in the room behind the stage. All of which has made Harpers a favourite haunt of local neo-hippie jam bands.
Disabled: toilet.

House of Blues

96 Winthrop Street, at John F Kennedy Street, Cambridge (491 2583). Harvard T. **Open** *shows* 9pm-1am Mon-Wed, Sun; 10pm-2am Thur-Sat. **Admission** $6-$22. **Credit** AmEx, Disc, MC, V. **Map 4 B2/3**

A cramped but cosy spot in an alley off Harvard Square, this is the house that blues built. Real-life juke-joint troubadours pass through regularly, and Fat Possum's roster – especially RL Burnside – draw better crowds than many rock stars. The restaurant is downstairs, the ticket counter's in the basement and the blues is in the attic, in a folksy, unpretentious room adorned with folk art commemorating the founders and innovators of the Delta and beyond. *See also p152* **Restaurants & Cafés**.
Disabled: toilet.

Jacque's Cabaret

79 Broadway (426 8902). Arlington T. **Open** 11am-midnight Mon-Sat; noon-midnight Sun. **Admission** $4-$6. **No credit cards. Map 5 F5**

Even though it's just steps away from the bustling Theater District, Jacque's has remained a well-kept secret and a bastion of surrealism. Local punk and glam acts discovered this seedy transvestite hangout a couple of years ago and began gigging alongside the drag lip-synch acts. The basement has since been 'renovated', but art exhibitions and art-rock bands ranging from the Dambuilders or Six Finger Satellite to out-of-town avant-rockers like Be-Non, Oneida, and Rhythm Activism, have yet to reform the place's warped ambience. *See also p193* **Gay & Lesbian Boston**.
Disabled: toilet.

Johnny D's Uptown Restaurant & Music Club

17 Holland Street, Davis Square, Somerville (776 2004). Davis T. **Open** 11.30am-1am Mon-Fri; 9am-1am Sat. **Admission** $6-$15. **Credit** AmEx, Disc, MC, V.

This is the city's best roots-rock club, family-owned and a favourite hangout for knowledgeable enthusiasts of all stripes. It has played host to a comeback-bound Ronnie Spector, honkytonk heroes such as Billy Joe Shaver and Junior Brown, and revivalists like the Squirrel Nut Zippers-associated Andrew Bird. The acts are presented in a lounge/restaurant setting, so get there early and get a table. There's a dance floor right in front of the stage for spectators – and to accommodate the club's weekly swing nights, which were a staple well before the Zippers learned to Charleston. Once this has been filled, you'll have to squeeze in behind the bar.

Website: www.johnnyds.com

Karma Club

See p202 for listings.

Although it seems to change décor every month, Karma's upmarket atmosphere – a hotchpotch of visual references to Arabian nights – remains intact. The room was undergoing renovation when we went to press, but that hasn't stopped visiting rock luminaries Motley Crue from showing up after their own gigs to hang out in the VIP Mambo Lounge. Girls Against Boys, Sunny Day Real Estate, Grant Lee Buffalo and the Jesus and Mary Chain have played here. The club's Wednesday-night drum 'n' bass events are famous and attract the likes of Grooverider and Goldie as guest DJs. Oh, and when Neil Finn played, he brought along his pal Eddie Vedder. Consider the room officially blessed.

Kendall Café Alehouse & Grill

233 Cardinal Medeiros Avenue, at Bristol Street, Cambridge (661 0993). Kendall/MIT T. **Open** 4pm-1am Mon-Thur; noon-1am Fri; 3pm-1am Sat. **Admission** free-$5. **Credit** MC, V. **Map 4 D3**

A comfortable, compact acoustic room with an insider's taste in singer-songwriters, the Kendall has played host to some pretty big names: from local pop titans such as Letters to Cleo and the Gravel Pit to 'secret' gigs by Elvis Costello and Elton John lyricist Bernie Taupin. The club was also ahead of the trend in booking monthly 'residencies' for out-of-town acts: it took an early chance on a then-unknown Alaskan chick named Jewel, for instance. Also the unofficial home of Boston's 'Hellcountry' scene, which tends to be a little more raucous and eclectic than elsewhere.

Kirkland Café

421-27 Washington Street, at Beacon Street, Somerville (491 9640). Harvard T. **Open** 7pm-1am daily. **Admission** $3-$8. **Credit** MC, V. **Map 4 C2**

Towards the end of the week (usually Thursdays and Fridays) the Kirkland becomes Club Bohemia, home to a steadfastly anachronistic scene surviving from the glory days of the Real Kids. It's heavy on garage-damaged pop and rock 'n' roll, with occasional rockabilly and surf nights. Blue-collar to the bone and utterly immune to the trends and trade-winds of tastemakers, the Kirkland has the kind of hootenanny atmosphere that evolves only in places where payday still means something.

Disabled: toilet.

Lansdowne Street Music Hall

36 Lansdowne Street, behind Fenway Park (536 2100). Fenway or Kenmore T. **Open** 9pm-2am daily. **Admission** $3-$10. **Credit** AmEx, Disc, MC, V. **Map 3 D5**

Locals will probably be calling it Mama Kin for years to come, but in January 1999 Boston rock heavyweights Aerosmith took that name off the marquee, stripped the joint of all its Aerosmith memorabilia, and sold off their share of this venue on the Landsdowne Street nightclub strip. Not that this should change things much – Aerosmith played here only twice, and the band never made a habit of more casual visits. There are rumours that the larger venue next door, **Avalon** (*see p201 and p204*), may annex part of the club, but for the time being its three rooms remain intact. The smaller front room hosts mostly local bands; there's a larger room next door for national cult-level types (avant-soundtrack guy Ryuichi Sakamoto, electra-folkie Beth Orton); and upstairs, the Playhouse occasionally hosts theatre (including a memorable run of *Jesus Christ Superstar* with Gary Cherone in the title role), but usually settles for singer-songwriters looking for a cabaret setting.

Disabled: toilet.

The **Lizard Lounge** *in Cambridge.*

Linwood Grille

69 Kilmarnock Street, at Boylston Street (267 8644). Fenway T. **Open** 10am-2am Mon-Sat; noon-2am Sun. **Admission** $5. **Credit** MC, V. **Map 3 D6**

When Boston's world-famous punk landmark the Rathskellar closed down a few years ago, the soundman and a bunch of the regulars moved a few blocks away to this slightly larger urban roadhouse at the back of Fenway Park. During the season it remains a Red Sox bar, but it has taken over the Rat's specialities – the local heavy metal, garage-punk and surf scenes – and has also played host to bands such as Nashville Pussy, Zeke and the Demolition Doll Rods. Recent expansion has added a new stage, an increased capacity and a much better sound system. Cheap beer, a couple of pool tables and dedicated regulars make this one of the last real sinister rock 'n' roll dives in town – and that's a compliment.

Website: www.spy_dog.com/linwood/home.html

Lizard Lounge

1667 Massachusetts Avenue, at Harvard Street, Cambridge (547 0759). Harvard T. **Open** 9pm-2am daily. **Admission** $3-$7. **No credit cards. Map 4 B/C 2/3**

Situated just below a bustling restaurant, this renovated basement was opened by folks who wanted to emulate the classy, in-the-round set-up of a Nashville club. It's the kind of room where you can choose from several great Martinis and catch deft, independent singer-songwriters. But its real strength is its ecleticism. Former Berlin Airlift guy Rick Berlin runs a Warholian/Brechtian cabaret night; also worth checking out is the monthly Club d'Elf series (*see p123*). *See also* **Cambridge Common**, *p123* **Pubs & Bars**.

Middle East

480 Massachusetts Avenue, at Brookline Street, Cambridge (497 0576). Central T. **Open** 11am-1am Mon-Wed, Sun; 11am-2am Thur-Sat. **Admission** $5-$8. **Credit** AmEx, DC, Disc, MC, V. **Map 4 C/D3/4**

This is Boston's musical heart. Low-key and friendly, it's a unique mix of all-round artistic and cultural endeavour where you're just as likely to run into the former mayor as,

Festivals & the indie jazz scene

Boston's indie jazz scene blossoms with unpredictable regularity. Jazz often finds its way into the indie rock stronghold the **Middle East** (*pictured below*) and the **Green Street Grill** (*see page 206 and page 204*). Top-flight avant-garde acts also often show up at the **Zeitgeist Gallery** (312 Broadway Street, Cambridge; 876 2182). Names that rarely, if ever, find their way into the mainstream environs of the Regattabar and Scullers show up here and at local community centres, churches and colleges (consult the *Boston Phoenix* and the Calendar section of the *Boston Globe*, both available on Thursdays, for complete concert information).

Such performers enhance a tradition of experimentalism that's peculiar to Boston, although several of them boast international reputations. Joe Morris has virtually invented his own vocabulary on the electric guitar. Joe Maneri is a reed player and innovator in microtonal composition (and long-time New England Conservatory faculty member) who has fronted small ensembles with his son Matt, an equally imposing electric violinist. Together they've recorded several albums for ECM.

There are other names in new jazz to keep an eye out for, including the Either/Orchestra, Charlie Kohlhase, Debris, Saturnalia, Jeff Song, Bhob Rainey and Raphé Malik. For the past two Octobers, a three-day '**Autumn Uprising**' festival has presented some of the strongest of these players (441 0563/www.members.aol.com/tautology3). An impressive two-day **Asian-American Creative Music Festival** (577 1400/www.home. sprynet.com/sprynet/exnihilo/) has featured locals such as Song and the Indo-jazz ensemble Natraj, as well as imported talent from San Francisco such as Fred Ho and Jon Jang. The **Boston Creative Music Alliance** (in addition to co-producing the Asian-American Festival) presents a mix of Boston and New York adventurers in various venues between January and April, and between September and December. Recent seasons have included David S Ware, Joe Morris, Marty Ehrlich, Mark Helias and Ned Rothenberg (contact Gillian Levine on 868 3172 for more information).

For excellent free concerts, check newspaper listings for the **New England Conservatory** (*see page 218* **The Performing Arts**), where impressive musicians such as George Russell, Ran Blake, Fred Hersch, Allan Chase and Dominique Eade often give faculty recitals. Finally, the **Boston Globe Jazz Festival** happens every June at the Hatch Memorial Shell (information 929 2649). Although it sometimes presents an interesting concentration of artists over a one-week period, the newspaper seems to have an ambivalent attitude toward the cost and promotion of the event. In any case, it's hardly something to make travel plans around. Unlike Montreal, New Orleans or San Francisco, Boston still does not support a major jazz fest.

say, Peter Wolf. It's a favourite with local heroes such as Helium and Come as well as national tastemakers such as Built to Spill, June of '44, Pavement, Sleater-Kinney and Hovercraft. It regularly hosts punk, ska, jazz and lots in-between. The Bakery has free music seven nights a week (not to mention belly dancing) in a restaurant setting. The upstairs room presents up-and-coming locals and indie cult faves. The downstairs room, a converted bowling alley, is frequently packed to the gills with shows you just won't see anywhere else. The *Boston Phoenix* recently named the place the 'Best Place to Get Mistaken for a Rock Star', because it's the place rock stars go when they're not rocking, and because it's tough to tell the regulars from the folks on stage.
Disabled: toilet. Website: www.mideastclub.com

Midway Café

3496 Washington Street, near Williams Street, Jamaica Plain (524 9038). Forest Hills T. **Open** noon-2am daily. **Admission** Fri, Sat $2-$4. **No credit cards**.
The neighbourhood is one of the last bohemian territories left in Boston and the only thing it lacks is more venues like the Midway. A tiny local, it nonetheless boasts an amazing array of talent that's heavy on country, surf and rockabilly, and an audience of old-time townies and cheap-rent-seeking artistic types. Expect to see a full-blown Teddy crowd if you go to see the Cranktones – unquestionably the best roots-rockabilly in town. Scandinavian Merseybeat specialists the Kaisers and raucous West Coast tiki-surf cats the Bomboras have turned up on occasion.

O'Brien's

3 Harvard Avenue, between Brighton Avenue & Cambridge Street, Allston (782 6245). Harvard Ave T. **Open** noon-1am daily. **Admission** $4. **No credit cards**. **Map 4 A5**
The student ghettos of Allston have long harboured a tremendous punk/hardcore/metal scene, which traditionally congregated at such long-forgotten joints as Bunratty's and Molly's. The rent's gone up, Bunratty's is now a slick Euro café, and the only spot left for loud rock 'n' roll is this tiny Irish bar, whose other attractions include a big-screen TV. Always in danger of being closed down for overcrowding (its legal capacity is around 50), O'Brien's suffers from patchy booking and lack of publicity. But you can still find big-draw local bands such as Roadsaw, Scissorfight, Honkeyball and Cathode playing to their friends and regulars on good nights.

Paradise Rock Club

967 Commonwealth Avenue, at Babock Street (box office 562 8800/recorded information 562 8804). Pleasant St T. **Open** *box office* noon-6pm Mon-Fri; 3pm-6pm Sat; *club* from 7/8pm Wed-Sat. **Admission** $8-$20. **Credit** AmEx, MC, V.
If you've just heard their first single on the radio, they'll probably play here soon; and if they're playing the Centrum, chances are they were here a couple of years ago. U2, INXS and Alanis Morissette all played formative gigs here, but Paradise is most recently famous for being the place where Patriots QB Drew Bledsoe went stage-diving at an Everclear show, injuring a patron and setting off a string of lawsuits.
Disabled: toilet. Website: www.blackstone-presents.com/paradise.html

Plough & Stars

See p124 **Pubs & Bars** *for listings.*
An early location for the long-running 'Helldorado' series run by ubiquitous scenester Billy Ruane, the Plough is a blue-collar Irish pub by day and a cosy roots-pop nook at night. Morphine got their start here and Mark Sandman's alter-ego jazz-surf band the Hypnosonics occasionally appear. Recovering indie-rockers doing country or the singer-song-writing thing (or occasionally the surf-rockabilly thing) are a favourite attraction.

Roxy

See p200 for listings.
A 1930s ballroom that until recently served solely as a chic dance club, the Roxy still had enough old-time appeal beneath the neon to make it the natural choice to spearhead the swing revival. A huge dancefloor cordoned off by brass railings and an exquisite balcony inspired legions to come all gussied up for the Squirrel Nut Zippers, Cherry Poppin' Daddies, Brian Setzer and Big Bad Voodoo Daddy. Independent promoters seeking refuge from the long arm of the Don Law/SFX booking empire have also used it to present acts as varied as Jon Spencer, Pavement, Tricky, Nick Cave, John Cale and Billy Bragg.

TT the Bear's Place

10 Brookline Street, at Central Square, Cambridge (492 2327). Central T. **Open** 7pm-midnight Mon; 6pm-1am Tue-Sun. **Admission** $3-$8. **Credit** AmEx, MC, V. **Map 4 C3**
If the corner of Mass Ave and Brookline Street is the most important block in Boston rock – the Middle East is just steps away – then this is where it started. TT's recently celebrated its 25th anniversary, but it would be hard to pin down a single defining identity – in a recent month you might have seen Moe Tucker, the Donnas and Edith Frost; but all manner of acts have played here, and it's a favourite of locals fluent in skewered pop and country. Though the club's now somewhat overshadowed by the Middle East, it still manages quite a few coups. Despite what are possibly the worst sightlines of any major club in Greater Boston, TT's has stubbornly remained a local favourite.
Disabled: toilet. Website: www.tiac.net/users/ttbears/

Wellfleet Beachcomber

Cahoon Hollow Beach, Wellfleet (1-508 349 6055). **Open** *Memorial day-Labor Day* noon-1am daily.
Boston rock's summer retreat. A quaint shack with an outdoor patio, it sits at the top of a sand dune that winds down to the ocean. There's music every weekend during the summer (phone during the season for details), augmented by weekend blowout 'Dune Tunes' – festivals that drag on by bonfire-light well into the morning.
Disabled: toilet. Website: www.thebeachcomber.com

Western Front

343 Western Avenue, near Central Square, Cambridge (492 7772). Central T. **Open** 5pm-1.30am Wed-Sun. **Admission** $3-$10. **No credit cards**. **Map 4 C3**
A hotspot for reggae and Caribbean music – with a little avant-jazz thrown in – recommended especially if you like music that feels lived in instead of just stared at. Recently the club has experimented with contemporary forms, bringing in dub genius Mad Professor and hosting a monthly hip hop/poetry/jazz open-mike night.

Jazz

Boston has produced its share of legendary clubs (the Stables, the Hi-Hat, George Wein's Storyville, and, more recently, the 1369 in Cambridge) as well as musicians (Harry Carney, Serge Chaloff, Roy Haynes, Johnny Hodges, Sam Rivers, Tony Williams). It even has what could be considered America's one true jazz university – the Berklee College of Music. But the live scene in the city always seems on the verge of extinction.

The renovated **Roxy** *gets into full swing on a Friday night. See above and page 200.*

Since the death of the twin Jazz Workshop/ Paul's Mall in the late 1970s, jazz has lived a nomadic existence. There are 'jazz nights' at various multi-purpose clubs and plenty of hotel jazz piano gigs, but few speciality venues. Instead, the music rides on the enthusiasm of fans-turned-entrepreneurs and non-profit making societies that produce concerts sporadically in a variety of borrowed venues, including churches, museums and libraries. But there are a slew of musicians living in Boston, at least a couple of conventional commercial venues and plenty of good jazz to be heard if you search.

Hotel lounges

It's impossible to talk about these clubs separately: together, they're the anchor of the Boston jazz scene, lending it a modicum of stability.

The Regattabar

Charles Hotel, 1 Bennett Street, at Harvard Square, Cambridge (661 5000). Harvard T. **Open** 7pm-1am Tue-Sat. **Admission** $8-$24. **Credit** AmEx, DC, MC, V. **Map 4 B2**

The Regattabar offers cocktail-table seating, reasonable covers, a menu of satisfying light snacks and an essential line-up of events. In a typical season, performers include Kenny Barron, Tommy Flanagan, Dave Holland, John Scofield and estimable local artists like Mili Bermejo or Dominique Eade. Non-jazz fare tends towards blues and Latin music. Like Scullers, the Regattabar's use is restricted by the hotel that owns it (both clubs also serve as function rooms for the hotels). The 'stage' is in a corner at floor level, under a low ceiling that restricts sightlines and consistent sound. Book a table close to the action if you can.
Disabled: toilet.

Scullers Jazz Club

Doubletree Guest Suites Hotel, 400 Soldiers Field Road, at River Street (562 4111). Central T. **Open** for shows only, phone for details. **Admission** $10-$30. **Credit** AmEx, DC, Disc, MC, V. **Map 4 B4**

High above the Charles River, on the Boston side, Scullers has a spectacular view of the water. Unfortunately, its location (at the intersection of two major thoroughfares) cuts it off from public transport and foot traffic. Again, there are light snacks, cocktail tables and a hefty line-up. Regulars include Kenny Garrett, Roy Haynes, Danilo Pérez (a teacher at Berklee) and David Sanchez. The club also books its share of 'smooth jazz', cabaret-pop and R&B such as New York Voices, the Persuasions and Lee Ritenour.
Disabled: toilet. Website: www.scullersjazz.com

Other venues

Bob the Chef's Café

See p138 **Restaurants & Cafés** *for listings.*

For years this South End restaurant has been a favourite late-night stop for excellent soul food. A few years ago it expanded, was renovated and introduced jazz nights (from 7.30pm Thur-Sat; admission is $2). The combo is worth a trip.

Lizard Lounge

See p206 for listings.

The Lizard is worth a visit if only to see one of Boston's homegrown phenomena, the Fringe, a sax, bass and drums trio of some 25 years standing, born of the free jazz of Coltrane, Coleman, Archie Shepp and Sam Rivers. These three virtuosi whip up a rock-like intensity every Monday night. Thursdays are often given over to bassist Mike Rivard's Club d'Elf, an electronica-and-jazz experiment that draws on a wealth of great local musicians. Sunday night poetry jams feature the expert backing of saxophonist/ poet/playwright Jeff Robinson and his trio.

Ryles Jazz Club

212 Hampshire Street, Inman Square, Cambridge (876 9330). Central T. **Open** 9pm-1am Tue-Thur; 7pm-2am Fri, Sat; 10am-3pm, 7pm-midnight, Sun. **Admission** free-$12. **Credit** AmEx, Disc, MC, V. **Map 4 D2**

There's jazz in the comfortable downstairs room here, with sandwiches and snacks (as well as a Sunday jazz brunch) and windows looking out onto Inman Square. Jazz trumpeter/promoter Frank Vardaros fills the room with his personal heroes, such as Maynard Ferguson and Arturo Sandoval, Dave Liebman and John Abercrombie. Upstairs there's Latin dancing as well as special theme nights for lesbians (*see p194* **Gay & Lesbian Boston**).
Website: www.rylesjazz.com

Wally's Café

427 Massachusetts Avenue, at Columbus Avenue (424 1408). Mass Ave T. **Open** 9am-2am Mon-Sat; noon-2am Sun. **Admission** free. **No credit cards. Map 3 E6**

This hole-in-the-wall has been legendary (at various addresses along Mass Ave) since 1947. Wally's is a haunt for students from Berklee and the New England Conservatory, and when former Berklee-ites like Roy Hargrove or Branford Marsalis drop in, you can see how the club has provided a rite of passage for generations of young players. Jazz is played from Tuesday to Sunday, with blues on Mondays.
Disabled: toilet.

Scullers Jazz Club, *anchor of the local scene.*

The Performing Arts

The lowdown on local comedy, theatre, dance and classical music.

The best of Boston's theatre scene is divided between the enormous and the tiny. Mid-range theatre has recently begun developing, but most successful plays are either enormous productions put on in the Theater District or tiny underground shows playing to less than 100 people a night. The gap between big and small is less marked in dance, where the Boston Ballet rules over the local dance world and most other pretenders to the throne are runners-up. In the same way, the Boston Symphony Orchestra dominates the classical music scene. Boston comedy is almost exclusively tiny, with even marquee players sharing the stage with local yokels (who are often funnier than the headliner).

Boston has firmly established itself on the performing arts map, though. Boston Ballet's annual performance of *The Nutcracker* is one of the most popular in the world, the American Repertory Theatre has premièred works by writers such as David Mamet and August Wilson, and the city has spawned more than its fair share of stand-up comics.

TICKETS

Getting tickets means either travelling to a venue and buying them from the box office, or shelling out some extra dough to buy them over the phone. That probably means dealing with the nightmare that is **Ticketmaster** (931 2000). Expect long delays, impossible conversations and a booking fee, but at least you'll get seats. Seeking to provide an alternative to the evils of Ticketmaster is the local **NEXT Ticketing** (423 6398), a company that has tried really hard to make things better and now operates a system that is inexplicably every bit as bad as that at Ticketmaster.

When your search for tickets seems impossible but you don't want to seek out touts (scalpers), try **Back Bay Ticket** (40 Dalton Street, at Boylston Street; 536 9666). Sometimes the company can make the impossible happen. For last-minute and discounted tickets, the place to go is **BosTix** (723 5181). There are three locations, at Copley Square and Faneuil Hall in Boston and at 1350 Massachusetts Avenue, at Harvard Square in Cambridge. Every day, last-minute tickets to selected theatre, music and dance performances go on sale at 11am at these booths. Tickets are half price and you can only buy them on the day of performance. You can also buy full-priced tickets for advance shows at these locations (be warned that it's a Ticketmaster outlet) and you have to pay in cash, no matter what you're purchasing.

Theatre

Listings for theatres start on page 213.

Like many cities, Boston devotes an entire neighbourhood to its theatres. The Boylston Street area, known as the Theater District, is where you'll find the big guns, and the biggest in town is the **Wang Center for the Performing Arts**, which seats 3,700 and has reigned as the regional heavy-hitter ever since it opened in 1924. Home to the Boston Ballet, large plays, a few mass-appeal concerts and occasional movie screenings, the Wang's calendar runs the gamut of the art world. The centre sees performances that range from Mikhail Baryshnikov to *Miss Saigon* or Tori Amos. Movies here are especially fantastic – shown on the biggest screen in the area – and the choices are always top-notch, whether they are Sean Connery films, the *Star Wars* trilogy or MGM classics.

Right next door to the Wang is the **Shubert Theatre**, the last remnant of a national chain of theatres owned or operated by the impresario Shubert brothers. Since 1910, this has been the place to catch big musicals when they hit town, from *South Pacific* in the 1940s to *Rent* in the 1990s. Having undergone a full-scale renovation in 1996, the theatre is poised to attract even better shows, especially now that it has joined forces with the Wang.

Another good place for watching big musicals is at the **Colonial Theatre**. Built in 1900, it's the oldest continuously-operated theatre in Boston. The fan-shaped auditorium layout means there's scarcely a bad seat in the house, which is also the case at the **Wilbur Theatre** nearby.

The line-up doesn't change much at the **Charles Playhouse**, but that doesn't seem to bother anyone. On one stage, mind-blowing pop

The Blue Man Group: stalwarts of the **Charles Playhouse**. *See page 213.*

culture performance artists the Blue Man Group can be seen. The other stage hosts the semi-improvised comic murder-mystery *Shear Madness*, which has somehow managed to become the longest-running non-musical in American theatrical history. Still small, but on the rise and worth looking out for, are relative newcomers Boston Theatre Works, who perform at the **Tremont Theater**.

Staying in Boston but moving beyond the Theater District is one of the mid-range theatres, the **Lyric Stage**. As a response to escalating ticket prices elsewhere, the Lyric began staging major productions at cheaper rates, and has become the oldest resident professional theatre company in the city. The **Actors Workshop** provides a more traditional angle on modern theatre, minus the shock and surprise. A little further away in Brighton, the **Publick Theater** has staged both classics and children's theatre since being founded in 1971 and the shows are made all the more interesting by being performed outside in Christian Herter Park.

The **Boston Center for the Arts** encompasses four different companies, each with its own individual programme and philosophy. The SpeakEasy Stage Company and Pilgrim Theater put on small-scale, intimate, contemporary shows that are more left-of-centre than more traditional Broadway hits. The Theater Offensive doesn't necessarily try to be offensive, although you'll certainly find it so if you're a homophobe – most plays centre around gay and lesbian issues. And the Súgán Theater Company performs predominately Irish works in BCA's Black Box Theatre. The BCA also includes the century-old **Cyclorama**, an enormous round open space that plays host to various receptions, functions and occasional performances (*see page 68* **Sightseeing**).

One of the top companies in town is Boston University's resident **Huntington Theatre Company**, which performs at the University Theater and draws 150,000 viewers a year. Founded in 1982, the Huntington has built a high-profile reputation by balancing a schedule of musicals, new works and theatre classics. The company has premièred countless works over the years, including plays by Tom Stoppard and Willa Cather, and enjoys a reputation as a fairly traditional theatre troupe.

Not at all traditional, and possibly the best theatre company in the area, is based a few miles away in Cambridge. Since 1963, the **American Repertory Theatre** (ART) has broken new ground, working with artists like playwright David Mamet and novelist/playwright Don DeLillo. Some critics dismiss the ART as being too 'out there', but it's hard to argue with the pair of Pulitzers the company earned in 1983 and 1985. It performs at the **Loeb Drama Center** at Harvard University. Nearby is the **Hasty Pudding Theatre**, which hosts ART shows as well as performances by Harvard students and local amateur theatre companies.

If you really want avant-garde, try **Mobius**. A combination of art gallery and performance space founded in 1977, Mobius is devoted mainly to the sort of dance, theatre and performance art that isn't ready for primetime and doesn't have much desire to get there. More than 100 local artists perform at Mobius each year, and the space is described as 'a laboratory for artists experimenting at the boundaries of their disciplines' – which says it all.

The suburbs also house lots of great small theatres. In Newton, there's the **New Repertory Theatre**, which began in 1984 and has improved steadily over the past few years. Then there's the **Jewish Theater of New England** and Somerville's **Peabody House Theater Co-operative** which features small productions by up-and-coming local talent. And **TheatreZone** is working hard to revitalise the oft-maligned city of Chelsea through off-beat works performed at various locations, as well as by running theatre programmes for children.

OUTSIDE BOSTON

Since 1978, one of the largest theatre companies outside Boston has been the **Merrimack Repertory Theater** in Lowell, who perform in Liberty Hall at Lowell Memorial Auditorium (50 East Merrimack Street; 1-508 484 3926). In Newburyport, there's the **Firehouse Center for the Performing & Visual Arts** (1 Market Square, Newburyport; 1-978 462 7336), which features small-scale, local productions. New Bedford's **Zeiterion Theatre** (684 Purchase Street; 1-508 994 2900) hosts jazz and pop concerts but occasionally stages shows, too. And if you're willing to make the trek all the way to Beverly, the **North Shore Music Theatre** (62 Dunham Road, Beverly; 1-978 922 8500) puts on large productions in a small way.

For a completely different theatrical experience, try the **Boston Rock Opera** (10 Cameron Avenue, at Massachusetts Avenue, Somerville; 623 6533), which was founded in 1993 and performs in various local nightclubs. Shows feature local rockers, from small bands to bigger names. The production of *Jesus Christ Superstar* in 1998, for example, starred Gary Cherone (formerly of Extreme, now of Van Halen) and Kay Hanley (Letters to Cleo), as well as various local talents. Other past performances have included a play by the Kinks' Ray Davies and of course, *The Rocky Horror Picture Show*.

Actors Workshop

40 Boylston Street, between Washington & Tremont Streets (423 7313). Boylston T. **Open** *box office* 9am-7pm Mon-Fri; 10am-7pm Sat. **Tickets** $10-$20. **No credit cards. Map 5 G5**

American Repertory Theatre/ Loeb Drama Center

Harvard University, 64 Brattle Street, at Hilliard Street, Cambridge (547 8300). Harvard T. **Open** *box office* 10am-5pm Mon; 10am-7.30pm Tue-Sun. **Tickets** $23-$55. **Credit** AmEx, MC, V. **Map 4 B2**
Disabled: toilet.

Boston Center for the Arts

539 Tremont Street, at Clarendon Street (426 5000). Back Bay or Copley T. **Open** 9am-5pm Mon-Fri. **Tickets** $10-$20. **Credit** MC, V. **Map 5 F6**
Disabled: toilet.

Charles Playhouse

74 Warrenton Street, at Stuart Street (426 6912). Boylston or NE Medical Center T. **Open** *box office* 10am-6pm Mon, Tue; 10am-8pm Wed, Thur; 10am-9pm Fri, Sat; noon-6pm Sun. **Tickets** $39-$49. **Credit** AmEx, MC, V. **Map 3 G5**
Website: www.blueman.com

Colonial Theatre

106 Boylston Street, at Tremont Street (426 9366). Boylston T. **Open** *box office* 10am-6pm Mon-Sat; noon-6pm Sun. **Tickets** $25-$75. **Credit** AmEx, MC, V. **Map 3 G5**
Disabled: toilet. Website: www.broadwayinboston.com

Hasty Pudding Theatre

12 Holyoke Street, at Mount Auburn Street, Cambridge (495 5205). Harvard T. **Open** *box office* 10am-5pm Mon; 10am-7.30pm Tue-Sun. **Tickets** prices vary according to performance. **Credit** MC, V. **Map 4 B2/3**

Huntington Theatre Company/ Boston University Theater

264 Huntington Avenue, at Massachusetts Avenue (266 0800). Symphony T. **Open** *box office* 11am-5pm Mon-Fri; noon-4pm Sat, Sun. **Tickets** $10-$54.50. **Credit** AmEx, Disc, MC, V. **Map 3 E6**
Disabled: toilet.

Jewish Theater of New England

Leventhal-Sidman Jewish Community Center, 333 Nahanton Street, Newton (965 5226). Newton Centre T. **Open** *box office* noon-5pm Tue-Thur. **Tickets** prices vary according to performance. **Credit** MC, V.
Disabled: toilet.

Lyric Stage

YWCA Building, 140 Clarendon Street, Copley Square (437 7172). Arlington or Back Bay T. **Open** *box office* 11am-5pm Tue; noon-performance Wed-Sun. **Tickets** $24-$30. **Credit** AmEx, Disc, MC, V. **Map 3 G5**

Mobius

354 Congress Street, at Dorchester Avenue (542 7416). South Station T. **Open** *box office* half hour before performance. **Tickets** $4-$12. **No credit cards. Map 5 H5**

New Repertory Theatre

54 Lincoln Street, at Walnut Street, Newton (332 1646). Newton Highlands T. **Open** *box office* 10am-6pm Mon-Fri. **Tickets** $22-$28. **Credit** AmEx, MC, V.

Peabody House Theater Co-operative

Elizabeth Peabody House, 277 Broadway, at Route 28, Somerville (625 1300). Sullivan Square T. **Open** *box office* 10am-5pm Mon-Fri. **Tickets** $10-$14. **No credit cards.**

Publick Theater

Christian Herter Park, 1175 Soldiers Field Road, Brighton (782 5425). Harvard Square T, then 86 bus. **Open** *box office* noon-7pm Tue-Sun. **Tickets** $15-$30. **Credit** MC, V.

Shubert Theatre

265 Tremont Street, at Stuart Street (482 9393). NE Medical Center T. **Open** *box office* 10am-6pm Mon-Sat. **Tickets** $15-$60. **Credit** AmEx, MC, V. **Map 5 G5**
Disabled: toilet.

TheatreZone
189 Winnisimmet Street, Chelsea, near Broadway (887 2336). Bus 111. **Open** 10am-6pm daily. **Tickets** $10-$12. **Credit** MC, V.
Website: www.theatrezone.org

Tremont Theater
276 Tremont Street, next to the Wang Center (338 4274). Boylston T. **Open** *box office* 9am-5pm Mon-Fri. **Tickets** $14-$19. **Credit** AmEx, Disc, MC, V. **Map 5 G5**
Disabled: toilet. Website: www.bostontheatreworks.com

Wang Center for the Performing Arts
270 Tremont Street, at Stuart Street (box office 482 9393/Boston Ballet 695 6950/1-800 447 7400). NE Medical Center T. **Open** *box office* 10am-6pm Mon-Sat. **Tickets** $15-$60. **Credit** AmEx, MC, V. **Map 5 G5**
Disabled: toilet. Website: www.boston.com/wangcenter

Wilbur Theatre
246 Tremont Street, at Stuart Street (423 4008). Boylston or NE Medical Center T. **Open** *box office* 10am-6pm Mon-Sat; noon-6pm Sun. **Tickets** vary according to performance. **Credit** AmEx, MC, V. **Map 5 G5**
Disabled: toilet. Website: www.broadwayandboston.com

Comedy

Boston has a reputation as a comedy hotspot and successful comics the city has spawned range from the hugely high-profile (Jay Leno) to the mainstream bizarre (Steven Wright), the collegiate vitriolic (Denis Leary) and the not-recognisable-by-name-but-you'd-know-him-if-you-saw-him (Lenny Clarke). The venues where most of these people started out have since closed; the current breeding-ground for tomorrow's big names is **Nick's Comedy Stop** in the Theater District. It's true that most of the comics here favour raunch for raunch's sake and a lot just aren't even funny. But sometimes you may come across a hidden gem and be left gasping for air.

Once a comic starts getting a reputation and some notoriety, they might serve as an opening act for one of the nationally-known comedians that play the **Comedy Connection**. This is just about the only place in town to see the big guns of the laugh circuit, who may or may not be worth it. Further out, the **Comedy Palace** at Grill 93 in Andover programmes a decent mix of up-and-comers and national has-beens. For group performance, there's the improvisational comedy stylings of ImprovBoston who whip up something off-the-cuff every weekend at the **Back Alley Theater**. And alternative comedy has a home in Boston, too, namely at the **Comedy Studio** in Harvard Square.

Back Alley Theater
1253 Cambridge Street, at Beacon Street, Cambridge (576 1253). Central T. **Open** from 8pm Fri, Sat; 2pm Sun. **Admission** free-$12. **Credit** MC, V. **Map 5 G4**

Comedy Connection
Upstairs at Faneuil Hall, at Quincy Market (248 9700). Gov't Center T. **Open** 9am-10pm daily. **Admission** $8-$20. **Credit** AmEx, MC, V. **Map 5 G4**

Comedy Palace
Grill 93, River Road, Andover (1-888 865 2844). **Open** 8-10pm Thur; 9-10.30pm Fri; 8-10.30pm Sat, Sun. **Tickets** $8-$12. **Credit** AmEx, MC, V.
Disabled: toilet.

Comedy Studio
Hong Kong Restaurant, 1236 Massachusetts Avenue, at Bow Street, Cambridge (661 6507). Harvard T. **Open** from 8pm Thur-Sun. **Admission** $3-$7. **No credit cards. Map 4 B2/3**

Nick's Comedy Stop
100 Warrenton Street, at Stuart Street (482 0930). Boylston T. **Open** 7pm-2am Thur-Sat. **Admission** $10-$14. **Credit** AmEx, MC, V. **Map 5 G5**

Dance

One of the world's most popular productions of Tchaikovsky's *The Nutcracker* is danced by the **Boston Ballet**, who are based at the **Wang Center for the Performing Arts** *(see above)*. The Boston Ballet was founded in 1963 and began performing *The Nutcracker* two years later under the direction of the legendary Boston Pops conductor Arthur Fiedler. But the company is no one-trick pony and draws a yearly audience of over 242,000, who flock to see their mostly mainstream classical productions.

Another less prestigious but still significant dance troupe is the **Ballet Theatre of Boston**, founded in 1986 by artistic director José Mateo. The troupe has an in-house choreographer who produces original works as well as new interpretations of the classics and the company performs at the **Emerson Majestic Theatre**.

Ever since 1980, **Dance Umbrella** has been a forum for contemporary and culturally diverse dance, and has clocked up 55 world premières over the years. Past performers have ranged from Hip Hop Boston to the Trinity Irish Dance Company and Bill T Jones. Another interesting cultural mix can be found courtesy of the **Impulse Dance Company**. Their *Hip Hop Over Swan Pond* should give you an idea of the kind of genre-bending the company goes in for.

In Cambridge there's the **Dance Complex**, which hosts luminous artists-in-residence who teach classes and then perform for the masses. And in nearby Central Square, the **Green Street Studios** offer small-scale dance performances as well as local theatre.

Dance Complex
536 Massachusetts Avenue, at Brookline Street, Cambridge (547 9363). Central T. **Open** *box office* 9am-9pm Mon-Fri; 9am-6pm Sat; 9am-5pm Sun. **Tickets** $10-$15. **No credit cards. Map 4 D3**
Disabled: toilet.

Laszlo Berdo and Jennifer Gelfand perform Boston Ballet's annual 'Nutty Nutcracker'.

Dance Umbrella

515 Washington Street, at West Street (482 7570). Downtown Crossing T. **Open** *box office* 9am-5pm Mon-Fri. **Tickets** $28-$65. **Credit** AmEx, MC, V. **Map 5 G5**

Emerson Majestic Theatre

219 Tremont Street, at Boylston Street (box office 824 8000/Ballet Theatre of Boston 262 0961). Boylston T. **Open** *box office* 9am-6pm Mon-Fri; 10am-2pm Sat. **Tickets** $15-$65. **Credit** AmEx, MC, V. **Map 5 G5**
Disabled: toilet.

Green Street Studios

185 Green Street, at Central Square, Cambridge (864 3191). Central T. **Open** *box office* 8.30am-6.30pm daily. **Tickets** $10-$15. **No credit cards. Map 4 C3**

Impulse Dance Company

179 Massachusetts Avenue, at Boylston Street (536 6989). Hynes/ICA or Massachusetts Avenue T. **Open** *box office* noon-9pm Mon-Sat. **Tickets** $10-$25. **No credit cards. Map 3 E5**

Classical music & opera

In the Puritan seventeenth century, the only form of music permitted in Boston was psalm-singing. As late as the 1960s it was against the law to play a saxophone in a club in Cambridge, as it was considered to be the devil's instrument. Things have improved considerably, but the Puritan streak still applies to the classical world as much as it does to the 'devil's music' of blues and pop. At least, that's one explanation as to why classical music in Boston is dominated by the wealthy **Boston Symphony Orchestra** (BSO, founded in 1881), while opera has often been barely represented at all. Compare Boston to New York, for example, where the Metropolitan Opera has long dominated the scene, despite the eminence of the New York Philharmonic.

Boston's musical funding traditionally came from the Brahmins of Beacon Hill, who preferred the symphony orchestra to the vulgarities of opera. The original Boston Opera House, built in 1909, was demolished in 1958. Sarah Caldwell's Opera Company of Boston, known for its aesthetic vision and fiscal precariousness, foundered in the 1980s and has not been revived since. Peter Sellars made a brief Boston foray – and disappeared again (though not before producing a stunning *Marriage of Figaro,* among other productions). These days, the BSO is the dominant classical music institution. But Boston is also an international centre for early music and period instrument study and performance. In addition, many esteemed contemporary composers (Arthur Berger, Gunther Schuller and John Harbison among them) have based themselves in Boston, with its rich academic scene, so new music ensembles also flourish.

Bankboston Celebrity Series

(Information 482 6661). **Tickets** $25-$68.
Credit AmEx, MC, V.

The Celebrity Series began in 1938 with the likes of Kirsten Flagstad, Marian Anderson, the Ballet Russe de Monte Carlo and Rudolf Serkin. These days the organisation books more than 70 events between October and May each year in venues such as **Jordan Hall**, **Symphony Hall** (*see p216-7*) and the mammoth **Wang Center** (*see p214*). Performers include all manner of classical musicians (the St Petersburg Philharmonic, Reneé Fleming, Murray Perahia),

Seiji Ozawa celebrates 25 years with the **Boston Symphony Orchestra**.

dancers (Mark Morris, the American Ballet Theatre), jazz exponents (Wynton Marsalis or the Lincoln Center Jazz Orchestra), and unclassifiables such as the Chieftains or Kodo drummers.

Boston Lyric Opera

(Information 542 6772/bookings 482 9393/1-800 447 7400). **Tickets** $25-$98. **Credit** AmEx, MC, V.

These days, for fully-staged productions, Boston opera-lovers depend on the Boston Lyric Opera, which mounts three operas a year, sometimes drawing brilliant young singers (such as Lorraine Hunt in Handel's *Xerxes* and Dominique Labelle in Verdi's *La Traviata*) to sometimes uneven productions. In 1998 the Lyric moved from the tiny Emerson Majestic Theater (a 976-seater, owned by the dramatic arts oriented Emerson College) to the 1,550-seater **Shubert Theatre** (*see p213*). The Lyric has established financial solvency and managerial stability since its founding in 1976 and in the 1998-9 season was reporting a 72% subscriber rate (*Opera America* called it 'the fastest growing opera company in America'). The Lyric has stated as its mission the fostering of the 'next generation' of opera talent and in 1998 it appointed experienced opera and theatre director Leon Major to the new post of artistic director, a move that bodes well for the BLO's artistic as well as financial future.

Boston Philharmonic

(Information 496 2222). **Tickets** $12-$60. **Credit** AmEx, MC, V.

The Philharmonic prides itself on its mix of freelance professionals, students and amateurs who play side by side, while Boston audiences value it as a clear alternative to the BSO. The orchestra has been lead since its inception in 1978 by conductor Benjamin Zander. Zander's podium style is flamboyant, his interpretations sometimes idiosyncratic (he's gained some notoriety for championing Beethoven's original warp-speed tempo markings). But he's a serious, deeply respected musician and the Philharmonic's performances, especially of Mahler, are highly regarded and Zander's proponents would even install him at the BSO, replacing Ozawa. Performances are at **Jordan Hall**, **Symphony Hall** (*see below*), and Cambridge's **Sanders Theatre** (45 Quincy Street, Cambridge; 496 2222). It's always worth getting there early to hear Zander's colourful pre-concert lectures.

Boston Pops

(Information 266 1492/bookings 226 1200). **Tickets** $24-$75. **Credit** AmEx, Disc, DC, MC, V.

The Boston Pops are BSO-lite. During the summer season, while the BSO performs at Tanglewood, the seats of **Symphony Hall** (*see below*) are removed and replaced with large circular tables where champagne and snacks are served to the accompaniment of popular classics played by the Pops. The orchestra hosts an array of guest artists, such as James Taylor, Bonnie Raitt, Mary Chapin Carpenter and Victor Borges. It was conductor Arthur Fiedler who originally put the Pops on the international map, inaugurating the huge Fourth of July celebrations at the Hatch Memorial Shell, producing a series of popular recordings and getting national television exposure with *Evening at Pops*. He was followed as conductor by soundtrack composer John Williams (1980-93) and by the young and dynamic Keith Lockhart in 1995.

Boston Symphony Orchestra & Symphony Hall

301 Massachusetts Avenue, at Huntington Avenue (information 266 1492/bookings 226 1200). Symphony or Hynes/ICA T. **Open** *box office* 10am-6pm Mon-Sat. **Tickets** $24-$75. **Credit** AmEx, Disc, MC, V. **Map 3 E6**

The BSO has a long and venerable history, but it really came into its own under the stewardship of Serge Koussevitzky, music director from 1924 to 1949. It was Koussevitzky who established the BSO's summer home, the **Tanglewood Music Center** in the Berkshires (*see chapter* **Trips Out of Town**) as an artistic mecca – both for the training of young musicians (Koussevitzky's most famous personal protégé was the young Leonard Bernstein) and for the development of new music. In fact, Koussevitzky not only drilled the orchestra in the classical repertoire, but commissioned a significant number of new works, among them pieces by Bartok, Stravinsky and Copland.

Seiji Ozawa, the BSO's 13th music director, celebrated his 25th anniversary with the orchestra in the 1998-1999 season, a longevity that equals Koussevitzky's and rivals the careers of any number of international conductors (one of Ozawa's teachers, Leonard Bernstein, lead the New York Philharmonic for 11 years; another, Herbert von Karajan, was with the Berlin Philharmonic for more than 30).

However, although Ozawa is a national hero in his native Japan, in Boston both critics and the orchestra have been ambivalent in their attitude towards him. Ozawa's weakness remains the standard German Romantic repertoire. He's at his best with French and modern composers, gave a stirring rendition of Strauss's *Salome* several seasons ago (with Hildegard Behrens singing the title role) and has been growing into Mahler. The BSO players, it goes almost without saying, are top notch and sometimes Ozawa gets brilliant performances out of them (the orchestra's annual trips to Carnegie Hall in New York are invariably big hits). They also deliver good performances for guest conductors like Bernard Haitink (Principal Guest Conductor since 1995) and Simon Rattle.

The 2,600-seat Symphony Hall is an acoustical and architectural marvel. It was designed by the New York firm McKim, Mead & White and completed in 1900; if you're a classical music lover, you'll want to visit it for a performance by the BSO (between October and April), the Boston Pops or one of the many touring companies that pass through town. *Disabled: toilet.*

Emmanuel Music

Emmanuel Church, 15 Newbury Street (536 3356). Arlington T. **Tickets** from $15.50. **Credit** MC, V. **Map 5 F5**

Craig Smith (best known for his Mozart opera collaborations with stage director Peter Sellars) is another highly regarded Boston conductor. His Emmanuel Music group draws from the cream of Boston's musical crop and delivers compelling concert performances of Mozart's operas, religious choral works on Sunday mornings, and an ambitious, multi-season 'complete Schubert' series.

Jordan Hall

290 Huntington Avenue, at Gainsborough Street (536 2412). Mass Ave or Symphony T. **Open** *box office* 10am-6pm Mon-Fri; noon-6pm Sat. **Tickets** free-$100. **Credit** Disc, MC, V. **Map 3 E6**

Many of Boston's music groups stage concerts at the New England Conservatory's Jordan Hall (just down the street from Symphony Hall) and it's worth a visit, to catch either a performance in the Celebrity Series or one of the many New England Conservatory free faculty/student recitals. The hall's acoustics have traditionally outshone those of Symphony Hall. It was designed and built in 1903 by architect Edmund Wheelwright, with a distinctive horseshoe curved arrangement of its 1,000 seats, and since opening has been the place to hear vocal and piano recitals as well as chamber music. While superstars such as Horowitz, Arrau, Ohlsson and Pollini have been forced, by virtue of their popularity, to play at Symphony Hall, other audiences get the treat of hearing Peter Serkin, Dawn Upshaw and the Juilliard String Quartet at Jordan. In 1995, the hall underwent a major renovation. Some have claimed that, despite precautions and state-of-the-art acoustical consultation, the hall's perfect balance has been ruined – that brass blares and *pianissimo* blurs. It's an arguable point. Jordan is still a jewel of a concert hall.

New music

With the wealth of universities in the Boston area and the number of established composers teaching at them, it follows that all those composers are going to need groups to play their music (they can't depend on the BSO). Here's a sample of who to watch out for.

Composer and BU faculty member Theodore Antoniou guides BU's resident contemporary music ensemble **Alea III** (353 3349) through its annual series of engrossing concerts featuring old and new music, while Boulez, Schoenberg and Copland are mixed with estimable Boston composers like Mario Davidovsky, John Harbison and Scott Wheeler by the **Auros Group for New Music** (323 3430).

Boston Musica Viva (354 6910) music director Richard Pittman schedules a balanced mix of twentieth-century works, from Prokofiev and Schoenberg to Carter and Harbison, and various world premières. BMV (founded in 1969) also makes conscious efforts to include 'world music' influences like gamelan and Latin in their programmes.

Music director of **Collage New Music** (325 5200) David Hoose is one of the most respected new music conductors in Boston. In a typical four-concert season series, Collage performs a well-programmed mix of pieces by established composers (Babbitt, Carter, Copland, Thomson) as well as world premières.

A collective of composers and players began the group called **Dinosaur Annex** (482 3852), and they continue to present thoughtful programmes of their own and other people's music, including works by Babbitt, Davidovsky, Schuller, Arthur Berger, Ezra Sims and artistic director Scott Wheeler.

Schools

Boston Conservatory

8 The Fenway (536 6340). Hynes/ICA T. **Open** *box office* 9am-5pm Mon-Fri. **Tickets** free-$20. **Credit** AmEx, Disc, MC, V. **Map 3 D6**

Located in the Fenway area, the Conservatory (founded in 1867) presents a full calendar of performances, including the Boston Conservatory Chamber Players, Wind Ensemble, and Orchestra. Guest piano recitalists in the past have included Andrew Rangell and Mykola Suk.
Website: www.bostonconservatory.edu

Boston University School for the Arts

855 Commonwealth Avenue, near Boston University Bridge (353 3350). BU West T. **Open** *box office* 9am-5pm Mon-Fri. **Tickets** free-$15. **Credit** AmEx, MC, V.

Free faculty recitals include performances by early music keyboard specialist Mark Kroll, conductor David Hoose, and resident ensembles such as the Atlantic Brass Quintet, Muir String Quartet and Alea III contemporary music ensemble (*see above*). Student performances by the Boston University Opera Institute are also highly regarded.

Longy School of Music

1 Follen Street, Cambridge (876 0956). Harvard T. **Open** *box office* 9am-5pm Mon-Fri. **Tickets** free-$15. **Credit** MC, V. **Map 4 B2**

Founded in 1915 by Boston Symphony oboist Georges Longy, the school's faculty has since included Nadia Boulanger and the esteemed violinist Roman Totenberg among its directors. It offers a good programme of concerts,

Rob Kapilow conducts at **Jordan Hall**. *See page 217.*

especially during its annual 'September Fest' in the intimate Edward M Pickman Concert Hall, just outside Harvard Square.

New England Conservatory

290 Huntington Avenue, at St Botolph Street (585 1100). Mass Ave T. **Open** *box office* 9am-5pm Mon-Fri. **Tickets** free-$100. **Credit** Disc, MC, V. **Map 3 E6**

The big daddy of Boston music schools, founded in 1867, boasts a $33-million endowment and credits itself with supplying 44 per cent of the players of the BSO from its faculty. For the average concert-goer, that means a year-round calendar of excellent free faculty and student recitals, often given in NEC's **Jordan Hall** (*see p217*).

Website: newenglandconservatory.edu

Early music

Boston Baroque

(Information 484 9200).

Harpsichordist and conductor Martin Pearlman founded this group as Banchetto Musicale in 1973. It's renowned for concerts and recordings that première period instrument performances of Monteverdi, Mozart, Handel and Bach. Most performances take place in **Jordan Hall** (*see p217*).

Boston Cecelia

1773 Beacon Street, at Dean Road, Brookline (232 4540). Dean Rd T. **Open** *box office* 9am-5pm Mon-Fri. **Tickets** $11-$54. **Credit** MC, V.

Donald Teeters conducted this group's inaugural concert on 21 November 1968, to honour the patron saint of music. One of the most respected choral groups in town, the group mixes its speciality, Handel, with premières of new work, rarely performed pieces and concert performances of opera.

Boston Early Music Festival

(Information 661 1812).

The Boston Early Music Festival & Exhibition is a biennial June event featuring exhibitions, performances and at least one blow-out full-dress international production 'centrepiece performance' of a Baroque opera (in 1997 it was Luigi Rossi's *L'Orfeo*, in 1999 Francesco Cavalli's *Ercole Amante*). Annually, the BEMF presents seven-concert series during the regular season, drawing on an international cast such as Sequentia, Hesperion XX Trio, the Tallis Scholars, the Anonymous Four, Romanesca and the Boston-area based Musicians of the Old Post Road. Programmes take place in a variety of concert halls and churches.

Handel and Haydn Society

Horticultural Hall, 300 Massachusetts Avenue, at Huntington Avenue (266 3605). Symphony T. **Date** 10am-6pm Mon-Fri. **Tickets** $20-$60. **Credit** AmEx, Disc, MC, V. **Map 3 E6**

The name almost says it all. Artistic director Christopher Hogwood leads the self-styled 'Premier Chorus and Period Orchestra' of America in H&H as well as smatterings of Bach, Beethoven and others, with annual jazz crossover concerts featuring guests such as Dave Brubeck and the Modern Jazz Quartet.

Isabella Stewart Gardner Museum

See p90 **Museums & Galleries** *for listings.*

You can combine your museum-stop at this stunning Renaissance palazzo with a concert-stop on Sundays. The series includes premières of new works as well as performances by some of the most respected musicians in Boston and special guest artists such as Musicians from Marlboro and the Chamber Music Society of the Lincoln Center.

Museum of Fine Arts

See p90 **Museums & Galleries** *for listings.*

The MFA's concert series specialises in early music and the Baroque, with performances by the resident early music Museum Trio and recent guest artists such as cellist Pieter Wispelwey, soprano Sharon Baker and the vocal sextet Lionheart. The Valentine's Day concert of classic Broadway pop with soprano Nancy Armstrong and local baritone Robert Honeysucker has become an annual favourite.

Sport & Fitness

Where to watch and where to play in a town that takes its sport seriously. Very seriously.

Spectator sports

Washington has its politics, New York City has its urban arts and sophistication, and Boston has its sports teams. In this blue-collar city, following the ups and downs of big-money spectator sports is a passionate way of life. Each of the major professional teams – the Red Sox, Celtics, Bruins and New England Patriots – have their dedicated (some might say rabid) fans. In recent years, the Patriots football team has won new converts thanks to a 1997 visit to the Super Bowl. Football genius Bill Parcells was responsible for the team's turnaround, and his defection to the New York Jets just weeks after the Super Bowl loss remains a sore point among many fans. A Patriots/Jets rivalry has sprung up as a result, and matches between the two teams pack many sports bars with patrons devouring tuna sandwiches (Parcells' nickname is 'the Tuna').

Boston also has a professional soccer team, the New England Revolution, but the local faithful have yet to take to the kick game. College sports are also popular, especially Boston College football and basketball. Harvard/Yale football games always draw a crowd, but mostly from out-of-town alumni.

INFORMATION & TICKETS

For local sporting information, look no further than the two daily newspapers, the *Boston Globe* and the *Boston Herald*. Both have nationally-recognised sports sections that report on professional goings-on in great detail; the *Globe* also publishes daily television and radio broadcasts of games and sport talk shows; it has a free pro **sports score information line** (265 6600). The easiest way to get tickets is to phone or visit the box office of the team you want to see.

Auto racing

If you like your fun loud and oily, make a special visit to one of the many stock car and drag racing speedways located in New England. Most are within an hour's drive of the city; some are further.

New England Dragway

Route 27, Epping, NH (1-603 679 8001). **Open** *Apr-Oct* 5-9pm Wed, Fri; 9am-5pm Sat, Sun. **Tickets** $10-$25. **No credit cards.**
Both motorcycle and auto drag racing.
Disabled: toilet.

New Hampshire International Speedway

1122 Route 106 North, Loudon, NH (1-603 783 4744). **Open** 8am-5pm Mon-Fri. **Tickets** $35-$75. **Credit** Disc, MC, V.
New Hampshire International Speedway hosts motocycle and auto racing.
Disabled: toilet. Website: www.nhis.com

Riverside Park Speedway

Route 159, Agawam, MA (1-413 786 9300). **Open** 9am-5pm Mon-Fri. **Tickets** $20-$35. **Credit** AmEx, Disc, MC, V.
NASCAR racing, and on select Sundays demolition derbies.
Disabled: toilet.

Seekonk Speedway

Route 6, Seekonk, MA (1-508 336 9959). **Racing** *May-Sept* 6pm Sat; *Oct* second weekend. **Tickets** $12. **Credit** (telephone bookings only) MC, V.
The Seekonk hosts pro-stock, sportsman, street-stock and Formula 4 racing, as well as truck racing.
Disabled: toilet.
Website: www.seekonkspeedway.com

Stafford Motor Speedway

Route 140, Stafford Springs, CT (1-860 684 2783). **Racing** *Apr-Sept* 7pm Fri. **Tickets** $2-$12.50. **Credit** AmEx, MC, V.
Hosts NASCAR racing. It also has motorcycle, monster truck racing and off-road racing. If you're really enthusiastic, take advantage of the free overnight parking available from the evening of a race.
Disabled: toilet. Website: www.staffordspeedway.com

Waterford Speedbowl

Route 85, Waterford, CT (1-860 442 1585). **Racing** *Apr-Oct* 6pm Sat. **Tickets** $16-$17. **Credit** AmEx, Disc, MC, V.
The Waterford hosts modified-, late model-, stock, and mini-stock car racing.
Disabled: toilet.

Baseball

Boston is home to the **Boston Red Sox** and loyal fans are said to be members of the 'Red Sox Nation'. Despite disappointing devoted fans year after year with failed attempts to win the World Series or even just achieve a division win, the fans keep coming back to **Fenway Park**. *Boston Globe* columnist Dan Shaughnessy penned an excellent history of the team *The Curse of the Bambino* (*see page 274* **Further Reading**) which posits that the Sox will never win another title because the team cursed itself by trading Babe Ruth to the New York Yankees (*see page 224*). No harm seems to come from just attending a game, however.

The baseball season runs from April to October. Tickets are usually available at Fenway Park on game day although it may be difficult to get tickets for a Red Sox/Yankees face off (the rivalry dates back to the Babe's trade to New York). Tickets to games with the Toronto Blue Jays are also tough to find thanks to longtime BoSox pitcher and Cy Young Award winner Roger Clemens's 1996 defection up north. Tickets can also be purchased by calling the Fenway Park bookings line.

Fenway Park

4 Yawkey Way (267 9440/bookings line 267 1700/tours May-Sept 236 6666). Kenmore T. **Open** *Oct-Mar* 9am-5pm Mon-Fri; *Apr-Sept* 9am-5pm daily. **Rates** *tours* $3-$5; *tickets* $12-$35. **Credit** AmEx, Disc, MC, V. **Map 3 D5/6**
Disabled: toilet.

Basketball

Boston fans are still mourning the retirement of basketball legend Larry Bird and the demolition of the beloved Boston Garden, which nurtured 16 championship-winning **Celtics** teams. (The team now plays in the bland **FleetCenter**; die-hard fans hate the venue but the new arena is actually a much more comfortable place in which to watch a game.) But luckily the excitement returned two years ago with the hiring of coach Rick Pitino. Pitino has yet to turn the losing team around, but he ignited the masses by coaching the bottom-of-the-barrel Celtics to a win over the world-champion Chicago Bulls and Michael Jordan in the 1997/98 season opener. After contract machinations between owners and the players' union delayed the start of the 1998/99 season, it remains to be seen what Patino can do with the new Celtics. The bottom line is, you can still get tickets to these games, but this may change soon.

FleetCenter

1 Causeway Street, at North Station (624 1000). North Station T. **Open** *box office* 11am-7pm daily. **Tickets** $18-$28. **Credit** AmEx, DC, Disc, MC, V. **Map 5 G3**
Disabled: toilet. Website: www.fleetcenter.com

Dog & horse racing

Raynham/Tauntan Greyhound Park

1958 Broadway, Raynham, MA (1-508 824 4071). **Racing** 1pm daily. **Admission** $1.50. **No credit cards.**
Daily dog racing.
Disabled: toilet.

Rockingham Park

Rockingham Park Boulevard, Salem, NH (1-603 898 2311). **Open** noon-11pm daily. **Admission** $1. **No credit cards.**
Rockingham Park offers simulcast horse racing as well as live racing. For information on Salem, *see chapter* **Trips Out of Town**.
Disabled: toilet.

Suffolk Downs

111 Waldermar Avenue (the junction of routes 1A & 145), East Boston, MA (567 3900). **Racing** *Sept-June* 12.45pm Mon, Wed, Sat; *simulcast* noon-midnight daily. **Admission** free. **Credit** AmEx, MC, V.
Live racing takes place on a seasonal basis but the track is open daily for simulcast racing.
Disabled: toilet.

Wonderland Park

190 VFW Parkway, Revere, MA (1-781 284 1300). **Racing** 7.25pm daily; 5pm Tue, Sat; *simulcast* from 12.30pm daily. **Admission** $2. **Credit** *dining only* MC, V.
Wonderland Park offers dog racing and broadcasts of simulcast racing from Hong Kong.
Disabled: toilet.

Football

The **New England Patriots** used to be the laughing-stock of professional sport in Boston. The team regularly lost week after week by embarrassingly large margins. The low point came in 1990 when a female sportswriter for the *Boston Herald* accused several players of sexually harassing her in the locker room. But then local businessman Bob Kraft bought the franchise and hired Bill Parcells to turn the team around. Within three years, Parcells had coached his players to the Super Bowl. Today, Boston is filled with born-again Patriots fans. The multi-year signing of major quarterback talent Drew Bledsoe hasn't

hurt, either. Parcells is long gone (he switched to division rival the New York Jets just weeks after losing to the Green Bay Packers in the Super Bowl) but Bledsoe's still around. It's almost impossible to get tickets to a Patriots game (they play at **Foxboro Stadium**), but you can catch the excitement by watching a game in one of Boston's many sports bars (try **Daisy Buchanan's**, for example: *see page 116* **Pubs & Bars**).

Foxboro Stadium

60 Washington Street, Foxboro (931 2222/1-800 543 1776). **Tickets** $25-$50. **Credit** AmEx, MC, V.
Disabled: toilet.

Ice hockey

Like the Patriots and the Celtics, the **Boston Bruins** recently hired a big-name coach by recruiting Pat Burns from arch rivals the Montreal Canadians. He has yet to score big in terms of a division win (much less a Stanley Cup), but he has added excitement to the game. Not that Bruins fans were much in need of it. Unlike fickle Patriots and Celtics fans, who attend games in big numbers only when the players are racking up wins, the Bruins faithful are there in their black and yellow jerseys, game in, game out, regardless of team performance. Tickets are not available for every game; phone the **FleetCenter** to get them (*see page 220*).

Marathon running

The 100-year-old **Boston Marathon** takes place every April on Patriot's Day (*see page 38* **Boston by Season**), which is a relatively obscure holiday marking Paul Revere's famous ride through the colonies warning that the British were coming. The city more or less shuts down on the day of the race to prepare for the arrival of 37,500 runners (a figure that doesn't include the number of unregistered runners who jump into the race) and tens of thousands of spectators. Great views of the runners can be had in the last four miles of the race, which take place in Boston. It finishes at Copley Square but the area is always mobbed. If you walk a mile or so from Copley you can cheer in the winners in slightly less crowded conditions.

Polo

If you want a taste of sporting action combined with high class tailgating (think wine and cheese as opposed to beer and chips), a trip to the **Myopia Polo Grounds** in Hamilton, Massachusetts is a must (Route 1A). Polo matches are held every Sunday at 3pm throughout the summer and tickets cost $5. Phone 1-978 468 7956 for details.

Line up for a spot of boating on the Charles.

Soccer

The **New England Revolution** (www.anyrevolution.com) play in **Foxboro Stadium** (*see above*), also home to the New England Patriots, but the team doesn't enjoy anything close to the popularity that the Patriots do. Which means you'll always be able to get a ticket ($10-$25). Phone the stadium for details.

Active sports

Nearly everyone works out in Boston. This is probably because Boston descended from a community of Puritans whose work-based culture of self denial has passed down through the centuries. This is probably a good thing, though it can be disconcerting to find yourself on a stairmaster working out next to an older man who's sporting a huge gut and displaying all the signs of an imminent heart attack. But that's the city's charm: Boston is utterly lacking in glam culture, so that everyone, regardless of where they tip the scales, feels comfortable attending aerobics classes or lifting weights.

GENERAL INFORMATION

Metro Sports magazine, a free regional publication available in most sports shops, publishes information about outdoor activities. *New England Runner*, available on newsstands for $3.95, is an excellent resource for local road races and multisport events. The *Boston Globe* also publishes activities listings on Saturdays, but it's an incomplete directory of weekend events. If you've left some of your sporting equipment or clothing behind, check out **City Sports** (480 Boylston Street, between Berkeley & Clarendon Streets; 267 3900), a shop with several locations throughout the city and surrounding areas.

Boating & sailing

Wannabe Ahabs will find plenty to do within the city, though you should be warned: water traffic on the Charles River and within Boston Harbor gets very congested on sunny summer days.

Boston Harbor Sailing Club

200 High Street, at Rowes Wharf (345 9202). Aquarium T. **Open** 9am-5pm Mon-Fri.
Rental $75-$387 per hour; $710-$2,318 per week.
Lessons *per day* $499, plus materials; *cruising course* $799, plus materials. **Credit** AmEx, MC, V.
Map 5 H4
Disabled: toilet. Website: www.by-the-sea.com/bhsclub/

Boston Sailing Center

54 Lewis Wharf, at Atlantic Avenue (227 4198). Aquarium or Haymarket T. **Open** *2 Nov-14 Apr* 9am-5pm Mon-Fri; 10am-4pm Sat; *15 Apr-1 Nov* 9am-sunset daily. **Charters** $100. **Lessons** from $520.
Credit MC, V.
Map 5 H3/4
Website: www.bostonsailingcenter.com

Babe who?

In truth, nobody in baseball really believes in the Curse of the Bambino – well, not *that* many people. But it's one hell of a story. When you've got as much history against you as the Red Sox have, every late-season collapse, every play-off series defeat, even every addition to the regular season 'loss' column, potentially adds to the mythology surrounding the most famous jinx in the history of sport.

It all began in 1919, when the Red Sox's owner, Harry Frazee, got into mild financial trouble when a few of his theatre productions didn't do as well as expected. To ease his bank balance, Frazee sold a player to the hated New York Yankees for $100,000 cash and a loan to pay the mortgage on the team's stadium, Fenway Park. Not much to write home about under normal circumstances. But the player in question was Babe Ruth, and so began the Curse. Ruth went on to lead the Yankees to their first World Series a few years later and became the greatest player the game has ever seen. Since the trade, New York have won the American League 35 times and the World Series on 24 occasions (including a sweep of San Diego in 1998). Boston have won just four of the former, and none of the latter.

They've certainly come close, but therein lies the Curse. For just when it seems as though the Red Sox are going to banish history forever, something fantastic, memorable or just downright ludicrous occurs. Take 1946, when the Sox took a three to two lead in the Series. After losing game six, St Louis stole game seven and the championship when St Louis outfielder Enos Slaughter incredibly scored the winning run all the way from first base, on a single to centerfield in the bottom of the eighth. Or 1967, when the Sox again lost in game seven of the Series, again against St Louis. Or 1975, when Joe Morgan blooped a broken-bat single into centre with – you guessed it – two outs in the ninth inning of game seven, giving Cincinatti the World Series.

Or, of course, 1986, and one of the greatest games in baseball history. With a lead of 5-3, and two outs in the tenth inning, this would surely be the Sox's year. Until, that is, with the Sox one out away from victory, the Mets put together two singles off Calvin Schiraldi. Even then, though, Schiraldi quickly got two strikes on Ray Knight. The Red Sox were one strike away from their first World Series in 68 years. Knight broke his bat on the next pitch, but – of course – it fell in for a single. Gary Carter scored from second, and Kevin Mitchell took third base. 5-4.

Now the Sox brought in Bob Stanley from the bullpen. Just as Schiraldi had done five minutes earlier, Stanley got two quick strikes on the batter, Mookie Wilson. One strike from the Series. Again. Stanley threw a ball outside. Wilson fouled off another strike. Still, one strike. The Series.

Stanley's next pitch sailed maybe six inches off the plate, but the ball still squeaked past Sox catcher Rich Gedman. Mitchell darted home from third base with the tieing run, and Boston had somehow contrived to blow it again. It hardly came as a great surprise when, five pitches later, ageing first baseman Bill Buckner let a soft grounder from Wilson go straight through his legs for the most famous fielding cock-up in baseball history. Knight scored from second with the winning run, the Mets took the game 6-5 and won the anti-climactic decider two nights later to clinch the Series.

Since then, the Sox haven't even got close. However, 1998 was their best year for some time. The addition to the pitching staff of Pedro Martinez lifted the team, while the re-emergence of Bret Saberhagen and the improved control exhibited by knuckleballer Tim Wakefield meant the Sox had three 15-game winners in 1998. The batting, though, looks less secure in the long term: though the team batted a fine .280 in 1998, third in the American League, the average was artificially boosted by slugger Mo Vaughn, whose .337 average was second in the American League, and young shortshop Nomar Garciaparra, whose sophomore season – .323 average, 35 homers and a team-leading 122 RBIs – was as good as anyone could have reasonably expected. Aside from these two, though, none of the team's regular hitters reached a .280 average, let alone .300, and with Vaughn (who also led the team with 40 homers in '98) joining the Anaheim Angels in the off-season, the team may struggle to repeat its successes of 1998.

With the team in a state of flux, though, at least Fenway Park is secure – for now. Boston's stadium, with its intimate atmosphere and 37-foot-high (11-metre) left-field wall – the Green Monster – is surely the most unique in baseball. If you've never seen a baseball game before, Fenway Park is the perfect place to get started. On 13 July 1999, it hosts the All-Star Game, an annual celebratory baseball bonanza where the two teams – one from each league – are, in the main, picked by fans across

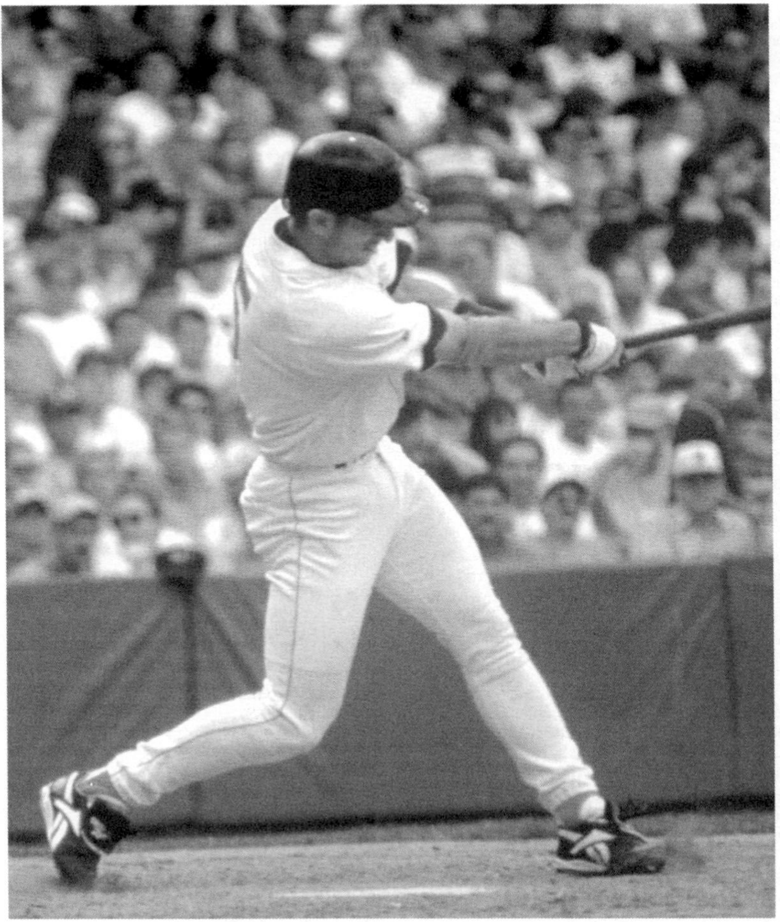

Boston shortstop Nomar Garciaparra, one of the best young hitters in baseball.

America. For the preceding week, Boston will go baseball crazy, with tons of special events and exhibits.

But in the grand scheme of things, none of this really matters. The Red Sox could sign Greg Maddux, Kevin Brown, Mark McGwire, Sammy Sosa, Mike Piazza, Tony Gwynn or any current All-Star, and it wouldn't mean a thing. Because until the sports priests carry out a serious and legitimate baseball exorcism in Fenway Park, the Curse of the Bambino will prevent the Sox from reaching the ultimate plane and winning the World Series. Just don't talk about it in Boston.

Community Boating

21 David G Mugar Way, on the banks of the Charles River, between the Hatch Shell & the Longfellow Bridge (523 1038). Charles/MGH T. **Open** *1 Apr-31 Oct* 1pm-sunset Mon-Fri; 9am-sunset Sat, Sun. **Membership** *2-day pass* $50; *45-day pass* $75. **Credit** MC, V. **Map 5 F4**

Community Boating hires out sailing boats, kayaks and windsurfers. *See also page 78* **Sightseeing**.
Disabled: toilet.

Bowling

Lanes & Games

195 Concord Turnpike (Route 2), Cambridge (876 5533). Alewife T. **Open** 9am-midnight daily. **Admission** $2.60-$3. **No credit cards.**

An urban hipster's haven.

Boston Bowl Family Fun Center

820 Morrissey Boulevard, Dorchester (825 3800). Bus 20. **Open** 24 hours daily. **Rates** *10-pin bowl* $1.50-$3.30; *shoes* $1.65. **Credit** MC, V.

A blue-collar hang out.
Disabled: toilet.

Sacco's Bowl-Haven

45 Day Street, Somerville (776 0552). Davis T. **Open** 9.30am-midnight Mon-Fri; 10am-midnight Sat; noon-midnight Sun. **Rates** *per string* $1.85-$2; *shoes* $1; *pool* $7.50 per hour. **No credit cards.**

Sacco's Bowl-Haven attracts a mix of blue-collar types and urban hipsters.

Camping

Boston is within an hour's drive of fantastic camping in state forests as well as the Green and White National Forests. The **Appalachian Mountain Club** (5 Joy Street, at Beacon Street; 523 0636) is an excellent resource on New England camping. *See also chapter* **Trips Out of Town**.

Cycling

Pedestrians and drivers loathe bike messengers and – by default – recreational cyclists the world over, and Boston is no exception. That said, there are plenty of dedicated trails that are good for both cyclists and in-line skaters. *See page 265* **Directory** for more information on these.

There are plenty of places where you can rent bikes or blades across the Boston area. Some, such as **Back Bay Bikes and Boards** (336 Newbury Street; 247 2336) do both (*see also below* **In-line skating/rollerblading**). For bike rentals in Boston, try **Community Bicycle Supply** in the South End (496 Tremont Street; 542 8623), or the **Inter-national Bicycle Center** in Allston (89 Brighton Avenue; 783 5804). In Cambridge and Somerville, there's the **Bicycle Workshop** (259 Massachusetts Avenue, Cambridge; 876 6555) or **WheelWorks** (145 Elm Street, Somerville; 776 2100). The latter also stocks *Ride*, a locally-produced 'zine chronicling the New England racing scene.

Fitness centres & gyms

YWCA

140 Clarendon Street, at Stuart Street (351 7600). Back Bay T. **Open** 8am-7pm Mon-Fri. **Membership** $50 per year; $10 drop-in fee. **Credit** MC, V. **Map 5 F5**
Disabled: toilet.

Metropolitan Health Club

209 Columbus Avenue, at Berkeley Street (536 3006). Back Bay T. **Open** 6-11pm Mon-Fri; 8am-9pm Sat; 9am-9pm Sun. **Membership** $55 per month, $12 drop-in fee. **Credit** AmEx, Disc, MC, V. **Map 5 F5**
Disabled: toilet.

Health Works Fitness Center for Women

441 Stuart Street, at Dartmouth Street (859 7700). Back Bay or Copley T. **Open** 6am-10pm Mon-Fri; 8am-7pm Sat, Sun. **Rates** $12 drop-in fee. **Credit** MC, V. **Map 3 F5**
Disabled: toilet.

Golf courses

The following are public courses.

Fresh Pond Golf Course

691 Huron Avenue, at Fresh Pond Parkway, Cambridge (349 6282). Alewife T. **Open** *Apr-Nov* 5.30am-dusk daily. **Rates** $16-$29. **No credit cards.**
Disabled: toilet.

George Wright Golf Course

420 West Street, Hyde Park (361 8313). Bus 50. **Open** 5.30am-9pm daily. **Rates** $12-$27. **Credit** MC, V.

Leo J Martin Memorial Golf Course

190 Park Road, Weston (1-781 894 4903). Riverside T. **Open** *18 Apr-20 Nov* dawn-dusk daily. **Rates** $10-$20. **Credit** MC, V.

Newton Commonwealth Golf Course

212 Kenrick Street, Newton (630 1971). Boston College T. **Open** dawn-dusk daily. **Rates** $10-$30. **Credit** MC, V.
Disabled: toilet.

Ponkapoag Golf Course

2167 Washington Street, Canton, MA (1-781 828 4242). **Open** 6am-3pm Mon-Fri. **Rates** $17-$20. **Credit** MC, V.
Disabled: toilet.

Putterham Meadows Golf Course

1281 West Roxbury Parkway, Brookline (730 2078/2079). Chestnut Hill T. **Open** dawn-dusk daily. **Rates** $22-$32; *lessons* $35 per half hour. **Credit** AmEx, MC, V.

Lessons

Will J Devine Gold Club

Franklin Park, 1 Circuit Drive, Dorchester (265 4084). Bus 22. **Open** dawn-dusk daily. **Rates** $11-$25. **Credit** AmEx, Disc, MC, V.

This is the second-oldest public course in America.

In-line skating/rollerblading

If you like to skate, you've come to the right place. Boston and nearby cities offer a plethora of paved trails and roadways for the inveterate eight-wheeler. Both novices and experienced skaters

There's no going off the rails on Boston's bike trails. See also page 265 **Directory**.

should check out the Charles River Bike Path or the Minuteman Bike Trail (*see page 265* **Directory**). If you want to get in a good workout, hit the trail before 10am on weekend mornings, otherwise you'll run into major traffic – all the other runners, walkers, skaters and bikers.

If you want to hire or buy blades, try the **Beacon Hill Skate Shop** (135 Charles Street; 482 7400). *See also above* **Cycling**.

Pool & billiards

It's not uncommon to find a pool table plunked down in the middle (or off to one corner) of a Boston bar. But if you really want to play, check out the **Boston Billiard Club** (126 Brookline Avenue; 536 7665). Also worth visiting are **Sully's Billiards** in Allston (445 Cambridge Street; 254 9851) and **Flattop Johnny's** in Cambridge (1 Kendall Square; 494 9565).

Racquetball (squash)

Boston Athletic Center

653 Summer Street, at D Street (269 4300). South Station T. **Open** 5.30am-11pm Mon-Fri; 8am-8pm Sat, Sun. **Rates** $8-$15. **Credit** AmEx, Disc, MC, V.
Map 3 H/J 5/6
Disabled: toilet.

Rowing

Charles River Canoe and Kayak

2401 Commonwealth Avenue, Newton (965 5110). Riverside T. **Open** *1 Apr-31 Oct* 10am-sunset Mon-Fri; 9am-sunset Sat, Sun. **Rates** *rental* $9-$10 per hour. **Credit** Disc, MC, V.

Running

Local runners flock to the Minuteman Bike Path and the Charles River Bike Path at the weekend (*see page 265* **Directory**), but both are especially good for those wanting a long run: the Charles River Bike Path provides an 18-mile (29-kilometre) round trip on knee-forgiving asphalt, and you can get in a 22-mile (35-kilometre) run if you do the Minuteman trail both ways, starting at Davis Square in Somerville (with the added bonus that the miles are marked on the path). To run off the beaten path, however, check out the trails in the 2,060-acre (834-hectare) **Middlesex Fells Reservation** (off Route 28 in Malden, Medford, Stoneham & Winchester; 1-781-322-2851).

The annual **Boston Marathon** is held in April (*see page 38* **Boston by Season**). Although you must meet a time qualification in a previous race to register officially, the race sees its fair share of illegal entries every year. Unlike, say, the New York Marathon, it's pretty easy to jump into the Boston Marathon. The **Tufts Healthplan 10K** for women is held on Columbus Day (11 October) and usually attracts big-name racers. Phone 1-888 767 7223 for details.

Skateboarding

Folks who work for the skateboard magazine *Thrasher* love Boston. With its cobblestoned streets, cracked sidewalks and numerous handrails, stairs, curb cuts and ledges all concentrated within a small space, Boston is a great place in which to skate.

In addition to the parks listed below, the **Metropolitan District Commission (MDC)** playground in Brighton (between Soldiers Field Road and the Charles River) features rolling concrete banks and other great obstacles. The area in front of the **Boston Medical Center** (near the intersection of Massachusetts and Harrison Avenues) has enormous curved brick banks that attract skateboarders from all over the city and the **Christian Science** complex on Huntington Avenue (*see page 66* **Sightseeing**) is another good spot. *See also page 271* **Directory**.

Maximus Skate Park

324 Rindge Avenue, at Massachusetts Avenue, Cambridge (576 4723). Alewife T. **Open** noon-8pm daily. **Rates** $10 per day. **Credit** AmEx, Disc, MC, V.

Eight Ball Skate Park

Route 140, Bellingham (1-508 966 3613). **Open** 3pm-9pm Tue-Fri; 1pm-8pm Sat, Sun. **Rates** $4-$10. **Credit** MC, V.

Underground Snowboards

860 Commonwealth Avenue, at Boston University, Brookline (232 8680). BU West T. **Open** 10am-9pm Mon-Fri; 9.30am-6pm Sat; noon-5pm Sun. **Credit** AmEx, Disc, MC, V.

Skiing

Aficionados of the sport have been known to make fun of New England skiing, with its rocky trails and slushy snow, but there's some good downhill action to be had in the northern states. In the last decade most New England resorts – including the big ones, **Killington**, **Sunday River** and **Sugarbush** – have brought the art of snow making to a new level. In other words, as long as the temperature co-operates, there will be snow to ski on, regardless of snowfall. It's possible for road warriors to zip up Route 93 North to **Loon Mountain** on the Kancamagus Highway or to **Cannon Mountain** in Franconia Notch Parkway, both in New Hampshire, for a day trip's worth of skiing, but you'll thank yourself if you set aside a weekend for the excursion. *See page 253* **Trips Out of Town** for more details.

For those who can't afford to leave the city, try the **Blue Hills** (4001 Washington Street, Milton, MA; 1-781 828 7300). It's not the most challenging terrain and snow conditions are entirely dependent on the weather, but it's just a 15-minute drive from Boston and you can get in a few runs in an afternoon if that's what you're after.

The **Ski Market** (860 Commonwealth Avenue, near Boston University Bridge; 731 6100) not only sells all sorts of ski and snowboard gear, but can be used as a resource for New England skiing and local events.

Swimming

By July and August the ocean has warmed up enough to go swimming. Boston and its environs have a number of beaches run by the **Metropolitan District Commission** (727 9547); the New England coastline is also dotted with beautiful strips of sand and sparkling blue water.

Good local beaches include **Carson Beach**, at Day Boulevard, South Boston, **Castle Island**, also in South Boston, **Revere Beach**, on Revere Beach Parkway, and the beach at **Lynn**, on the northeast edge of Greater Boston.

If you'd rather visit a pond, you're in luck. If you're willing to travel, you can visit Walden Pond in Concord, the site where Henry David Thoreau penned *Walden* (*see page 235* **Trips Out of Town**).

The Metropolitan District Commission also operates **public pools** in the Boston area. These are open daily from late June to early September; phone 727 1300 to find out the location of your nearest pool.

Tennis

Public tennis courts in Boston are available on a first-come, first-served basis. The City of Boston operates a number of them, as does the Metropolitan District Commission. The most centrally-located court is on **Boston Common**, on Beacon Street (phone the Parks Recreation Department on 635 4505 to book it). For complete listings, consult the phone book or contact the MDC (*see above* **Swimming**).

Trips Out of Town

Trips Out of Town

A visit to Boston wouldn't be complete without a sample of the surrounding area: read on for the highlights of the six states of New England.

Because Boston, the 'Hub City', is at the geographical heart of New England, a three- or four-hour drive out of town in any direction takes you into what is, culturally and historically, the richest part of the American landscape. The physical landscape has its share of splendour, too.

The cities and towns surrounding Boston tend to be extremely conscious of their historical heritage and, since a good part of their livelihood often springs from the tourism that history generates, they diligently preserve the traces of the past. The carefully tended landmarks at Plymouth and Salem, the painstaking restorations at Mystic Seaport and Old Sturbidge, and the grand mansions of Newport are all an easy day's excursion from Boston.

The high level of literacy that is part of the New England tradition and the proliferation of colleges and universities across the region generate a grand array of musical and artistic events throughout the warmer months. Massachusetts alone has classical music at Tanglewood, dance at Jacob's Pillow and theatre at Williamstown. Newport, Rhode Island has jazz, blues and folk festivals and Burlington, Vermont has a major reggae gathering.

In the realm of natural beauty, the New England countryside has drawn urbanites at least since the day Henry David Thoreau beat it out of Concord and set up his shack at Walden Pond. And since the environmental consciousness he spawned runs strong in New England to this day, that landscape is near-sacred. The Green Mountains of Vermont, the White Mountains of New Hampshire, the Berkshires in Massachusetts and Connecticut's Litchfield Hills offer touring, lodging and recreation facilities that run the gamut from grand resort hotels to rustic country inns and quaint B&Bs. Hiking and cycling are major local pastimes in spring, summer and fall; skiers arrive from all over the USA in the winter. The seashore along Cape Cod, the islands of Nantucket and Martha's Vineyard and the rugged, rocky Maine coast rank high in the pantheon of great American vistas. Every direction out of Boston has its share of rewards.

Hotel chains

For those who want predictable accommodation and prices, all the major hotel chains do business extensively throughout New England. For recommended lodging en route, see the relevant sections in this chapter.

Best Western (1-800 528 1234)
Comfort Inns (1-800 228 5150)
Days Inn (1-800 222 3297)
Holiday Inn (1-800 465 4329)
Howard Johnson (1-800 654 2000)
Hyatt (1-800 233 1234)
Marriott (1-800 228 9290)
Motel 6 (1-800 466 8356)
Quality Inns (1-800 228 5151)
Radisson (1-800 333 3333)
Ramada Inn (1-800 272 6232)
Red Roof (1-800 843 7663)
Super 8 (1-800 800 8000)
Travelodge (1-800 255 3050)

TRANSPORT

The classic New England farmer's rejoinder to the confused tourist is 'you can't get there from here!'. He's wrong. As the oldest continually settled part of the American continent, New England's network of roadways is extensive and well-maintained. Rent a car and you'll find that the terrors of Boston traffic are but a grotesque anomaly, and if you venture into rural New England, the courtesy and diffidence of the motorists may actually confuse you.

Boston has branches of all the major car rental firms, plus a number of smaller, local outfits (*see page 264* **Directory**). The latters' cars won't look quite as flash but are a good deal cheaper. When shopping around, ask if the rates include tax (often quite high) and insurance. And you might want to visit a branch of the **AAA** to stock up on maps and get help on planning your trip (*see page 264* **Directory**).

Public transport in New England may not be up to European standards but is still better than average for the USA. Rail services – whether MBTA Commuter Rail or Amtrak – run frequently along the main urban corridors throughout most of the day and into the evening, and the region is

A New England point of hue

The turning of the leaves in New England is one of the touchstones of American life, right up there with mom and apple pie. Every fall the normally sedate countryside explodes in a brief but dramatic pageant of colour that natives catalogue by the year and store in memory like vintage wines in a cellar.

The emergence of the colours with the turn of the seasons results from changes in leaf chemistry produced by shorter daylight hours and cooler temperatures. As the leaves shut down chlorophyll production, first the yellow of carotenes then the red of sugars comes to the fore. At the very last, only the brown of tannins remains. Warm, sunny days and moderately cool nights make for the most pronounced palette. Leaves directly exposed to the sun tend toward red, those in the shade toward yellow. The salting of highways occasionally results in the phenomenon of trees with one side a blaze of colour and the other still green.

New England's forests are particularly colourful because of their concentrations of aspen, hickory, birch and ash – for gold and yellow – and maples and oaks – for orange and red. The deep carpet of evergreen in the more northern part of the mix makes for a stunning contrast.

For Vermont, New Hampshire and western Massachusetts particularly, this is peak tourist season – the invasion of the leaf peepers. Road traffic slows to a crawl on the state and local roadways (so much the better for the packs of touring cyclists) and the trails are full of backpackers. If you plan to visit the New England countryside in foliage season – generally mid-September to mid-October – make your arrangements well in advance. Months in advance.

You may want to simplify the process by using one of the many foliage touring services, which come in a variety of formats. Go by bus with **TLC Tours** (1-800 624 4216), by bicycle with **Vermont Bicycle Tours** (1-800 453 8680), on foot with **New England Hiking Holidays** (1-800 869 0949) or up in the air with **Balloons Over New England** (1-800 788 5562). A good online source for these providers and a wealth of further information can be found at **New England.com** (www.newengland. com). All of the New England states have separate numbers for reports on local foliage conditions:

Connecticut (1-800 282 6863)
Maine (1-800 533 9595)
Massachusetts (1-800 632 8038)
New Hampshire (1-800 262 6660)
Rhode Island (1-800 556 2484)
Vermont (1-800 837 6668)

blanketed by bus services. Public transport within the larger cities is quite good, but many of the most interesting destinations are small towns, so you'll need a car to explore these. Also, much of the flavour of New England is best sampled by merely driving along its back roads.

If you're a keen cyclist, head for Cape Cod, the Berkshires, the Maine coast, the lake region of New Hampshire or anywhere in Vermont – all of which have wonderful biking terrain.

Trains

Amtrak runs along two branches between New Haven, Connecticut and Boston, as well as up the Connecticut River Valley and across northern Vermont. The **Massachusetts Bay Transportation Authority (MBTA)** runs regular Commuter Rail train services to most destinations within half an hour of Boston, from Plymouth in the south to Cape Ann in the north.

Amtrak

(Information 1-800 872 7245/482 36603).
Trains depart from South Station, 700 Atlantic Avenue and Back Bay Station, 145 Dartmouth Street.
Website: www.amtrak.com

MBTA Communter Rail

(Information 222 3200).
Trains depart from North Station, Causeway Street and South Station, 700 Atlantic Avenue.
Website: www.mbta.com

Buses

The **South Station Transportation Center** (700 Atlantic Avenue, at Summer Street in the South End) is the main depot for regional bus services. Major companies that run services to greater New England include **Greyhound**, **Bonanza** and **Peter Pan**. For details of other services, *see page* 263 **Directory**.

Bonanza

Information (1-800 556 3815).

Greyhound

Information (1-800 231 2222).
Website www.greyhound.com

Peter Pan

Information (1-800 237 8747).

The colonial circuit

These sites are America's great secular shrines. Just as you don't go to Mecca without ogling the Kabaa, you don't pass through the Massachusetts Bay Colony without paying homage to the founding families.

Plymouth

Plymouth Rock may not be the very spot where the Pilgrims landed, but it's come to be taken as fact. Even so, it has been moved several times over the years, broken in two on one such occasion, and only came to rest at its present location in 1867. The rock itself is rather unimpressive, especially compared to the monstrous, neo-classical monument that guards and dwarfs it. A replica of the ship the Pilgrims rode in on is docked close at hand. **Mayflower II** (State Pier, Water Street; 1-508 746 1622; open daily March-November) is a full-scale version of the original, with a staff of performers in seventeenth-century garb who recount the tale of the Pilgrims' struggles.

Plymouth itself is full of narrow streets and seventeenth- and eighteenth-century houses, most of which are open to the public, appropriately furnished and staffed by guides in period costume. If you can stomach any more silver-buckled shoes and big black hats, truck on over to the **Plimoth Plantation** (Warren Avenue, off Route 3A South at Exit 4; 1-508 746 1622; open daily March-November), where an in-depth re-creation of the original 1627 settlement includes a village full of actors who speak, work, play, eat and breathe as authentic a re-enactment of seventeenth-century life as is humanly possible.

Where to stay & eat

Dining in Plymouth is a briny business. Join the locals for the inexpensive, top-notch fish and shellfish at the **Lobster Hut** (Town Wharf; 1-508 746 2270), a self-service affair with an outstanding view. Stare down your fear of cholesterol and order one of the seafood rolls – fried scallops, clams or shrimps in a bun. Or go a bit more upmarket at **Issac's**, which offers another great ocean view and more elaborate seafood preparations (114 Water Street; 1-508 830 0001).

Plymouth has a number of serviceable, if undistinguished motels within convenient reach of downtown and its attractions. A more pleasant and quieter choice, one with its own private beach, is the **Pilgrim Sands Motel** (150 Warren Avenue; 1-800 729 72637; rooms $60-$130), a few miles out of town but just a short walk from the Plimoth Plantation. For a B&B near the harbour, try the **Mabbett House** (7 Cushman Street; 1-800 572 7829; rooms $100-$180), a fine old colonial residence tastefully furnished with a collection of European antiques.

Getting there

Plymouth is an hour south of Boston by train, or about halfway to Cape Cod if you're driving, so you can make a daytrip out of a visit, or catch it on the fly. There are numerous organised tours of the area. Phone the **Plymouth Chamber of Commerce** (*see below*) for more details.

By car

Plymouth is 40 miles (64km) southeast of Boston on the I-93 (Southeast Expressway) to Route 3. Take Exit 6 (roughly 45 minutes' drive, depending on the traffic).

By bus or rail

Plymouth is an hour by train from Boston. **MBTA Commuter Rail** (*see p231*) runs daily services from South Station. Buses also leave from South Station.

Tourist information

Plymouth Chamber of Commerce

225 Water Street, Plymouth (1-508 830 1620).
Open 9am-5pm daily.
Website www.plymouthchamber.com

Plymouth Visitors' Center

130 Water Street, Plymouth (1-508 747 7533/1-800 872 1620). **Open** *summer* 9am-5pm Mon-Fri, 9am-7pm Sat, Sun; *winter* 9am-5pm Mon-Sat.

Salem & Marblehead

If any town ever made a silk purse out of a sow's ear, it's Salem. While there's more to its history than the notorious witchcraft trials of 1692, that event still colours its name more than 300 years later. The residents, however, have managed to turn a black mark into both a local industry and a curious point of pride, or at least an identity. Both the city's police cars and the local paper sport caricatures of witch's profiles as their logos.

Witchcraft-related points of interest include the **Witch House** (310½ Essex Street; 1-508 744 0180; open daily), where some 200 unfortunates were questioned about their supposed dealings with Old Scratch, the **Salem Wax Museum** (288 Derby Street; 1-508 740 2929/www.salem waxmuseum.com; open daily), and the **Salem Witch Museum** (19½ Washington Square; 1-978 744 1692/www.salemwitchmuseum.com; open daily), which features a very thorough and scary 3D mixed-media re-enactment of the Puritan hysteria.

Old downtown Salem, off the Common, is a National Historic District and has a wealth of architecturally interesting streets. In the heart of the area is the **Peabody Essex Museum** (*see page 96* **Museums & Galleries**), founded by the East India Maritime Company in the late-

A pressing engagement at the **Salem Witch Museum**. *See page 232.*

eighteenth century, when Salem was at the peak of its glory and dominated the shipping trade to China. The Peabody collection documents the history of whaling and merchant shipping, and features a vast collection of exhibits from the sailors' travels; the Essex Institute serves as the local historical society.

A more fully fleshed out representation of Salem's seagoing past is found aboard the **Friendship** (docked at Central Wharf, at the end of Derby Street; 1-978 740 1660; closed for reconstruction until 2000), a full-scale replica of a three-masted 1797 East India merchant ship. It is docked at the end of Derby Street, amid the nine-acre (3.6-hectare) **Salem Maritime National Historic Site** (174 Derby Street; 1-978 740 1660; open daily), which offers tours of reconstructions of wharves, warehouses and stores of the time, as well as the old Customs House where Nathaniel Hawthorne worked before the publication of *The Scarlet Letter*.

Salem's most famous native son, Hawthorne took the inspiration for his other great novel from the **House of the Seven Gables** (54 Turner Street; 1-978 744 0991; open daily), a seventeenth-century building that, like so many others in town, is stuffed with period furniture and staffed by guides in period costume. (For more on Hawthorne, *see chapter* **Literary Boston**.) There's more of the same at the **Pioneer Village** (Forest River Park, West Avenue; 1-978 745 0525; open daily), where the whole Puritan settlement of 1630 has been recreated.

Nearby **Marblehead**, on the south shore of Salem Bay, is another significant eighteenth-century shipping centre with a well-preserved historic district of ancient houses and winding streets, and a spectacular coastal setting. The municipal offices at **Abbott Hall** (180 Washington Street; 1-781 631 0528; open Mon-Fri) contain the original copy of the oft-reproduced painting *Spirit of '76*, with the iconic Revolutionary fife and drum threesome. Marblehead styles itself as the 'Yachting Capital of America', and **Race Week**, at the end of July, is a highlight of American sailing competition; throughout the rest of the season, boats of every description ply the outer harbour and waterways.

Where to stay & eat

Salem has dining options of various sorts along Pickering Wharf, where there's a great view of the seascape. **Chase House** (Pickering Wharf; 1-978 744 0000) serves traditional New England seafood; or you can dine in the building where Alexander Graham Bell conducted some of his early telephone experiments, the **Lyceum Bar & Grill** (43 Church Street; 1-978 745 7665), which offers contemporary American cuisine in refined surroundings.

Lodging in Salem, besides the usual hotel chains, features a range of more colourful possibilities. There are several historic choices at **Salem Inn** (7 Summer Street; 1-800 446 2995; rooms $119-$270), a complex of two ships' captains' homes both on the National Register of

Historic Places, and the recently refurbished 1874 **Peabody House**. The **Hawthorne Hotel** (18 Washington Square West; 1-978 744 4080; rooms $104-$285), while not as old as its name suggests, offers a full hotel service in the grand manner, is close to all the sights, is nicely furnished and maintained, and reasonably priced for all that. You can save some money a little further off the Common at the **Amelia Payson B&B** (16 Winter Street; 1-978 744 8304; rooms $75-$130) – an 1845 Greek Revival structure with a piano in the parlour. Or save even more at the **Coach House Inn** (284 Lafayette Street; 1-800 688 8689; rooms $80-$130), another nineteenth-century ship's captain's mansion, elegantly fashioned.

Lodging downtown in Marblehead can be a bit pricey, though it may be worth it at the likes of the **Harbor Light Inn** (58 Washington Street; 1-781 631 1069; rooms $125-$245), whose two refurbished eighteenth-century buildings offer an intriguing mix of history and modern convenience. Local dining may not be outstanding but decent fare and a fine view can be had nearby at both the **Barnacle** (141 Front Street; 1-781 631 4236) and the **Driftwood** (63 Front Street; 1-781 631 1145).

Getting there

By car

Salem is 16 miles (26km) north of Boston. Take Route 193N to Exit 37A (195N) onto Route 128N and follow the signs. The journey can take anything from 30 minutes to an hour, depending on traffic. Marblehead is 5 miles (8km) closer to Boston.

By bus, boat or rail

The journey to Salem by rail takes half an hour by **MBTA Commuter Rail** (*see p231*) out of North Station. **Harbor Express** (376 8417) runs a daily ferry service to Salem from Pickering Wharf; the journey takes an hour. Buses 441 and 442 run from outside Haymarket T to Marblehead daily; the journey takes just under an hour.

Tourist information

Salem National Visitors' Center

2 New Liberty Street, Salem (1-978 740 1650).
Open 9am-5pm daily.

Lexington & Concord

These two Boston suburbs are inextricably linked in the historical imagination as the scene of the first skirmishes of the American Revolution. Paul Revere rode through here with the famous warning that King George's Redcoats were coming in search of arms caches. A group of the American colonists' Minutemen interrupted their procession at Lexington Green and suffered eight deaths for their troubles (*see page 8* **History**). The tables were turned at Concord's North Bridge, the British troops began a long, bloody withdrawal to Boston, and the gloves were off.

Concord is further distinguished by its place in American letters: the epicentre of Transcenden-talism, the first great school of American literature and one that prefigured its enduring attraction to mysticism and the Orient. It was the residence in both life and death of Ralph Waldo Emerson, Henry David Thoreau, Louisa May Alcott and Nathaniel Hawthorne.

All the major sights of **Lexington** are centred around **Lexington Green**, a triangular plot anchored by the **Minuteman Statue** and dotted with markers and memorials of the day of battle. A diorama at the **Lexington Visitors' Center** (*see page 235*) outlines all the particulars of the event and there is a re-enactment of the affair every year on Patriots' Day, the Monday nearest 19 April (*see page 38* **Boston by Season**).

The **Lexington Historical Society** (1-781 862 1703) offers tours of three late seventeenth-century houses that figured significantly in the battle. The **Buckman Tavern** (1 Bedford Street; 1-781 852 5598; open daily March-October), directly on the Green, is where the Minutemen assembled in wait for the British and where they set up their field hospital. The **Hancock-Clarke House** (36 Hancock Street; 1-781 852 5598; open daily May-September), north of the Green, is where the rabble-rousers Samuel Adams and John Hancock had taken refuge from the king's men in Boston and where they were awakened in the night by Paul Revere and hustled out of town. About a mile east of the Green, the **Munroe Tavern** (1332 Massachusetts Avenue; 1-781 852 5598) served as the British command post during the fight and the assembly point for their retreat in the aftermath.

A broader take on American history is available at the **Museum of Our National Heritage** (*see page 96* **Museums & Galleries**) and at the **George Abbott Smith Museum** (7 Jason Street; 1-781 648 4300; open Mon-Fri), in nearby Arlington, which both offer rotating exhibitions on aspects of American society and popular culture.

Concord's share of historical sites includes the chief part of **Minute Man National Historical Park** (174 Liberty Street, off route 2A; 1-978 362 6944; open daily), where another Minuteman statue stands at one end of a reconstruction of the North Bridge and a plaque on the far bank recalls the British dead. The **North Bridge Visitors' Center** (*see page 235*) holds a diorama and a collection of Revolutionary War memorabilia and offers guided tours of the site. The Battle Road section of the park, lined with informational markers, stretches out along the first few miles of the British line of retreat to Lexington and Boston. The **Minute Man National Historical Park Visitors' Center**

is located about a mile east of the North Bridge site (*see below*).

The landmarks of Concord's days as an intellectual beacon reflect how remarkably condensed its gathering of genius was. Within a few short blocks you'll find a group of homes that once contained an unparalleled flowering of American literary genius. All the buildings contain carefully preserved artefacts of their inhabitants and are open to the touring public, though schedules vary and most of them are closed in the winter (*see page 28* **Literary Boston**).

The essayist Ralph Waldo Emerson, the key figure in the Transcendentalist movement, lived for most of his life at 28 Cambridge Turnpike (**Ralph Waldo Emerson House** 1-978 369 2236; open Thur-Sun, April-October). The steep colonial roof of the **Old Manse** (269 Monument Street; 1-978 369 3909; open daily) sheltered both Emerson and Nathaniel Hawthorne at different times, and the stories the house inspired were Hawthorne's first claim to fame. The **Orchard House** (399 Lexington Road; 1-978 369 4118; open daily) was home to the educator Bronson Alcott, another prominent Transcendentalist, though its best-known resident was his daughter Louisa May, who wrote *Little Women* here. She also lived for a time at the **Wayside** (455 Lexington Road; 1-978 369 6975), where Hawthorne later came to spend his final years.

The living embodiment of Transcendentalist practice, the first hippie and the father of environmentalism, Henry David Thoreau set up shop south of town on Route 126 at **Walden Pond**. The original one-room cabin, where he sought to live the simple life, is long since gone – only a pile of stones marks the spot – but the well-conserved **Walden Pond State Reservation** (915 Walden Street; 1-978 369 3254; open daily) that now encompasses the area still affords the kind of swimming and hiking that the native seer advocated. If you must, you can visit one of the two full-size, exactly furnished replicas of the original cabin, one near the reservation parking lot and the other in town, at the **Thoreau Lyceum**, which also houses a collection of the naturalist's letters and memorabilia and is situated at the **Concord Museum** (*see page 93* **Museums & Galleries**).

Where to stay & eat

Dining and lodging in Lexington is pretty much limited to the usual franchises and chains. Concord has two inns downtown with a fair amount of history: the nineteenth-century **Hawthorne** (462 Lexington Road; 1-978 369 5610; rooms $85-$225) and the eighteenth-century **Colonial Inn** (48 Monument Square; 1-978 369 9200; rooms $135-$189), both of them a bit pricey.

The **Minuteman Statue**, *Lexington (p234).*

Getting there

By car

Lexington is 9 miles (14.4km) northwest of Boston on Route 128 (I-95). Concord is 18 miles (29km) northwest of Boston and 6 miles (9.7km) west of Lexington. Take Route 2A from Lexington, or Route 2 from Boston.

By bus & rail

The **MBTA Commuter Rail** (*see p231*) service covers both towns, Lexington by bus only, Concord by train only. Awkwardly, there is no public transport connection between the two. Both services leave from North Station.

Tourist information

Minute Man National Historical Park Visitors' Center

174 Liberty Street, off Route 2A, Lexington (1-978 362 6944). **Open** 9am-4pm daily.

Lexington Visitors' Center

Lexington Green, 1875 Massachusetts Avenue, Lexington (1-781 862 1450). **Open** 9am-5pm daily.

North Bridge Visitors' Center

174 Liberty Street, North Bridge (1-978 369 6993). **Open** 9am-4pm daily.

Maritime Massachusetts

Cape Ann

A brusque neck of land perched in the Atlantic, Cape Ann is Cape Cod's rugged twin. Like its sister, it has a generous share of sandy beaches, but it's granite and stone that make it distinctive. High, rocky ledges loom over the coastline and much of the landscape shows the wear of glaciation and the terminal moraine left in the last glacier's wake.

This is maritime Massachusetts at its most rigorous, a place where the sea has been serious business since the earliest days of settlement. **Gloucester**, the main town, with its magnificently sheltered harbour, has been a centre of the fishing industry since 1623. The first fishing schooners were designed and built here and it was the world's chief fishing port in the nineteenth century. While the industry has faded in recent years, Gloucester is still a significant processing centre for factory fishing fleets.

Some 10,000 Gloucestermen are said to have died at sea over the years and the town's tribute to them, the bronze statue popularly known as 'the Man at the Wheel', stands guard on the harbour promenade, just off Western Avenue. For more information on this hazardous occupation contact the **Cape Ann Historical Museum** (27 Pleasant Street; 1-978 283 0455; open Tue-Sun except February), which is dedicated to maritime and other aspects of local history *(see page 93* **Museums & Galleries**).

Those who have a taste for kitsch on a truly monumental scale should take Route 127 south of town, then turn down Hesperus Avenue to **Hammond Castle** (80 Hesperus Avenue; 1-978 283 2080; open Sat, Sun, May-September), a full-scale stone replica of a medieval castle, complete with drawbridge, built to order for an eccentric inventor and multi-millionaire of the 1920s. The castle's whimsical view takes in the reef of Norman's Woe, cited in Longfellow's poem *Wreck of the Hesperus*, though the Hesperus sank elsewhere and Longfellow had never seen the place.

The town of **Rockport**, further east on the Cape, takes its name from the granite quarries that were long its chief income. Rockport's sedate charms have drawn tourists since the 1840s and it is home to a long-established artist's colony. The artists come to drink in the views of the ocean and of weatherworn houses on narrow streets. One old lobster shack on the town wharf is so frequently depicted by artists that it's known locally as 'Motif Number One'.

For an interesting trip north of Cape Ann take Routes 133 and 1A to **Newburyport**, an old maritime centre that boasts many fine Federal-style mansions. Stop along the way at **Woodman's** (126 Rear Main Street; 1-800 649 1773) in Essex, a big old barn of a place where that New England staple the fried clam was invented in 1916. Prices are low, portions are huge, and the hand-lettered signs and picnic table seating make Woodman's a regional classic. You can also take a peek at **Ipswich**, which has the largest extant collection of seventeenth-century houses in America.

After Newburyport, head out over the causeway to **Plum Island**, where a national wildlife refuge includes seven miles (11.3 kilometres) of wide, sandy beach. The dunes and marshes serve as waystation to tens of thousands of migratory geese and ducks and permanent home to hundreds of other species of flora and fauna. Among the best beaches on Cape Ann proper are **Wingaersheek Beach**, on the north shore, and **Good Harbor** and **Long Beach**, on the south. South of Gloucester, at **Rafe's Chasm Park**, the granite ledges open to a chasm 200 feet (61 metres) long and 60 feet (18.3 metres) deep, where the tides often produce some striking sights and sounds. East of town, **Pebble Beach** offers an unusual shoreline of timeworn stones stretching far to the horizon. **Singing Beach**, some 15 miles (24 kilometres) west of Newburyport, is another local favourite.

Where to stay

Gloucester came late to tourism so lodgings tend to be in contemporary motel style. More interesting choices include Rockport's **Addison Choate Inn** (49 Broadway; 1-800 245 7543; rooms $95-$140), a Greek Revival house from the 1850s, and the **Inn on Cove Hill** (37 Mount Pleasant Street; 1-978 546 2701; rooms $71-$101), a Federal-style structure from the 1790s, reputedly built with the proceeds from a discovered cache of pirates' loot. Phone the **Cape Ann Chamber of Commerce**'s hotel hotline for last-minute bookings (*see page 237*). For dining, **Evie's Rudder** (73 Rocky Neck Avenue; 1-978 283 7967; closed in winter) in the heart of the Rocky Neck Art Colony, features a moderately-priced, eclectic menu, quirky bric-à-brac décor and a festive atmosphere. The **White Rainbow** (65 Main Street; 1-978 281 0017) is a more expensive choice, with nouvelle American dishes served by candlelight.

Getting there

By car

Gloucester is 30 miles (48km) northeast of Boston on Route 1 or I-93; Rockport is 40 miles (64km) from Boston, and 7 miles (11.3km) north of Gloucester on Routes 127 or 127A.

By bus & rail

MBTA Commuter Rail (*see p231*) runs trains to Gloucester from North Station. The bus service on the Cape Ann peninsula is run by the **Cape Ann Transportation Authority** (CATA; 1-978 283 7916).

Tourist information

Cape Ann Chamber of Commerce

33 Commercial Street, Gloucester (1-978 283 1601/ hotel hotline 1-800 321 0133). **Open** 8am-5pm Mon-Fri.

Cape Cod

For many New Englanders, the only true cape is the one named after the fish that was long the salty staff of regional life – Cape Cod. A spit of sand 65 miles (105 kilometres) long that curls out into the Atlantic like a bodybuilder's flexed arm, the Cape was born of the sand deposits left in the last glacier's retreat. Because the Cape has no bedrock and is so exposed to wind and current, sections of its coastline still change radically from year to year.

Provincetown, snug in the Cape's fist, is where the Pilgrims first set foot on the continent and where they drew up the Mayflower Compact that laid the foundations of their government. The Puritans might not be too happy about what has come in their wake – one of the oldest centres of openly gay life in the USA and a summertime honky-tonk that blankets the Cape with millions of visitors every summer.

If possible, visit the area during the off-season, when its essential nature and quieter charms are better appreciated. Although many Cape businesses close by late fall, you'll have the dunes and beaches to yourself and find lodging at bargain rates.

Sandwich, on the upper Cape, dates back to 1637 and is the oldest permanent settlement on Cape Cod. During the nineteenth century it became a centre of the American glass-making industry, the local artisans' ovens fuelled by the plentiful surrounding scrub brush. The town's **Glass Museum** (129 Main Street; 1-508 888 0251; open daily) contains a wealth of sparkling examples of the work of those craftsmen.

Not far away, the **Heritage Plantation** (67 Grove Street, 1-508 888 3300; open April-October) is a hodge-podge of objects ranging from antique cars to Currier & Ives prints and antique firearms. It includes several museums and a Shaker barn built on 76 acres (30.5 hectares) of grounds, and

Whale watching

Environmentalism is deeply ingrained throughout New England, partly because the natives have seen how easily nature can be ravaged. The depletion of fishing stocks in the North Atlantic in the 1970s is a prime example. In the hard times that followed, residents of many seaside towns drew on their new awareness, flavoured it with a pinch of traditional Yankee resourcefulness and, making a virtue of necessity, introduced something new to the tourist trade – whale watching.

Some form of this recreation has gone on in the region at least since the 1950s, but in the last 20 years it has become a major phenomenon – every New England state, except landlocked Vermont, offers a taste of it. Most of the activity is concentrated along coastal Massachusetts and Maine, because of their proximity to the **Stellwagen Bank**, a prime feeding ground for whales of all species. It's a rare voyage that fails to finds at least a handful of the giants at play, and often the show is so lively that it seems as if they have a bit of the ham in them. Their brainy cousin dolphins frequently take the stage as well.

The viewing runs from late spring to early autumn, since the North Atlantic is notoriously rough in the colder months. It's a lengthy voyage

out, however – more than 20 miles (32 kilometres) to the main stage – and warm clothes and waterproof covering is a good idea at any time of year.

Whale watching cruises include the **East India Co.** (57 Wharf Street; 1-978 741 0434) in Salem; **Cape Ann Whale Watch** (415 Main Street; 1-800 877 5110) in Gloucester, on Cape Ann; **Dolphin Fleet** (MacMillan Wharf; 1-800 826 9300), in Provincetown, on Cape Cod; and the ships **Indian** (1-207 967 5912) and **Nautilus** (1-207 967 5595) in Kennebunkport, Maine.

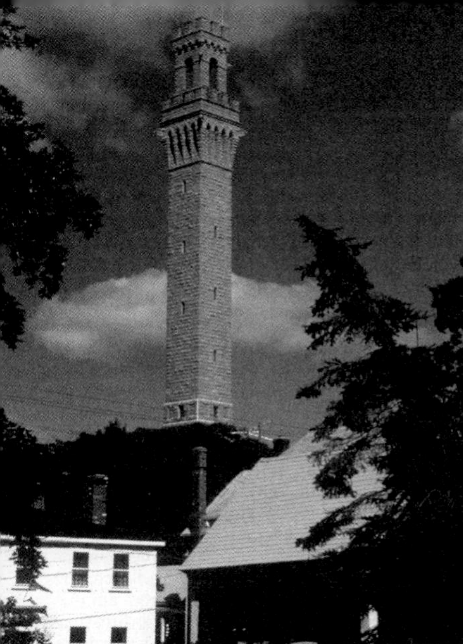

Pilgrim Monument, *Provincetown (p239).*

offers children free jitney rides and a turn-of-the-century carousel.

Woods Hole, on the Cape's far southwest tip, is one of the world's great centres of maritime research. The **Woods Hole Oceanographic Institute** (15 School Street; 1-508 289 2663; open April-December), which assembled the team that, in 1985, located the remains of the *Titanic*, has a group of exhibitions on the subject of undersea exploration. The more visitor-friendly **Marine Biological Laboratory** (100 Water Street; 508 289 7623; open Mon-Sat) offers weekend guided tours and a slide show in the summer months. The **National Marine Fisheries Aquarium** (Albatross Street; 1-508 495 2000; open Mon-Fri) has an aquarium that also includes hands-on installations.

Hyannis, halfway out on the Upper Cape, is the transport hub of the area, with rail and airport services and ferries to both Nantucket and Martha's Vineyard. It came to the forefront of popular awareness as the summer resort home of the Kennedy clan and remains inseparably linked to visions of a suntanned JFK at the tiller of a skiff. The family compound is walled off from view south of town in Hyannisport but there's an extensive photographic display at the **JFK Hyannis Museum** (397 Main Street; 1-508 790 3077; open Wed-Sat).

Development in this part of the Cape has been schizophrenic. Towns on the north shore, by Cape Cod Bay, have been more successful in avoiding the congestion and commercialisation of the south, by Nantucket Sound. North across the dunes, for example, the village of **Barnstable** presents a quiet alternative to the sprawl of Hyannis, with a number of well-preserved historic buildings. These include the **Sturgis Library** (6A Main Street; 1-508 362 6636; open daily), the country's oldest library, and the **West Parish Meetinghouse** (Routes 6A and 149; 1-508 362 8624), its oldest Congregational church.

Brewster is another north shore town that has retained most of its original charm. It hosts three museums, including the long-defunct **Stony Brook Grist Mill** (830 Stony Brook Road; 1-508 896 6745; open Tue, Fri, Sat in May and June; Fri in July and August), now dedicated to the topic of early manufacture, the **Cape Cod Museum of Natural History** (869 Route A; 1-800 479 3867; open daily), and the **New England Fire and History Museum** (1439 Main Street; 508 896 5711; open Mon-Fri mid-October to mid-May), which houses an extensive collection of early fire-fighting equipment.

Chatham is a chic little town at Cape Cod's elbow that has been continuously settled since the mid-seventeenth century. In its earliest days, Chatham's perch on the shipping lanes made it a favourite location for 'moon-cussers', bands of pirate wreckers who roamed the beaches with false lights that led boats aground to be pillaged. Chatham's most prominent landmark today is one that guides sailors back safe from the sea, the **Chatham Light**. The town still plays host to a substantial population of fishermen and it accommodates the tourist trade in genteel style with an interesting collection of crafts and antiques shops downtown.

For a glimpse of primal New England, head south of town past the Chatham Light onto **Morris Island** and take the ferry to the **Monomoy Island National Wildlife Refuge**. This barrier island, born out of a hurricane some 40 years ago, serves as a stopover point for bird migration in the Atlantic Flyway and as nesting at the **Morris Island Visitors' Center** (*see page 240*).

From here north to Provincetown – the lower Cape – the Atlantic Coast of Cape Cod comprises the **Cape Cod National Seashore**, 28,000 acres (11,240 hectares) of dunes, cliffs, scrub, trails, marsh and unspoilt beaches. The southernmost of these, **Nauset Beach**, outside the town of East Orleans, offers the best surf and draws the youngest, liveliest crowd. For information on biking and hiking and a general introduction to the seashore's natural wonders, stop at the **Salt Pond Visitors' Center** in Eastham or the **Province Lands Visitors' Center** in Provincetown (*see page 240*).

This last, narrow stretch of the Cape has escaped most of the horrors of over-commercialisation. **Wellfleet Harbor**, on the Bay side,

Visit out of season and you'll have the dunes and beaches of the Cape to yourself.

encloses the 1,000-acre (401.5-hectare) **Wellfleet Bay Wildlife Sanctuary** (291 State Highway; Route 6A; 1-508 349 2615; open daily May-October; Tue-Sun November-April), where the **Massachusetts Audubon Society** sponsors tours and lectures and (for a fee) allows camping. Both Wellfleet and nearby Truro have developed reputations as artists' and writers' retreats. Edna Saint Vincent Millay and Edmund Wilson lived in Wellfleet in the 1920s; Edward Hopper liked the bleak light of the high dunes outside Truro.

Provincetown has the same kind of laissez-faire attitude found at America's other end of the earth, Key West, and the rowdy character typical of all seaports. Norman Mailer, a longtime resident, liked to refer to it as 'the Wild East', a place where anything goes when it comes to personal style.

The town has been a magnet to literary types since the turn of the century, when summer refugees from Greenwich Village such as John Reed and Eugene O'Neill first made their way north. John Dos Passos, Sinclair Lewis, Tennessee Williams and Jack Kerouac followed in their footsteps over the years. Mailer is the greatest of the literary lions currently associated with the scene; his novel *Tough Guys Don't Dance* was set here. The novel's hero braves the heights of local landmark **Pilgrim Monument**, a 252-foot-high (77-metre) granite tower in the middle of the downtown area.

The special light of the ocean air around Provincetown has inspired visual artists as well. The **Provincetown Art Association and Museum** (460 Commercial Street; 1-508 487 1750; open daily in summer; Sat and Sun in winter) has offered exhibitions, lectures and classes since 1914. Painters such as Hans Hoffman, Milton Avery, Marsden Hartley and Robert Motherwell are among the modern masters who have lived and worked here. Their work can be seen at old school galleries such as **Julie Heller** (2 Gosnold Street; 1-508 487 2169; open by appointment) and **Berta Walker** (208 Bradford Street; 1-508 487 6411; open by appointment), while **DNA** (288 Bradford Street; 1-508 487 7700; open daily in the summer) shows more daring, recent work.

Where to stay & eat

Lodging is extremely varied the whole length of Cape Cod. The rule of thumb is that the quieter towns on the Cape Cod Bay side of the peninsula are more interesting and relaxing. Rates tend to drop the further down the Cape you are from Provincetown, though there are bargains there too, if you book well in advance. And of course, off-season rates drop precipitously (and the Cape has a wonderful austerity once the tourists have gone).

Far down on the Cape's shoulder, in Sandwich, the 1837 Federal **Village Inn** (4 Jarves Street; 1-800 922 9989; rooms $75-$105) counts a charming wrap-around porch among its amenities. Mid-Cape, in Barnstable, the **Beechwood** (2839 Route 6A, 1-800 609 6618; rooms $90-$170) nestles among the trees after which it's named and includes a full breakfast in its rate. Chatham's historical district has a number of carefully-restored, period-furnished mid-nineteenth-century inns, though they can be expensive in season. Wellfleet is a good place to find inexpensive, if undistinguished, alternatives on the lower Cape. On the other side, the eighteenth-century Colonial **High Brewster Inn** (964 Satucket Road, Brewster; 1-508 896 3636; rooms $90-$210) has beautiful gardens and a rural setting.

If you must be where the action is, Provincetown's most luxurious lodging (with prices to match) is the **Brass Key** (67 Bradford Street; 1-800 842 9858; rooms $100-$325), while the Colonial-style **Fairbanks** (90 Bradford Street; 1-800 324 7265/1-508 487 0386; rooms $50-$195) offers lower prices and more history. Out of the centre, the rugged charm of the **White Horse** (500 Commercial Street; 1-508 487 1790; rooms $50-$75, studio apartments $90-$125) is a penny-saver's delight.

Dining in Provincetown runs the gamut. Upmarket interpretations of New American cuisine are the order of the day at **Front Street** (230 Commercial Street; 1-508 487 9715); decent contemporary Italian food can be had at reasonable prices at the venerable **Ciro and Sal's** (4 Kiley Court; 1-508 487 0049); and stylish light fare can be had at **Café Heaven** (199 Commercial Street; 1-508 487 9639). The drive back to Wellfleet is worthwhile for dinner at **Aesop's Tables** (316 Main Street; 1-508 349 6450; closed in the winter), which shows a specially inventive touch with fresh local ingredients. Phone ahead wherever you go, as off-season hours are unpredictable and sometimes non-existent.

Provincetown has a significant Portuguese community, emigrés from the Azores who came to work the fishing boats. Their cuisine is served in interesting surroundings at **The Moors** (5 Bradford Street; 1-508 487 0840), known for its spicy way with swordfish and pork. Or simply grab a loaf of fresh Portuguese sweet bread from the **Provincetown Portuguese Bakery** (299 Commercial Street; 1-508 487 1803) and take a stroll downtown.

Getting there

By car

Cape Cod's gateway, Sagamore Bridge, is 30 miles (48.3km) southeast of Boston on Route 3, the most direct route.

By bus & rail

The **Plymouth and Brockton Bus** (1-508 771 6191) operates every hour from Boston's South Station to Hyannis and then on to Provincetown. The **Cape Cod Regional Transit Authority** (1-800 352 7155) and **Bonanza** (*see p231*) cover the mid-Cape region by bus. Provincetown runs local shuttle bus services in town during the summer months.

By boat

Bay State Cruises (457 1428) runs a daily ferry service from Boston to Provincetown in the summer months and on weekends in spring and autumn. The journey to Provincetown takes 3 hours and boats depart from Commonwealth Pier.

Tourist information

Cape Cod Chamber of Commerce

Junction of Routes 6 and 122, Hyannis (1-508 362 3225). **Open** 9am-5pm daily.

Morris Island Visitors' Center

Route 6, Chatham, Morris Island (1-508 945 0594). **Open** *summer* 9am-5pm daily; *winter* 9am-5pm Mon-Sat.

Province Lands Visitors' Center

Race Point, Provincetown (1-508 487 1256). **Open** *summer* 9am-5pm daily; *winter* 9am-4.30pm daily.

Salt Pond Visitors' Center

Route 6, Eastham (1-508 255 3421). **Open** *summer* 9am-5pm daily; *winter* 9am-4.30pm daily.

Martha's Vineyard, Nantucket & New Bedford

The rocky offshore twins of Martha's Vineyard and Nantucket sprang from the same glacial activity that created Cape Cod just 12,000 years ago. The history of both islands and the nearby port of New Bedford, on the mainland, is inextricable from the history of whaling. New Bedford remains a working commercial fishing port but the islands now live off the tourist trade.

Nantucket was the early leader in the whaling business but, as the ships grew larger, **New Bedford**, with its deep harbour, came to displace it. In its prime it was the source of all light: the port through which flowed the oil that lit the lamps of the day. Though that glory faded with the rise of the petroleum industry, the city has done an outstanding job of preserving its history in four separate historic districts.

The intricate, exhausting rigours and many terrors of the whaler's trade are documented in the **Whaling Museum** (15 Broad Street; 1-508 228 1894; open daily) in the heart of the 16 square blocks of the historic waterfront district. A few cobblestoned steps across the way is the **Seamen's Bethel** (15 Johnny Cake Hill; 1-508 992 3295; open daily), where Father Marple's fiery sermon rang in the ears of Moby Dick's Ishmael.

The first recreational use of **Martha's Vineyard** was for Methodist camp meetings in the summer of 1835. Summer residents now include glitterati such as Spike Lee, Walter Cronkite, Carly Simon and Bill Clinton.

Of the Vineyard's main towns, **Edgartown** is the largest and oldest. A walk along the harbourside, past the stately captains' mansions on Water Street, reveals the prosperity they brought back from the sea. The island's historical society here keeps the **Vineyard Historical Museum** (59 School Street; 1-508 627 4441; open Tue-Sat in

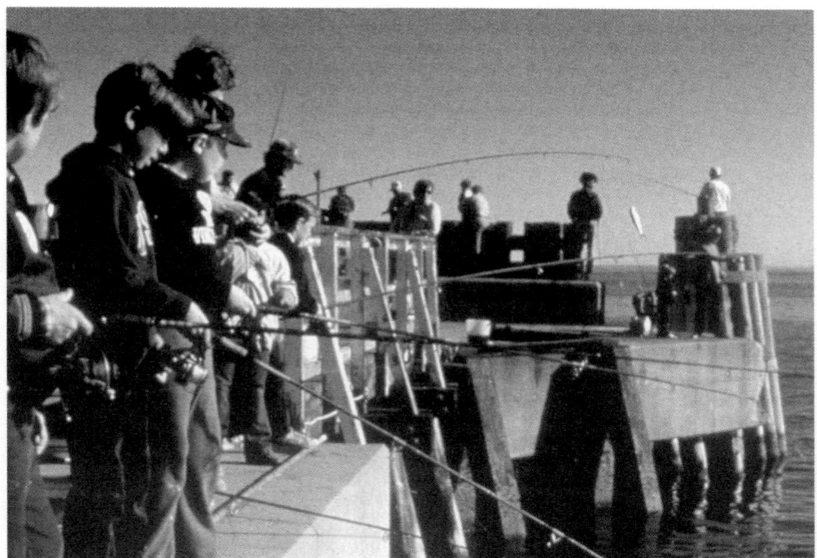
Fishing from the pier at **Oak Bluffs** *on Martha's Vineyard.*

summer, Wed-Sat in winter) replete with scrimshaw, ships' models and other artefacts of local history.

Oak Bluffs, where the religious gathered, has a sweet collection of Victorian 'gingerbread' cottages (1 Trinity Park; 1-508 693 7784) and the wonderful 1876 **Flying Horses Carousel** (33 Circuit Avenue; 1-508 693 9481), reputedly the country's oldest. A premier example of American folk art, it operates until 10pm for a dollar a ride throughout the summer. Stick to Oak Bluffs for the island's liveliest late-night action, too, chiefly at the **Atlantic Connection** (124 Circuit Avenue; 1-508 693 7129), where celebrity-spotting is part of the fun, and the **Ritz** (1 Circuit Avenue; 1-508 693 9851) for live blues.

Vineyard Haven (also known as Tisbury), on the north coast, was long the island's chief port and is where the old colonial atmosphere is best preserved. **Gay Head**, on the western tip, is unusual for its large resident Native American population. **Gay Head Beach**, outside town, is famous for dramatic mile-long cliffs of multi-coloured clay and the great views from the trails above them.

Nantucket has a reputation as the Vineyard's prim little sister and it strives to keep it that way. First settled by religious refugees from the Puritan colony, it was the world's foremost whaling port throughout the eighteenth century. Even in the long period of decline that followed, the picturesque island was a favourite summer retreat for well-to-do holidaymakers.

When, after World War II, an explosion of middle-class tourism threatened to trouble Nantucket's quiet charm, the locals rose up in the cause of historic preservation. They established the first official historic district in New England and enacted an especially strict zoning and housing code. New construction in most of Nantucket is carefully regulated to blend harmoniously with the past. This is the home of colonial retro.

Not surprisingly, the **Nantucket Historical Association** (15 Broad Street, 1-508 228 1894; open daily) offers a well-organised tour of Nantucket town's historic district. Highlights include the **Jethro Coffin House**, a seventeenth-century saltbox that is the island's oldest building, the last of the town's eighteenth-century mills, and the **Old Gaol**, a very civilised one, it is said, from which prisoners were allowed home for the night. A visit to the **Whaling Museum** is also part of the tour. Housed in an old whale oil candle factory, its collection includes the giant skeleton of a finback whale and a premier collection of whaling art and artefacts.

Where to stay & eat

As a result of the celebrities on Martha's Vineyard, the bluebloods on Nantucket, the tourists and the need to import most produce, good dining on Martha's Vineyard and Nantucket is not cheap. If

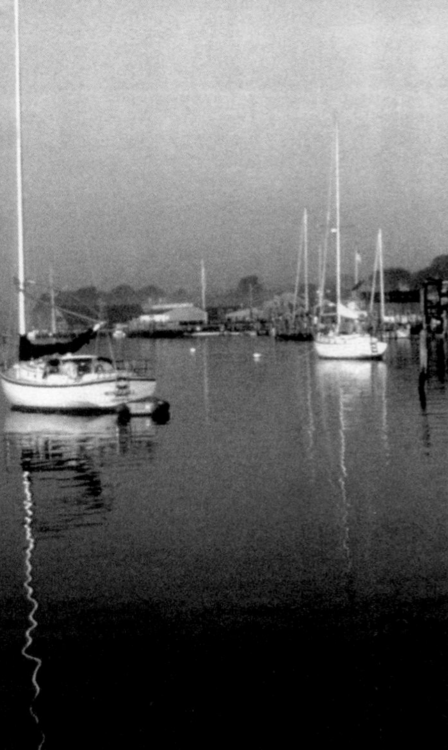

The aptly-named **Vineyard Haven** *(p241).*

(p241)

you take the plunge on Martha's Vineyard, **Savoir Fare** (14 Church Street, Edgartown; 1-508 627 9864; closed in winter), does New American food that drew Bill Clinton when he was last in the vicinity; **L'Etoile** (27 South Summer Street, Edgartown; 1-508 627 5187) has a renowned contemporary French menu. And love it or loathe it, the tourist-packed **Black Dog Tavern** (Beach Street Exit, Vineyard Haven; 1-508 693 9223) is a good place to load up on a huge breakfast or watch the sunset. On Nantucket, the classy village of Siasconset contains **Chanticleer** (9 New Street; 1-508 257 6231), where you'll pay through the nose for great classic French cuisine and an outstanding wine list.

Lodging is not cheap anywhere on Martha's Vineyard in season. A reasonable blend of comfort and convenience at relatively modest prices can be found in Edgartown at the **Victorian Inn** (24 South Water Street; 1-508 627 4784; rooms $105-$325), a former whaling captain's home, and in Oak Bluffs at **Oak House** (Sea View Avenue; 1-508 693 4187), a beachside Victorian house.

Prices run even higher among the swells of Nantucket, but the local landmark, **Jared Coffin House** (29 Broad Street; 1-800 248 2405; rooms $65-$210), is not too exorbitant and packed with history. Nantucket, fortunately, has a wealth of B&Bs listed through services such as **Nantucket Accommodations** (1-508 228 9559).

Getting there

By boat

The most common way to get to both Martha's Vineyard and Nantucket is by ferry. The **Massachusetts Steamship Authority** (1-508 477 8600) has an all-year-round service from two Cape Cod locations: Woods Hole to Martha's Vineyard takes 45 minutes, and Hyannis to Nantucket takes 2 hours.

There are also several privately run ferries that run from the Cape to the Vineyard in the summer: **Island Queen** (1-508 548 4800) and **Pied Piper** (1-508 548 9400) run from Falmouth; **Hy-Line** (1-508 778 2600) from Hyannis; and the **Schamonchi** (1-508 997 1688) runs from New Bedford. Hy-Line also has a summer service to Nantucket.

By car, bus & air

Check with the ferry services about transporting cars to the islands, since there are restrictions at different times of the year. There's little call to take one, anyway. Both islands have extensive shuttle bus services during most of the year courtesy of the **Martha's Vineyard Transit Authority** (1-508 627 7448) and the **Nantucket Regional Transit Authority** (1-508 228 7025). Both islands are suitable for cycling, especially tiny Nantucket, and bike paths are plentiful. Besides, all the major car rental firms are found in force, if you really need to drive. Better yet, rent a moped. They're extremely popular (even if the locals have mixed feelings about them).

You can fly with **Cape Air** (1-508 771 6944) from Boston to Hyannis, Provincetown, Martha's Vineyard or Nantucket.

Tourist information

Martha's Vineyard Chamber of Commerce

Vineyard Haven, Martha's Vineyard (1-508 693 0085). **Open** 9am-5pm Mon-Fri.

Nantucket Island Chamber of Commerce

48 Main Street, Nantucket (1-508 228 1700). **Open** 9am-5pm Mon-Fri.

The mild, mild west

The farmlands of the Connecticut River Valley mark the beginning of western Massachusetts. It's also known as the Pioneer Valley, for it was America's first frontier. Most of the valley was once the floor of a vast glacial lake that stretched from central Connecticut far north into Vermont and New Hampshire, and the remains of that sediment-rich floor make the soil exceptionally fertile, particularly for New England.

The soil drew the first colonists, despite a major Native American presence, and some bloody history

The Vineyard's **Gay Head**, *famous for its dramatic cliff-top views. See page 241.*

ensued. But those days are long past. Time and superior armaments honed what was wild Indian frontier to the early Puritans. The archetypal pristine New England town, with its village green and white-steepled church, flowered here and the American ideal – a society of independent farmers and artisans – blossomed.

Nineteenth-century entrepreneurs harnessed the river to power the mills of early industry, and factory life still marks the cities of the lower valley, though not always for the best (*see page 254* **Dark satanic villes**). Local manufacturing fell on hard times in the years after World War II and has never fully recovered. Still, the wealth those mills generated endowed a number of highly regarded colleges that give the area much of its character.

Pioneer Valley

The towns of the Pioneer Valley are about 90 miles (145 kilometres) west of Boston. The quickest way to get there is along the Mass Turnpike (I-90), but the valley can also be reached from the north by way of Route 2. That's the path the early colonists took, following the Indian markings along what was then the **Mohawk Trail**.

The first white settlement was the town of **Deerfield** (just southwest of Greenfield), where the indigenous people's attachment to the land proved very strong. Inter-tribal warfare and waves of epidemic had almost destroyed the Pocumtuck tribe that had occupied the site for several thousand years, but they returned to contest the European invasion fiercely. Twice in Deerfield's early years the whites were overwhelmed in battle and the town abandoned. The first occasion was during King Philip's War, in the 1670s, after which the land lay vacant for seven years. The second occurred early in the course of the French and Indian wars, when the town was raided and burned to the ground, and the survivors marched off several hundred epic miles into captivity in Quebec.

Tokens of these struggles and other aspects of the period are on display at the village museum, **Memorial Hall** (8 Memorial Street, Deerfield; 1-413 774 3768; open 9.30am-4.30pm daily, May-October). The building dates back to 1798, when it first served as part of the elite private school, Deerfield Academy. Much of the rest of the town is of similar age and has been carefully preserved, not as a replica, but as something close to a living shrine to pre-industrial life. The heart of town, known only as 'The Street', is almost entirely composed of houses dating from the eighteenth and nineteenth centuries. Most of them are still in use, but 14 of them are open to the general public. Tours are conducted by **Historic Deerfield** (Hall Tavern, The Street, Deerfield; 1-413 774 5581; open daily) and period-style lodging is available at the **Deerfield Inn** (81 Old Main Street; 1-800 926 3865; rooms $147-$242), which dates from 1884.

A short drive east of Deerfield on Route 2 is the town of **Shelburne Falls**, where a local women's group maintains the **Bridge of Flowers**, a 40-foot long (12-metre) former trolley bridge whose burden now is a rainbow of flower beds. It's a singularly delightful example of roadside America. Among the town's other charms is the **Copper Angel Restaurant** (2 State Street; 1-413 625 2727), which has a menu featuring many inventive vegetarian dishes and a whimsically 'heavenly' ambience.

The drive south through the valley can follow the interstate, I-91, but the more interesting and scenic route is along the older back roads. A leisurely hour's drive will take you to a unique cluster of small college towns with outsize cultural vitality.

Amherst alone nurtures three institutions. The most prestigious is **Amherst College** (100 Bolt Wood Avenue; 1-413 542 2000), a small, liberal arts college in the classic mode. It dates from 1821 when it included the lexicographer Noah Webster among its original trustees. More recently, the bard of New England, Robert Frost, was a long-time faculty member. To the north is the immense campus and 25,000-strong student body of 'U-Mass', the **University of Massachusetts** (Massachusetts Avenue; 1-413 545 0306), whose most famous alumnus – the basketball genius Julius Irving (Dr J) – took no doctorate but holds the title just the same. In the hills south of town is **Hampshire College** (Route 116; 1-413 549 4600), which has an experimental orientation and a counterculture air.

Further south, along Route 116, the town of **South Hadley** consists almost entirely of **Mount Holyoke College** (1-413 538 2000). Founded in 1837, this was the first women's college in the United States and is the oldest of the 'Seven Sisters', the elite women's schools that were the counterpart of the formerly all-male Ivy League. 'The Belle of Amherst', Emily Dickinson, was among Mount Holyoke's first graduates, but it was in the town to the north that she was born and spent most of her life. The **Dickinson Homestead** (280 Main Street, Amherst; 1-413 542 8161; reservations for tours recommended), where she spent the final 30 years of her life in seclusion, is now a National Historic Monument.

Another of the Seven Sisters, **Smith College** (1-413 584 2700), is located a little to the northwest, in the city of **Northampton**. The largest women's liberal arts school in the nation, Smith's redbrick quadrangles cover a good deal of the downtown area.

Northampton's one-time mayor and most famous resident was the 30th US president, the consummate Yankee Calvin 'Silent Cal' Coolidge. When, in the days before his terms in the White House, Coolidge moved to Boston to serve as Governor of Massachusetts, the frugal New Englander rented a hotel room there and left his family in Northampton. The great Coolidge quip is his reply to the lady who bet she could pry three words from him: 'You lose'.

Northampton has been continuously settled for more than 300 years. It has had a placid history for the most part, but is interesting for the storm of religious frenzy that erupted in the 1740s under the direction of the charismatic preacher Jonathan Edwards. The full pageant of the area's past can be studied in the period homes restored and maintained by **Historic Northampton** (46 Bridge Street; 1-413 584 6011).

All the local colleges sponsor museums, galleries and individual cultural events that are open to the public, so there's generally something of interest happening every day of the week. There's even one of the very few museums in the world devoted to comics, the **Words and Pictures Museum** (*see page 93* **Museums & Galleries**). And with the youthful population in and around these ivory tower villages, there's also a wealth of interesting shops, clubs, bars and eating establishments.

TRAVELLING FURTHER SOUTH

The southernmost portion of the Pioneer Valley is less refined and its two chief towns are industrial centres. **Holyoke** is a planned industrial city that was once an important papermaking centre. Though it has fallen on tough times, the glory days are recounted at the exhibition centre at **Heritage State Park** (221 Appleton Street; 1-413 534 1723; open Tue-Sun).

Situated further south, **Springfield** has managed much better. It remains the largest city in western Massachusetts and a significant manufacturing centre. The US military bought small arms from here from Revolutionary times up until the Vietnam War and, in the 1800s, the city was famous for the Springfield Rifle. The **Armory** (1 Armory Square; 1-413 734 8551; open Wed-Sun) was closed in 1968 and now houses a museum dedicated to the history of small arms. Another American mechanical device that has gone out of production and passed into the valhalla of cult veneration is the Indian Motorcycle. Forget about Harleys; cognoscenti will want to visit the **Indian Motorcycle Museum** (33 Hendee Street; 1-413 737 2624; open daily).

But Springfield's most successful and enduring product is a game. It was in Springfield that Dr James Naismith, looking for a form of indoor sport suitable to the long New England winters, suspended two wicker baskets at either end of a gymnasium floor. The game has come a long way since 1891 and every loving detail and curiosity of its history is explored at the **Basketball Hall of Fame** (*see page 96* **Museums & Galleries**).

If you want to get the most outrageously large dose of ersatz Americana anywhere outside of Williamsburg, make a detour 30 miles (48 kilometres) east of Springfield on I-90 and travel a few miles south on I-84 to **Sturbridge**. Adjoining Sturbridge you'll find **Old Sturbridge Village** (1 Old Sturbridge Road; 1-800 733 1830; open daily), a 200-acre (80-hectare) living museum to which more than 40 nineteenth-century buildings from all over New England have been moved, fully restored and populated with costumed interpreters who re-enact the everyday life of rural 1830s New England. For a chance to buy some Americana of your own, the nearby village of **Brimfield** (on Route 20) hosts a series of monster antique shows throughout the summer. Phone **Brimfield Antiques & Collectables Fair** (1-413 283 2418) for details and a brochure.

Where to stay & eat

Both towns offer centrally located lodgings: in Northampton, the **Hotel Northampton** (36 King Street; 1-413 584 3100; rooms $130-$190) and the **Lord Jeffrey Inn** (30 Bolton Avenue; 1-413 253 2576; rooms $69-$168) in Amherst, are both local landmarks, and neither is particularly expensive. Most of the nightlife is in Northampton. The **Iron Horse** (20 Center Street; 1-413 584 0610) is a well-established venue with an eclectic range of live music; **Pearl Street** (10 Pearl Street; 1-413 584 0610) is primarily a dance club.

A cosmopolitan array of good food at undergraduate prices abounds in the north of the valley around the towns of Amherst and Northampton. In Amherst, try **Judie's** (51 North Pleasant Street; 1-413 253 3491) for light American fare. In Northampton, the **Eastside Grill** (19 Strong Avenue; 1-413 586 3347) specialises in spicy Cajun dishes while **La Cazuela** (7 Old South Street; 1-413 586 0400) serves decent Mexican food.

Getting there

By car

The Pioneer Valley is 90 miles (145km) west of Boston, along the Mass Turnpike (I-90). Route 2 is the most scenic way to explore the Mohawk Trail.

By bus

Greyhound links Boston and Springfield; **Peter Pan** and **Bonanza** both operate between Boston and the major towns of western Massachusetts (*see p231 for all three*). The **Pioneer Valley Transit Authority** (1-413 781 7882) provides local transport in the area.

Tourist information

Amherst Area Chamber of Commerce

400 Main Street, Amherst (1-413 253 0700).
Open 8am-4.30pm Mon-Fri.

Greater Northampton Chamber of Commerce

99 Pleasant Street, Northampton (1-413 584 1900).
Open 9am-5pm Mon-Fri.

Greater Springfield Convention & Visitors' Bureau

1500 Main Street, Springfield (1-413 787 1548).
Open 8.30am-5pm Mon-Fri.

The Berkshires

High and rugged enough to give the land character, low and gentle enough to make it accessible, the Berkshires make westernmost Massachusetts a most inviting retreat. Like the Pioneer Valley, the area has gone through stages of farming settlement and factory growth. It's distinct, however, as the playground for many years of the elite and the intelligentsia of both New York and Boston: Hawthorne and Melville picnicked here; Henry James dropped in on Edith Wharton. The Gilded Age's plutocrats built so many of their elaborate 'summer cottages' here that the Berkshires were labelled 'inland Newport'. The residue of all that money and culture is the theatre, dance and music festivals the region is known for today.

Williamstown, near both the New York and Vermont state lines, is the home of **Williams College** (880 Main Street; 1-413 597 3131), another of New England's fine, small, liberal arts schools – the 'little Ivies'. The 200-year-old college has some interesting architecture and a good museum of art, but the town's aesthetic gem is the **Clark Art Institute** (225 South Street; 1-413 458 9545; open daily July, August; Tue-Sun September-June), which numbers more than 30 Renoirs in its collection. Then there's the **Williamstown Theater Festival** (1-413 597 3400), a summer-long extravaganza that does everything from classical drama to contemporary experimentation.

Picnicking at the annual **Tanglewood** *music festival.*

Further south, **Pittsfield** is the region's largest city, and its geographic and governmental centre – but not much to look at, nevertheless. It does hold a few points of interest however, and rather a strange brew at that. **Hancock Shaker Village** (1-800 817 1137; open daily), 5 miles (8 kilometres) out of town, at the intersection of Routes 20 and 41, is a restoration of what was an American Shaker community between 1790 and 1960. The austere life and beautifully spare crafts of the Shakers are demonstrated, thankfully without the rigmarole of period costume and assumed identity. Just outside town is **Arrowhead** (780 Holmes Road; 1-413 442 1793; open daily), a place for all lovers of literature to fall prostrate. Here, from 1850 to 1863, Herman Melville lived, schmoozed with Nathaniel Hawthorne, peered into the soul of man and the eye of god, and wrote a book about a whale. The **Berkshire Museum** (39 South Street, Pittsfield; 1-413 443 7171; open daily July, August; Tue-Sun September-June) is right in town, though its sensibility is all over the place: local history, glowing rocks, stuffed birds, Babylonian tablets, live fish in the basement and an art-house cinema all feature. Oh, and there's a mummy.

Lenox, Lee and Stockbridge cluster along Route 7 – above, on and below I-90 respectively. **Lenox** is gorgeous: a sumptuously tended village of gracious old homes and well-manicured lawns under immense old oaks. **Stockbridge** is cut from the same silken cloth, trimmed with piping of bohemian funk. **Lee** is working class: an old paper-making town – and it shows. Each of them is a summer home for one of the muses.

Lenox's star attraction is the famed summer-long series of concerts at **Tanglewood** (information 266 1492), a 500-acre (200-hectare) estate south of town, on Route 183. Conductor Seiji Ozawa and the Boston Symphony Orchestra lead the annual charge, with guest reinforcements from everyone who's anyone in classical music. The 5,000-seat 'Shed' hosts performers of the jazz and pop stripe too. Long before the music started, Nathaniel Hawthorne stayed here long enough to write his children's classic, *Tanglewood Tales*.

Another literary landmark is Edith Wharton's 'cottage', **The Mount** (2 Plunkett Street; 1-413 637 1899; open daily May-November). Here, in the early years of the century, Dame Edith entertained her peers among the ruling class: all the better to dissect them in *The Age of Innocence*. Nowadays, the **Shakespeare & Company** troupe (1-413 637 3353) performs here from late May to early November.

Lee is the centre of the dance universe for ten weeks every summer, at the **Jacob's Pillow Dance Festival** (1-413 243 0745), 10 miles (16 kilometres) east of town on Route 20. The nation's foremost such event, the 'Pillow' stems jointly from the mama and papa of all modern dance, Martha Graham and Ted Shawn. Besides the usual giants of contemporary dance strutting on the main stage, genre groups take their turn and fledglings deliver works-in-progress free on the lawns.

Stockbridge hosts the **Berkshire Theater Festival** (1-413 298 5576) from late June until late August. The main stage, in a 100-year-old Stanford White 'casino', attracts top-flight thespians in productions of the classics; a newer stage, the Unicorn, shows new and experimental work. And because Norman Rockwell lived for more than 30 years in this town (whose appearance embodies the ideal of his clean-cut vision), Stockbridge contains the mother can of American corn. For better or worse, the **Norman Rockwell Museum** (*see page 96* **Museums & Galleries**) holds the highest concentration of the artist's work anywhere outside the morgue of the *Saturday Evening Post*. Go and see it, and repent of your cynicism.

Where to stay & eat

Lodging in the Berkshires is varied. Lovely **Lenox** has a slew of moderately pricey, venerable old inns, in the centre around Church and Walker Streets. **Stockbridge** holds the pre-eminent example of the species, the **Red Lion** (30 Main Street, Stockbridge; 1-413 298 5545; rooms $72-$175), which is not that more expensive than other options. For cheaper rates, phone the **Berkshire Visitors' Bureau** (*see below*) about local motels and B&Bs. There are many available if you book well in advance.

The **Church Street Café** (65 Church Street; 1-413 637 2745), in the heart of Lenox, is a local favourite for reasonably-priced nouvelle American cooking. For variety, as well as economy, drive the extra few miles to **West Stockbridge** and the **Truc Orient Express** (3 Harris Street; 1-413 232 4204) and sample the delicate fare of Vietnam.

Getting there

By car

The Berkshires are a good three hours' drive west of Boston on the Mass Pike (I-90) – the distance to Pittsfield is 134 miles (216km). It takes longer on the lesser roads but you get a better sense of the country. If you're continuing on from the Pioneer Valley, consider taking Route 9 from Northampton to Pittsfield, or Route 2 through Shelburne Falls along the Mohawk Trail to Williamstown, both of which are well-maintained roads. Route 7 is the Berkshires' main street, the only highway running the length of the region from north to south.

By bus

As for the Pioneer Valley (*see p245*).

Tourist information

Berkshire Visitors' Bureau

Berkshire Common, West Street, Pittsfield (1-413 443 9186). **Open** 8.30am-5pm Mon-Fri.

Schismatistan

The settlers went south and west to escape the Puritans, who some thought too strict and some too lax. In little Rhode Island, the smallest of the states, founder Roger Williams was radical enough to insist on complete freedom of conscience, separation of church and state and respect for Native Americans. Connecticut's settlers were of two minds. One faction, centred around Hartford, advocated a more democratic system than the Bay Colony's. Another group, Puritans who left England late and, in their super-orthodoxy, found the first arrivals in Massachusetts grown too liberal, came to New Haven and instituted a theocracy based on Mosaic law. The two parts were soon joined but a relatively mild form of government was preserved.

These promising beginnings did nothing to prevent some unpleasant behaviour. Enlightened Rhode Island – with hundreds of miles of shoreline and great natural harbours – turned to the sea and took up the slave trade. By the 1700s, the wealthy families of the colony were waited upon by several thousand captive Africans. Connecticut played less of a role, but the port of New London also handled its share of human cargo.

Both states developed along the same lines as the mother colony. Shipping dominated the early days, heavy industry the nineteenth century, industrial decline the twentieth. Both states have major centres of culture and higher learning; both have significant enclaves of wealth. Off the major highways, both states have unspoiled vistas of great natural beauty.

Rhode Island

The city of **Providence**, less than an hour south of Boston on I-95, is the capital of Rhode Island and has been a major shipping and manufacturing centre for 200 years. The city's College Hill area is home to **Brown University** and the **Rhode Island School of Design (RISD)**. Brown has an innovative course of instruction and a reputation as the hippest of the Ivies; RISD (known as 'rizdee'), a hotbed of avant-garde arts training, was where David Byrne assembled the Talking Heads. **RISD's Museum of Art** (224 Benefit Street; 1-401 454 6100; open daily) has a strong collection of Impressionist work. **Benefit Street**, downtown along the river, hosts a concentration of eighteenth- and nineteenth-century houses restored and open to the public courtesy of the **Providence Preservation Society** (1-401 831 7440). **Federal Hill**, the venerable Italian neighbourhood on the west side of town, is where Raymond Patriarca, long-time *capo dei capi* of the New England mob, resided for many years until his recent (natural) death.

Newport, another 30 miles (48.3 kilometres) south of Providence, on Route 114, was in its early years a commercial seaport to rival New York and Boston. It later turned from frigates to pleasure yachts and its name remains synonymous with upper crust luxury. As in the Berkshires, the summer mansions of the local aristos were known as 'cottages', many of which can be seen in a tour along **Bellevue Street**, offered by the **Newport Preservation Society** (424 Bellevue Avenue; 1-401 847 1000/www.newportmansions.org). The tour also includes **Hammersmith Farm** (further out on the peninsula), which was Jackie Kennedy's childhood summer home, as well as the site of her and Jack's wedding reception and is a trove of Kennedy memorabilia.

A nice reflection of local history is the fact that Newport, as a haven of tolerance, contains America's oldest surviving synagogue, the **Touro Synagogue** (72 Touro Street; 1-401 847 4794; tours Mon-Fri, Sun, at 2pm), and as a haven of leisure hosts the **Tennis Hall of Fame** (194 Bellvue Avenue; 1-401 849 3990; open daily). Newport's summer music scene has lost the stature of the days when Dylan's electric antics stunned the faithful, but August still sees the **Ben & Jerry's Folk Festival** and the **JVC Jazz Festival** (phone 1-401 847 3700 for details of both).

Block Island, 12 miles (19.3 kilometres) off the coast of Rhode Island, is a favourite destination for tourists wanting to get away from it all. Apart from the little village of **Old Harbor** with its fine old Victorian inns, this former pirates' lair has nothing for the visitor but sun, sand, dune and beach. Summertime ferry services run from Newport and Providence and year-round services from Point Judith, Rhode Island. Phone 1-401 783 4613 for fares and schedules.

Where to stay & eat

Lodging at the **Biltmore** (Kennedy Plaza; 1-800 294 7709; rooms $120-$390) in Providence is not cheap but is good value for money. The art deco façade dates from 1922 and the location couldn't be more central. In the historic district, the **Old Court** (144 Benefit Street; 1-401 751 2002; rooms $110-$145) is less expensive; the building's almost 100 years old and contains a menagerie of period furniture. Newport has many historic lodgings.

Hammersmith Farm: *one of Newport's modest 'cottages'.*

Two interesting, very reasonably priced choices in the heart of town are **Melville House** (39 Clarke Street; 1-401 847 0640; rooms $85-$165) and the **Mill Street Inn** (75 Mill Street; 1-800 392 1316; rooms $85-$325), the latter housed within the walls of a turn-of-the-century sawmill. For B&Bs throughout the state, phone **Bed & Breakfast of Rhode Island** (1-800 828 0000).

Providence has a wide range of dining choices. **Al Forno** (577 S Main Street; 1-401 273 9760) is famous for wood-grilling pizza and an inventive Tuscan-style menu. A moderately priced alternative with traditional southern Italian fare is **Angela's Civita Farnese** (141 Atwells Avenue; 1-401 621 8171), in the Federal Hill neighbourhood. **Capital Grille** (1 Cookson Place; 1-401 521 5600) is another upmarket choice – a steak, chops and seafood house in the old Providence train station.

In Newport, the **White Horse Tavern** (Marlborough and Farewell Streets; 1-401 849 3600) claims to be the oldest operating tavern in the country, dating back more than 300 years. It's open for dinner only, with rather expensive black-tie service, high-end New American cuisine and a top-notch wine list. Jackets are required for men. The **Music Hall Café** (250 Thames Street; 1-401 848 2520) is a casual alternative with inexpensive Tex-Mex food.

Getting there

By car

Providence, Rhode Island is 50 miles (80.5km) from Boston along the I-95.

By bus or rail

Bonanza links Boston to Providence by bus; **Amtrak** by rail (*see p231 for both*). Buses operating locally are run by the **Rhode Island Public Transportation Authority** (RIPTA; 1-401 781 9400).

Tourist information

Block Island Chamber of Commerce

Water Street, Block Island (1-401 466 2982).
Open *summer* 10am-5pm Mon-Sat, 10am-3pm Sun; *winter* 10am-5pm Mon-Sat.

Newport County Convention & Visitors' Bureau

23 America's Cup Avenue, Newport (1-401 849 8048).
Open 9am-5pm Mon-Fri.

Greater Providence Convention & Visitors' Bureau

1 West Exchange Street, Providence (1-401 274 1636).
Open 9am-5.30pm daily.

Connecticut

There are several points of interest clustered around the mouth of the Thames River, in Connecticut's southeastern corner. The town of **Mystic** is an old whaling and shipbuilding centre that has converted 17 acres (6.8 hectares) of its waterfront into the **Mystic Seaport Museum** (75 Greenmanville Avenue; 1-860 572 0711; open daily), a complex of ships, shops, homes and wharves where the life and crafts of nineteenth-century maritime New England are preserved and re-enacted. More than 400 period crafts are on display, and the repair and restoration of new additions to the collection are part of the show.

Groton, just a few miles west on I-95, is a one-horse town, that horse being the nuclear submarine. The home of General Electric's Electric Boat division and a major US Navy submarine base, it has been the scene of frequent political demonstrations in the past, but both the protests and their source have faded in the post-Cold War era. The original of these undersea monsters, the *USS Nautilus*, is on display at the **Submarine Force Museum** (Crystal Lake Road; 1-800 343 0079; open Mon, Wed-Sun). **New London** (further east still and directly on the Thames), is the home of the **US Coast Guard Academy** (15 Mohegan Avenue; 1-860 444 8444), which is open to the public on rare occasions.

North of these coastal towns, on either shore of the Thames, are two anomalous outcroppings of Las Vegas-style recreation. The remnants of two local Native American tribes have opened competing casinos in the towns of **Ledyard** and **Uncasville**. The former is the home of **Foxwoods** (39 Norwich Westerly Road; 1-860 885 3000; open 24-hours daily), run by the Mashantucket Pequot tribe; the latter is home to **Mohegan Sun** (1 Mohegan Sun Boulevard; 1-860 204 8000), run by the Mohegans. Both of them do a booming business all year round, drawing gamblers from across the northeasern USA. The Pequots make a big thing of the huge sums they donate to the preservation of Native American arts and culture, primarily at their own **Pequot Museum and Research Center** (Route 2; 1-860 396 6800; open daily).

The city of **New Haven**, about an hour's drive to the east, on Long Island Sound, is best known as the home of **Yale University**. Harvard's traditional rival, and something of a conservative counterpoint to the latter's liberalism, Yale has a number of cultural institutions that welcome the public. The **Yale Art Gallery** (1111 Chapel Street; 1-203 432 0600; open Tue-Sun) is strong on French Impressionist and American Abstract Expressionist work; the **Yale Center for British Art** (1080 Chapel Street; 1-203 432 2800; open Tue-Sun) includes fine examples of Hogarth, Constable, Reynolds and Turner; the **Peabody Museum of Natural History** (170 Whitney Avenue; 1-203 432 5050; open Tue-Sun) holds more than nine million specimens from a whole range of sciences and world cultures. The city neighbourhoods around the campus have the eclectic assortment of clubs, bars, restaurants, shops and theatres one would expect, given the educated population of the area.

The **Nook Farm** neighbourhood, on the east side of town, contains two literary landmarks. Samuel Clemens took the swag he'd earned under a pen name and purchased an immense, and immensely overwrought, Gothic mansion now known as the **Mark Twain House** (351 Farmington Avenue; 1-860 247 0998; open daily) in which he lived with his family from 1873 to 1897. At the same time, nearby at 77 Forest Street, the author of the anti-slavery novel *Uncle Tom's Cabin* lived in what is now called the **Harriet Beecher Stowe House** (1-860 525 9317; open Tue-Sun October, November, January-June; daily June-September, December). Both houses have been restored, are packed with period artefacts and author memorabilia and have guided tours.

The far northwestern corner of Connecticut is an attractive slice of bucolic New England that goes by the name of **Litchfield Hills**. It has a certain cachet as one of the further reaches of settlement for well-to-do New Yorkers, but since the rustic flavour is what drew them, the village greens are undisturbed and the forest lies thick on the land. It's a bit of a drive from Boston – about three hours – but the area has all the charm of the Berkshires with the advantage of even less tourist development.

Where to stay

The **Inn at Mystic** (Routes 27 and 1; 1-800 237 2415; rooms $65-$250) is outside town but a great place to stay for a wonderful ocean view. In **New Haven**, the **Three Chimneys Inn** (1201 Chapel Street; 1-203 789 1201; rooms $149-$189) is a restored Victorian lodging that's moderately expensive but about what you'd expect for an 'old Eli' (Yale) traditional lodging. **Litchfield**, in the hills of the same name, has the **Tollgate Hill** (Route 202 at Tollgate Road; 1-800 445 3903; rooms $90-$175), a 250-year-old tavern and stagecoach stop situated on 10 tree-lined acres (4 hectares). For B&Bs in the Litchfield Hills, contact the local **Travel Council** (*see below*).

Getting there

By car

The mouth of the Thames River is about two hours' drive from Boston, west on the Mass Pike (I-90) and south on I-395. New Haven is 142 miles (229km) from Boston: take the Mass Pike and then the I-84 and I-91 at Sturbridge.

By bus or rail

Greyhound and **Bonanza** both serve the area by bus; **Amtrak** stops at Mystic and New Haven (*see p231 for all three*).

Tourist information

Litchfield Hills Travel Council

Telephone enquiries (1-860 567 4506).

Taciturnia

Stones. They're famous for them – stony fields, stony mountains, stony people. The land and the people of the northeast's northeast are perfectly matched in austerity and honesty.

The White Mountains of New Hampshire, having withstood 75 million fewer years of erosion than their neighbours, the Green Mountains of Vermont, stand taller and straighter as a result. What wear they've seen, however, has been enough to uncover the granite cores whose colour gives them their name. Perhaps it's the 'Granite State's' stubborn soil and long, harsh winters that have laid bare the similar core in the native character. What other state has a motto to match their ornery injunction: 'live free or die'?

Maine's stones stand along the sea, on the rocky coastline where most of its population lives. It's a vast state, so big that the rest of New England could fit inside it, and much of the inland region is untamed wilderness. Holidaying there is more of an expedition than a daytrip. So out of the way it's almost out of the USA, Maine supports a strong Green Party and a governor who disdains all political affiliation. Rock-ribbed, yes, but with unconventional inclinations.

New Hampshire

New Hampshire has an attractive string of beaches and state parks along its brief stretch of coast, but its most distinctive natural features are inland and high above sea level. The jewel of its coast is the city of **Portsmouth**, which has a recent veneer of chic and a deep layer of history. First settled in 1623, it was known, enchantingly, as 'Strawberry Banke', for the wild fruit that grew there in abundance. In the old downtown area a museum district of the same name surrounds **Market Square** and walking tours of its eighteenth-century houses are available through the **New Hampshire Chamber of Commerce** (*see page 252*). The local citizenry, whose foresight prevented the destruction of the area for 'urban redevelopment' in the 1950s, have transformed **Strawberry Banke** into a lively shopping district as well, with a variety of crafts' shops and eating spots.

On the far side of the state and about two hours northwest of Boston on I-93 and I-89 is **Hanover**, New Hampshire's other attractive urban centre. **Dartmouth College** (1-603 646 1110) was founded here in 1769, with a charter from George III 'for the instruction of the youth of Indian tribes', and the school still provides special scholarships for Native Americans. The school's **Hood Museum** and **Hopkins Center for the Arts** sponsor a variety of interesting

New Hampshire's granite-faced **'Old Man of the Mountain'**. *See page 252.*

lectures and events, but the most striking work of art on campus is in the basement of the **Baker Memorial Library**, where the Mexican muralist Jose Clemente Orozco painted the immense *Epic of Western Civilization* while teaching here in the 1930s.

The lakes region of central New Hampshire is dominated by the melodically named **Lake Winnipesaukee**, a body of water shaped like some odd experiment in fractal geometry. There's no shortage of stunning views along its 180-mile (290-kilometre) shoreline, but none that will give you a true sense of the lake's size. **Laconia** and the neighbouring lakeside village of **Weirs Beach** (dubbed 'the Coney Island of New Hampshire', for its boardwalk, arcades and rides) are best known to the public for the annual mid-June uproar of **Motorcycle Week**, in which tens of thousands of two-wheeled 'hog' fanatics from all over the nation pull into town and burn equal amounts of beer and gasoline far into the night. The festivities devolved into a massive street brawl in the summer of 1965, but the typical leather boy these days is a stockbroker on a weekend lark – more wannabe than wild one.

There's a more sedate version of American weirdness in **Moultonborough**, on the north side of the lake, where a sinuous, seemingly endless access road leads up through several thousand acres of wooded mountainside to a turn-of-the-century millionaire's folly known as **Castle in the Clouds** (Route 171; 1-800 729 2468; open daily June-October). Tours of this elaborate, stone-walled Xanadu and its grounds are available in season. Those who want to stop the madness should check into any of the towns a few miles away to the northwest, around **Squam Lake**, the 'golden pond' where Hepburn and Fonda starred in the movie of the same name.

The **White Mountains**, spread out over three quarters of a million acres of the state's northern panhandle, are New England's most rugged heights and New Hampshire's pride and defining characteristic. **Conway**, near the Maine state line off Route 16, is the traditional gateway to the area and the terminus of the now-defunct rail service that opened the mountains to tourism. Nowadays, **Lincoln**, off I-93, is more quickly accessible. Either way, the drive between the two towns along the **Kancamagus Highway** (Route 112) offers countless great views of mountain and waterfall. Further north on the interstate, outside **Franconia Notch** (they don't have 'passes' or – heaven forbid – 'gaps' here) is the state totem, the **Old Man of the Mountain**. This 40-foot high (12-metre) granite profile, the product of wind and water erosion, was the inspiration for Hawthorne's story 'The Great Stone Face'. Though it has come to have sacred status among the citizenry, PT Barnum once dared offer to buy it.

Northeast of the notch, on Route 3, is the town of **Bretton Woods**, where, in 1944, the powers that were established the Old World Order – the International Monetary Fund and the World Bank. Even mightier forces rage a little further to the east, atop New England's tallest peak, **Mount Washington**, where weather conditions of Antarctic intensity prevail and over 200-mile-an-hour (322 kilometre-an-hour) winds (the world's strongest) are regularly recorded. The peak is accessible by trail, **Cog Railway** (1-800 922 8825) and roadway, but those 'This Car Climbed Mount Washington' bumper stickers are no idle boast – jalopies and junkers need not apply.

Where to stay

Staying in Portsmouth's historic district is expensive, but lodgings such as **Bow Street Inn** (121 Bow Street; 1-603 431 7760; rooms $99-$114) are undistinguished but relatively cheap. Up in the lake country, **Red Hill Inn** (Route 25B; 1-800 573 3445; rooms $105-$175), in Center Harbor, is reasonably priced, with a good restaurant. In the White Mountains, **Mount Washington Hotel** (Route 302; 1-800 258 0330; rooms $245-$1195) is decidedly pricey but positively reeks of history, faded glamour and power – this is where the Bretton Woods International Monetary Conference was held.

Getting there

By car

The lakes region of New Hampshire is two hours north of Boston (roughly 100 miles/160km); take the Laconia exit off I-93. Conway, in the White Mountains, is about 3 hours north of Boston (150 miles/240km), off Route 16.

By bus

Concord Trailways (1-603 228 3300) operates services across New Hampshire.

Tourist information

New Hampshire Chamber of Commerce

500 Market Street, Portsmouth (1-603 436 1118).
Open 10am-6.30pm Mon-Fri.

Maine

Maine's south coast is a land of old fishing villages and sandy beaches, similar to the Massachusetts shore. The twin towns of Kennebunk and Kennebunkport are the most famous names in the area, chiefly because of the latter's connection to the 41st president, George Herbert Walker Bush. The seaside resort of **Kennebunkport** evinces the preppy atmosphere appropriate to the former president; neighbouring **Kennebunk** has a more proletarian and commercial air. Both towns have their share of history and historic homes. Kennebunkport plays host to the **Seashore Trolley Museum** (Log Cabin Road; 1-207 967 2800; open daily May-October), where a collection of almost 200 electric streetcars is displayed, vintage and contemporary, from around the world, including a 'Desire' from New Orleans. The town of **Old Orchard Beach** – half an hour further up the coast – features seven miles (11.3 kilometres) of beach and a touch of honky-tonk along the pier; its **Palace Playland** amusement park includes a Ferris wheel and a working, turn-of-the-century carousel.

Portland is Maine's largest city, though still none too large, with a population of 65,000. It has some outsize culture and cool, partly because of its fine natural setting, bound as it is on three sides by water, and partly because of a strong local historic preservation movement. An added influence is the presence of a sizable academic community, the 10,000 students of the **University of Southern Maine** and the small but intense **Maine College of Art**.

The city was settled in 1623 but much of it burned to the ground in the Great Fire of 1866. The cobblestoned streets of the **Old Port Exchange**, the city's downtown historic district, are lined with numerous fine examples of the Victorian architecture that rose in the fire's wake. After dark the port lights up in a different kind of blaze, from the heat of young bodies in the thicket of the district's restaurants, bars and clubs. For highbrow pursuits, the **Portland Museum of Art** (7 Congress Square; 1-207 775 6148; open Tue-Sun May-October) has, in addition to the Payson collection of Impressionist work, a strong selection of paintings by Edward

The white stuff

New England skiing doesn't offer the expansive terrain of Europe's Alps or the American Rockies but it does have history and charm. And while New England's weather can be wet and unpredictable, the sciences of snowmaking and grooming have been perfected there, so good skiing is available with or without Mother Nature's co-operation.

Skiing has been a staple of the local tourist industry since the 1930s, when the first rope tow in America was set up on a steep hillside meadow in Woodstock, Vermont. Most of the region's leading ski resorts are still located in Vermont, but enthusiasts have good options in New Hampshire and Maine as well. Downhill skiing is the most popular form, but there are plenty of opportunities for cross-country touring as well. Stratton Mountain, in Vermont, claims bragging rights as the birthplace of snowboarding, and there is space for boarding at the bigger resorts (Sugarbush's slopes are unrestricted), but Yankee skiing is more trad than rad.

Now in its sixtieth year, **Stowe** (1-800 253 4754), on the slopes of Vermont's highest peak, Mount Mansfield, is a winter resort complex that has become synonymous with luxurious living and high style. The mountain's Front Four of expert trails are legendary for their challenge, but beginners will find plenty of options there as well. Stowe is also one of Vermont's better locations for cross-country skiing. For après-ski dining, Stowe village is unrivalled in its quality and variety.

Killington (1-800 621 6867), about 60 miles (96 kilometres) south of Stowe, is the largest skiing operation in Vermont and also has a range of difficulty that makes it suitable for all visitors. Without a nearby village to retire to, the nightlife is confined to the mountain's amenities but it's lively enough. The fine dining at nearby **Hemingway's** (Route 4; 1-802 422 3886; four-course set meal $50) has made it the only four-star restaurant in the state.

Sugarbush (1-800 537 8427), in Vermont's Mad River Valley, provides gentler skiing for the most part, and is definitely less lively at night. The towns of the valley have more than their share of scenery and charm, however, and preserve something closer to the original Vermont ski ambience.

In New Hampshire, the resort of **Wildcat** (1-800 255 6439/1-603 466 3326), situated in the heart of the White Mountain National Forest, has remained particularly unspoilt. Most of the trails are relatively difficult, and the winds coming off Mount Washington can be a real test, but the scenery is outstanding and the prices beat those of the larger resorts. New Hampshire has good cross-country trails at the **Black Mountain** resort in Jackson (1-603 383 4490) and **Mount Washington** (1-800 282 5220).

In Maine, **Sunday River** (1-207 824 3000) is without a lot of flashy amenities, but it's big enough to accommodate visitors in the very height of season and the crews maintain a consistently high quality of surface. More dynamic terrain and a higher degree of challenge are available at **Sugarloaf** (1-800 843 5623), further into the Maine interior.

Other resorts worth investigating include: **Wacheusett Mountain** in Princeton, MA (1-800 754 1234/1-978 464 2300); **Attitash** in Bartlett, NH (1-603 374 2368); **Loon Mountain**, on the Kancamagus Highway, NH (1-603 745 8111); **Mount Sunapee** in Newbury, NH (1-603 763 2356); **Pat's Peak** in Henniker, NH (1-603 428 3245); **Waterville Valley**, NH (1-603 236 8311); **Cannon Mountain** in Franconia Notch Parkway, Franconia, NH (1-603 823 5563); **Mad River Glen** in Waitsfield, VT (1-802 496 3551); **Mount Snow**, VT (1-802 464 3333); **Okemo** in Ludlow, VT (1-802 228 4041); **Pico** in Killington, VT (1-802 422 3333); and **Stratton Ski Resort**, VT (1-802 297 2200).

Hopper, Andrew Wyeth and Winslow Homer, especially for his seascapes.

Maine is so big that, once beyond Portland to get to the headlands north of Casco Bay where the real Maine begins, is a three-hour drive from Boston. The satellite roads off Route 1, for hundreds of miles north of here, lead to unspoiled coastal villages of ice-cold waters and granite-bouldered beaches. Those along the **Boothbay Peninsula**, about an hour north of Portland, are the best known, but others, and usually those furthest north, offer the purest examples of old Maine life. Off the coast, in the **Penobscot Bay**, about five hours out of Boston, is the especially virginal and attractive **Deer Isle**, summer home to the highly regarded **Haystack Mountain School of Crafts** (1-207 348 2306). Even further north is **Mount Desert Isle** and its **Acadia National Park** (off Route 3, Bar Harbor; 1-207 288 3338) which is a full day's drive out of Boston, but offers some truly unparalleled coastline – a combination of pounding surf, jagged rock and

Dark satanic villes

In the course of the nineteenth century, New England was transformed from a land of fishermen, sailors and farmers to one of factory hands. The village green of the country town and the seaside docks of the shipping port gave way to the red-brick factory and worker housing of the New England mill town.

The older livelihoods had their shortcomings. The soil was never really all that good and the growing season was short. Whaling was immensely profitable, but the birth of the petroleum industry replaced whale oil with kerosene. The clipper ship's predominance faded with the arrival of the steam engine.

New England's salvation was the factory. The region was rich in fast-running rivers and streams, and as early as the 1780s wealthy merchant shipping families began to harness that water power for the manufacture of textiles. The fledgling industry was crippled, however, by a British monopoly of the advanced technology of the day. It took two acts of industrial espionage for the fledgling industry to gather strength.

The first took place in Pawtucket, Rhode Island, on the banks of the Blackstone River, where a young Englishman named Samuel Slater, working from memory, managed to replicate the first model in America of the Arkwright power spinning frame, for the production of yarn. The second bit of larceny was accomplished by Francis Cabot Lowell (a resonant Massachusetts name), who travelled to England for the express purpose of studying the Cartwright power loom for the production of cloth, and, in another demonstration of prodigious memory, successfully constructed the first American copy of the machine in a Waltham mill on the Charles River in Massachusetts.

Lowell is best known for the town that bears his name and that served as the original model for the company towns that sprouted up as the Industrial Revolution spread throughout New England. Lowell was built from scratch on the Merrimack River over the course of a few years in the 1820s and included mills, stores, housing, churches and canals. It was a benevolent autocracy at first, with a working population recruited from the small towns of rural New England. Decently housed, relatively well-paid and ceaselessly counselled in the virtues of Christian temperance, the 'Lowell girls' became an icon of enlightened capitalism.

Touring the canals of **Lowell**, *Massachusetts.*

Sampling the wares at the **Boott Cotton Mills Museum**.

This worker's paradise collapsed, however, as the industry burgeoned and seized on an arriving population of European immigrants from the 1840s onward. Throughout the post-Civil War era and into the early twentieth century, the mill towns of New England became a landscape as grim as its counterpart of the time in the north of England. At the same time, this harsh system produced some monumental feats of production. Particularly with the advent of steam power and the introduction of precision-tooled, interchangeable parts, New England became the cradle of American industry of every sort, from firearms to clockmaking, furniture, clothing and shoes.

The mill towns faded in the twentieth century and underwent near-total decay after World War II. Cheap labour and the absence of trade unions, first in the American South and then in the Third World, were too much for the bosses to resist – the factories either closed down or relocated. But in one of the peculiar ironies of American life, the old mills have lately begun to be resuscitated and transformed. Historic preservationists and yuppie-minded real estate developers have refurbished sites such as Lowell and the giant Amoskeag Mills in Manchester, New Hampshire, which have become flavour of the moment for artists' housing and high-tech industry.

Places of interest

American Clock and Watch Museum

100 Maple Street, Bristol, Connecticut (1-860 583 6070). **Open** *1 Apr-6 Dec* 10am-5pm daily; or by appointment.

American Precision Museum

196 Main Street, Windsor, Vermont (1-802 674 5781).
Open *May-Nov* 9am-5pm Mon-Sat; 10am-4pm Sat, Sun.

Boott Cotton Mills Museum

See p93 **Museums & Galleries** *for listings.*

Slater Mill Historic Site

67 Roosevelt Avenue, Pawtucket, Rhode Island (1-401 725 8638). **Open** phone for details of daily tours.

unbroken pine forest. The isle's chief town, **Bar Harbor**, has a touch of tourist tack these days, but also a hint of its time as an elite resort of the late nineteenth century.

Where to stay & eat

If you're looking for somewhere to stay on the south coast, save yourself a few dollars and forego Kennebunkport for **Kennebunk**, where the **Kennebunk Inn** (45 Main Street; 1-207 985 3351; rooms $65-$135) offers the charm it has accumulated since 1799, at much lower rates than can be found in the glitzier seaside town. In **Portland**, the **Regency** (20 Milk Street; 1-800 727 3436; rooms $119-$199) is right in the historic district (for which you'll pay a premium), while the **Pomegranate Inn** (49 Neal Street; 1-800 356 0408; rooms $95-$175), west of the downtown area, is a bit cheaper and delivers a bright mix of nineteenth-century and contemporary colour.

The outstanding dining choice in Kennebunkport is the **White Barn Inn** (37 Beach Avenue; 1-207 967 2321), where inspired interpretations of classic New England dishes are offered in the rustic elegance of a refurbished country barn. Dining in Portland is varied and inventive. In addition to a wealth of ethnic spots, **Street and Co** (33 Wharf Street; 1-207 775 0887) does upmarket contemporary seafood in a converted industrial building, while **Fresh Market** (43 Exchange Street; 1-207 773 7146) offers decent, inexpensive pastas, cafeteria-style.

Getting there

By car

Kennebunk and Kennebunkport are about 90 minutes north of Boston on the I-95 (roughly 80 miles/129km).

By air

Several airlines serve Portland International Jetport, including Delta, United Airlines and Continental. *See page 263* **Directory** for details of these and other major airlines.

Tourist information

Maine Office of Tourism

Telephone enquiries (1-800 533 9595).
Website: www.visitmaine.com

Moose encounters

Coming down a mountain road and seeing a vehicle pulled over up ahead, its driver peering intently out from behind the steering wheel into the woods, one does the same. And there, wonder of wonders, stands, not too far off, a momma moose, indifferent to her human audience and placidly nursing two young.

This was not a common occurrence in New England, outside the deep Maine woods and far north of New Hampshire, just 15 years ago. Today, however, as far south and west as central Vermont, the roads through the high gaps have the familiar icon of the 'deer crossing' sign joined by that of a bigger, shaggier ungulate – *Alces americana*, the North American moose. And those signs are well heeded – the moose is a big mo'fo'. With bulls running the height of an NBA centre at the shoulders and equal in weight to three team players, you can bet the car insurance lobby leaned hard on the legislature to get those signs up pronto.

Big as they are however, there is something irresistibly endearing about these brunette behemoths. Maybe it's the ungainly structure, with all that tower of muscle gaining mass, against all physics and logic, building upwards and forwards through the block of chest and shoulder, then out into the camel-like snout with the downhanging goatee, all of it crowned with the swept-back forest of multi-pronged horn. That must be it: all that awesome power above those spindly legs. And then there's the air of calm. Unafraid of humans or anything else that lives in the woods – why, they probably like us! We sure like them (though they've reappeared in such numbers that, sad to say, several states now authorise annual moose hunts). Maybe it's the fond childhood TV memories of *Rocky and Bullwinkle* – whatever, just run a web search on the keyword 'moose' and see what happens. There's a veritable cult out there.

It would seem that visitors to central New England owe their increased chances of moose encounters to the activities of Canada's Hydro Quebec electric company, who have destroyed enough moose environment in recent years to drive increasing numbers of them south across the border.

Contact the **Vermont Fish and Wildlife Department** (1-802 241 3700) or the **New Hampshire Food and Wildlife Department** (1-603 271 3211) for information on likely moose zones. In the state of Maine, professional moose watch guides come and go – phone the **Maine Office of Tourism** (*see above*) for the most up-to-date details.

Vermont villages are at their most splendid in the autumn.

Ecotopia east

Vermont

The closest parts of Vermont are a two-hour drive from Boston, and many of the most interesting parts of the state are three hours or more away. It's worth the trek. Visually and culturally, there is no place else like it.

Enter Vermont from the south and the **Green Mountains** billow up slowly in greeting. It's the perfect, gentle backdrop to the easy pace of the small towns in this part of the country, where the manners of another age linger on. **Brattleboro**, off the I-91, the major settlement closest to Boston, is more representative of contemporary Vermont. Its roots are atypical too, in that, because of its location on the Connecticut River, it was an industrial centre in the nineteenth century. That

The Republic

'The gods of the hills are not the gods of the valleys', proclaimed Ethan Allen, and it still rings true. Vermont is different, the natives tell you, and it's their proudest claim. They also like to say that 'Vermont is what America was', and there's something to that, too.

It's a poor state for the most part. The Green Mountains that are its chief defining characteristic are the northernmost arm of the Appalachians, and the hardscrabble farms and windworn faces of traditional Vermont would not be out of place in the high reaches of west Virginia and east Kentucky. The state carries a veneer of modernisation from the tourist trade and the chic of urban expatriates, but the heart of Vermont remains in its dairy farms, with their cheddar cheese and maple syrup, and its small towns, with their high-steepled churches and village greens.

Vermonters have lived in defiance of the ways of the flatlander since the first days of colonial settlement. It's an attitude born out of triumph over the difficult terrain they inhabit. The Green Mountains are among the oldest on earth, and eons of wear have left them with a strange, gnarled beauty. But the soil is poor, outside of the river valleys and the shores of Lake Champlain, and even the aboriginal Abenaki Indians limited their settlement to the lowlands.

It was the lure of furs that first brought both Indians and Europeans to the hills, and from 1630 on there were 150 years of armed struggle for control of the territory, at one time or another involving the Abenaki, the Iroquois, the English, the French and the Dutch. While the area passed into English control at the conclusion of the French and Indian Wars, both the colonies of New York and New Hampshire laid claim to it.

This political ambiguity bred a taste for anarchy in Vermont's first white settlers. Most of them had come up the Connecticut River from southern New England to land granted by the governor of New Hampshire. When the Crown ruled that New York had sovereignty, the settlers found themselves harassed by the New York sheriff's posses, surveyors and real estate agents. Resistance coalesced around the Green Mountain Boys, a rough band of sharpshooters led by brothers Ethan and Ira Allen, the Romulus and Remus of the hills.

This militia fended off the New Yorkers and then turned that experience to use against King George himself. Though they played a significant role in several of the colonists' victories in the American Revolution, New Yorkers' resentment of the cantankerous ways of the Allens and their followers barred Vermont's admission to the union of former colonies. The Vermonters retaliated by declaring themselves an independent republic.

The republic flirted with the idea of a separate peace with the English and played with the idea of a Greater Vermont including portions of New York and New Hampshire. Those states, in turn, contemplated partition of the unruly hill country, and, at one point, the Continental Congress debated an invasion. The ill feeling survived the Revolution, and it was not until 1791 that Vermont joined the union, the 14th state (and the first to abolish slavery).

This contentious history left Vermonters with an enduring taste for independence and anti-authoritarianism. If the state remained a bastion of rural conservatism and rock-ribbed Republicanism until recent years, and though it remains, racially, the whitest state in the union, it's still a remarkably tolerant and common-sensical place. (It was Vermont's Republican senator George Aiken who suggested, in the midst of the Vietnam War, that the United States simply declare victory and go home.)

Vermont's gorgeous landscape and live-and-let-live mentality has made it irresistibly attractive to aesthetes and bohemians from the cities of the northeast. Long a favoured summer retreat of writers and artists, it became one of America's prime breeding grounds for counter-culture communities of the 1960s and 1970s.

Most of the hippie communes have come and gone, but their impact on the general culture is unmistakable. Vermont's most renowned export, Ben & Jerry's Ice Cream, with its psychedelic packaging and tithing to 'politically correct' causes, shows unmistakable traces of its counterculture origins. Cities such as Burlington, Brattleboro and especially the state capital, Montpelier, overflow with shops and businesses devoted to music, arts and crafts, New Age practices, health food and vegetarian businesses. A significant gay and lesbian population is present and out.

All the currents of culture and history that make Vermont unique came together recently in the Fred Tuttle senatorial campaign of 1998. Tuttle, a 79-year-old retired dairy farmer, raised and spent all of $16 to defeat a former Massachusetts millionaire who moved to the Green Mountains for the sole purpose of buying his way into the state Republican party's senatorial nomination.

One of Vermont's most famous exports.

The cagey Tuttle, whose campaign statements read like woodshed Zen, came to represent a way of life more authentic than that of the modern world. He seemed the very embodiment of the old-time Vermonter, the close-mouthed bumpkin whose simple ways and earthy wisdom easily outfox the glib city slicker. It was as if he'd walked out of one of the classic Vermont tales:

City Slicker (asking directions): Do you know how to get to X?
Farmer: Nope.
City Slicker: Do you know how to get to Y?
Farmer: Nope.
City Slicker: Do you know how to get to Z?
Farmer: Nope.
City Slicker: You don't know much, do you?
Farmer: Nope. But I ain't lost.

Or:

City Slicker: How come you have so many cows up here?
Farmer: We prefer 'em.

Tuttle capitalised on Vermonters' resentment of arrogant out-of-staters (the rule of thumb is that one must spend ten winters in Vermont before one can begin to claim native status) and swept the newcomer from the field. He trumped his opponent in one debate by challenging him to correctly pronounce the names of the Vermont towns of Calais ('Kallus') and Leicester ('Leester'). His one big fundraising dinner was a nickel-a-plate affair that was trumpeted as the cheapest opportunity anyone would ever have to buy influence in Washington.

The appeal of Tuttle's campaign was in no way undercut by the fact that it was the brainchild of another former Massachusettian, a fortysomething media-savvy film-maker who'd made Tuttle the subject of a 1996 mockumentary called 'Man With a Plan'. In fact, the marriage of rustic ways and urban sophistication perfectly captured the nature of contemporary Vermont.

Even though Tuttle made it plain he had no intention of working to defeat the Democratic incumbent in the general election and, in fact, intended to vote for him, the state Republican organisation had the good sense to respect this stampede of indigenous feeling and step out of the way. The bandwagon proved strong enough that politicians of every stripe in totally unrelated campaigns clambered aboard, stumbling over one another in the rush to broadcast the age and depth of their Vermont roots.

The most amazing example of Vermont's difference is a nice Jewish boy from Brooklyn, New York, one Bernard 'Bernie' Sanders, now in his fifth term as Vermont's Congressperson in the US House of Representatives. The difference, and the amazement, is that Sanders is an avowed socialist, a phenomenon unknown in the USA since before the days of Joe McCarthy.

A quietly charismatic former writer and teacher, Sanders was elected mayor of the city of Burlington in the 1980s with the support of a group called the Progressive Coalition, more popularly known as the Sanderistas. The city enjoyed an economic boom under his administration and came to be regularly voted one of America's most livable cities.

While Sanders makes no secret of his socialist philosophy, his formal label is 'independent', a word easier on the ears of his fellow Vermonters, and one that resonates with their own stubborn inclinations. The Green Mountains these days show a streak of red.

prosperity faded and left it ripe for post-1960s gentrification. Consequently, as throughout the state, Brattleboro today vibrates with countercultural lifestyles and politics and its old downtown area of winding, riverside streets is a warren of crafts shops and creative cuisine.

Bennington, nestled in a broad bowl in the foothills of the state's southwest corner, is a good introduction to the more classic, mellow Vermont. It was Ethan Allen's mountain redoubt when he first made a name for himself as leader of the resistance to the New York landlords' attempts to stake claims in the Green Mountains (*see page 258* **The Republic**). What the Albany sheriffs knew as the 'Bennington Mob' had, within a few years, lead the attack on Fort Ticonderog as the 'Green Mountain Boys' – it was among the colonists' first key victories. The **Battle Monument** outside town refers to another colonial triumph, however, in which regular forces beat back a British attempt to capture a significant arms store in the area. Another American hero associated with the town is the painter and longtime resident Grandma Moses, 30 of whose primitive landscapes are on display at the **Bennington Museum** (West Main Street; 1-802 447 1571; open daily). Another of the Seven Sisters, **Bennington College**, is here too; its students (before co-education) were famous for a penchant for black leotards and an artsy cast of mind.

The drive north from Bennington along Route 7 leads through a good many representative small Vermont towns, each with their village green and white-steepled church, and through a broad swath of gorgeous, rolling mountain country. A photographer's delight all year round, it's especially prime when the leaves turn in late September and early October (*see page 231* **A New England point of hue**). **Arlington** and **Manchester**, on the southern stretch of the drive, both have charming old inns and some intriguing shops. **Rutland**, about an hour north, is a sad, shabby exception to the state's charm. **Middlebury**, however, half an hour north again, displays all the old virtues and has the added energy of **Middlebury College**, another fine, small liberal arts institution.

Some of Vermont's most recent cultural developments can be appreciated about 20 miles (32 kilometres) over the back roads east of Middlebury, outside the little town of **Hancock**, off Route 100; here the state's longest-running 1960s community survives and thrives. **Quarry Hill** (1-802 767 3902) and its **North Hollow Day School** have come a long way since the longhairs first huddled in a ramshackle farmhouse, eating brown rice and veg. They're still vegetarian, but the group's primary income these days stems from software development. Visitors are welcome if they call in advance and adhere to the group's dogma: 1) Don't hit kids 2) We can put up with you if you can put up with us 3) No dishes in the sink. An understanding of the unity of all living beings is recommended but not mandatory. No drugs.

Another half-hour up Route 7 from Middlebury is **Burlington**, 'Lake Champlain's Queen City'. This is Vermont's Big Apple, and it's booming. The economy is fuelled by the presence of the University of Vermont, nearby IBM and an assortment of other high-tech outfits. The heart of downtown, **Church Street Marketplace**, is a four-block-long pedestrian mall of tasteful shops, several bookstores and varied dining options. The town has a lively bar scene and musical choices ranging from DJ Spooky to Doc Watson and Yo-Yo Ma. The view over Lake Champlain at sunset is a dream. Even the crumbling **Old North End** is on the verge of gentrification. All this and socialism (sort of) too – Congressperson Bernie Sanders' Progressive Coalition still holds City Hall. What's not to like? (Though oldtimers might say, 'I have a feeling we're not in Vermont any more'.)

Where to stay

The **Arlington Inn** (Route 7A; 1-800 443 9442; rooms $250-$490), a few miles north of Bennington, is an 1848 Greek Revival mansion in one of the area's loveliest small towns. Just outside Middlebury, the cheaper **Waybury Inn** (Route 124, off Route 7; 1-800 348 1810; $80-$115) has bargain rates. It's so representative of the species that it served as the model for the inn operated by the Bob Newhart character in the TV show of the same name that chronicled the misadventures of an urban refugee in search of country simplicity. South of Burlington, the **Inn at Shelburne Farms** (Harbor Road, Shelburne; 1-802 985 8498; rooms $95-$300) is an immense Edwardian mansion that dates from 1899 and rests on an estate of almost 1,000 acres (401 hectares). Pricey, but not as much of a splurge as you'd expect.

Getting there

By car

Brattleboro, the settlement closest to Boston, is roughly two hours' drive from the city via the Mass Pike (I-90) and I-91 (116 miles/187km). Bennington is an hour west along Route 9 off the Brattleboro exit off I-91, roughly three hours from Boston.

By bus or rail

Vermont Transit (1-802 254 6066) serves Brattleboro from Boston's South Station twice daily. **Amtrak** (*see p231*) operates services to Burlington (Essex Junction) and Brattleboro.

Tourist information

Bennington Area Chamber of Commerce

Veterans' Memorial Drive, Route 7 (1-802 447 3311).
Open 9am-5pm Mon-Fri.

Brattleboro Visitors' Information Bureau

Putney Road, Battleboro (1-802 257 1112).
Open 9am-5pm Mon-Fri.

Directory

Directory

For information on abbreviations used in this guide, *see page vi* **About the Guide**.

If you're phoning from outside Boston, dial 1 and the area code 617 before any of the numbers listed below, unless otherwise stated. All 1-800 numbers can be dialled free of charge from within the USA, although bear in mind that some hotels add a surcharge for the use of their phones, whatever number you call.

Getting Around

To & from the airport

Logan International Airport

(Information 561 1800/Logan Airport Ground Transportation 1-800 235 6426).

Boston's Logan International Airport is located on a spit of reclaimed land to the east of the city, and is just 3 miles (5km) from the downtown area. The airport's five terminals are lettered A to E and connected by a shuttle bus that also runs to Airport T station. By 2003 Logan will be considerably bigger, particularly the international terminal; the work is currently underway.

By bus

Seven bus companies provide a non-stop transfer between the airport and South Station near downtown Boston. They are Bonanza, CNJ, Conquer, Trailways, Peter Pan, Plymouth & Brockton and Vermont Transit. The fare is $6 one way.

Buses leave from all five of the airport's terminals every 15 to 30 minutes between 7.15am and 10.15pm Monday to Friday (with an additional 6.25am service at weekends and on public holidays). The last bus leaves an hour later, at 11.15pm. Departures from South Station are between 5.55am and 9.15pm Monday to Friday, and 5.20am and 9pm on Saturday and Sunday. They leave the station from Gate 25.

Logan Express (1-800 235 6426) runs a bus service from the airport to Braintree, Framingham and Woburn. One-way fares cost $8 on weekdays, Monday to Friday, and $6 on Saturdays.

By taxi or limousine

Taxis are available outside the airport's baggage claim area. A cab ride to downtown Boston costs $15-$20 and about $23 to Cambridge, with an extra $1 toll for travelling through the Sumner Tunnel from Logan to Boston. Station wagons, taxis with disabled access and credit card taxis are all available upon request. For a list of reputable firms *see page 264*.

If you want to travel in style, advance booking can be made with **Carey Limousine** (623 8700) and the **Commonwealth Limousine Service** (787 5575).

By boat

Travelling by boat is the most pleasant way of getting to and from the airport and is certainly a good way to say farewell to the city.

The **Logan Water Shuttle** (1-800 235 6426) connects the free terminal shuttle bus with Boston's Rowes Wharf (6am-8pm Mon-Fri; 10am-11pm Sat; 10am-8pm Sun; $10 one way). The journey takes approximately seven minutes.

Harbor Express runs a similar service between the airport, the southern suburb of Quincy and Long Wharf, in downtown Boston near the Marriott Hotel. Phone 376 8417 for the schedule. **City Water Taxis** (422 0392) operates between 1 April and 15 October ($5-$10) and takes passengers from the airport to the World Trade Center, Congress Street (near South Station), Long Wharf (for Government Center and the North End), North Station and Charlestown, among other stops.

By T

The **Massachusetts Bay Transport Authority** or MBTA operates the local subway system known as the 'T'. Access to Airport station is by the Blue Line, which runs from State/Citizen's Bank or Government Center stations – the journey takes about 15 minutes. Airport shuttle buses numbers 22 and 33 take passengers from the airline terminals to the T station. Photocopied T maps are available from information booths in terminals A, C and E. *See also page 263* **Public Transport**.

Disabled travel

Airport Handicap Van

(561 1769).

Airport Handicap Van is a service that runs between the airport and various hotels to Wood Island T stop (as there is no disabled access at Airport T stop). Phone the above number for details. *See also p266* **Directory A-Z**.

Left luggage

If you want to leave your luggage at the airport there are lockers available, but allow plenty of time to access your luggage before your flight departure. You will need to pass through security to get to your lockers and you should make sure you have plenty of change.

A small- to medium-sized locker costs 75¢ per half hour with a maximum charge of $4.50 for 24 hours, and a large locker costs $1.25 per half hour with a maximum charge of $7.50 for 24 hours.

Package Express
Fifth Floor, South Station Transportation Center, 700 Atlantic Avenue, at Summer Street (526 1842). South Station T.
Open 7.30am-8pm Mon-Fri; 8am-6pm Sat, Sun. **Rates** $3 per piece, per day; $5 overnight.
No credit cards.
Map 5 G5
Luggage storage at South Station.

Major international airlines

There are 39 airlines operating out of Logan Airport, including those listed below. For domestic and other international airlines consult the *Yellow Pages*.

Aer Lingus
1-800 223 6537
Air Atlantic
1-800 426 7000
Air France
1-800 237 2747
Alitalia
1-800 223 5730
American Airlines
1-800 433 7300
British Airways
1-800 247 9297
Business Express/ DeltaConnection
1-800 345 3400
Canadian Airlines
1-800 426 7000
KLM
1-800 374 7747
Lufthansa
1-800 645 3880
Qantas
1-800 227 4500
Swissair
1-800 221 4750
United Airlines
1-800 241 6522
Virgin Atlantic
1-800 862 8621

Public transport

Public transport in the Boston area is run by the **MBTA** and consists of the T, Commuter Rail and buses.

Money-saving 'Visitor's Passports' are available for one-day ($5), three-day ($9) or weekly ($18) use, providing unlimited travel on the T and MBTA buses. For those planning longer stays, monthly passes are available for $27. Passes can be bought at Airport, Government Center, Harvard, Alewife and Riverside T stations and North Station, South Station and Back Bay Station, as well as at the Boston Common and Prudential Center tourist information booths (*see page 273*).

MBTA
(Information 222 3200/1-800 392 6100/pass program 222 5218/ complaints 222 5215).
Website: www.mbta.com

The T

The subway, or T, was America's first and is efficient, cheap and easy to use. Tokens costs 85¢ (40¢ for under-12s; 20¢ for senior citizens), though a trip on one of the Green or Red Line surface extensions can cost up to $2.25 (you pay the driver).

Trains run from 5.15am to 12.30am Monday to Saturday and from 6am to 12.30am on Sundays. Free subway maps are available from major stations such as Harvard, Government Center, North Station, Back Bay, South Station and Park Street. 'Outbound' and 'inbound' services often have different subway entrances: the direction is in relation to Park Street.

Not many Bostonians (and even fewer visitors) know that each branch colour was chosen to reflect a characteristic of the area that each line covers. The Green Line, for example, was named in honour of the Emerald Necklace, the chain of parks and woods that links Boston and the western suburbs. The Red Line, serving Harvard, pays homage to the Harvard Crimsons, the university's football team. The Blue Line is supposed to mirror the colour of the waterfront, and the Orange Line runs along Washington Street, originally known as Orange Street after William of Orange, king of England between 1689 and 1702.

Bus services

The MBTA runs around 150 bus routes in Boston and the suburbs. The flat fare is 60¢ (15¢ for senior citizens), and payment has to be in exact change (one of the reasons it's worth buying a Visitor's Passport).

Buses run from 5.30am to 1am daily. Routes and timetables are available from major T stops or the MBTA central office (10 Park Plaza, 120 Boylston Street).

Most out-of-town services depart from the **South Station Transportation Center** (700 Atlantic Avenue), which is served by the following bus companies:

Bonanza
(720 4110/1-800 556 3815)
For services to Cape Cod.
Greyhound
(526 1801/1-800 231 2222)
For national services.
Peter Pan
(426 7838/1-800 237 8747)
For travel routes in and around the Massachusetts area.
Concord Trailways
(426 8080)
For buses to New Hampshire and Maine.
Plymouth & Brockton
(773 9401)
For buses to Plymouth and Brockton.
Vermont Transit
(1-800 451 3292)
For buses to Vermont.

Rail services

Boston has three main train stations: **South Station** (700 Atlantic Avenue, at Summer Street), **Back Bay Station** (145 Dartmouth Street, at Stuart Street) and **North Station** (Causeway Street, at Friend Street).

MBTA Commuter Rail runs from North Station and South Station, serving the Greater Boston area and Massachusetts as far as Providence, Rhode Island. The national rail service **Amtrak** (1-800 872 7245/www.amtrak.com) runs from South Station and Back Bay Station.

Taxis & limousines

Taxis can be hailed on the street at any time, providing, of course, that you can find one available. This becomes particularly difficult after 1am, when public transport has closed down for the night. Taxi ranks can be found near major hotels, outside main train stations and in Harvard Square, Cambridge.

Regular meter fares begin at $1.50 for the first quarter of a mile and then 25¢ for each eighth of a mile thereafter.

If you have a complaint about a taxi service phone the police department's **Hackney Hotline** on 536 8294.

The following local taxi companies offer a 24-hour service and most accept major credit cards but it is always best to phone to check first):

All Area Taxi
(536 2000)
Bay State Taxi Service
(566 5000)
Checker Taxi
(536 7000)
Independent Taxi Operators Association
(268 1313/426 8700)
Red & White Cab
(242 8000)

The **Boston Cab Association** (262 2227/536 5010) also has limousines (*see also page 262*), **Boston Coach** (387 7676) has vans, coaches, limousines and cars, and if you use **Town Taxi** (536 5000) you might end up being chauffeured by 'Boston's Best Taxi Driver' Bobby Uzdavinis (voted so by *Boston Magazine*).

Lost property

MBTA

The MBTA lost and found department is divided into different sections for each form of transport. If you lose something on a **bus** phone 222 5202 (24 hours daily, but you can only pick up valuable items between 9am and 6pm daily).

Phone 222 3600 for property lost on **Commuter Rail** (6.30am to midnight Monday to Saturday; 7.30am to 11.30pm on Sunday). Each T line has a different number:
Blue Line (222 5522);
Green Line (222 5220);
Orange Line (222 5404);
and **Red Line** (222 5321). All are open 24 hours daily.

Taxis

If you lose something in a taxi, phone the police department's **Hackney Hotline** (536 8294). It's open 24 hours a day.

Driving

Until the 'Big Dig' (*see page 16* **Boston Today**) is completed, driving in Boston is not recommended, but if you must drive, here is some of the information that you may need:

The three main highways that lead into town are the I-95, the I-93 (the Central Artery), which runs all the way to Vermont, and the I-90 (the Massachusetts Turnpike, or 'Mass Pike'), which is the route taken to and from New York.

The speed limit on most major highways is 55 miles per hour. On sections of the Mass Pike this goes up to 65 miles per hour. Elsewhere in Boston, speed limits range from 20 to 50 miles per hour.

The **American Automobile Association** or **AAA** (1-800 222 4357) can provide members with maps on request. Some clubs – including the AA and RAC in the UK – have reciprocal arrangements with the AAA, which also entitles you to discounts at certain sights, museums and hotels. The AAA offers a free towing service to members (except on the privately-run Mass Pike, which has its own patrol cars to aid breakdowns).

State law requires the wearing of seat belts. It's also a finable offense to scatter litter when driving: throwing a wrapper out of a car window could set you back up to $1,000 or cost you your right to drive in the USA.

Car rental

If you want to hire a car, check whether an international driver's licence will be required, as some rental companies insist on both a foreign and international licence (available from the AAA, *see above*).

Many companies also require that a licencee to be over 25 years of age, and all insist on payment with a major credit card. If you're driving with children under the age of five they must be in the back seat in an approved child-safety restraint.

Car rental rarely includes insurance, so check what you are covered for when renting a vehicle. Major rental companies include:

Alamo
(1-800 327 9633)
Avis
(1-800 831 2847/1-800 331 1212)
Budget
(1-800 527 0700)

Biking & blading in Boston

Americans and cycling are not supposed to mix. That's the traditional view, and in many American cities the appearance of a cyclist on the streets would almost be worthy of a newspaper report. Not in Boston. True, the most significant biking population is the city's many students, but office workers also commute by bike – especially along the 17-mile (27-kilometre) **Paul Dudley White** cycle path, which runs on both sides of the Charles River from near the Science Museum as far as Watertown, upriver in the west.

Yes, Boston even has dedicated cycle routes. And those routes also serve rollerbladers, or in-line skaters. The river path is arguably the nicest place to skate or cycle in Boston, giving you a great view of the city and Cambridge.

Its width and quality varies though. At its worst, the route simply follows the sidewalk, right next to the road, and also has to cross several main thoroughfares. However, from around the Longfellow Bridge on the south side to the Boston University Bridge, it is uninterrupted, high-quality tarmac. And on the other side of the river, skaters get extra space on Sundays between April and October, because the authorities close Memorial Drive from the Eliot Bridge in Cambridge as far as Western Avenue.

Another high-quality route, slightly further out of town, is the ten-mile (16-kilometre) **Minuteman Trail**, which starts near the Alewife T stop and runs out to the historic site of Lexington (*see page 229* **Trips Out of Town**) and on to Bedford. The downside of this route is that at weekends it gets very busy, it can be totally packed with other cyclists, bladers and pedestrians, not all of whom seem prepared to share the limited space.

The **Southwest Corridor** offers an easy four-mile (six-kilometre) ride from the South End around Dartmouth Street into Roxbury, along the **Pierre Lallement Bicycle Path**. It's named after the Frenchman who is generally credited with inventing the bicycle. He died broke in Boston in the late nineteenth century.

If you have a whole day, take a picturesque ride along the old harbour, starting in South Boston at Fort Independence Park and heading for the John F Kennedy Library & Museum. Other biking and skating areas include the **Fresh Pond** reservoir in Cambridge and **Franklin Park**, between Dorchester and Roxbury, which has four-and-a-half miles (seven kilometres) of paved paths (*see page 41* **Sightseeing**).

For off-road trails, you don't have to go too far. In the **Blue Hills State Reservation**, south of Boston, there are miles of mountain bike trails. From downtown, it's about a 40-minute cycle ride to get there. Phone the **Metropolitan District Commission** (727 5114) for details.

For really serious mountain biking, check out the **White Mountain National Forest** in neighbouring New Hampshire (*see page 229* **Trips Out of Town**).

If you want to explore the Boston area by bike – a good idea – go out and buy *Boston's Bike Map* ($4.25), available in most cycle shops (*see page 226* **Sport & Fitness**) and also in many bookshops (*see page 219* **Shops & Services**). As well as a comprehensive map of every bike route in Boston, Cambridge, Brookline and surrounding districts, it has a wealth of information on the back, ranging from bike shop contact details, cycle organisations, tips on taking bikes on public transport and advice on dealing with the nutters who drive cars around Boston.

If you buy an MBTA 'Bikes on the T' pass ($5), you can take your bike on Commuter Rail and Orange and Red T services during off-peak hours. Phone the MBTA on 722 5000 for details.

For bike and blade hire *see chapter* **Sport & Fitness**.

Bicycling laws

The same traffic laws apply as for motor vehicles. Always ride with the flow of traffic and in single file. Lights are required from half an hour after sunset to half an hour before sunrise; children aged 12 and under are required to wear a helmet; no children aged under 12 months are allowed to ride as passenges and children aged between 12 months and four years, or weighing less than 40 pounds (18 kilogrammes), must be carried in an approved child-carrier.

Dollar
(1-800 800 4000)
Hertz
(1-800 654 3131)
National
(1-800 227 7368)

Parking

Parking is difficult, if not all-but impossible, in Boston. The number of spaces is trimmed by about five per cent each year, as the city has yet to comply with the Clean Air Act standards. What spaces do exist are metered and only available to non-residents for up to two hours between 8am and 6pm. A fine can cost $20 and retrieving a towed car more than $50. If you do get a ticket, phone the **Boston Office of the Parking Clerk** (635 4410).

The wisest thing to do with a car is leave it in a parking lot and walk. Boston's two main car parks are under **Boston Common** (on Charles Street, directly opposite the Public Garden; 954 2096) and under the **Prudential Center** (800 Boylston Street; 267 1002), which offers a discount on parking if you make a purchase at one of the shops in the mall above.

Other garages can be found at: **Government Center** (50 New Sudbury Street, at Congress Street; 227 0385), the **New England Aquarium** (70 East India Row, off Atlantic Avenue; 723 1731) and at **Zero Post Office Square**, Congress Street (423 1430).

Breakdown services

The **AAA** (1-800 222 4357) offers a 24-hour breakdown service (*see page 264*).

24-hour petrol stations

Bowdoin Square Exxon

239 Cambridge Street, at Blossom Street (523 3394). **Credit** AmEx, Disc, MC, V. **Map 5 F4**

Fenway Texaco Service

1241 Boylston Street, at Ipswich Street (247 7905). **Credit** AmEx, Disc, MC, V.

Directory A-Z

Business

Business libraries

Baker Library

Soldiers Field, off North Harvard Street, Allston (495 6040). Harvard T. **Open** 8am-11pm Mon-Thur; 8am-6pm Fri; 10am-6pm Sat; noon-11pm Sun. **Credit** AmEx, MC, V. **Map 4 A3**
Harvard Graduate School of Business, Management and the Social Sciences will provide access to the Baker Library for a fee of $50 per day.
Disabled: toilet. Website: library.hbs.edu

Dewey Library

30 Wadsworth Street, between Main Street & Memorial Drive (253 5677). Kendall/MIT T. **Open** 8.30am-11pm Mon-Thur; 8.30am-7pm Fri; 11am-6pm Sat; 1-9pm Sun. **Map 4 E4**
MIT's Dewey Library can also provide business, management and social sciences information.
Disabled: toilet.

Kirstein Business Branch of Boston Public Library

20 City Hall Avenue, off School Street (523 0860). State/Citizen's Bank T. **Open** 9am-5pm Mon-Fri. **Map 5 G4**
This is not only the most comprehensive Boston library specialising in management and business resources but also the first place to turn to for business information.

Pardee Library

595 Commonwealth Avenue, at Kenmore Square (353 4301). Kenmore T. **Open** 8am-10.45pm Mon-Thur; 8am-8.45pm Fri; 10am-5.45pm Sat; noon-10.45pm Sun. **Map 3 D5**
The Pardee Library is Boston University's management library but is also open to the general public.

Convention centres

Bayside Exposition Center

200 Mount Vernon Street, at Morrissey Boulevard (474 6000). JFK/UMass T. **Open** 8.30am-5pm Mon-Fri.
Disabled: toilet. Website: www.bayside.expo.com

Hynes Convention Center

900 Boylston Street, at Gloucester Street (954 2000). Hynes/ICA T. **Open** 9am-5pm Mon-Fri. **Map 3 E5**
Disabled: toilet.

World Trade Center

164 Northern Avenue, at Seaport Lane (385 5000/1-800 367 9822). South Station T. **Open** depends on functions. **Map 3 J5**
Disabled: toilet. Website: www.wtcb.com

Courier services

Local and national messenger services include:

DHL Worldwide Express

600 Windsor Place, at South Street, Somerville (1-800 225 5345). Lechmere T. **Open** 24 hours daily. **Credit** AmEx, Disc, MC, V. **Map 4 D2**

Federal Express

775 Summer Street, at Atlantic Avenue (1-800 463 3339). South Station T. **Open** 9am-9pm Mon-Sat. **Credit** Disc, MC, V. **Map 5 G5**

Symplex Courier Systems

189 North Street, at North Square (523 9500). Haymarket T. **Open** 24 hours daily. **Credit** AmEx, MC, V. **Map 5 G3**

US Postal Service

Fort Point Station, 25 Dorchester Avenue, behind South Station (1-800 222 1811). South Station T. **Open** 24 hours daily. **Credit** AmEx, Disc, MC, V. **Map 5 G5**

Office services

Kinkos

10 Post Office Square, at Milk Street (482 4400). Downtown Crossing T. **Open** 24 hours daily. **Rates** *computer rental* $12 per hour; *design* $20 per hour. **Credit** AmEx, DC, Disc, MC, V. **Map 5 G4**
Kinkos offers computer rental, printing, faxing and mailing services and is open all night. What more could you want?
Website: www.kinkos.com

Branches: 2 Center Plaza (973 9000); 1 Mifflin Place, Cambridge (497 0125); 178 Dartmouth Street (262 6188).

Sir Speedy

20 Province Street, at School Street (227 2237). State/Citizen's Bank T. **Open** 8.30am-5.30pm Mon-Fri. **Credit** AmEx, MC, V. **Map 5 G4**

Copying, printing, desktop publishing, binding and graphic design services are all available here.

Branches: 827 Boylston Street (267 9711); 76 Batterymarch Street (451 6491); 77 North Washington Street (523 7656); 711 Atlantic Avenue (426 3434); 1 Kendall Square, Cambridge (494 0255).

Copying

Copy Cop

815 Boylston Street, opposite Prudential Tower (267 9267). Prudential T. **Open** 24 hours daily. **Credit** AmEx, Disc, MC, V. **Map 3 E5**

Branches: 601 Boylston Street (267 7448); 260 Washington Street (367 3370).

Gnomon Copy

325 Huntington Avenue, at Gainsborough Street (536 4600). Mass Ave T. **Open** 7.30am-8.30pm Mon-Thur; 10am-6pm Sat. **Credit** MC, V. **Map 3 E6**

Secretarial

Secretarial Express Plus

(442 8693/pmim@concentric.net). **Open** 9am-8pm Mon-Fri. **No credit cards.**

A team of secretaries and website designers are on offer here: phone for details of their services.

Website: www.citysoft.com/secretarial-exp

Translation services

Harvard Translations

815 Somerville Avenue, at Porter Square (868 6080). Porter T. **Open** 9am-5.30pm Mon-Fri. **No credit cards. Map 4 B1**

JKW International

Third floor, 143 Newbury Street, at Dartmouth Street (859 8600). Copley T. **Open** 9am-5pm Mon-Fri. **Credit** AmEx, MC, V. **Map 3 F5**

JKW International offers translation and interpreting services for all major languages. It also provides a multi-lingual secretarial service. Phone for further details.

Consulates

All embassies are located in Washington, DC. Consulate offices based in Boston include the following:

Canada

Suite 400, 3 Copley Place, at Huntingdon Avenue (262 3760). Copley T. **Map 3 F5**

Republic of Ireland

Third floor, 535 Boylston Street, at Clarendon Street (267 9330). Copley T. **Map 3 F5**

United Kingdom

25th floor, Federal Reserve Plaza, 600 Atlantic Avenue, opposite South Station (248 9555). South Station T. **Map 5 G5**

Website: www.britain-info.org

Consumer information

Better Business Bureau

(426 9000).

A non-profit public service organisation that offers a message service. If you are interested in receiving information on a particular company (and know their address) or wish to file a complaint, you can phone the above number.

Website: www.bos.bbb.org

Office of Consumer Affairs and Business Regulation

(727 7780).

If you have a complaint to make regarding your consumer rights or a query regarding your responsibilities, OCABR should be able to help. Arbitration services for home improvement and car purchase are provided, as well as basic information on the Boston marketplace. Though the organisation doesn't offer mediation or legal services, it will refer you to local groups that do.

Website: www.consumer.com/consumer

Customs & immigration

Standard immigration regulations apply to all visitors. Be prepared to queue when you arrive at immigration for anything up to an hour. During your flight, you will be handed an immigration form and a customs declaration form to be presented when you land at the airport.

Expect to explain the nature of your visit (business and/or pleasure). If you don't have a return ticket and are planning a long visit, you will be questioned closely.

US Customs allows visitors to bring in $100 worth of gifts duty free ($400 for returning Americans), 200 cigarettes (one carton) or 50 cigars and one litre of spirits (liquor).

Any amount of currency can be brought into the USA, but a form, available from the airport, must be filled in for anything over $10,000. Prescription drugs must be clearly marked (and visitors should be prepared to produce a written prescription upon request). No meat, meat products, seeds, plants or fruit can be taken through customs. For more detailed information on agricultural produce and customs phone the **US Department of Agriculture** (1-301 734 8295).

UK Customs & Excise allows returning travellers to bring in £145 worth of gifts and goods and an unlimited amount of money, as long as you can prove it's yours.

For further information contact the following services:

Office of Immigration and Naturalisation

First floor, John F Kennedy Building (565 3879). Gov't Center T. **Open** 7am-3pm Mon-Fri. **Map 5 G4**

US Customs Service

1201 Constitution Avenue Northwest, Washington, DC 20229 (1-202 927 6724).

Disabled travellers

Boston is generally well equipped for disabled travellers. Hotels must provide accessible rooms, museums and street curbs have ramps for wheelchairs and buses on some routes are wheelchair accessible. However it's always best to phone first to double-check.

Transportation Access Passes (TAP) entitle the disabled passenger to reduced fares on public transport. Passes are available for $3 from the **MBTA Senior and Access Pass Program Office** (Back Bay Station, 145 Dartmouth Street, at Columbus Avenue; 222 5123), and applications must be completed by a licensed health-care professional. The office also supplies a map that shows disabled access points to the T. For information on access to more than 200 local arts and entertainment facilities contact **Very Special Arts** (Massachusetts China Trade Center, 2 Boylston Street, at Tremont Street; 350 7713/ www.vsamass.org).

Access Tours
(1-781 322 1610/1-800 557 2047).
Access arrange special tours for the disabled. You can either book your travel through them or take part in one of their pre-packaged tours, ranging from weekend trips to Foxwood to one-week tours of Greater Boston.

Lift Bus Program
(1-800 543 8287).
For queries about bus access.

Massachusetts Office on Disability
(727 7440/1-800 642 0249).
A good source for enquiries on rights enforcement, building access and other information useful for disabled travellers.

Mobility International USA
PO Box 10767, 97440 USA (1-541 343 1284).
Mobility International USA offers workshops and exchanges lasting from two to four weeks situated throughout the USA. Activities available include living with families, disability rights training workshops, team-building and leadership seminars.
Website: www.miusa.org

Society for the Advancement of Travellers with Handicaps
Suite 610, 347 Fifth Avenue, New York, NY 10016 (1-212 447 7284).
SATH offers advice for members and publishes *Open World,* a magazine focusing on disabled travel. It costs $13 for a year's subscription.
Website: www.sath.org

Electricity

The United States uses a 110-120V, 60-cycle AC voltage, rather than the 220-240V, 50-cycle AC voltage used in Europe. Laptops and most travel appliances are dual voltage and will work in the US and in Europe, but do check before you plug them in. You will also need an adaptor for North American sockets; they can be bought at airports, pharmacies and department stores.

E-mail & websites

Boston is renowned for its IT industry, so getting on-line is not a problem. The best way to check your e-mail when you're away is to either use one of the public libraries with on-line facilities or to pay for the use of a computer at a cybercafé or at **Kinkos** (*see page 266*).

To check your e-mail while travelling, set up a free e-mail account at **Yahoo** (www.mail.yahoo.com), **MailCity** (www.mailcity.com) or **Hotmail** (www.hotmail.com). It might even be worth registering with all three just in case one is down when you log on.

For hotels that offer modem or dataport facilities so you can check mail using a laptop, *see chapter* **Accommodation**. Be warned that modem configurations for the United States telephone systems may be different from their European counterparts.

For a list of the best of Boston's websites *see page 196* **Media**.

Cybersmith
42 Church Street, at Massachusetts Avenue (492 5857). Harvard T. **Open** 10am-10pm Mon-Thur; 10am-midnight Fri, Sat; 11am-8pm Sun.
Credit AmEx, Disc, MC, V.
Map 4 B2
In amongst the VR machines and coffee cups at Cybersmith are both Macs and PCs. On-line services cost from $9.95 per hour or $24.95 for four hours.
Disabled: toilet.
Website: www.cybersmith.com

Emergencies

Ambulance, Fire, Police
(911).

Massachusetts State Police
(1-508 820 2300).

Health & medical

Within the United States you will have to pay for any emergency treatment you might need. Contact the emergency number on your travel insurance before seeking treatment if you can, and you will be directed to a hospital that will deal directly with your insurance company.

Clinics/hospitals

Below are some of Boston's major hospitals, most with 24-hour emergency departments.

Beth Israel Deaconess Medical Center
330 Brookline Avenue, at Longwood Avenue (667 3759). Longwood T.
Open 10am-8pm Mon-Fri; 10am-6pm Sat, Sun.

Brigham and Women's Hospital
75 Francis Street, between Huntingdon & Brookline Avenues (732 5500/1-800 294 9999). Brigham Circle T. **Open** 24 hours daily.

New England Medical Center
750 Washington Street, at Kneeland Street (636 5000/referral service 636 9700). NE Medical Center T.
Open 24 hours daily.
Map 5 G5

Children's Hospital
300 Longwood Avenue, at Brookline Avenue (355 6000/355 6611). Longwood Avenue T.
Open *telephone enquiries* 24 hours daily.

Franciscan Children's Hospital and Rehabilitation Center

30 Warren Street, at Commonwealth Avenue (254 3806). Warren Street T. **Open** 24 hours daily.

Massachusetts General Hospital

55 Fruit Street, at Cambridge Street (726 2000). Charles/MGH T. **Open** 24 hours daily. **Map 5 F4**

Mount Auburn Hospital

330 Mount Auburn Street, at Memorial Drive (492 3500). Harvard T. **Open** 24 hours daily. **Map 4 A2**

Cambridge Health Alliance

1493 Cambridge Street, at Maple Avenue (498 1000). Harvard T, then 69 bus. **Open** by appointment only. **Map 4 C2**

Dentists

Metropolitan District Dental Society

(1-508 651 3521). **Open** 9am-4pm Mon-Fri.

Tufts Dental School

1 Kneeland Street, at Washington Street (636 6828). NE Medical Center T. **Open** *emergency walk-in clinic* 9am-10.30pm Mon-Fri. **Map 5 G5**

Dental Referral Service

(1-800 917 6453). **Open** 8am-8pm Mon-Fri.

Pharmacies (24-hour)

CVS

155-7 Charles Street, at Cambridge Street (523 1028). Charles/MGH T. **Open** *pharmacy* 7am-midnight daily; *store* 24 hours daily. **Credit** AmEx, Disc, MC, V. **Map 5 F4**

There are branches throughout town: check the phone book or phone the number above to find the location of your nearest.

Alternative medicine

Langer Chiropractic Group

1446 Cambridge Street, at Beacon Street, Cambridge (492 1754). Harvard T. **Open** by appointment Mon-Thur. **Credit** AmEx, Disc, MC, V. **Map 4 D2**

Dr Langer is a specialist in chiropractic therapy, physiotherapy and massage. A same-day emergency service is also available.

Market Street Health

214 Market Street, at North Beacon Street, Brighton (787 3511). Harvard T, then 86 bus/Alewife T. **Open** *telephone enquiries* 9am-2pm Mon-Fri. **No credit cards**.

Market Street Health has been in practice for 16 years and offers a wide variety of complementary medicine and holistic therapies. These include acupuncture, colon hydrotherapy, chiropractic therapy, homeopathy, Chinese medicine, flotation, comprehensive massage and yoga.

Disabled: toilet.

New England School of Acupuncture

34 Chestnut Street, Watertown (926 4271). Central T, then 70 bus. **Open** 9am-7.30pm Mon-Fri; 9am-3pm Sat. **Credit** varies.

The oldest college of acupuncture and Oriental medicine in the country offers acupuncture, herbal medicine treatments and shiatsu.

Disabled: toilet.

Helplines & agencies

AIDS Hotline

(1-800 235 2331/536 7733). **Open** 9am-7pm Mon-Fri; 10am-2pm Sat.

AIDS Hotline offers telephone advice from counsellors on emotional issues, testing and insurance, as well as referral to support groups for legal assistance, mental health support and financial advice.

Alcoholics Anonymous

(426 9444). **Open** 9am-9pm Mon-Sat; noon-9pm Sun.

Volunteers (recovered alcoholics who have been through the programme) offer counselling and referral to other helplines, detox houses and AA meetings.

Battered Women's Hotline

(661 7203). **Open** 24 hours daily.

Trained volunteers offer over-the-phone counselling, referral and refuge information for women who are subject to abuse.

Beth Israel Deaconess Health Information Line

(667 5356). **Open** 24 hours daily.

The line provides answers to health questions by a trained nurse or where necessary provides referral to a doctor.

Child-at-Risk Hotline

(1-800 792 5200). **Open** 24 hours daily.

An emergency service provided by the department of Social Services. The hotline will refer concerned adults or abused children to other agencies.

Drug & Alcohol Hotlines

(445 1500/1-800 327 5050). **Open** 24 hours daily.

Information and education on substance abuse, referrals to detoxification centres within Massachusetts and advice on who to phone for out-of-state information.

Rape Crisis

(492 7273). **Open** 24 hours daily.

Rape Crisis is a hotline that takes messages from people who have suffered sexual abuse. A trained counsellor will phone back, usually within five minutes.

Samaritans

(247 0220). **Open** 24 hours daily.

A telephone befriending service. Trained volunteers offer confidential advice about emotional problems.

Samariteens

(1-800 252 8336). **Open** 24 hours daily.

A hotline that offers the same service as the Samaritans, but for teenage callers. Between 2pm-11pm daily, the line is staffed by teen volunteers.

STD

(1-800 227 8922). **Open** 8am-11pm Mon-Fri.

Provides advice on how to get education and information on HIV and AIDS, with referral for financial advice, support groups, legal assistance and mental health support.

Insurance

It's advisable to take out comprehensive insurance cover before travelling in the United States: it's almost impossible to arrange once you are there. Make sure that you have adequate health cover since medical expenses can be high. *See page 268* **Health & medical** for a list of Boston's hospitals and clinics.

Libraries

For a list of libraries with good business departments *see page 266* **Business**.

Boston Public Library

700 Boylston Street, at Copley Square (536 5400). Copley T. **Open** *general library & research* 9am-9pm Mon-Thur; 9am-5pm Fri, Sat; 1pm-5pm Sun; *print department,*

rare books & manuscripts (Oct-May) 9am-5pm Mon-Fri; *young adults' room* (Oct-May) 9am-5pm Mon-Sat; 1-5pm Sun.
Map 3 F5
Branches: 25 Parmenter Street (227 8135); 685 Tremont Street (536 8241); 151 Cambridge Street (523 3957).

Liquor laws

The legal drinking age is 21 and Boston is serious about checking photo identification. Not all forms of out-of-state identification are accepted so it is best to carry your passport with you if you are likely to want a drink or to buy one from a liquor store. Alcohol is sold in liquor stores and a few supermarkets and convenience stores, but it is illegal to purchase alcohol on Sundays unless from a bar or restaurant, or in the period between Thanksgiving and New Year.

Money

Each dollar (buck) is divided into 100 cents. Coins range from copper pennies or cents (1¢), to silver nickels (5¢), dimes (10¢) and quarters (25¢). Half-dollar and dollar coins do exist, but are rarely used (a new $1 coin is scheduled to go into circulation by the year 2000).

In an attempt to clamp down on forgeries, changes have been made to the design of paper money and a new $20 bill is now in circulation (the re-design of other denominations is to follow soon, although the old bills will remain legal tender indefinitely). Notes come in six denominations – $1, $5, $10, $20, $50 and $100, though the $100 bill is not universally accepted.

Banks & bureaux de change

Most banks are open from 9am to 5pm Monday to Friday, and some are open from 9am to noon on Saturday.

You can obtain cash on a credit card account from certain banks. Check with your credit card company before you leave, and be prepared to pay interest rates that vary daily.

Bank Boston
100 Federal Street, at Summer Street (556 6050). South Station T.
Open 8.30am-5pm Mon-Fri.
Map 5 G5
Bank Boston also has currency exchange booths at Terminal C (569 1172) and Terminal E (567 2313) of Logan Airport.

Boston Bank of Commerce
133 Federal Street, at Summer Street (556 6050). South Station T.
Open 9am-5pm Mon-Fri.
Map 5 G5

Thomas Cook Currency Services
(1-800 287 7362).
Phone for the latest exchange rates and the location of your nearest Thomas Cook branch.

Western Union
(1-800 325 6000).
Western Union is still the most reliable way to get money wired from one country to another.

ATMs

Automated Teller Machines (ATMs) or cashpoints are easy to find. Most machines will accept American Express, MasterCard and Visa credit cards and selected debit cards, provided you know your Personal Identification Number (PIN), but you will be charged interest for drawing out cash. Check with your credit card company or bank for details of charges before leaving.

If you want to find out where the nearest ATM is, phone **Plus ATM Location Service** (1-800 843 7587) and follow the recorded instructions, or try **Cirrus** (1-800 424 7787).

If you have desensitised the magnetic strip on your card or have forgotten your PIN number, most banks will dispense cash to cardholders with valid photo identification.

Credit cards

Many hotels, car rental agencies and airlines require payment by credit card and most major cards are accepted in restaurants, petrol stations, some taxi cabs and shops, but it is always best to check first.

The five main credit cards accepted in the United States are **American Express**, **Discover**, **Diners' Club**, **MasterCard** and **Visa**.

Lost or stolen credit cards

American Express
1-800 221 7282

Discover
1-800 347 2683

MasterCard
1-800 307 7309

Visa
1-800 336 8472

Lost or stolen travellers' cheques

American Express
1-800 221 7282

Thomas Cook
1-800 223 7373

Visa
1-800 227 6811

Tax

In Massachusetts, food, prescription drugs, newspapers and clothing under the value of $175 are all exempt from state tax but a five per cent tax is levied on almost everything else. Lodging tax is 9.7 per cent, meal tax is five per cent and there is also a variable tax on booze.

Postal services

Post office opening hours in Boston are usually 9am-5pm Monday to Friday with the exception of the city's main post office, which is open 24 hours a day.

Fort Point Station
25 Dorchester Avenue, behind South Station (654 5325). South Station T.
Open 24 hours daily.
Map 5 G5

Poste Restante

If you have no definite address while you are travelling and want to pick up your post when you are away, have it sent Poste Restante to the main post office c/o General Delivery, Fort Point Station, Boston, MA 02205. Proof of identity is needed when picking up mail.

Stamps

A standard letter costs 60¢ to send to Europe and 32¢ within the United States.

Public toilets/restrooms

Public toilets in Boston are few and far between. Your best bet is to buy a drink from a bar or café so you can use their facilities.

However, there are public toilets in the Cambridge Side Galleria, Copley Place, Prudential Center and Quincy Marketplace shopping areas.

Religion

Here are just a few of the many places of worship in Boston and nearby. Check the *Yellow Pages* for a more detailed list.

Baptist

First Baptist Church of Boston
110 Commonwealth Avenue, at Clarendon Street (267 3148). Copley T. **Open** 11am-2pm Mon-Fri. **Service** 11am Sun.
Map 3 F5

Twelfth Baptist Church
160 Warren Street, at Moreland Street, Roxbury (442 7855). Dudley T. **Open** 10.30am-5pm Mon-Fri; 10am-5pm Sat; 2pm-5pm Sun.
Service 10.45am Sun.
Disabled: toilet.

Catholic

Cathedral of the Holy Cross
1400 Washington Street, at Union Park (542 5682). NE Medical Center T. **Services** *English* 9am Mon-Sat; 8am, 11am Sun; *Spanish* 9am Sun; 7pm Sun; 7pm Tue, Thur.
Map 3 F6

Sacred Heart Church
49 Sixth Street, at Otis Street, Cambridge (547 0399). Harvard T, then 69 bus. **Services** 9am Mon, Wed-Fri; 6.30am Tue; 7.30am Sun.
Map 4 E3
Disabled: toilet.

Episcopal

Christian Science Church
215 Massachusetts Avenue, at Huntington Avenue (450 2000). Symphony T. **Services** 7.30pm Wed; 10am, 7.30pm Sun.
Map 3 E6

Church of the Advent
30 Brimmer Street, at Mount Vernon Street (523 2377). Charles/MGH T. **Services** 7.30am Mon, Tue, Thur, Fri; 6pm Wed; 9am Sat; 8am, 9am, 11am Sun.
Map 5 F4
Disabled: toilet.

Old North Church (Christ Church)
193 Salem Street, at Hull Street (523 6676). Haymarket T. **Services** 9am Wed; 9am, 11am, 5pm Sun.
Map 5 G/H3

Jewish

Jewish Religious Information Services
117 Tremont Street, at Boylston Street (426 2139). Boylston T.
Open 9am-4pm Mon-Thur.
Map 5 G5
Jewish Religious Information Services provides referral to other organisations, temples and synagogues as well as advice on kosher foods and restaurants.

Temple Israel
Longwood Avenue, at Plymouth Street (566 3960). Longwood T.
Services 5.45pm Fri; 9am, 10.30am Sat.
Disabled: toilet.

Methodist

Old West Church
131 Cambridge Street, at Staniford Street (227 5088). Gov't Center T.
Service 11am Sun.
Map 5 G4

Muslim

Islamic Society of Boston
204 Prospect Street, at Massachusetts Avenue, Cambridge (876 3546). Central T.
Services 6am, 1pm, 2.45pm, 5.04pm, 7.30pm, daily.
Map 4 C3
The Islamic Society acts both as a religious organisation and an information service.
Disabled: toilet.

Presbyterian

Church of the Covenant
67 Newbury Street, at Berkeley Street (266 7480). Arlington or Copley T. **Services** 10am Sun.
Map 3 F5
Disabled: toilet.

Quaker

Beacon Hill Friends House
6 Chestnut Street, at Charles Street (227 9118). Park St or Charles/MGH T. **Open** *office* 9am-5pm Mon-Fri; *meetings* 10.30am Sun.
Map 5 F4
The Friends House also has rooms for rent (in the Quaker style) for $50-$75 per night.
Disabled: toilet.

Safety

Boston is one of the safest cities in the United States. However, as in any big city, it's wise to be aware of the basic safety precautions. Don't fumble with your map or wallet in public; always plan where you're going and walk with brisk confidence; avoid walking alone at night; avoid parking in questionable areas (if in doubt, use valet parking when you can) and keep your car doors locked when parked and while driving.

Central Boston is generally well lit, but pedestrians should probably avoid Boston Common, the Public Gardens and the walkways along the Charles River after dark. It's also useful to know that the couple of blocks along Washington Street, between Avery and Stuart Streets, are known as the Combat Zone – and that is not a fashion statement.

Smoking

The Boston Public Health Commission recently implemented a citywide ban on smoking in restaurants: for the full story, *see page 117* **Pubs & Bars**.

Students & study

As Boston has the world's largest number of colleges and universities per square mile (and that's not including Cambridge), the choices for study are many. The city is a great place to be a student with loads of student activities, and there are a wide variety of courses and summer schools on offer each year.

For further details *see chapter* **Campus Culture**.

Telephones

The United States telephone system is privately run, mainly by AT&T and Bell Atlantic. This means that rates vary considerably – especially for long-distance or international calls, although most local calls in Boston cost 25¢.

Emergency
Dial **911** for police, fire or medical emergency services.
Operator
Dial **0**.
International operator
Dial **00**.
Directory enquiries: local
Dial **411**.
Directory enquiries: national
Dial **1** + **area code** + **555 1212** (if you don't know the area code, dial the operator).
Toll-free numbers
These generally start with **1-800** or **1-888**.
Speaking clock
Dial 637 1234.

Massachusetts area codes

Boston **617**
Boston suburbs **781**
North, north coast and Cape Ann **978**
South Coast, Cape Cod and the Islands **508**

How to dial

Direct dial calls

If you are using a payphone and will be paying for the call with change, dial 1 + area code (if outside Boston) + phone number. An operator or recorded message will tell you how much change to deposit. If you are using a phone card to pay for the call, follow the instructions on the card. For local calls, deposit 25¢ and dial the number.

Collect calls

For reverse-charge calls, dial **0** + area code + number.

International calls

Dial **011** followed by the country code. If you need operator assistance with international calls, dial **00**.

UK **44**
New Zealand **64**
Australia **61**
Germany **49**
Japan **81**

Hotel phones

Most hotels add a (usually hefty) surcharge for the use of their phones: often it is cheaper to use a phone card or credit card (especially when making international calls).

Phone cards

Telephone cards – usually the best option for making international calls – can be purchased at a variety of outlets, including Visitors' Centers (*see below*) and **CVS** pharmacies (*see page 269*).

Time & date

Massachusetts operates on **Eastern Standard Time**, which is five hours behind Greenwich Mean Time and one hour ahead of Central Time (from Manitoba to Texas), two hours ahead of Mountain Time (Alberta to Arizona and New Mexico) and three hours ahead of Pacific Time (California).

Daylight Saving Time is observed from the first Sunday in April to the last Sunday in October, when clocks are turned forward one hour.

In the USA, dates are written in month, day and year order; so 12/5/99 is the 5th December 1999, not 12th May.

Tipping

Unlike in Europe, tipping is a way of life in the USA: many of the local labour force rely on gratuities for part of their income, so you should tip accordingly. As a rough guide, tip bartenders ten to 15 per cent; bellhops/porters at least $1 per piece; cab drivers 15 to 20 per cent, cloakroom attendants $1 per garment; food delivery staff and hairdressers 15 to 20 per cent; hotel maids $1 a night; hotel concièrges $3-$5; restaurants 15 to 20 per cent and valet parking attendants $1-$3.

Tourist information

Boston National Historical Park Service

15 State Street, at Congress Street (242 5642). State/Citizen's Bank T. **Open** *early June-6 Sept* 9am-6pm, *7 Sept-late May* 9am-5pm, daily.
Map 5 G4
A useful source for information on Boston and New England; there's also a bookshop.
Disabled: toilet.

Cambridge Office of Tourism

Office 352, 18 Brattle Street, at Mount Auburn Street, Cambridge (441 2884/1-800 862 5678). Harvard T. **Open** 9am-5pm Mon-Fri.
Map 4 B2
For general inquiries on Cambridge. The office also publishes the *Cambridge Visitor Guide,* which has information on local accommodation, sights and attractions as well as maps, a seasonal calendar of events and a walking tour map. The office also runs **Visitor Information Center** in Harvard Square (*see p273*), which has a touch-screen service to help you find your way around Cambridge.
Website: www.cambridge-usa.org

Greater Boston Convention & Visitors' Bureau

2 Copley Place, Suite 105, Boston, MA 02116 (536 4100/1-888 733 2678). **Open** (telephone enquiries) 8.30am-5pm Mon-Fri.

Average temperatures

	°C	°F		°C	°F
Jan	-6 to 2	22 to 36	**July**	18 to 27	65 to 82
Feb	-6 to 3	22 to 38	**Aug**	18 to 26	65 to 80
Mar	-0.5 to 8	31 to 46	**Sept**	13 to 23	56 to 73
Apr	4 to 13	40 to 56	**Oct**	8 to 17	46 to 63
May	10 to 19	50 to 67	**Nov**	3 to 11	38 to 52
June	15 to 24	59 to 76	**Dec**	-3 to 4	27 to 40

The Greater Boston Convention & Visitor's Bureau (GBCVB) provides information on attractions, restaurants, performing arts and nightlife, shopping and travel services. Its website is also fairly comprehensive. The main office operates as a telephone information service, but the bureau also runs Visitor Information Centers at various locations in the city (*see below*).
Website: www.bostonusa.com

Massachusetts Office of Travel and Tourism

(727 3201/recorded information 1-800 447 6277/UK office 0171 978 7429). **Open** *Boston office* 8.45am-5pm Mon-Fri; *UK office* 9am-5pm Mon-Fri.
The Office of Travel and Tourism has a telephone information service and also publishes a free magazine called *Getaway Guide,* which includes information about attractions and lodgings, a map and a seasonal calendar of events covering the state of Massachusetts.
Website: www.mass-vacation.com

Traveler's Aid Society

17 East Street, at Atlantic Avenue (542 7286). South Station T.
Open 8.30am-5pm Mon-Fri.
Map 5 G5
The Traveler's Aid Society is a non profit-making social service agency that has been helping travellers since 1920. Although most of the organisation's work is with homeless families, volunteers also provide information on Boston and will help out stranded travellers.
Branches: Logan Airport, Terminal E (567 5385); Amtrak booth, South Station (737 2880).

Visitor Information Centers

Boston Common
147 Tremont Street (426 3115/advance information 1-800 888 5515). Park Street T.
Open 9am-5pm Mon-Fri.
Map 5 G4

Prudential Center
Between Boylston Street & Huntington Avenue (advance information 1-800 888 5515). Prudential or Hynes/ICA T.
Open 9am-5pm daily.
Map 3 E6

Cambridge Information Booth
Harvard Square (497 1630). Harvard T. **Open** 9am-5pm Mon-Sat.
Map 4 B2

Visas

Under the Visa Waiver Scheme, citizens of the UK, Japan and all West European countries (except for Ireland, Portugal, Greece and the Vatican City) do not need a visa for stays in the United States of less than 90 days (business or pleasure) – as long as they have a passport that is valid for the full 90-day period and a return or onward ticket. An open standby ticket is acceptable. Some restrictions apply: if you have previously been turned down for a visa, for example.

The US Embassy in London provides a reasonably comprehensive recorded message for general visa enquiries from British citizens (phone 0898 200290 or check the website at www.travel. state.gov).

Canadians and Mexicans do not need visas, but they may be asked for proof of their citizenship. All other travellers, including those from Australia and New Zealand, must have a visa; contact your nearest United States embassy or consulate for more information. In general, it's best to send in your application at least three weeks before you plan to travel. Visas required more urgently should be applied for via a travel agent.

Vocabulary

For a list of Boston colloquialisms, *see* **Local Lingo** *page 18* **Boston Today**.

Weather

Boston's weather is so unpredictable, seasons have been known to change four times in one day. Deciding what to wear can be difficult, but as long as you wear layers and carry a waterproof, you're (literally) covered for all eventualities.

There's no doubt that winter is very cold, however – largely due to the sea breeze. The proximity of the ocean also accounts for the high humidity levels in the summer (with averages of 56 to 76 per cent). The average annual rainfall is 43 inches (109 centimetres), most of which seems to fall in March.

Weather forecast

Phone **936 1234** or **637 1212** to check the daily temperature. Or check the Massachusetts weather on the web at: www.rainorshine.com

Directory

Further Reading

Non-fiction

Charles Bahne: *The Complete Guide to Boston's Freedom Trail*
Engaging historical account of the stories behind the sights.
Jack Beatty: *The Rascal King: The Life and Times of James Michael Curley, 1874-1958*
Thoroughly researched biography of the charismatic Boston mayor and a good reference to big city politics in the US.
Helen Byers: *Kidding Around Boston: What to Do, Where to Go, and How to Have Fun in Boston*
A parents' guide to keeping kids happy in Beantown.
Robert Campbell and Peter Vanderwarker: *Cityscapes of Boston*
Photographic history of the evolution of the city juxtaposing old and new pictures of it.
Marty Carlock: *A Guide to Public Art in Greater Boston: From Newburyport to Plymouth*
An overview of the area's best public art.
Kevin T Dame and Rioji Yoshida: *Fenway in Your Pocket: The Red Sox Fan's Guide to Fenway Park*
The title says it all.
Peter Davison: *The Fading Smile: Poets in Boston from Robert Lowell to Sylvia Plath*
The lives and work of Boston's mid-twentieth century poets.
David Hackett Fischer: *Paul Revere's Ride*
Account of the legendary ride to Lexington, related as a historical narrative.
Sebastian Junger: *The Perfect Storm*
Gripping account of a crew of Gloucester fishermen caught up in the 'Hallowe'en Gale' in the North Atlantic in 1991.
Ronald P Formisano: *Boston Against Busing: Race, Class and Ethnicity in the 1960s and 1970s*
The story of the bitter fight over busing that divided the city.
Barney Frank: *Improper Bostonians: Lesbian and Gay History from the Puritans to Playland*
Comprehensive history of homosexuality in Boston.
Doris Kearns Goodwin: *The Fitzgeralds and the Kennedys: An American Saga*
The story behind America's answer to royalty.
Jan Holtz Kay: *Lost Boston*
Acclaimed pictorial essay of the city.
Walt Kelley: *What They Never Told You About Boston (Or What They Did That Were Lies)*
Local cabbie's humourous collection of facts about the city.
J Anthony Lukas: *Common Ground: A Turbulent Decade in the Lives of Three American Families*
The 1970's busing crisis, through the eyes of an Irish-American, a black and a white middle-class family.
Robert S Morse: *25 Mountain Bike Tours in Massachusetts: From the Connecticut River to the Atlantic Coast*
For the ambitious recreational biker.
Shaun O'Connell: *Imagining Boston: A Literary Landscape*
Overview of literary Boston, from Emerson and Thoreau to Mailer and Dickenson.
William P Quinn: *Shipwrecks Around Boston*
Guide to the famous and not-so-famous wrecks that lie in the waters off the city.
Douglass Shand-Tucci: *The Art of Scandal: The Life and Times of Isabella Stewart Gardner*
Biography of Boston's famous patron of the arts and the inspiration behind Isabel Archer in *Portrait of a Lady.*
Dan Shaughnessy: *The Curse of the Bambino*
Entertaining look at the Red Sox 'curse' by local sports journo.

Fiction & poetry

James Carroll: *The City Below*
Historical novel based on the lives of two Irish brothers from Charlestown.
Nathaniel Hawthorne: *The Scarlet Letter* and *The House of the Seven Gables*
Two American – and New England – classics.
George V Higgins: *The Friends of Eddie Coyle*
Bestselling potboiler by a Boston prosecutor who knows his stuff.
William Dean Howells: *The Rise of Silas Lapham*
Late nineteenth-century tale of a Vermont businessman's attempt to become part of the Boston Brahmin.
Henry James: *The Bostonians*
The tale of Varena Tarrant, James' Boston feminist.
Henry Wadsworth Longfellow: *The Works of Henry Wadsworth Longfellow*
Includes the famous 'Paul Revere's Ride'.
Robert Lowell: *Life Studies* and *For the Union Dead*
The poet's account of growing up privileged in Boston and hating it.
Stephen McCauley: *The Object of My Affection, The Easy Way Out* and *The Man of the House*
Funny novels set in Cambridge, depicting the lives of gay and straight characters.
Robert McCloskey: *Make Way for Ducklings*
The classic children's tale about ducks on Boston Common.
Herman Melville: *Moby Dick*
Melville's nineteenth-century romance of the sea – a quintessential American novel.
Barbara Neely: *Blanche Cleans Up*
Political potboiler told from the perspective of an African-American working woman.
Robert B Parker: *The Godwulf Manuscript*
First in a series of mystery novels set in Boston.
George Santayana: *The Last Puritan*
Brilliant memoir in the form of a novel set around Boston, in which the protagonist comes to grips with Puritanism.
Henry David Thoreau: *Walden*
The Transcendentalist's most famous work, written while living in isolation in a cabin over two years, two months and two days.
John Updike: *Roger's Version*
The writer's updated version of *The Scarlet Letter.*
Various: *Cape Cod Stories*
Collection of short stories from the Cape, Nantucket and Martha's Vineyard by authors such as Edgar Allan Poe, Paul Theroux, John Updike, Sylvia Plath and Kurt Vonnegut.
William F Weld: *Mackerel by Moonlight*
Political thriller set in Boston and written by a former Massachusetts governor.

Index

Note: *Numbers in bold indicate the section giving key information on the topic; italics indicate illustrations.*

b

Advertisers' Index

Please refer to the relevant sections for addresses/telephone numbers

Maps

Place of interest and/or entertainment

Railway stations

Subway

Parks

Hospitals/universities

Neighbourhood .... BACK BAY

Street Index

Map 1
0
40 miles
0
50 km
© Copyright Time Out Group 1999
VERMONT
White Mountains
MAINE
NEW HAMPSHIRE
MASSACHUSETTS
CONNECTICUT
RHODE ISLAND
ATLANTIC OCEAN
To Burlington
To Rutland
To Brattleboro & the Green Mountains
To the Berkshires
To New York
Waterville
Augusta
Montpelier
Franconia Notch
Lincoln
Conway
Lewiston
Auburn
Casco Bay
Portland
Hanover
Lake Winnipesaukee
Laconia
Old Orchard Beach
Biddeford
Kennebunk
Kennebunkport
Connecticut River
Concord
Portsmouth
Manchester
Keene
Newburyport
Plum Island
Nashua
Lawrence
Ipswich
Rockport
Cape Ann
Gloucester
Shelburne Falls
Greenfield
Deerfield
Pioneer Valley
Salem
Marblehead
Lexington
Logan International Airport
Concord
See Map 2
Walden Pond
BOSTON
Massachusetts Bay
See Map 7
Amherst
Northampton
Worcester
Holyoke
Provincetown
Truro
Brimfield
Sturbridge
Springfield
Plymouth
Wellfleet
Cape Cod Bay
Eastham
Brewster
Sandwich
Barnstable
Providence
Fall River
Chatham
Hyannis
Hartford
New Bedford
Monomoy National Wildlife Refuge
Buzzards Bay
Woods Hole
Nantucket Sound
Oak Bluffs
Newport
Vineyard Haven
Edgartown
Gay Head
Nantucket
Martha's Vineyard
Uncasville
Mystic
Groton
New London
Nantucket Island
Block Island
91
89
93
95
202
190
90
290
495
84
395

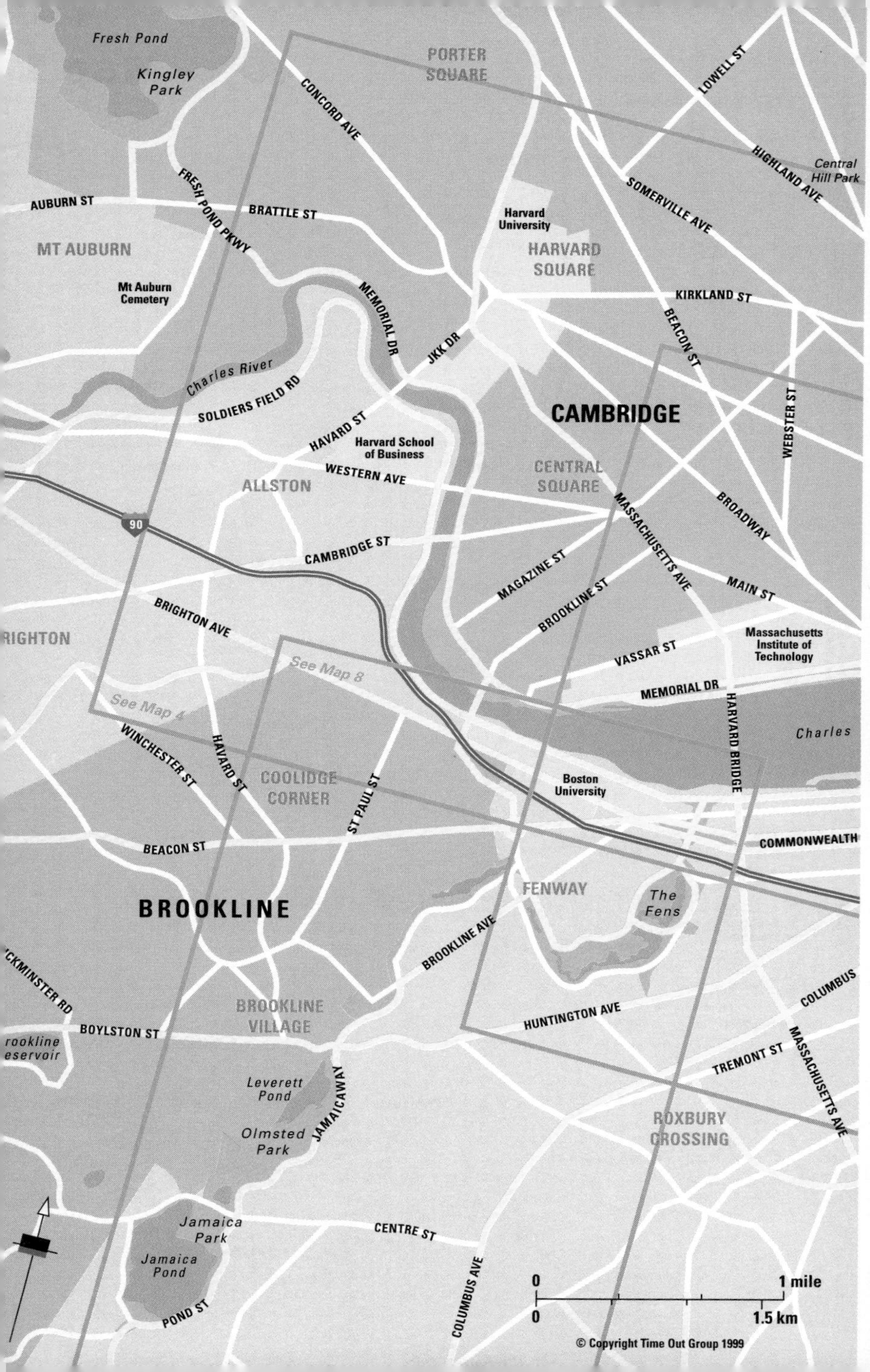
Fresh Pond
Kingley Park
PORTER SQUARE
CONCORD AVE
LOWELL ST
HIGHLAND AVE
Central Hill Park
SOMERVILLE AVE
FRESH POND PKWY
AUBURN ST
BRATTLE ST
Harvard University
MT AUBURN
HARVARD SQUARE
Mt Auburn Cemetery
MEMORIAL DR
KIRKLAND ST
BEACON ST
JKK DR
Charles River
SOLDIERS FIELD RD
CAMBRIDGE
WEBSTER ST
HAVARD ST
Harvard School of Business
WESTERN AVE
CENTRAL SQUARE
ALLSTON
MASSACHUSETTS AVE
BROADWAY
90
CAMBRIDGE ST
MAGAZINE ST
BROOKLINE ST
MAIN ST
BRIGHTON AVE
RIGHTON
Massachusetts Institute of Technology
VASSAR ST
See Map 8
MEMORIAL DR
See Map 4
HARVARD BRIDGE
Charles
WINCHESTER ST
HAVARD ST
COOLIDGE CORNER
ST PAUL ST
Boston University
BEACON ST
COMMONWEALTH
FENWAY
The Fens
BROOKLINE
BROOKLINE AVE
CKMINSTER RD
BROOKLINE VILLAGE
HUNTINGTON AVE
COLUMBUS
BOYLSTON ST
rookline eservoir
TREMONT ST
MASSACHUSETTS AVE
Leverett Pond
JAMAICAWAY
ROXBURY CROSSING
Olmsted Park
Jamaica Park
CENTRE ST
Jamaica Pond
COLUMBUS AVE
POND ST
0
1 mile
0
1.5 km

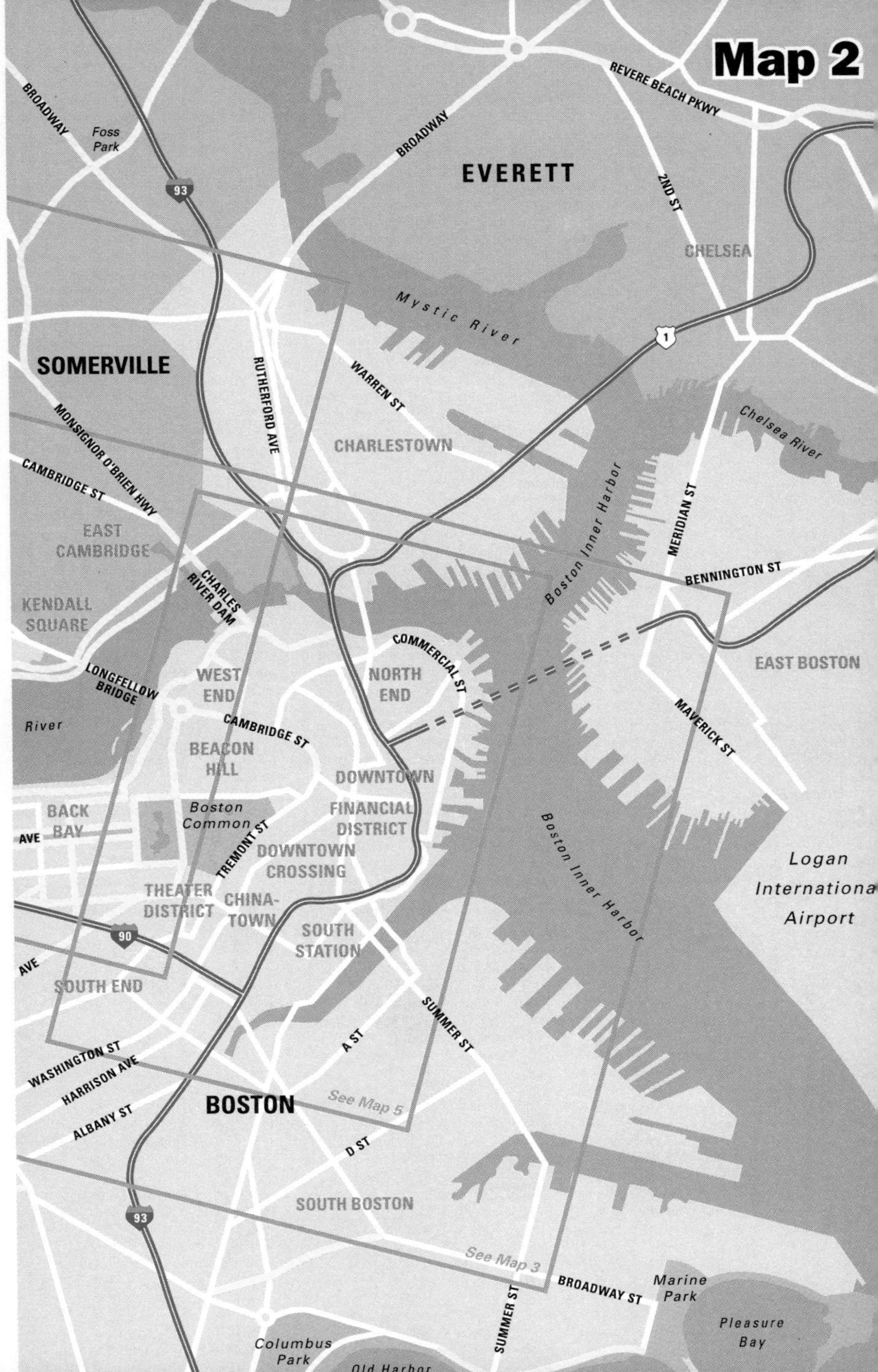

Map 2
REVERE BEACH PKWY
BROADWAY
Foss Park
BROADWAY
EVERETT
2ND ST
CHELSEA
Mystic River
SOMERVILLE
RUTHERFORD AVE
WARREN ST
MONSIGNOR O'BRIEN HWY
CHARLESTOWN
Chelsea River
CAMBRIDGE ST
MERIDIAN ST
EAST CAMBRIDGE
Boston Inner Harbor
CHARLES RIVER DAM
BENNINGTON ST
KENDALL SQUARE
EAST BOSTON
COMMERCIAL ST
LONGFELLOW BRIDGE
WEST END
NORTH END
MAVERICK ST
River
CAMBRIDGE ST
BEACON HILL
DOWNTOWN
BACK BAY
Boston Common
FINANCIAL DISTRICT
AVE
TREMONT ST
DOWNTOWN CROSSING
Boston Inner Harbor
Logan International Airport
THEATER DISTRICT
CHINA-TOWN
SOUTH STATION
AVE
SOUTH END
SUMMER ST
WASHINGTON ST
A ST
HARRISON AVE
ALBANY ST
BOSTON
See Map 5
D ST
SOUTH BOSTON
See Map 3
BROADWAY ST
Marine Park
SUMMER ST
Pleasure Bay
Columbus Park
Old Harbor

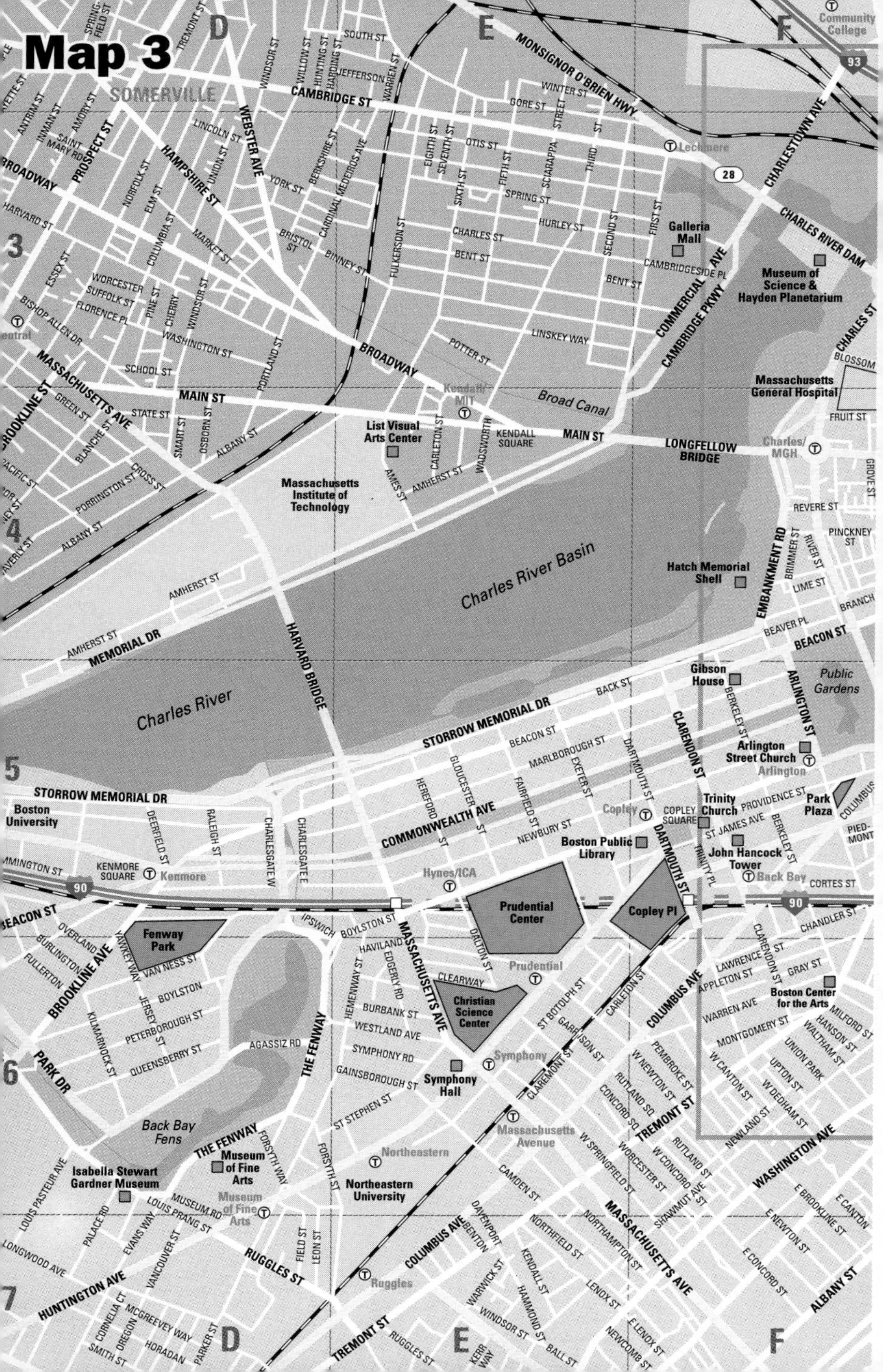
Map 3
D
E
F
SOMERVILLE
Community College
93
MONSIGNOR O'BRIEN HWY
CAMBRIDGE ST
SOUTH ST
JEFFERSON
WINTER ST
GORE ST
OTIS ST
SPRING ST
HURLEY ST
CHARLES ST
BENT ST
Lechmere
28
CHARLESTOWN AVE
CHARLES RIVER DAM
Galleria Mall
CAMBRIDGESIDE PL
Museum of Science & Hayden Planetarium
COMMERCIAL AVE
CAMBRIDGE PKWY
LINSKEY WAY
POTTER ST
BROADWAY
HAMPSHIRE ST
PROSPECT ST
WEBSTER AVE
MASSACHUSETTS AVE
MAIN ST
Broad Canal
Kendall/MIT
KENDALL SQUARE
LONGFELLOW BRIDGE
Charles/MGH
Massachusetts General Hospital
BLOSSOM
FRUIT ST
List Visual Arts Center
Massachusetts Institute of Technology
AMHERST ST
MEMORIAL DR
Charles River Basin
Charles River
HARVARD BRIDGE
Hatch Memorial Shell
EMBANKMENT RD
REVERE ST
PINCKNEY ST
BEACON ST
Public Gardens
Gibson House
STORROW MEMORIAL DR
ARLINGTON ST
CLARENDON ST
Arlington Street Church
Arlington
Park Plaza
Boston University
COMMONWEALTH AVE
Copley
COPLEY SQUARE
Trinity Church
Boston Public Library
John Hancock Tower
KENMORE SQUARE
Kenmore
Hynes/ICA
Back Bay
90
Prudential Center
Copley Pl
Fenway Park
BOYLSTON ST
BROOKLINE AVE
Prudential
Christian Science Center
Boston Center for the Arts
COLUMBUS AVE
THE FENWAY
Symphony
Symphony Hall
TREMONT ST
Massachusetts Avenue
PARK DR
Back Bay Fens
Museum of Fine Arts
Isabella Stewart Gardner Museum
Northeastern
Northeastern University
WASHINGTON AVE
RUGGLES ST
HUNTINGTON AVE
Ruggles
ALBANY ST

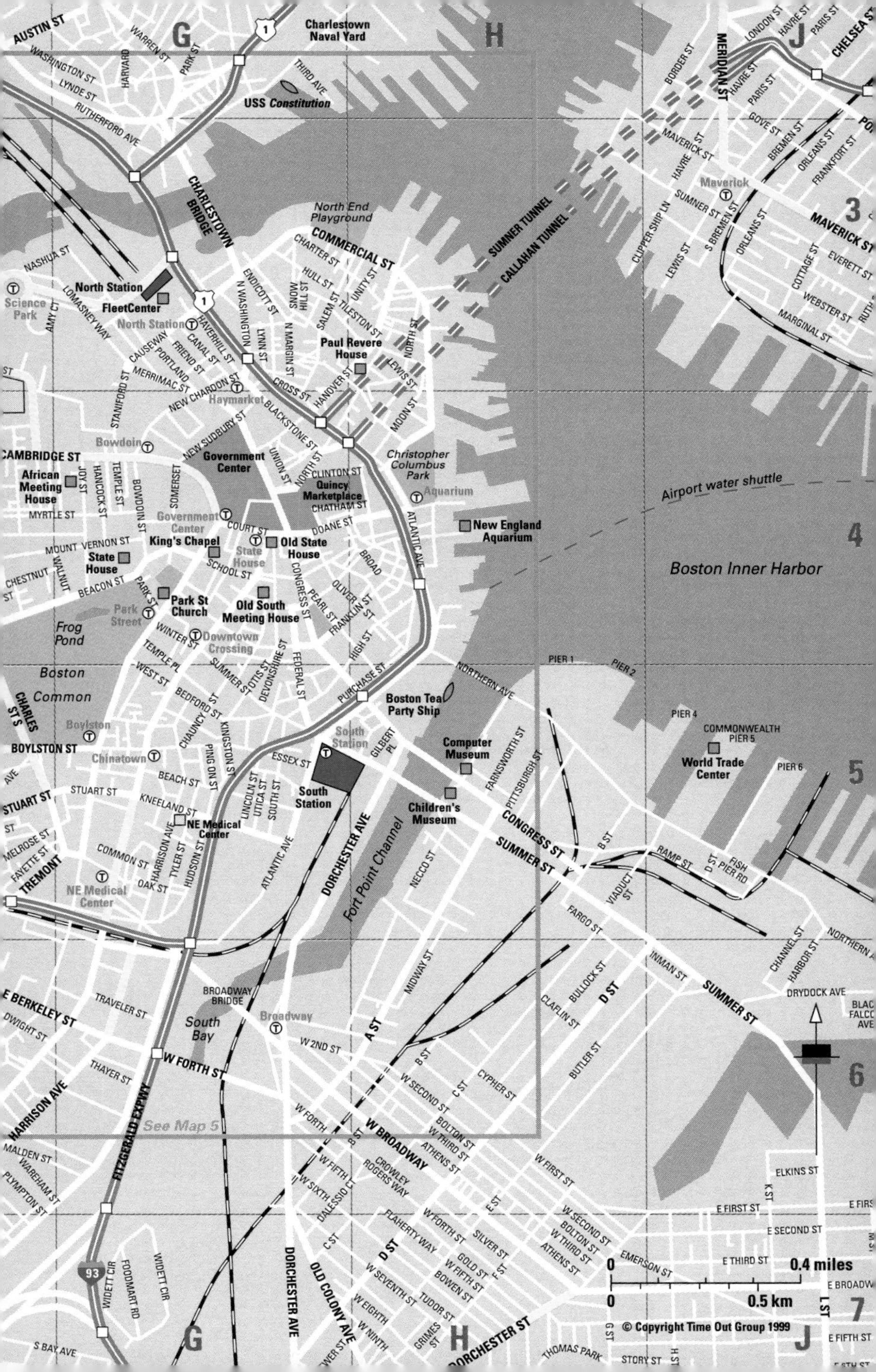
G
H
J
3
4
5
6
7
Charlestown Naval Yard
USS Constitution
AUSTIN ST
WARREN ST
WASHINGTON ST
HARVARD
PARK ST
LYNDE ST
RUTHERFORD AVE
THIRD AVE
CHARLESTOWN BRIDGE
North End Playground
COMMERCIAL ST
CHARTER ST
HULL ST
UNITY ST
SALEM ST
TILESTON ST
ENDICOTT ST
N WASHINGTON
NASHUA ST
North Station
FleetCenter
Science Park
LOMASNEY WAY
AMY CT
CAUSEWAY
FRIEND ST
CANAL ST
HAVERHILL ST
PORTLAND
MERRIMAC ST
NEW CHARDON ST
Haymarket
STANIFORD ST
LYNN ST
N MARGIN ST
Paul Revere House
NORTH ST
LEWIS ST
HANOVER ST
CROSS ST
MOON ST
BLACKSTONE ST
NEW SUDBURY ST
Bowdoin
CAMBRIDGE ST
Government Center
UNION ST
NORTH ST
CLINTON ST
Quincy Marketplace
CHATHAM ST
Christopher Columbus Park
Aquarium
African Meeting House
JOY ST
HANCOCK ST
TEMPLE ST
BOWDOIN ST
SOMERSET
MYRTLE ST
COURT ST
DOANE ST
ATLANTIC AVE
New England Aquarium
MOUNT VERNON ST
King's Chapel
State House
Old State House
BROAD
State House
CHESTNUT
WALNUT
BEACON ST
SCHOOL ST
CONGRESS ST
Boston Inner Harbor
Airport water shuttle
PARK ST
Park St Church
Old South Meeting House
OLIVER ST
PEARL ST
FRANKLIN ST
Park Street
Frog Pond
WINTER ST
Downtown Crossing
TEMPLE PL
HIGH ST
WEST ST
SUMMER ST
OTIS ST
DEVONSHIRE ST
FEDERAL ST
PURCHASE ST
Boston Common
CHARLES ST S
BEDFORD ST
CHAUNCY ST
KINGSTON ST
Boylston
BOYLSTON ST
Chinatown
PING ON ST
ESSEX ST
South Station
GILBERT PL
Boston Tea Party Ship
NORTHERN AVE
PIER 1
PIER 2
PIER 4
COMMONWEALTH PIER 5
World Trade Center
PIER 6
Computer Museum
FARNSWORTH ST
PITTSBURGH ST
Children's Museum
BEACH ST
STUART ST
KNEELAND ST
LINCOLN ST
UTICA ST
SOUTH ST
NE Medical Center
HARRISON AVE
TYLER ST
HUDSON ST
MELROSE ST
FAYETTE ST
TREMONT
COMMON ST
OAK ST
NE Medical Center
ATLANTIC AVE
DORCHESTER AVE
Fort Point Channel
NECCO ST
CONGRESS ST
SUMMER ST
B ST
RAMP ST
D ST
FISH PIER RD
VIADUCT ST
FARGO ST
INMAN ST
CHANNEL ST
HARBOR ST
NORTHERN AVE
DRYDOCK AVE
BLACK FALCON AVE
BULLOCK ST
D ST
CLAFLIN ST
SUMMER ST
MIDWAY ST
BROADWAY BRIDGE
E BERKELEY ST
TRAVELER ST
DWIGHT ST
South Bay
Broadway
W 2ND ST
A ST
B ST
W FORTH ST
THAYER ST
FITZGERALD EXPWY
HARRISON AVE
See Map 5
W SECOND ST
C ST
CYPHER ST
BUTLER ST
W FORTH
B ST
W BROADWAY
BOLTON ST
W THIRD ST
ATHENS ST
W FIRST ST
MALDEN ST
WAREHAM ST
PLYMPTON ST
W FIFTH
CROWLEY ROGERS WAY
W SIXTH
DALESSIO CT
ELKINS ST
K ST
E FIRST ST
E SECOND ST
E ST
W SECOND ST
BOLTON ST
W THIRD ST
ATHENS ST
C ST
D ST
FLAHERTY WAY
W FORTH ST
SILVER ST
GOLD ST
W FIFTH ST
BOWEN ST
F ST
EMERSON ST
E THIRD ST
E BROADW
W SEVENTH ST
TUDOR ST
W EIGHTH
W NINTH
GRIMES ST
DORCHESTER AVE
OLD COLONY AVE
DORCHESTER ST
THOMAS PARK
STORY ST
G ST
H ST
L ST
E FIFTH ST
93
WIDETT CIR
FOODMART RD
WIDETT CIR
S BAY AVE
LONDON ST
HAVRE ST
PARIS ST
CHELSEA ST
MERIDIAN ST
BORDER ST
HAVRE ST
PARIS ST
GOVE ST
MAVERICK ST
BREMEN ST
ORLEANS ST
FRANKFORT ST
Maverick
SUMNER ST
S BREMEN ST
CLIPPER SHIP LN
LEWIS ST
HAVRE
MAVERICK ST
EVERETT ST
COTTAGE ST
WEBSTER ST
MARGINAL ST
SUMNER TUNNEL
CALLAHAN TUNNEL
0
0.4 miles
0
0.5 km
© Copyright Time Out Group 1999

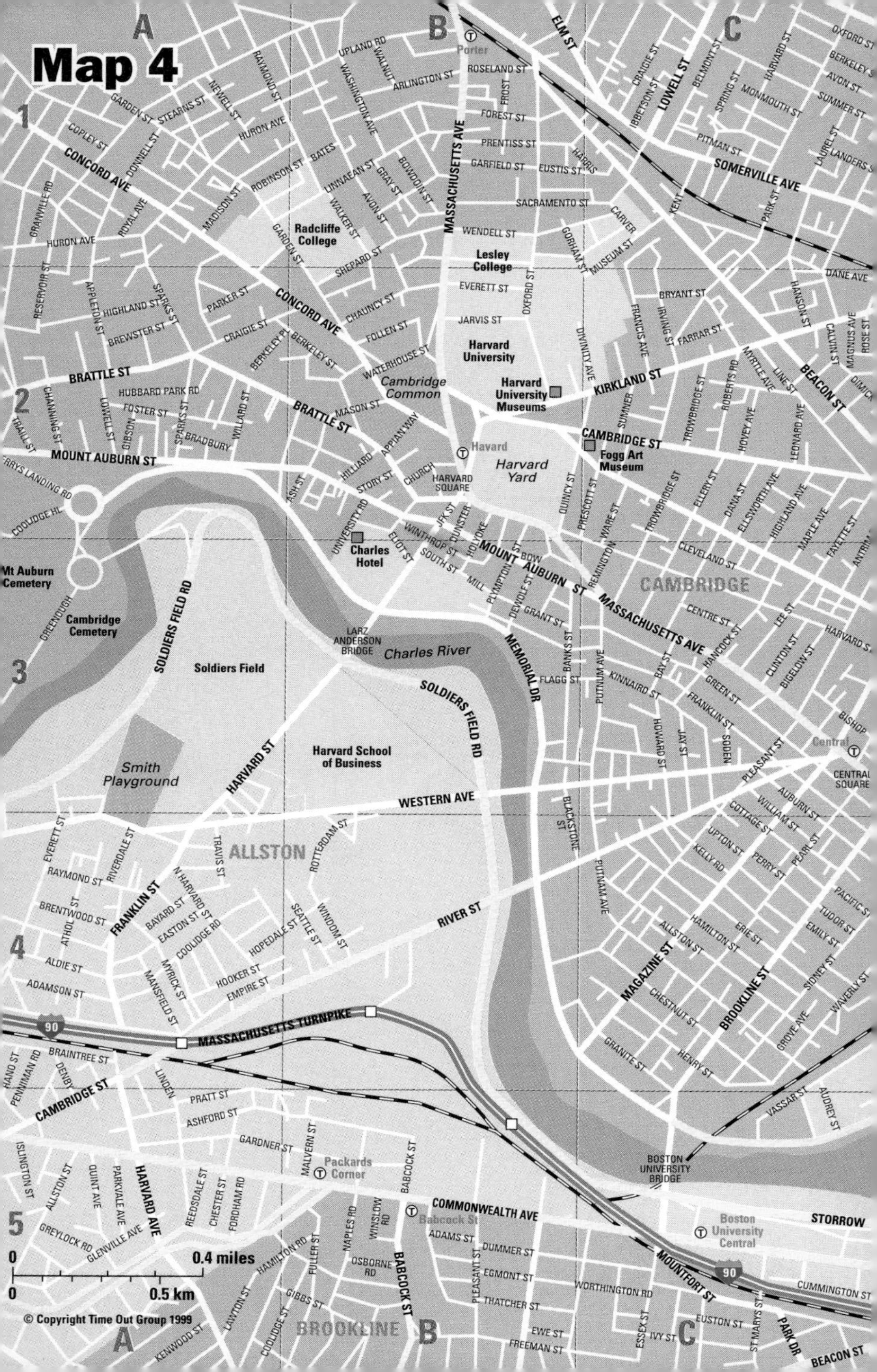
Map 4
A
B
C
1
2
3
4
5
Porter
Harvard
Central
Packards Corner
Babcock St
Boston University Central
Radcliffe College
Lesley College
Harvard University
Harvard University Museums
Cambridge Common
Harvard Yard
Fogg Art Museum
Harvard Square
Charles Hotel
Mt Auburn Cemetery
Cambridge Cemetery
Larz Anderson Bridge
Charles River
Soldiers Field
Harvard School of Business
Smith Playground
ALLSTON
CAMBRIDGE
BROOKLINE
Central Square
Boston University Bridge
Massachusetts Turnpike
Massachusetts Ave
Concord Ave
Brattle St
Mount Auburn St
Kirkland St
Cambridge St
Memorial Dr
Soldiers Field Rd
Western Ave
River St
Harvard St
Franklin St
Commonwealth Ave
Storrow
Mountfort St
Magazine St
Brookline St
Somerville Ave
Beacon St
Harvard Ave
Babcock St
Park Dr
0
0.4 miles
0
0.5 km

D
E
F
1
2
3
4
5
SOMERVILLE
Central Hill Park
HIGHLAND AVE
MEDFORD ST
MCGRATH HWY
BROADWAY
EVERETT AVE
RUSH ST
CUTTER ST
WEBSTER ST
CROSS ST
FLINT ST
GLEN ST
OLIVER ST
FOUNTAIN AVE
TUFTS ST
ALSTON ST
KNOWLTON ST
FRANKLIN ST
FRANKLIN AVE
MYRTLE ST
FLORENCE ST
PINCKNEY ST
LINCOLN AVE
PERKINS ST
MOUNT PLEASANT
CALDWELL ST
PARKER ST
BRIGHTON ST
CRESCENT
CAMBRIDGE ST
DORRANCE
ARLINGTON AVE
BEACHAM
SEVER ST
SPICE
MAIN ST
BALDWIN ST
CHAPPIE ST
RUSSELL PL
RUSSELL ST
AUBURN ST
OAK ST
ALLEN PL
STREET D
STREET A
LINCOLN ST
DUNSTABLE ST
Community College
AUSTIN ST
GILMAN ST
GRAND VIEW
SUMMIT AVE
HAMLET ST
BOSTON ST
MUNROE ST
COLUMBUS AVE
PRESCOTT ST
PUTNAM ST
VINAL AVE
QUINCY ST
CHURCH ST
BOW ST
WARREN
STONE AVE
LAKE ST
WASHINGTON ST
NEW WASHINGTON ST
FIRST AVE
INNER BELT RD
JOY ST
LINWOOD ST
POPLAR ST
CHESTNUT ST
EVERETT
ROSSMORE ST
MANSFIELD ST
MERRIAM ST
ALLEN ST
LINDEN ST
PERRY ST
LINCOLN PKWY
CLARK ST
ADRIAN ST
NEWTON
CONCORD AVE
OAK ST
DICKINSON
SPRINGFIELD ST
HOUGHTON
PROSPECT ST
TREMONT ST
WEBSTER AVE
WINDSOR ST
WILLOW ST
HUNTING ST
HARDING ST
SOUTH ST
PORTER
WARREN ST
MEDFORD ST
93
28
Millers River
MONSIGNOR O'BRIEN HWY
WINTER ST
GORE ST
CAMBRIDGE ST
OTIS ST
EIGHTH ST
SEVENTH ST
FIFTH ST
SCIARAPPA STREET
THIRD ST
Lechmere
INMAN SQUARE
INMAN ST
AMORY ST
SAINT MARY RD
HAMPSHIRE ST
LINCOLN ST
BERKSHIRE ST
CARDINAL MEDEIROS AVE
YORK ST
SIXTH ST
SPRING ST
HURLEY ST
SECOND ST
FIRST ST
Galleria Mall
CHARLESTOWN AVE
CHARLES RIVER DAM
Charles River
BROADWAY
NORFOLK ST
ELM ST
COLUMBIA ST
UNION ST
MARKET ST
BRISTOL
BINNEY ST
CHARLES ST
BENT ST
CAMBRIDGESIDE PL
COMMERCIAL AVE
Museum of Science & Hayden Planetarium
Science Park
ESSEX ST
WORCESTER
SUFFOLK ST
PINE ST
CHERRY
WASHINGTON ST
WINDSOR ST
ALLEN DR
ROGERS ST
BENT ST
FULKERSON ST
CAMBRIDGE PKWY
CHARLES ST
LINSKEY WAY
POTTER ST
BLOSSOM ST
SCHOOL ST
PORTLAND ST
Massachusetts General Hospital
GREEN ST
MAIN ST
STATE ST
SMART ST
OSBORN ST
PELHAM
Kendall/MIT
Broad Canal
FRUIT ST
List Visual Arts Center
CARLETON ST
WADSWORTH
KENDALL SQUARE
MAIN ST
LONGFELLOW BRIDGE
Charles/MGH
CAMBRIDGE ST
AMES ST
AMHERST ST
GROVE ST
PHILLIPS
CROSS ST
PORRINGTON ST
ALBANY ST
Massachusetts Institute of Technology
REVERE ST
PINCKNEY ST
MOUNT VERNON S
EMBANKMENT RD
BRIMMER ST
RIVER ST
Charles River Basin
Hatch Memorial Shell
LIME ST
BRANCH ST
AMHERST ST
AMHERST ST
MEMORIAL DR
HARVARD BRIDGE
BEACON ST
Boston Commo
Gibson House
BERKELEY
ARLINGTON ST
Public Gardens
BACK ST
DARTMOUTH ST
CLARENDON ST
STORROW MEMORIAL DR
BEACON ST
MARLBOROUGH ST
Charles River
Arlington Street Church
Arlington
BOYLSTO
GLOUCESTER ST
EXETER ST
FAIRFIELD ST
HEREFORD ST
MEMORIAL DR
BACK ST
Boston University
DEERFIELD ST
RALEIGH ST
CHARLESGATE W
CHARLESGATE E
MASSACHUSETTS AVE
COMMONWEALTH AVE
NEWBURY ST
Copley
COPLEY SQUARE
Trinity Church
PROVIDENCE
ST JAMES AVE
BERKELEY ST
Park Plaza
COLUMBUS AVE
STUART ST
PIEDMONT ST
MELROSE ST
FAYETTE ST
Boston Public Library
DARTMOUTH
John Hancock Tower
SHERBORN
KENMORE SQUARE
Kenmore
Hynes/ICA
Prudential Center
CORTES ST
90
BOYLSTON ST
CHANDLER ST

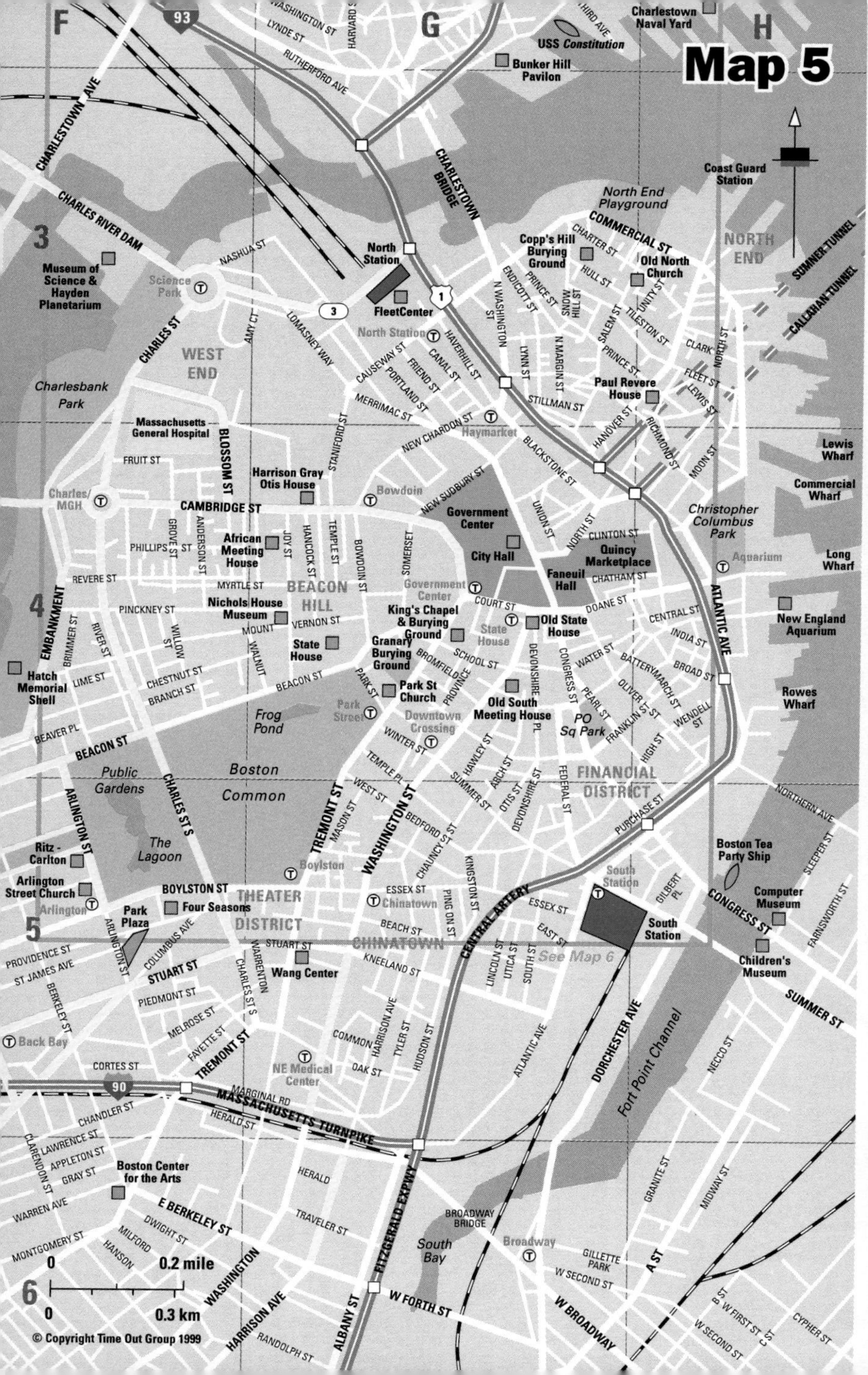

Map 5
Charlestown Naval Yard
USS Constitution
Bunker Hill Pavilon
Coast Guard Station
North End Playground
Copp's Hill Burying Ground
Old North Church
NORTH END
Museum of Science & Hayden Planetarium
Science Park
North Station
FleetCenter
WEST END
Charlesbank Park
Paul Revere House
Massachusetts General Hospital
Haymarket
Lewis Wharf
Commercial Wharf
Harrison Gray Otis House
Bowdoin
Charles/ MGH
Government Center
Christopher Columbus Park
African Meeting House
City Hall
Quincy Marketplace
Faneuil Hall
Aquarium
Long Wharf
BEACON HILL
Nichols House Museum
King's Chapel & Burying Ground
Old State House
State House
New England Aquarium
Granary Burying Ground
Hatch Memorial Shell
Park St Church
Old South Meeting House
Park Street
Downtown Crossing
PO Sq Park
Rowes Wharf
Frog Pond
Public Gardens
Boston Common
FINANCIAL DISTRICT
The Lagoon
Boston Tea Party Ship
Ritz - Carlton
Arlington Street Church
Arlington
Boylston
South Station
Park Plaza
Four Seasons
THEATER DISTRICT
Chinatown
Computer Museum
CHINATOWN
See Map 6
Children's Museum
Wang Center
Back Bay
NE Medical Center
Fort Point Channel
Boston Center for the Arts
South Bay
Broadway
MASSACHUSETTS TURNPIKE
CENTRAL ARTERY
FITZGERALD EXPWY
0 0.2 mile
0 0.3 km

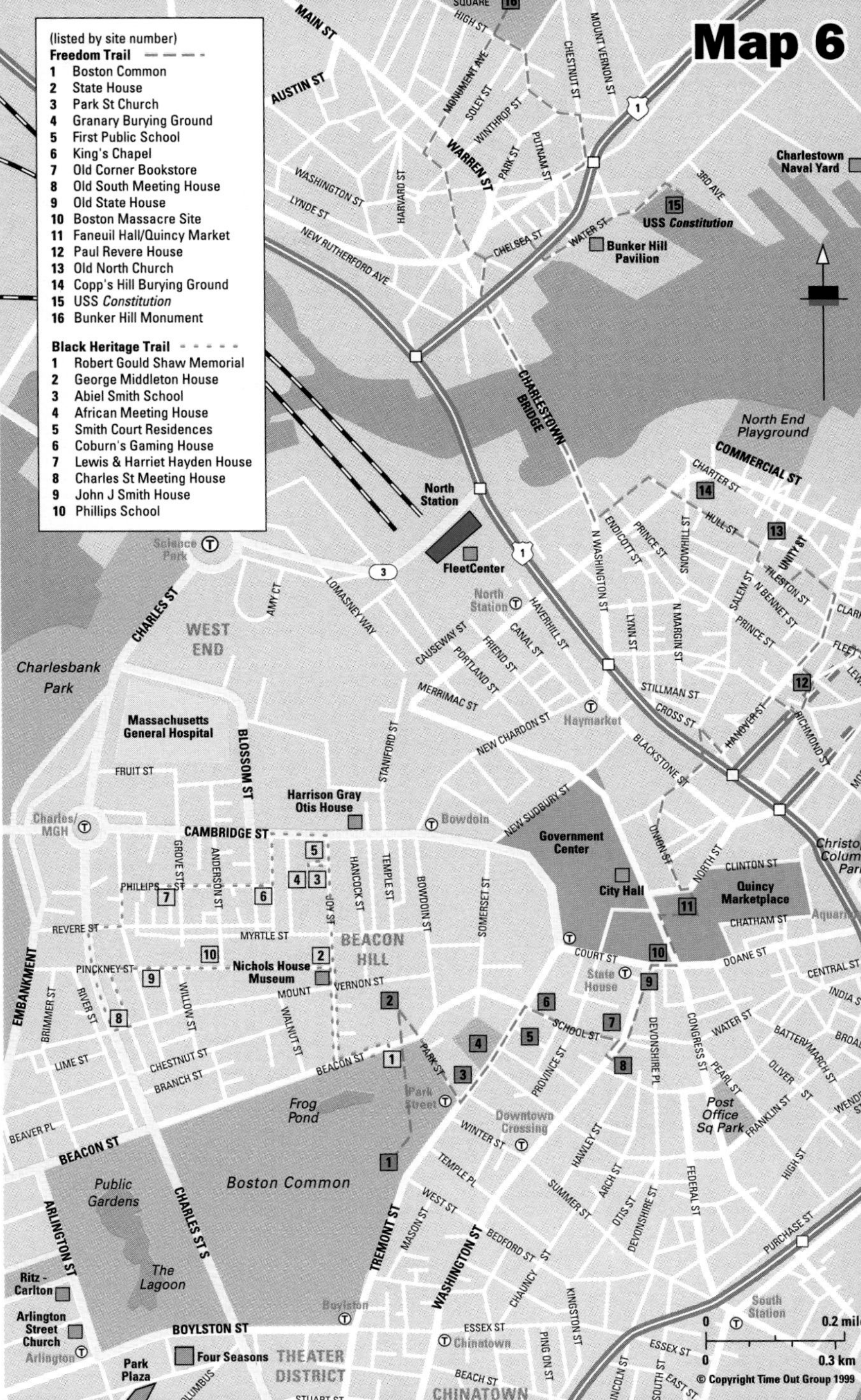
Map 6
(listed by site number)
Freedom Trail
1 Boston Common
2 State House
3 Park St Church
4 Granary Burying Ground
5 First Public School
6 King's Chapel
7 Old Corner Bookstore
8 Old South Meeting House
9 Old State House
10 Boston Massacre Site
11 Faneuil Hall/Quincy Market
12 Paul Revere House
13 Old North Church
14 Copp's Hill Burying Ground
15 USS Constitution
16 Bunker Hill Monument
Black Heritage Trail
1 Robert Gould Shaw Memorial
2 George Middleton House
3 Abiel Smith School
4 African Meeting House
5 Smith Court Residences
6 Coburn's Gaming House
7 Lewis & Harriet Hayden House
8 Charles St Meeting House
9 John J Smith House
10 Phillips School
Monument Square
Charlestown Naval Yard
USS Constitution
Bunker Hill Pavilion
North End Playground
North Station
FleetCenter
Science Park
West End
Charlesbank Park
Massachusetts General Hospital
Harrison Gray Otis House
Government Center
City Hall
Quincy Marketplace
Christopher Columbus Park
Beacon Hill
Nichols House Museum
State House
Frog Pond
Boston Common
Public Gardens
The Lagoon
Ritz - Carlton
Arlington Street Church
Four Seasons
Park Plaza
Theater District
Chinatown
Downtown Crossing
Post Office Sq Park
South Station
0 0.2 mile
0 0.3 km
© Copyright Time Out Group 1999

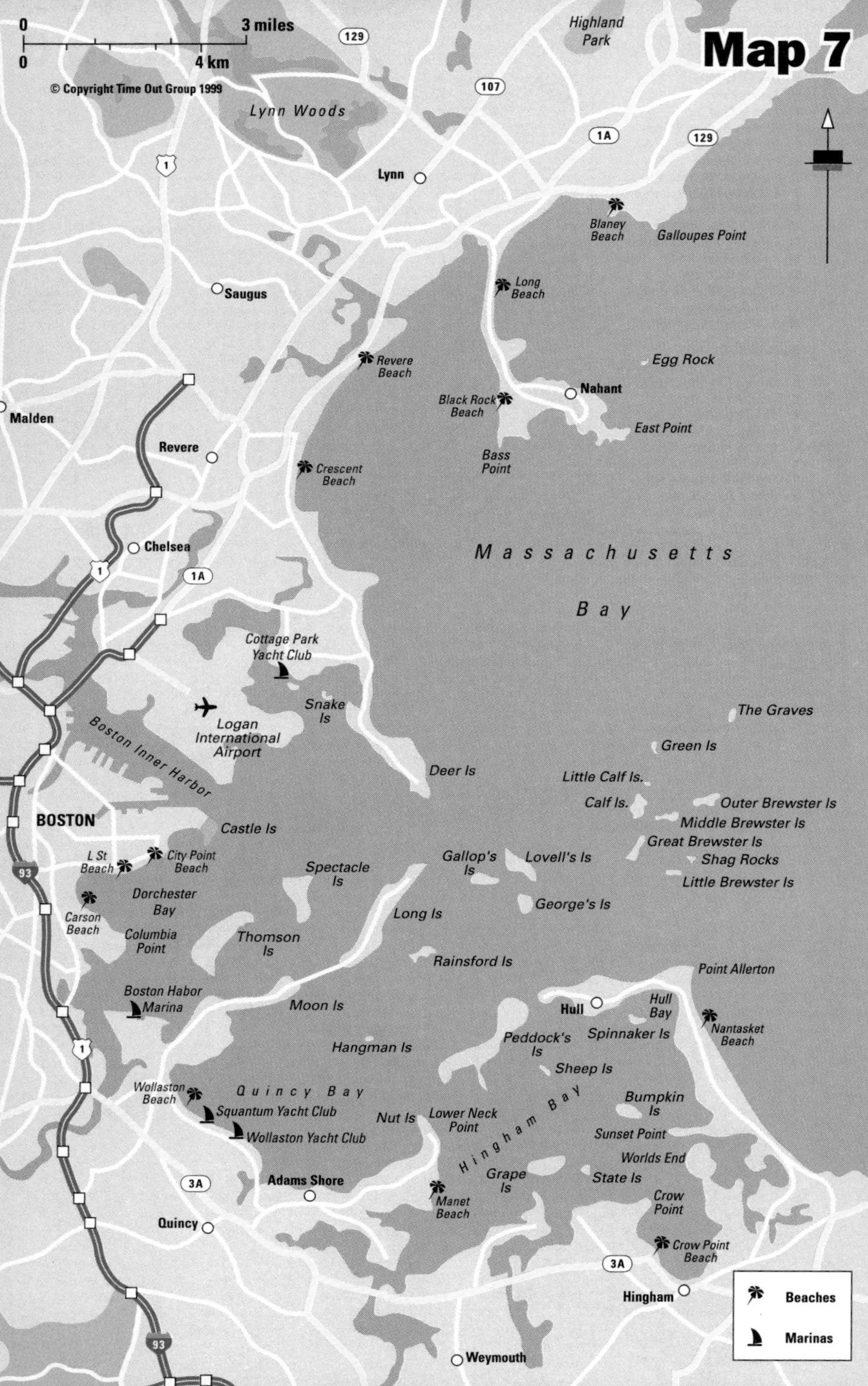
Map 7
0
3 miles
0
4 km
© Copyright Time Out Group 1999
129
Highland Park
107
Lynn Woods
1A
129
1
Lynn
Blaney Beach
Galloupes Point
Saugus
Long Beach
Revere Beach
Egg Rock
Nahant
Black Rock Beach
East Point
Malden
Revere
Bass Point
Crescent Beach
Chelsea
Massachusetts Bay
1
1A
Cottage Park Yacht Club
Snake Is
Logan International Airport
Boston Inner Harbor
The Graves
Green Is
Deer Is
Little Calf Is.
Calf Is.
Outer Brewster Is
BOSTON
Middle Brewster Is
Castle Is
Great Brewster Is
L St Beach
City Point Beach
Gallop's Is
Lovell's Is
Shag Rocks
Spectacle Is
Little Brewster Is
93
Dorchester Bay
Carson Beach
George's Is
Long Is
Columbia Point
Thomson Is
Rainsford Is
Point Allerton
Boston Habor Marina
Moon Is
Hull
Hull Bay
Nantasket Beach
Peddock's Is
Spinnaker Is
1
Hangman Is
Sheep Is
Wollaston Beach
Quincy Bay
Bumpkin Is
Squantum Yacht Club
Nut Is
Lower Neck Point
Hingham Bay
Wollaston Yacht Club
Sunset Point
Worlds End
3A
Adams Shore
Grape Is
State Is
Manet Beach
Crow Point
Quincy
Crow Point Beach
3A
Hingham
Beaches
Marinas
93
Weymouth

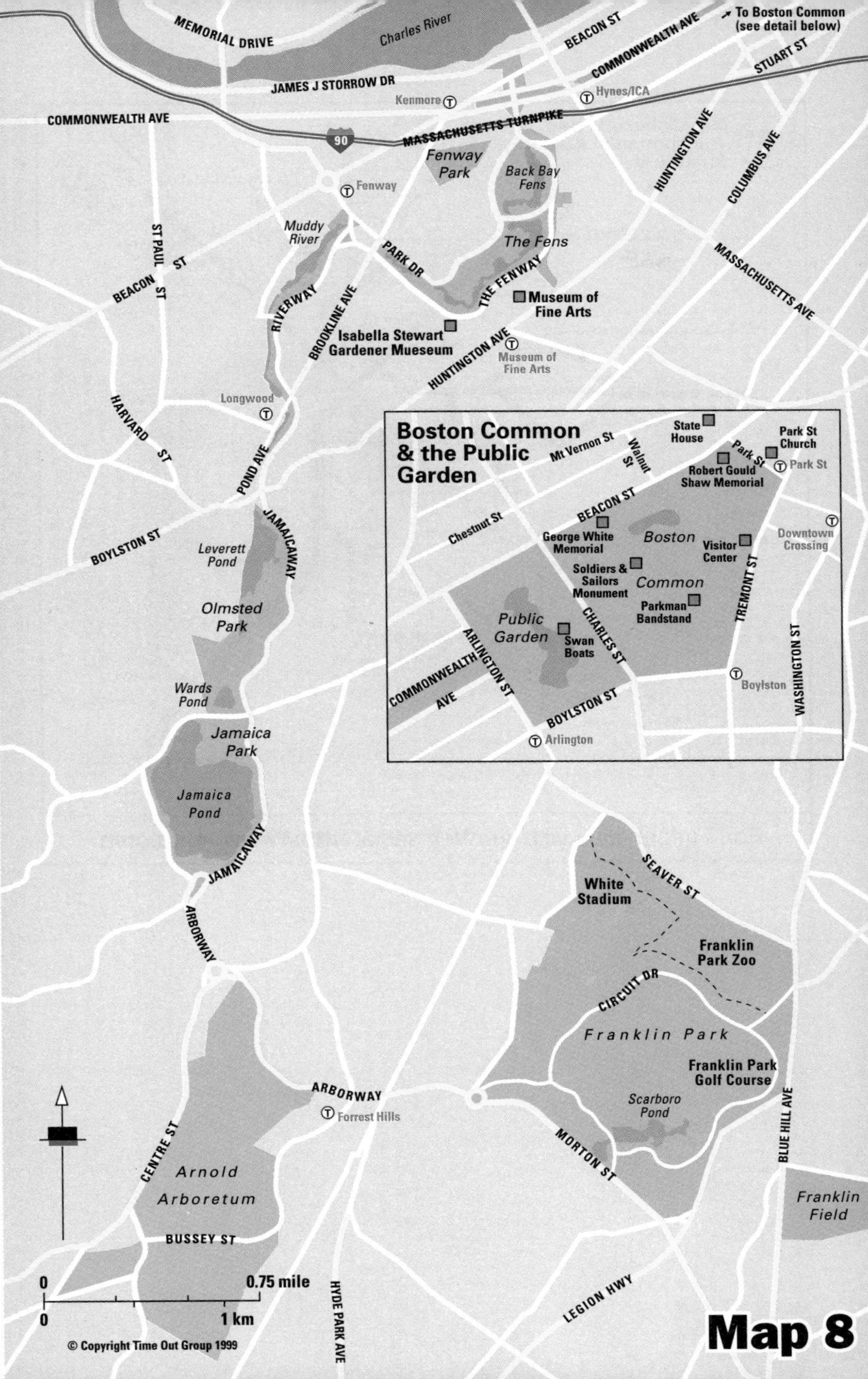

Memorial Drive
Charles River
James J Storrow Dr
Beacon St
Commonwealth Ave
To Boston Common (see detail below)
Stuart St
Kenmore
Hynes/ICA
Commonwealth Ave
Massachusetts Turnpike
90
Fenway Park
Back Bay Fens
Fenway
Huntington Ave
Columbus Ave
Muddy River
St Paul St
The Fens
Park Dr
Massachusetts Ave
Beacon St
Riverway
Brookline Ave
The Fenway
Museum of Fine Arts
Isabella Stewart Gardener Mueseum
Huntington Ave
Museum of Fine Arts
Longwood
Harvard St
Pond Ave
Boston Common & the Public Garden
Mt Vernon St
Walnut St
State House
Park St Church
Park St
Park St
Robert Gould Shaw Memorial
Beacon St
Chestnut St
George White Memorial
Boston Common
Visitor Center
Downtown Crossing
Soldiers & Sailors Monument
Tremont St
Parkman Bandstand
Public Garden
Swan Boats
Charles St
Arlington St
Commonwealth Ave
Boylston St
Boylston
Washington St
Arlington
Boylston St
Jamaicaway
Leverett Pond
Olmsted Park
Wards Pond
Jamaica Park
Jamaica Pond
Jamaicaway
Arborway
Seaver St
White Stadium
Franklin Park Zoo
Circuit Dr
Franklin Park
Franklin Park Golf Course
Arborway
Forrest Hills
Scarboro Pond
Centre St
Morton St
Blue Hill Ave
Arnold Arboretum
Franklin Field
Bussey St
0
0.75 mile
0
1 km
Legion Hwy
Hyde Park Ave
© Copyright Time Out Group 1999
Map 8

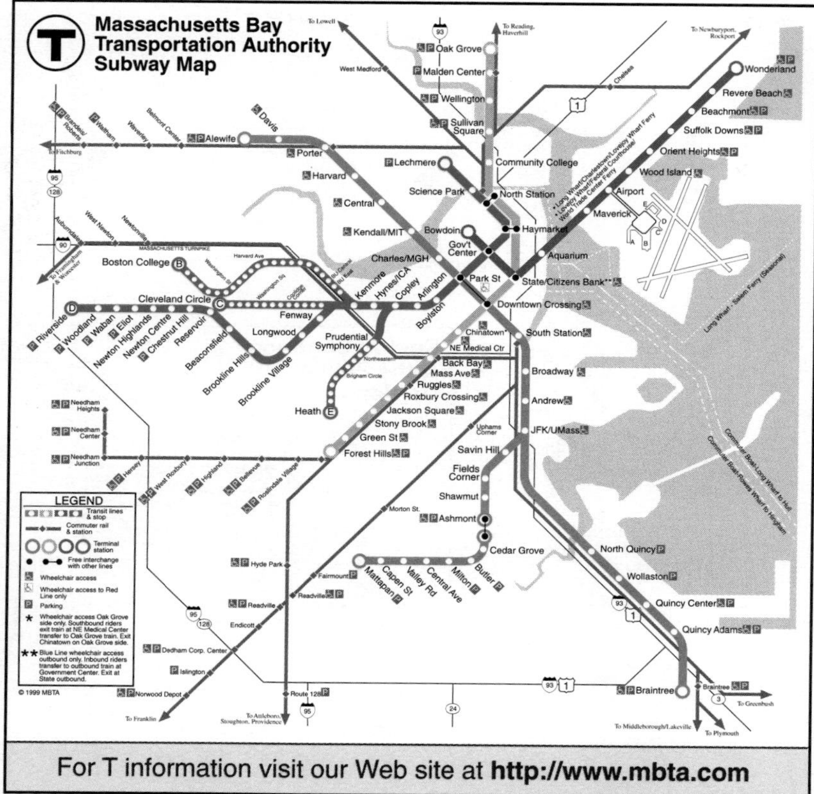

Massachusetts Bay Transportation Authority Subway Map
To Lowell
To Reading, Haverhill
To Newburyport, Rockport
Oak Grove
Malden Center
Wellington
Sullivan Square
Community College
West Medford
Chelsea
Wonderland
Revere Beach
Beachmont
Suffolk Downs
Orient Heights
Wood Island
Airport
Maverick
Brandeis/Roberts
Waltham
Waverley
Belmont Center
Alewife
Davis
Porter
Harvard
Central
Kendall/MIT
Charles/MGH
To Fitchburg
Lechmere
Science Park
North Station
Haymarket
Bowdoin
Gov't Center
Aquarium
State/Citizens Bank**
Park St
Downtown Crossing
Chinatown*
NE Medical Ctr
South Station
Long Wharf/Charlestown/Lovejoy Wharf Ferry
Lovejoy Wharf/Federal Courthouse/World Trade Center Ferry
Long Wharf - Salem Ferry (Seasonal)
Auburndale
West Newton
Newtonville
MASSACHUSETTS TURNPIKE
To Framingham & Worcester
Boston College
Harvard Ave
Washington St
Washington Sq
Coolidge Corner
BU Central
BU East
Kenmore
Hynes/ICA
Copley
Arlington
Boylston
Cleveland Circle
Fenway
Longwood
Prudential
Symphony
Northeastern
Brigham Circle
Heath
Riverside
Woodland
Waban
Eliot
Newton Highlands
Newton Centre
Chestnut Hill
Reservoir
Beaconsfield
Brookline Hills
Brookline Village
Back Bay
Mass Ave
Ruggles
Roxbury Crossing
Jackson Square
Stony Brook
Green St
Forest Hills
Broadway
Andrew
JFK/UMass
Uphams Corner
Savin Hill
Fields Corner
Shawmut
Ashmont
Cedar Grove
Butler
Milton
Central Ave
Valley Rd
Capen St
Mattapan
Morton St.
Needham Heights
Needham Center
Needham Junction
Hersey
West Roxbury
Highland
Bellevue
Roslindale Village
Commuter Boat-Long Wharf to Hull
Commuter Boat-Rowes Wharf to Hingham
North Quincy
Wollaston
Quincy Center
Quincy Adams
Braintree
To Greenbush
To Middleborough/Lakeville
To Plymouth
Hyde Park
Fairmount
Readville
Endicott
Dedham Corp. Center
Islington
Norwood Depot
Route 128
To Franklin
To Attleboro, Stoughton, Providence
LEGEND
Transit lines & stop
Commuter rail & station
Terminal station
Free interchange with other lines
Wheelchair access
Wheelchair access to Red Line only
Parking
* Wheelchair access Oak Grove side only. Southbound riders exit train at NE Medical Center transfer to Oak Grove train. Exit Chinatown on Oak Grove side.
** Blue Line wheelchair access outbound only. Inbound riders transfer to outbound train at Government Center. Exit at State outbound.
© 1999 MBTA
For T information visit our Web site at http://www.mbta.com

Time Out Boston Guide Please let us know what you think

(FIRST EDITION)

About this guide...

1. How useful did you find the following sections?

	Very	Fairly	Not very	
Boston In Context	❑	❑	❑	(5)
Sightseeing	❑	❑	❑	(6)
Accommodation	❑	❑	❑	(7)
Eating & Drinking	❑	❑	❑	(8)
Shopping	❑	❑	❑	(9)
Arts & Entertainment	❑	❑	❑	(10)
Trips	❑	❑	❑	(11)
Directory	❑	❑	❑	(12)
Maps	❑	❑	❑	(13)

2. Did you travel to Boston: (17)

Alone? ❑ With partner? ❑
As part of group? ❑ With children? ❑
On business? ❑ I Live here. ❑

3. How long was your trip to Boston? (18)

Less than three days ❑
Three days to one week ❑
One to two weeks ❑
Over two weeks ❑

4. Did you visit any other destinations in the USA? If so, which ones?

5. Where did you get additional travel information from? (19)

Tourist Board ❑
Internet ❑
Travel agents ❑
Another guide book (please specify)

Other

(20/22)

6. Is there anything you'd like us to cover in greater depth?

7. Are there any places that should/should not be included in the guide?

8. How many other people have used this guide? (23)

none❑ 1❑ 2❑ 3❑ 4❑ 5+❑

About other Time Out publications...

9. Have you ever bought/used Time Out magazine? (24)

Yes ❑ No ❑

10. Have you bought any other Time Out City Guides? (25)

Yes ❑ No ❑

If yes, which ones?

(26/28)

11. Have you ever bought/used other Time Out publications? (29)

Yes ❑ No ❑

If yes, which ones? (30)

Film Guide ❑
Kids Out magazine ❑
London Eating & Drinking Guide ❑
London Pubs & Bars Guide ❑
London Visitors' Guide ❑
ici Londres ❑
Paris Eating & Drinking Guide ❑
Paris Free Guide ❑
London Shopping Guide ❑
Student Guide ❑
Book of Country Walks ❑
Book of London Walks ❑

(31)

Book of New York Short Stories ❑
Time Out New York magazine ❑
Time Out Roma ❑
Time Out Diary ❑
www.timeout.com ❑

About you...

12. First name:

Surname:

Address:

Postcode:

13. Year of birth (32)

14. Sex: male ❑ female ❑ (43)

15. Are you: (44)

employed full-time ❑
employed part-time ❑
self-employed ❑
unemployed ❑
student ❑
homemaker ❑

16. At the moment do you earn: (45)

under £10,000 ❑
over 10,000 and up to £14,999 ❑
over £15,000 and up to £19,999 ❑
over £20,000 and up to £24,999 ❑
over £25,000 and up to £39,999 ❑
over £40,000 and up to £49,999 ❑
over £50,000 ❑

❑ Please tick here if you don't want to receive further information on related promotions or products.

Time Out Guides

FREEPOST 20 (WC3187)
LONDON
W1E 0DQ

AFFIX
STAMP
HERE

Penguin Direct
Penguin Books Ltd
Bath Road
Harmondsworth
West Drayton
Middlesex
UB7 0DA